The Software Developer's Guide
Third Edition

Whil Hentzen

Hentzenwerke Publishing

Published by:
Hentzenwerke Publishing
980 East Circle Drive
Whitefish Bay WI 53217 USA

Hentzenwerke Publishing books are available through booksellers and directly from the
publisher. Contact Hentzenwerke Publishing at:
414.332.9876
414.332.9463 (fax)
www.hentzenwerke.com
books@hentzenwerke.com

The Software Developer's Guide, Third Edition
    By Whil Hentzen
    Technical Editor: Patricia A. Nowak
    Copy Editor: Farion Grove

ISBN: 1-930919-00-X

Manufactured in the United States of America.

Our Contract with You, The Reader

In which we, the folks who make up Hentzenwerke Publishing, describe what you, the reader, can expect from this book and from us.

Hi there!

I've been writing professionally (in other words, eventually getting a paycheck for my scribbles) since 1974, and writing about software development since 1992. As an author, I've worked with a half-dozen different publishers and corresponded with thousands of readers over the years. As a software developer and all-around geek, I've also acquired a library of more than 100 computer and software-related books.

Thus, when I donned the publisher's cap five years ago to produce the *1997 Developer's Guide,* I had some pretty good ideas of what I liked (and didn't like) from publishers, what readers liked and didn't like, and what I, as a reader, liked and didn't like.

Now, with our new titles for 2002, we're entering our fifth season. (For those who are keeping track, the '97 DevGuide was our first, albeit abbreviated, season, the batch of six "Essentials" for Visual FoxPro 6.0 in 1999 was our second, and, in keeping with the sports analogy, the books we published in 2000 and 2001 comprised our third and fourth.)

John Wooden, the famed UCLA basketball coach, posited that teams aren't consistent; they're always getting better—or worse. We'd like to get better…

One of my goals for this season is to build a closer relationship with you, the reader. In order for us to do this, you've got to know what you should expect from us.

- You have the right to expect that your order will be processed quickly and correctly, and that your book will be delivered to you in new condition.

- You have the right to expect that the content of your book is technically accurate and up-to-date, that the explanations are clear, and that the layout is easy to read and follow without a lot of fluff or nonsense.

- You have the right to expect access to source code, errata, FAQs, and other information that's relevant to the book via our Web site.

- You have the right to expect an electronic version of your printed book to be available via our Web site.

- You have the right to expect that, if you report errors to us, your report will be responded to promptly, and that the appropriate notice will be included in the errata and/or FAQs for the book.

Naturally, there are some limits that we bump up against. There are humans involved, and they make mistakes. A book of 500 pages contains, on average, 150,000 words and several megabytes of source code. It's not possible to edit and re-edit multiple times to catch every last misspelling and typo, nor is it possible to test the source code on every permutation of development environment and operating system—and still price the book affordably.

Once printed, bindings break, ink gets smeared, signatures get missed during binding. On the delivery side, Web sites go down, packages get lost in the mail.

Nonetheless, we'll make our best effort to correct these problems—once you let us know about them.

In return, when you have a question or run into a problem, we ask that you first consult the errata and/or FAQs for your book on our Web site. If you don't find the answer there, please e-mail us at **books@hentzenwerke.com** with as much information and detail as possible, including 1) the steps to reproduce the problem, 2) what happened, and 3) what you expected to happen, together with 4) any other relevant information.

I'd like to stress that we need you to communicate questions and problems clearly. For example…

- "Your downloads don't work" isn't enough information for us to help you. "I get a 404 error when I click on the **Download Source Code** link on **www.hentzenwerke.com/book/downloads.html**" is something we can help you with.

- "The code in Chapter 10 caused an error" again isn't enough information. "I performed the following steps to run the source code program DisplayTest.PRG in Chapter 10, and I received an error that said 'Variable m.liCounter not found'" is something we can help you with.

We'll do our best to get back to you within a couple of days, either with an answer or at least an acknowledgement that we've received your inquiry and that we're working on it.

On behalf of the authors, technical editors, copy editors, layout artists, graphical artists, indexers, and all the other folks who have worked to put this book in your hands, I'd like to thank you for purchasing this book, and I hope that it will prove to be a valuable addition to your technical library. Please let us know what you think about this book—we're looking forward to hearing from you.

As Groucho Marx once observed, "Outside of a dog, a book is a man's best friend. Inside of a dog, it's too dark to read."

Whil Hentzen
Hentzenwerke Publishing
July 2002

List of Chapters

Table of Contents

Chapter 3: Types of Processes   23

Chapter 4: Choosing a Process   39

Chapter 7: Positioning 83

Chapter 8: Marketing 99

Chapter 19: Scenarios Encountered During the Specification Process

Acknowledgements

Writing one book could be considered a fluke. A second—perhaps a mistake. A third? Perhaps a moment of weakness. But *DevGuide 3* is the eighth ISBN to have my name attached to it. This could be considered to be a trend.

Nonetheless, just because I've done it before doesn't make it any easier; as many of you who have been waiting patiently for this book may suspect, it may even be more difficult. And as difficult as it was, it would have even been *more* difficult without the help and support of many people.

First, as always, my wife, my partner, my lover, my best friend... yes, all the same person... Linda. Our relationship has survived many events over 25 years, and as I write these words, it appears it will survive yet another book. Next, my kids—many more than the last time I wrote an acknowledgement—Jackie, Alex, Wolfie, Sammi, and Griffin. Perhaps part of the reason this book took so long was that I spent time with them over the past couple of years instead of pushing them off "to work on my book."

Patty Nowak has been as patient a soul as I can imagine; indeed, there were many times when I thought she'd return a phone call simply with hysterical laughter. She's asked many tough questions—some to which I still don't have the answers. That bodes well for another edition, although I'm not telling anybody about it for a long, long time.

Over the past 12 years, the FoxForum Irregulars have provided an overabundance of feedback; indeed, many of the war stories in this book have come directly or indirectly from late nights swapping tales at various software development conferences.

This business has always been known for the "feast or famine" cycle; these past few years have exaggerated those cycles to the point that you never know who's going to go out of business tomorrow. As a result, many developers have taken full advantage to make hay while the sun is shining; I've relied on Ted Roche, Steve Sawyer, and Roxanne Seibert for their insights about the development process, but unfortunately they weren't available enough because of these business cycles. Perhaps they'll have more time in the future, although I don't want to wish a famine cycle upon them that would create that time.

Ken Hawkins and Ron Effertz, names from the distant past, neck in neck for the title of "Best Manger I've Ever Had," also influenced me more than they know. And the folks at Geneer, possibly the best software development firm in the country, but who was still subject to the economic crushes over the past few years, and whose passing was just chronicled earlier this month.

And I don't want to forget J.Geils, despite their busy schedule during the second week of August 1969.

Finally, who and what kept me up and motivated during those late nights while the tome was being assembled? Proof positive that you don't ever want to drive with me while I'm in charge of the CD changer: B.B. King, Brooks and Dunn, Hole, Queensryche, and, of course, Twisted Sister. Now more than ever, the truth hurts.

Software will always be better when written at 105 decibels.

—Whil Hentzen

About the Author

Whil Hentzen

Whil Hentzen is President of Hentzenwerke Corporation, a Milwaukee-based firm that has specialized in developing strategic database applications for Fortune 2000 firms in the manufacturing, financial, and healthcare industries since 1984. The firm has customers throughout the United States and in more than two dozen foreign countries. Hentzenwerke has hosted the semi-annual Great Lakes Great Database Workshop since 1994. Whil also owns Hentzenwerke Publishing, a technical book publisher that specializes in high-end software development topics. Started in 1996, HWP has produced dozens of books covering various aspects of software development.

Whil has written and spoken extensively about software development. He has been a Microsoft MVP (Most Valuable Professional) since 1994 for his contributions to the Microsoft development community. He has also been editor of *FoxTalk*, Pinnacle Publishing's high-end technical journal for FoxPro, since 1996. He is the author of books about Visual Studio (*Visual FoxPro 6.0 Fundamentals*), Visual FoxPro (*Programming Visual FoxPro 3.0*), FoxPro (*Rapid Application Development with FoxPro 2.6*), and custom software development (*The Software Developer's Guide, Third Edition*), was technical editor for *The Pros Talk Visual FoxPro 3.0*, published by Microsoft Press, and has contributed chapters to several other books.

In 1999, Microsoft contracted with Whil to create the Certification Exam for Visual FoxPro 6.0 Distributed Applications. The exam is now live and has been taken by developers worldwide to help them achieve Microsoft Certified Solution Developer status.

Whil has presented more than 70 papers at conferences throughout North America and Europe, including the Microsoft Visual FoxPro DevCon, the German National DevCon, Conference to the Max (The Netherlands), the Spanish National DevCon, Database & Client/Server World, FoxTeach, the FoxPro Users Conference, and the Mid-Atlantic Database Workshop.

In 2001, he received the first Visual FoxPro Lifetime Achievement Award from Microsoft for his contributions to the community over the past decade. Whil has a B.S. in Mechanical Engineering from Rose-Hulman Institute of Technology, named as the United States' top independent engineering school in 1999 through 2002 by *U.S. News & World Report*. He served on RHIT's Commission on the Future from 1993 to 1998.

Whil has been heavily involved in community services throughout his life. He served as president of the Clifton Track Club, the 1,000-member Cincinnati-based running club, from 1983 to 1985; was president of the Greater Cincinnati PC Users Group from 1985 to 1987; and was on the board of CISE, the small business branch of the Greater Cincinnati Chamber of Commerce, from 1986 to 1988. After moving to Milwaukee, he assembled the popular annual race booklet for the Badgerland Striders Running Club from 1991 through 1996, and was president of the Milwaukee Association of FoxPro Developers from 1993 to 1998.

He currently spends his spare time with his wife and five kids and volunteering for the local school district. He is an avid distance runner, having logged nearly 50,000 miles lifetime, and, pending recovery from a severe injury a few years ago, hopes for one more shot at a sub-15-minute 5,000-meter clocking before age and common sense close the door on that activity.

You can reach Whil at whil@hentzenwerke.com, or at 414.332.9876.

Patricia A. Nowak

Patricia A. Nowak has spent the past several years as a solution developer, specializing in custom applications for consumer finance and automotive manufacturing clients. Over the years Patricia has held a variety of roles on these projects, from project manager to lead developer to "process person." The past six years she has focused on automotive finance applications for Latin America market clients and has the distinction of knowing far more about Argentine tax law than any non-native has a right to know. Patricia was also a founding member of the Fox User Group in Detroit and served as the organization's newsletter editor for six years.

Patricia makes her home in Detroit's western suburbs but is happiest "up north" among northern Michigan's beautiful lakes, where she enjoys hiking, biking, wind surfing, and skiing.

How to Download the Files

Hentzenwerke Publishing generally provides two sets of files to accompany its books. The first is the source code referenced throughout the text. Note that some books do not have source code; in those cases, a placeholder file is provided in lieu of the source code in order to alert you of the fact. The second is the e-book version (or versions) of the book. Depending on the book, we provide e-books in either the compiled HTML Help (.CHM) format, Adobe Acrobat (.PDF) format, or both. Here's how to get them.

Both the source code and e-book file(s) are available for download from the Hentzenwerke Web site. In order to obtain them, follow these instructions:

1. Point your Web browser to **www.hentzenwerke.com**.

2. Look for the link that says "Download"

3. A page describing the download process will appear. This page has two sections:

- **Section 1:** If you were issued a username/password directly from Hentzenwerke Publishing, you can enter them into this page.

- **Section 2:** If you did not receive a username/password from Hentzenwerke Publishing, don't worry! Just enter your e-mail alias and look for the question about your book. Note that you'll need your physical book when you answer the question.

4. A page that lists the hyperlinks for the appropriate downloads will appear.

Note that the e-book file(s) are covered by the same copyright laws as the printed book. Reproduction and/or distribution of these files is against the law.

If you have questions or problems, the fastest way to get a response is to e-mail us at **books@hentzenwerke.com**.

Icons used in this book

 Indicates that the referenced material is available for download at
www.hentzenwerke.com.

 Indicates information of special interest, related topics, important notes,
or version issues.

 Indicates a "War Story."

Introduction

Where I tell you what you're going to get out of this book.

When I wrote the first edition of this book in August of 1996, I set out to solve a specific problem.

The problem was that highly skilled developers faced an artificial barrier to their income increasing with their skill level, even more so than other professions that rely on a combination of hourly rate and billable hours.

In accounting, a highly skilled CPA might be 2x, 3x, 4x as productive as your run-of-the mill CPA. In software, it's common for a highly skilled developer to be 10x, 20x—I've even heard of multiples of 40x—more productive. That's times, not percent. Yes, doing in an hour what an everyday developer does in a week.

The problem is that the highly skilled developer can't bill an hourly rate of 40 times more than an everyday developer. The best they can hope for is 50-100% more—if an average developer billed $75, a highly skilled one could bill at $100, $125, $150. Maybe.

The solution was to bill for results, not hours. If a highly skilled developer could produce a project that would take an average developer a week, in an hour, and then bill for a fixed price—the same amount that the average developer would have charged for the week of work. The customer gets the same product and pays the same price—and the highly skilled developer gets compensated for their high level of skills.

DevGuide 97 and *DevGuide 99* showed you how to make this happen for an individual developer and for a small development shop. However, there were three requirements that had to be met for a fixed price project to be successful. These were:

1. A well defined specification—so you know what to produce.

2. A level of skill and process—so you know how to do it.

3. A history of past performance—so you know how much to charge because you know how long it took last time.

But not all applications met these requirements. There are simply some projects that won't fit into this particular mold.

This, the Third Edition of *The Software Developer's Guide*, widens the scope of the original charter, and deals with projects where the requirements for a fixed price project were not able to be met. I'll discuss the variety of development processes, including traditional Structured Development, Rapid Application Development, and even Agile Processes, such as Extreme Programming.

Then I'll revisit the original questions—how much and how long—and attempt to answer them again, for each of these processes, as best as can be done. I use this caveat because, despite the surfacing of new processes, the same requirements must be met to provide a fixed price for a project; just because you're using a new development process doesn't mean that you can suddenly suspend the laws of physics and economics.

In doing so, though, I've expanded on many of the existing topics, both for new processes as well as additional ways of looking at traditional means. And, at the same time, I've been able to tighten up and reorganize my thinking for some existing topics. As a result, I've added nearly 200 pages of material to a book that some already felt was without peer.

One other thing that I've added to this book is relevant quotes to lead into each chapter. Our initial charge, gladly accepted by my technical editor, Patty Nowak, was to restrict the quotes to movies starring Harrison Ford, Mel Gibson, or Sean Connery. Much to my dismay, she insisted upon adding Richard Gere. And once the barn door was open a little, well, a precedent was set—we gradually broadened the scope (yes, yet another example of scope creep) to include the Star Wars galaxy, and then just about anything we liked.

The scariest part of this whole process was discovering how many times a quote from "Dumb and Dumber" seemed applicable. We're not exactly sure what message this is giving us, but you might want to keep it in mind as you're undertaking the adventure of software development in what a friend from Down Under calls the "naughties."

Section I:

About
Development

Software development takes many shapes and forms because there are a lot of variables in the game. There are different types of developers, different types of projects, and different types of processes. However, not every type of developer maps well to every type of project, nor to every type of process. Not every project is a good candidate for every type of process. And not every process is a good candidate for every project.

Your job as a software developer is not to simply slam out code, but to deliver the whole enchilada. And that starts with picking the projects that you (and your team) can be successful at, and continues with picking the right process for the type of developer you are and the type of project you're working on.

You can't perform this mixing and matching properly, however, without knowing what the options are. This section will delineate the various types of developers, projects, and processes, and help you decide which types of projects are right for you (and your team). Finally, you'll learn how to choose, in concert with your customer, which processes are appropriate candidates for the project in question, and then come to agreement on the process to use.

When you're done with this section, you'll have the wherewithal to evaluate a customer's situation, make the appropriate choice, and pitch that choice to the customer successfully. You may even decide to make the choice yourself, and simply present one option to the customer.

Chapter 1
Types of Developers

"There are two types of people. Those who divide people into two types, and those who don't."—Anonymous

There are many types of developers—from the freelance programmer working off a card table in the corner of the bedroom in his apartment for non-profits in his one-horse town, to the globe-trotting professional in the $2,000 suit masterminding complex distributed applications with hundreds of thousands of users. Each type of developer is best suited to handle some types of projects but not others, and the same goes for types of processes. You need to know which category you fall into so that you can match yourself with the right types of projects and processes.

The first edition of this book was targeted at a specific group—independent developers who needed a manual for running their software development business. The scope of the second edition grew to include small development shops, and started to address the issues of corporate developers. This edition expands the scope some, but more so, discretely identifies those groups so that you can classify yourself and defines traits that can help you choose projects and processes in a more appropriate fashion.

But there are many more types of developers than just those three categories; indeed, they come in all shapes and sizes. In technical terms, this is a multi-dimensional set of variables. So how do you categorize such a group? Usually you pick one attribute, and work through the range of possible values in the domain of that attribute. In other words, if you're categorizing humans by appearance, you pick an attribute such as hair color, and work your way from transparent (bald) to white, yellow, light brown, dark brown, and on to black. Within each of those colors, you then describe other attributes, such as height, weight, gender, eye color, and so on.

But "type" of software developer doesn't just mean the people themselves but the work unit in which they are involved—the group in which the people themselves work. Thus, the attribute has been chosen for us—the number of people in the work group. I'll vary that, and then discuss other attributes, such as work environment, types of disciplines and work, for each value.

The independent developer

Given the complexity of software development in today's world, it may be surprising to some that there are still a large number of sole practitioners in the development field. Indeed, in the early '90s, many pundits predicted the disappearance of the independent by the year 2000. Fortunately, this hasn't been the case.

The independent developer is a single individual, operating either as a sole proprietor, a Sub-S Corporation, or even an LLC (limited liability corporation). They may work on a single project at a time, and those projects may be many months, or even years long. These situations are much like having a steady job, with additional benefits of higher pay and more flexibility. In these cases, it becomes important for the independent to follow both the letter and the spirit of the law to stay independent, and not be declared an employee of a long-term client.

Other independents multi-task, always keeping several projects going at the same time, interspersing short jobs (a day or a week) with longer ones. The benefit to keeping multiple projects running at the same time is that should one wind down or go bad suddenly, the developer doesn't have all her eggs in the same basket; the remaining projects act as a safety net. The downside is that there is inevitably some downtime involved in switching from one project to another, and in gaining new projects (and customers).

Some independents specialize in a certain discipline, such as programming with a specific language or consulting on the use of a certain technology. Other independents get their start working for smaller companies, putting together a specific application, and then often end up becoming a pseudo-IS department for their customers, providing advice, support, and general consulting in addition to the development of custom applications. And still others never specialize in a single area, instead preferring to be the jack-of-all-trades. In this book, we're primarily concerned with independents who make the majority, if not all, of their living doing software development.

Independents may base their operations in the home, in a corner of the living room, a spare bedroom, the den, or a room over the garage. If home isn't conducive to setting up shop, they may lease space in an office building. The independent developer may prefer to work at the office, or may work on-site with a customer as often as possible.

The partnership

Eventually, many independent developers get so busy that they can't handle the work by themselves anymore—either because of time constraints or because of a lack of knowledge. One way out of this dilemma is to hook up with an equal as a partner. This partnership may take the form of two equals—both technically strong, either in the same area or in different, complementary areas. Or it may take the form of a technical person and a business person.

Once there's more than one mouth to feed, it becomes much more important to have multiple revenue streams coming in through the form of multiple projects, preferably with multiple customers. The issue of determining whether one is self-employed or an employee of the customer becomes moot quickly.

Some partnerships focus on a single discipline, while others form a partnership in order to broaden their reach through the acquisition of capabilities they don't already possess. In both cases, the partners' activities run the gamut of strict software development projects through a range of activities, including general consulting.

The partnership most often takes up residence in a formal office, although more and more "virtual partnerships" are formed by two or more people who all work in separate locations, or gather at one person's house when needed. Still, the existence of a real office doesn't mean that the customer's site is forsworn—it's not uncommon to have much of the work done on site at a customer.

The small development shop

The alternative for an independent developer to going into partnership with another person is to hire employees. Once the initial decision to add staff has been made, it's relatively simple to go to three, four, and more employees.

A shop with two, three, or four developers, and perhaps a couple of support staff, can undertake larger projects, but at the same time, has more demands on getting the work in the door in order to meet payroll and the overhead associated with non-billable personnel and an office. The company usually still has a couple of bread-and-butter customers (or projects) that provide the majority of the work that sustains the company.

A multi-developer shop can still specialize in a single discipline, such as a single language—indeed, shops with a half-dozen or a dozen employees may still all rely on a single tool for their work.

A small development shop such as this most likely operates out of an office, and adds the trappings of an administrative assistant or office manager and perhaps some technical support staff.

The large development shop

As a development shop grows, there comes a time where it's so big that the company is no longer subject to the success of a single project or keeping a single customer. I once heard this described by a principal of a 50+ developer shop like so: "When we were small, if we fell on hard times or a tight month, the three partners would forgo our paychecks that month so that we could pay the company bills. Now, our combined salaries are such a small part of the company's operations that it wouldn't do us any good anymore."

You can think of this type of operation—15, 25, 50 developers, with dozens or more customers and projects—as having reached critical mass. Many small companies rely on a sugar-daddy customer for a disproportionate amount of their income, but eventually reach the stage where losing the revenues of the single largest customer would be an inconvenience rather than a major disaster or a crippling blow. This is critical mass.

This isn't always the case—one of the advantages of a larger development shop is the wide range of resources (simple manpower as well as technical knowledge) that can be brought to bear on a single project. As a result, it's still possible for a 50-person shop to have a single bread-and-butter customer for whose project 10, 15 or more developers are assigned.

A development shop of this size has grown beyond a single level of reports—the president or managing partner is no longer directly responsible for every employee. The company may be organized around development tools and languages, where one group produces C++ apps, another does Java, and a third does VB and SQL Server projects, each group having its own manager. Another possible structure is organized around functional areas, such as analysis/design, development, testing, and implementation.

A third possibility is industry focus—insurance, manufacturing, finance, and so on. We've even seen large shops where teams are pulled together on a project-by-project basis, where personnel are pulled together from a variety of disciplines to put together a project— and a fluid structure where teams come together for a specific gig, and then are disbanded when the project ships.

There are a number of huge companies that do development of very large projects—ones in the millions of dollars, requiring tens of thousands of hours. These types of organizations can often be categorized in the same breath as the "large development shops" that I've just spoken of, since even the largest of projects still needs to be broken down into more manageable subsystems.

To be fair, though, these types of organizations are beyond the scope of this book.

The small company developer

There are hundreds of thousands of small companies where the information systems needs of the entire company all rest on the shoulders of one or a handful of individuals. This person may bear the title of IS manager, or systems manager, or PC coordinator, or any other number of monikers. But whatever they're called, they're responsible for the whole kit and caboodle— from ordering and installing computers to keeping software up-to-date to managing the network day-to-day to procuring or writing applications.

These applications often range from macros running in Lotus 1-2-3 or Microsoft Word, to kludging together data transfer bridges to make stand-alone third-party applications talk to each other, to department-level or company-wide applications in Access or Xbase, to writing a front end for their Oracle or SQL Server database.

These developers usually have had no formal training, and often have been thrown into the job by virtue of there being no one else, and they seemed to do an okay job when were asked to automate some task when they weren't busy fighting a fire somewhere else.

The large company developer

Much like the difference between a small development shop, where a developer is likely to wear multiple hats, and the large development shop, where a developer is a small cog in a large machine, the large company developer is characterized by having a single, specific role in the application development process.

A large company will have the resources—and the need—to create separate positions for separate jobs. One person will be responsible for the day-to-day network management, a second (and third and fourth) for supporting the users, and still others to handle the hardware infrastructure, such as upgrading machines and installing new ones.

Application development will often fall into a separate department, where one's role will be that of a junior programmer, senior programmer, analyst, tester, or similar types of discrete roles.

The consultancy

There's another type of information systems consulting company that isn't focused strictly on building applications. The regional, national, or multi-national consultancy provides a wide range of consulting services to companies through its defined region.

These services typically range from specific application development all the way through management consulting; the emphasis is most often on billable hours per consultant per time period. In some organizations, delivering a product is way down on the priority list. You may have seen the commercial where the consultants recommend a course of action to a business manager, whereby he turns around and agrees with their recommendations, and asks them to implement. They fall over themselves laughing, saying, "Oh, gosh, you don't understand. We don't actually *do* anything."

Strictly speaking, they do have "deliverables"—position papers, recommendations for one strategy over another, that sort of thing. Given the huge amount of hype in our business these days, these types of studies and analysis can be very valuable—if the consultant actually sticks his neck out and takes a stand. On the other hand, it's often easier to recommend a course of action when you don't have to make it work yourself.

This type of organization isn't covered in this book at all.

Conclusion

The type of developer you are, or development shop you're in, isn't, in and of itself, that important. But when put in context of the other variables, knowing yourself will become important. Let's look at the types of software development projects next.

Chapter 2
Types of Gigs

"What kind of music do you usually have here?"—Elwood Blues
*"Oh, we have both kinds—country **and** western."—Claire*
  —Blues Brothers

There are almost as many types of software projects ("gigs") as there are customers, each again with similarities and differences. You may be offered many different types of assignments. Original development, rewrites, version 2.0 development, maintenance, troubleshooting, audits, and hourly consulting all differ in the skills and resources they require, and in the benefits and risks involved. In this section, we look at the different types of engagements, and talk about the characteristics and advantages and disadvantages of each. Finally, I remind you that this book is about developing software applications—not the broad range of work elsewhere.

The field of "computers" is so broad that it nearly defies quantification. My grandmother-in-law once cornered me at a family gathering and complained, "You're in computers, aren't you? Well, a couple of weeks ago, the computer at our office just stopped working. Can you tell me why that happened?" No description of what type of computer—mainframe terminal or personal computer—much less details on what specifically was happening, but since I was "in computers," I was expected to be able to troubleshoot the problem.

In order to put what I do—developing custom applications using a specific tool or suite of tools—in proper perspective, I often use the following explanation with those not in the field to illustrate how limited my expertise is. "The weekly trade magazine *Computerworld* is usually 150-200 pages long, in 11x17 tabloid format. It covers the full range of the computer industry. On page 63, in the lower right corner, every couple of weeks or so, there's an article on what I do. The rest of the page, and the other 150-200 pages, I don't have hardly anything to do with."

Even within this narrow discipline of software development, though, there's a wide range of potential projects, from a brand-new application to be developed from scratch, to routine maintenance on an application written by someone a long time ago in a galaxy far away. Each of these types of gigs has peculiarities that you need to understand.

Original development

My favorite mode. In my opinion, there is nothing quite like the thrill of taking out a blank sheet of paper and creating a brand-new application from scratch. The purest form of application development is the brand-new app, where the customer pulls out a file folder full of ideas, memos, scribblings, and notes on the backs of napkins, and you start with a clean sheet. No legacy data, no existing expectations from users comfortable with the old system, no preconceived notions about "we've always done it this way."

Definition

In this situation, a customer needs a new application, either to automate a process that is currently being done manually, or to automate a new process—one that didn't previously exist. An example of the first type is that of a company that used to hand-type its invoices from hand-written quotes, but now wants to create its quotes on a computer, and wants the information on the quote to create an invoice automatically.

An example of the second kind would be when a business adopts a new process or develops a new capability. For example, a magazine company is used to collecting articles, editing them, and collating them into a print publication, and has information systems that track the subscriptions, article submissions, authors, and payments. They decide to expand to the Internet, and now need a new mechanism for tracking downloads of articles and payment to authors on a per-download basis.

Skills required

Original development requires a broad range of skills, starting with analysis of the business or process to be automated, and continuing with the possible re-engineering of the business or process and the design of the application. Then, of course, there's the actual development—programming as well as assembling modules and components—and winding up with testing, installation, and deployment.

These skills don't all have to reside with one person, though. As projects get more involved, in fact, it's doubtful that one person will possess them all or even be able to possess them all.

Time span

The time span of an original development project can vary greatly—from just a couple of weeks for something small and straightforward, to many months or years for a complex application. Some would argue that a time span of more than six months to a year for a project indicates that the project should be broken down into more than one project; whether this is appropriate for a specific project—well, the answer is, "It depends." Generally, breaking down a project into smaller, bite-sized chunks will make it more manageable, and easier to show progress. True, there may be additional expense due to having to construct additional interfaces between the modules, but the flip side is that these smaller, less complex pieces will be easier to work with and maintain.

Location

The location at which original development can be done is very flexible, and may vary according to the phase of the project. Some developers do all their work on-site, either preferring the proximity of the customer's personnel, or being required to be on-site by the customer. Other developers do most of their work off-site, preferring more control over the environment. With an off-site location comes freedom as to hours and the ability to juggle multiple projects within short time spans—it's a rare situation when a customer will let you work on someone else's project while you're on their site. Often, off-site development still requires some on-site time, usually on the front end for analysis and design meetings and the back end during testing, installation, and deployment, but interim progress report meetings are also often done in person.

Pros and cons

The upside to new application development is that there is no old application against which it will be compared. If you're currently in a new relationship with a person who'd just spent a long time in their previous relationship, you're likely familiar with the inevitable comparison with the old and familiar "my old boy/girlfriend never did that" refrain. The other upside is, as I've mentioned, that for many developers, one of the most interesting parts of the job is the ability to create something from nothing, and nowhere is that more possible than with a brand-new application.

The chief downside is that customer expectations need to be managed extremely carefully. Since there isn't a point of reference (with an existing application that's either being replaced or being added on to), customers often have idealistic (that's French for "unrealistic") expectations in their heads. They've undoubtedly spent a lot of time thinking of this new application, and may have fallen into the trap of building it up to be more than it really will be.

Another downside is that, up until recently, there seemed to be fewer and fewer clean slates around upon which we can write an original, brilliant application. But that's what the commissioner of the U.S. Patent Office said in 1897—"Everything worthwhile has already been invented."

This isn't really the case—as new platforms and technologies appear, there are opportunities for brand-new applications. The Internet, handheld devices, home networks, wireless, biometrics… these are some current targets for a slew of new apps.

Application rewrite

Nearly as good as original development is replacing an application with a new version. This is different from upgrading an existing application with new features (see "Version 2.0 development" next).

Definition

In this scenario, the customer has an existing application and needs to have it replaced. One common reason for replacement is that the existing functionality is so outmoded that mapping the current business processes to the application requires increasing amounts of non-productive effort. An application that had a single mechanism of shipping inventory to customers hard-coded in the order entry module may now require multiple workarounds due to an increasing variety of shipping and delivery options. Or a business may have simply evolved so significantly that so many new functions are required that adding them all into the existing application would be more complicated than rewriting the application from scratch—much like tearing down a house and building from scratch can be less expensive than trying to fix up an existing shack.

Another reason for a rewrite is that the customer desires a suite of features that can't be included simply by upgrading the current application. Use of components like ActiveX controls that provide sophisticated user interfaces or the need to output to a variety of sources, including fax, e-mail, PDF, and HTML, are examples of features that can't be provided simply by updating a character-based application.

Finally, the customer may need to deploy the application on a new platform, such as Windows or the Internet. Any of you who are involved in moving a DOS-based application to Windows or Web-enabling a customer's business have already seen this in action.

To be sure, each of these specific examples wouldn't in and of itself require a complete application rewrite, but when several of these are combined, a compelling argument can often be made for the rewrite.

Skills required

The same skills as those required for original development are needed here—with a healthy dose of political deftness. After all, it's easy to knock down someone else's work when given the opportunity to replace it, but you never know who has invested—financially as well as emotionally—in the existing app.

Finally, as with rewrites, you may also need to be able to handle legacy systems— importing data from previous versions or other systems that were used in the past.

Time span

The time span for a rewrite can be similar to that of original development. It may seem that there is an opportunity for time-savings since the customers may have a clearer idea of what they want, since they've got a concrete, well-known point of reference to work from, instead of just a consultant waving his arms and drawing scribbles on a white board. On the other hand, the developer needs to spent more time with the existing application—it's not uncommon for a customer to assume that a feature that was in the old app will magically reappear in the new one, even though it's not been discussed or documented anywhere throughout the specification process. It's incumbent upon the developer to thoroughly understand the old application first. Without that, you might as well be starting from scratch.

The structure of the old application may also inhibit the rewrite from being broken up into smaller, more manageable pieces.

Location

The attributes of the application being rewritten as well as the requirements of the customer dictate whether the work has to be done on-site or can be done off-site. In some situations, the application is portable (this is particularly true for vertical market applications) and so off-site development is possible. In other situations, the application being replaced has to communicate with other applications or components that aren't available off-site, or contains sensitive data or algorithms that can't be taken off-site.

Pros and cons

The good news is that oftentimes the customer's expectations have been, er, adjusted to a more reasonable level after having been through the development process once. They now understand that there aren't any silver bullets or magic potions. They are also much more likely to know what they want, what works, and what doesn't.

On the other hand, though, it may take a while to accept the fact that a complete rewrite is necessary. Sometimes a customer will come to you knowing full-well that they want the old application redone, or that while they don't want it redone, they'll have to bite the bullet and do it anyway.

Often, though, this is a conclusion that takes a while to arrive at. They'll first say they want a few tweaks to the existing application, and then a few more, and then a brand-new feature that's fairly tricky, and then a change that will require some fundamental changes to the underlying infrastructure... All of a sudden, you're looking at some major work, and you have to tell them it'd be easier to tear down the whole building and start over again.

In either case, the customer's expectations still need to be managed. Customers are often surprised to find that a rewrite will cost more than the original program—not realizing that the rewrite usually isn't a simple replacement, but a significant reworking as well as representing substantial improvements over the existing system.

Another common issue is the expectation of "it worked like this in the old one." For example, with old character-based applications, there were often a multitude of keyboard shortcuts to provide accelerated paths for experienced users. Those keyboard shortcuts may not be practical, or even possible, in a GUI-based or Web-based application, causing some initial frustration for new users. Users will cling to the old ways of doing things and it will take time to convert them to new ways.

Version 2.0 development

Further along the lifecycle of an application is that of a "dot-zero" release—a major upgrade to an existing application.

Definition

Sometimes the existing application is in pretty good shape—it just needs a lot of new goodies. The framework is sound, and the basic functionality still serves the company well. They just need more—just as if you were going to build an addition to a house you already loved, because you had no place for the twins that arrived home from the hospital last week.

There is no clear distinction between a "version 2.0" project and simple maintenance—as witnessed by the ".0" releases from various software manufacturers, one firm's bug fix or functionality tweak is another company's major feature.

Often you'll be asked back in to upgrade an application of yours to a new .0 release; in these cases, you are already familiar with the company's business, the application's functionality, and the code base upon which it was built.

In other cases, you'll be asked to update an application that was created by someone else—either another firm that is no longer available to do the work, or that the customer doesn't want to work with anymore, or internal staff who no longer have the time or who have moved on.

Skills required

Many of the same skills as those required for original development and rewrites are needed here, along with possibly one more: the ability to spelunk through existing code and determine what someone else has done—with or without accompanying documentation.

There may or may not be a time element involved; if the upgrade has been promised at a certain time, or if there are other time pressures, you may find yourself under additional pressure to complete and ship the upgrade.

Since upgrades are typically shorter projects, you'll probably be working on more than one project at a time. Thus, you'll also need to be able to juggle multiple projects, and be able to attend to more details than if you were just working on one project. Thus, you'll need to stay an expert on this entire project—the old system as well as the new parts—and other projects that you're working on at the same time.

Finally, as with rewrites, you may also need to be able to handle legacy systems—importing data from previous versions or other systems that were used in the past.

Time span

The time span for an upgrade is typically much shorter than the original project. This means that you'll probably want to have several projects running at the same time, since an upgrade isn't the same type of "sugar daddy" that a brand-new app or rewrite can be.

At the same time, a shorter delivery schedule means you'll be able to provide "instant gratification" to a customer. A new project that takes 9 or 12 or 18 months can seem to drag out forever—an upgrade may run just a couple of months. Before the customer knows it, their new version is ready.

Location

Similar to a rewrite, the attributes of the application being upgraded as well as the requirements of the customer dictate whether the work has to be done on-site or can be done off-site. Many of the same parameters apply, but more so.

For example, an upgrade to a live application may require access to other systems that are currently running and installed, and that aren't portable. In this situation, you're going to need to do the majority of your development on-site. Purists may argue that proper development techniques would require that a completely duplicate test environment be set up, but that isn't always possible or practical. For example, if your application is just reading data from another system, it may be realistic to do development and testing against that live data set.

The same goes for upgrades of applications that are security-conscious or otherwise require access to information that can't be taken off-site. It may be impossible (or just very, very impractical) to create a model of another system that interfaces with the application just for the sake of the developer's convenience in developing off-site.

Another reason that an upgrade may need to be developed on-site is that a larger percentage of the development effort is in the installation and deployment, since integration with the existing systems requires regression testing that isn't needed with the rollout of a brand-new app.

Of course, this isn't always true—upgrading an application that is intended to be portable, or of a part of a distributed application, where the location of the application's components are geographically dispersed, means that the development doesn't have to be tied to a specific location.

Pros and cons

While it doesn't contain the same verve of a brand-new app or a rewrite, a major upgrade provides the opportunity to add "cool new features" that weren't in the budget (or the imagination) earlier. Furthermore, as programmers, many of us are by nature perfectionists, but the pressure of shipping often means that we don't get to take care of the "fit and finish" as much as we'd like to. A major upgrade often allows you the chance to smooth out some rough edges and clean up little annoyances that have been bugging you (and/or your customer).

In an awful lot of cases, though, we find we are dealing with applications that may have started out on a sound footing, but have been modified, mutated, upgraded, dragged through conversion programs, moved from 10-year-old code bases, to the point where a full rewrite is needed but can't be afforded. In these cases, trade-offs and compromises are dealt with daily, and it's never as much fun working with limited resources as when you have a seemingly unlimited pot 'o money.

Another upside with an upgrade is that the client has taken ownership of the old version in a way that is not possible with a brand-new system, and thus is much more likely to know what they want, what works, and what doesn't. The flip side of this is that, as always, their eyes may be bigger than their stomachs. Clients are often surprised to find that version 2.0 will cost as much as, if not double, what version 1.0 cost years ago.

It can also end up that work is underestimated more in this type of application than in other situations because you think it will be easy to slap in a new feature—but it often ends up being more complex. Along these same lines, testing is frequently way underestimated in this situation—because these types of systems often have code that is difficult to spelunk and modules that have a high degree of interaction between them.

Maintenance

In many cases, an existing application suits the company just fine. Well, just as soon as these two or three "little" problems can get fixed. Given the transient nature of our profession, the original programmer is many times nowhere to be found, and so a new developer is brought in to do the work.

Definition

Software development maintenance is the work done between ".0" releases—small bug fixes, tweaks to existing features, minor enhancements, or additional reports. I differentiate this work from the troubleshooting (covered later), as this work involves expanding the capabilities of an original system, perhaps adding additional reports, or rearranging form elements, but not making significant changes to either the data or application structure. If the problems are more bugs, crashes, or major design flaws, I consider the work more of a troubleshooting nature.

You can think of maintenance as the routine work necessary to keep an application up and running—just as with a house, there are always small repairs to be done and little items to be fixed up or changed.

Skills required

The range of skills required during maintenance now diverges significantly from earlier types of development discussed. First, the analysis and design skills are really not required at all. Many companies look at maintenance as belonging to that of a journeyman programmer—find the bug, fix the code, and get out.

A better than average knowledge of the language or tool used is helpful, because you're often spending a significant amount of time figuring out what's going wrong, or what the last programmer did, than you are actually doing the work.

Another important skill involves interpersonal relationships—the maintenance phase of software development can involve testy customers more often than brand-new apps where everyone is full of excitement and optimism about the new toy they're going to build.

Time span

Maintenance, by definition, doesn't take that long—the scope of maintenance work is simply a set of small changes and fixes. This is a good place to mention that there's a proper way to approach maintenance.

If you're responsible for ongoing maintenance work on an application, it's easy to fall into the following trap without realizing it through the following scenario. The customer asks for a change, you make it, and you install the new program. Then they ask for another change, and you stop what you were doing, make the change, and install the new fix again. And again, and again, and again. Your time gets eaten up with very little to show for it.

With smaller systems, it's much more efficient to gather a group of changes, make them all at once, and then deliver and install a ".1" version. Your time will be more efficiently used and your customer will appreciate it as well. I've had instances where I've been requested to deliver a new release of an application three or four days in a row, because the customer receives a new executable, and finds another thing they want changed within hours of beginning use of it. If you're working with a customer who is used to picking up the phone, requesting a change, and expecting it to be delivered the next day, you may have to work with them to evolve your process. You might want to track every change request regardless of size (I discuss details on doing this in Chapter 24, "Bug Reporting and Application Feedback," and Chapter 27, "Change Orders"). With each change, provide an estimate, and wait for the customer to approve the work. Then work with the customer to group the changes into a release (a defined list of features with a version number) that has its own testing and delivery.

By having a defined process of tracking and releasing everything at once (a release might include new enhancements as well as maintenance and bug fixes), there is a lot less of the "onesey-twosey" requests sneaking in and your not getting recognized or paid for the effort.

My shop had this problem with a couple of customers, one for whom we developed a major version 2.0 application, and another for whom we developed a series of 15 or so separate, but interconnected applications. We had to move both of these customers onto a tracking system so that we could group change requests and actually get work done instead of constantly delivering upgrades to put out the "fire of the moment."

Once we did this, we stopped having the problem of our customers beating on us about why some feature wasn't getting implemented or some bug wasn't fixed. We could explain it was because they were also requesting us to do all this little stuff instead… and here is the log to prove it. Once they learned how to work with us on the tracking database, they actually liked seeing what was being done—they felt a new sense of control over their application and they started to help define releases. Because they do have to sign off to have something implemented, they now pay attention and participate in what is going on.

It also reduced conflicts between different users, because there were no surprises when a new feature went in and the person who requested it was happy but it stomped on some other user in another department. It improved our customer relations significantly and eliminated surprises.

Location

Maintenance is subject to the same considerations as the previous types of development discussed—if it's possible to have a complete copy of the app off-site, then maintenance can be done off-site as well. The one danger that becomes more important to consider is the "small fix" that is performed on-site and implemented without proper testing. We've all heard stories of how making "one small change" brought down a whole system because proper regression testing wasn't performed.

Pros and cons

Maintenance is often the work given to junior programmers—no design or analysis, just rooting around in someone else's code to fix the mess they left behind, or to make routine, uninteresting changes. And you sometimes have to put up with an irritated customer at the same time. But some people thrive on this work—the challenge of hunting down an arcane bug or touching up something "just so" is what they live for.

Maintenance is largely undefined, and as such isn't part of the charter of this book, so I won't be addressing it after Chapter 4, "Choosing a Process."

Troubleshooting

On the same level, but definitely a different beast, is software development troubleshooting.

Definition

Troubleshooting is the homeowner's equivalent of calling the plumber in the middle of the night because there's water leaking from the upstairs bathroom, it's already ruined most of the furniture in the living room, and it's making its way to the bookcases in the den.

When an application blows up, stops working, or starts spewing out garbage, this is the time the troubleshooting developer gets called in. I have seen huge magnitudes of difference in the abilities of programmers to troubleshoot and fix problems. I consider troubleshooting to be a high art—a combination of intuitive grasp of the system design, excellent memory for all the complex inter-relationships of a complex system, the dogged determination to work through tough problems, and the ability to become "one with the machine," a Vulcan Mind Meld with an application, a Pinball Wizard of bits and bytes.

A colleague of mine relates this classic troubleshooting story:

One of our top developers got called in on a problem with a fairly complex application he had written a year before. All the basic data was correct, but on one report, incorrect values appeared in one column. The client was trying to compare the equivalent of apples and oranges, and the report required a complex grouping, sequencing, and rolling-up of the data. The problem came from a data modeling decision made years before, a decision that was a choice between different ways to store and accumulate data, but it meant that this particular column of information was very difficult to calculate.

The system had been in live production for nearly a year, and a major change to the system, with the requisite testing, was not in the best interests of the client. Also, since this error occurred only rarely, and had not significantly affected the customer's business, great effort to fix it was not called for. The developer pored over the data design documents, the source code, and the specifications, and browsed a copy of the live data to understand all of the permutations of the problem. The developer came up with, considered, and rejected four different approaches to solving the problem before arriving at the optimal change.

He opened the pre-processing program for the report, and changed two lines of code—one that created a temporary index on a working cursor, and the second that searched that index—recompiled the application, tested the change, regression tested the app, and shipped it to the client. Net work: about three and a half days. Amount of time saved over the other alternatives: about three weeks. Result: happy client.

Skills required

Troubleshooting skills range even further afield than those of a maintenance programmer—an excellent—or even better!—command of the language or tool is essential, but so is the ability to mollify an upset customer. Akin to a brilliant physician with no bedside skills, a troubleshooter without corresponding people skills shortchanges himself as well as the customer.

You've probably heard the story of the fellow who takes his expensive, high-tech car into the auto mechanic because of a funny noise emanating from the engine compartment. The mechanic listens to the engine for a few minutes, opens the hood, reaches in with a screwdriver, and turns a screw a half-turn. The noise is gone. The mechanic hands the owner a bill for $75, and the owner goes ballistic. "$75 for turning a screw a half-turn?" "No, I only charged you $0.35 for turning the screw. The $74.65 was for knowing which screw to turn, and how far to turn it."

Same thing goes for the developer involved in troubleshooting projects—it's knowing where to look inside the hundreds or thousands of programs, and, once the program responsible is found, what line in that program to change to fix the program—not actually just typing a new line of code.

Time span

The time span for a troubleshooting gig can vary widely—from a half hour, similar to listening to the engine and turning a screw a half-turn, to days or weeks, where you turn off the water, tear out the entire ceiling, find the rotten pipe, replace all the plumbing piping and fixtures, and then rebuild the ceiling and damages below.

Location

By definition, the trouble is coming from a live system. Given that you probably aren't there when problems are occurring, you'll have to either troubleshoot remotely or make an on-site visit. If it's involving hardware, on-site may be more likely, while with software, there are a lot of tools and communication devices to rely on. And an experienced troubleshooter asking the right questions ("Is the computer plugged in? Is it turned on? Is the monitor turned on?") may make all the difference in the world.

Pros and cons

Troubleshooting can be exciting work—but that's another way of saying "stressful." I know of one fellow who plays the developer's version of Red Adair—the fellow who puts out oil field fires all over the world. Our friend thinks nothing of getting a noon-time call from a client in trouble, and being on a plane with two associates, headed for another continent, just hours later. In fact, he lives for it!

On the other hand, wearing a pager, carrying two cell phones, and being available 25 hours a day isn't for everybody. Some folks need a normal life, free from workplace pressures while they take their kids to the park or play cards with the neighbors.

Troubleshooters—assuming they can fix the problem—get to play hero, and receive a hero's accolades. Of course, they may also end up, like Charlie Brown, the goat if they can't get the job done.

Troubleshooting, by definition, is unstructured, and as such isn't part of the charter of this book, so I won't be addressing it after Chapter 4, "Choosing a Process."

Audits

Every once in a while, a customer asks you in to "take a look at our current system and tell us what you think." This situation, the application audit, more so than most, is fraught with peril, but with the increased risk, comes a sizable potential reward.

Definition

A specialized type of consulting, an audit has a specific deliverable—a written evaluation of an existing piece of software. This often is part of the evaluation of an existing system that is being considered for upgrade, conversion, or replacement, and the outcome of the audit may play a large part in the decision of what to do with the current system.

Skills required

A wide range of skills—from the ability to review a business's processes and determine whether the application matches those processes, to the nitty-gritty of spelunking through directories full of aged, arcane files and examining code—is needed to properly perform an audit.

As with a rewrite, auditing an existing application also requires political skills to walk that fine line between telling the truth and offending the customer.

Time span

An audit is a quick job, usually requiring anywhere from a couple of hours to a full day of work, but rarely more than that.

Location

The audit is usually conducted at the customer's site, as their live application is the target of the audit.

Pros and cons

An audit is tricky to pull off successfully. One reason is because of the balance you have to strike between telling the truth about the state of the app and being cognizant of the investment that the company has made in the app—they don't want to be told that they spent money foolishly or needlessly.

 Another reason is that the auditor is in a precarious position in terms of being objective. Most often, the audit is brought up as an aside to the sales process of other work. Thus, the results of an audit can appear to be self-serving. If you trash the app too much, it can appear that you're just trying to garner more work for yourself. On the other hand, if you sugarcoat the results, you may be stuck with working on an application that you actually feel should be replaced or rewritten. Appendix A (included in the downloads) covers the application audit in full detail, and thus it won't be addressed further in the body of this book.

Hourly consulting

There are situations where the work that needs to be done can either be a mishmash of requirements—some bug fixes, some new features, some upgrades, some changes—but there isn't a discrete deliverable anywhere in sight. In these cases, what the customer wants is a body on-site to work on an hourly basis until the tasks are completed or they've run out of money. About the only way to describe the deliverable is "Do what I tell you to do and stop when I tell you to stop."

This type of work often goes well past the realm of software development. For example, it may include training or mentoring work—helping to show others how to develop applications or acting as a "Mr. Wizard" for programmers who have questions. It may also expand into general computer consulting—setting up and troubleshooting computer networks, installing and configuring software, or any number of other computer-related tasks.

As a result, this work is done on an hourly basis, and as such, doesn't fit in with the charter of this book. Indeed, it really doesn't even require more explanation. Again, I won't be addressing it after Chapter 4, "Choosing a Process."

Chapter 3
Types of Processes

"There is more than one way to skin a cat, and the approach you take depends on how much of the cat you want left. It also depends on whether you're after the cat or the skin."—Anonymous

Just as the earlier editions of this book were targeted at a specific group of developers, they were also targeted at a specific type of process—the so-called waterfall method. But not all development fits into this one method, any more than all developers are the same or all development is the same. In this chapter, I'll discuss what your options are for developing a custom software application.

The processes for software development make up a spectrum not unlike the color spectrum. In the color spectrum, colors evolve from red to orange to yellow to green to blue. However, there is no specific point that you can define as "blue" or "yellow"—there are many shades of yellow, some that are full of orange, and others with a markedly greenish tint. Nonetheless, if I tell you that I'll pick you up in a yellow car, you know roughly what to look for. My car might be a bright yellow taxicab, or a washed-out-yellow Civic, or a mustard-yellow Corvette—but you know I won't be showing up in a black Grand Prix or a white mini-van. The term "yellow" defines a range of possibilities.

Similarly, the software development processes range from highly structured methodologies at one end to free-form, every-man-for-himself cowboys hacking at the other. In between the two end-points are types of processes—Rapid Application Development and Extreme Programming, to name two—that, like colors, don't identify an exact point in the spectrum, but rather serve as markers for areas along the spectrum.

Different processes have different requirements, both from the customer's point of view as well as with respect to the developer. As the software developer, you'll be charged with determining which type of process is most appropriate for a given situation. In order to do so, you need to be familiar with what the possible processes are in the first place.

Structured development (the waterfall method)

Structured development, or the waterfall method, gets its name from a visual interpretation of the process. A waterfall starts in one place, and then descends to a second level, and then a third, and then a fourth, but never goes back to a previous level.

The waterfall method of software development follows the same path. It starts out with an analysis of the problem, determining the requirements of the solution, and then moves on to a design of the solution, then the development (programming) of the design, then the testing, repair, and modification based on the testing, and, finally, the implementation.

In many cases, each of these functions is performed by a different person; indeed, many times by separate groups or departments. Each step must end before the next one begins, and the customer must sign off on successful completion of the stage via a formal acceptance process before the next step begins.

This process came about early on in the computer age because it was the only possible way to develop software back then, and because the people doing it were trained in other disciplines and had backgrounds in other industries where this process was the norm.

The first programmers were actually hardware engineers who needed to develop software so they could test their hardware. They were used to the analysis/design/build/test/implement cycle because that's how they built the hardware.

In addition, the CPU cycle was precious, and the tools for iterative development didn't exist. You simply didn't have the luxury to slap together a program and run it, counting on the compiler to catch your bugs and errors in design—you needed to take care of those things before ever submitting your program to be run.

The advantage of the waterfall method is that it can produce solid, reliable applications that do what they are designed to do, particularly for applications that are relatively static. Furthermore, given an experienced team with a history of development, the time and dollars required to build an application can be determined with reasonable accuracy once the specification has been completed.

There are four primary downsides to the waterfall method. The first is that it takes a long time, and for much of that time, no apparent progress is made. The analysis and design meetings can seem to take forever, and then, once programming has started, there aren't many deliverables for a while.

The second is that the waterfall method doesn't provide much flexibility for change. Once the design has been completed and programming has started, modifications as a result of new requirements being discovered can't simply be added on the fly. Ordinarily, modifications are handled through a formal "Change Order" process that in and of itself can be time-consuming.

However, over time more and more tools have become available to help complete various portions of the process, and it seems that the more automation that's been introduced into the waterfall method, the more willing our users are to go back and change something that was done in an earlier phase. So, in a way, these automated tools have enabled a type of iteration that wasn't practical years ago. For example, it is easier to go back and change a database structure because of the use of some CASE tool, so 1) the team is more willing to make such a change, and 2) the customer is willing to do it because it no longer has such a negative impact to cost and schedule.

The third downside is that the waterfall method requires a level of discipline and sophistication that is hard to imbue in the PC culture. The personal computer enabled rapid iteration of projects—but since they were, in the beginning, "small" projects, they escaped notice of the formal disciplinarians in software development. Then PCs became powerful enough to do "real" applications, and the industry responded by trying to put processes that were good for mainframe projects onto small "PC" projects. When we realized we needed something, we slapped on that proven old waterfall method—now we are trying to find a happy medium where relatively small projects follow a process, and that process ideally can enable the team to meet the needs of the e-economy pressures and needs but not burden it with mountains of administration.

The fourth downfall is that the structured development process can tend to shut out users from partaking in the development process, and thus a sense of ownership isn't fostered as well as with other methodologies.

Note that many people refer to the waterfall method as "structured development," and that's how I'll refer to it in the rest of this book.

Rapid Application Development (RAD)

In a formal sense, "RAD" was coined by James Martin in the 1970s as a result of his research on software engineering. It refers to a specific approach regarding application development. In the three decades since, though, the term has been mutated in every conceivable way to the point that it's unrecognizable and virtually useless, except as a generic moniker for "cool and fast" by marketing folks.

In a rough sense, though, we can use RAD as a catch-all term for the next step in the evolution away from the waterfall method of application development. In the traditional waterfall approach, users are consulted only during the initial analysis phase. Design, developing, testing, and deployment are executed in series, and the users don't see the developer's work until the application is deployed. This, of course, makes it difficult, and very expensive, to implement changes as well as compensate for changing requirements, miscommunication, and other mistakes.

Instead of waiting to finish one phase of the development process before proceeding on to the next, what if you sketched out a rough design, and then built a prototype that acted as a model for the design? And you incorporated user input and feedback during that process? Then, with that prototype, you'd gather more formal feedback, and go back to the analysis and design phases, and improve them. You'd retool the prototype, incorporating the feedback and new features in your design.

This process, iterating between analysis, design, and prototyping, would continue until you reached one of several milestones—the improvements and changes being suggested in each pass would gradually become smaller and smaller until they could be ignored or postponed to another release, or until you ran out of time or money and had to move to programming and implementation.

The prototype application becomes an aid to analysis and design by giving the users a concrete basis on which to evaluate the performance of the application, rather than abstract diagrams and descriptions.

Depending on the type of application being built, a significant portion of the programming may have already been done during the prototyping as well.

Benefits of RAD

The prime advantage of RAD is that you get a product that is much more likely to match the users' requirements because they get to "see and touch" their application—actually working with a prototype is much different from looking at screen shots or text-based descriptions. It is also possible to get an application up and running more quickly than with the traditional waterfall method because the analysis and design can be done faster with the users' help during the prototyping, and because some of the development can be done in parallel.

But there's much more to it than that. Let's investigate the many benefits of RAD.

Customer ownership

When your users are working alongside you during the development and prototyping of the system, instead of simply listing requirements, watching you ride off, and wondering what you're going to come back with, and when, they're much more inclined to take ownership of the system.

A number of years ago, I built a system that was going to replace a DOS-based application that the company's sales reps had all been using for eight or nine years. The old system had been developed in house by a developer whose office was right down the hall from the IS director. The system was widely liked in part because it was "their" system—not something bought off the shelf or otherwise acquired.

When the company decided to contract out for the replacement, there was some nervousness as to whether the system would be as well accepted by the reps. As a result, the IS manager and the VP of sales both participated in RAD meetings every Friday throughout the winter and spring as the system was being prototyped.

When questions later came up about "the system," the two were quick to mention that it wasn't just "the system," but "our new system." The two, in fact, took some delight at customizing and enhancing pieces of the system, schmaltzing up demos for grand announcement, and acquiring doo-dads that went along with the system, such as mouse pads with the system's logo and golf shirts designed for each sales rep with the name of the system above the chest pocket.

It was very clearly "their" system even though an outside shop had developed it.

You will likely find that it is easier to engage their participation—you may even find that you can get them to do legwork more easily, because it's *their* system.

Knowledgeable users

In the same vein, when users are involved in the development process, they more quickly and more fully internalize the functionality because, after all, they were the ones who determined what that functionality would be, and had a direct hand in determining how that functionality was going to be implemented.

In the system mentioned in the previous section, the IS manager and VP of sales both led internal training classes for the sales reps and sales support staff. Since they were intimately familiar with the system, they were fully capable of showing others how to use it. And they're leading the class.

Depending on your user community, you may even be able to find people who will actually *read* your specifications and documentation (gasp!), and write the final user documentation as well.

Better testers

The third advantage to using the RAD process for this particular system was that these two individuals were also the initial beta testers, and they were able to catch bugs that involved major functionality immediately. For example, one of the modules had a price calculation screen that involved a number of very complex calculations. Since they both knew the business that the system was modeling and the system, they were able to match up expected results with actual results for a wide variety of scenarios—something that a casual ("Oh, we gotta do some more stupid testing today") tester would likely not have been able to do as thoroughly.

You'll likely find with your users that since they have taken ownership of the system from the beginning, it's in their own interest to make sure it works properly. Think about how you treat the acquisition of a brand-new car of your own vs. when you get in a rental car. You're much more likely to examine every knob and button before you drive off in your own new car. With a rental, you'll adjust the seat, make sure you know where the essential controls are, and then take off. Similarly, you're much more likely to park in an out-of-the-way spot with your brand-new car than a rental that's a couple of years old.

Same thing here—since the system isn't simply being "dumped" on them, they're going to take care of it—starting with making sure it works properly from the get-go. They'll be involved in the user acceptance testing from the start—including helping write the tests to make sure they fairly stress the system.

Multiple champions

When your users are involved from the beginning in the design and development, you'll likely not have to work as hard to "sell" the system to the user community because having people involved along the way will generate excitement. Part of that excitement will translate into your acquiring additional champions.

As I said in the beginning, you should always have a champion for your system in the user community or at the customer's site. If you're the only proponent for the system, it's near a sure bet that the first instance of complication will cause enough trouble for the system to be waylaid or abandoned altogether.

In the opposite fashion, the more champions you acquire along the way during development, the more likely that problems you encounter will not cause a derailment of your system.

Reduced fears

As the number of users who buy into the system increases, the number of fears in the user community in total goes down. Not only will the new converts not have the fears that typically accompany a new system, but the remaining "unconverted" will have their fears lessened as well, since they'll see a larger and larger number of people who are not worried about the impact of the new system.

Ease of data migration

If your system requires any sort of data migration, that process is more likely to be successful if you have users who can bridge knowledge of the old and new systems.

I have never run into a customer who actually understands what their current data looks like, or truly knows what's in it. There's always garbage in some fields, legacy fields that have never been removed, and even whole sets of garbage records that end up hanging around. As a result, if they don't truly understand their data, how are *you* going to write a conversion routine that actually works? You're going to need their help in making those decisions about how to deal with fields that contain unexpected or invalid data as well as records that shouldn't be in the system.

Better communication

No matter what type of development process you use, you're going to have to provide regular status reports to your user base or customer. Even if you're working on-site and you are in constant communication, you'll need to document your progress for a couple of reasons.

First, except when you're directly working with the president or owner of the company, those documents serve as a vehicle for your contacts to communicate to their bosses. If you don't provide status reports, your contacts will have to create them themselves, and that's going to mean extra work for them, and it's possible that the information will not be reported accurately.

Second, you'll need documentation of your progress along the way for your own records—so you can track what you're actually doing, not what you think you're doing. Remember the adage, "That which gets measured gets accomplished." If you're not measuring what you're getting done, it's too easy to fool yourself about your progress. And many a developer has moved along a "great" relationship with a customer, thinking it's okay to skip progress reports, only to be brought up short all of a sudden by a suddenly unhappy customer who demands to see the results. Don't mistake a comfortable and easygoing working relationship as tacit permission to slack off on part of your job.

Finally, in order to determine your price, as you'll learn in Chapter 17, "Calculating Time and Cost for a Specification," you need to have collected a history of your costs, which is driven in part by these status reports.

The benefit of a RAD process is not that you can skip these reports—you still need to do them, but your users or customers will have a better sense of and confidence in where you're at.

More realistic expectations

Finally, as the users work with you during the development of the prototype, you'll have ongoing opportunities to set their expectations properly—and, if you remember, that's the name of the game in this business. They're far more likely to be happy with what they get because they'll have been asking for it all along. It's a lot more difficult for your kids or your spouse to complain about the results of a shopping trip if they accompanied you on the trip than if you went alone, right? Same thing here. It's more difficult for a customer to be unhappy about the functionality and operation of a system that they've had a hand in developing than if they feel you did it all by yourself.

They'll also get a better feel for how long it takes to accomplish your work, and as they see your progress, they can better gauge how many additional things they should ask for and how long it will take you to respond.

Disadvantages of RAD

There are disadvantages, too, though. One disadvantage is that it can be tempting to prototype well past the point of diminishing returns, and never get the job done. Once users see how easy it is to make a few little changes to the prototype, it's possible for them to request iteration after iteration, in search of the "perfect" application. At some point, you'll have to say "good enough" and postpone future requests for a subsequent version.

Another disadvantage is that it's easy for customers to perceive that you're nearly done with the app simply on the basis of a few prototype screens, and it can be a difficult challenge to convince them otherwise.

Agile Methodologies

"Agile Methodologies" is a loose term that refers to any number of a variety of ultra-rapid software development techniques. They all draw from the same pool of techniques and thought processes—pair programming, immediate turnaround of small modules, writing code to small test plans that were created before the coding started, and so on.

The first Agile Methodology (AM), and probably the most mature (all of three or four years old now) was "Extreme Programming" (XP). XP is a development style created and popularized by Kent Beck as the natural evolution to RAD in answer to the faster and faster turnaround cycles demanded by the "Internet generation" of software development—vague and ever-changing requirements combined with incessant pressure to deliver "yesterday."

Its core premise is that of starting a software project with a minimalist design that is put into production immediately, and that evolves constantly to add needed functionality. The development is carried out by a pair of programmers in front of one screen, with short turnaround times, who integrate and test the whole system several times a day, and write unit tests before the modules they are to be run on, and keep those tests running at all times.

Obviously, this is a radical departure from even advanced RAD techniques of rapid design and prototyping iterations, but given the history of software development—50 years and we're still in the Stone Age—XP has gained a number of adherents who are still looking for a better way to develop applications.

The advantage of XP is that the application is put into production very quickly—no waiting for six months or a year before the user sees anything concrete. As a result, this saves time and money. By definition, an application that is ready in a month will cost less than one that is ready in a year. Additionally, features that aren't absolutely necessary are delayed until "later," and thus don't produce a cost.

The disadvantage of XP is that it requires, er, extreme discipline. Many developers will attempt to mimic XP but only implement part of the process. This is like learning to swim with one arm and one leg "tied behind your back."

There is a contingent of developers who wonder if, generally, Agile Methodologies are more ideally suited to applications that do not "do data." If you think of some early Web sites where the database back end consisted of three tables, it's easy to see where this approach could work beautifully. But it's easy to wonder how effective this approach would be if you needed to have any significant data behind it. Are Web developers still working in this manner today? Could you realistically go about this incremental a design and have a data structure worth anything?

It's difficult enough to convert a well-designed data structure to a new schema and not have huge holes or major problems after you're done, given that the philosophy behind Agile Methodologies—write a bit of code, test a bit of code, install a bit of code—pretty much requires wholesale changes to data structures on an ongoing basis.

Agile Methodologies have only been around a few years, and so can still be considered "on probation," although that pronouncement will surely earn me nasty e-mails from avid supporters of one or more of the techniques. The jury is still out on whether these are going to be good for the long haul. Still, for certain types of projects, an Agile Methodology might just be the ticket.

Benefits of Agile Methodologies

All methodologies are intended to manage risk. Structured programming/Big Design is a stern reaction to CLHASWH (discussed later in this chapter) approaches, often termed "Cowboy Coding," and attempts to manage risk by concentrating on the analysis and design phases so as to reduce to a manageable certainty the actual construction of the software. Ideally, the uncertainty of construction can be reduced to the point where the client can be quoted a fixed price and a firm delivery date by, some would say, nitpicking the details to death. In this extreme attempt to control and manage the process, the process takes precedence over delivering value, driving up costs and slowing the development process.

All software development has four major variables: resources (the people, money, and materials required), scope (what is the system expected to do when completed), time (how long it takes to complete the system), and quality (does the system do what it is expected to do).

In practice, quality is not really a variable subject to manipulation, as shortcuts that sacrifice quality for the sake of limiting costs (resources) or time-to-completion actually add to these other variables in the long term. As a result, one should regard quality as a fixed value in relation to the other three.

That said, you might consider that Agile Methodologies deal with quality in a different way than the other processes. The best definition of quality that I've ever run into has been simply "fitness for use." A rough-cast two-penny nail that you pick up at a hardware store may be of sufficient quality if you're building a doghouse in the backyard, but a finely crafted machine bolt may still not be of sufficient quality if you're using it on a space shuttle.

This "fitness for use" has two basic components: quality of design and quality of production. The design has to address the use issue, while the production has to meet the specifications of the design. A square wheel may be machined and produced perfectly to specifications (high quality), but its design (a device to enable a vehicle to travel over ground via an axle) is poor (low quality). An oblong wheel that was designed as a round wheel— the design was better quality but the production was poorer quality—would end up being a better solution.

Agile Methodologies can do a better job to produce the production of the solution, at the risk of a poorer design, because the system is being built in small pieces and thus the big picture may not be addressed until too late.

How Agile Methodologies deal with risk

Each of these variables represents certain dimensions of risk, and both structured programming and RAD fail, in some ways, to adequately manage those risks. Agile Methodologies, in general, attempt to address these issues by recognizing certain truths about the development process. As you read through this list, you should either be nodding your head knowingly, or underlining these points in bold:

- The user never has a clear idea of the requirements for the system, and determining these requirements is a process of discovery rather than documentation.

- The user will always require changes to the system during development.

- The user shouldn't be making technical decisions; developers should not make business decisions.

- The user is interested in features, not program modules.

- The user wants to see tangible results as soon as possible.

These truths create the following risks.

- The risk that the customer will spend more than they planned, wait longer than they want to, and end up with something that doesn't meet their needs.

- The risk that the developers will commit to a deadline or cost estimate on which they can't deliver.

- The risk that the developers will need to incorporate some new technology that they're uncertain of, and could jeopardize cost and delivery estimates.

- The risk that the customer will continually request changes to completed program code, delaying and/or significantly complicating the construction process.

- The risk that the overhead associated with the project will help the project feed upon itself, creating a monster of scope creep and turning the project into a death-march.

- The risk that non-technical managers will get involved in making technical decisions.

Agile Methodologies deal with these risks differently than other methodologies in that AMs were created specifically to deal with these risks head-on. Structured development was devised for the convenience of the programmer, not the customer. RAD moved along the route to an extent, and AM attempts to deal with software development methodologies to solve the customer's problem, not the programmer's problems. The others were created for the programmer's convenience. Here's how AMs deal with the risks, and attempt to compensate for the failures of other methodologies.

Risk 1: Cost overrun/extended time frame/failure to meet needs

Because the analysis and design phase of structured programming is highly uncertain (it's not unheard of for this phase to drag on for years), both the cost and time-to-completion for this phase are also uncertain. The risk is that the client will spend more than they planned, wait longer than they want to, and end up with something that *still* doesn't meet their needs. AM addresses this risk by providing something immediately, and at minimal cost, that explicitly meets the most important needs of the moment.

Risk 2: Failure to meet cost/time frame promises

With both structured development and RAD, at some point the developer quotes price and time delivery numbers, and then is committed to meet those. Given the great difficulty most development shops have in quoting reasonable numbers for these parameters (hence, this book!), it's highly likely that those numbers will not be met. AM addresses this risk by breaking down the deliverables into small entities where an overrun is less likely and doesn't have as significant an impact; reasons for overshoots can be incorporated into future deliveries in a continuous feedback loop, reducing the risk as the project progresses.

Risk 3: Incorporation of untested technology

The introduction of untested technology creates a brand-new risk: moving the system development from an engineering project to a research and development project. As a result, cost quotes become cost estimates, and not very good ones at that. Delivery quotes are similarly out the window.

AMs address this risk in the same fashion as the aforementioned Risk 1 by breaking down the deliverables into small entities, where an overrun can be contained in a small environment so that it can be studied and the rest of the project can be rescoped and measured accordingly.

Risk 4: Change requests

The analysis and design phase can span so much time that the client's business model, supply and/or distribution chains, internal organization, market, and competitors can all change during this process. This further adds to the cost and time uncertainty of this part of the project. Once analysis and design has been completed and the project has moved to the construction phase, changes may (nay, will) continue to occur, and can negatively affect code quality. The risk is that the client will continually request changes to completed program code, delaying and/or significantly complicating the construction process. AMs address this risk, again, by providing something immediately, before requirements have had time to change.

Risk 5: Process focus creates a death-march

Structured programming/Big Design can become so mired in the process that the actual delivery of working program code that meets the client's needs becomes secondary, and the analysis and design and the documentation seen as integral to the process consumes so many resources that there isn't enough left to bring the process to completion. In addition, the process actually assists in the addition of new requirements, such that the project feeds upon itself, and the process ends up encouraging scope creep instead of reducing it. The process can be complicated by numerous repetitive forms to complete, and multiple sign-offs for every requirement and specification. The risk is that the project will turn into a death-march driven by unchecked scope creep.

AMs attempt to address this risk by minimizing overhead and process constraints, instead focusing on delivery of usable functionality in short order.

Risk 6: Span of control

One of the supposed benefits of structured programming is that it allows non-programmer project managers to control a process in which they can't actively participate. There is often distrust or anxiety on the part of the client, and this can extend to the analysts and project managers who don't really understand software construction, and thus eventually also begin to distrust the developers. Bureaucratic procedures are put in place in an attempt to control the propeller-heads in development, which further slows the process and increases costs.

AMs attempt to address this risk by creating small work units where the individuals best suited for each task actually perform those tasks.

Dealing with how long and how much

The major risk factor that Agile Methodologies do not address (but handle in a manner that's often acceptable to the customer) is the age-old questions "How long?" and "How much?"

Proponents of AMs argue that these questions cannot be answered—ever—until the customer can explicitly describe what it is that is going in "the shopping basket," any more than the shopping clerk at the grocery store can tally up your bill until he sees what's in the basket. The attempt to create that explicit answer, given the ethereal nature of software development and the nature of the truths listed earlier in this section, will be met with failure until we have better tools and processes.

Proponents of AMs will argue that Agile Methodologies handle this failure in a manner that's often acceptable to the customer. Whether you agree, of course, is up to you, and depends on the situation you're involved in. The bottom line is that the customer has the final say in how well the answers to "How long?" and "How much?" need to be defined.

Comparison of Agile Methodologies with structured programming

Before proceeding with a description of how an Agile Methodology works, a discussion of the variety of AMs that exist is required. With a half-dozen books on the marketplace, Kent Beck's Extreme Programming is probably the most mature and most fully articulated of the Agile Methodologies. Others include, but are not limited to, Feature Driven Design, Adaptive Software Development, and Crystal Clear Methodology. This is not to say that XP should be the only methodology to employ. You may find that some of the practices of other Agile Methodologies represent a better fit for your shop, your clients, or your projects. However, because of the completeness of the XP model, its practices will more directly influence the remaining discussion.

Agile Methodologies differ from structured programming in one very significant way. Structured programming uses the waterfall model, and even RAD processes rely on a two-step process: specification, then development. Agile Methodologies use an iterative process from the very beginning—building a spec for a small piece of the application all the way through to delivering it, and then starting again with another spec for the next piece. The assumption of the waterfall model (as befits the engineering paradigm on which it's based) is that the development team is dealing with a static problem. However, software development is rarely dealing with a static problem.

A friend of mine once likened software development to changing the tires on a moving car. While all processes start with identification of the client's needs and a list of requirements, both structured programming and RAD processes then proceed to defining specifications and designing the entire system. Agile Methodologies, on the other hand, tend to formulate the requirements as a list of specific desired features, prioritize this list, and employ a cycle of specification, design, implementation, and delivery of each feature before proceeding to the next.

The goal of this approach is to accommodate (and even encourage) refinement, correction, and change of the requirements and specifications during the development process. As pointed out earlier, the customer's needs often change during development. Again, it's a normal and expected part of the process. The customer's needs also change as they're exposed to a working system; automation (or re-automation) of a process often changes the process, and gaps in the specifications and requirements often become apparent when the client has the opportunity to "test drive" a system.

The role of requirements and specifications

While the way in which it is expressed differs, defining the customer's need and collecting requirements is a central first step in both structured programming and an Agile Methodology.

This defines the scope of the project, and is the single most important tool for keeping the scope manageable within the constraints of the customer's budget and deadlines. Kent Beck has written that you can give your client the choice of two of the three "negotiable" variables (quality is non-negotiable): scope, cost, and time. The developers pick the third.

Defining the "wish list" scope, and then determining how much of this can be accomplished within the time or cost constraints, is the mechanism by which this most important variable is managed. If the customer wants to expand the scope, the developers can tell the client how this will affect cost or time-to-completion estimates. If the customer wants to limit cost, the developers can tell the customer what has to be trimmed from the scope. With an Agile Methodology, because the list of features is always prioritized (and re-prioritized as needed), it's usually clear that the items at the end of the list are the ones that need to go.

Specifications are also common to both approaches. This is what documents the business logic, the user interface, the work flow, and the data presentation and data collection rules for the system.

However, while both approaches rely on requirements and specifications, their role in the process is different. First, in an Agile Methodology, requirements documents and specifications are usually much less formal than in RAD processes, and certainly less than in structured programming. Their role is to facilitate communication, not control—the developers understand what the customer expects, and the customer understands what the developers are committing to deliver. Theoretically, requirements and specs could even be hand-written on index cards or the backs of envelopes. If forms are used, it is only to streamline the process, not to enforce rules about what blanks must be filled in.

Also, while requirements collection is a "first step" in the process in both structured development and Agile Methodologies, in Agile Methodologies it is revisited and manipulated at every opportunity—requirements collection is a process of discovery, not documentation. In an Agile Methodology, the requirements are used as the central mechanism for directing the development process, defining deliverables, and ensuring that the process delivers value.

As mentioned earlier, this process also continually tests how the customer values each feature. As new features are added to the list during development, the list must be re-prioritized. The choice of feature A vs. feature B is a binary decision. If added features require changes in the cost or time-to-completion estimates, or if other features must be postponed to another phase of the project or another fiscal year, the customer is forced to re-examine the value they place on each feature. Is adding feature A worth giving up feature B? Is adding a new feature worth delaying delivery by an estimated month, or adding $10,000 to the estimated cost?

To function as the central guiding force in an agile process, the requirements are prioritized, and the requirement at the top of the list is then fleshed out by the developers in cooperation with the client into detailed specifications, and the requirement is coded and delivered for the client's approval in a very short time period—usually 2-4 weeks. This process is repeated for each requirement on the list until the system is completed to the client's satisfaction.

This iterative process is the first of the two central components of an Agile Methodology, and is common to all of the Agile Methodologies with which we're familiar. The requirements can take different forms. XP uses the term "User Stories." Crystal Clear Methodology uses "Use Cases." Feature Driven Development uses a list of features. In all cases, the requirement unit is something that 1) defines a significant feature of value to the customer, and 2) is something that can be implemented in a very short time period, usually 2-4 weeks. Note that there is no relation between features and what we as developers think of as modules. The difference is one of point of view. Modules are how we see the internal organization of the system; features are how the customer sees the system's functionality.

This distinction between features and modules is important. For instance, if you're working on a system that requires an order-entry component, as a developer you're likely to get sidetracked by all of the supporting modules that are required to maintain the data that the order entry component will require—customers, vendors, products, pricing, and so on. This can take weeks in itself, and when you finally get to the order-entry component, you might discover that the specifications for some of these supporting modules were insufficient or poorly understood—a one-to-many relationship between two data entities is discovered to be a many-to-many relationship, making one of the supporting maintenance modules incorrect. Thus, instead of getting sidetracked in this manner, you recognize that the customer is most interested in that order-entry component, and concentrate on getting that piece right, and only then are you free to concentrate on the supporting modules.

Because the requirements collection is defined as customer-defined features, all of which are more or less the same "size" in terms of difficulty to implement, it's often easier for the customer to prioritize all of these features. Recognizing that this can still present problems to some customer, XP places each feature (what they call a "User Story") on an index card, and the customer is asked to arrange them on a conference table in order of importance.

A friend of mine once had a customer who, when presented with a list of features on a whiteboard, would make a list of priority numbers next to each feature. They all had "1" written next to them, but some had "1+", "1++", or circles and underlines to indicate relative importance. In other words, the customer considered all of the features important, and resisted the attempt to prioritize. Index cards arranged on a conference table forces prioritization. Even though that particular customer would probably start stacking cards in the No. 1 position, their position in the stack still indicates a priority.

The assumption here is that the system will be constructed beginning with the most important features, and progressing first through the "must have" features, then through the "important but secondary" features, and finally through the "nice to have" features. This allows the customer to rest assured that even if the budget and time resources are consumed faster than anticipated, the system will at least meet their most pressing needs. The developers too get to play a role in this prioritization process, by moving up in the priority list those features that represent significant technical risk—usually those features that require use of new or otherwise unfamiliar technologies. This allows the developers the comfort of knowing that those unfamiliar and possibly difficult features won't pile up at the end of the process.

Estimating time and costs and billing

I mentioned earlier that XP and other Agile Methodologies don't do a very good job of estimating time and costs. This is true when you're considering the entire system. However, when you're looking at each individual module, it's a different story. Because part of the strength of Agile Methodologies is that they accommodate constant change, estimating these two important numbers is difficult when considering the entire project. On the other hand,

Agile Methodologies do allow low-risk commitments to delivery date and cost for each iteration. I say "low risk" because the commitments are to a small unit of the whole project. The cost of being wrong is thus proportionately less, and there is ample opportunity to improve during the project.

Requirements collection to develop the prioritized feature list for the entire system is a very open-ended process, and must be billed hourly. This provides an incentive to the customer to ensure that their employees do their part to keep this process moving. However, the developers share this burden, requiring them to manage this process and do their part to keep the client focused and on track to complete this phase of the project as efficiently as possible. As developers, we're out to deliver maximum value, and allowing a meeting to drift to discussion of the performance of the local sports teams or last night's sitcom episode while our clock is running does not fulfill this responsibility very well. It's tricky to get a client back on track once this thread drift occurs—the first few times. But as with anything, with practice you'll be able to get them marching again in short order.

Once this feature list is completed to everyone's satisfaction, regardless of what medium was used to document the process, the list becomes a deliverable and the client is billed for this work.

Similarly, the first step of each iteration is compiling the specifications or manufacturing instructions for the feature being implemented. Again, this is a smaller, but no less open-ended process, and must be billed hourly. However, once the manufacturing instructions are complete, you can determine how many people you are going to devote to this iteration, and commit to a fixed price and delivery date in writing. The client has a document that describes what you've committed to completing, and you have a recipe to use over the next 2-4 weeks to deliver it.

When the feature is completed, the latest build of the system is delivered to the customer for their review (along with the source code if that is part of your agreement), and it's accompanied by an invoice that details the hours spent compiling the manufacturing instructions, the cost for those hours, a description of the feature that was implemented, and the agreed-upon cost for that feature.

You might employ a "Specifications Document" that allows you to quickly wrap up a specification meeting and get to work on the actual construction of an iteration. This document can identify the participants in the specification meetings and the dates of the meetings, and will serve to inform the customer right away what they'll be billed for this work—both the hourly work to develop the specification, as well as the fixed cost for the finished feature when delivered.

Code Like Hell And See What Happens (CLHASWH)

Finally, migrating to the far end of the spectrum extends this trend of less design while getting your hands on the keyboard quicker and results in the "Code Like Hell And See What Happens" approach.

Every developer has heard the joke where the pointy-haired boss from "Dilbert" says to his team of programmers, "I'll find out what the users want. In the meantime, while you're waiting, you guys start coding." Unfortunately, like many stereotypes, this one has its roots too firmly planted in reality to be funny.

Sadly enough, and, unfortunately, encouraged by a lot of cowboy programmers, the first thing many companies expect to see upon engaging a software developer is some programs. Sounds reasonable enough, right? You hired a programmer, you should get some programs.

The advantage of CLH is immediate gratification—the engagement starts at 8 AM, and programs start to appear at 9:30 or 10 that morning. The disadvantage is that the programs produced are poorly designed, badly constructed, don't meet more than a superficial set of user requirements, and can't be maintained with less than a superhuman effort. By the time these problems are discovered, though, the CLH programmer is long gone, ready to wreak the same havoc on another unsuspecting customer.

Conclusion

Like the color spectrum, the choices of process available to the software developer range from the tightly structured process to the cowboy style of coding. They each have their place, but it's important to understand the pros and cons of each, and which type you're best suited for, for a particular application and set of customer requirements. And it's even more important to be able to communicate the resulting expectations to your customer.

Chapter 4
Choosing a Process

"You must choose wisely."—Guardian of the Holy Grail
  —Indiana Jones and the Last Crusade

Now that I've identified the types of projects and processes that make up the gamut of software development, it's time to discuss how to mix and match them. When you first talk to a customer, they probably don't know any of this. It's likely that all they know is that they want some software development work—of some sort—done. It's up to you to determine what type of project they've got, and to either educate them as to the available possibilities, or just choose yourself and present the best option to them. But you need to know what the options are first, and then you have to know how to present them to your customer. That's what I'm going to cover in this chapter.

The purpose of this chapter is two-fold. First, it's to show you how to choose a development process—what things to consider, and what options you have. But that's the easy part and, frankly, one that you may not need that much help with.

The second purpose of this chapter is to help you deal with your customer during this process. In some situations, you'll choose yourself, and then simply make a proposal to the customer. Particularly if you've got a certified process, you may not be able to offer them any flexibility, because you would stand to lose your certification.

In other cases, you'll present several possibilities, and work with the customer to choose. In both of these situations, though, it can get tricky—not every customer has all that much common sense. It's easy for you to decide yourself—but not quite as easy to maintain the strength of your conviction when you're looking at a six-figure project, but the customer is being irrational or asking for unreasonable things.

In many cases, you should work hard to have your customer understand what your process is and why it benefits them. If you can show them this much organization, you will likely blow them away.

It's very easy for a customer to want to pick and choose pieces of various processes, as if they were ordering from a smorgasbord. You and I both know it doesn't work like that, but they don't, and, often, they don't care, either. So it can become a contentious meeting, and you have to be able to argue first, rationally, about why one thing will work and another will not, and then be able to stand your ground and just say No if they insist on an irrational decision.

I wish I had a nickel for every story where the development group got suckered into a fixed-price job without having a fixed spec. In most of the cases, the sales guy got the client to sign the contract, gave them a number of, say, $245,000, and the only details were a two-page memo describing a vague idea of an e-commerce or distributed sales processing system.

So that's what I'm going to do—provide you with ammunition if it comes down to a confrontation.

Before I begin, though, I need to mention that this chapter is not an exact flow chart where I ask a series of Yes/No questions and lead you to the magic answer. There is too much variability and imprecision in software development, not to mention your varied experience level, which I cannot gauge, for that to work. Instead, what I can do is present and organize a number of considerations that you can use to help organize your own thoughts and make a better choice.

I also want to mention here that you don't want to play newbie teacher with this process. I'm referring to the brand-new teacher who reads the lesson the night before presenting it to the class. Read this entire book before undertaking this choosing process. If you choose based solely on what you've read so far, you're going to miss the details later on that you'll need to make the best choice. Read the whole book so you understand the whole process, not just the overview presented here. Then read this section a second time to get the choosing process fresh in your mind again.

Type of project

Part of your role as a software developer, assuming you're part of the initial meetings with the customer, is to provide analysis of the customer's situation and then propose a solution. Since this book is about software development, it would be logical to assume that the fundamental solution is going to be a piece of software.

That may or may not be true, but determining that either a new or upgraded piece of software is indeed the answer is a fairly easy conclusion to reach. The next decision, though, is much more difficult, because the variables that come into play in making the decision are more complex, but also because explaining the choices to the customer is significantly more difficult.

I'll cover the initial contacts with the customer in the next few chapters, but first it's time to discuss how to do the analysis yourself so that you're prepared when you come into contact with the customer.

Generally, a customer doesn't really care about buying software. They care about solving a problem they're having, and figure that some sort of computer hardware/software combination is the way to do it. Given the pervasiveness of computers, they've probably given this some thought and so have an idea of the type of software they need. Furthermore, in that they've contacted you—a specialist in development software—it's likely that they understand that they're looking for custom software of some sort, but not necessarily.

Thus, the first question you'll have to ask is what they're looking for. Do they want you to write a new software application for them? Do they want you to modify, upgrade, convert, or replace an existing application? Do they want you to simply provide some sort of up-to-now unspecified services to solve a problem (or problems) they're currently having with their current software?

Closely aligned with this question are the dual issues of time and budget. You'll need to determine what type of time frame and what size budget they've got in mind at the same time that you're asking about the type of software development services they want.

A customer may not know the answers to these three questions—type of development, time span, and budget—or they may not be, particularly in the case of budget, willing to share them with you. I'll cover specific strategies for helping them determine these answers, or in the case of a reticent customer, getting this information out of them, in the chapters on The Initial Contact and The Sales Call.

For now, though, I'll assume that I've got at least rough ideas of the answers.

Type of process

At this stage of the relationship, the table is usually wide open for possibilities, so it's the best time to provide the customer with the possible routes to take during this process. In order to do so, you need to know what the possibilities are up front, so that you can guide the customer appropriately.

As described in the previous chapter, you have basically four choices: structured development, some sort of RAD approach, XP, or simply "CLH." Which one you choose depends on your own abilities as well as the requirements of your customer.

Your own abilities

Naturally, I mean "you" in the big-picture sense—if you're a sole practitioner, the first person singular is appropriate, but if you're part of a bigger shop, I'm referring to the whole group involved in the project.

You have to ask yourself: Do you have the ability to handle the type of project and perform the type of process involved? XP requires a two-developer team in front of the computer, while a waterfall process for a very large project requires significant experience in analysis and design.

Customer requirements and attributes

What are the specific attributes of your customer? Each customer has specific priorities, requirements, and abilities that will help you narrow in on one possibility and remove others from contention.

Do they have a fixed budget?

Believe it or not, not all customers have a fixed budget for a project. They may have a business need so pressing that the price, no matter what it is (within some sort of reason), is miniscule compared to the alternative, or that the upside is so large that the price pales.

For example, back in 1999, some companies found themselves behind the eight-ball as the end of the year approached due to software that was not Year 2000 compliant. For these folks, whether the project cost was $40,000 or $400,000 didn't really matter—the alternative was shutting down on January 1, and either losing more than that in sales each day, or even watching the company fold.

This can also be true if they must meet some sort of government compliance (taxation, emissions level tracking…) or adhere to legal requirements—they have little or no choice about what can be done and sometimes only slightly more choice over how it can be done.

Another example is more cheerful. You may be able to save a company significant amounts of money due to the automation of a specific function or task—compared to the $300,000 to $500,000 a year that the company will save, whether the cost of your application is $80,000 or $120,000 doesn't really matter a great deal.

Do they have a fixed deadline?

As mentioned earlier, a looming deadline may be paramount. The deadline may be imposed from outside, and thus be non-negotiable, such as the Year 2000 target date was. On the other hand, it may be imposed from outside, but while not non-negotiable, still be a fixed deadline that represents an opportunity. For example, an application that has to go live concurrently with the start of a sports season could potentially wait until next year, but the lost opportunities from missing a full year may make that no choice at all. The league certainly isn't going to postpone a sports season simply because some software programmer missed their deadline.

A deadline may also be imposed from within. A vice president wants the application done before he goes on vacation. The application has to be shown at the annual sales convention although it has nothing to do with the sales convention. The system has to be ready so it can integrate with the upgrade of the network planned six months from now. And so on.

Finally, the deadline may be reasonable, or not. In the case of an unreasonable deadline, the customer is usually loath to sacrifice any other part of the project, preferring the sacrifice to come from the developer's hide. As you well know, the sacrifice will eventually be made from the project, either in terms of features or quality.

Some deadlines are just silly; the result of an executive trying to throw his weight around. Other deadlines are important, but not life-threatening. Still others are critical. Thus, speed of development and deployment may be the first priority, ahead of budget, features, and quality.

How critical is quality?

As much as every company would like to think that quality is "Job One," most often it takes a backseat to budget, deadlines, and other constraints. Applications that have known bugs can often be worked around through other mechanisms, and that may be a more efficient route in getting the application shipped. For instance, an order entry system may have an error in the calculation used to produce a subtotal when more than two credit memos show up on the same invoice. However, this particular situation may happen so rarely that the customer decides it's not worth spending a half-day or a day trying to track the problem down.

In some cases, though, quality is paramount, and other requirements are clearly secondary. Software for the space shuttle, as well as medical devices and other mission-critical applications—24-hour-a-day financial trading systems and online order entry systems are two that come to mind—requires a very high degree of reliability. It is likely that a sole programmer with a Code Like Hell approach wouldn't be successful with this type of system.

The point is that shipping is a feature. It can be beneficial to release software even if there are known issues because they are not so critical that they will do harm, and the other features the users will get are so beneficial that the software should be released, and then you work on resolving the problems in a subsequent release. For some applications, of course. Can you picture mission control radioing the Apollo spacecraft: "Neil, take your time on the moon. We aren't quite done coding the landing sequence. We'll upload a new BIOS to you when we're ready."

How involved do they want to be?

Companies have different capabilities for wanting to be, and being able to be, involved in the development process. And these are two different things. A company may want to be intimately involved, but lack the capabilities, either know-how or resources or political acumen, to do so successfully. You've probably heard the line, when a developer is asked how long a task will take, "Two days. Or five if you stand behind me and second guess everything I do."

At the same time, you might decide that you want to have at the very least some minimal level of customer involvement, but if you have to legislate that, well, it's difficult to legislate an attitude.

Find out whether they want to be involved during the process, and, if so, what personnel they have available, and to what extent.

How involved can they be?

Once a customer has indicated they want to be involved, and has proposed their personnel, find out the skill level of those people, and whether they are appropriate matches.

How well defined is the project?

Some projects are extremely well defined, to the point that the major portion of the work is actually just writing the code and testing it. Many other projects, though, are still in the dream stage—where the customer has ideas of what they want, and a folder full of screenshots of other applications that do what they want ("except for this one thing here").

Do they have an appreciation for software development? Do they buy in?

Some customers are fairly sophisticated in terms of software development—they've been through this before, or may even be veteran developers themselves. Others, on the other hand, want nothing to do with it—preferring that you pull a rabbit out of your hat at the end of the project. And still others go so far as to disdain the process, thinking it trivial or unimportant. (Ed Esber, president of Ashton-Tate, the folks responsible for dBASE, earned the enmity of all of his technical employees in the late 1980s when he declared that his programming staff was no more important to the company than the janitors.)

Beyond the question of whether or not you want to work with a company with this attitude, you should consider whether you *can* work with them.

Considerations for choosing

As I mentioned earlier, there isn't a rigorous flow chart of how to choose which process; rather, I can offer some guidelines and considerations.

The first consideration is the company itself—the organization and culture. For example, a highly regimented company where all decisions are passed through committee upon committee may well freak out if you suggest an Agile Methodology, while a "dot-com" organization may easily choke on the structure and formal processes required with a waterfall process.

Consider how your customer runs their own business—specifically in terms of how they ensure quality in their own products. Do they have highly structured engineering and quality control departments, or do they shoot from the hip, accepting shoddy quality and the resulting ongoing loss of customers and requirements for replacing bad units simply as a cost of doing business?

Structured development

Structured development is best when:

- The project is large and/or very complex.

- The customer has a high level of requirements already defined.

- They have a fixed budget.

- They have a fixed, but not rushed, time frame.

- They have a high need for quality.

- They do not want or need to be involved during the development.

- They do not have a high level of sophistication (note that the reverse is not true—a high level of sophistication does not preclude the use of structured development).

Rapid Application Development

RAD is best when:

- The customer has a high level of requirements already defined, although this could be less than structured development.

- They do not have a fixed budget.

- They have a fixed, but not rushed, time frame.

- They have a high need for quality.

- They do want to and can be involved during the development.

- They have a high level of sophistication.

Extreme Programming

XP is best when:

- The customer does not have a high level of requirements already defined.

- They do not have a fixed budget.

- They have a rushed time frame.

- They have a high need for quality.

- They do want to and can be involved during the development.

- They have a high level of sophistication or a high level of acceptance of iteration.

Code Like Hell And See What Happens

CLHASWH is never best. However, it may be the only route to take given a customer's particular requirements. I'll discuss how to protect yourself from the inevitable problems that arise from using this type of process in later chapters.

Conclusion

You'll need to read this whole book first before making the choice. This section is here to introduce you to the spectrum of development processes. You have to get more involved in each of them before you can advise a customer. You need to understand what you're getting into.

Section II:

Starting
Out

Remember when you started programming in the visual environment?

It wasn't as easy as loading your development tool or programming language editor, writing some code, and then compiling and running it. You had to find the form designer, and figure out how to place visual controls on the form, and where to put code that would execute in any one of a thousand places, and how to manipulate one control from another. And then you had to find how to run that form, and how to attach it to a menu, or how to call another form from it, and how to run reports, and how to handle contention when more than one user wanted to get at the same data at the same time.

There often didn't seem to be any rhyme or reason to the process. Unlike procedural programming, where Line One logically led to Line Two, visual programming seemed to be made up of a lot of disjointed pieces that all interacted with each other on the same level as opposed to an obvious hierarchy. Eventually, of course, you figured it out, or you had someone show you how, or you found a book that had an example that was pretty close to what you wanted to do.

Starting and running a software development shop is much the same—lots of stuff to learn that doesn't seem to follow one step after another. If you're considering a move into software development as an independent, this section will show you how to get started. First, I'll discuss some issues that you should consider before making the move. Then, once I've failed to dissuade you from making the jump, I'll give you a road map for preparing for the life and work of an independent, and show you how to set yourself up to maximize your chances for success. This is the information I wish I'd had when I started.

Chapter 5
Are You Ready?

"Ready, fire, aim!"—Anonymous

This chapter begins at the beginning—before you start a jump into the world of the independent software developer. Custom software development as an independent is very hard work, and you need to gain a significant advantage over your current situation for the change to be worthwhile. In this chapter, I'll explore various factors you'll need to take into consideration before you quit your day job and become a one-man shop.

There's a classic Doonesbury cartoon where Mike is telling his elementary-school-age daughter what he did during the day. "First, I watched some C-SPAN. Then I answered the mail, downloaded some files, and, finally, untangled the phone cord." "Wow, Daddy!" she responds. "Well, don't be fooled, honey. The life of a consultant isn't always so glamorous."

Just like Mike's daughter, your expectations of what the life of a consultant is like may not be completely realistic. You may hear of consultants making $100, $125, $150 or more per hour. You do the mental math—2,000 hours a year times whatever hourly rate you're thinking of, and *voilà!* You're suddenly picking out the color of your Ferrari and deciding which type of Jacuzzi you want on your yacht.

Well, it's not that easy. You don't want to quit your day job simply because you think you're going to be able to take off early Friday afternoons, stop dealing with a dopey boss, and rake in dollar bills by the bushel baskets.

Deciding to make the jump

Just as with any decision, you'll want to weigh the pros and cons to becoming an independent. And, since this is a bigger decision than, say, buying stonewashed vs. black jeans, it bears a lot of scrutiny. After all, you're talking about how you're going to make your living, support your family (if you have one), and change your career path.

In the next few pages, I'll lay out some pros and cons for you. You can evaluate them yourself, prioritizing them as appropriate for your situation. I would suggest that you do so, and then lay the page aside for a bit—a few days, a week, or more—and then look at the list again. Once the heat of the battle has subsided, look at the list again, and re-evaluate whether or not you've fairly judged the items. What may have looked attractive two weeks ago when you were fed up with a pointy-haired boss may not be as compelling an argument for ditching your job now.

People buy things because they are dissatisfied with the status quo. They're in pain—they're hungry, so they buy food. They're cold, so they buy clothes. They're bored, so they buy entertainment.

Similarly, people make changes because the status quo isn't satisfying anymore. However, in this case, it's not just because they're in pain—the human condition is to continually, forever, endeavor to improve one's position and stage in life. You're certainly not considering a new job in order to make things worse for yourself, are you? Even if you're considering leaving your current job in order to escape a bad scene, it comes right down to trying to improve your lot in life.

Let's assume that you have a 9-5 (ha ha!) position as an employee for a company. I'll lay out some good reasons—and bad reasons—for making the move.

Making the move

Why do you want to move?

Many people quit a job because they're running away and not running toward a situation. While the purpose of this book—or even this chapter—is not to provide career advice, I'd be remiss if I didn't at least mention this idea. The grass isn't always greener, though it may seem that way during a bad spell at your current job.

> *A fellow murdered his wife and her lover. He was leaving town, having gotten away with it so far, but was pulled over. The officer, well known to the man, may or may not even have known about the murders, and might have pulled the car over for something else altogether. The man had a gun on the seat next to him. The murderer's quandary was whether to shoot the cop and try to escape, shoot himself and be done with it all, or give up without a fight. He gave himself up. Asked later about his decision, the fellow explained, "I had to know what happened next."*
>
> *The moral of this story is that you can always decide to quit tomorrow—don't make the decision during an emotional rush.*

No matter how bad something seems at your current position, remember two things. First, it could get better. And, second, it could get worse. The point is that it's generally a bad idea to make a job change from an emotional point of view. Rash decisions rarely pay off.

Good reasons

The best reason is because the change will help you better accomplish the goals you've set down for your life. If you haven't already, it would be a good idea to take stock of your life now and decide what you want to do with the rest of it. Richard Bolles' *What Color is Your Parachute* has been the classic job-hunter's manual for more than 30 years, and his advice is still as valid today as it was when he first penned the words.

Let's examine what some of these good reasons might be.

Compensation: "Show me the money!"

Most of us work because we need the money. As an independent consultant, you have the potential to make more money. Note that this isn't a given—and there are plenty of consultants out there who return to the employee-for-hire world because they, for one reason or another, didn't make the big bucks they thought they would.

But when you work for someone else, you can pretty much count on your paycheck each payday. With the consulting life, "payday" often becomes "pray-day"—you pray that the check from a customer arrives before you have to make the house payment or put a deposit on your son's braces.

On the other hand, as your own boss, you have nearly unlimited potential. Many of us know of a peer who "started his own company," worked like crazy for a while, and then sold the shop to another company and retired while his kids were still in grade school.

Freedom: "But I have weekends off."
In the movie *Arthur*, Dudley Moore, the scion of a wealthy family, is asked what he "does." He responds, "I play tennis, I race cars, and I fondle women." And then, as if needing to justify such demands, he adds, "But I have weekends off, and I am my own boss."

The ability to schedule your own time is, in my mind, the key benefit to being an independent consultant. Money comes and money goes (particularly with a house, a spouse, and kids), but the ability to control when you do whatever it is you do is paramount to achieving job (and life) satisfaction.

Control: "I am my own boss."
Similar to the previous reason, being able to decide which projects you take on is an important benefit to being self-employed. If you're just starting out, you may feel compelled to take on every project that shows up at your door—but eventually, most consultants end up with more work than they can handle. At this point, you're in the catbird's seat—being able to pick and choose what jobs you want to undertake.

The reasons you pick a particular job vary, of course—one fairly boring gig may pay exceedingly well, while another won't prove to be terribly profitable, but it gets your foot in the door of a company, or a technology, that you want to be involved with.

Job security: "Do you feel lucky?"
There's another aspect of being your own boss, and that's that you can't be fired in the same way as when you're an employee of another company. It sounds funny to use "job security" as an advantage, but if you set up your consultant practice properly, you should always have several projects going at the same time. Then, if one suddenly shuts down, you've still got others to work on. You may experience some "downtime," but more often than not, your other projects will be more than happy that you have additional time for them. Just be sure, of course, to keep looking for another gig to keep your plate full.

New projects: "Said something about a new line of work."
Another advantage to going independent is the possibility of greater access to the types of projects you want to work on. The situation of many employees reminds me of the quandary of the fruit-cart owner at the end of *LadyKillers* once his cart has been upended in a brawl: "He said something about a new line of work." You may be limited to the types of projects you can work on when employed by someone else, or you may be forced by corporate circumstances to work on projects you're not interested in—the only thing in your way when you're independent is your own ability to do the work and the availability of projects in that area.

It's not unusual for an employer to maintain a number of systems in "legacy" mode, written in a language several generations old, and do minimal maintenance on those systems. If you're employed with such a firm, you may be chomping at the bit to work in the newest hyper XMVR meta-language development tool, but not see an opportunity at your current employer. If it doesn't look like that will happen at your current firm, that may be a good reason to look around. Bear in mind, however, that they don't call it the bleeding edge for nothing. While you don't want to be stuck in some backwater where all you know how to do is maintain the same old system, you may not want to be too far out on the edge.

Bad reasons

There are lots of bad reasons to leave a job as well as to become a consultant. Some are germane to any job change, and the rest revolve around unrealistic expectations of the consulting lifestyle ("I'll save the world, get the girl, and be home in time for dinner!").

Avoiding bad situations: "Run away!"

As King Arthur and his band of merry men found in *Monty Python and the Holy Grail*, simply running away from a bad situation rarely helped them—they found themselves in another mess as soon as they turned around. It's tempting to think, when confronted with a problem at your day job, that you won't have the same problem as a consultant.

For example, "I won't have to deal with those dunderheads once I'm on my own." True, you won't have to deal with *those* dunderheads, but you'll have to deal with a whole new bunch, sometimes a different bunch each week, like a bad sitcom.

Perhaps you're thinking that you want to get away from all the red tape and bureaucratic paperwork and just do what you love—development. And you're absolutely right—you'll have all the time you want to crank out software—as soon as you fill out the time sheet from yesterday, and send out the invoices for the work you did last week, and handle the month's financial statements and quarterly tax filings, and renew business licenses, and find the warranty on the printer that just went belly up, and review the specifications for the work you're about to undertake, and review the contract for the new project you hope you win next week.

Furthermore, when you're a full-time employee, your employer has some constraints when it comes to removing you. As a result, you can get away with certain behavior that, while a nuisance to your employer, isn't enough for them to wage war and terminate you. A customer is under no such restrictions. All you need is one bad meeting with a customer, and you'll find that six-month project you were working on has been shelved while they find someone else to take your place.

Compensation: "Show me the money!"

Just because you have the potential to make more money doesn't mean you will. You have two parts of the income statement to manage as a consultant. First, there's the income side. What if you just don't find the work? When you're a consultant, technical skills are just part of the game. You need to be able to find—and obtain—projects. And you have to perform so that they keep you on for the life of the project—and the next one, and the one after that.

What if you do a lot of work for a customer that goes out of business, or stiffs you? The landscape is littered with many former consultants who got left holding a $10,000 or $20,000 or $30,000 invoice, and a customer standing behind his $500/hour lawyer saying, "So sue me!"

It doesn't take too many of these projects to put you in a hole from which you'll never recover. You need to be able to generate the business and then collect the income for that work—two tasks that are significantly different from writing specs, cutting code, and picking up a paycheck every other Friday.

And sooner or later you'll realize that the week you were going to take off to work on the garage, or take the kids to Wally World, or the four days at a developer's conference—all the time you're away, you're not working, and so you're not earning.

Keeping the money: "How much did you blow this time?"

The other side of the income statement has expenses on it. Benefits for a full-time employee can account for as much as 40% of salary—many new consultants are shocked to see $500 or $1,000 going out the door each month for health insurance, for example. When your computer breaks, you don't just call IS for a new one—you have to rummage through your stack of credit cards to see if there's one with enough room to pay for a new machine.

It's not just the big expenses, though—it's also $75 for a laser toner cartridge, $10 for pens, $50 for postage, and a whole host of other items that can—and will—add up quickly.

Finally, together with your income, you have to manage all this—you've suddenly become a part-time accountant, or you've got to find one to do the work for you.

Support staff: "Who *are* all these people?"

This issue comes and goes with the times. With the staff reductions that have been carried out at companies around the world in the late 1990s and then again in the early 2000s, this is not as big an issue as it was years ago, but it's still a factor. As an independent consultant, you're responsible for *everything*. Not just the production of work—you expected that. But when your phone service disappears in the middle of a rush project, you're going to be dealing with the phone company until it's repaired. When it's time to mail a letter, or make a copy, or proofread a proposal, or find a new Internet connection—the burden is on you to do so; there isn't a secretary or a fellow co-worker to lean on.

You'll want to minimize the "stuff" you'll need to support, especially at first. If you don't need your own Web site, domain, mail server, collating and stapling photocopy machine, fax machine, custom phone answering machine, and office at first, think of all the time you'll save not spending the time to buy, install, learn to use, fix, maintain, repair, and replace these things. Until you get to the point that you decide to bring on other consultants, you do everything from answer the phone to take out the trash. So don't set yourself up to have more to do than you absolutely have to.

Managing your time: "The best thing is I get to do all this from home!"

The corporate world subconsciously provides discipline for you to manage your time and your work. You've got a boss to whom you must answer and, in some fashion or another, deliver the goods. Once out on your own, there's no one standing by the door to make sure you get to work at 8 AM, or to stop you from yakking on the phone for half the morning, or to keep you from taking off at 3 PM to go for a ride or a swim.

Some people just don't have the level of self-discipline necessary to get their work done without someone managing them. A customer isn't going to micro-manage—they're just going to find out that you didn't meet the deadline you promised, and that after three weeks, you're now three weeks behind. It's a very rare customer who will put up with a miss like that more than about once.

But it's not just your development work that must be timely. While the customer is certainly No. 1, you're in this for the money, right? So sending out those invoices is No. 1, too. Along with chasing down those slow-to-pay customers. Naturally, you can't do invoicing without data, so filling out timesheets is No. 1. And you'll need to pay taxes, and regularly monitor whether or not you're profitable. So accounting is No. 1.

And there's always the possibility that this gig won't work out, so you'd better make sure that you've got potential customers on the line as well. So marketing gets on your To Do list. Where? Why, No. 1, of course.

So, here, you have to know yourself. There are many time-management systems out there, and I can't tell you what will work for you. Some people like juggling many projects using 15-minute time slices, while others prefer long stretches of uninterrupted time. I just want you to realize that, while the customer probably wants and expects you full time, your business needs attention, too. "Taking care of business" in the evening and on weekends after the phones stop ringing may be a workable solution for a while, but it's not a tenable long-term solution. Your family and, indeed, you yourself also need attention.

Crunching the numbers

Now that you've gotten an overview of the pros and cons, it's time to cover the specifics. First, let's look at the numbers—both from the income side as well as the expenses you can expect to see as a consultant.

Income

Income comes from two pieces of data: the number of "widgets" produced and the price per "widget." Most consultants, starting out, charge by the hour, either until they've got enough experience to consider alternative forms of pricing or unless they've got a specific type of project where a different pricing mechanism is appropriate. As a result, with respect to a consultant, the widget is most often an hour of work, and the price for that widget is the consultant's hourly rate. Thus, your income will be determined by how many hours you work, and the rate you charge per hour.

Setting your hourly rate

Setting your hourly rate is the source of much angst and frustration, and, unfortunately, there isn't a cookie-cutter recipe for doing so.

You want to take care when setting your rate, of course, because it's going to be the prime determinant of how much you'll be able to make in a year. Giving up $10 an hour will add up to $10,000 or more over the period of a year.

The correct rate will also help you acquire the business you want. If you set your rate too high, customers will look elsewhere. Unless you've got incredible credentials and a proven track record, it'll be nearly impossible to get a customer to pay significantly above market rates. If you set your rate too low, however, not only will you shortchange yourself, but you'll also look amateurish in the eyes of prospective customers. You've looked askance at a remarkably low price for something yourself, haven't you? Customers will wonder why your price is so low as well.

Like almost everything I say in this book, there's a flip side to this as well. Setting your rate higher is also a statement that you believe you deliver work of higher value. A software vendor friend had a terrible time breaking into a new market, until he raised his rates considerably. You may also see a beneficial effect in that raising your rates may more quickly drive off some of the more difficult penny-wise, pound-foolish customers.

There are several factors that enter into the process of setting your rate:

What are other consultants in your area (geographic and expertise) charging? An Oracle developer in San Francisco or London may well charge $200 an hour, while the going rate for an Access developer in Albany, New York, or Brasilia, Brazil, may only be $50 per hour. This factor just gives you a range with which to work—in the same region, there are usually developers charging a range of rates, where the top rate may be two to four times the bottom number. For instance, in Dallas, Texas, you could easily find Visual Basic developers charging anywhere from $35 to more than $100 an hour.

Once you've determined what the generally accepted range of fees is, it's time to evaluate your own skill set, and place yourself in that spectrum appropriately. One common mistake that many new consultants make is undervaluing their skills just because they're new at being independent. Don't forget that the majority of your time will be spent with customers doing analysis and design, or in front of a monitor—both of which, presumably, you've done plenty of already.

On the other hand, there are additional skills that are peculiar to the independent life, and you'll need to take the fact that you're not an experienced *independent* developer into account.

Finally, it's time to look at your own particular circumstance—how much money do you actually need yourself? As mentioned earlier, it's a mistake to assume that you'll be able to bill your hourly rate for 2,000 hours a year (40 hours a week * 50 weeks a year).

You want me to work How Many Hours?

If you're going to try to maintain a sane lifestyle, you can start your calculations with 2,080 potential work hours a year—40 hours a week and 52 weeks a year.

Now that you've got that number in mind, it's time to start nibbling away at it. You may have heard that experienced consultants usually figure on being able to bill 1,000 hours in a year. Sure, you can work your tail off, and if you get lucky, you might collect 1,500 hours; brand-new associates wanting to make partner at a law or accounting firm may ratchet that number close to 2,000. In both of these cases, however, there is still a large amount of non-billable time that must accounted for—and it doesn't come free.

Remember the vacations you want to take? Holidays during the year? Two weeks of vacation plus 10 paid holidays a year takes you down to 48 working weeks immediately. How about a couple of conferences that you normally attend? And throw in maybe a week of sick time. That's another three weeks, so the number of billable weeks is now down to 45. At 40 hours a week, that comes out to 1,800 hours. But what goes into that 40 hours? It's not all billable.

First, unless you've got more business than you know what to do with, you're going to be looking for business. This can include cold calling, attending industry functions and chamber of commerce gatherings to schmooze, responding to government RFQs, assembling marketing literature, or designing your Web page. You'll go on sales calls for which the customer doesn't expect to pay, and provide technical support and answer questions for free in order to generate good will. None of it, of course, is billable time.

Next, you're going to take care of a myriad of administrative, financial, and legal details. An hour's meeting with the lawyer to set up the corporation may not seem like much, but throw in a trip to the office supply store and some drive time, and you've suddenly lost a half-day. Each day you'll spend some time answering the phone, wading through e-mail, getting the mail from the Post Office box, and so on. And each week or month you're going to have to send out invoices, go to the bank, pay bills, clean the office, and so on. Again, nothing by itself is a huge matter, but it adds up, and it's all non-billable.

Finally, you'll be your own IS and technical support department now. You'll have to keep your phone and computer equipment running, install your own software, upgrade equipment, reinstall software (often, over and over), and, these days, maintain your own Web site. You'll also still be reading the current industry rags, going through a book now and then, and attending half-day seminars on this technology or that new set of buzzwords.

This was just part of the job when you had a corporate job—now, it's time you spend that you don't get to bill for. In other words, that half-day you spent installing the new set of development tools (and figuring out why your e-mail client no longer works) just cost you $400 in lost income.

I hope that you are starting to see that billing just half time each week is going to look pretty good. That ends up being less than 1,000 hours a year.

So let's start over again. First of all, you probably have this nagging suspicion that you're not going to become a successful independent developer on 40 hours a week and get seven weeks off each year. So some of your here-to-fore known as "free" time ends up going to the company. Evenings, weekends, early mornings—whatever your style is, figure on at least 50 hours a week devoted to your new job.

Setting a goal of 25 billable hours for each of those 45 billable weeks, then, is a reasonable and attainable goal. That's a little over 1,100 hours. Enough to make a living, but without going crazy or driving your family out.

What's the total income?

Now that we have this target of 1,100 hours (to make the math easy), let's figure out what your rate must be—at a minimum.

First, make some assumptions about what the range of rates you can possibly charge is—in a typical Midwestern city in the United States, that's $50 to $100. You can use those rates as bookends to figure your expected income—$55,000 to $110,000. That's a pretty broad range, but it's a starting point.

Now on to the part of the story where we take it away.

Expenses

You can break down expenses several ways. One way is to separate startup vs. ongoing; another is equipment and hard goods vs. services. Since the bottom line of expenses is that you're going to be paying for them, it might make the most sense to break outgoing dollars into three groups: startup, ongoing and future, and one-time categories. Ongoing expenses are those that you can expect and budget for each month, while one-time expenses are those that show up only occasionally.

Startup

Like it or not, even though you're running a service business, you're going to have to pony up some cash right away. Since many new consultants start by working out of their home, I'll bypass the additional expenses of setting up an outside office for the time being. Even working out of your house or apartment, though, you'll need some basic items.

The first is a place to work. This includes a desk, a chair, bookshelves, a filing cabinet, a computer, a printer, a business telephone, some means of receiving faxes, and so on. Most of this you probably already have, but there are two pieces that you should give careful consideration to.

The first is a good quality chair and a suitable work surface. Hopefully you'll be spending lots of time at your desk—working!—and it's foolish to scrimp on a chair, ruining your back and your posture for just a few hundred dollars. The second is a fireproof filing cabinet or safe. You don't need to store every scrap of paper in there, but your really important papers— tax returns, incorporation papers, certificates of insurance, contracts, and so on—should go in there. You might also keep your most recent backup in there as well (although you should always have a complete backup off-site as well!).

You'll also need startup office supplies—toner, fax paper, staples, pens, pencils, and whatever else you use on a daily basis. It's handy to have a bit more than you need—for instance, I always keep a spare toner cartridge around, so that when the current one runs low, I don't have to run out for one immediately. Besides, the cartridge has the bad habit of running out at 3 AM while you're printing the final copy of the proposal for the big 8 AM meeting with the customer.

Another set of startup expenses includes legal and accounting fees. It's a good idea to have your lawyer and accountant work together to make sure that there are no loose ends that each party thought the other had taken care of.

If you're planning on using your home computer or family computer for work, you may think that you're all set. After you've slaved away on it for a week or two, you may rethink that strategy. First, a computer that seemed absolutely fine for occasional use may suddenly become the next best thing to a boat anchor once you're depending on it day in and day out. If the family is expecting to use it, you may find yourself giving up access—or at least being bugged to—at critically busy times.

Also, that home computer that seemed to be half luxury, half plaything is now the source of your livelihood. If something happens to it—a bad hard disk, a fried motherboard, or any number of other minor catastrophes—you will find yourself crippled and unable to perform for your customers.

As a result, you should give serious thought to a new computer that you will use strictly for business, and expect to rely on the home computer as a backup. It only takes a couple of days of downtime before you realize you'd have been better off with a spare machine. Don't forget to budget for software that you'll need, as well as technical support plans. You may be used to having access to subscriptions at the office—you'll need your own subscriptions for at least some periodicals. These expenses all come at once as you're setting up.

Along with all of these, you may need to provide a deposit for certain expenses. Common are deposits for a business phone, an Internet connection, insurance, and a Yellow Pages ad.

Ongoing

These are the bills that are going to be showing up in the mailbox every month, quarter, or year.

The first bill that should be showing up is your salary. For a start, use the salary at your previous job. You may want to bump it up—after all, isn't one of the reasons you want to go independent to make more money?

Traditional monthly expenses include miscellaneous office supplies, your telephone and Internet bills, advertising, and postage. If you're claiming your office as a home office expense for tax purposes (again, get professional advice on this), you may want to allocate monthly payments for your share of the rent.

Quarterly and yearly bills often include insurance and professional fees. You may only expect to get a bill from the accountant or lawyer once a year, but if you budget quarterly, the annual bite won't be as bad.

And many of your startup costs will end up being annual bills—subscriptions, software updates, and so on.

You'll also have to plan for paying your own taxes. This can be a shocker to many people. You are of course aware of withholding taxes—the difference between your gross and net paychecks (not including other deductions like retirement plans or health insurance). But your employer also ponies up extra monies that you never see. Once you're self-employed, you'll need to send the government that money yourself. And it's not insignificant—figure an additional 15-20% of your gross income, depending on where you live.

Depending on how you set up your consultant business, you may pay the government each month, or you may get to submit a quarterly estimated income tax. Your accountant can advise you on the details—but the important thing to remember is that as a self-employed individual, you're responsible for calculating and filing all of your own taxes, and for doing it when the government expects you to. Don't play fast and loose with the taxes you owe, either by postponing or neglecting them—the government is a ruthless and tireless creditor.

One-time

This is really a misnomer, because this category covers "all the other expenses." For example, conference registrations, new computer equipment, new software, replacements for things that break or wear out, and other "one-time" expenses that don't occur regularly, but that do come up regularly.

For instance, you should plan on replacing your computer every two years or so. You may want to stretch it to three according to your own personal inclination, but it's quite an unfortunate circumstance if you find you need a new $4,000 machine just as you run into a slow period of work and can't afford it.

The result

I'll leave it to you to fill in the exact numbers for each of these items, but here's a running start.

First, recognize two things about the list of expenses. In your zeal to make sure you've got everything covered, you've probably put more in there than you'll actually spend. But at the same time, there will be expenses that you can't anticipate that will show up. All in all, these two factors will likely net out—so your expense number is probably a good start.

Second, it's hard to set an hourly rate even with all this information. The expenses will tell you what your income *has* to be, at a minimum. You may choose to go higher than that. If your hourly rate is too low to support your projected expenses, then you've got another think coming.

You may find this all to be too much work, and be tempted to skip the whole exercise. That would be a "bad" idea. Try this quick-and-dirty calculation. Take your current gross income, and multiply it by 150%. Then add another $5,000 to $15,000, depending on how much gear and stuff you already have. That's what you'll need to budget for—as a minimum.

It behooves you to put together a budget for your first two years of independence. You can be assured your actual numbers won't match your budget too closely—you'll get a break on health insurance and save thousands of dollars there, or your hard drive will fail and you'll need to pop for a costly repair a year before you'd planned on buying a new machine.

Whatever happens, it's better to plan conservatively, and have some money left over at the end of the year than to find that you failed to budget for numerous expenses, or that you were far too optimistic in terms of income, and find yourself considerably worse off, or even in debt, at the end of the year.

One of my friends was told by her financial advisor to set aside 8% of her gross fees each month for "incidentals" during the first year and 5% each succeeding year. It's paid off well for her so far.

Finally, recognize that the budget is not a fixed document, but rather a living being. Consider revising the entire two-year project plan as your circumstances change. Update it as you better understand your expenses, and can better predict your income. Every three months is a good target for this exercise. Any more often and you'll be buffeted by one-time expenses that hit in a particular month; less frequently and it'll do you successively less good. As you go through this exercise each time, remember that you're not just interested in the current set of facts and numbers, but the assumptions that gave rise to the estimates in the first place. Can you learn to make better assumptions? That's the goal.

Avoid over-optimism, a programmer's Achilles heel, and don't spend so much time noodling that you forget to make money.

Cataloging the skills

Money isn't the only thing you need to be concerned about, however. The skills you need as an independent consultant are not the same as those needed to be a staff programmer or corporate consultant. Before you take the leap, consider whether or not you've got the following skills.

Technical analysis and design

As an independent software developer, you'll most likely be expected to deliver a complete solution—starting with the analysis of the problem and design of the solution. If you've never done this work before, you'll need to acquire these skills in a hurry.

Technical programming skills

Most likely you're considering a jump into the independent consulting life because you've developed a great deal of experience with the part of the process known as "cutting code."

This is where you have the design of the solution in hand, and it's up to you to create the application itself.

This skill is at the same time more and less important than it was when you were a cog in a bigger machine. It's more important because being able to do the job right now means more money in your pocket—you're getting paid for being competent at your profession, not simply for filling a chair and eventually arriving at a solution. Back in the corporate world, it often didn't matter whether you took four hours or four days to accomplish a task—as an independent, the more you can get done in a given unit of time, the better off you'll be.

Many of a consultant's assignments are clean-up operations, where a previous consultant or employee came up with some "clever" way to make something work, a way that seemed to work at the time, but that failed to thrive in the long run. Your job as an independent consultant is to know the industry best practices and use them, quickly and efficiently.

While your customer may not be able to tell whether it should take three hours or four hours to accomplish a task, you'll often run into situations where "I can't bill the client for all that time"—the fewer incidences of this you have, the happier both you and your customer will be.

To some extent, in the bigger scheme of things, your competency as a programmer is less important because it's just one of many things you'll be doing as an independent software developer. You'll likely only spend 50-75% of your billable time—which means 25-33% of your work day—actually cutting code, compared to the majority of your day when you were an employee. But, at the same time, the coding effort is what the customer will live with for years after you're gone, so you can't get by with mediocre skills.

Testing

Ah, what can I say about testing? Why, I'll pontificate with bland, sweeping generalizations like every software developer does, right? (Well, until Chapter 25, "Testing—Who Does It?" where I cover it seriously.) It's difficult to generalize about testing since the environment that you are considering leaving could vary greatly. For instance, you could have been responsible for all your own testing, after which your work was placed into production immediately. At the other end of the spectrum, you might have had virtually no responsibility for testing, leaving that up to a separate QA department.

As an independent, however, you'll be responsible for the final quality of the delivery of your work, and your customer will expect that testing is one of the services you have provided, either personally, or through an employee or a subcontractor. As the saying goes, the second worst person in the world to test your code is you (the first being, of course, your mother, who never wants to find anything wrong with her kid). Nonetheless, you'll be faced with three options: Test your work yourself, have someone (other than the customer) test it for you, or write perfect code.

You won't have a QA department to back you up, as you might have had as a corporate developer. You will have to aim for a higher standard of quality in your deliverables, as a customer is unlikely to pay for much that doesn't work. Unlike in-house development, where you may have had a couple of tries to get it right, you'll have to do better in this league.

And don't think that you'll be able to get away with letting the customer take responsibility for testing—even if they offer. I'll explain why in Chapter 25, "Testing—Who Does It?"

Your skill as a programmer, in this case, can be complementary to your skill as a tester. The better a programmer you are, the worse a tester you can very well be, and vice versa. The fundamental question to ask yourself, however, is, "Can I—somehow—deliver applications without a lot of bugs and that meet the customer's level of expectations?"

Delivery

Delivery, funny enough, is a skill unto itself. Under the term "delivery" I'm grouping a number of items—the packaging of an application, the delivery and installation at a customer's site, and the training and ancillary support services required until the application is successfully deployed.

As an independent, you may be called upon to provide all of these services. In many cases packaging isn't quite as big a deal as it has been in the past. Nowadays, packaging can be as simple as running the Setup Wizard, compressing the resulting files into a single ZIP file, and placing the ZIP file on your FTP site for download by your customer, as opposed to having to cut multiple floppy disks and hand deliver them to your customer's site.

However, the rest of the delivery process involves many "soft" skills, including helping your users through the installation process, training some or many users to use your application, and answering the inevitable questions that come up while your customers are using their new application.

Delivery is a critical period in the life of the application. Despite the best analysis and design, despite great development and quality assurance, if the customer doesn't understand how to use the application, or why they would want to, the application will be a big flop. I've seen six-figure budget applications slowly fade away or just end up on the shelf—simply because the application couldn't be sold to the users.

Communication

Communication skills take many forms; indeed, the term can mean nearly anything you want it to mean. For our purposes here, I'm going to define communication as having three complementary pieces to it.

Listening

The first is listening. One of the invisible handicaps most developers suffer from is that they're usually pretty smart. This can be a handicap because after a lifetime of being thought of as Brainiac, a developer learns, subconsciously, to dismiss the opinions and thoughts of others.

As an independent consultant, you'll often be exposed to people with a broad range of brainpower. There'll be your counterpart in the IS department, who may either feel kinship with another "geek" or animosity toward a potential competitor. There'll be somebody in sales, a personable, yet seemingly none-too-bright representative—until you find out they've talked you into all sorts of unbelievable situations. Upper management will often be part of the mix—you may meet a doddering figurehead, still around only because of inertia and a secret manila folder with unusual photographs of the CEO, or your link to the executive suite may be a cagey, "crazy like a fox" power broker, wise well beyond her years.

Walking into a room with these folks and assuming you're the smartest kid on the block is not a mistake—letting everyone else know this is. As a result, if you keep your mouth shut and let the others open up, you'll be in a better position than if you run roughshod over everyone else.

Listening can be a valuable skill during each phase of the development process. Here's one example. When you are first interviewing a customer to understand what it is that they are after, the best thing you can do is to let them talk. Your job is to hear what they have to say, and repeat it back to them.

In this exercise, you get to verbalize what you think the customer has said, and they get to hear that you do understand their problem, and you get them to confirm that you understand. It's amazing how smart the customer thinks you are when you simply parrot their words back to them.

You'll have other opportunities where you can present your proposals and thoughts and editorial comments, but at this point, let the customer know that you are listening and understand what they are saying. Prodding this conversation along with "So what do you expect that I could do for you?" and "Have you considered a budget figure for this project?" and "Have you got a specific deadline for this work?" along with some of the other questions covered in Chapter 11, "The Sales Call," will often get you a surprising amount of information. But you have to *listen* for it.

Now, how do you tell whether you've got listening skills? There's not really a test that you can take that'll tell you how your listening skills rate. However, you're not completely without resources either. Chances are that over the years, you've received a number of job evaluations—search through them carefully, ignore all the sanctimonious drivel that usually ends up on your job review, and look for a few keywords about how your listening skills rate. If you see the same types of phrases—"needs to work on," "could be better at," and so on—over and over, it's time to pick up some coaching, or at least a self-help book, on listening.

Talking

The flip side of listening, of course, is talking. As many a pundit has noted, you have two ears but only one mouth; nonetheless, your customer isn't paying you simply to listen. At some point, they're going to want to hear back from you. This form of communication has two parts, actually.

The first facet of talking with the customer is the ability to verbalize what you're thinking. People (er, that's us) often have trouble getting across what they're thinking because their mind is moving several times faster than the listener is comprehending. A second problem for technical people is the tendency to slip into "geek talk"—drilling down into the details of the problem and proposing solutions wrapped in acronyms and buzzwords. In addition to reviewing job evaluation comments as discussed earlier, you can get a feel for whether or not you're a good communicator by how the other person reacts. Little or no response, or, worse, a plain dumb look on the listener's face often means that you're not getting through to him.

The second facet of talking to the customer is that of persuasion. As a consultant, you'll often have to present a solution that conflicts with the status quo or the solution proposed by another party. In this case, you'll have to persuade the group involved in the project that your solution is the better choice.

By this time in your life, you should have a gut feeling as to whether you're good at this. Do you have a history of delivering stellar solutions, only to have them shot down by "the suits" down the hall? Do your solutions appear to be accepted, but never quite get around to being implemented? If your answer is "Yes" to either of these questions, you may have fewer skills in this area than you'd like to admit. Again, know your strengths and weaknesses, and work on the weaker areas.

Writing

Written communication plays the same role as talking—it's just the non-verbal version of providing information back to the client.

A consultant or person on their own or in a small company must have good written communication skills. In a larger organization it is easier to hide such a deficiency—other team members do the writing, or perhaps you have a tech writer/editor. But for those who struggle getting a written point across, this absence can become a critical road block and they have to figure out a way to get past it by themselves or with some help.

Pieces of the pie

A subtle danger lies ahead for a successful independent software developer—the maintenance trap. I first read about this in the prelude to Alan Schwartz's excellent "Models of Maintainability" treatise in Winchell's *FoxPro 2.x: A Developer's Guide* by M&T Press.

The problem occurs when the amount of time required to provide maintenance of existing, satisfied customers consumes all of your available time, leaving no time to do new, custom development (the cool stuff). If you've played your cards right, you will have a couple of customers, and be building a couple of applications concurrently, using your freedom as an independent consultant to time-slice between customers. In all likelihood, one will finish before the other, and you'll start on a third.

In many cases, that first customer will be able to use their application with little, if any, involvement from you, and you'll stay busy building your second and third applications. All of your time is still spent building new applications. Eventually, though, that first customer will have a request for maintenance—perhaps a simple question, or a quick modification, or more extensive enhancements and changes. And when you finish the second and third applications, the scenario will repeat itself.

The slice of the pie you have for new applications has now shrunk, as you are now committed to spending part of your time maintaining those applications. This state of affairs folds in upon itself, until you've built so many applications that you're spending all of your time maintaining them, and you have no time for new projects.

Paradoxically, this happens as you're hitting your stride as a developer; your reputation has grown, and you're getting busier and busier with new work as well.

There is no clear-cut solution to this situation, but there are some options. One is to become a maintenance programmer, in essence, becoming bound to your legacy applications. Generally, this isn't a wise choice, as those applications will eventually have to be upgraded or replaced, and if you haven't kept your skills up-to-date, you won't be in the running for the new work, and you'll be out of a job.

Another solution is to hire staff to help you take care of the maintenance; oftentimes a junior or less skilled programmer or developer can do the maintenance of a project less expensively while, at the same time, it provides a valuable learning curve for them. Indeed, many times the growth of a one-man shop into a multiple-developer company is caused specifically by this situation.

A third possibility is to simply refuse to do maintenance, either explicitly, or covertly by raising your rates to the point that the customer goes elsewhere for ongoing support. This is generally not a winning proposition, because it's likely they won't be coming back to you for future projects.

A different way of not doing maintenance work is to put the monkey on the customer's back—but to make that part of your strategy from the beginning. Sometimes called "technology transfer," part of the delivery of the application is the delivery of the source code and the training of the customer's personnel on how to access and maintain the application themselves.

You may feel that you're again in danger of losing new work by following a technology transfer strategy, but if it's done properly, that won't be the case at all. What I've done in many cases is explain to the customer that my role with them is to do the "heavy lifting" during the application development stage, but that it's a better fit if I turn the project over to them when it's finished, so that they can continue on with the "fit and finish," such as reports and minor tweaks and modifications that are often requested.

You need to qualify the customers for whom this strategy will work early in the game. They need to have technical people on board with the aptitude and interest to take on the maintenance and enhancement role. This doesn't work with many "end user" companies, but it can be ideal for those with an IS staff. You get to do all of the cool, new innovative development work, and customer insiders get an inside track on watching the "Pro from Dover" do the heavy lifting and then take over ownership to do the upkeep that we would see as dull but that they see as secure. Everybody wins.

> *I'll make use of the analogy of putting up a building throughout this book, and here's the first example. Many companies own their own physical buildings, and, accordingly, have their own maintenance staff whose job it is to keep the building in good shape. However, the company didn't rely on their own maintenance staff to build the building, nor do they expect their maintenance crew to put major additions on the facility, or to build new buildings on the grounds.*
>
> *Instead, they'll contract out with a firm whose business is to erect new buildings and perform major construction on existing structures. Once they're done, they'll turn over the blueprints, plans, and other documentation to the maintenance staff of the company. It's not the construction company's role to perform "minor" construction tasks like cutting new doorways in walls, hanging light fixtures, or replacing floor and ceiling surfaces—it's the maintenance crew's. Once the building is done, the construction company exits, and the maintenance crew will then be in position to perform maintenance and attend to the building's upkeep.*

Conclusion

It may sound like this gig as an independent is an impossible task—only a superman could possibly have skills that range from the analysis and design of technical solutions to the business acumen to profitably continue to the political adroitness to handle the maze of customer personalities. But this situation is similar to that of a basketball player. When you're out on the playground scrapping with whoever walks onto the court, you can get away with imperfections in your game. And when you're part of a big corporate team, you've got backup and other resources that you can rely on.

When you're an independent, though, you're in the big leagues. You can't get away with a bad left-handed dribble or an inability to shoot from past 15 feet. You don't have to be the best at every single skill, and, depending on your skills in other areas, you might even be able to get away with mediocre performance. Witness Shaquille O'Neal at the free line some time. But while a one-trick pony might make it in the college ranks or the corporate world, where there's lots of backup, it's likely not going to be enough when you're on your own.

Ted Roche tells the story of two guys he knew who quit their day jobs to follow their dreams. They opened up a computer store many, many years ago, selling a brand of computer you've probably never heard of. They knocked themselves out for years, working late, starting early, scrimping pennies. They had the greatest customer service and the best attitudes. They would do anything to make sure the customer was satisfied. They soared within their industry, gaining a worldwide reputation, mingling with the movers and shakers of the industry, influencing the direction of many products, and still keeping all of their customers satisfied.

The machine, however, eventually flopped, the industry collapsed, and they barely got out with their shirts. In seven years, the business had cost them everything, but in the end they were lucky enough to pay off the second mortgages, refill the retirement funds they'd emptied, and pay back most of the loans. They went back into the world, but with no regrets. The ride had been worth it. May your experience be as spiritually fulfilling for you.

Chapter 6
What You'll Need

"I feel a need... a need for speed."—Maverick to Goose
—Top Gun

So you've decided to open shop as a software developer. You might be going at this as an independent, or perhaps you've been charged with starting a software development department at a company. You could go in blind and unprepared, but wouldn't it be better to start your first day with a plan and a toolbox full of goodies? In this chapter, I'll provide a list of things you'll need to make your first few months as painless as possible. As with the previous chapter, those of you who are already in the biz may find information here that's useful to see if you're missing anything, or if there are places where you can buttress your current plan.

While this chapter seems to continue Chapter 5's theme of preparing someone for going out into the world of independent consulting, it's actually broader than that. There are more than a few of you out there who are all of a sudden responsible, either formally or informally, for starting a software development department at a company. This chapter's for you as well.

Starting a service business, either on your own or under the umbrella of a host company, would seem to require little to no preparation. After all, the customer is buying what you've got in your head, and what you can do for them—and, particularly in software development, there's not a lot of "gear" required. The joke has long been "A computer and $30 worth of business cards, and you're a computer consultant!" Given that there are a lot of folks out there with this mindset, you can do yourself an immediate favor by being better prepared than those folks. "Being prepared" has two parts to it.

The first part is in your own mind—do you know exactly what you're going to be doing? And how you're going to go about it? Probably not. But the clearer a picture you have, the better off you're going to be. Some consultants run under the "AFAB" (Anything For A Buck) banner—one day they're writing a new module for an existing application, the next they're troubleshooting some data corruption, the third they're training, and the fourth they're doing design for a brand-new application.

This is okay, mind you, if that's what you intend on doing. But there are a lot of opportunities out there—it's easy to get whipped back and forth from one type of work to another to a third. The problem with this is that you never develop a core competency or in-depth expertise at one thing.

A corollary to this has to do with being efficient in your work. Software development is tough enough when you know what you're doing. Spending a lot of time learning the ropes, assembling materials each time you need to meet with a potential customer, making decisions about how you're going to organize or structure a process, or reworking something when you come across a different way is wasteful. You could better spend that time actually billing, couldn't you?

The second part is the public face you present—to your customers, to potential employees, to business partners, and to anyone else you deal with. The better prepared you are, the more comfortable your customer is going to be. Even if you're a wizard and know your stuff cold, if you appear to bumble through design meetings, presentations, and the general process, your customer will lose confidence. This can cause them to question your judgment, give them reason to question your invoices (always a problem!), and possibly move on to the seemingly greener pastures of another consultant.

Let's look at what you need.

Decide what you're going to do

The first thing you'll need is a clear picture of what you're going to do and how you're going to do it.

What services are you going to provide?

This can be a tricky question when you're starting out because you may be in a position where you can't be all that choosy. If you're moving into the independent world because you've got a big project already lined up, then this decision has been, in large part, already made for you—you're going to provide the services that this customer wants. This isn't completely true, though, because you and your customer may have different ideas about what you're going to do for them, or the initial set of expectations may evolve as the project progresses.

For example, you may be "hired on" to put together a new application for your customer. Mid-way through, however, their system manager quits, or their aging MRP system starts to die, or any number of other catastrophes rear up. Since you're in the thick of things—and possibly the only "computer guy" available—they turn to you for help. It may be "just for these one or two things," or they may dump the whole project on your shoulders—"Put the application you're building on hold and fight this fire until we've got a replacement/solution lined up." All of a sudden you end up spending four months performing one or more tasks for which you're neither trained nor prepared, or really all that interested in doing.

If you're just starting out, on the other hand, it's tempting to say "yes" to each potential project that comes along, and, indeed, it might be necessary. It's easy to spread yourself too thin if you do this, though, and never get really ready, or good, at any single type of work.

So what kinds of work could you do? Here are a few choices just in the software development field:

Hourly consulting. Some projects are amorphous, with a lot of tasks that cross boundaries. There's some new stuff to build, some retrofitting, an interface or two to design, and so on. And, frankly, perhaps being a jack of all trades is more to your liking—some people like sitting in front of a monitor all day long, crafting the most gorgeous programs, being left alone for the majority of their time, but others can't stand the solitude—they need the constant buzz of human interaction, and fire-fighting often provides that.

Building new software applications for internal use. More and more, companies are realizing that their business relies on software—and they have more and more custom internal applications that they run their business on. A company often has a mishmash of systems, and decides to throw one out and replace it with one built from scratch. Shortly after this decision, though, they realize that they don't have, or no longer have, the resources to develop that replacement themselves. At this point they'll search for an outside resource to do the work for them.

This work often entails the whole enchilada—from analysis and design, through programming, and even help with testing, implementation, and training. In my case, this is what I do nearly to the exclusion of all other work: "We build apps from womb to tomb."

Building software products for companies for resale. Similar to the previous choice, the critical difference is that internal applications can often be rolled out and implemented a piece at a time, while a product has to be delivered as a whole entity. Sure, in some cases a product can be split into multiple modules, and each module can be delivered separately, but the whole module needs to be completely finished.

Second, quality control for internal applications is often not as demanding as it is for an application that is sent to a third party who is paying for it. The folks in the Inventory Management department can deal with the fact that the last batch of reports hasn't been finished yet, and that they have to click through a couple of error messages each time they want to run the outdated materials handling routine. When you've deployed an application to 50, a couple hundred, or several thousand sites, the tech support related to dealing with those issues will be overwhelming, or will even kill the sale of the product.

Adding on to existing applications. Not everyone has the luxury of, or the interest in, starting out with a clean sheet of paper. Some people like getting into the guts of an existing application, figuring out what it does, tweaking it, adding hooks to call new routines or modules, and so on. This type of development requires knowledge of the existing application as well as the tool(s) it was built with, or a facility for learning a new toolset on the fly. It also requires a certain type of political adroitness in working with the installed base of users to extend their application without upsetting their current processes.

Interfacing among multiple applications. A specialized type of software development involves building interfaces among applications that weren't designed to share data, or whose mechanism for sharing is awkward, incomplete, or just doesn't work as advertised. There's an entire skill set required for spelunking through undocumented file formats, converting data from one format to another, building real time services that detect changes to data and feed it to another application, and the like.

Converting applications from one version, or platform, to another. Updating an application from one version to another is usually posed as "just a simple conversion," but it often becomes a complete rewrite as the customer learns about the new capabilities that the new version has, and realizes that this is a golden opportunity to add new features and change existing functionality that they never really liked anyway.

However, unlike building a new application from scratch, the customer comes with a huge preconceived notion of functionality that's going to show up in the new version. It's a common scenario for the customer to hand over a couple of floppy disks that contain the original program (in compiled form, no less), and expect you to completely understand the application within a few days. Yes, including each of the magic formulas and the undocumented knowledge that Ctrl-Alt-F4, when in the Add Customer screen, brings up a credit calculator that isn't used anywhere else or described in any of the Help or documentation.

Analysis and design only. Sometimes a company has the internal firepower to cut code all day long—but needs outside talent to get the project going and designed. Here, you'd be brought in for your analysis and design skills, tasked with determining what the application will do and putting together the specification, with the intent to turn over the programming and implementation to another group.

Just like a doctor who brings in a specialist for a second opinion, or a dentist who sends you to an oral surgeon for a root canal, specialization in this type of work offers a chance to become extremely skilled and offer a great deal of value, and it can be lucrative as well.

Custom programming from existing design specs. Some people don't like the analysis and design. Yes, it happens. Some people like Brussels sprouts too. Go figure. In some shops, software development is highly compartmentalized. One department or group interfaces with the users, and creates design documents that are turned over to "the programmers." And this is where you come in—they contract out to you, and your mission is to turn those design documents into code. You may even have the luxury of writing code but not having to implement that application—that function would be turned over to yet a third group.

Each of these types of work requires a different mix of skills, and you'll want to tailor your modus operandi accordingly. This is difficult to do if you don't know what type of work you are looking for.

Where do you want to work?

The next thing you should get clear in your own mind is where you want to work. Other than Hawaii, that is.

Some people like to work on-site—at the customer's location—while others would much rather work at home, visiting the customer on occasion when required. There is no right answer—this is completely a matter of personal preference—but if you have one preference, you need to know it and make sure that you can indeed operate that way, and that you can explain why to your customers as well.

Some customers prefer to have you on-site all the time. It's not uncommon for you to be asked to be on-site for a specified period of time "just in case we need you" even though you don't have a specific assignment or task to accomplish. Other reasons range from an installation and development environment that would make it nearly impossible for you to take "a copy" of their environment back home with you to a dynamic situation that changes so often that frequent, unscheduled face to face communication is necessary.

When on-site, you can be faced with a widely varying environment. I've been in situations where we were sat down in a half-finished cubicle next to the copier and across from the vending machines. On the desk was a 14-inch monitor with a poor refresh rate, attached to a four-year-old computer with the cover off and a hard disk that was on the brink of failure. Each morning I had to wipe the desk down from the grit that had fallen from the broken ceiling tiles above, and then said a short prayer that the work I'd done the day before ("We don't allow our consultants access to the network!") was still intact.

But I've also had experiences where the first, second, and third questions were "What do you need?", staff and management were available whenever I needed, and I was fed royally from sunup to sundown. I was the "expert from afar," and they were going to pamper me as much as possible in order to make my stay as productive as possible.

And if you work on-site 40 hours a week, when are you going to have time to run your own business? If your customer expects you to be on-site during the entire week, you're pretty much forced to tend to your own matters during off hours—evenings, weekends, holidays, and so on. (I'm assuming you know that when at a client's site, you work for that client, and that client only, right?)

Of course, this may be an advantage—forcing you to keep your billable hours up. If you're one of those who have trouble managing their own time, having an outside influence make sure that you don't spend all of Monday and half of Tuesday untangling the phone cord can be a very good thing indeed.

On the other hand, if you work off-site, you have complete control over your environment, or at least as much control as anyone has. You can set up your network and your machines as you like, have the tools you need and want, work the hours you want, wear the clothes you want, well, get the idea?

This is my preferred mode of operation, as I can schedule work to mesh with the rest of my day, instead of having to create strict demarcations of "I'm working now and I shan't do anything else" and "I'm not working now and thus shan't let work enter my consciousness t'all." Life just doesn't work like that, so why force an artificial distinction?

This comes with a couple of requirements. The first is that you have to set expectations with your customers about when you are reachable. If you want to take off in the middle of the day to read to your first-grader at school, or go wind surfing on Fridays, or whatever, that's fine. Just make sure that your customers understand when they're going to be able to get hold of you.

The second caveat is to make sure that you are, in actuality, reachable at those times. Customers are unique creatures—each one has a different set of expectations. I've worked with some customers who have a phone glued to their ear, and seem to have some deep-seated need to make voice contact with you each day. Other customers dismiss the phone except for the most urgent of circumstances, preferring to wait until the weekly meeting to communicate. And yet other customers depend on e-mail exclusively; I've received more than one message complaining, "Talk? You mean, like, on the phone?"

What type of company/industry do you want to work with?

You'll also want to have an idea of what types of companies or industries you want to work with. Do you feel more comfortable working at the headquarters of Fortune 500 multi-nationals? Small, home-grown manufacturers where the president of the company still knows the name of every person in the factory? Perhaps you like government agencies, or non-profits. Steady, conservative firms that have been around for ages? Or fast-growing companies whose systems go out-of-date faster than their telephone directory?

Each of these types of companies has a particular personality, and along with that come requirements and expectations. Think of the last few places you've worked—both the good and the bad—and list the attributes of the companies that you liked and disliked. Put all that together to form a profile of the ideal company you'd like to work with.

Do you plan to do it all yourself?

Think ahead for a bit. Do you want to stay independent—that is, a solo operator—for good? Or do you plan on adding staff as soon as you can find work for them? How you go about finding business, indeed, the actual business you find, will vary according to the answer to this question. Your role will also vary—in the former, you'll be everything from master developer to trash collector. In the latter, you'll want to delegate certain tasks as soon as possible, keeping just what you yourself have to do on your own To Do list.

In short, if you plan on adding employees, you'll need to do three things. First, you'll want to prospect for business more often, and go after larger jobs to ensure there is enough work for your company. Second, you'll need to formalize processes and procedures sooner rather than later, and when I say formalize, I mean it—you won't be able to make it up as you go if you're trying to make sure that everyone in your company is doing things the same way. And, finally, you'll have to budget time—considerably more time than you think—in recruiting, training, and retaining people.

When you look at this list of things to do, you have to ask yourself, "Is this why I got into this business?" Many developers have looked at themselves one day after growing a company to 5, 10, 20, 50 people, and realized that they're many times removed from what got them into the business in the first place—the love of developing applications.

On the other hand, the challenge of running a software development shop with many people is a fascinating intellectual puzzle, requiring equal parts of technical acumen and people/management skills. To some, this is the best job of all.

How much money do you want to make?
Again, there seems to be an obvious answer to this question—"More than Bill Gates"—but there is a serious reason for asking.

As an independent, your income requirements and expectations have a significant impact on your style and mode of work. There are tradeoffs between the type of work you do, the lifestyle you want, and your potential income. Let's take two typical situations.

As an hourly consultant, working on a large, multi-year project on-site at a large, wealthy customer, you will probably be able to enjoy a reasonably high rate per hour, and your billable hours per week will be maximized. On the other hand, your freedom to come and go as you please, to set your own hours, and to run the show will in many cases be quite limited.

Conversely, as the sole developer working as an occasional troubleshooter and maintenance programmer for a small non-profit agency, your billable rate will probably be lower, and your billable hours may not be nearly as voluminous or regular as in the first situation. However, you could well have more freedom, the run of the place, the ability to set your own hours, and you'll have the job satisfaction that comes with being the guru upon whom everyone depends.

Of course, both of these situations can be circumvented to some extent. In the second case, for example, you could use additional projects to keep your billable hours up and work extra hours to make up for the low hourly rate.

Once you've made these decisions, you'll need to get a handle on the actual dollars you need to bring in to stay afloat, and how much you'd ideally like to bring in. I'll cover this in more detail shortly when I cover the budget.

How do you want to get paid?
Finally, you'll have to decide how to get paid. This topic is one that developers (and people in many other businesses as well) seem to have an inordinate amount of trouble with. After all, you did the work—why would anyone not want to pay you for it? They should be so grateful, in fact, that they'll beg you to take their money, right?

Obviously, it doesn't quite work like that. And trouble in this area can cause fundamental problems in the rest of your business—after all, making money is the primary reason you're doing this in the first place. Many a consultant has ended up back in the ranks of the "employed by someone else" simply because they weren't able to get the money in the door.

There are three basic schemes for getting paid. The first is to bill hourly, and invoice periodically for the hours you've worked. The trick here is to make sure that you don't wait too long to bill, and don't let the due date wander too far out in the future. Ideally, you should bill every week or two, and get paid within 7-10 days. You may be asked to bill once a month, with terms of 30-45 days, but that's very definitely not a good idea. You could end up working for two solid months or more, only to find out that the customer is going to play fast and loose with paying you, or, worse, simply refuse to pay at all. By billing often and getting paid quickly, you reduce your exposure.

The second scheme is to bill upon completion of certain points. This can work well for projects that have clearly defined milestones—both for you, as it gives you incentive to get the job done for the customer, and for the customer, as they can see what they're paying for. You should still get paid regularly, and quickly. Instead of setting one huge milestone months or longer in the future, break the project down so that you have deliverables that you can reach every week or two, and, again, make your terms 7-10 days.

The third scheme is to use a retainer. In this situation, you get your money up front, and then the work you do is applied to that payment. After you've worked so that the money is used up (or, rather, nearly used up), you send out another invoice, and repeat the process. The important feature about this process is that you have committed to working that many hours for your customer—they have "rights" to your time.

This works well for you, in that you get your money quicker than any other means, and, if properly executed, it works well for the customer too, since they now have dibs on your time and can ensure that their work will have priority over other customer projects that may come along.

Set the ground rules yourself!

Once you've made the decisions about these items, you're in a position to set down the ground rules for your customer. If you don't, the customer will, and their rules might not be ones you care for all that much. It's much better to optimize the situation to your liking as much as you can.

Here's a concrete example—travel time, and whether or not to charge for it. In every online forum I've ever been on, the issue of charging for it comes up over and over again. In the olden days when I was scraping for every gig I could dig up, I didn't charge for travel time, thinking that doing so might jeopardize the deal. Now that I'm older and, er, more tired of driving, I want to get paid for that time. Even though the customer sees that he agreed to it, he may not have read the Engagement Letter that closely, and thus missed that part—and now he's questioning it. How do you explain your billing for travel time to the customer? After all, he feels it's not productive time for him—you're not really getting any work done for him while you're in the car.

The fact of the matter is that, while you may not be directly creating for them since you're, hopefully, paying attention to the road, your time is being spent on their behalf—

driving to them. If you weren't traveling to their site, you could be spending that time doing work for another customer and, presumably, getting paid for it.

It's even easier to see this if you're billing for an employee's time. Suppose an employee spends four hours of an eight-hour day traveling. You're paying your employee for that entire day, so you need to get paid for all that time—not just the actual four hours on-site.

If you're a corporate developer, a similar situation comes up—if you have to account for your time, and you're traveling to another location (whether it's on the other end of the building or a factory in another part of the city), you need to account for that time—and since the time is dedicated to that project, it needs to go to that project.

Depending on the level of sophistication of the corporate time-tracking system, of course, you may even have subcategories for a project, including productive (design or programming) time and non-productive (travel and admin) time. But it all still needs to be applied to the project.

Define your methods and methodologies

Once you've decided what type of work you want to go after, you need to define your methods and practices. And that, presumably, is why you're reading this book. You've probably got some ideas already; combine those with the things you find in this book that apply to you and your situation, and you'll be all set to put this section together.

The reason you need to do this work now is so that you can explain to your potential customers how you do what you do. Simply waving your hands, looking down your nose at them, and proclaiming, "It's technical—you wouldn't understand" isn't going to cut it. They're more likely going to select you as their consultant if you can clearly and concisely explain your process to them, and what part they're expected to play in it.

The benefit doesn't stop at the sales call, though. Software development is most likely new to your customer; and even if it isn't, software development performed with a professional methodology almost assuredly is. As a result, you'll have to explain to them, over and over, how things work—what your roles and responsibilities are, and what theirs are. If you don't know this yourself, cold, you're not going to be successful when you explain it to them.

Define your billable and non-billable activities

At some point in every consultant's career, they're going to get a call from a customer, and the voice on the other end of the phone is going to say, "Why are you billing us for this?"

If you define, up front, before you begin, what activities you perform that are billable, and which are not, you will have a better chance of surviving that phone call with your invoice still intact. If you don't, you open up the possibility for negotiation not only for that item, but also for every other item you ever try to invoice for.

Customers, both because of naivete as well as chutzpah, will come up with the most outlandish excuses why they don't feel they should pay for one thing or another. And in some cases, if you have not figured out where you stand on certain issues, you may not be certain whether you should be billing them yourself.

For example, do you bill for travel time to and from a customer's office? If so, how much? Your regular hourly rate, or a different rate? Does it depend on how you travel? Is your rate different if you're driving (and thus unable to do anything else) as opposed to taking the train or flying (where, presumably, you can be working on a laptop or reading something)? If your engagement runs overnight, do you bill for eight hours or at a rate per day? If you leave in the afternoon for a multiple-day trip that starts with a customer meeting the following morning, how do you handle billing for that partial day?

Do you bill for meetings? Do you bill for time spent in a reception area, waiting for someone to come out and escort you back to their offices? What if you're in a meeting, and the other participants get called away for a while? Do you bill for that time you're waiting for them to return?

Suppose you forget materials when you're visiting the customer, and have to make a second trip back—do you bill for that time? For the travel time?

What about bugs? Do you charge for fixing bugs? What about enhancements that the customer thought were already specified in their documents, but never made it to the formal spec? What about issues that were discussed verbally but never put down in writing?

Suppose their IS department gives you the wrong information, and you perform work based on that information. Later you have to rework or throw out something. Is that billable?

This isn't an exhaustive list, but it'll give you a good start. Having this list will help you keep from giving away your time when your customer starts pressing you and you're not sure where to draw the line. Most everyone likes to get something for nothing, and some folks like to get everything for nothing. Be aware that you could get involved with someone who wants to squeeze you for service after service—for free. Having this list will help you know, and give you confidence, to say "no" when it's appropriate.

Put together a portfolio

In certain worlds, a portfolio is *de rigueur*—an advertising exec or artist wouldn't think of going to see a customer (or to a job interview) without one of those oversized leather satchels that contain copies of their greatest and showiest projects.

I've also run across individuals who have collected samples of their work in a binder to show prospective employers—I saw one so-called "I Love Me" book and hired the person on the spot.

Why shouldn't you have a portfolio of your work—samples of projects you've done, together with descriptions of how you do your work—to show prospective customers? Most consultants and consulting firms have a glossy brochure, a few business cards, and a glib line of, er, salesmanship as their own tools in a sales call.

You may not want to bring a laptop computer with you; sometimes that can get distracting when you call up a live application, and there may be reasons why you can't actually demonstrate an application you've done for someone else. And, as Murphy would attest, the demo or live app that was working perfectly an hour ago when you tried it at home is as often as not going to blow up in front of the customer during that first sales call.

However, you can bring screen shots, and with the inexpensive color ink-jet printers available these days, you can put together a sample of screens and reports that'll make any red-blooded geek salivate. Many customers like to see what the "look and feel" of your applications is like, as well as seeing a variety of possible interfaces. All too often, they're still stuck in a character-based world, and it's reassuring for them to see samples of modern graphical and browser-based interfaces. And one of your samples might have similarity to what they're looking for—"An inventory management system that tracks both stock and custom assemblies? Sure, we did something like that here."

But don't stop there. You're going to want to show them how you do what you do, and what tools you use to get there. For instance, you might start out with the form you fill out as part of the initial sales call—showing them that you're organized and rigorous about asking for and tracking information from the get-go.

You could also show them a sample Engagement Letter, a Functional Specification, and Change Orders for the specification. Of course, everyone has those, right? You'll want to tour them through the development process as well. Samples of your bug-tracking form, weekly defect reports, testing checklists, and other paperwork will show your customer that you know what you're doing, and that you've got a documented process that you follow. Given the haphazard way that most software is developed, this portfolio will set your customer considerably more at ease—and, should they be evaluating more than one developer, will put a significant burden on the next person who walks through their door! You're competing for that customer—the more barriers to entry you can create for your competition, the better!

This may seem like a lot of work, and some of it may seem pretty vague right now. Rest assured that I don't expect you to put this book down and crank all this out before you go on to the next chapter. The rest of this book will show you each of these pieces, plus a great deal more, in detail. I'm just showing you a quick roadmap here. I myself have gone a couple steps further than this sample portfolio, of course—I use this book as part of my portfolio when I talk to potential customers!

Create a budget and a business plan

Let's just pretend that you were going to start a company that manufactured widgets, and you needed a bank loan to get started. You'd write up a business plan and present that to your banker as part of your loan request. Then, six months later, and a year later, you'd update the business plan and present it to your banker to show him how you're doing, and what you've done with the money, and why you need more, or an extension of the terms, or whatever.

This business plan isn't just a tool for soliciting money from your banker, though. It should be a tool you use to run your business. In fact, you don't even need to apply for a loan in order to write up a business plan—you should put the plan together regardless. Interestingly enough, I have friends who have gone through this exercise, and then took their business plan to a banker—and were approved for $150,000!

As I've said before, this business plan is merely a first guess at what you're going to do—reality will most likely be considerably different. However, with a business plan, you can re-evaluate and make mid-course corrections to stay on track. It's much easier to make small adjustments frequently than to try to make a major change well down the road, only to find yourself incapable of doing so.

For example, suppose you've budgeted $350 a month for phone service. If you don't budget, but just have this idea of "about $350" in your head, it's all too easy to watch months go by, and suddenly end up with a $9,000 phone expense at the end of the year. Boom—you've spent $5,000 more than you intended, and that's $5,000 that is no longer in your own paycheck.

Suppose, on the other hand, you map out a formal budget, with "$400" in each cell for the entire year, and check your actual phone bill against your budget each month. The first month comes in at $700, and the second comes in at $800, and you can already tell that you'd better do something. You're only over by $650, not $5,000, a much more manageable number. Of course, there are all sorts of things that may happen at this point—you may realize that your initial figures were way too optimistic, or that you had several extraordinary expenses that won't be happening again. In any case, it's better to find out now than in another 10 months when it's too late to repair a year of wild spending.

Contents of a business plan

There are as many types of business plans as there are businesses, of course, and there isn't any single "generally accepted business plan format" that you are required, or advised, to follow. But a business plan is really just a grand "To-do" list, narrowed down for your business.

First, decide on your goals. Since the primary goal of a business is to make money, you'd think you'd start out with a budget, but that's not exactly correct. You start out with an idea of what you're going to do to make money. You define the product or service that you're going to sell, and you describe it in some detail.

Next, you define the marketplace in which you're competing, in terms of other companies and other products/services, and place yourself in there. Describe how you are going to be positioned in the market.

The third part is to describe how you're going to sell what you've got. This is critical—you can be loosey-goosey about the first two parts, but you must have a clear idea of who you're going to sell to, how you're going to do it, and how many of them are going to buy. This, after all, is going to create the top half of your budget—the income side.

With software development, this is a little different than if you were selling shoes ("145 pairs a day") or dental services ("12 cleanings, 7 fillings, and 2 general exams a day"). Nonetheless, you have to pin down just exactly how you're going to obtain projects, how big those projects are going to be, how many projects you can do at the same time, what your hourly rate is going to be, and how many hours a week you're going to have to work to produce the work to support those projects. Note that the hours you work each week have to include both billable hours that generate income as well as the non-billable hours you have to deal with.

Sure, it's still a wild-assed guess—how can you tell if you're going to land one $100,000 project next Tuesday, or if you're going to run into a series of small jobs, each running $8,000, or fall somewhere in the middle? No one knows. Nonetheless, you have to throw the dart and make a guess. A month later you take a look at this guess, and revise it—hopefully to the better.

This third part has to include the specific tasks you're going to perform in order to produce those numbers. If your guess is three $50,000 projects for the year, that's fine. But what—exactly what—are you going to do to make that happen? Are you going to cold call 10 people each morning? Run an ad in the local shopper? Go to four Chamber of Commerce meetings each week? And from those actions, what do you expect the results to be?

Suppose you decide you're going to make 10 calls a day. That's 50 calls a week, or 800 calls each four-month period. One of those has to result in a $50,000 project. But you should figure that you're not going to have 799 "No" calls and then the 800th will magically say, "Yes!" Instead, you'll make 800 calls, and only talk to a live human on 200 of them. Of those

200, you'll have an actual conversation with 50. Of those, 10 will be interested, 6 will turn into sales calls, 3 will turn into proposals, and 1 will turn into that $50,000 job.

If these are your numbers, but you end up selling four $50,000 jobs after only 110 calls, then you know you need to scale back your calling plan, because you're going to be overwhelmed by work before you make it halfway through your list. On the other hand, if the numbers turn out worse, then you'll have to ratchet up the number of calls you make each day, or find an additional avenue of marketing.

> *When I started my first company—a PC software training company in the early '80s—my wife picked up the local business phone directory and started "smiling and dialing." By the time she'd made it through the D's, we'd landed four good-sized training gigs—one at Avon, one at Burke, one at Cincinnati Metro, and one at Drackett.*
>
> *This was clearly a trend, so I quit my daytime job, and we rented an office and started hiring people. And then didn't pick up another training contract until the M's.*
>
> *Fortunately, the contracts already in place were enough to go on, and several other sizable jobs showed up later in the alphabet. However, be aware that business trends can be fickle. Andrew Grove has postulated that "Only the Paranoid Survive"—while true, just remember, just because you're paranoid doesn't mean you're guaranteed to survive!*

Whatever route you take, the important thing is to write down your plan, see how reality matches your plan, and then make adjustments accordingly.

Two business plan tips

The first tip is to be conservative when putting together your plan. It's a lot easier to recover from a conservative mistake than an optimistic one. If you were assuming that you'd spend $1,000 a month on phone and ISP service, but you find a deal and end up only spending $400, this mistake isn't going to hurt you. If you had the numbers reversed, the additional $7,200 of expense for the year could make a significant negative impact on your business.

It's not just numbers, though, that should receive your conservative attention. You'll make many other assumptions that may not prove valid. For instance, suppose one of your marketing projects is to hold a series of free seminars on emerging technologies to develop leads. What if you plan a seminar on the release of a new product, but the manufacturer postpones release for three months—or a year? Suddenly the potential value of that seminar goes way down—but you may still have to pony up the cash for the space you reserved, and you won't be getting the leads you expected.

The second tip is to define your services in detail. This is not the place to be terse! When you sell a product, you define your product in great detail—features, prices, options, target customers, target markets, and so on. Your service is your knowledge, so first define what you know. Are you an expert (or, maybe, an intermediate?) with a particular development tool? Do you have experience with more than one tool?

Remember, you're not trying to sell someone here—you're trying to quantify your own capabilities. Listing "Programming character graphics with Borland Pascal '87" isn't going to do you any good.

Your knowledge isn't based solely on development tools, though. What about business knowledge? Perhaps you have a lot of experience in the garment manufacturing industry, or food processing. Define specifically what you know—this knowledge becomes one of your products that you can offer for sale.

Finally, you want to define how you implement your knowledge—your processes—so, as I've said before, document what you know about the software development process. There are a lot of coding cowboys out there—offering software development processes as one of your services will set you apart from the competition.

Contents of a budget

Not only does a marketing plan produce income numbers, of course, it also produces expenses. And, even more so, the successful marketing plan produces work, which produces even more expenses. So it's time to look at the budget.

A budget is actually just one section of your business plan, but it's often the only part that people formally write up. You've done budgets before (hopefully!)—pull out your trusty spreadsheet, and create a list of income and expenses down the first column. Extend them out for 12 months, calculate the totals for each row as well as the differences for each month and the total year, and you're all done.

Well, not that fast. Putting numbers in a spreadsheet is easy. And, as any venture capitalist will tell you, the numbers don't mean anything. What VCs look for are the reasons behind the numbers. For example, suppose you put down $350 a month for phone expenses. How did you arrive at that number? Does it include an initial deposit? Do you have past experience with business phone expenses? Do you have an idea how many local and long distance calls you'll make each month?

Indeed, the most important part of the budget is not the numbers—it's the footnotes below that explain how each number was arrived at. If you have documented your assumptions, you can then revise the numbers intelligently when you find out how good (or bad) your assumptions were. Next year, when you make up the next budget, you'll be in a position to then produce a more accurate budget, based on your history and your experience this year.

The assumptions aren't the only important part of your budget, though. Look at the 14th column (it's the one where you've totaled each row). Do those numbers make sense? For example, picking on phone expenses again, suppose the yearly total is $13,000 (it could happen—between an ISDN line, business line, fax line, cellular service, and chatty friends on the other end of the country). Does that make business sense to you? If you've budgeted income of $120,000, does it make sense to spend 10% of that on phone service? Or does it make sense to revisit those assumptions, and do some work on saving money in this area?

When you see that you've budgeted $2,200 on subscriptions, and you look across the room and see them all gathering dust because you haven't had time to read any of them for the past four months, does it make sense? Is it possible that you could drop a few of them, and instead buy a compilation CD at the end of the year for a fraction of the price?

Company structure

Part of the business plan is how you're going to be legally, and financially organized. You'll want to decide your company structure—sole proprietor, partnership, Sub-S corporation, LLC, regular corporation—and then determine what you'll need to do to set it up—and, more importantly, to maintain it. Remember that the goal of a business is to make money, so you need to take a few days to thoroughly understand what you'll need to do come tax return time.

List your initial resources

Now that you've got your plan, take a look around and see what you've got. You might have already done this when creating your budget—perhaps you've already got a business phone line, so you don't have to budget for a deposit for a business line. Or you've just plunked down $499 for a three-year subscription to *GeekWorld*, so that line in your budget will be blank for a while.

Isn't this a lot of work?

You may be overwhelmed by the amount of work described in this chapter—all before you land your first customer or receive your first check.

Don't be afraid to put a lot of work into this. Professional ballplayers—the very best in the world—still spend the majority of their time practicing. And they don't practice behind-the-back slam-dunks or Hail Mary passes from the 50-yard line—they practice the fundamentals—100 free throw shots every morning or an hour of batting practice after calisthenics.

And you're just a rookie—so practice for you is that much more important. Each time you review how you present yourself, what you do, why you do it, you're practicing—so when you land in front of a customer, they'll assume you've been doing this for years.

Each time you make a pass at your materials, plans, documents, and such, you'll find holes in your practices and assumptions that are better found now than when you're two months into a yearlong gig with a customer.

Also, you'll be able to reuse much of what you put together for your business plan—your marketing materials and your Web site will rely on this information.

And, frankly, building this business plan is a great exercise in determining whether you've really got what it takes. If you can't map out a strategy for your business's future, then you probably won't do well with many of the non-coding related skills that will secure your future income.

Jumping off for practice

Now that you've got it all together, it's time to get real, sort of. As soon as you're ready for business, start making sales calls—as many as possible. Chase down every single lead that you run across, and make the sales call as if your livelihood depended on it. Don't worry about whether you really want the business or not. Why would you go on a sales call for a project that you don't want? Because, as with everything, practice is essential to becoming skilled.

By making these "practice" sales calls, you'll become more and more comfortable in this foreign territory. You'll run into many different scenarios and environments, find out what types of questions a potential customer will ask, and learn how to respond. Much better to flub your lines in front of someone whose business you don't need than to mess up while pitching to a critical client.

> *I remember the first "sales call" I went on, just a couple years out of college. A customer for whom I had done some spreadsheet training wanted me to develop a complex spreadsheet for them. I got all dressed up in my best suit to interview the assistant controller (the contact at the customer), and left 45 minutes later, dripping wet. He had grilled me up and down, left and right about my background, skills, the approach I'd take, and 100 other things. All for a custom spreadsheet that was going to cost less than $1,000. I still picture him going home that night and having a good laugh with his wife: "You shoulda seen the kid who came in today to do that rate calculation spreadsheet!"*

You may remember *MAD Magazine*'s regular feature "Snappy Answers to Stupid Questions," where the cartoon set up a situation typical of daily life, and provided smart-ass answers that you "wish you had thought of then." You can't possibly anticipate every question that a customer will ask you, or what situations you'll find yourself in, but the more practice you have, the more likely you'll have learned how to respond in those situations. And the more comfortable you are, the better off both you and your customer are going to be.

Chapter 7
Positioning

"Your friend seems to be quite a mercenary. I wonder if he cares about anyone—or anything—at all?"—Princess Leia to Luke Skywalker, about Han Solo
"I care!"—Luke Skywalker
  —Star Wars, A New Hope

Positioning is the placement of your product or service in relation to your competition in the marketplace. Avis Rent-A-Car's slogan, "We're #2—we try harder" is a well-known example. Positioning allows you to differentiate yourself from your competition, and differentiation is what gets you the business in the first place, lets you charge premium prices, and generally lets you run things your way. And positioning is where expectations are first set.

Expectations are set the first time your customer hears of your company. If you're looking through the Yellow Pages for a rental car company, and you run across a company named "Rent-A-Wreck," you have already formed an impression, and have developed a set of expectations that you will subconsciously carry with you when dealing with this company. For example, you would likely expect to pay rock-bottom prices, you would expect to find older cars not exactly in the prime of life, and you would expect service from a caustic, gum-smacking, cigarette-smoking woman with big hair along the lines of a Carol Burnett comedy sketch.

If, on the other hand, you ran across a company named "Executive Motorcar Leasing, Limited," you would expect a high level of service, high quality, brand-new cars, and prices to match.

Simply by choosing a name, each of these companies has staked out a share of mind with you, and developed a set of expectations. This combination of share of mind and initial expectations positions the company in relation to others in the industry.

Positioning: The basics

Business consists of a number of disciplines, such as marketing, sales, research and development, manufacturing, finance, service, support, transportation, and so on. Depending on the maturity level of the business and the position of the business on the supply-demand curve, each of these disciplines may be more or less emphasized.

For example, in a highly competitive, mature market such as consumer goods, marketing and finance are very important. Marketing is important because differentiating a product in a field where there are many similar products requires a great deal of attention. Finance is important because often the profit margins in the business are small, and so it's important to keep track of one's pennies—those pennies may be the difference between staying in business and failing.

In the custom software development industry, on the other hand, there is more demand than supply, so in many cases all the marketing that needs to be done is simply standing up, waving one's arms, yelling "I write code! I write code!" and waiting for the crowd to bury you.

Thus, you may not know a lot, if anything, about positioning. Here are the basics.

What is positioning?

Positioning is the placement of your product or service in relation to those of your competition in the market that you are serving. (From now on, I'm going to use the term "product" to mean both "product and service.") That sounds like one of those textbook definitions that you had to memorize in school, and forgot soon after. But there are some ideas in that definition that we need to explore further.

In a practical sense, positioning allows you to differentiate yourself from the competition. Differentiation is what gets you the business, lets you charge premium prices, and allows you to be more proactive in running your business. Conversely, when the product you're offering is perceived as "just like all the others" and therefore a commodity, you'll have a tougher time selling. Buyers have no specific motivation to choose you over the other guys, and if they do choose you, they have no reason to pay premium prices, and you'll likely find yourself reacting to the competition's moves instead of vice versa.

Another advantage to positioning is that you get first crack at setting expectations for your customers, and this holds true whether you're an independent or work in a company's software development department. In both cases, your customers really don't care about you— they have a problem to solve, and they're hoping that you—the computer guy—can solve it for them. It's up to you to communicate the types of problems you can solve, how you go about doing so, and, just as importantly, which types of problems you can't solve.

A well-known example of positioning has been the rallying cry, "We're #2," for a certain company for years. You already know I'm talking about Avis. Why would anyone in their right mind boast that they're losing the race? Because it attracts the attention and sympathy of America's Everyman, who loves to back the underdog. It's also a position that no one else can claim. It also stakes out the high ground in an area that's extremely valuable—customer service. "We're #2, so we have to try harder" implies that you'll get better care than by going to the market leader or any other participant in the business.

Another classic example of positioning is Apple's "A computer for the rest of us." Again, this is positioning for a perceived consumer product. This campaign was targeted at individuals, not corporations—but, surprisingly enough, a large percentage of corporations have people working there.

In order to successfully position your product, you need to answer a few questions.

What do you sell?

First and foremost, what is it that you think you're selling or, in the case of corporate developers, offering? A disconcerting number of software developers are in the "AFAB" business—"Anything For A Buck." Yes, when the mortgage payment is due in four days and you don't have a lick of work, most anything from installing network cards to changing printer ribbons sounds awfully attractive. And on the corporate side, although you'd like the luxury of being able to develop cool new apps all day long, your boss may not see it the same way. But if you don't have a goal for the type of work you'd like to do, then you'll never get there. You may have to pick up a few less-than-completely-desirable jobs along the way, but, if you identify your position and keep emphasizing it, you'll eventually be able to pick and choose among jobs and do what you want to do.

You need to be very clear, in your own mind, about what it is that you're offering. If, by the time you're reading this, you're still not clear, then go back to the last two chapters and work on this until you are clear. Face it—if you're not clear in your own mind, you will fail when you try to set specific expectations in your customer's mind.

Is the answer to this question some variant of "I write custom database applications," or would you like to have a bit more room to provide a wider breadth of services or a greater depth in a specialization? Do you want to provide ongoing support and maintenance? Do you want to modify standardized accounting software packages? Do you want to upgrade custom applications written by other developers who have long since disappeared? Would you like to do training? Are you interested in providing additional pieces to the IT puzzle—setting up networks, tweaking installs, setting up communications, or any number of other services that your customer may need?

Identifying what it is you sell—or, more likely, what you want to sell—doesn't mean you're prohibited from doing anything else. However, you'll be building yourself around your greatest strengths and those things that interest you the most.

Be clear that you know what you want to offer before you talk to your first customer, and be able to identify it in 25 words or less. If you can't tell someone at a cocktail party what you do in two or three sentences, you don't have a clear idea yet.

What are they buying?
Customers are often so focused on their own situation that they're not paying attention to you. To them, all computer folk are the same. The industry is still new enough that many people don't understand that there are specialties and subspecialties, just as with medicine, law, and other similar professions. It is up to you to determine what it is that they think they're buying.

I once delivered a custom application to a customer, and after installing it on their network and handing them a set of original diskettes, they asked, "But where's the box?" They thought that they were buying a piece of software—just like in the store—and didn't realize that there was a difference between a $99 word processor from Computer City and a $20,000 custom application.

For this reason, you should ask the customer straight out, "Are you looking for us to write custom software for you?" How they answer this question will give you the information you need to continue.

If they look at you with a quizzical look in their eye, and answer with the business equivalent of "Well, duh…" then you're on the right track. They understand, to a large extent, what they're getting into—in fact, they might have even done this before.

But if they start to talk around the question, or hesitate, or continue to talk without answering, they might not understand exactly what it is that you're offering.

What are they really buying?

What you do and what your customers buy are two different things. Maybe you've heard the old adage "People don't buy quarter-inch drill bits. They buy the ability to make quarter-inch holes." Along the same lines, as much as it might hurt your feelings, people aren't all that interested in buying your software. They've got a problem to solve, and they're hoping, yes, praying, that your custom application will solve that problem.

On a grander scale, though, it's not the application that will solve that problem—it's you (and your company or department) that will solve it.

Sure, they said they wanted a piece of custom software. But they really have a business problem to solve. Perhaps they want to provide wider access to the sales figures, and on a more timely basis. Or they want to let their field reps calculate quotes on the fly, instead of having to send faxes into headquarters. Maybe their customers want more details on their bills. And so on.

Custom software development is a pretty exciting business. I can't imagine selling electric motors or designing struts for a vehicle's undercarriage for the rest of my life. (Well, except perhaps for a few fleeting moments during the fourth reinstall of Windows before noon one day.) As a result, it's easy to go into a meeting with a potential customer and after listening for a few minutes, start jabbering on about "We could do this" or "I can do that" without really listening to what they're looking for.

The best way to avoid this scenario is to keep your mouth shut, except when asking questions. If you listen carefully enough, and ask enough questions, you'll eventually be able to discover what it is they're really interested in.

In Chapter 11, "The Sales Call," I'll discuss what questions to ask the customer in order to pin them down about exactly what it is they're really buying.

Why do they buy it?

Why do people buy? Fundamentally, people buy things because they're dissatisfied with the status quo. More succinctly, they're in pain, and they expect their purchase to ease or remove that pain. Money is generally considered to be the scarcest of scarce resources, and so people are rather particular about parting with it. (Although, when you think about it, you can always get more money, but you can't turn back the clock.) As a result, they're very demanding about expecting results when spending money.

Think about the last few things you bought. In each case, if you reflect carefully, your purchase was aimed at removing some sort of pain. You were hungry, so you bought a burger and fries at that fine cafe named "EAT." When you were done, you weren't hungry anymore. However, your eye hurts from the fistfight with the regulars at "EAT," so you bought a bottle of disinfectant. You also found that you were a mite chilly from the new holes torn in your shirt, again from that fight with the boys from "EAT," so your third purchase, a new shirt and sweater, eased that pain. Get the idea?

What types of pain could someone be experiencing that would cause them to buy custom software from you? (No, I'm not advocating the application of torture to get them to buy... That comes during acceptance testing when you have to deal with some whiny creep who keeps complaining about "bugs" when he hasn't taken the time to read the specs to find out what the system is designed to do!) As a custom software developer, you're probably selling to companies, and so you really have to convince the people in those companies to sign the purchase order. They won't do so unless they're convinced that your software will ease their pain.

They might have a legitimate business reason. For example, they may want to provide IVR (Interactive Voice Response) access to part of their database so that patients can find out the status of their prescription without having to talk to a human, thus providing 24-hour service while at the same time reducing labor costs. And, conveniently, they want you to provide the programs that will do so.

But, funny enough, people are human, and as a result (you can quote me on this), one of the biggest mistakes you can make is to assume that people will act rationally in a business setting. There are a lot of not so obvious reasons ("illogical") that someone would buy custom software from you:

- He needs to get his boss off his back.

- She wants to boast to the others in her golf foursome.

- He needs to impress a customer.

- She wants to show the guy in the adjoining department that she had enough power to get their MIS project approved while he didn't.

- He wants to keep his budget from shrinking next year, so he's going to make up some project that will use up the remaining budget for this year.

- They don't want to do the work themselves.

- They convinced the boss that they are too busy to take this on—don't want work cutting into their golf game.

- They want someone to blame.

- They want to "acquire" your ideas.

- You are also working for their competition and they think you will be a good source of information.

- No one believes them, so if they hire a consultant to say the same thing it might actually get done.

The list is endless.

The one thing people don't want to happen upon the purchase of an item is to end up even more unhappy than they were when you started. Even more than becoming the hero, they don't want to become the goat. So pain avoidance is a significant part of the equation.

How does this insight on why people buy things help you determine your positioning? The original answer to the earlier question of "What do you sell?" was "Custom database applications." It might be more beneficial for you to realize that you're really selling peace of mind, or a week of freedom from the boss, or the route to a bigger office. If you can decide what it is that you really sell, then you're well on the way to developing a position.

Jewelry is another example of "What you're buying isn't really what you're buying," and how positioning helps jewelers sell to their customers. All jewelers sell essentially the same stuff—and it all comes from the same two blocks of wholesalers in New York City. Sounds like a commodity if there ever was one.

In Milwaukee, there are a number of "chain" jewelry stores that cater to the middle of the market. They position themselves as "the friendly neighborhood jeweler" or the one where "the low prices are worth the drive out to the country" or as having the "largest selection in town." But each of these jewelers is essentially targeting the same group of customers.

But there's another jeweler in town, however, that has been around for a century, and has been, from the get-go, the city's most exclusive and expensive jeweler.

Instead of selling regular jewelry, they are selling the glamour of their store's reputation. Price is never mentioned; simply receiving a box with their emblem on it is guaranteed to send a woman's heart a-flutter. They're not selling jewelry—they're selling a piece of the Rich and Famous.

Who else could they buy it from?

Unless you're a monopoly (and there isn't such a thing as a monopoly in the computer business, now is there?), your customers have a choice about how to solve their problem.

This doesn't always mean that they can walk down the street and buy from Hank, the neighborhood software developer. But there is often more than one way to skin a cat. And whether you're after the skin or the cat plays a large part in which way you choose.

First, they may be able to go to a competitor who offers similar services, or, at least, a competitor who they perceive to offer similar services. In this increasingly global, connected world, you may find yourself competing not only with other local developers, but with large consulting firms moving down-market and with off-shore development houses as well—sometimes all on the same engagement.

Second, they may be able to go to a different source that can provide many (if not all) of the services in need. Just because you're a corporate developer, don't assume that you're their only source. A department may be able to outsource the development of their new software project, or they may be able to hire someone who can do most of what they need using an end-user tool.

In addition, some types of development, particularly when they can be done using end-user tools, don't require a professional software developer as a player. Other types of development may place a higher premium on specific industry or technical knowledge—such as mathematical forecasting or document publishing—than on the software development process.

Third, they may be able to figure out a different way to solve their actual problem, other than buying custom software. For instance, suppose they're looking for a way to handle a huge influx of orders caused by the introduction of a new product. Instead of buying custom software, they may just add another row of desks to the army of clerks on the seventh floor, and handle the overflow by throwing bodies at it.

Finally, perhaps their need simply isn't that critical, and they can afford to wait. The pain may subside of its own accord.

So don't bet that you're their only solution.

Why do they buy it from you?

Ready to have your ego deflated? The answer to this question often does that.

The full text of this question is actually "Why do people buy from you and not someone else?" In other words, what distinguishing characteristics do you have? Unfortunately, you're the worst person to answer this question, right? Partly because it's hard to be objective, and partly because 99% of what you are going to say is probably something out of a Dilbert cartoon:

- "Because our quality is better!"

- "Because we have the best people!"

- "Because our customer service is excellent!"

- "Because we are focused on total quality management in a team while delivering 100% customer satisfaction."

Unfortunately, more often than not, the answer is something like, "You had the biggest ad in the Yellow Pages," "You were closer than the other guys we called," "No one answered the phone when we called our regular programmer," or even, "You were the first company that happened to be open."

How do you determine the real answer to this question? Sure, you can hire a market research firm to do the objective questioning for you, but that's probably not a great choice. First, it's expensive. And second, if you're like most software developers, you don't have a customer list numbering in the thousands—or even the hundreds. As a result, the sample size isn't big enough for a market research firm to draw valid conclusions.

Instead, go back through the list of projects you've done over the past 5 or 10 years (or less, if you don't have that much experience)—yes, even the ones you'd rather forget—and ask yourself how the initial contact was made. And at that time, what were their other choices? (This is an excellent question to record as part of the initial interview or phone call, by the way. I cover more ideas on what to collect during the initial interview in Chapter 10, "The Initial Contact.") Given that information, you can make some guesses about the general nature of why your customers are buying from you.

Then it's just up to you to decide whether you like the answer, or, if not, what you want the answer to be, and to take corresponding action.

Determining your competitive advantage

What is your competitive advantage?

This begs the assumption that you have one. There is so much demand for our services that it's entirely possible that you're still in the middle of the crowd—no distinguishing characteristic, no specialty or advantage that helps you consistently win projects, but still happily busy working day to day.

And that's not necessarily bad. You can live a long time in the middle of the pack. It's just that having an edge makes your life more profitable and more fun. Perhaps you do have a competitive advantage, but you're simply not aware of it. Here's how you can try to determine what it is.

Take out a large sheet of paper and list as many characteristics about developers that customers would be interested in (or horrified about) as you can. This list might include professional appearance items like suits or jeans, business cards with raised lettering or with smears from the HP III that they were printed on, fancy offices or someone's garage. Or it may be technical things like presence on beta test teams of current products, access to industry resources, and years of expertise in the field. Does the firm answer the phone within two rings, do they have an after-hours number, and do they have a receptionist or a scratchy answering machine?

Once you're done with this list, put yourself firmly in the shoes of someone who is on the hunt for custom software, and review the items—are they truly things that would concern this prospective buyer?

Then call a dozen of your competitors (or have an associate do it for you) and find out how they rate—or if they even make the list. Eventually you'll find a number of similarities and a few differences. Finally, rank yourself on the same list (or have some associates do it for you), and see where you stand. If you like what you see, you have just positioned yourself competitively against them. If you don't like what you see, you've now got the ingredients for developing a positioning plan—which, of course, should be part of your business plan.

Before you get all fired up about trumpeting the differences between you and the other guys, remember that the advantage or the difference that you're trying to project has to be important to the customer. If your primary distinguishing characteristic is that you always wear gym shorts and a propeller beanie when you work, it's entirely possible that most customers aren't going to care.

Why corporate IS departments should be interested in positioning

I want to emphasize that this discussion isn't just for independent developers. Corporate developers may also want to consider positioning themselves. Just because you have a lock on the work coming to you doesn't mean you're necessarily going to want all of it.

You may want your organization to funnel IT projects through you before they go outside for help, so that you have the "right of first refusal" and are in a position to cherry pick the good projects, and shunt off less desirable projects to others. Positioning in this environment will help you identify your department to your customer base inside the organization as to what your expertise is, and what it isn't, so that you get the good stuff first.

Samples of positioning

P.T. Barnum once said, "If you can't describe your idea on the back of a business card, you don't have a clear idea of what it is." In this section, I'll describe some ways that you can differentiate yourself from the developer down the street, or down the row of cubicles.

How can your potential customers tell that you're different from the next developer who's going to walk in the door? Everybody has a beard (well, maybe not some of the women), everybody looks like a geek (well, again, maybe not some of the women), and everybody can recite the 10 most obvious inconsistencies in the first episode of ST:TNG (yes, even the women).

A successful positioning

Would you like to be let in on a secret—how I developed an unbeatable answer to this last question? As I mentioned in the introduction, I started developing PC applications in 1982 with dBASE II on a 64K PC. My first company was based in Cincinnati, and I used dBASE for a number of years. I sold that company in the late '80s and moved my family back to my hometown of Milwaukee. When I started up again, I was the new guy in town with a few skills but no contacts and no leads. As a result, the first thing I did was call up each of the current developers in town and ask to subcontract, in order to get started and move some bucks into my wallet.

After making 20 or 30 calls, I came to one incredible conclusion about all of those developers: They were all the same. I couldn't tell one from the next from the third. If any of them are reading this, they're thinking that I probably skipped over their name, but that's okay. The point is that after a week of cold calling competitors in my own business, I couldn't tell any of them apart. And if I couldn't, potential customers couldn't either.

I was worried that I would walk into a prospective customer's site and as soon as I left, they'd forget my name and call the next guy on the list. So I asked myself, "What is going to make me stand out from the other 20 developers in the phone book?" Other than showering regularly, that is. After pondering the question for a while, I turned it around and put myself in the place of the customer. "So why are you different from the three others we've interviewed this week?"

The only answer I could come up with was to develop professional credentials that would set me apart. But how?

The software development industry, while a profession like accounting or medicine, has one distinguishing characteristic: All one has to do to become an "expert" is buy a PC, print up some business cards, and learn some jargon. You don't have to go to med school for a decade, you don't have to pass the bar exam or become a CPA. Furthermore, there are precious few avenues to obtain any sort of credibility, and most developers don't even do that.

So my next step was to develop a set of public credentials such as speaking engagements, writing articles, being active on the CompuServe forums, and so on. I did this to be regarded as somewhat of an expert in the field. I've been very fortunate to gain the visibility I have, and a couple of great breaks have fallen my way, but all in all, the positioning was a very calculated move.

Once I achieved that, it was easy to stand out from the competition. More than once I've gone to prospects to discuss potential development, and brought along copies of things I've written. The competition doesn't stand much of a chance when the customer finds out that they've been learning from a book that you, the customer's other potential vendor, have written.

This doesn't mean that my company wins every contract. If I were to walk in the door of a MIS director's office and find out that I look just like the bully who used to beat that director up every day at lunch, well, it won't matter how impressive my curriculum vitae is—I'm not going to get the job.

Well, enough of my "I Love Me" story. The point is that positioning yourself in the market—as I did with language expertise—enables you to win jobs and command higher margins than you would otherwise be able to.

First, let me address the question already on the tip of your tongue: "You just told us how you did it, and now anyone can do the same thing. Don't you feel stupid for giving away your secret?" The answer to this is pretty easy. It's "No."

There are lots of languages and tools around, and I certainly don't have a monopoly. Publishing and speaking at conferences as a means of developing credibility are time-honored techniques used in many industries. While developing language expertise in 1991 was certainly easier than it is today, it's not impossible as we watch 2002 disappear in the rear view mirror. There are a few caveats, however.

First of all, it takes a great deal of time to develop extensive expertise in a specific language, and time is not a resource we have an abundance of anymore. The frequent revision cycle of our tools makes a large investment in a single development environment more and more difficult, and if it's accomplished, the credential is fleeting—you need to continually make the investment as new versions come out. That's something that many are not willing to do.

Second, as tools become more complex, they depend on other tools as well, and the more tools that are thrown into the mix, the more difficult it is to develop mastery.

Third, while it's valuable, visibility is not a substitute for competence. Being able to write a paper or skillfully present materials in a 75-minute demonstration is not the same as developing a 3,000-hour application.

How can you differentiate yourself from your competition? Let me count the ways.

Expertise with a tool

Although I've just played the doom-and-gloom guy about developing expertise in a particular language, this area is still wide open. Consider becoming the world's best on a particular product, to the absolute exclusion of everything else. Additionally, become comfortable with absolutely everything under the sun regarding that product, so that when the customer calls, you're in a position to do whatever they ask.

Naturally, there is a downside to this approach. Suppose you achieve the top of the heap, and six months later, the product is sold off or discontinued. You may feel that you've put yourself at the end of a very fragile limb, but frankly, there's still a lot of value in your position.

First of all, there is likely still a lot of maintenance work (as well as some new work) for those firms that have made a significant investment in development in that product. They'll continue to need support from someone. As other developers who also specialize in this language begin to drift away, you'll find yourself continually in demand.

Second, contrast yourself with another developer who, similarly, is a "one-trick pony" but doesn't have the expertise or credentials that you have. I've seen this several times—the high-end developers still keep busy; those at the bottom of the food chain starve.

You've heard the joke "What did the COBOL programmer say to the SmallTalk programmer?"—"Would you like fries with that, sir?" Fortunately, this dig is fairly far off base. COBOL programmers had themselves a field day during the Y2K countdown, and they will continue to be in demand for some time to come. Who will suffer first? The COBOL programmer with expertise and credentials or the COBOL programmer simply with expertise?

Expertise within an industry or market

You don't have to identify a specific tool, though. You may decide to specialize on the platform, or the mechanism of delivery. The Internet, obviously, is hot. And while the "Internet" isn't a "language," expertise with the mechanism is helping a lot of developers do very well. Palm development is another area, and within that, wireless expertise.

Process expertise

Another area of expertise can focus down to a single phase or aspect of the software development process. Some consultants make their living by being really, really, *really* good at one thing, such as user interface design, object-oriented analysis, or testing. Rather than wading through the entire minefield of software development, these people are called into a team as the subject matter authority on one particular aspect of the job.

The positive side of this type of positioning is that it can be crystal clear what you do and what you do not do, and you can often charge a premium—much like the doctor who specializes in, say, pediatric brain surgery can charge more than your "run-of-the-mill" surgeon. You will need to keep up with every source of late-breaking news in your field— subscribing to all of the journals, attending the conferences, monitoring the online forums— but, in exchange, you get to focus on that one thing that you love. The downsides with such a highly focused specialty are the risk of your techniques becoming obsolete, the challenges of establishing your credentials sufficiently to put food on the table, and competing in a smaller marketplace.

Outsourcing expertise

Outsourcing is one of those terms that occasionally pops up on the cover of *Business Week* as the business management fad of the month. It's well beyond me to predict whether or not the long-term trend is toward outsourcing or not. It's entirely possible that in another 10 years the popular business magazines will predict the doom of outsourcing as companies learn to properly manage internally.

Or maybe not.

In any case, there's definitely a need for firms who specialize in outsourcing custom software applications. Realize, however, that this service is different from simply being an independent programmer, or from the "body shop" that parks people on chairs for months on end. Just as outsourcing payroll processing or disaster recovery services involve a complete package of services, outsourcing custom application development entails the whole suite of services from analysis and design, through specifications, program development, testing, installation, training, and maintenance.

Depending on the size of the application, a single developer may be able to wear all of these hats, but not always. If you have the expertise—and the desire—to do so, there's a world of opportunity in this niche.

Selling before the chasm (leading edge expertise)

In his landmark book, *Crossing the Chasm*, Geoffrey Moore described a phenomenon of high technology marketing that has spelled doom for many firms in high-tech businesses.

The scenario plays out like this. A firm introduces a new product, and gets a landslide of business with little or no marketing. Somewhere during the flurry of activity, somebody in management realizes that if sales continue, the firm will soon be overrun with business. As a result, the firm expands, adding executives from outside the industry, opening sales offices, building new factories, hiring additional staff, and a whole host of other activities appropriate for a firm that's in the middle of a tenfold increase in sales.

And then they wait for the initial surge of orders to become a flood—for which they are now prepared.

And they wait. And wait.

Pretty soon cash has dried up. Executives used to commanding large forces of staff are starting to lay people off. Management blames Sales for poor sales, and accuses them of sitting on their backsides. Sales blames Marketing for doing a lousy job, and Marketing blames both R&D for not coming out with a new version fast enough, and the factory for failing to fix the faults of the current version.

Sooner than is really believable, the company fails. What went wrong?

The problem is that initially, the company was selling to one market, but to sustain its growth, the company needed to begin selling to another market, and didn't recognize the difference.

The market for a high-technology product can be split up into a bell curve. The leading slope of the bell curve is made up of early adopters—those who are willing to put up with the inadequacies of a new product in exchange for an early competitive advantage, or simply the thrill of playing with something new. This group of early adopters creates the initial surge of orders.

The steep upslope of the bell curve is made up of a second group—a group who, while interested in early adoption of technology, are also going to demand a business rationale for getting involved. And the marketing to this group is significantly different from the marketing done to the early adopters. However, the firm didn't recognize this difference, and tried to sell to the second group in the same manner. That attempt failed, and sales actually fell instead of increasing. This difference is referred to as "the chasm," and Moore's book is about how to change marketing techniques from the first group to the second.

The rest of the bell curve is made up of several more segments, each with its own particular characteristics and requirements as well.

Why is this important to you? Because you may find a place in the technologies that you work with where you can sell to one of these groups—specifically, to the early adopters. Their needs are particularly demanding—they want to be coddled and taken care of in terms of being made to feel important. They're getting "in on the ground floor" and it's critical to make sure they feel that they're special.

Knowing this, you may be able to develop an expertise and a facility for working with these types of customers. And once you've developed a reputation for being "high-tech" and "ahead of the curve" (difficult as it may be in the computer industry), you can make that capability a differentiating factor and position yourself accordingly.

Customer service orientation

Perhaps your answer lies in the non-technical arena: 24-hour, on-call service, or offices in multiple cities to handle customers with multiple sites. However, if this is your tact, you don't want to assume you know the level of service you customer wants/needs. Sometimes it is obvious—they are open 24x7 so they will need the system supported 24x7. But other times it may not be clear to you what they want/need. You need to discuss with the client what their needs are to make sure you can deliver what they want/need. You want to understand what your client considers to be "good service" so you understand their expectations.

Company demographic specialization

Markets aren't simply groupings by industry anymore. Just as the "soccer mom" demographic became popular with the political campaign committees a few years back, businesses can be sliced and diced in many flavors in order to target a specific niche.

However, for custom software developers, the size of a company can be a compelling demographic.

Selling to a Fortune 100 company has its specific challenges—the IT executives at those firms are sought after by large numbers of vendors. You need to be able to develop specific skills to sell to that market, but if you can, you've got an edge on all the others who don't have those skills.

On the other hand, while it may seem that an 11-person "mom and pop" company would not be a likely target for a developer trying to sell customer applications starting at $50,000 or more, that's not entirely true. A number of firms in the medical business, for example, are essentially middlemen for processing claims data—and their entire business revolves around information processing. A $50,000 application may not be unrealistic for a firm with a $400,000 payroll that does nothing but manipulate data.

Furthermore, small firms typically don't have the need for (or the ability to pay for) a full-time MIS person. Or, if they do, that person is often tied up with mundane, day-to-day tasks like debugging formulas in spreadsheets, figuring out why the printer keeps getting jammed, and installing new NICs in the machines that the owner "got a deal on from a friend" last weekend.

It takes a certain kind of personality, as well as the need to be more of a "jack of all trades," to be able to deal with smaller businesses. But that's exactly what you're looking for—being able to differentiate yourself by describing the services you excel at providing for small firms.

Geographic orientation

Similar to vertical market expertise, consider casting your net in a regionally specific area. Does your region have more than one commonly used language, such as Quebec in Canada? Does the region have a high concentration of industry or a set of needs that are peculiar to that area?

What about servicing the rural areas from a metropolitan base? There are lots of large manufacturing companies located in small communities, and they typically "come to the big city" for their legal and accounting help. Why shouldn't they come to the "big city" for their software development services as well? A lot of firms, when developing marketing lists, ignore companies that aren't inside the city limits. If you fish in areas that other fishermen tend to ignore, your odds of success will likely be better.

Vertical market orientation

The next possibility for positioning that you could look at would be to focus on customer needs instead of your capabilities. Languages and products come and go, but experts in a specific field can make a living for as long as that field is around. Do you know more about the Laundromat, used car, or fresh produce business than anyone else within 100 miles? If you know everything there is to know about providing pricing data to manufacturer reps, you're going to be able to go in against the competition that is learning about the business for the first time, and clean their clock.

In fact, positioning yourself as an expert in a specific vertical tool is an excellent idea, because your ability now transcends the requirement of being an expert in a language. You can say, "Yes, I've written 17 applications that deal with pricing data for manufacturers reps," and the competitor is going to stutter, "Yeah, uh, I think I can do one of those."

You may be an expert in Paradox 4 or Visual Basic 6.0, but as soon as the new release comes out, *voilà!*—you're a rookie just like everyone else again. On the other hand, if you know tons and tons about medical data, and the new version comes out, you still know tons and tons about medical data. (Thanks to my friend Miriam Davis for making this point so clear.) Meanwhile, the other guy is trying to learn the new version like you are and still doesn't have any vertical expertise. (Naturally, you have to be considerate of specific customer knowledge, trade secrets, and the like, but there's still a lot of room to maneuver and still respect the confidentiality of firms for whom you work.)

The positioning of a corporate IS department

The preceding discussion is all fine and good for the independent developer, but if you're a corporate developer, you may be left wanting. "Sure, an independent can turn down business, but we can't—we're captive to our company." In some cases, that may be true, but more than likely, you've still got some room to maneuver.

The first possibility is to, with the help of corporate management, explicitly state what your department's mission is. Perhaps you need to split IS into two parts—one being software research and development, and the other being operations, production support, and help desk technical support—so that you don't have people manning the help desk and trying to design and develop internal software applications at the same time.

Once you've got a dedicated software development group, more or less, it's time to focus on the types of development they'll do. For instance, I know of many companies that define for their users which platforms and tools they'll support, and if a user decides to install an application that's not on the "approved" list, they're on their own. The same can go for writing apps—if your internal development group standardizes on Oracle and C++, when a user department comes asking for modifications to a custom Visual Basic application, you can point them to the "approved" list.

The second possibility is when management doesn't provide this ability, and expects you to support anything and everything that shows up under the tree. In this case, you may be able to subconsciously position your department by assigning priorities to incoming jobs according to your preference. Eventually your department will get a reputation for "Awww, they only do Delphi in IS—if we want Java, we're going to have to find our own help."

Be careful how far you take this position, however, as it can be a two-edged sword. Refusing to support the evolving needs of the company can spell the death knell for you. The IS departments who ignored the users and concentrated on their COBOL applications on the mainframe brought about the PC revolution, and it's this kind of attitude that is causing management to consider outsourcing their operations.

You may also be able to direct the type of work that comes in by designing processes and procedures that fit better with the type of work you want to do. For example, suppose you want your department to specialize in internal client/server apps, and you don't want to do small, department-level LAN apps. Set up your processes so that they're tailored for the client-server jobs. The LAN applications will take longer and require a bunch of paperwork or meetings that may be unnecessary.

Conclusion

One last word about positioning. Part of the reason for this book is to suggest and publish a standard methodology for managing the acquisition and development of custom applications. Because there is no standard methodology like those in the medical, legal, or financial fields, anyone can buy a PC and call themselves an expert. By providing a set of guidelines or generally accepted practices, I'm hoping to create some common groundwork for application development.

So, from that perspective, this whole book is a case study in positioning. Think about it.

Chapter 8
Marketing

"You can have Spam, Spam, Spam, Eggs and Spam."
 —Monty Python

Marketing is the process where you make the customer aware of your products or services, and convince them to prefer your product or service to those of the competition. Sales, which I'll cover shortly, is the process of converting an interest in your widget to a sale of your widget. In other words, marketing is the advance team for sales.

If you are reading this chapter in the hopes of finding the Holy Grail to marketing, the magic answer, the trick to making a million dollars next week, well, today is your lucky day. Out of the thousands of books written on marketing over the past 50 years, I alone have found the answer, and I'm going to share it with you.

Bob Kehoe, a friend of mine and co-founder of RDI Software Technologies (now known as Geneer) in Chicago, is fond of saying, "Marketing: nothing works." What he means is that none of the traditional avenues toward marketing—Yellow Pages ads, newspaper ads, direct mailing, cold calling—none of them work for software providers like they do for providers of consumer goods. If you sell automobiles, you can run a series of ads on the radio or TV, and expect a certain return on your dollar. If you provide snow-plowing services or sell life insurance, you can do a direct mail piece and find a predictable amount of business coming in over the transom within a given amount of time.

But custom software is one of those weird beasts. It's not like selling vacuum cleaners or industrial tubing or any number of other hard goods. It's more like selling accounting services. You can't just "smile and dial" like a stockbroker. You need to make a lot of personal contacts, collect references, and wait a long time. Don't expect to go into business, run a few ads or send out a mailing, and be swimming in business as if you were a pet shop. That's what Bob is saying.

So, how do you go about picking up new business? How do software companies grow if they don't have the means to market? And how do you, as a corporate developer, package the products and services you offer so that the rest of the company knows what you're doing?

What is marketing?

Whittling down the entire expanse of the sales process into a couple of pat phrases such as "marketing" and "selling" is kind of like saying there are basically two types of computers—big ones and small ones. Thousands of books and seminars have been put together on the various pieces of the sales process, with nearly as many techniques, methodologies, and gimmicks. But fundamentally, it all boils down to four things: Locate prospects with a reasonably good chance that they could be buyers of your products/services, make a prospect aware of your product, get them to prefer it to other choices, and then provide the means for them to purchase it. Marketing is the first of the two parts of this process—locating a prospect and making them aware of your product.

Types of marketing

Marketing takes many forms, but can be boiled down into three basic types. First, image marketing is what the multi-nationals do when they sponsor an event or a cause. This typically builds company or brand-name awareness, but without the direct sales message (image marketing lacks the "Buy XYZ because it's 10% faster" message). The second type—brand marketing—focuses on a specific category of product for which you want to differentiate your product. And the third—product specific marketing—is often targeted toward a particular audience, and is focused on a specific offering.

General image marketing

With image marketing, all you see is a company's logo or their name. Instead of trying to promote or push a specific product or service, they're simply displaying their name in conjunction with a "good cause" or a "memorable event" in the hope that you will come to view that firm in a positive light.

Sponsors of public television are a good example of image marketing. "'The Beauty of the Wilderness, Part 7' is funded in part by the Monolithic Oil Company and the Omnipresent Computer Corporation."

Then, when it comes time to choose a new computer system or buy gasoline, these two firms hope that you'll ignore the salesman from R-Computers-R-More-Reliable and drive past the Environmentally Friendly Gasoline Shoppe.

Or, for another example, "What kind of sneaker do I want? Oh, I don't know. What are my choices? Nike or Reebok? Hmmm, never heard of Reebok—let's try the Nikes."

Another reason for image marketing is to attempt to offset past (or potential future) negative publicity surrounding other activities of the company. I'm sure you can easily think of firms engaged in this practice without me slamming them as well.

Image marketing is expensive, obviously, since there is nearly no chance of ringing up a sale as a direct result of the expenditure. Therefore, given scarce resources, this avenue is one you probably won't want (or need) to avail yourself of in a big way. Nonetheless, you may still be able to keep your name in front of the appropriate peer groups without extraordinary outlays.

For instance, sponsoring a refreshment break each year at the same developer's conference is a way to directly put your name in front of a large number of potential customers, employees, and business partners.

Another example would be, if your local user group wants to send out a flyer to announce a big meeting but can't afford the mailing costs, to offer to pick them up in exchange for a blurb saying "Postage paid for by Space Age Programming" and a tip of the hat during the business announcements at the meeting.

If your group is already involved in a charitable event, see if you can get the local paper to cover the 100% successful blood drive (even if there were only two of you), or provide all of your employees with matching company T-shirts for a charity walk.

Brand marketing

An offshoot of image marketing is brand marketing. It's the plethora of signs you see ringing the ballparks each spring and summer and the flashing logos covering indoor scoreboards. There are no direct sales messages; the hope of the marketing department when they let loose with their million dollar budgets is that you'll remember their product of service instead of the other guy.

Brand marketing is most widely used when you have a relatively homogenous product (for example, a set of athletic shoes of which any would be acceptable to play tennis in) and you try and build a "brand" that tells your buyers this one is somehow better, you will play more like Sampras or a Williams sister—when in actuality many/any of them would be useful for your purpose.

When you establish a brand, you then can start to charge a premium because the brand supposedly gives the consumer some value. Clorox is a tremendous example of brand marketing—they can charge a premium and they have the same stuff in their bottle as "no name bleach," yet people would pay more for it.

For a software services company, establishing a company image, while expensive, can be worthwhile, but brand marketing for software services is probably an avenue that you won't want to waste your money on.

Product/service marketing

The third type of marketing actively promotes a specific product or service, together with information that is intended to make you prefer that product or service to an alternative. This is the most targeted, the most direct, and the bridge between marketing and sales. Here, you dangle the bait ("Save Now!", "Limited Time Offer") and set the hook ("Call Before Midnight Tonight!", "Visit Our Web site at www.SpaceAgeProgramming.com").

Thus, when you see an ad that states "The Monolithic Long Distance Phone Company's Friends, Pals, and Distant Acquaintances Program will save you 10% over Bob's Phone Company's rates," you're seeing product/service marketing in action.

Target of marketing

There are lots of consumers out there—most of them being people. Marketing can be targeted to any combination of these people, but there are three general target groups.

Customers

Here is where your dollars are going to make the most difference—getting the word out to specific groups of potential customers. This can take the form of advertising in ways that expose your company to specific types of companies you want to reach. It may also mean sending mailings to select groups of companies that may be more interested in what you have to offer than the average firm.

Peers

You can also increase awareness by marketing specifically in your industry. In the software development business, there is a lot of cross-pollination. While you may not think it's wise or appropriate to advertise to your competitors, remember that firms may be your competitors one day and your partners the next—or vice versa. Furthermore, while your primary objective may be to attract business, remember that customers aren't the only resource you'll want to attract to your firm. Employees are another—and being visible in your community of peers is a good way to present yourself as an attractive employer.

Community

These are more of the general broadcast messages, where you want to get your name out there, perhaps educate a few potential customers, but get the neighbors to know what you do, in case they, someone they know, or the uncle of the sister of the former high school boyfriend is looking for just the service you offer. Community marketing can be product, brand, or image marketing.

Community marketing can be done in a shotgun approach—such as a firm that sponsors the Olympic Games—or it can be more targeted—sponsoring the local village fair. Thus, a kind of subset of image marketing is marketing to the community. This includes any type of involvement with a geographic area, and most probably does not include specific product information dissemination.

Purpose of marketing

It is important to remember that the purpose of marketing is to develop, first, awareness of your firm and its products, and second, to (hopefully) encourage preference—where a potential buyer becomes predisposed to purchasing from you instead of another firm.

As a result, the measurement of your marketing efforts should not be delineated in "dollars sold this month"—that would be a measure of a sales department. Rather, you should be tracking inquiries as the direct measure of your marketing efforts. If you're so inclined, you can even qualify a lead as to how likely the prospect is to buy, and thus determine which marketing efforts result in the best bang for the buck.

I'll discuss this in more detail later, but every inquiry your firm receives should be tracked—why they're contacting you, how they heard of you, what they're looking for, and how likely they are to buy.

Let me reiterate—you are not trying to sell a product through a marketing brochure or direct mail campaign or whatever other means you might employ. All you're trying to do is to get them to call you for more information. Once they call, then it's time for the sales process to kick in. It's just like a resume; you'll never get a job from that piece of paper, but if you get the interview, the resume has done its job.

Develop awareness

The average consumer is bombarded with thousands of marketing messages a day, and it starts earlier and earlier. How many of you have a kid whose first cognitive action in the car was to recognize the golden arches of McDonalds? (And how many of you cringed when it happened?) The marketing folks at McDonald's have done their job—developing awareness in a kid not yet two years old.

You're looking for a similar type of recognition—when you introduce yourself to someone, and they respond, "Oh yeah, I've heard of your firm." Of course, if that person is your daughter's gym teacher, that recognition may not mean a lot, but you never know—the gym teacher's spouse may be the IS manager at MegaMetal Manufacturing.

The keys to developing awareness, if you don't have a couple hundred million to spend next month, are repetition and consistency.

The message

You only have a few seconds to get across an image about your company to prospective customers. You do this by creating a "message" that synopsizes what you want that image to be.

Remember when I said you should be able to distill the mission statement for your business in two or three sentences—that if you can't write down what you do on the back of a business card, you don't have a clear idea? Then, later, I said that you should be able to identify your competitive position in a similar manner.

You can use these two blurbs to define this message. Your message should support your marketing position and be appropriate for the type of marketing you are doing.

Repetition

It's often said that a student of a foreign language needs to "experience" a word 17 times before internalizing it. The first time a future customer sees your name, perhaps in a newspaper "business short" announcing a promotion, it probably won't register. The second time they chance upon your name, say, in the Yellow Pages, you're still not on the radar. But after you or members of your company have written articles in their favorite journals, helped raise money for the local charity, spoken at a local Chamber of Commerce event, and sponsored the ice cream night for the kid's soccer league, why, suddenly it seems like you are everywhere—a part of the community, and obviously (by inference) a trusted resource.

Consistency

As far as consistency, your ends will be better served if all of your materials look like they came from the same place. It can be more expensive than you like to have someone put together a complete company portfolio—logo, stationery, envelopes, business cards, and the like, but there are ways for even those on a tight budget to do so. You might try connecting with a part-time graphic artist who is spending time at home with small children, for example.

Seek and listen to the advice of a good marketing professional, whether you hire someone yourself, or just borrow the wisdom from the local library. Find a good, sharp image that is easily recognizable, works well as an electronic file (GIF format), and faxes and scans well. Match the image to the product you are selling. Bankers like solid, block-of-granite type stuff, while small Web entrepreneurs may want something "swooshier." If you're selling creativity, have a creative logo. If you're selling reliability, look like part of the establishment.

Once you've acquired a set of materials, use them consistently throughout—put the same logo and message on your Web site, on your brochures, in ads, and so on.

Encourage preference

The second half of a marketing campaign is to cause the potential customer to prefer your product to the competition's. Thus, with the exception of image marketing, your marketing message can, and should, include a benefit that comes along with the product.

It's easier to think of these benefits for concrete goods like automobiles, diamonds, or malt liquor (you might recall the parody where the marketing slogan "Gets you there faster!"

was jokingly proposed for all three products at the same time), but it's not impossible to do so for professional services.

Remember when you were going through the exercise of determining your competitive advantage in the previous chapter? WHAT? YOU DIDN'T DO IT? Time to put this book down and do it now—knowing what your competitive advantage is will make it easier to devise marketing that pushes your customer to prefer your company over the other one.

What are some examples of encouraging preference that make sense for a software development company? Time to market might be one example—being able to turn around projects quickly is a "feature" that most customers desire of their software developers. High quality—measurably better than the competition—is another benefit that could prove attractive to a potential customer. And 24-hour service and availability might be an advantage to a third group of customers.

Just be sure that the benefit you push is one that's important to your customers, and one that you can deliver on.

The difference between marketing and selling

Selling, then, is asking for the order once they've called. Well, maybe you ask for the order. There may be folks you don't want to work with for one reason or another. For instance, their project may be too small—or too big—for it to make sense for you to take it on. Or their corporate culture may not mesh with yours. I once worked with a firm that had an extremely high level of "in-your-face" interpersonal interaction—between employees as well as with vendors, and even customers. They weren't trying to be insulting or obnoxious (although it certainly came across that way). It was simply the style laid down by their founder many years ago. If the culture of a potential customer differs too far from your own, if you don't feel you would be comfortable working with that customer, well, consider giving it a pass.

But once you start selling, what then? The sales process for services such as those provided by lawyers, architects, and software developers is decidedly different from the process for selling cars, sneakers, or tree-trimming. It evolves around a "consultative" approach instead of the "shoving it down their throat" fashion.

Your goal is to ease (or remove) the specific pain that caused them to pursue a purchase of custom software.

The marketing of a corporate IS department

Every once in a while, the manager of an IT department will convene a meeting of their group and proclaim, "We need to start marketing ourselves within the company." At this pronouncement, all of the attendees who are not in direct eye contact with the manager will roll their eyes, raise their eyebrows at others across the table, and inwardly think, "Yeah, right!"

I can see both sides to this story. On the one hand, this really does sound like politics gone out of control—a manager has decided to build a fiefdom, and the goals of the company end up in second place.

On the other hand, there is often so much "noise" inside a company—from the personnel department, the sales groups, the product development team, and so on—that it's easy for potential "customers" to forget about the MIS department, and just assume that "those guys in the glass house wouldn't have a clue about what we need."

Promotional materials

Promotional materials are, in one sense, more important to a firm that sells services since there are no visible reminders of their product. This is the same way with other consumables. Automobiles and refrigerators and athletic shoes have constant reminders all around you. But a piece of custom software is, for all intents and purposes, invisible except to the person actually using it.

As a result, you may decide that additional effort spent toward producing valuable promotional materials is worthwhile.

Company name

If you're starting to choose a company name, I have one pet peeve to share with you. Company names that have System and Compu and Micro and Consulting and other "high-tech" buzz words in there—you can't tell them apart, folks. The other type of name that drives me crazy is ABC Consulting. You know, somebody's initials. Or even worse—AAAAA Consulting. I apologize to those of you who have already done this, but I simply can't tell them apart—and so I don't think new customers can either. Of course, if you're already in business, then your customers know you and your company name doesn't really matter.

I'm rather partial to my company name; a moniker that was chosen with a lot of consideration and forethought.

I wanted a name that was different and that people would be able to recognize immediately. I searched for a couple of years looking for one. The image I wanted was a parody of all those great big huge conglomerates where they have giant smoke stacks belching tons of toxins into the air. You know, like Pittsburgh around 1900. All these big companies in Germany and the United States have names like Cameron Iron Works, the Rouge River Works, and so on. I was a lone computer consultant and thought the use of the same idea would be unique. That's how "Works" came about. In Germany, it's called Werke, so I tied that together with my last name and everyone can recognize this name instantly.

I came up with my company name while I was still working somewhere else—at a large manufacturing company. I had "H WERKE" put on my license plate while I was still employed there. Somebody at the factory asked me what it stood for. I couldn't really tell him that it was going to be my company name, so I created this great big long story, with the advance sell on it that "You're gonna love this, this is a really funny story!" I delivered the punch line and said, "Isn't that great, isn't that too funny?" when in reality, the story made no sense and wasn't funny at all. He smiled half-heartedly and nodded, "Uh, yeah, sure," and quickly walked away. I didn't have to worry about anyone else at the plant asking what the license plate meant.

The downside of this is that no one can pronounce it correctly, and that sometimes causes problems—particularly when they're doing a search on the Web.

Another clever name is Michel Fournier's company name. I was at FoxPro DevCon in 1992 with Ted Roche, and Michel was looking for a company name. We were bouncing back and forth various names, and suddenly Ted came up with the idea of Fournier Transformation, a take-off on the mathematical term. Very clever and very cool.

More well-named companies include Toni Taylor's company in Arizona—Taylor Made Software—and the California firm that makes Macintosh software, Abra Macdabra. RDI

Software Technologies recently changed their name to "Geneer" (pronounced like the last two syllables in "Engineer"). Recognizable and unique.

Once in a while there is a chance to have a really cool name. If you have one, it makes a whole world of difference.

Rules about company names

Okay, maybe these aren't rules—just my own firmly held beliefs. I'll explain the reasons and you can decide whether you agree.

First, a name shouldn't be too long. In the olden days, that meant nothing more than 32 characters. If it was more, people weren't able to print it on a mailing label (yes, some people still use dot matrix printers). Some consulting firms are really famous for doing this. They have the names of all five principals and then append a descriptive term like "Environmental Consulting Corporation, Inc." to the end. This name will never fit anywhere—any time they try to enter the company's name into a computer, when they try to print reports, or even display it on a sign for a trade show.

Avoid acronyms. MLB Consulting Inc.—who knows what MLB stands for, and even worse, who cares? There are so many acronymic firms that nobody is going to take the time to remember what yours stands for. It's also really easy to get confused between yours and another one that is very similar, particularly if the other firm's acronym is easily recognizable.

There's a company in Milwaukee that had a regular company name, and it was shortened to an acronym of its initials during the '70s when that was trendy. Ten years later, the trendiness wore off, and the company changed their name again, adding two words that were represented by the last two letters in the acronym—making their name redundant. How silly!

There's a networking firm in Chicago that started life as "Tower Lakes Computing" and is now "TLC Networks." I'd hate to compete with them if my company were named "TCL Networking." Wouldn't you automatically change "TCL" to "TLC"—just because the phrase "tender loving care" is so well known?

There are two schools of thought regarding whether your company name should include the type of work your firm does. On the one hand, it helps customers recognize your firm and helps identify what you do. Who the heck could figure out what "Hentzenwerke" offers? The most likely guess would be some sort of metal-bending, right? "AAA Mortgage Guarantors" easily identifies the firm and what they do, and if you're trying to buy hand saws, you can skip past them in the Yellow Pages.

On the other hand, should I decide to evolve from custom software development to R&D in mathematical algorithms used in encryption products, I don't have to change my company's name. Meanwhile, the folks at AAA Mortgage Guarantors have to do some fast-talking to explain why they're now trying to sell you stocks and bonds too.

A few years ago, you needed to consider the geographic reach of your firm—the more common the name, the more likely you'll run into conflicts as you expand geographically. There may only be one SoftPro Software in your city—but I'll bet there are a couple dozen throughout the United States, and likely several more in other English-speaking countries. But you could ignore the possibility if you were comfortable staying in your own city.

Nowadays, though, you need to consider international reach, if for no other reason that whether or not the ".com" version of your company name is available. If you wanted to pick "Data Base Specialists," there may be only one in your city, but that name is definitely going to be taken on the Web.

Additionally, consider the hassle of typing a URL that consists of a unique name. "Milwaukee Database Programming Specialists" may be unique worldwide, but do you really want to force customers to type all that into the address bar of their browsers? And do you expect them to remember the abbreviation "MDPS.com" or "MilwaukeeDPS.com" or something similar?

Logo

Common wisdom about logos has flip-flopped several times over the past few decades, and will undoubtedly do so again and again. There are several general variations on company logos, and none of them really matter unless you're going to spend tens of millions of dollars advertising your firm around the world.

The first variation is to incorporate your name in a specialized logo type. The famous red cursive handwriting for Coca-Cola has been around for decades, and is widely recognized,

The second variation is to create a logo from your company's initials. GE and IBM come to mind immediately—you can't separate the lettering of the cursive GE logo (see the top of a light bulb if you don't remember) or the horizontal stripes of the IBM logo.

The third variation is to create a symbol that is supposed to stand for the company, but has nothing really to do with it. The famous AT&T "Death Star" logo—a blue circle with a circle in the upper corner of the circle that resembled the half-finished Death Star of the first Star Wars movie—gained thousands of converts, and critics, as soon as it came out. The red "drippy coffee cup stain" of Lucent, the renamed Bell Labs, is another well-known example of spending millions of dollars for nearly nothing.

Business cards

You're not going to believe how much I'm going to talk about a simple 2"x 3" piece of paper. And you'll probably shake your head when I go on and on about the most trivial of points. I guess it's because while I don't think that glossy four-color literature is important for a lot of small software development firms, I'm convinced that everyone should have a good business card.

You can buy a little piece of software to print your business cards from your laser printer. And they usually look pretty bad. This is not the first impression you want to give somebody. It costs $50 to print 1,000 one-color thermograph (raised lettering) business cards. Have a graphic designer set your fonts for you if you're not comfortable doing it yourself. You can get a student at the local community college or graphic design school to do this type of work very economically. If you pay a graphic artist $200 (that's high) to do it once, you will never have to do it again.

Make your cards look professional. Some people like to write a short story on their business cards. Other people like to use five colors. Others put a dozen logos on their card.

How do you determine when you've crossed the line? Try this trick. Collect business cards from other people—continuously. (I have never—in 20 years—thrown out a business card.) Then scan through other people's business cards and you will be amazed at the junk people hand out. Pretty soon you'll be horrified—"Oh my God, I was going to do one of those—it looks so trashy!" You want a card that suggests professionalism and a solid company. I look at the blue-chip companies like IBM, General Electric, EDS, Citigroup, and

Exxon. These are the professionals. You can learn a lot by examining other people's business cards for half an hour.

A rule of thumb for a business card: You should be able to put a quarter on the business card and not obscure any important information. You may catch the corner of a logo or something but the idea is "White space is your friend."

What do you put on your business card? When it comes to design, suddenly everyone wants to get in on the act. You don't write a novel. Instead, just use the facts. In fact, more and more, sparseness is a virtue, since people are using those machines that scan business cards into their computers more frequently these days.

Basic information

First, include your logo if you have one. People like pictures—they catch people's eyes. Second, include your name, company name, and mailing address. I've been including "USA" on our cards for the past few years. Yes, we do a fair amount of international business, but I think that it lends a bit of style as the millennium changed. Of course, you may think it just looks pretentious, and that's your privilege. Planet Earth, on the other hand, is still probably over the top for the next few years.

Identify the voice and fax numbers, including area code. Yes, I've seen more than one business card without an area code. If you have a direct dial phone number, put it by your name. You can also squish it in the corner and label it "Direct Dial." Make sure that, if you include a direct dial number, the number will be answered. If someone dials and nobody's there, well, that would be bad, wouldn't it?

You are a computer geek, so why in the world would you print a business card and not include your e-mail addresses? Wait, you don't have an e-mail address because it's too expensive? Umm, well, hmmm. Would you take your car to a repair shop that didn't have lifts or jack-stands? In the first part of this century, e-mail is a standard tool of the trade. If you don't have an e-mail address, get one.

Similarly, you will probably want to include your URL, although where to put it can vary. The legacy snail mail address takes two and a half lines—street, city/state/zip, country. Other pieces—voice, fax, e-mail, Web page—are one-line entries. If your company name is offset from the rest of the address, putting the URL right underneath is a pretty good bet.

Titles and logos

I'm not sure whether titles go on your business card, because I personally don't like titles—my employees have never had them. I was turned off when I met someone with a business card listing the titles, "Chief Executive Officer, President, and Chairman of the Board." No, this was not the guy who runs Exxon or General Electric—this particular company had nine employees. Titles were clearly somebody's ego trip.

At other companies, however, titles are used as (stop me if you've heard this before) positioning. So you might find yourself in a meeting with the "Director of Business Development," a "Senior Consultant," and the "Director of Development," whatever those titles mean. So, if you have one, your title goes under your name.

Let's see. You have a logo, name, and address of your company with phone numbers and direct dial numbers, and e-mail addresses. Then you have the name and title of the person on the card. It's getting crowded, isn't it? That is why I opted not to have titles and put the e-mail address with the name so there's still some white space on the card.

If you have authorization or certification logos from other companies, include them. But you'll want to be careful. Suddenly a card with "Authentic Certified Whatevers" from Microsoft, Borland, Sun, IBM, Novell, and Autodesk becomes a pamphlet and not a business card. Consider putting them on the back. You did work hard for them, after all, and they're definitely worth using if they set you apart from your competitor or establish an expertise in any given area.

Flip up cards

These are those cards that expand to twice their size when you open them up. I have always been intrigued by them but never got around to doing one. I just didn't feel the need to put a brochure in someone's hand every time I met somebody. The ones I've liked have come from retail stores. On the front they talk about what they do. On the inside they give pictures of products, hours, catchy descriptions, and maybe a map of their locations.

Material and color

Well, there's still more. Let's talk about the physical card itself. You can make your card any color you want as long as it is bright white. (Some people disagree with me; I've seen very attractive light gray cards with blue or red ink—it's your decision.) It should be a linen finish and classy looking. The linen finish is the one where you can see the lines of threads up and down. They present an established appearance. You may go to see a customer wearing jeans and a "Java Rules!" T-shirt, but when you hand them a proper card, they'll receive and remember a subtle message of care and quality.

The difference in cost between a boring, badly done card and a high-quality card is just a few dollars. Spend it here. It's the difference between wearing a dark gray suit, white shirt, and tie or wearing a wide lapel suit that went out of date two years ago, a dark shirt, and a tie that doesn't quite match. It might have been trendy a few years ago but not anymore.

Probably the most interesting card I have ever seen was the card of a guy who worked with grain elevator operators. He was dealing with people who were basically filthy all of the time because they loaded trucks, barges, and other transportation vehicles. He needed to get his card in people's hands, but many times, the recipient would just stuff a card in a pocket and forget about it.

That night, the recipient's wife would wash the clothes and all the other cards that the elevator operator had stuffed into his pocked became little balls of fuzz. But this fellow's cards were made out of a velum material, like the stuff they made drawings out of in the old drawing board days. These cards could not be destroyed! As a result, his customers didn't lose his number nearly as often as they lost his competitors'.

There was a downside to these cards—you couldn't write on this material. So if you were talking to him and wanted to jot a note down, his card was not the place to do it. But I think this was fairly trivial given the other advantages.

Orientation

Do you print the card vertically or horizontally? You can do some very nice, good-looking things with portrait cards, but people put cards in a box or Rolodex and page through them. If yours is horizontal it won't match up, and won't play well with the other boys and girls. You may think it will stand out, but I've found that people will say, "Oh, this guy! I hate his card!"

The primary purpose of a business card is to enable the other person to contact you again at a later date. If you can do something to subtly catch his interest at the same time, all the better. If you do something stupid or cheap, your card will probably end up in the nearest receptacle. And the difference between novel and stupid is in the eyes of your beholders, so think long and hard before being radical or cute.

Multi-lingual cards

As our world becomes more and more global, more and more people do business in multiple countries, and it is not uncommon to find non-U.S. business people with cards that have their information in their native language on one side and in English on the other. Even in parts of the United States, some savvy people have the flip side printed in Spanish.

Stationery and other printed collateral

In these days of e-mail, faxes, cellular phones, wireless PDAs, and the like, it seems like no one sends letters anymore. Nonetheless, you'll probably need to do so once in a while. Your stationery, fax header sheet, brochures, Web site, and other visually available materials should look like they all came from the same place.

If you make the design simple, you can scan your logo and artwork into your computer, and produce documents right from your computer without having to hunt down stationery and insert it into the printer. You might also consider staying away from long vertical or horizontal lines in the artwork—if the paper goes into the printer crooked, the output can be much more easily skewed, and it doesn't look as good.

Faxes are also rough on horizontal rules, turning them into stairsteps or failing to reproduce them at all.

Brochures

Here's the bad news: No one will read them. Pages and pages of tiny text telling the world how great you are. They won't read it. They will look at it, and as long as the front page doesn't have any typos, they will put it aside. Is it really worth it to spend a lot of time and resources to design a brochure, and then spend thousands of dollars for a big fancy four-color job? Maybe not.

My guiding principle has been to make sure literature doesn't put the customer to sleep. I don't want it to be boring. A lot of firms make their brochures look like lawyer brochures. A bunch of guys in suits sitting at a large table with stacks of books behind them. This doesn't tell me why these people are better than everybody else. What is the problem they can solve?

You can't put any of those "We're dedicated to quality" phrases in your brochures. "Our people are our best asset. We invest in our people" and all of those platitudes. Oh yeah? Says who? Everybody puts them in there and nobody believes them. Don't try to sell your products and services directly in your brochure. The brochure is simply a means to get the customer to call you for more information. Pique their interest, perhaps encourage them to prefer you over the other guys a bit, and that's all you can hope for.

So, how do you distinguish yourself? What is it that you do that no one else does? This has to be a measurable item. I just spent a chapter on this topic—use your brochure and other materials to document your distinctive competence. If you have expertise in a specific industry, it's a good idea to have a page dedicated to describing the applications you have done. People will read that because they can relate to it. If you have specific skills, again, that will garner attention as well. Instead of using a traditional brochure, consider using a "fact sheet" or "case study" of past jobs and projects.

Finally, don't forget your call to action. In other words, tell them what you want them to do, such as call or write.

Brochures vs. CD-ROMs

A couple years ago I considered the idea of compiling a few sample applications that we'd done and putting them on a CD to send to customers instead of trying to convey the same story via a brochure.

Two and a half years later, it turns out that I still haven't done this. There are a couple of reasons why. First, the tools we use move too rapidly; by the time we've shipped an application and have it in a format ready to present, the tools have moved on. Don't you feel a bit embarrassed when you see sales literature for "the latest greatest" tool of some sort or another—and the screen shots are all in Windows 95, or, worse, Windows 3.1 or DOS?

Second, a fair number of our applications (and, of course, all of the coolest apps) are considered to be competitive advantages of our customers, and, thus, they don't want them paraded about for the world to see. While I'd like to be able to show more, well, they paid for it, so they get to choose on this front.

Finally, putting together this type of CD is a lot of work. We're simply not big enough to warrant a lot of time on this type of project yet.

However, that doesn't mean this is a bad idea—just that it hasn't yet been applicable for us. These days you can buy a CD-ROM writer for $99.95 or so (if your computer doesn't already come with one), and blanks are really inexpensive. Besides being more distinctive, this path is much more cost effective than spending thousands for another "me-too" brochure.

Presentations and slideshows

The rules of presentations are pretty simple.

First, tell them what you're gonna tell them, then you tell them, and then you tell them what you told them. Heard that one before? Good. Repetition makes a point stick. Your first slide should have your company name, the name of your presentation, your phone number, and maybe the URL of your Web site. Have the first slide displayed on the screen as soon as people start arriving, so people will know they've come to the right place. Furthermore, many also start to take notes, and since you're not talking yet, they'll be able to start out their notes with some great info—how to contact you. At the end of the presentation, you'll have a "Thank you!" or "Questions?" slide with… yes, your company name and phone number again.

In between the beginning and the end are the main slides. People like to know what comes next, so show them an outline and give them some time estimates for the material you're going to cover. Repeat the outline, briefly, throughout the presentation, so the attendees can follow where you are—much like the maps that showed where the adventurers were in "Around the World in 80 Days."

PowerPoint has a good outlining function built in, and we use it to ensure the presentation is logical, orderly, and flows well. PowerPoint also comes with a set of templates you can use to start to organize your thoughts into a cohesive presentation.

So what do you present? We do a variety of presentations—ranging from presenting papers at technical conferences and speaking at the local user groups, to teaching computer novices and selling products and services to potential customers. Each of these can have a slightly different pitch, a different tone, and needs to be sharpened to make that specific type of point. Our teaching slides have a goal such as "When you complete this session, you will be able to register and test servers in a DCOM environment." Our selling slides have a goal as well—namely, "When you have finished seeing these slides, you will understand what our service offerings are, why you want them, and what your next action should be."

Web sites and other online advertising

Web sites have evolved considerably, even since the last edition of this book just a couple of years ago. Nowadays, a Web site isn't just considered a cool part of the marketing package; it's often considered the first point of contact. With more and more people having high-speed access (that means instant availability) both at work and at home, it's getting easier to navigate a browser than to pick up the phone.

Make sure you know why you're building a Web site. How many people are going to buy a $250,000 custom development project from you because they were surfing around and suddenly saw your page? I would say approximately zero. Remember, "Nothing works." However, some of my colleagues' experiences have been different—the largest gig ever at a former employer was landed just exactly that way. Regardless who is correct, it is nice if you can direct a potential customer to your Web site instead of sending them literature (that is, if they are so inclined). It is easier to update your Web page than your literature, so you could use your Web page as an extension of your literature. Also, since about 100 gazillion people are using the Internet, your Web page might just show up in someone's search engine—perhaps as likely as them stumbling over your Yellow Pages ad in the Des Moines phone book.

It's very easy to say, "Hey, I'll just spend a whole bunch of time on this Web site because it's fun to do, it's cool, it's intellectually challenging to see what we can do," and so on. Suddenly you've chewed up hundreds of hours and what's the benefit? Where are you going to get a payback for that time? Keep sharp on this one, because it's an easy trap to fall into. Web sites are extremely costly to set up if you want to do it right.

On the other hand, if you're using your Web site as a learning tool, that's okay. But be sure that you've identified this up front.

If you want people to come back, you have to keep changing the content. How often? My personal opinion is at least once a week. (And those of you who spent the better part of six months looking at our old, unchanging Web site are probably giggling right now.) But that's a high-maintenance task, and frankly, is it worth it to you? If you're looking for your site to be an extension of your literature, it should be updated at least monthly. If you want to have people come back and visit the site over and over again, then you need to have something compelling on the site. And compelling means new.

If, on the other hand, you want to use your pages as a fairly static business directory entry—"Here's who I am, what I do, how to contact me, and on the next page is a catalog of products or services"—that's also a legitimate use. Just don't expect a lot of return traffic!

Marketing avenues and techniques

There are dozens of marketing avenues for you—many of them destinations that can suck the money out of your bank account with no hope of any return on the investment. Let's look at each one, and evaluate each one.

Advertising

Traditional advertising is pretty much a no-win situation for the custom software developer. Here are the primary mechanisms.

Television, radio, newspapers

These media are frightfully expensive for the small shop. If you're looking at a daily paper in a medium-sized city like Milwaukee, Memphis, or Oklahoma City, an ad that's two columns by four inches in the Sunday paper and one day in the daily paper will run close to $1,000 per week. And that's if you are using a frequency contract, which means you have to commit to a certain number of inches or a certain number of dollars. It would be significantly more on an ad-by-ad basis. If you look in the paper to see who else is advertising, you will see stockbrokers, transmission people, and local computer suppliers like "PC's R Us." Not too many service firms.

Radio may run $50 to $75 per half-minute spot in the same city. So if you're running a 30-second spot at non-prime time four times a day, you're looking at $700 to $1,000 a week as well. TV? If you're reading this book, you can't afford prime time TV, and do you really want to compete with the 2 AM infomercials? You might consider research into cable TV, but your advertising positioning would need to be highly targeted—perhaps as a sponsor of a "Tech-Talk" style of show.

I guess you can look at the lack of advertising as being a glass that's either half empty or half full. It's an opportunity because no one else is doing it, therefore you'll stand out. On the other hand, why isn't anyone else doing it? Perhaps because it doesn't work.

You need to have a healthy marketing budget to withstand that type of expense. However, you don't have to sell a lot from one of those ads. A campaign that runs $5,000 only has to sell a couple of jobs in order to make that back. On the other hand, if you are an individual or two-person shop, $5,000 is a lot of money if you don't get any responses. And don't expect to have the phone ringing off the hook after your first ad.

And consider your target market. If you are after one of the 300 CIOs and IS Managers in the area, broadcasting to the 3 million viewers in your local metropolitan market is an awful lot of wasted bandwidth.

Yellow Pages

Not many people look in the Yellow Pages for custom work. Generally, those who let their fingers do the walking either 1) don't have any contacts in the playing field, or 2) don't even understand the playing field. They look in the Yellow Pages for a diskette duplicating service or someone to repair their broken driveway. They ask friends and associates about a software developer.

If you're considering the Yellow Pages, be aware that the sales folk at most directory companies have honed their sales techniques to the extent that a used-car salesperson could learn some lessons. You have to be careful. You can usually work a deal where they will give you the next higher "thing" (size of ad, size of typeface, additional color) for little or no additional cost. The following year, however, they will be sure to charge you for running that same advertisement, and try to get you to upgrade to the next "thing" for just a few pennies more. Nobody ever wants to decrease their ad size the following year, and so this is a nearly guaranteed method to increase your cost year after year.

We have countered this technique over the past few years by asking for something else free. We were going to pay for bold, so we said we wanted extra large type this year. The next year we were ready to pay for bold and extra large type, and so we asked for a picture. It costs them very little to give in on this, and we're always getting more for our money. If our ad size is going to get bigger, we might as well take advantage of the fact that they will do this. And every few years we drop our ad size down significantly, so as to level the playing field again. Otherwise, we'd end up paying thousands a month just because we didn't know any better.

A scam to watch out for is their "Make sure to put 'See Us in the Yellow Pages' in all of your literature" line. Why would you, in your own literature, refer someone to the Yellow Pages where your competition is advertising?

Once you start advertising in one Yellow Pages directory, you'll have to watch out for solicitations from other directories that appear to be the same publication. There are multiple Yellow Pages and when you list in one, they want you listed in all. It is very easy to suddenly get hooked into a bill for several hundred or thousand dollars every month.

Make sure you get a camera-ready copy of what they are going to print. They have a tendency to be really lousy at taking what you give them and actually doing something with it.

Amazingly enough, despite the pessimism voiced in this section, we do have an ad in the Yellow Pages every year. It's aggravating—we're very clear in our ad that all we do is custom software development. And we still get calls from 14-year-olds wanting to buy a copy of Doom. Or somebody wanting help writing a WordPerfect macro, and they really think we ought to do it for free because, after all, aren't we the ones who wrote that program?

But over the past seven or eight years, we have picked up a few customers, and we're running a positive balance with respect to money in and out on this section of the ledger. For about $5,000 a year ($400/month), you can run several reasonable-sized ads. You only have to sell one job to recoup that, and you never know when one of those jobs will become a long-standing customer worth $10,000 or $20,000 a year.

Direct mail

It is very hard to sell professional services using direct mail. Would you buy services from a heart surgeon who mailed you a letter? I think not. You must have an extremely compelling message and be able to do it over and over again to have a winning record at direct mail. A lot of people figure since they have a computer, they can print out a bunch of names and addresses, slap together something in their desktop publisher, and they have a direct mail piece. Unfortunately, it's going to look like they did it themselves.

So now that you're convinced that an hour with PageMaker doesn't qualify as a marketing campaign, what types of activities are worth considering?

If you have a specialty in a specific industry segment, you can buy mailing lists (or research them yourself through the public library) and target a mailing to those companies. By explaining precisely what benefits you have provided for other firms in their industry, you can grab their attention quickly. The companies who didn't replace their systems a few years ago due to Year 2000 problems are starting to consider it now, given the whammy of DOS systems really not cutting it anymore.

Again, I'm not saying that finding business through direct mail is impossible, but it's difficult. If you are going to go the direct mail route, either hire a professional or at least get a couple of books on how to do it right. There are ways to make it happen.

Cold calls

Arguably the single biggest waste of time you could ever spend—particularly for selling professional services—is time spent cold-calling. You could be giving away money and half the people you called would still hang up on you. So if you're the prime mover in your company, you should spend your time doing other things.

Once you start growing—and need to feed the beast more and more frequently—cold-calling can become a worthwhile activity. You'll need targeted lists of potential customers, scripts for someone to follow, and an individual who can take telephones getting slammed down on his ear all day. But, unlike encyclopedias or life insurance, you potentially only have to make a couple of sales a month.

Internet job sites

A number of developers say that they have received a lot of business by responding to requests for help on the Internet. These messages are usually via newsgroups or bulletin boards. There are a number of sites, often tool-specific, that also provide access to job hunting (both full-time and contract work) mechanisms.

Newsletters and "e-newsletters"

I have mixed feelings about newsletters. On the one hand, how many of us need more paper on our desks? Don't we have enough to read already? I believe that a lot of potential customers feel the same way.

On the other hand, a well designed and written newsletter, produced on a regular basis and targeted at a group of likely candidates, is an excellent method for developing an ongoing relationship. If you focus on a vertical market, your newsletter can discuss problems and potential solutions—some (but not all) of which may include work that you can do for them.

Depending on your clientele, you may consider faxing instead of mailing, or even e-mailing a regular missive, both of which are considerably less expensive, and may reach the target more often than "another piece of mail."

Employment ads

You might consider contacting the firms advertising for full-time or part-time programmers in the Help Wanted section of the local newspaper. On the one hand, you know that they have a need—how much more targeted could you get? On the other hand, some of the ads will ask that responses be sent to the Human Resources department—and your pitch will undoubtedly get tossed. And some companies are only interested in hiring a full-time employee—"If I wanted a contractor, I would have looked for one, dammit!" and <click> goes the phone. But this is a low-resource, highly focused avenue for finding leads.

Some firms do this religiously. Other companies avoid it like the plague. Your choice depends on the amount of time you have and your personal preferences.

Professional affiliations

Not that many years ago, one of my colleagues found himself facing unemployment, as his company closed their main offices. One night at an unemployment support group, Ted got to hear one of those inspirational speakers do his thing on how he had pulled himself up by his bootstraps. "Network, network, network" was this man's mantra.

Everyone you know knows someone who knows someone who wants the kind of work that you do. Without being a boor about it, you want to make sure that everyone you know is aware of what it is you do, so they can tell their friends, and so on.

One of the best ways to get this kind of information circulating is to make speeches and presentations whenever possible. If you belong to Toastmasters, your local Chamber of Commerce, computer user groups, whatever—take the opportunity to place yourself center stage and put on an entertaining, educational presentation. And don't forget to mention what it is you do for a living. For money. For people like them. And encourage them to tell their friends.

So what do you do?

Given the way I've shot down nearly all of these possible marketing routes, you may be inclined to put this book down, toss your hands up in despair, and say, "I'm going to go start making bricks." What do you do? The answer is: Do It All. That's a little bit facetious, but you have to be prepared to explore more than one avenue. You are not going to be able to drop 20,000 pieces of direct mail and expect a windfall. You have to do direct mail, advertising, get your name in the paper, and so on. You need to be seen in a number of places.

The single most important trick to marketing is consistency. People have to see your name over and over. Who are some of the biggest marketers? Who has the biggest marketing budgets in the world? Companies we all know: Toyota, GM, Coca-Cola, Kimberly Clark, Proctor and Gamble. You would think that Coke—the best known trademark in the world—would never have to advertise again. But that's precisely why they continue to advertise—so they stay the best known.

Nothing works. But nothing fails, either. Every time someone learns your name, your business, your services, it's a step in the right direction for your marketing effort.

Conclusion

That about wraps up this section—I've given you a framework for deciding whether or not you should consider the independent consulting life, and then provided a plan of action you should follow to get started.

Now it's time to get into the middle of the action. In the next section, I'll cover the first big question of software development—how do I get the business I want?

Section III:

The Initial Contact

"Nothing happens until somebody sells something." A very wise, very old man told me this one day. He then told me the same thing a few weeks later, and then two days after that, and again, again, again, incessantly. He could get away with it, because he was my dad.

And he was right.

Software developers often don't have to worry about selling. People come to developers with a desperate look in their eyes, begging for their bacon to be saved. It's a seller's market. But there's a difference between scraping by and doing it right, and between staying busy and doing the work that you want to do. Attention to selling will pay huge dividends—better margins, higher profits, more sleep at night, a day off once in a while, even a chance to go out on a date with your spouse.

In this section, I will discuss the development of a basic marketing strategy. A great deal of a company's success, aside from having a client base, is having focused on a point on the horizon to steer by or aim toward. The ability to adhere to this strategy, while still maintaining a certain amount of flexibility to adjust to changes in the business or programming environment, is key.

Here's the process for selling customer software development.

Chapter 9
Setting Expectations

"Do you expect me to talk, Goldfinger?"—James Bond
"Why, no, Mr. Bond. I expect you to die."—Auric Goldfinger
  —Goldfinger

If there is one single idea you should take away from this book, it is that of setting expectations. All the problems in the world between two reasonably intelligent and rational individuals can be avoided if the two parties have the same expectations and those expectations are met. It's when expectations do not match, or when they are not met, that problems can (and most often, do) occur.

Expectations are the cornerstone of any relationship, be it personal or professional. Think about your own life, and review relationships that worked in the past, or are working now. Then, consider relationships that are not working (or haven't worked in the past)—and recall why they failed.

This book is primarily focused on how you develop, communicate, and manage your client's expectations. Not only is it to your advantage to develop the expectations for your customer, but it also is your job. You are the expert, after all. While you are doing so, of course, you'll have to communicate to them that simply because they have an expectation doesn't mean it will be met. They may tell you, "I expect this project to be done in two weeks and to cost $49." It's also part of your job to manage their expectations.

In short, it is your job to communicate to your customers what your expectations of them are, to determine what their expectations are, and to meld those expectations into one common set.

The nice thing about telling customers that you want them to put their expectations on the table is that this is terminology that they understand. If you tell them that they need to assemble a "List of High-Level Requirements," or to "Identify the Affected Operations," their eyes will glaze over and you'll get nowhere. Instead, you guide them through identifying their expectations, keeping the design documents that you're going to use in mind. When you provide these finished documents to the customer, they'll see the material is familiar to them.

The first rule is that expectations must be mutually understood—both parties must have the same understanding of what is expected of each party. The second rule is that, after they are understood, the expectations must be met. Let's examine both of these in more detail.

Expectations must be mutually understood

If two sports teams were competing in a contest presumed to be governed by a single set of rules, but each team was actually playing under a different set of rules, there most likely would be significant conflict, and the game probably wouldn't be finished without multiple arrests.

This may seem like a fairly trivial concept, and it is. It's putting the concept into practice that is difficult. Making sure that two sports teams have the same expectations is easy—the rules are written down in a rulebook that is widely distributed and ingrained in the players' lives from the day they begin the sport. Everyone knows you're not supposed to hold a basketball under your arm and run down the court—that's "traveling," and it's been illegal in virtually every game of basketball ever played in the past 75 years. The rule is well documented and understood by everyone involved.

On the other hand, putting the cereal boxes on top of the refrigerator is not a widely accepted practice in my house. Everyone in the house is either at least five feet tall (and thus can reach the cereal) or can move the stepstool to the fridge. The refrigerator is not built-in (so there's empty space above the appliance), and I've been doing it since I was a kid. But, just because I've been doing it since I was seven years old doesn't mean anything. It's not a well-documented practice, and it's not been done by everyone involved (i.e., my wife Linda). Therefore, while I might expect to find the cereal on top of the fridge, it's not going to be there, because the person who buys the cereal (Linda) puts it in the cabinet next to the sink. However, not only do I think the top of the fridge is a great place to put the cereal, I'm used to putting it there, and I do so without thinking.

Here, we have a case where expectations are not mutually understood, and there will be conflict (if not outright tears and bloodshed—Linda's tears and my blood) when she finds the cereal on top of the fridge tomorrow morning.

This may seem to be a stupid example, but I'm pretty sure you can come up with a recent conflict in your own household based on just as silly a situation. Toothpaste cap on or off? Throw the laundry in the basket or leave it under the sink? Put the dandelion digger away or leave it on the windowsill? Put your car keys in the same place every single time or put them down where it's convenient? You get the picture.

And this is an easily communicated situation where the rule is black and white—"The cereal goes in the cupboard." No vagueness caused by varying interpretations. No shades of gray creating an atmosphere of mistrust. The cereal goes here, period.

Misunderstandings in software development are even more likely. Contrast my cereal box crisis with the intricacies of communicating the behavior of a complex user interface, or an ill-defined data structure being downloaded from a mainframe, or who is responsible for that last pass at testing. It's obvious that misunderstood expectations are pretty easy to come across.

Expectations must be met

Okay, so I have finally gotten it through my skull that Linda expects me to put the cereal in the cupboard. We both have the same expectation, and have agreed that the top of the fridge is where we collect dust, not cereal boxes. But suppose in the excitement that accompanies the shipping of this book, I forget, and the Corn Flakes appear up there next Wednesday. That's likely to cause conflict, unless we can do something about it. There are two possible solutions—either alter my behavior so that it positively does not happen again, or change the expectations so that Linda understands and expects me to forget once in a while.

Notice that the two fundamental rules have not been changed—the expectations must still be mutually understood, and they must be met.

An example of setting expectations

A hardware manufacturer of PC peripherals once wrote up a document about expectations in response to an increasing flood of complaints about their service and support policies. In it, they discussed the difficulties in testing their $39 device with all of the thousands (tens of thousands?) of machine configurations, and explained what they thought reasonable expectations of a purchaser of said $39 device should be—and what they shouldn't be.

For example, if the device failed to work with a machine, the customer should expect to have access to a page of "Frequently Asked Questions" where the customer could troubleshoot their problem. The customer could also expect to have their money refunded if they couldn't get the device to work. They should not expect to be able to spend an hour on the phone with a technician, free of charge, or to have a service representative make an on-site service call for free.

To you and me, the expectation of having a service representative make an on-site visit to troubleshoot a problem with a device that cost as much as a couple cases of soda seems pretty ridiculous; but clearly, the manufacturer had run into that situation enough times that they had to spell it out.

Expectations peculiar to software development

Users expect software to be delivered on time, under budget, and completely bug-free. Even the state-of-the-art system that they want to have installed before the components used to build it have been released by the software manufacturer.

An editorial in *Computing Canada* in mid-1997 stated:

"IT projects are not engineering projects. Software research is a better description. In engineering, a repeatable process is applied to a problem such as building a bridge. The technology stays the same, the tools stay the same, and the process stays the same. If any of these changes, the bridge goes over budget. With software projects, the technology changes every project, the tools change every project, and the process is in a continuous state of flux. Add to this mix that what is likely being built is the automation of a likely poorly understood process. All that should be known is that with all unknowns, any estimates are educated guesses."

Is this news to you? Of course not. We all live in this world.

But how many of your customers have this expectation? *None of them.* They don't understand. They haven't reinstalled the operating system four times only to find that the video driver for the card on the machine is outdated and mislabeled. They haven't followed the documentation step by step in order to sync the remote data with the master copy, only to find that the typographic error in step 5 meant that you actually overwrote your master copy with old data instead of the other way around. They haven't wrestled with immature technology marketed by guys in $2,000 suits as "state-of-the-art" and "being used by all of your competitors" only to find that the key link between two components is buggy and won't be fixed until the next release. It still works well enough for the demos, after all.

Even if your customers did understand, they most likely wouldn't agree. They don't care about your problems—and rightfully so—they have a business to run, and if you're not going to provide them with the widget they need, they'll go down the street to someone else who will.

And if they did agree, they still wouldn't have an incentive to accept and put up with *your* problems. It's hard work, and that means it's too easily postponed.

So it's your job to develop a set of expectations that they can understand and agree to. Once that's done (and it's an arduous process), it's your job to perform to that set of expectations. And it's your job to continue to remind them what those mutually agreed upon expectations are, and to communicate how you are meeting those expectations.

It's also to your advantage to do this. By doing so, you determine the ground rules, and so you can tailor them as you need so that your life is easier. For example, take the issue of how to document defects. If you provide your customers with a Bug Reporting form and instructions on how to fill it out, you are dictating to them what you want. They may resist in the beginning, but they'll find out that eventually their life will be easier because you aren't refusing to fix ill-documented bugs or repeatedly asking for additional clarification.

If you wait for them to do so, you'll likely get a mess—an ill-defined or undefined process that is easier for them, up front, to do, but will make your life harder and interfere with your ability to respond to them in a way that is satisfactory to either of you.

How to make expectations happen

Explaining how the process works to them right at the beginning establishes the first expectation from both sides. You tell them that you have a predefined methodology that you have used successfully in the past, and that this methodology is used to control time and dollars, and to produce a quality product that they are satisfied with.

From your side, you're telling them that you expect to follow your process—that you're not going to wing it or throw parts of the process out the window to satisfy a whim on their part. On their side, they can expect to see a method emerge from the madness of analysis and design, and that there is a reason behind many of the seemingly unnecessary tasks involved.

Getting expectations out of people always seems to be either very easy or very hard. And typically, when it is easy, the person has been through a software project before that followed a meaningful methodology. If the person hasn't, though, it can be very hard, and you'll have to pay close attention to everything they say in order to determine what their real expectations are.

And this is what I'm going to do throughout this book—discuss ways to describe what your expectations are to the other party, whether that other party is a customer, a department manager requesting an application, a co-developer, or an employee.

Chapter 10
The Initial Contact

"We meet the right sort, this will work. We get some buckaroo..."—Marko Raimus
—The Hunt for Red October

Your PC beeps—another e-mail. An acquaintance sits down next to you at your fourth-grader's soccer game. A scrap of paper is slipped under the door at 5:01 Friday afternoon. A request for a quotation comes in mail. The Bat Phone rings. Or a man in a gray flannel suit bursts through the door, staggers into your office, clutching a gunshot wound, and with his last dying breath, gasps out, "I want you to build an app for my wife." It's now your move. What do you do? At some point, you're probably going to have to talk to someone—and that's where you can start setting expectations and communicating your competitive advantage. This chapter discusses how to handle that initial contact with a prospective customer.

At the start of a relationship with a potential customer, the primary goal is not simply to get the job. Rather, your mission is to both position yourself in their eyes so that you can win the business *if you want*—and at the same time, to determine whether or not you do indeed want to win the business.

Ten percent of the firms in the world are ones that you simply don't want to work for under any circumstances. They could be highly dysfunctional. Modern lore describes the company that bought laptops and Ethernet cards for all of their employees, and then fastened the computers to desks to prevent theft, and wouldn't allow access to the network for non-managerial employees for fear of hacking sensitive data. There are lots of companies in the world. Do you really have to work with one this completely clueless?

Or perhaps they're just unreasonable. You've run into the type—always wanting $20 worth of services for $9.99—and they'll wait 90 days to pay you, and expect you to pick up the check or they'll charge you for mailing it.

A third possibility is that they're simply dishonest. There are a thousand scams—like the one where a company places a few small orders and pays on time in order to develop credit worthiness, and then places a huge order and disappears without paying the bill. There's really no protecting yourself against a firm that's out to intentionally bilk you. At the same time, you should trust your gut feeling.

It's a small percentage, so I don't want to spook you, but still, given this uncertainty, it's wise to go into every new business relationship with a "seller beware" attitude.

Where the phone call comes from

As the introduction indicates, the initial contact can take any one of many forms—phone calls, e-mails, letters, even a physical contact at a weekend event. But for the purposes of this chapter, I'm going to assume that at some point, you either get a phone call, or you have the opportunity to make a phone call to the person interested in your services as a custom software developer.

This means that I'm not going to address those situations where some monolithic government agency has sent you a 300-page Demand For Quotation that must be filled out in triplicate and submitted to a faceless agency hundreds of miles away. These types of organizations don't understand that you can't buy custom software with the same process that you use when buying $500 hammers or $28,000 toilet seats.

Not all is lost, however, if you get one of these government packages on your desk. I've worked with several government agencies where the staff was extremely reasonable and worked very hard within their rules to make good custom software happen. The bottom line was that in these cases, a "phone call" still happened.

The phone call form

 The phone call form is a single piece of paper that is used to track all of the important information about the prospect. This form is used regardless of who initiates the call. A sample Phone Call form is included in the *DevGuide* downloads.

At my company, every person who is capable of answering a phone has a stack of these forms at their desk. Not filling one out when a new prospect calls is about as grievous an action as one can commit at the shop.

I've been asked why this form, in the 21st century, is still a piece of paper. Well, actually, the call log can be called up on the computer, and usually is. But it's wise to have a form around just in case. Why? Call me old-fashioned. You won't buy that? Okay, it's because the phone rings at the most inopportune times. You know—you're the only one who's not on the phone, and you're 10 minutes into installing a new piece of software. Or you've just logged off and grabbed your keys, ready for a long weekend. Are you going to make the caller wait "until I finish installing this new service pack" or "until I log on to my computer?"

The form has three sections. The top part is for general demographic information about the prospect (name, address, and so on). The second part covers their environment and what they are looking for in terms of services from us. Finally, the bottom is where we track the disposition of the project and what we're supposed to do.

Who are they?

This section allows you to capture all the necessary information you would need as far as working with and contacting someone.

Today's date

We date everything. (Restraint on your part from making wisecracks at this point would be appreciated.) Nothing is more frustrating than finding a phone call form without a date on it—how recent is this? We track what dates things happened during the progress of a project, and the date of the call is the starting point for any project.

Caller's name

We try to get both their first and last name, although sometimes they won't provide this. "I'm the only Helen in this department," comes the response. If they're adamant, I'll let it go, figuring that I'll get their name on a future go-around. Be sure to mark the lack of a last name so that if you, at the end of the call, need to send them something, you can ask for their full name.

Be sure to get it spelled properly as well. If you think you know, you can ask: "And 'Olson' is spelled with two O's, correct?"

Whenever someone refuses to give me their last name, I'm always tempted to send mail to "Helen NoLastName," but, I've never had the courage.

Caller's title or position

This is trickier, but it's important. I've gotten calls from $7.00/hour clerks and from Executive Vice Presidents of MIS for multinational corporations. You have to be a bit sensitive here, and sometimes titles don't mean that much, but it's essential information to gather.

You have to be careful of your time, and you need to be able to identify the decision maker as soon as possible. The last thing you want to do is drive 50 minutes for an appointment with this person only to find out you're doing little more than dropping off literature or trying to sell to a Second Assistant to the Executive Secretary of Somebody Vaguely Unimportant.

If they don't volunteer the information right away, which they often don't, I'll usually try something like, "Are you one of the developers at SAMRC?" Once in a while one of those delightful individuals overflowing with social graces will answer, "Uh, no" and not go any further, but most of the time they'll fill in the blank, at least to some extent.

Of course, just because they give you a "Lead Project Manager" type of title doesn't mean they have decision-making authority, but it gives you a place to start.

Company name/address

This is pretty self-explanatory, but I do want to point out that you should ask whether an acronym is the full name of the company or just a nickname. It's frustrating to try to look up the company in the phone book or other directory, and not find "SAMRC" listed, since that's just what the employees call it—the full name is Space Age Materials Research Corporation.

Depending on the nature of the call, I'll sometimes look up the company name while I'm talking to the person, and then I can confirm their address. "Oh, yes, Space Age Materials Research Corporation. You're on Bellmer Road, right?" This makes the caller feel more important and that they're being listened to—either you already know something about the company, or you've taken the time to look them up. Not all that many people pay this much attention.

If they give you a PO Box number, try to get a street address at the same time. Imagine having someone else in your company take down all the information and set up an appointment for you at 8 AM one morning. You take the phone call form with you the night before, and at 7:15 the next morning you discover all you've got is a PO Box. Their offices don't open until 8, you can't find the company name in the phone book, but no matter how you slice it, you're going to look bad showing up at 9:05.

Company business

If you already know what they do, fill it in. Otherwise, ask. Simply asking "What do you do at Materials Research Corporation?" is all you need to say. Finding out what business they're in can potentially provide a segue into a more fulfilling conversation. "You dump toxic chemicals into fish hatcheries? Well, that's excellent! We've done two applications where we tracked what was dumped into municipal swimming pools—and so we know a lot about that business."

Phone number/fax number

Again, this should be trivial, but I never rely on waiting to get this information at an in-person sales call. It's nice to have their phone number with you for any number of reasons. Same goes for the fax number—once you've got it, you don't have to ask again. Don't forget the area code—more and more metropolitan areas are getting multiple area codes. Just because the location is only eight miles away doesn't mean it's in the same area code.

What about pagers and cell phones? I generally don't ask at this stage, as few of our conversations tend to be Right Now Very Urgent. Perhaps when we get into the weekend when we go live with the system, we might need to make such arrangements. I don't carry a pager, and I never give my cell phone number out to people because I never have it on. I only use it for outgoing calls. If I'm out of the office, chances are I'm not going to be available, and on the off chance that I am, I'm most likely not going to be able to have a meaningful, technical discussion with someone—while riding my bike or changing lanes on the freeway.

Thus, most of the time, a call to my cell phone would result in an unsatisfactory communication. Accordingly, I don't ask for theirs either. Your experience and preference may differ.

E-mail address of the caller

There is a lot of information that can be exchanged asynchronously, and e-mail is the perfect medium for doing so. However, be sure to note how often they check their e-mail. Some people have it piped to their desk throughout the work day, but others have to dial up and thus may only get it once or twice a day—or ever less frequently. Voice mail, on the other hand, is usually picked up frequently.

Hours and availability

It's not uncommon to run into someone who works from home part of the time, or who shuttles from one office to another. If that's the case, you may need to note when they're available at which location.

How did they hear of your company?

If you recall, you just spent billions of dollars in the last chapter on marketing. Wouldn't it be nice to track which marketing mechanisms are actually providing leads? We can go back through our call logs and tally up how every customer we've worked with initially found out about us.

What if they won't give you this information?

It's sometimes tricky to get all of this information—when someone is window shopping or just kicking tires, they might not want to identify themselves fully.

Usually this reticence is due to the expectation that, once you have their name and phone number, you'll dog them to the ends of the earth, trying to snare that sale. You've probably run into firms that operate like that yourself, and if you haven't, I could sic a few of them on you, if you like. This doesn't often happen in our business, though, since developers are by nature not that type, and our business doesn't lend itself to that high-pressure methodology.

If they refuse, I'll typically talk with them for a couple of minutes, and ask again. If they're still looking for more information but are unwilling to identify themselves, I'll explain, bluntly, that my time is just as valuable as theirs, and I don't spend my time with people who won't tell me who they are.

I've found that this works pretty well. Why should I spend 20 or 30 minutes with someone who won't tell me who they are? What are they trying to hide? I'll talk to anyone for a minute or two, but if they're so distrusting up front, it bodes poorly for a long-term relationship.

What do they want?

As I discussed in the section on Yellow Pages advertising, you will get calls from the most clueless of folk. This section actually gets filled out before the name and address section, because, frankly, if they're looking to buy a copy of an accounting package, I don't care who they are—they'll just get sent to a reseller immediately.

Thus, it's important to identify exactly what they want as soon as you can. We often ask people bluntly, "Are you looking for someone to develop custom software for your company?" It may seem a bit brusque, but it's really not insulting, and it presents an extremely clear situation to the caller.

There are three possible answers. First, they might know what they want—and they want custom software developed for them. These are good calls. Second, they may simply answer "No"—because they're looking for a real estate management package, "Under $300, if possible." The third possibility is that they're not sure, in which case you get to start earning that exorbitant salary of yours.

In this third scenario, they've usually not described the problem to themselves yet, and so they'll just start rambling to you about their situation and how tough things are. You, then, get to play 20 Questions, and these are described in more detail in the next section.

Our phone call form has three check boxes—one for each of these three possibilities, although, of course, if they don't want custom software developed, we usually don't get around to filling out the rest of the form.

Types of custom software development

Even if writing custom software is the only thing you do, there are four kinds of software development services you can potentially offer.

In the first case, they don't have a system, but know they want one. In my opinion, this is the plum of the profession—starting from a clean slate.

The next kind would be making modifications to an existing system. To me, this is the least attractive, because there are very few systems that were both put together well, and then kept up-to-date correctly. Trying to modify code written by someone else who didn't understand the system they were trying to build and didn't have a good grounding with the tools they were attempting to use is a job best left for someone else.

On the other hand, you may like the puzzle. You could well find that neither the original developers nor the client knew enough about the business to design it right the first time. In many cases, thus, you'd find that the second go-round can produce much greater success, and a very happy client. In any case, offering to do such work can be a foot in the door, even if another path is selected as the final solution.

The third type of service is to upgrade an existing application, or parts of it, using an existing design or set of data structures. This doesn't happen often, but when it does, it's because the users have very specific requirements (or think they know something about software development, and thus insist on forcing their conditions on the developer as a show of power).

Finally, there's the possibility that the user doesn't know what to do, and thus starts at the beginning—asking you to evaluate their existing application in order to determine where to go next.

Thus, to make sure we don't go in with an initial misunderstanding, we have check boxes for each of these possibilities on our phone call form.

Environment

Here's where we try to get a handle on the size and scope of the project, and that's important because pretty soon, they're going to ask, "How much is this going to cost?"

What are some of the boundary conditions you can find out about? First, who's going to use it? How many people? What skill level(s) do they possess? Where (geographically) are they located? (Is everyone in the same cubicle farm on the fourth floor, or are they spread out across three continents?) What is the environment—operating system(s), hardware, networks? What are the company's plans for changes to these answers over the next couple of years?

These aren't commitments, but by asking about the environment that the application has to live in, you get a chance to get an idea of some of the expectations, and assess whether you have the skill set for the job. Obviously, an application that has to be running 24/7 because it's monitoring medical equipment at a hospital will have higher requirements than a tool used to estimate pension benefits once a year.

Budget and timeframe

Tricky question, this, and for several reasons. First, many companies like to keep their cards close to the vest. They somehow feel that by offering a number, that answer will somehow magically become the floor for all future discussions. As a result, they can be threatened by a direct question like "How much do you want to spend?" So we work around to that answer by first asking "Do you have a budget for this project yet?" They can say, "We have no idea how much this is going to cost" or "Yes, but we'd rather not say quite yet" or, sometimes, even "We've got a budget of $37,000."

The second thing we do to "soften the blow" is to ask about a timeframe along with a budget. Later on in this book I'll discuss a twist on the old adage "Fast, good, cheap: Pick any two." But for the time being, it's important for the customer to realize that timeframe is just as important as budget—they may have all the money in the world, but if they want the first module delivered next week, they may be disappointed. Similarly, if they're really cramped for funds but have a flexible delivery date, we may be able to work something out.

If they don't have a clue about how much this is going to cost, perhaps it's because they haven't gone through an in-depth examination about what they want. In that case, I explain that it's part of my job to help them determine the costs that different scenarios can involve. Just like someone who is building a house for the first time, they may well be ignorant of software development costs. Nonetheless, it's the rare individual or company who has carte blanche to develop software (or build a house). Somewhere, somehow, someone has got some sort of idea, and so I try to pull that out of them: "Are you thinking about $10,000? $100,000? $1,000,000?" That's enough of a range for anyone to be able to come up with an initial guess.

The final result may be two or three times their original number, but at least we have something to start with.

The other question I might ask here, especially if the customer is being particularly opaque about their budget, is to ask how this software will make them money. People don't build software just for the fun of it (well, not too often, in my experience), so there's some cost they are avoiding, some process they are enhancing, or some new service they will be offering that will make them money. If they know how much they are going to make or save, work through a brief microeconomics lesson on ROI with them, and now we have a ballpark budget figure to talk about.

I'm really reluctant to continue talking with someone who is, at this point, still unwilling to provide any kind of a number, and so we nudge them along some more.

One approach I've used successfully is to anecdotally explain that "Well, I like to get an idea of where the project might stand. I still run into people who think they can get a piece of custom software written for a thousand dollars." I once did this with a company looking for some fairly straightforward estimating software but with a few tricky hooks into their existing accounting software, only to be met with the reply, "Oh, we weren't looking to spend nearly *that* much!"

Evidently his accounting software cost $159 (sound familiar?), and he thought that a "custom application" might run two or three times that. I then explained that a custom software application to do the work he thought he was looking for could run anywhere from $20,000 to $50,000, and suggested he run down to the local store to see if he could find something closer to his price range.

If they still refuse to provide a number, then I might offer to do some initial consulting—in order to help them develop an idea of the size and scope of their project. Alternatively, I might simply suggest that they do some more internal research about what they're looking for, and then offer to contact them later.

Who else are they evaluating?

This is also a tricky question to ask, but the answer can be pretty interesting as well. Again, you're trying to be careful with their time. Occasionally they will spill the beans that they've really already picked a developer, and are just making a couple of other calls to satisfy some rule or another (particularly with government jobs that have to be bid out).

Why waste your time if they've made it clear that they've already made up their mind?

Of course, never bad-mouth the competition—even if you have to hold your hand over the phone while you burst out laughing about whom they're considering. Every company has their own special niche in this world—and there are undoubtedly places where your competition will fare better than you would.

If asked my opinion of another company, I usually try a three-phase approach. First, I soft-pedal my opinion. Next, I try to find something good about them, even if it means damning the other company with faint praise. Finally, I close with "I don't know that I'm qualified to talk about someone else's company—I can tell you what we do, and give you as much information as possible so that you can talk to them as well and then make the decision that makes sense for your company and situation."

A very brief description, highlighting those areas where you know your competition is weak and you shine—your experience with this industry, track record, time in business, stability—can introduce sufficient doubt to get a potential customer to re-examine their criteria.

Hopefully they will see that my company has its act together much more than the competition, and that makes the prospect's decision that much easier.

What happened to the original developer?

If they've already got some sort of software in place, this is a very important question. You're in the initial evaluation stage, and here's where you get to start determining whether or not you want to work with this company. There is probably a very good reason that they're not using the original developer. He quit, got transferred, disappeared, or died. She's working on another project. He's become a manager. This version of the project is so big they need an outside firm to manage it. And so on.

There are also a few reasons that aren't as good, and, in these cases, you usually will have to read between the lines. "Our previous contractor doesn't return our phone calls anymore." (Translation: We haven't paid his last two invoices.) "Our contractor didn't understand our business needs." (Translation: We changed the rules on her faster than she could type.) "We need some fresh blood on this project." (Translation: We've beaten every one else to death with stupid ideas and they won't listen to us anymore.) And so on.

Be careful. Sometimes a parting of the ways is the original developer's fault, but there are a number of companies that seem to have gone through every developer in town because they insist on an unreasonable working relationship.

Conclusion

Again, to sum up, they need to be able to spell out that they want us to write (or modify) custom software for them. If they can't get this through in two to four sentences, then they're not clear enough in their own minds about what they want, and trying to continue through the intricate process of analysis and design is likely going to be beyond them.

What is the next step?

The third part of our phone call form is one of those "Internal Use Only" types of areas. It's where we determine what the next step is. Since this form may be handed from one person to another, it's important to be specific about what is going to happen next. And since it's on the form, it's a good reminder that we have to confirm with the caller what they're expecting as well.

The first possibility is that no action is required because there isn't any work available for us. This is the case when the caller was trying to buy a copy of Doom or some new printer cartridges. Although most of the form isn't filled out, we still keep it. If we find out we're getting 75 calls a day from people who want to buy a replacement copy of MultiMate (the '80s word processor, not the breeding program for Holstein cows), perhaps it signifies a new opportunity for us. Or maybe it just means that some of our marketing materials are ill targeted or badly assembled.

The second possibility is when the caller was indeed kicking tires, and specifically says, "We'll call you." Some sales folks would cringe at my response, saying, "Always make sure you call them back and follow up," but that's because most of them are selling into a market crowded with competition. I've found that most software developers have more work than they can handle, and so they don't have to chase after prospects that aren't actively interested. And I personally hate the feeling that I'm nagging someone, so if they want to take the initiative to pursue me, that's fine.

Although I'm reticent to nag someone, that doesn't mean I won't try to follow up. Thus, at my company we always offer to give them a call back when it's convenient or appropriate. If they specifically say, "*No!*" then we check the previous box. If they aren't actively interested, but wouldn't mind a follow-up call, we check the third box—to follow up at a requested date and time.

As an aside, I'd like to mention that this technique—taking sort of a laid back approach to following up with a prospect—stops once they sign on the dotted line. As soon as they become a paying customer, it's our responsibility—perhaps the most important thing we can do—to be proactive about maintaining communication with them.

The fourth possible choice is when there is active interest, and the next move is theirs. For example, perhaps they're going to assemble some materials that they want to send you, or they're going to have their boss call when she gets back into town next week, or whatever.

The fifth possible choice is when they want you to do something—send materials, for example—or when you've offered to do something specific, like providing a referral.

I've saved the best for last—when they want to meet with you—a real, live, honest-to-goodness sales call. In this case, you'll want to make sure you have the date and time correct, as well as the address and any special directions if you're meeting at their place.

A typical phone call

Now that you've got this form ready to fill out, you're waiting for the phone to ring. What happens when it does?

Remember that you have two goals that the caller may not be aware of. The first is to determine whether there is a match between you and the prospect. This isn't the same as finding out what they want—in this case, you're looking for all those potential clues that spell "This prospect is trouble" and that warn you away from the prospect. The second goal is to avoid wasting time—spending time with someone who is obviously not a match.

Of course, there is that third item on your To Do list during the call—listening to them and finding out what they want.

Put yourself in their shoes—and remember that those shoes may be pretty ragged and torn. They may be having difficulty clarifying what it is that they're looking for—perhaps they're frustrated, their boss has mandated that they fix the problem, and they've finally found someone who may be able to work magic for them. Or perhaps they're going through the motions because the search is part of their job, but they'd really much rather be doing something else.

So your job is to help them communicate while, at the same time, letting them begin to set expectations of what they want from you—and what their role in this relationship will be.

It's also worthwhile to point out now that this could well be an uncomfortable process for your caller—they're potentially going to be parting with a great deal of money, and they're afraid of making a bad choice. And most people are completely unfamiliar with the process of buying custom software.

You've likely bought several cars, and you probably still take a great deal of time choosing what you want, making sure you get the best price, and that you've chosen a dealer that you think you'll be happy with. And all that pressure comes from buying a car—something that's easy to understand and for which there's a huge amount of knowledge and support. The angst accompanying the purchase of custom software can be much greater. Be sure to keep your caller at ease as best you can—make it easy for them to maneuver through this process.

Get them on track right away

Brrrring! It rings! And someone on the other end says that they're looking for a programmer, or they have an application that they're having trouble with, or something along those lines. They'll usually start into the nuts and bolts of the system, or perhaps begin to describe what problems they're having—even before they've identified themselves.

As I've said before, as soon as you can, get them to confirm that they're looking for software development services—even if you have to ask them flat out, "Are you looking for us to develop software for you?"

Many times, that direct question will stop them for a second, and you then have the opportunity to take control of the conversation and guide it so that you get all the information you need (while still letting them spill their guts, of course).

I've found that at this point, many people are willing to let you provide a little structure. "You're looking for software development? Well, gosh—cuz that's what we do here! And this is how this all works…" This is a great way to launch into an explanation of the process (with somewhat better grammar, perhaps). Here's how you could go about this:

"Well, first I'd like to get a couple pieces of data in case the phone company decides to terminate our conversation unexpectedly. Then I'd like to find out about your company and your software development needs. Finally, I can explain how we navigate through this process of software development, and then you can decide if you think there's a fit and if we may be able to provide some services for your firm."

Notice that this allows you to get your form filled out quickly, and get on to the important part—what it is they're looking for.

Get your phone call form filled out

If the prospect starts rambling, it can be difficult to get them to answer your questions or to explain how things work. What I've found works best is to let themselves get tired, and when they stop to catch their breath, ask them if you could ask them a few questions.

"Well, tell you what. This sounds like something that we might able to help you out with. Could I interrupt for a minute and ask a couple questions here?" Hardly anyone is going to take offense at this request, and now you're in a position to take control.

Ask them to do their homework

In the event that they're interested in buying custom software, it's time to get serious—and see how serious they are as well. Just because they have a budget and they've identified what it is they want doesn't mean that checks are going to start flowing your way. Plenty of people would like as much free consultation done up front as they can get away with. Just as you've tried to guard against the time-waster on the phone, you'll need to double your guard against those folks who get a hook into you.

I've found the best way to watch out for these types is to find out whether they're willing to invest their time up front as well.

My terms are that I'll make a single sales call at no charge, but after that, the clock starts ticking. But I'd rather not spend all my time on sales calls that end up being dead ends, so I ask them to do some homework in preparation for the sales call visit. If they're not interested, then I'm not either.

This homework consists of helping them to give me enough information so I can answer the inevitable question, "How much is this going to cost?" One of the goals of the sales call is to determine the size and scope of the project, and thus be able to give them a rough ballpark of the dollars and hours involved.

Regardless of whether you eventually go for fixed price or time and materials pricing, the customer is going to want to have an idea of the size of the bill, both for the design and for the finished system. The sooner you can give them a number—and the rationale behind that number—the more comfortable the customer is going to be. Ask yourself, how long would you work with an architect before getting an idea of how much that new home is going to cost?

This request for the customer to do their homework so that the "How much?" question can be answered in a single meeting works for projects up to, say, low six figures. Past that, the scope is so large that it's going to take more than a single meeting to even pin down the big picture.

Now, what does this homework look like?

I'll ask them to provide a list of all the things they want this system to do, to indicate whether this would be a "data entry" function, a "running a report" function, or an "execute a process and sit back while it runs" function. I'll also ask them to prioritize these functions—into "gotta have," "need pretty badly," and "it sure would be nice if" categories.

If they're so disposed, I'll ask them to try to lay out their data tables by thinking in terms of a series of spreadsheets. Most everyone knows what a spreadsheet is nowadays, and it's easy to map a spreadsheet to a fairly normalized set of tables. They can help out a fair amount by identifying each major entity (which would each go into a separate spreadsheet), and the primary keys (the one column in the spreadsheet that would make each row unique). They can even identify the foreign keys—what column in one spreadsheet would link it to another.

Many prospects enjoy getting involved to this degree, and appreciate being brought into the "inner circle" as this appears to do. Instead of shooing them away ("It's technical—you wouldn't understand"), you achieve more buy-in. You'll also quickly find out some valuable clues about the personalities involved. The one user who produces a beautifully formatted and printed series of spreadsheet mockups for the tables of his component of the system may be a good candidate for beta testing later on.

Sometimes this request is too advanced—they don't know how to even begin thinking of "screens" or "reports"—and so I'll step back a bit, and ask them to write down "operations you want to be able to do." By getting them to talk about the business in their terms and perhaps even do some diagramming on how the business flows, they can provide the structure needed for use cases and such. Everyone loves to talk about themselves in one way or another.

Ask whether they already have some process information—even simple operations manuals—anything that will provide some structure for you and give you a head start on their business terms. A glossary of terms—sometimes very key in larger organizations or companies in certain industries that tend to develop their own lingo—will be very helpful in that the terms themselves are often the "players." Even within the same industry, competitors may use the same term differently, so the more you can learn about what's specific to your customer will help you become productive more quickly.

They may resist by claiming they don't have the time. In this case, I hold off on scheduling a visit until they can make the time. It's pretty easy to explain that meeting with them would be a waste of time until they can do their homework for the meeting, and, in fact, I'm trying to save them some money. If they want me to visit before they're ready, they'll have to meet with me again once they've pulled their materials together—and the clock is running for that second meeting. Much better to get a bit of work done for free, wouldn't you say?

If they're simply unwilling to do this, then I'm probably not going to waste my time visiting them—it tells me that they're not serious. Of course, I wouldn't phrase it that way— rather, I'd suggest that perhaps they're not quite ready, but when they get closer to wanting to bring me in, I'd be happy to do so.

"What can we do to prepare?"

Experienced or insightful prospects will value both their own time and yours, and will ask, "What can we do to prepare for our meeting?" I love these kinds of prospects! The trick here is to give them a list of things you're going to want to know, and that they might have to do a bit of research on, but not one that is so long that they won't get it done.

I use this checklist for a second reason—to help get them organized, and to make sure I write down the answers to a number of important questions whose answers are already well-known well to the customer, but are easily overlooked by the developer in his haste to get to the project itself.

Close the conversation

Make sure that both you and the caller understand what the next step is. You've already got this big blank area on your phone call form waiting for you, so it's easy to remember. Just repeat what you understand the next step is to your caller, and you'll be all set.

Follow-up to a phone call

Once you're done with a phone call (this might have just taken 5 or 10 minutes), what do you do? Hopefully, not much. You're not getting paid yet, so the less work you have to do now, the better.

However, "not much" doesn't equate to "nothing." You may have a list of "To-do" items resulting from the phone call—gathering materials you offered to show them at the sales call, for example. You should also pull together an agenda, and send it along with any materials you promised. Many customers won't know where to start with their homework, and so you'll probably need to send them samples.

Agenda for the meeting

The sales call can be a chaotic meeting, with introductions of the players, a demonstration of the current application, and piles of folders with documentation and lists of ideas for "the new version"—it can be overwhelming. Not having a game plan puts you at risk for losing control of the meeting, spending too much time, getting sidetracked on unimportant issues, and generally making poor use of the time spent with them. And this bodes poorly for you—if you can't manage a simple sales call, how are they going to feel about entrusting the management and development of a custom software application to you? Worse, how are you actually going to pull it off?

In the next chapter, I'll go over the sales call in detail, and from that, you'll be able to put together how you want to structure your own sales calls. Once you've done so, you'll be able to put together a generic agenda for a sales call meeting. You'll want to send this to your potential customer ahead of time so that they know what to expect.

Send the agenda plus other materials

Of course, just because you've gathered all of the materials doesn't mean you're done. You'll want to get them to your potential customer as well—and the sooner you do so, the better. First, it makes you look sharp—that you're on the ball and attentive to their needs. Second, there's less chance you'll forget. And third, if they've requested sample documents to help them with their homework, the sooner you get the material to them, the more time they will have to prepare for the meeting.

Twists for the corporate IS department

If you're working in a corporate IS department, this process usually becomes shortened—nearly beyond recognition, in some cases. It's not uncommon for the phone call to last all of 30 seconds—enough for the user department to ask you to a meeting at 1 PM that afternoon, and at that meeting they'll ask you to deliver a first prototype before they go home for the night.

Obviously, you won't have to go through all of the pieces of the phone call form—you may well have all the demographic information you need, for instance. You probably won't have to worry about some of the background information, such as "What happened to the original developer?" Everyone heard all about him the few days after he was shown the door.

On the other hand, you may need to get some information. For example, depending on the size of your company, you may need directions to where they are located—Building 45, third floor, past the demo showroom. You might also need charge codes against which you'll log your time, and you may need to get approval to do work from both their department head as well as your own manager. Just because their ID badge has the same company logo as yours doesn't mean they're not above a bit of subterfuge to get something done under the table, or off the books.

Regardless of these issues, you'll still want to be very clear about what the user department is looking for. You'll still want to ask them, "You are asking me to write custom software for you, right?" It's still possible to over-engineer a solution, or put together an application that is inappropriate for the environment. In fact, it can be even more likely, in an environment where your cost is "internal." And, just as in the independent world, applications only get bigger—they never get smaller. Thus, at first glance, you may think you can short-circuit the process, because the "We can whip this out in a few days—a week at most" application often turns into an application that half of the company ends up using.

And since you're not necessarily worried about the meter running, you may change the way you approach "homework." One of my colleagues asks the user to start by describing the business and not the application. By keeping them away from design—thinking of "screens" and "reports"—she saves a lot of headaches later because they don't really do a very good job putting them together, and she then has to play diplomat in order to get rid of their stuff and give them a decently designed app. Also, as object-oriented techniques play a larger role in the systems, having them think in terms of the business does usually align nicely to OO design, so no longer does she have to do as much translation between business and code.

Chapter 11
The Sales Call

"You had me at hello."—Dorothy
  —Jerry McGuire

In one of his early comedy albums, Bill Cosby hypothesized that graduation from a karate class was not the ultimate goal of taking such a class. Rather, he said, "Eventually, you want to get attacked." In a similar vein, while the goal of marketing is initially to get phone calls, ultimately, it's to make a sales call. More so than the phone call, an in-person visit is your best chance to set expectations while at the same time determining whether you want the job. This chapter covers the in-person sales call in detail.

Call me old-fashioned, but I still think software development requires face-to-face contact. The endeavor you're about to undertake is hard work, full of stress, and often gets touchy. Having a face to attach to a voice— the personal contact—makes getting through those tough times a lot easier.

This works in both directions. How often have you said, "You don't look anything like I pictured, based on what you sound like?" The gruff, coarse voice on the phone may belong to Santa's twin brother, or a taller version of your older sister. It's easier to put yourself in their shoes if you've met with them face to face.

Likewise, remember that we're scary folks. Programmers aren't like normal people—well, on average. Sure, there are a few of you who go to baseball games and teach your kids to ride a two-wheeler on the weekend. But there are a disproportionate number in our business who, to put it delicately, lack some fundamental social skills. And in this stressful situation—the spending of a large amount of money for something they can't touch or feel, or even understand very well—people are inclined to fear the worst.

Meeting you in person can help put those fears to rest. (Or, I suppose, intensify them to the point that they don't leave their house for a year.) When they find out you're a human being just like most of the other people at their company, they'll relax and be able to focus on the matter at hand: assisting you in developing good software.

Purpose

Going into a sales call without a clear set of goals in mind is a waste of time. You should have four items foremost in your mind.

First, you want to determine whether or not there's a match between you and the prospect. Next, you want to get your arms around the size and scope of the project, in at least some rough fashion. The primary purpose of this is so that you can provide some reasonable answer to the inevitable question—"How much is this going to cost?"—but this information will also be needed so that you can make a decision as to which type of process and payment mechanism is best suited for this project.

The third item is to explain to the prospect how the custom software development business works, and to either propose the type of process and payment mechanism you've selected, or to suggest the options and work out with the customer which is best. And finally, the last is to, if you want to, sell the prospect on having you do a specification for the project they're contemplating.

Identify the likelihood of a match

The sales guys argue that the purpose of the sales call is to get the job, but it's not. You first want to determine whether you want the job and, if that is the case, then you want to do the sales thing—actually work to get the job. This is called "qualifying the prospect." Custom software is in high demand and the available suppliers are scarce, so it's not difficult to find people who want the product you supply. Finding people who have reasonable expectations, who are going to be good to work with, and, yes, who have money, is not quite as easy.

You've already weeded out some of those folks who are obviously not a match during the phone call, but due to the ethereal nature of our business, it's not possible to winnow out everyone.

As my friend Ed Leafe has said, "It is better to be sad that you lost the work than to be sad that you got it." The gain you realize from a good job is much smaller than the potential loss you can incur from a bad job—much like short selling in the stock market has significantly more risk than simply buying stock. The most you can gain from a good job is a healthy profit—but if a job goes south, you can lose your company. It pays to be very careful when doing the initial courtship with a new customer.

Once you've got a handle on them, it's your job to convince them that you can do the work they want done, and you'll spend the rest of the sales call doing so. By your actions as well as your words, you'll set expectations—you want to talk and act so that the expectations they develop are appropriate for the job, so that they are not disappointed in the long run.

Remember, most likely, this customer has not bought custom software before, so they may well have a set of expectations that are unreasonable or impossible. And no matter how skilled you are, or how good a Joe they are otherwise, if they leave this meeting harboring a false set of hopes, the relationship can turn ugly in short order.

First pass at identifying size and scope

The previous section focused on you—what your goals are during the sales call. Don't be fooled into thinking that what you want matters. If you eventually decide to work with this company, they are going to be the one making the decisions and writing the checks, so you need to take care of them all the while. It's just that there's a lot more going on inside your head than what the prospect may perceive.

After the customer gets past the "Are we comfortable with this programmer" stage from their own point of view, they'll want to know the answer to two questions: "How much is this going to cost me?" and "Can you have it finished sometime late next week?" At the same time, you're going to have to answer the question, "What type of process and payment mechanism is going to be best for this project?"

If you can provide a good, albeit very rough, answer to the first two questions to your customer, and garner enough information so you can answer the third question to yourself, you'll make your prospect more comfortable and enhance the possibility of putting together a relationship.

This part of the sales call usually takes the longest—you'll spend time with them reviewing what they're looking for, all the while asking questions and gathering information so you can determine the answers to these questions yourself.

Pitch the price and best process

Once you've determined what the approximate price and best process to use are, it's time to deliver the news to the customer. These two issues are very much interrelated. And there are two approaches to take.

The first is when the customer asks, "So, how much?" Note that they won't word the question exactly like this—more likely, they'll have spent anywhere from 20 minutes to a couple of hours describing what they're looking for, and then they'll say, "Well, naturally, we won't hold you to this answer, but can you give us a ballpark figure for this project?" No matter what you say, they'll remember the number you give them. If you try to remind them later that they promised not to hold you to this preliminary number, they'll always respond with "Yes, but…" and deliver some incredible rationalization (or irrationalization?) as to why that promise is no longer valid.

The second approach is when they don't ask, "How much?" You can take this as a sign that they either aren't interested, or have something up their sleeve such that the price is inconsequential. Customers *always* want to know how much during the sales call; if they don't, you have to watch out! For this reason, if they don't bring up price, don't heave a sigh of relief and think that you're getting away with something—cuz you aren't. Bring up the question yourself, and see how they react.

In both cases, you need to cover a broader ground than just giving them a dollar figure. You may propose a single development process, and not let them have another choice, because their circumstances preclude any other choices. Or you may propose that the two of you work out the choice of development process together.

I'll explain how to do this later in this chapter.

Sell them on the next step

The last item on your internal "To-do" list will be to close the meeting and confirm the next steps. What those steps are depend on 1) whether or not you want the gig (and they want you), and 2) what type of process you've decided on.

If you don't want the job, you need to excuse yourself gracefully from further consideration—sort of the same as claiming that you have to stay home Friday night because you were going to wash your hair. Well, maybe a bit less transparently than that. And if they don't want you, they may come right out and say so ("We are looking for someone who <fill in a condition>") or they may let you down gently, such as with a line like "We'll have to do some more research and will get back to you."

Assuming that the two of you want to continue together, the next step depends on the type of process you've decided on.

If you're going with a process that involves a specification, then the software development project is divided into two pieces. Just like a building, a custom software application requires a blueprint to be used during its construction.

Taking the building construction analogy a step further, a blueprint is designed by an architect. And that architect may or may not be involved with the actual construction of the structure. Similarly, my firm always proposes the development of a specification as a service separate from the development of the application itself.

This approach gives the customer peace of mind. They feel that if they're not happy with your work after a certain point, they can walk away from you and go somewhere else—providing them with a safety valve.

Thus, remember that you are trying to sell them on doing a specification, not on the whole programming job. If they like the spec, then the development will come naturally. I've found it's a rare occurrence to write a complete specification and then have the customer go elsewhere for the development itself. During the sales call, don't look so far out in the future that you lose sight of the short-term goal.

On the other hand, if the gig doesn't involve a spec, then it's time to get rolling with development. Even then, however, it doesn't mean that you head on back to the shop, create a new directory on your development machine, and start slinging code. First, you'll need to formalize the relationship—including the specifics of this type of process—with an Engagement Letter, and then you'll need to meet with them to determine *something* about the application they want.

Note that a prospect who wants you to start coding before specifications have been developed—but do it for a fixed price—is a prospect better left on the mountainside to die a slow, miserable death. Hopefully you've weeded that type out early on!

Goals vs. agenda

There is a lot happening on several levels during the sales call, much like a blind date. On the surface, the two of you are getting acquainted, and after some pleasantries, talking business and maybe talking a bit of tech. Under the surface, you're checking out the customer, and, hopefully, they're doing the same to you. It can be easy to get sidetracked during the actual visit, so I just want to mention again that the previous four sections are items on your internal "To-do" list. The actual agenda of the sales call, which I cover later in this chapter, can be significantly different!

Where to meet

As much as it is a hassle for you, the sales call should always be made at the customer's location. I'll discuss the other options as well, but this has been my experience—meeting first at their place of business has the most advantages all the way around.

Pros and cons of "Their Place"

There are four reasons for meeting at their place.

First, it's a natural courtesy, and most people expect it. They're the customer; you're the vendor, and so you do the legwork.

Second, many times, the customer will want you to look at files, programs, printouts, and so on. There is usually no practical way to do this if they have to pack up everything and bring it to your office. Even if they try, they're more than likely to forget something.

They may also want you to look at their existing applications and systems, and those may not be portable.

Furthermore, you may need to (or they may want you to) meet with other people who don't have to be available for the entire meeting. It's terribly inconvenient for them to bring additional people along in this situation.

The third reason is that you need to scout out the territory. There's a lot you can learn from the digs a customer resides in. First of all, by visiting them, you'll find out a lot more clearly how big or small they are. You will also find out the general atmosphere of the company—are they just basically nice people? I learned a long time ago that there is a percentage of people in the world who simply aren't very nice, and I decided not to do business with them. Let them make the lives of my competition miserable, not mine.

Next, does it feel like the company is on solid ground? Do they have a frugal image, or have they spent enough money to make their people reasonably comfortable? If people are stacked two to a cubicle (no, that's not just in Dilbert's imagination) and the building is in disrepair, could the company be in financial trouble, or are they just grossly stingy with funds? If so, could this be a sign that they're going to try to nickel and dime you? If a company is going to spend $10,000, $25,000, or $50,000 on an application, a cheap mentality isn't going to be conducive to a good working relationship.

You'll also get a feel for how the company operates. The reason you're there, generally, is because they've got a problem and they want you to solve it. Is it possible that the problem is not one that the implementation of a software application will fix, but rather it's an operational problem and automating it will simply make the same mess in a shorter period of time?

The computer environment is another aspect of the company that you'll be able to see with your own eyes. Over the phone, they may have described that they've got "pretty much new computers" with "a brand-new network." Once on-site, though, you see machines with filthy keyboards and dust-laden screens, no-name system units with the covers off, and a laser printer balancing on a stack of books while you're stepping over network cabling strung across hallways.

This tells you two things. One is that either they're lying to you, or their definition of "new" comes from a dictionary you've not seen before. The other is that you may be in for a couple of challenges that you hadn't expected—many a developer has wasted time trouble-shooting a supposed programming problem only to find out that cheap NICs are dropping packets.

Finally, you have some control over when the meeting ends. If worse comes to worst, you can simply walk out. A bit more graciously than that, hopefully, but it's difficult to leave your own office to terminate a meeting.

This much said, meeting at their place isn't always the answer. It's possible that your contact isn't well organized, or that they fool themselves into thinking they're more organized than they really are. In this case, they will often fail to prepare properly or as completely as they would if they had to pack up the whole show and take it on the road.

Second, the company culture may be such that interruptions are the natural order of the day. It's possible to get an hour's worth of work done in a four-hour meeting in this type of place. It still may be valuable to meet in such an atmosphere, if for no other reason than to learn this, and to then account for it during future work. But if you really have to be efficient, then perhaps another location is the answer.

Pros and cons of "Your Place"

Suppose the prospect wants to (or even demands to) meet at your place? They may want to check you out just as much as you want to check them out. And, if you've implemented some of the ideas discussed later on in this book, you should be proud of your place, and want to show it off. However, you might consider postponing that for a future meeting, if possible.

Second, they may also realize that they're not going to get any work done in their own office, and prefer to get off-site.

If they're a long distance away, they also might feel uncomfortable asking you to spend the better part of a day traveling to and fro, particularly if the sales call is fairly speculative.

There could also be a hidden reason—suppose your office is downtown, and they want to go shopping for the holidays. They can combine a business trip with pleasure, and perhaps even get their company to pay for lunch and parking. (I've had it happen more than once!)

On the other hand, just as with their site, you'll have to control interruptions and other demands on your time—and you'll want to make sure you are as prepared for the meeting as you would be if you visited them.

If you work out of your house, there are a whole host of additional issues involved in having a customer visit you where you live. First of all, you may not want to have to keep the house, filled with children and their accessories, in a constant state of readiness. Second, offices, while they can be lavish or not, reflect the business. A customer may make judgments about you based on your home that would be inappropriate. Finally, you (and they) may simply be uncomfortable holding a business meeting at your home.

Pros and cons of "A Neutral Place"

In some cases, neither your digs nor theirs may work out. I dislike meeting in, say, a restaurant, for a whole list of reasons. It's generally an awkward atmosphere—just about the time you're starting to discuss some critical or touchy issue, the server stops by with another annoying question. They'll often try to hurry you through your meal. There isn't enough table space to spread things out. And try to find a plug for a computer, much less the tabletop space for that as well. And if you've got more than two people, no one can see the screen of a notebook anyway—do you really want to bring an LCD panel or separate monitor into a restaurant?

Bottom line—if it's the only way to go, it beats missing the opportunity to talk to them, but keep this option at the bottom of your list.

What to wear

One of the longer threads in memory on CompuServe's FoxUser forum was titled "Dress for Client?" In the thread, the poster asked whether it was necessary to get dressed up to go to a client for a 10-minute visit that consisted of picking up a new set of data files and installing a new report.

Of course, as many threads on CompuServe do, this one eventually degenerated into unrelated topics, such as the discussion of what items men keep in their pockets that women keep in their purses (one friend said he kept a comb in his left rear pocket, to which I thought,

"Braggart!"). But the gist of the thread dealt with whether or not dressy attire was required, recommended, or simply superfluous.

I have conflicting emotions on this topic. First and foremost is the desire to make the customer feel comfortable. If the customer could possibly be offended by what you're wearing, then it's a mistake. This, of course, goes both ways. Perhaps your prospect is at a downtown bank—you'd want to get dressed up because, more than likely, the bank employees still respect a formal dress code. Your prospect may not care themselves, but what if their boss happens by? Better to err on the side of caution.

On the other hand, it's been known to happen that a consultant wearing a $2,000 suit can offend the employees in a factory environment where "dressed up" means buttoning a shirt and washing their hands. You wouldn't want your prospect to feel you were "slumming" when you were visiting their office.

The second issue I personally deal with is that I'm really selfish, and that extends to wanting to be able to choose what I wear, instead of having another entity dictate to me what the uniform shall be. But that's just me. Fortunately, more and more, a casual dress code has become commonplace, and I've been able to survive with a corporate clientele and still not change out of dress slacks and polo shirts for the past couple years.

Of course, your mileage may vary. Here are some options.

A suit

Although the heading says "A suit," I'm really talking about "dressing up." Now, you may ask, "What constitutes 'dressing up' for the customer?" To my way of thinking, you can wear anything you want, as long as, for men, it's a dark suit, white shirt, and conservative patterned tie, and for women, it's essentially the same, a suit with hose and pumps, and a white or light-colored blouse. I read that *Dress for Success* book back when I was an impressionable young weenie, and I've never been able to shake those inclinations. Of course, depending on the time of year, the suggestions laid down may be personally inappropriate. If you've got hair down past your shoulders, wearing a suit and tie looks more out of place than if you were to don a leisure suit.

Perhaps you could break these rules if you were in Hollywood (flashy suits and fast cars) or Miami (Hawaiian shirts and fast cars), but not in the rest of America.

Business casual

A lot has been made of "Casual Days" in corporate America over the past few years, and some of it is beginning to spread to other parts of the world. It's important to note that "casual" doesn't mean the same thing everywhere. At a manufacturing plant, "casual" may truly mean anything but bike shorts, halters, and flip-flops. At the headquarters of a multi-national, "casual" may mean dress slacks, dress shirts, shined shoes, and the related accessories. In other words—just no tie and jacket.

Don't just assume that you can wear a pair of Levi's and a T-shirt asking, "Have you hugged your ISP today?" when your customer tells you "We've got a casual dress code here."

Programmer casual

One of my favorite anecdotes has to do with "programmer casual." One day in the financial district of a large American city, two of my friends met for lunch. One was on a sales call from a nearby city, meeting with high-level executives on a mid-six figure application, and was wearing a blue suit, white shirt, and Ivy League tie. The other was visiting the city on a different business venture, had hair half-way down his back, had gone unshaven for, well, more than a couple of days, and sported the latest "in your face" admonition of a sneaker manufacturer on a T-shirt worn over a ratty pair of jeans and worn sandals. Said the one more casually dressed, "Gee <name>. People pay me for what I *know*."

While this actually happened, remember that the clothes you're comfortable in while programming may take the idea of "casual dress" too far for a customer. While I will go to outrageous lengths to avoid having to wear a suit myself, at the other end, a shirt with some sort of collar, pants without tears, holes, or marks, and clean shoes are a minimum.

Again, your perspective and environment may dictate a different level.

The point to dressing to see a customer is that what you wear should not detract from the message that you are delivering—in fact, what you wear should be invisible to the customer, so they can concentrate completely on the content of your message. If you're in doubt, dress up. You can always take off a tie or jacket if you've overdressed.

What to bring

You can divide potential things to bring to a sales call into two categories—supporting materials for your company, and demonstration materials such as sample apps.

Materials

Gosh, I'm simply appalled at the number of people who go on a sales call and forget to bring a business card, a notepad, or literature about their company. Not when they don't have them, but when they do, and just forget. How can you ever walk out of the office without a few business cards and a pad of paper?

If you're one of those who never seems to have everything in place, consider putting together a "Things to take to meetings" checklist, and keep a file folder stocked with these items.

You might consider keeping a stack of business cards, a pen, and a legal pad in your car's glove compartment—as a friend does—so that if you run into someone as you're driving to the beach in your swim trunks, you still have the gear to take notes and make a contact.

And, finally, remember that portfolio I mentioned back in Chapter 6, "What You'll Need"? The sales call is why you put it together in the first place!

A PC

Keep the goodies—particularly the newest gadgets you've picked up—to a minimum. You may want to bring a PC to demonstrate some of your applications, but don't get sidetracked showing all the cool things you can do. Customers want to talk about themselves, not you.

Furthermore, they probably won't understand much of what you show them anyway. It's hard to successfully demonstrate anything but the most trivial of applications in a short period of time.

It's also possible that they will focus on extraneous details ("How did you get the title to turn blue?" or "What's that red thingy in the middle of your keyboard?") instead of the business problem being solved. Why expose yourself to that possibility? There will be time later for demonstrating work you've done in the past.

The agenda—your game plan for the meeting

It's very important that you have a plan for the meeting. I usually try to hold a sales call to between an hour and a half and two hours, but I've been on sales calls that took five hours or longer. These don't do you any good—neither you nor the prospect can remember half of what goes on in a meeting that lasts that long, and it usually takes that long because one or both parties is disorganized or easily distracted, or the customer is trying to get some consulting done for free.

You must control the meeting—that's what a sales call is, after all, a meeting. And your best weapon for doing so is to have an agenda. In fact, the best way to control the meeting with an agenda is to fax the agenda to the prospect in advance.

They'll want to show you what they've got. You'll have some questions. They'll want to talk for hours. You'll want to see examples of things they're talking about. They'll think up more things while they're talking. You'll discuss similar projects you've done. They'll have their eyes opened up to the myriad possibilities that two hours ago hadn't been considered. You'll point out some ideas. They'll ask some off-the-wall questions.

Obviously, the conversation could range all over the south forty. There isn't a single cookbook approach to making this an efficient, purposeful meeting, but there are two pieces to this meeting.

The first is the external plan—the agenda that you sent them—that provides structure to this meeting.

The second is a set of checklist items that you're going to want to answer yourself by the end of the meeting. These issues aren't necessarily things that you can bring up with a customer, but they're things you're going to want to keep in mind as you're going through the external plan.

The external plan consists of the following items:

- Reiterate the purpose of the meeting.

- What is their pain?

- What systems do they have?

- What do they want and what do they expect?

- What software tools do they have to go from current to desired?

- What is their budget?

- What is their timeframe?

- The sales pitch—you, dollars, time, and process.

- Agree on the next step.

Your internal agenda should include the following items:

- Who else are they talking to?

- How serious are they about this project?

- Realistically, what are your chances?

- How involved do they want to be during development?

- What's the decision-making process?

- Who is the champion for this project?

- What are the possible processes for this project, and which one is the best choice?

- If the champion doesn't hold the purse strings, who approves the dollars?

It's a tricky juggling act—making sure they adhere to the agenda is tough enough; keeping your own internal agenda in mind as well makes this process quite a challenge.

The external plan

Reiterate the purpose for them

This is a sales call—a get-acquainted meeting so that they can check you out, you can see what they've got cooking, and the two of you can determine whether there's possibly something that can be worked out between the two of you. So they're going to want to determine whether they're comfortable with you, whether they feel they can trust you, and whether or not you might have the technical and business savvy to help them.

Naturally, they'll be thinking along these lines, but they may well not have determined just how they're going to make that determination. More often than not, it comes down to "They sounded like they knew what they were talking about." But in our business, it's not that difficult to sound like you know what you're talking about—all you have to do, really, is be at least one full chapter further along in the "buzz word textbook" than the other guy.

Since most anyone who walks in the prospect's door can yak about something vaguely technical for a while, you'll want to set yourself apart by explaining to them how they should evaluate you. You can tell them that not only are you going to learn about what they're looking for, but you will also explain how your firm works, and what they can come to expect from your company. And, finally, you'll tell them how you're going to go about sizing and scoping the application they're interested in. Remember that you gave them homework during that initial phone call, so they're already a little bit used to taking direction from you.

At the same time, as I've discussed, you're going to be evaluating them. Of course, you can't exactly say that to them. Instead, you'll want to couch your mission in terms of "seeing whether there's a fit between our firms." After all, it's entirely possible that they may have requirements that you can't meet. Those requirements might be to provide 24-hour on-call service, or to have expertise in an area of process control that you're not able to provide, or to do most of your work on the weekends. It may be that the job is too small for your firm—or too big. Another requirement might be that you'd have to be able to get along with a company populated with jerks, or to do $50,000 applications for $10,000.

No matter what the requirements, if you can't meet them, you should bow out. And that's what you're trying to determine—can you fulfill their requirements?

It's extremely important to remember—and to communicate—that this is *not* a problem-solving session—that type of intellectual work is what you get paid for!

Depending on the nature of the company and whom you're meeting with, you may want to tour the office, meet some people, and so on.

What is their pain?

This was briefly discussed in the previous chapter about the phone call. Again, the most important thing you can do is to define or pinpoint exactly what is causing them pain. If they can't describe it succinctly, do not let go until they can. This is your ultimate benchmark for determining whether the final product is a success.

Along these same lines, ask yourself, what is the customer's biggest fear, and what can you do to alleviate that fear? They really aren't all that interested in computer code or cool development tools—they've got a business to run and they want their problems solved. They may feel that computer programmers are weird and scary, so consider what you can do to put their mind at ease. You may not be able to ask them flat out "What can I do to make you less frightened?" but I've found a fair measure of success in asking similarly blunt questions. For example, "What else can I do to help make this project a success?" and "What critical success factors do you know about for this project already?"

What systems do they already have?

You'll need to check out current software, current hardware, and the ancillary things like manuals, source code, documentation, and so on. Yes, you've been over this on the phone, but it's easy for them to make assumptions about things during the "heat of the phone call" or to make mistakes. Your contact may not even have known the answers to these questions, but didn't want to admit so for one reason or another.

They may tell you that they have Windows 95, but, in actuality, they've got the box—still in shrink-wrap—or it's actually running, but only on the machines in Purchasing. That environment would kind of put a damper on the possibility of writing with a 32-bit development tool, wouldn't it?

The military's credo says to "Trust, but verify." Nonsense. Just verify.

When it comes to data, don't take their word for it. Get the documentation, and even more so, get samples. I wish I had a nickel for every time I was given file layouts or site maps that were six months out of date compared to the actual data sets.

What do they want and what do they expect?

This, of course, is the longest, and most important, part of the meeting.

Your goal is to get a rough idea of how big this system is and how they think it might work. Issues regarding whether or not the Company Type field can be filtered depending on who is using the system are irrelevant at this point, but it's usually the level of granularity the user wants to cover.

Begin this part of the meeting by reviewing their homework. This will do two things for you. First, if they've actually done it, you'll find out that they're, to some extent, serious. And second, if they've done it, whether or not they followed directions, and how much detail they've provided will tell you *how* serious they are as well as how technically savvy they are.

I once had a customer attempt to prototype some screen layouts in Visual C++—using a command button to represent every control on the form. Yes, that's right—there were about 100 command buttons on the form, representing text boxes, labels, check boxes, option buttons, and even command buttons. The customer had been shown, by a friend, how to draw a form using Visual C++, and how to put a command button on the form as well. The friend assumed that the customer would be able to extrapolate that knowledge so that he could put other controls on the form as well—but, obviously, that assumption was wrong. It took me two days to undo the damage done by the customer's friend and the customer's good intentions.

The work the customer has done gives you a place to start. It's interesting to note (although you can't tell the customer this) that the actual work they've done is not that important at this stage. For example (albeit a trivial example), they might have listed 15 screens in their system: Customer Add, Customer Edit, Customer Delete, Customer Query, and Customer Find, and the same five for Vendors and for Employees. More important is that they know they want the ability to perform a variety of maintenance tasks on three entities. How these tasks are specifically implemented isn't at issue yet. You're trying to get to the point where you've identified that the system basically consists of three entities and some fairly standard tasks for each of them.

By listening to them discuss what they've put together, you can also get an idea of their expectations—both the general level of their sophistication as well as specific functionality issues. They have probably already painted a picture in their mind of what this application is going to do, and they're probably going to have trouble explaining it all to you. Some things are going to be difficult to explain, and other things are just going to be "assumed"—"Doesn't all software work like that?"

I once had a customer who kept comparing the custom app I was putting together for them with Quicken. They were continually disappointed that the interface didn't sport every fancy feature that Quicken did. First, they assumed that since Quicken lets you do "X," and that since Quicken is a Windows application, every piece of software that runs on Windows should be able to do "X." Second, their general attitude was that since it's in Quicken, it's obviously possible, and since Quicken only cost $179, it couldn't have been very hard—so why don't you do that? Don't you know how?

It took several meetings to get it through to them that Quicken also cost more than the $120,000 budgeted for their application to develop—and that if they wanted to pay the same millions of dollars that Intuit spent on developing Quicken, it'd be no problem to duplicate any feature they wanted.

The point is that their expectations—no matter how unreasonable—were important to them, and until I was able to reconcile their expectations with reality, we were going to have conflict and someone was going to be unhappy.

The ideal would be for the prospect to have done their homework exactly as you had asked on the phone, and to be able to identify every screen, report, process, table, and external entity in the system in a 45-minute discussion. If you can do this, then when the "How much is this going to cost?" question rears its ugly head, you can cock your head to one side for a moment, and then give them an answer.

I've done this before, and, given a couple of caveats, it works remarkably well. First, the user has to have a very clear idea in their head of what they're expecting. For instance, they might want a complete rewrite of an existing system with a new tool or for a new platform, so they've already figured out the functionality they want. Or perhaps the prospect has recently joined the company and worked with a system at their old job that has given them a head start. In these types of cases, the user can very likely give you a rundown of what they're looking for in some detail.

Second, you have to have some experience in developing specifications and applications of this type. They may have an extremely detailed set of requirements, but if this is only the second intranet application you've developed, you're not going to be able to give them an answer. Of course, that's the case with costing out anything—if you haven't done it before, then you can't say—period.

However, if you do have some history, you can do it. I'll explain exactly how to determine a dollar figure to give the prospect later in this chapter.

What if they haven't done their homework, or, they've done it, but very badly? In either case, they're still going to have the same expectations by the end of the meeting—that they're going to get an idea of how big the system is, how much it's going to cost, and whether or not you have a clue about developing it.

In this scenario, I help them sketch out major entities and functions related to those entities. Then I go back and identify any other major tasks that aren't tied specifically to an entity. This process is reasonably quick, and I can capture a large percentage of the primary functionality quickly. From this I can make a guess at how many interfaces, reports, and processes might be needed, and that's what I'm looking for—a rough idea.

Naturally, this will change during the specification process, but what I've done is put a stake in the ground, so that when the scope of the project changes and they see more dollars than originally estimated, I can explicitly explain why. "We started out assuming a system with 10 primary screens, 15 supporting screens, six lookup screens, two dozen reports, and two posting processes. It's now grown to 23 primary screens, 31 supporting screens, eight lookups, three dozen reports, and still two posting processes. This is why we've exceeded our initial estimate."

Naturally you will need to keep them informed along the way about how the bill is growing. The point here is that by documenting, from project inception, how big the system is, you have a baseline that you can refer to later on.

It's easy for the meeting to get off track as soon as this topic is broached. Many developers have run into the user who fancies himself a system designer, and expends a great deal of effort doing what he thinks is a design. Unfortunately, the result is the equivalent of drawing every pane of glass in every window in the front elevation of a house, but never laying out a floor plan, much less deciding how many rooms or what type of electrical, plumbing, and HVAC systems are required.

This is why the assignment of homework over the phone is a good idea. It gives you control over the path of the design discussions, and sets the stage for what you want to get accomplished during this first meeting.

What tools do they have to go from current to desired?

How prepared are they to begin the design of a specification? Do they have a list of desired functionality? Sample screens? Report layouts? Descriptions of processes, operations, flow of work through the system? Or are you starting out with a blank sheet of paper?

Do they have any expectations of how you are going to do your analysis and design? Are they going to expect to be part of the technical design? In other words, are they simply going to read drafts of specifications and Ooh and Aah during prototype demos, or do they want access to the design and modeling tools along with your staff? If so, are they capable of using them?

What tools do they have? Are they going to have to upgrade existing hardware, buy new hardware, upgrade versions of software, install a new operating system, put in a better network?

What kind of shape is their data in? Can it be used as is? Converted from an existing system? Can the existing systems be used in any way? How might they go about a transition from the old data to the new data?

How rigorous are their current MIS procedures? Do they have the ability to audit the information they produce? What are their alternate plans for disaster recovery? Do they perform regular backups? Have they ever done a backup? Do they know what a backup is? Can they spell "backup"?

What is their budget?

Now is the time to find out how much they want to spend—really. They may have talked around the question on the phone, or given you a vague answer, or perhaps just not answered at all. Or perhaps you didn't ask. In any case, you need to know now.

If they say they don't have any idea, either they don't know what they are doing, or they are lying. A lot of people feel that by giving away a budget number, somehow, magically, the price of the project will be just a little bit over the budget number. So I don't ask them what the budget is, but whether they've got a budget—and what ballpark they're working in. If they say they don't even know what their ballpark is, then I suggest that they define the problem that this software system is going to solve very carefully. Then, they should figure out what the solution to that problem is worth to them.

If they don't even want to provide a ballpark figure, if they're not willing to provide even a rough idea, then I tell them that it's going to be more expensive in the long run. If I have to create something without knowing what parameters I'm working with, there's going to be some missteps as we discover where we want to head.

Would you hire an architect to design a house or a building, and refuse to give them any idea of your budget? Of course not. First of all, before you spent hundreds of thousands or millions of dollars on a building, you would have done some thinking about what it is you're trying to build. Is it a two-story cottage with a spare bedroom and 1.5 baths? Or a 10-story office building that's wired for the special needs that multi-national media companies have? And once you pinned down what it was you were trying to build, you'd do some homework to get an idea of what that might cost. If it turned out to be more than you could (or wanted to) afford, then you'd scale back your needs or find some more money somewhere.

But you wouldn't contract with an architect without doing a bit of this beforehand. If you absolutely had to start without having any idea, the architect's first duty would be to help you define your needs and explain, roughly, what they might cost.

Similarly, your prospect either has to give you some sort of idea about what they might want to spend or be able to spend, or contract with you in order to determine that information. A software developer, just like an architect or other professionals, has one resource that is scarce above all else—time. And thus you can't spend large amounts of your time on a project without getting paid.

Depending on how things feel at this point, you can offer to help them develop the budget, for a price, since they have no idea or aren't "current" on hardware pricing and software development. If they balk at your hourly rate for doing this, then it's definitely time to put on the walking shoes. If they don't balk, this will go a long way toward cementing their relationship with you.

What about the situation where they don't even know what they want to do? They just have this vague sense of dread that if they don't get this problem solved soon, they're going to be in bigger trouble than they are now. But they're not even exactly sure what the problem they're trying to solve is, or what the best approach will be.

You can then, instead of asking for a budget number that they've already determined, simply start developing away, with the explicit understanding that the final result may be the better part of an order of magnitude larger than they first thought. Yeah, I know they said they didn't have any idea—but, that's not really the case, is it?

When someone tells me they "have absolutely no idea," I work through the following exercise with them. First, I ask them if they think it will cost more than, say, $1,000. They usually say yes. Then I ask if they think it will cost less than $10 million. They again usually say yes. So then I suggest that they actually do have some idea. It may not be a really good idea, but they do have some sort of range. And from there, they can winnow down the range even more. Eventually they may get to some sort of figure that they can do something with, even if all they can do is roll their eyes and scream.

This little exercise can be done during the sales call, and help provide an answer to the "What's your budget" question.

Thus, if they don't know their budget, either walk away, or offer to help them determine what it might be. But you don't have to do it for free.

If they still refuse, then run away. They probably don't trust you and it does not bode well for a good relationship. Or they may have good intentions but are so ignorant of the process and unwilling to take your advice that they'll be nothing but headaches.

What is their timeframe?

Realize this about timeframes: They are almost never as ironclad as the customer makes them out to be. At the same time, *the customer almost never realizes this themselves*. I recall reading about a group of consultants brought in to finish a job, and they were given a drop-dead target date by which the system had to be up and running.

Upon starting the project, the consultants found that this deadline was the third such "non-negotiable, drop-dead deadline" for this particular project in the past year.

Most deadlines are arbitrarily imposed. Why? Because someone somewhere wants the project done before they go on vacation, because it's the end of the budgeting period, or because there's a big pow-wow in Las Vegas the following week and "wouldn't it be great if we could show this system to everyone there?"

Furthermore, most deadlines are usually unreasonable because someone who does not understand the scope or the complexity of the system imposed them. There are physical limits to the amount of work that can be done. Some people feel that by adding developers to a project, it can be done sooner. Generally, adding more developers to a late project only serves to make it later. See Frederick Brooks' *The Mythical Man-Month* for a complete discussion of this phenomenon.

It's not just the noodlehead in the corner office, however, who is to blame. Developers are part of the problem as well. How many times have you run into a situation where, each time previously, it's taken you a month to perform a given task, but you're still willing to bet the farm that "this time, it will be different." As a result, you'll estimate it will only take two and a half weeks. We're all optimists—assuming that for the first time in 37 projects, nothing will go wrong with the operating system, all of the tools will work as expected, no one on the team will quit in midstream, and the customer will never change their mind.

Nonetheless, you will have to deal with unreasonable expectations that are apparently cast in stone. The key is to manage and mold those expectations as early on in the project as possible—and the sales call is the best place to start.

I've found the best technique to use, upon hearing the target date for rollout, is to slap my knee and laugh loudly, hollering, "You want it *when*?" Well, okay, maybe I don't do this all that often. But you can help form a more reasonable expectation for delivery by playing detective about the initial request for a finish date. What is so important about this date—why does the project need to be done by then? Perhaps it's only part of the project that needs to be finished, or it has to be in good enough shape to be demonstrated, or an interface needs to be defined and complete, so that another project can be started.

I'll talk about dealing with deadlines in more detail later. The key is to find out what your prospect's expectations are now.

The sales pitch—you, dollars, time, and process

At some point, it's going to be a good idea to talk about who you are and what you do. You may have done this early on in the meeting, during introductions, but it's surprising how many potential customers want to jump right into the details of the project. I've found that if they're not ready to hear the "I Love Me" story early on, insisting that they listen to the whole spiel will either be boring or aggravating. And you don't want to bore or aggravate a potential customer in the first 10 minutes of a sales call.

Thus, another common time to tell them about you is once you've been able to hear about their company, needs, and project. During this whole time, you're doing rather little talking, simply asking pointed questions to show that you are interested and understand what they're talking about. It's tough to do sometimes, but be patient—you'll have your moment in the sun soon!

Naturally, you're going to want to spend the whole meeting along these lines, but, while it's fascinating material for you, the customer really doesn't care all that much. Sorry, but that's life in the big city.

You need to boil down your sales pitch into a couple of paragraphs, highlighting the key points that are going to be of interest to the folks on the other side of the desk. You may be impressed with yourself that you wrote a book on the newest snazzy development tool or that you just finished the install of an application that all of the leaders of the Free World use on a daily basis. And I probably would be too. But unless that accomplishment has specific bearing on the customer's situation, it's not worth more than about a sentence, primarily to illustrate that you've been around the block more than once or twice.

The big part of the "sales pitch" is what you do, more than what you say. Listening to them, asking the right questions, and taking care to make them feel comfortable that you can solve their problem—that's what's going to sell them. If you can show a little evidence along these lines, you'll be well off.

Once you're done with the personal sales pitch, you've established yourself as the expert (for the moment, anyway), and so while you've got their attention, take full advantage of it. Thus, it's time to move into the "Based on what you've told me and my experience with other applications, I'd recommend that..." part of the sales pitch.

There isn't a single way to go about this; it depends on the type of development process you're going to propose as well as what type of payment mechanism. I've found it usually ends up being one integrated discussion, all fitting under the heading of "Here is our recommendation."

For example, for a classic waterfall process application, you might say, "We recommend that we develop this application using a traditional waterfall development process. The first thing we'll do is create a complete Functional Specification. The price will be time and materials, and based on <list the factors here>, we estimate that it will take approximately <time> and <dollars>."

"Once we've finished the specification, we'll have a fixed price for the entire application. At this point, it's virtually impossible to provide an accurate estimate of the price for the entire application, because features and functions are likely going to change during the specification process. However, supposing that the information we have right now doesn't change, the application will cost approximately <dollars>."

This discussion is actually longer than the preceding example, but it gives you a rough idea of how the process and price and timeframe are all intertwined into one sales pitch.

I'll cover examples of how to word this discussion for other development processes in the sections of the book that cover those processes.

Decide what the next step is

This is done in two steps. First, you have to, internally, decide whether you want the project. If you do, then determine what the prospect would like to do. If it looks like they want to continue, I like to take out a fresh sheet of paper, write down "To Do" at the top, and then review what the prospect is expecting. This gives them yet another warm fuzzy that you will leave with a very clear idea of what they want, and helps them clarify in their own mind what they will be getting.

At the same time, here's your chance to commit them to action as well. During the meeting, they've undoubtedly come up with things that they're going to have to do research on, make decisions about, discuss with other people, and so forth. By writing down everyone's To Do list here, there's less of a chance of misunderstanding.

And I've found this helps me manage multiple projects better. It always seems really clear to me what the next step is when I leave a meeting. But by the time I get back to the office, unload the briefcase, yak with whoever is waiting for me, and sit down for work, it's easy to have forgotten half of it. And that's if I can get to it right away. If I've got another meeting or it's the end of the day, or something else pops up—who knows when I'll get back to it?

Some people even formalize this into a memo and will copy that document to everybody after the meeting. Whatever works for you and your situation.

Write it down, make sure everyone sees the same thing, and you'll be better off.

Your internal agenda

Now that I've covered the game plan as far as your prospect is concerned, I'll talk about you. You will want to get the answers to the following questions during the course of this initial meeting.

Who else are they talking to?

Believe it or not, you're probably not the only developer on the planet the customer is talking to. Better to find out who your competition is than to wander around blindly in a fog. You may wish to alter your message depending on whether your competition is the owner's nephew or a well-known consulting company.

Who is the champion?

A champion is the person at the firm who pushes the project along, ensuring that the rest of the company will buy in. This person should have fiscal responsibilities so they can authorize the funds. If that's not plausible, they should at least be knowledgeable about how much the company wants to spend on the project.

This person can also act as the fulcrum for decision-making about a variety of issues about the project, and act as the shepherd during development, testing, and installation.

Your job will be to make this champion look good. If you develop an adversarial relationship with the one person who is dedicated to waving the flag for the project, you might consider looking for another job.

If you don't have a champion, you don't have a prayer.

How serious are they?

While, hopefully, you've already determined this to some extent during the phone call, it's a waste of time to go on a sales call only to find out the prospect "was wondering if maybe we shouldn't start thinking about maybe looking at some other kind of system, sometime down the road. Maybe, that is."

However, yes, sometimes those tire-kickers do turn into business. One friend of mine has re-quoted an application annually for almost a decade—the original system was to be written in FoxBase in 1989—before it finally sold early in 1998—and was implemented in Visual FoxPro 6.0. The ongoing effort was worth it, though, because within three months, my friend sold three more installs of the same app to other divisions—all at the same price as the original!

But at the same time, you can't afford to keep updating a proposal for free every three months or two years. As I'm writing this book, I'm currently working with a prospect that has requested to start development work four times since the sales call. After each request, I send out a new Engagement Letter (described in the next chapter), and it sits on someone's desk for a few months. Then they get all excited again, but something trivial has changed, like the name of the department head, and they ask for a new Engagement Letter. But they never get around to actually making anything happen.

As you'll see, once the sales call is over, the meter starts running. No matter what—the meter starts running on the next meeting. Imagine the amount of time, non-billable, I could have wasted with these people had I not held to that rule, and they started asking me to "come in for just one more meeting."

Sure, some of you may be saying, "But another meeting may be just what you need to get them over the hump and get them to commit to the project." I can see that point. My philosophy is that many of us are busy enough that we don't have to coddle prospects like that. When they're ready to buy, they'll buy. But I'm not going to waste my time on folks who aren't ready yet. If they need assistance, they should pay for it.

So how do you determine whether they're serious? One way to tell is by whether or not your contact is prepared. Are they organized with the materials they said they'd have on the phone? Do they get constant interruptions? Do they have to look up information, call other people for additional information, or hunt through stacks of paper, mumbling, "I know it's in here somewhere?" How many others in the company are involved? And how critical is this system to the company?

How involved do they want to be with you?

There isn't a right or wrong answer here. I can think of some customers with whom I worked hand-in-glove during the development of an application—and I wished every second that they would go away. And I can also think of other customers that signed the Engagement Letter, read the specification, and didn't call again until I had a final build ready for them, but that I sure would have liked to have worked with more closely. And there are those who seemed to get involved at just the right level.

The danger sign you are looking for is one of those "gut feelings." Do they seem to be too involved—that they want to micro-manage every step, second-guess your every decision? Remember, you're the expert. If they're not going to take your advice, then perhaps you should fire them as a customer. It's a tough situation when you normalize a set of tables to the 21st normal form because the DBA at the customer's site insists on it, and then complains about the poor performance of the finished app.

At the other end of the spectrum, it's their application. I once had a customer who spent well into six figures on an application, but hardly looked at the modules as they were being delivered—they simply ran a couple of tests to see whether something really ran and paid the invoices.

At final delivery, they realized that they really didn't understand how the system worked, and ended up spending another 25% for changes to the system and additional training for their personnel—expenses that could have been cut down significantly had they been involved throughout the development.

What's the decision-making process?

It's always nice to be able to deal with the decision-maker directly, instead of having to present a proposal and then wait two weeks while it makes its way up and down the chain of command, or worse, while it wends its way through committee meetings.

However, you're not always that fortunate. Sometimes the decision-maker is too far removed from the front lines. It may be that the company's structure requires decisions of a certain dollar amount or impact to be made at a certain level, but the implementation is done by people with their hands on the day-to-day workings.

Other times, the company will play the negotiation game for all it's worth. This is a particular sore spot of mine. Just like you, I'm a busy guy. I don't want my people to spend time with some doofus in a big office who wants to see if he can squeeze another 2 percent off the price, or if he can get an extra day of training for free. Software development is too inexact a process for someone to get out the calculators, trying to shave pennies here and there. And if he's just trying to turn each discussion into a confrontation where he has to win and I have to lose, then I'd rather not play.

In any of these cases, the issue is to make sure you know what has to happen. If you're dealing with the decision-maker directly, you have quite an advantage—you can find out what hot buttons they have and react accordingly in a direct and immediate manner.

If you have to wait on a faceless decision-maker ("the Regional Vice-President who only visits every other Tuesday"), then you need to do the best job you can, and present your case advantageously. Remember the question about the champion? If you have a good champion, they will help you win the job—telling you what works and what doesn't work at that company and with the decision-making tree in particular. Your job, again, is to make your champion look good.

And if you're going into an adversarial relationship (and I would recommend against it), then you need to keep your nose clean, your I's dotted and T's crossed, and generally hew to all of those other clichés.

If you don't understand what the decision-making process is, and who it involves, then at worst, you'll lose the job for the wrong reasons, and at best, you'll spend a lot more time and energy barking up the wrong trees until you get the job. Like I mentioned earlier, you don't want to drive for 80 minutes for a sales call only to find out you've got the wrong person, and you end up dropping off literature and picking up an RFP that could just as easily have been mailed.

At the meeting

Now that you've got an idea of what needs to be done, I'll walk you through a typical sales call and discuss some of the things that may happen.

Introductions

When you meet people, make an extra effort to remember their names. It's a social skill that isn't expected as often in this business. When you receive a business card, actually look at it—if even for a couple of seconds—and examine the person's name and title. Of course, be sure that you've brought yours along as well.

In the absence of a business card exchange, you can often get away with repeating the person's name if it's uncommon or sounds as if it's pronounced in an unusual way. As soon as you can, write the person's name down—with the phonetic spelling. When I am in a meeting with more than two other people, I write down their names in a diagram that matches how they're seated, and then, if I have time, I add a physical attribute or two about them (blonde hair, looks like Herman Munster). That way, when I see them in another meeting but they have the audacity to sit in a different chair, I can call them by name again.

Get them on track and control the meeting

By providing an agenda and having an outline from their homework, you can often take charge of the meeting. Sometimes the prospect will expect to lead the meeting, but you can deflect that by speaking first, pulling out the agenda, and asking if they have anything to add.

It's a difficult situation when the prospect acts like the proverbial bull in a china shop and just charges into the meeting by showing you this great screen he "drew up last night and do you think it would be good to use for the main inquiry screen." Software development is a fascinating intellectual challenge, and many a user has been bitten by the bug. As a result, they become so involved in particular aspects of the project that they lose sight of the big picture—and this first sales call is dedicated to the big picture.

How do you wrest control from this type of person? Well, first ask yourself whether you really want to. In other words, are you going to be able to work with this person? You need to give them a few chances to take cues from you, but at some point, if they insist on running the meeting without agreeing to the agenda, then this relationship may not be for you. I know it probably wouldn't be for me.

At best, you'll spend more time than normal with this person, reeling them back in and getting back on track. That can be a considerable problem, both in terms of raw hours being built up as well as the continual distractions causing you to lose track and having to revisit issues. This person, by virtue of not wanting to listen to your expert advice, will pay more than they should have to. You'll want to consider that in your time and dollar estimates.

Existing functionality and new functionality

The majority of the meeting should be spent on two topics—evaluating their current application or system (it might be a manual process), and describing the major functionality desired in the new application.

Since the customer knows more about their company and application than you do, it's only natural to let them lead this process. However, you'll still have to keep them on track—nudging (or prodding, or forcing) them to move from one point to the next.

The trick is to keep them focused on the high-level requirements—much like the bullet points on the back of a package of commercial software. Once they start discussing specific functionality within a screen, they've gone too far, and it's time to move on to the next bullet point.

If they've done their homework properly, you should be able to move from one bullet point to the next consistently; more often, they've done a partial job, and you'll have to coach them along. It's important to remember that this list doesn't commit them to anything—you're simply documenting a starting point from which you can begin determining detailed requirements.

How much will this specification/application cost (in time and money)?

You'll almost never get through a sales call without having to deal with the question of "How much and when?" being posed by the prospect.

This is a tough issue—probably the toughest one in all of software development. The problem comes from a basic conflict—the prospect needs to know numbers so they can budget and plan. However, invariably, they have not defined what it is that they're going to buy well enough to get a price. It would be like expecting to get a price on a shopping cart full of food by simply looking at the items on the very top of the pile.

Given this basic dilemma, what can you do? Here's what I do—it seems to be the best compromise I've seen in nearly 20 years of building apps.

First, I explain that pricing anything requires a definition of what it is that the customer is buying. The more exact the price has to be, the more precise the definition of what it is they're going to buy must be.

Second, I explain that describing software, due to a number of factors, is very difficult and requires a number of iterations. What are these factors? First, software is abstract—it's not like a crate full of paper that you can touch and hold. Second, the tools used to create software are rapidly and continually changing, so we're in a constant state of R&D. And most businesses do not have the processes they wish to automate defined clearly. Finally, the iterative nature of software development lends itself to continual discovery—which by definition changes what is being developed.

The best that can be hoped for, then, is a series of estimates that get more and more accurate as the definition of the project becomes more and more detailed. First, I find out what the size and scope is, provide an estimate for the spec, and then a second, rougher estimate for the development is performed, based on the specification's size. As the spec changes, the estimate for the development is adjusted as well. When the spec is done, the development can be quoted accurately. If the spec isn't finished, then the development estimate is continually at risk.

This is like building a building. The first time you walk into an architect's office, they can probably give you some ballpark figures after asking you a dozen or two questions about the project. There are factors that can tilt this estimate one way or the other, but this initial estimate gives you a place to start. After each subsequent meeting with the architect, the price can be figured more accurately.

You can explain to your prospect that costs can vary for a couple of reasons. First, because the level of detail required to be exact is missing. Again, it's like a building. A skyscraper costs anywhere from $50 to $100 per square foot to build. It could be $200 if there are marble floors and working fireplaces in each office, or $25 if it's built in a depressed area with the absolute cheapest materials and a fair amount of finish left to the tenants. But these numbers don't mean anything if you don't know how many square feet the building will occupy. And these numbers still figure in a fairly tight range because building a structure is more of an engineering practice.

Remember, software development is still a lot of R&D. The tools are evolving, the tools break a lot, and there are few, if any, commonly accepted practices. Finally, the skills for a developer vary a great deal more than for the building trades, and thus the "cost per square foot" can vary greatly just because of a variance in the labor component.

The purpose of the homework, then, was to define the major items in the applications, so that I too could provide a ballpark estimate. This ballpark will become increasingly more accurate as I get into the nitty-gritty of the specification.

My company has developed many specifications over the years, and we have tracked our time to a fairly granular degree. As a result, we have enough history that we can now calculate how long it will take to develop an application and write the corresponding spec (and, thus, we know the cost) based on a list of screens, reports, and processes for the application.

For example, we have figured out that it costs, on average, $X per screen, $Y per report, and $Z per process. (I know that sounds very simplistic, but these numbers have been averaged out over a great many screens, reports, and processes—and they are, I stress to the customer, just averages that will get us into the ballpark.) We simply multiple those numbers by the number of screens, reports, and processes and provide an estimate for the development of the specification.

Naturally, the system will evolve from the initial guesses, but this is the starting point—it gives the customer the ballpark number they're looking for.

Then, as far as timeframe—you can figure out how many hours, roughly, are going to be required for the amount of money quoted, and you can then look at your company's schedule to estimate how you might fit that time into your workload.

The most critical point in all of this is to remember that whatever number you give the customer is the only number they'll ever remember. It doesn't matter how sincerely they promise "We won't hold you to this number." I can't count the number of times I've offered a "rough ballpark estimate" that suddenly became a fixed price at the next meeting.

This is why I insist on documenting even this ballpark estimate. Furthermore, I describe how it was arrived at, in writing, by listing every screen, report, and process that we discussed. That way, when the customer comes back four months later and wants to know why this initial $41,000 estimate has become more than $67,000 in invoices, I can point to what we initially started out with (14 screens, six reports, and two posting routines) and where we are currently (23 screens, nine reports, three posting routines, and a reconciliation process).

This process most closely aligns with the fixed price, waterfall methodology, but it's not limited to that. The ballpark number that you come up with may be enough to get the ball rolling, and the customer may want to begin developing the application through the Extreme Programming process next week. The final price won't be known until the project is over, but in that particular case, it's not necessary.

Since most people are still most comfortable with the fixed price, waterfall methodology, it's important to be explicit about how another pricing structure and development process is going to work, what the customer will get, and what their responsibilities are.

Come to closure and define the next step

At some point, you've either run out of agenda or you've run out of patience. Or perhaps the prospect has run out of time. At this point, it's time to determine whether or not you want to work with this customer.

If so, what I do is simply ask the customer what they want to do next. Although it's my decision to work with them, it's also their decision to work with me. If I want to, then it's up to them next.

If not, I explain that I don't think there's a good fit, for whatever reason, and terminate the meeting. I've found in most cases that the feeling is mutual—that if I don't want to (or can't) work with them, then most likely they're not going to want to either. Most likely you have a good business reason—you can't meet one or more of their expectations, either on delivery, cost, timeframe, expertise with tools, or expertise with their business or application. But there's often an undefineable sense of bad chemistry that both parties detect.

Even if you don't want to work with them because of a perceived personality conflict, you need a good business reason. You're liable to end up in court sooner or later if you turn down prospects because "I think you're kind of a jerk." I've found that simply saying "I don't feel we have the resources to do this project properly" works fine. Whether you want to explain those resources are time, expertise, or just personnel ("We don't have anyone on staff who could stand to work with you…") is up to you.

The next step

Supposing that you want to work with them, there are three possible avenues for the prospect to take.

Want an Engagement Letter for design

The optimal closing for the meeting will be a request by them for an Engagement Letter so that you can start performing work for them. If you're going to create a specification first, this Engagement Letter will include a ballpark estimate for the specification work, and, since they're now into the phase of spending money, they may have to get approval. If you're just going to start coding, it's twice as important to get them an Engagement Letter (some of you may know this as a "contract") that spells out the details of what services you're going perform.

It is a good idea to find out what hoops have to be jumped through at this point in order to get the Engagement Letter signed.

It can be aggravating to find out how little many people in larger companies know about the approval process for spending money. Over the years, I've had a surprisingly large number of people tell me with a straight face, "The money's already been approved" or "I can sign off on this" or "My boss said he'd sign it immediately." Then, of course, they find out the proposal has to go before some committee and it's going to be three months before I hear anything. Be skeptical.

Depending on the size of the application, there will likely be several layers of approval to go through before the application gets approved. There may be several layers of approval needed to even go ahead with the specification work. Your closing for the meeting should determine whether they want an Engagement Letter or if they have to get approval first.

Want additional consulting

In some cases, this sales call may have just opened up their eyes with regard to how much (well, how little) they know, and they might want you to come back, on a billable basis, just in order to help define their needs and to size and scope the system better.

In this case, you'll still need to produce an Engagement Letter—for the hourly consulting that they're requesting.

We'll get back to you

Yes, even though you may want to work with them, they may not want to, or be able to, turn around and say "Yes!" themselves. It could be that they're not interested, and are simply blowing you off in a nice fashion. Or perhaps they are interested, but aren't interested enough to make a commitment at the moment. Or perhaps the people you're meeting with don't have the authority to make a commitment themselves.

In any of these cases, play the part of Jimmy Stewart in "Harvey" and when they say, "We'll call you," directly ask, "When? Next Tuesday, about noon?" This way, you'll have a better idea of what to expect. You can also offer to follow up with them, but that decision depends on your personality.

The corporate IS department perspective

This whole chapter has been written from the point of view of an independent developer who is angling for the gig. What about the folks working in a corporate IS department, or the developer who wears multiple IS and related hats at a small company?

The big difference is that the corporate developer (I'll refer to both types of developers with the same term) usually doesn't get a chance to turn the potential customer down. That's not strictly true, and I'll discuss some options along those lines later in this section of the book, but for the time being, let's assume that you (the corporate developer) and your customer (other departments in your company) are stuck with each other.

Following the rest of this process is still a very good idea. Your goals are pretty much the same, although your internal motivation might be slightly different. As an independent, you're trying to avoid problems and make things go smoothly because you want to get paid. As a corporate developer, you generally have more latitude as far as the success of a project goes and still get paid.

Chapter 12
Scenarios Encountered
During the Sales Call

"There were rats, Dad. Big ones."—Indiana Jones to his father
  —Temple of Doom

Theory is all fine and good, but no matter how many books you read on the subject, sooner or later you're going to have to get on a bicycle yourself. All the reading in the world isn't a substitute for self-won experience. However, being prepared helps a great deal. In this chapter, I'll discuss a variety of scenarios that you could encounter during the sales process, and throw in a few war stories as well.

I don't think well on my feet. This may come as a surprise to people who have watched me in a meeting or in front of a group of people. More than once, people have commented on my ability to deal with unusual situations "on the fly." But it's all a smokescreen. There are two reasons I'm able to appear to think well on my feet.

First, I practice. I practice over and over again, examining different roles, trying out different possibilities—what if he said this? What if she did that? What if—what if—what if? Eventually, I've gone over enough different scenarios that the chances of running into something that takes me completely by surprise are slim.

And, second, I've done this long enough that I've seen a lot of situations before—and while I might not be the most original thinker, I can usually remember what to do in a situation when I encounter it again.

As a result, I've put together this chapter to help you "see situations" in advance, so that when you run into them yourself, they don't hit you completely cold. You might think of this chapter (and the corresponding chapters in other sections in the book) as *DevGuide*'s version of *Mad Magazine*'s "Snappy Comebacks to Stupid Questions."

A word about the tone of this chapter. It may seem overly pessimistic—you'll hear about liars and cheats and thieves and a whole host of other scoundrels. By the end, you may wonder whether you want to stay in this business. But the reason for this chapter is to help you deal with problems effectively—and thus, I have to discuss all those problems. Just as you may leave a self-defense class thinking that the entire population is out to get you, this chapter may leave you thinking that the whole business world is made up of crooks. It ain't so—but the consequences of dealing with a bad guy are extreme enough that you should be well prepared.

People not there

What if you arrive for a 10 AM meeting and at 10:33, you're still cooling your heels in the lobby? "He's in a meeting" or "She's still on the phone" is all you get from the receptionist. Or even better: Four instances of "He hasn't answered his page" over a period of 20 minutes. How long do you wait? I'm pretty hard-nosed about situations like these.

I can understand that your contact may have been called into a meeting by someone significantly higher up in the food chain. Or perhaps a previous meeting lasted much longer than was expected.

However, it's still incumbent on your contact to make arrangements for this type of exceptional situation. For example, your contact could interrupt the meeting for a minute so that they can arrange to have someone else greet you or ask you back another time. If the company's corporate culture dictates that your contact take an attitude of "They're only a salesman—you can let them wait," then you need to ask yourself how badly you want to work with this firm. I have a rule at my company—we don't work with jerks. Period. And we've turned down work with companies that treat their vendors poorly.

If you're stuck in the lobby for too long, don't be afraid to leave a message with the receptionist and then simply walk out. This begs the question, though, what is too long? It depends on the circumstances. If your contact was coming in from out of town, I might wait 45 minutes or more. (I always bring something to do—old magazines to catch up on, or other paperwork to review.) But if they've been on the phone for 15 minutes, I'd leave.

What happens next? It depends on what the reason was for their failing to meet with you. If there was a genuine emergency, you'd most likely hear about that from someone else the minute you walked in the door. Here, I'm talking about simple rudeness or poor time management where they're just late or they blew you off.

In these cases, I charge them for a subsequent meeting. When I talked to them on the phone, I told them that I'd make one call for free, but after that, the meter starts running. If they put me in such a position that they wouldn't even meet with me at a scheduled time, I'm not about to turn the other cheek.

This sounds all macho and such, but I can hear you wondering, "How do you actually get away with that?" I simply change the nature of the meeting from a "free sales call" to our first consultation. I suggest that perhaps, instead of simply meeting for a bit, we make this "a productive, working meeting." I propose that we'll actually get something of value done, be that more nitty-gritty sizing and scoping or an analysis of their existing systems. "And, of course, the meter starts running for this type of work. I'll send you an Engagement Letter that describes the services we'll provide, and we'll take it from there."

They may come back with, "Well, we'd still like to just sit down with you and kind of sort things out, on a no-charge basis, of course." If I feel they're jerking me around, I'll counter with, "I'm a pretty busy guy. I really don't have time to do this over and over again. It's much more efficient if we can get started on some work." At this point, you're kind of playing chicken with the prospect, but you're betting that they need you more than you need them, and remember that they're the ones who started this by being so incredibly discourteous in the first place.

People not prepared

More likely, but harder to put your finger on it, is when they show up on time—at least, their body does, but not their mind. It's up to you to determine how disorganized they are, and how badly their lack of preparation is going to harm the meeting. If it's merely going to turn a two-hour meeting into a three-hour one, you can probably bear the burden (and increase your estimates by 50% across the board). If, however, they're so unorganized or poorly prepared that you can't get through significant parts of the meeting, then you're better off terminating the meeting.

That's another reason to assign homework during the phone call—because they have a job to do as well. If they come to the meeting ill prepared—no homework—you can start to get an idea of how the relationship with them is going to go.

Didn't do their homework

Yeah, I've heard all the excuses. "My dog ate it." "The sun was in my eyes." "A robber stole it from me on the way to school." There are a few standard excuses that your prospect is likely to give you. Here's how to handle each one.

"I didn't understand what I was supposed to do"

This is easy—use the sales call to work through their homework with them. There's no problem here—your goal in the sales call is to size and scope the project, and by walking through their homework, you can do just that. An added benefit to this is that you're subconsciously demonstrating your competence to them.

Remember that each of the rest of these excuses may be a smokescreen for this one—they may be too embarrassed to admit that they didn't understand what you wanted, or that they didn't know how to do it. Give them an easy way out—a way to save face in front of their coworkers as well as in front of you.

"I didn't have time"

Take the same tact as with the previous excuse—do it during the sales call. You can't proceed any further until you can get this information, so you're going to have to do it now. Their homework is really just a structured approach to determining the answer to the question "What is this application going to do?"

However, you'll want to keep this in the back of your mind—if they were too busy for this first exercise, will they be too busy throughout the project? That doesn't necessarily queer the deal—but it's good to be aware of how much cooperation you may be getting throughout the life of the project.

"I don't think this is my job" or "This is what I pay you for"

This is quite a telling response, isn't it? It even more very clearly answers the question "How involved do they want to be?" If they want to pay me to do everything, I'm more than happy to—as long as I feel the relationship is still sound. Of course, at some point, they're going to have to get involved—at the minimum to approve the work that I've done.

"This isn't necessary" or "I didn't see any point in this"

This answer is more problematic. It probably hides insecurity on their part, so you'll have to walk gingerly, but at the same time, you want to make sure that you're running the show. I'm not going to tell my doctor how to operate, and I'm certainly going to give him as much information as he needs to help me. I expect the same attitude from the folks who are hiring me as an expert to help them. If they're not going to take my advice, then I'd rather not work with them at all.

I'd like to hear their reasoning—I'm always open to learning something new. But at the same time, I'm a little tired of listening to self-taught experts who figure that because they kept this old dBASE application running for a few years, they know more than any old consultant who might walk in the door.

There's always somebody who's going to tell you, "We don't need no stinkin' normalized tables" or some other truism—I'll let them give my competition gray hair.

Too many interruptions

What do you do if they don't let you finish a sentence without interrupting at least twice? I'm not going to coach you on people skills, but if they start badgering you too much, you can explain, "That would take more time to cover thoroughly than we have time for today."

"Come back for another meeting"

This is fairly common. "This sounds really good. My boss wasn't able to attend this meeting, but he'd like to meet you. Can you come back again next Wednesday?"

Arrrggghhhh! Why didn't they just schedule this sales call for next Wednesday, then? You know why, of course—the boss was using an underling as a foil. But should you have to waste your time on this ploy? It depends on your personal situation.

Depending on how I feel about the company, the job, and the people, I might try one of several approaches. The first, if I really, really want the job, is to suck it in and go for another meeting, free of charge.

The second approach is to "compromise" and offer to host the next meeting at my office, again, free of charge. In this case, the compromise is that they spend the travel time and effort, and all I'm out is the actual meeting time.

The third approach is to stand my ground and insist that from now on, the meter is running—and I made that clear on the phone. Of course, since they may not want to pay just for me to shake hands and make small talk for 15 minutes, I offer to make that a combination "sales call with the boss" and a working meeting where we start on the analysis and design.

It's all a matter of how badly you want the project.

The meeting that lasts forever

I once attended a sales call that started at 12:30 and lasted past 6 PM. Never again. What had happened was that they weren't exactly straightforward about the application they wanted done—they called me in on one application, but then trotted out three more during the course of the afternoon, each time promising that it was the last one. Well, I didn't catch on until they had started on the third app, and by that time, it was too late.

In retrospect, I'm not sure what could have been done differently. The meeting was out of town, so I was prepared to spend several hours there, but at the same time, I was thinking we'd have wrapped up by 4:00. Probably the best thing I could have done was to identify more clearly, up front, what the meeting was about, and then when a second project reared its head, take note of it with respect to the timeframe. Then, when the third project showed up on their desk at 3:50, I should have just called it quits, saying, "I wasn't prepared to stay much past 4—since this is the third project you've introduced today, why don't we handle that at our next meeting." And the next meeting, of course, would have been on the meter.

Wanting work done at the meeting

Sometimes people will try to get design or development work done during the sales call. I'm perfectly willing to demo a few things, and perhaps chat with them about a couple of items for a half hour, but that's about it. A proper sales call should take between an hour and two hours—if they try to stretch it much past that by getting into the design of the system, I'll conclude the meeting.

It's just a matter of indicating "That issue is really beyond the scope of this meeting" or "It's going to take a fair amount of time to answer that question—let's get back to our agenda, and I can spend more time answering that during an analysis and design meeting."

"I need to know how you calculated the price"

This one's really easy to deal with. Say "No."

This question usually comes about from one of three motivations. They could simply be intellectually curious about how this is priced. They may never have run into a software developer who used this kind of pricing before, and just want to know more.

Second, they're mistrusting, feeling that they're about to get ripped off since they don't have a lot of experience. Or, finally, they're under the misguided notion that they can assemble pieces of the application as if they were building blocks. (Someone has been reading that OOP marketing literature again—and believing it!)

I explain that, just as their manufacturing costs and pricing algorithms are proprietary to their company, so are our numbers. Sometimes they'll insist that they know the numbers so they can "design" their own system. "We need to know how much each screen and report costs, so we can add and subtract functionality to meet our budget." I explain that one can't buy custom software like it was canned fruit. There's a significant amount of integration between the parts. Period. If they're not willing to accept that answer, then let them work with someone else.

Watch your gut!

An editorial…

By now you've acquired a fair amount of information about their company and what they're like to work with. This is not like selling a car or a piece of capital equipment—where multiple sales calls are often required to get the business. Your time is your most precious resource—it's your raw materials—and they need to decide whether they want to go to the next step. You can't afford to visit again and again. At some point, they have to bring you on board to start doing work. This doesn't mean that once they go with you they are committed for the rest of their life, simply that they need to start paying you for your time.

At the same time, you need to decide whether you feel you are appropriate for the job and whether you feel comfortable with the company. You've listened to them for perhaps a couple of hours, asked questions and gotten a feel for what they're looking for and what they're expecting.

Watch your gut! If the little voice inside you is saying, "Oh, I don't know, there's something that feels bad about this," then pay attention! The worst thing to do is realize two months (and three overdue invoices) too late that you really shouldn't have taken this job.

Section IV:

Creating Specifications

At the end of the initial sales call, you'll either know what type of development process you're going to undertake, or you'll know that you need more information before you decide. In the latter case, you'll hopefully have signed the customer on for some preliminary consulting to determine this. In other cases, though, you and the customer have jointly agreed upon a development methodology.

This next section addresses the development and creation of specifications for the three basic types of processes—structured (waterfall), Rapid Application Development (RAD), and Agile Methodologies (such as XP). The first draft of this book divided those processes into separate sections, but I've found there were more similarities than differences, so I address specifications in one fluid discussion, digressing to cover something specific about a particular type of process as needed.

Remember that this section, like the rest of the book, should be read at least twice—once while you read through the whole book in order to acquaint yourself with the spectrum of software development processes so that you can better provide the appropriate solution to your customer, and then a second time in order to learn the specific tasks at hand.

Chapter 13
The Fundamental Premise
Behind Pricing Custom Software

"I'm going to need a fast car."
(Junior peels off bills from a money clip)
"A really fast car."
(More bills come off the clip)
"Faster... faster..."
(The clip is emptied of bills)
"Yeah, that's fast enough."
  —Burt Reynolds in Smokey and the Bandit

You wouldn't go into a grocery store, jam a bunch of stuff into a shopping cart, cover the top with your coat, and expect the clerk to tell you how much the contents is going to cost, would you? You wouldn't ask a homebuilder how much "a four bedroom, 3,000 square foot house on a half-acre lot" would cost, would you? And you wouldn't ask your doctor exactly how much he's going to charge for that experimental brain surgery, would you? Of course not. But this same situation—expecting a software developer to quote a fixed price without precisely specifying what the product is—is exactly what our customers do to us, time after time. This chapter will explain these dynamics and how to deal with them.

Before I begin the discussion of how to create a specification and determine the price for the application from that spec, I need to emphasize a critical point here.

A custom application is a "thing" that a company is going to purchase—just like a copier, a fleet of automobiles, a pallet of forgings, the transportation of a million gallons of oil from point A to point B, or 45 seconds of airtime during the Super Bowl.

And so they're going to want both a "price" and a "delivery date."

However, it's not as easy to quantify these attributes for a custom software application as it is for a crate that can be sized, weighed, lifted, and marked off on a receiving dockhand's checklist.

That's why we spend the time in the initial sales call with the customer to describe what the possible development scenarios—and available pricing mechanisms for each scenario—are.

Unfortunately, when a customer hears the gamut of potential development processes, they often stop listening after the phrase "fixed price" in conjunction with a structured development methodology. The other types of methodologies—RAD and Agile—sound foreign, weird, and thus are clearly good things to avoid. But this *structured development*—a business-like phrase—it sounds professional, proper, and when you raise the specter of being able to quote a fixed price for the application once the spec is done, why, is there any doubt that this is the best way to go?

Note that structured development and fixed price are not synonymous. The first is a necessary, but not sufficient, condition for the second. In other words, you can do structured development under any number of pricing schemes, but you can only do fixed price for structured development.

There are some very specific rules that must be followed if you're going to quote a fixed price—and most developers and customers alike ignore at least one of these, and often most if not all of them.

First of all, you must define what "it" is that the customer is buying. You can't quote a fixed price for an unknown quantity of goods or services. Period. This sounds logical, doesn't it? Yet I wish I had a nickel for every software development project that was given a fixed price even before the requirements gathering was done, much less a specification was done. Why does this happen?

It's a combination of greed and ignorance. One common scenario is when a project manager or sales type meets with a customer, feels pressure to make the sale, and makes a wild-ass guess about the size of the project. They'll take a look at what the customer has proposed, and wing a price based on that information—without evaluating what might be under the hood. Many times the price they quote will be wildly inflated, figuring that if the customer accepts the number, the firm will make a killing—a ton of money for what is obviously an easy project.

And then as the project development begins, and new requirements, features, and functions appear, the firm will add those to the project without additional charge, figuring that they've already got such a huge margin that they can afford to throw in a few freebies. What happens, of course, is that, even assuming that there was a margin to begin with, the add-ons quickly outpace the padding in the budget. However, the developer has set a precedent by throwing things in for free, and can't easily draw the line and start charging for changes at some seemingly arbitrary point.

The developer isn't all to blame, though. The customer often also thinks they're going to get something for nothing. They'll interpret a fixed price application as an "all-you-can-code buffet for $5.99." It's obvious that the development firm can't provide unlimited programming resources for a fixed price, but, the thinking goes in the customer's mind, that's their problem. They (the development shop) should have thought of that ahead of time.

Second, you must have the capability and expertise to produce that product or provide that service. This seems obvious—but again, the landscape is littered with the wrecks of software development projects where inexperienced programmers and managers were thrown into a project and expected to produce an application according to a predetermined budget and timeframe.

Third, you must have a history of your costs. You can't possibly quote a price for a product or service—no matter how well defined that service is—unless you kept track of what it cost you to make that product or service before. And thus you have to know what it cost you to make that product or provide that service before.

Fourth, you need to have knowledge of what might have changed since the last time you did this type of project. Unlike building roads in the desert, where the technology, the environment, and the people haven't changed all that much in the past 100 years, you are likely to be asked to implement an application in an environment drastically different from the environment you just deployed in a year ago.

Custom software development has a variety of unique dynamics that make each of these four pieces of information non-trivial and hard to obtain. Let's look at the troubles we're going to run into for each of them.

But first, again, you have to know what it is you're building. To repeat—you can't quote a fixed price for an unknown quantity of goods or services. Got it? And you have my permission to staple this to the forehead of your boss, your project manager, your customer—whoever needs to hear it.

If they want a fixed price, they have to define exactly what it is they're buying for that fixed price.

Define what "it" is

Let's start out with our first premise—we want to know "how much" and "when." I'm assuming that you understand that these are linked together. Since the work is a labor-intensive process, and the labor has a price per hour, time and dollars are inextricably linked. This doesn't mean that they're proportional, just that they're tightly coupled.

If you're delivering applications internally in a company, you may or may not have an obvious dollar figure attached to your work. Your department may charge out your time to other company departments, or the company may lump it all under a single "IT" umbrella. Nonetheless, you still have to know "how long" so that your manager can budget for manpower and, thus, compensation dollars, which eventually ends up becoming the same thing. The only difference is that you, personally, may not hand an invoice to your customer every couple of weeks.

So, you need to know exactly what it is you're providing to the customer. Unlike a bucket of car parts, however, the "things" you're delivering are much more ethereal. Essentially, the deliverables—the things your customer can "check off at the receiving dock"—are specific features or functionality. How do they get that functionality? By running your software during their business process—opening screens, entering data, pressing buttons, checking boxes, printing reports, transforming data from one format to another, and so on.

The user has to interact with the computer, make things happen, and get stuff out—and that's how we're going to look at it—screens, processes, and reports.

Not everything you're going to deliver will have been specifically asked for by the user— for example, a process to repair corrupted data might not be on your user's "wish list," but you could well decide to provide it as part of your standard umbrella of functions.

So our goal will be to create a description of what the user is going to "get"—and this is called a Functional Specification (FS). There are a few important things to note about an FS:

- It's a functional spec—not a technical spec. It describes what the user is getting—not how it's built underneath. Just as the brochure for an automobile describes what it will do—seat six comfortably, get 20 miles per gallon, and stop on a dime—but it doesn't describe how it's built—what types of ICs are in the trip computer or what the transmission components are made of. Those last few items would be covered in a technical spec—after all, engineering and quality control are going to need that information before they can manufacture the car.

- An FS actually serves four purposes, although the user will likely only see the first and last ones. The first purpose is the definition of what they're buying so they know how much it's going to cost. The second purpose is to define the requirements for the programmers so they can write the technical spec. The third is to provide the testing checklist—how are you going to verify that the system does what it is suppose to do unless you have defined—explicitly—what it is supposed to do? And, finally, it's a starting point for user materials, Help text, and training guides.

It is not a trivial exercise to create a Functional Specification. Why is this?

First, the business process is likely to be poorly understood, undocumented, and performed differently each time it's performed. Businesses are usually run and staffed by people, and people are not precise creatures. When you put these people into an ever-changing environment, as most businesses and industries are, it's only natural that the business process will be ill defined.

Second, people don't like to commit themselves to making decisions and blanket statements—"We always do it this way," for example. This condition is particularly true the more uncertain an individual is regarding how a business process works. People are afraid of making mistakes, and stating for the record—where it's going to be written down, and software built based on it—how something works. This puts them up against the wall. Furthermore, they're afraid that making a choice now will limit their choices in the future.

Third, people are generally lousy at describing how to do something. If you want a really concrete example, ask for directions. Your typical programmer excels at such a task, because their approach is to provide a logical, detailed description. Most people don't think in this fashion. Another telling example is to examine a defect report from a typical user. They'll skip steps, not write down error messages accurately, and not even fill out the form completely. It drives us crazy, but it's the way most people operate.

Finally, the people who do this type of work don't have a good set of tools to define, organize, and document the information we collect. We spend an inordinate amount of time dragging the information from the user, and more time organizing it and feeding it back to the user for confirmation, and then even more time putting the information in some sort of usable format. And each time we do this, we're making it up as we go. Sure, the final document might follow a fairly clear set of guidelines, but the fact that we get there at all is random chance—and there's very little to help us confirm that what we end up with is correct.

Traditionally, this work has been done by "analysts." Clearly, an analyst's skills must encompass both the technical as well as the social and political realms in a company.

An analyst has to be able to answer questions like "Is it reasonable to expect a system to perform process X?" At the same time, the analyst must be a skilled politician, working with a varied group of individuals, all with their own ideas and agendas, and be able to bring them to a consensus.

However, analysts are people too. They make mistakes, have their own biases, don't listen well, and perform with less than complete precision as well.

In some cases, analysts are generally paid more and are regarded with more esteem than the folks next in line—the programming staff—and rightly so. In many organizations, "analyst" is a promotion up from "programmer."

In other cases, the exact opposite may be true. Anyone who can code is a god and the rest of the staff just does paperwork—filling out forms and templates and generally not adding much value to the process other than lubrication and closure to each step.

Given this multitude of factors, it's no wonder that many programmers inwardly sigh with relief when their manager tells them, "This project is in a hurry—we don't have time for all that fancy design. Just start coding!"

Experience and capability

While it may seem that I'm overstating the obvious, a surprisingly large number of people attempt a project without the experience needed to do it. Okay, maybe it's not that surprising on the surface—after all, as the paradox goes, how are you going to get experience when you're inexperienced? What's surprising is that top management will send a completely inexperienced team—not just programmers, but analysts and project leaders—into battle and expect them to perform as if they were a highly trained machine.

Even this set of circumstances isn't as bad as it may sound. The problem comes when the individual (or team) without experience attempts to quote a fixed price when they don't have the expertise needed. Imagine if you were asked to quote a fixed price for building a skyscraper or a space shuttle. There'd be no way you'd be able to even get close—yet this is what customers and management expect inexperienced development teams to do each day.

This doesn't excuse you from taking on a project without the prerequisite experience—in fact, with today's rapidly shifting technological landscape, it's almost impossible not to run into this situation. You just can't quote a fixed price for the project. And when you're evaluating your experience, don't mistake one year of experience repeated five times for five years of experience.

A history of costs

Once you have defined what they want, you then need to reach into your bag of tricks. Why can a road-building company quote the production of a highway from one city to another and make money on it? Because they've done that sort of thing before, they kept track of what it cost in the past, and they have a wide enough range of experience to know which factors are the same and which are different.

Unfortunately, a number of factors make software development different from building roads. (And a good thing, too, because most of the developers I know would look pretty sad in a hard hat and an orange traffic vest.)

Most professionals who bill their time are reluctant to fill out time sheets or otherwise track their time with enough detail. There are two reasons for this. Developers, in particular, are often free spirits, and tend not to want to be pinned down about details. They flit from module to module—finishing up a control on one screen reminds them of something they think they missed on a second screen, so they open that one up for a few minutes, and that leads to a third. Fifteen minutes later they're back on the original screen—but how are they going to allocate time properly against each task?

Second, even when a developer is interested in (or at least not openly combative about) tracking their time, they likely have tools that are at best awkward to use, or more likely, just plain difficult to use. This is one of those cases where a shoemaker's kids get shod last. You would think that every developer on the planet would have some nifty little tool to track all of their time, assign it to the appropriate project, module and task, and then slice and dice it six ways from Sunday as desired. Unfortunately, the Holy Grail is still out there—we're still looking for the "record what I'm doing just by my thinking about it" time-tracking tool—and currently using a tool built in 1994 that we never seemed to get around to updating.

In a manufacturing environment, tracking is handled differently. A fellow with a white coat and a stopwatch wanders down to the factory floor and measures a variety of shop workers performing their tasks. From this data, the "time and motion expert" then comes up with a series of standards for performing each task, and then new projects are costed out using this data.

It's almost inconceivable to use this same technique for developing software. Measure how much time it takes to put a combo box on a form? Or to create a new view to a back-end database? I don't think so. However, it is still necessary to track time to a fairly discrete level in order to determine costs in the future—and it's prohibitive for anyone but the developer to do that tracking.

In short, most developers haven't tracked their costs of development to the level necessary to use that data to cost future projects.

Third, having a history of cost (or, indeed, any sort of metric) is only applicable if the next project will use that same technology and those same techniques—and if these things are well defined and documented. A road construction firm that has a wealth of data about building freeways in the desert is still ill equipped to provide a quote for a single-lane road going through a mountainous jungle.

Fourth, even if the technology stays the same, the components inevitably change. The developer becomes more knowledgeable and figures out a better way to do something. Or perhaps they get bored and decide to change the way they do something just for the sake of changes. This has the same effect as doing a new type of project, because there are still no historical costs associated with the new components.

Fifth, development on the PC platform is still immature and terribly lacking in rigor. Practices that are *de rigueur* in the "big iron" worlds are often greeted with amazement ("I never thought to do that before!") or, more often, disdain ("You don't understand—we don't have time to do all that testing here."). Test suites, formal test plans, version control, documented procedures for moving modules from development to test to product—these are all new concepts to the majority of PC developers.

As a result, due to an incomplete process, projected costs are incomplete as well. A project can run over because the process was poor or steps that needed to be taken were left out.

The next factor that contributes to a poor understanding of historical costs is the infantile level of the technology. You've undoubtedly had the experience of writing a pretty solid application, only to have the user ask for a change "here," and then watching your concrete structure turn into a house of cards. Each system is still more a work of art than a finely engineered machine, and costing for changes becomes proportionately more inexact.

Finally, except for at a small minority of development shops around the world, the whole development process is poorly defined and managed, so a complete and detailed history of costs means little. That project performance can't be repeated because the process isn't up to the task. Thus, just because X cost $100 last time doesn't mean it can be projected to cost $100 each of the next three times—because the process can't ensure X's repeatability.

Smart developers would go back to a project that has shipped and review what worked—and what didn't. Even a broad-brush overview would likely produce a number of areas where some attention or a change in methodology would be warranted. Of course, given the current state of the IT backlog, this is not likely to happen for the next 25 or 50 years. But it would still be a good idea.

Additional change factors

How many times do you do one app that is just about the same as one you did a while back? Occasionally it happens, but not often. After all, this is custom software—and by definition, each custom application is different from the last. And even when two systems could be similar, a developer often works hard to differentiate them, because sameness equates to boringness in a developer's mind. If you wanted to be bored, you'd work in a tollbooth.

So even if you had a complete and detailed history of your costs, and if you could control the process so that you repeat your performance so that projected costs were accurate, another suite of factors comes into play.

I'll label these factors as "outside influences" or "additional change factors."

The first has to do with the mindset of the user. Unlike a change to a machine or a house, a change to software doesn't require a physical item to be thrown out or remanufactured. Thus, the user assumes that changes to an application are easy—and will either (unknowingly) keep critical information from the developer or will trivialize the impact of possible changes they are aware of and not communicate those in time.

This is the equivalent of having built a bridge over a deep gorge, and just as the lines down the middle of the road are being painted, the "customer" mumbles something about needing to accommodate trucks with oversize loads like trees and house frames. And, now that he thinks about it, it doesn't look like the tight curve on the west approach to the bridge will provide enough room for those trucks to maneuver. The solution? Move the west end of the bridge downstream about 35 meters. Obviously, the "customer" for a bridge wouldn't do this, but a user for a piece of software would think nothing of making a similar request.

The other factor is that the technology changes daily, and sometimes more often than that. As a result, you are often putting a fair amount of R&D into a project. And by definition, you can't cost out R&D.

For any given project you can, and should, define what technology will be used for a specific solution, and hopefully you'll have a series of projects where you can spread the costs of ramping up on that new technology. Still, at some point you'll have to upgrade to the "latest and greatest" (or at least something somewhat newer). Some organizations decide to skip versions of software—deploying on Win95 but not Win98, on NT 3.51 but then waiting until Windows 2000. Deployment and training by themselves are so costly that it can often be more cost effective to wait a while.

When you're involved in the R&D process during a project, you can provide a budget, and decide to live with what you get when you run out of money, but you can't determine a fixed cost for an indeterminate result.

Factors that neither you nor your customer control can also play into this equation. For example, laws under which the company is regulated may change—sometimes without warning. Or something happens that's outside the realm of the application that you are working on, but that will eventually affect the app. The sale of the company, or the purchase of another company or another company's product lines, are two that come to mind immediately. Another is a change in the economy that invalidates the assumptions under which the application was developed. Remember when a barrel of oil was projected to cost $100 by the end of the 1990s?

Each of these factors has an impact on the work you're doing—making an accurate costing that much harder.

A fifth complicating factor

There's actually a fifth factor at work here that I didn't mention earlier in this chapter. We developers have a dirty little secret—we're eternal optimists. So what if the last 27 projects ran over budget, were delivered significantly late, and still didn't include all the functionality originally specified? It's a rare developer who won't assume that the 28th project will "be different." Why will this 28th project go perfectly? Well, because it's for a different department—"and those guys aren't jerks" (like the last 27 departments were). Or because "we're going to use a new tool, and 'based on what we've read in the trade journals, this new technology is going to make our testing cycle much shorter.'" Or because "our boss is giving us a new college kid who's going to do most of the coding, and he hasn't had time to learn any bad habits like the last three contractors we had." Or whatever the mantra of the month is.

The bottom line is that we're all too willing to acquiesce to a customer requesting a delivery or a budget or a feature set that, in a saner moment, we'd admit was pretty unreasonable to begin with—even if everything went well.

Pricing for Agile Methodologies

The implication of the preceding discussion is that the customer wants an estimated cost for the entire project before beginning. In many companies and corporate cultures, that's a reasonable and expected approach. However, it's not always the case.

Supposedly, established companies want to do a cost-benefit analysis on every dollar they spend, and that includes the monies they spend on custom software development. However, cost-benefit analysis is not an exact science—in many cases, it's not even evolved to a black art yet. As a result, companies don't know—they don't have *any* idea—what a new computer system or a new piece of software is worth to them. You've undoubtedly read some of the many studies that claim that the industrialized world's productivity, after spending a couple of trillion dollars over the past 20 years on technology, has barely budged.

As with any statistics, it's easy to let them paint any picture you want painted, but it sure seems to me that it'd be more difficult to spend that type of money and not realize any benefits, wouldn't it? I mean, as the saying goes, even a blind pig finds an acorn once in a while. Throwing all those dollars around, they just can't have all gone down the sewer.

Still, there's got to be a kernel of truth in those stories, and for me, the kernel is that many companies can't measure the value of a piece of technology—even after it's been put in place. What that means is that there's no way for them to determine in advance what a project is worth, what it's going to save them, so it's very difficult to put a price tag on it, saying, "We can't afford to spend more than $X." More likely, the price tag is going to come from a centralized budgeting process where IS is given a chunk of money, and it's up to the management to allocate those dollars.

What this means is that oftentimes a project has a budget, but the results of that project are nebulous. The customer doesn't have any way of determining how much each feature is worth, or even if it truly *needs* to be included. So, similar to building a house, custom software projects can be built with a "pot of money" and the development just needs to stop once the money runs out.

An Agile Methodology plays well in this arena.

The initial requirements collection is deliberately intended to break up the feature list into roughly equal-sized chunks that are prioritized according to importance to the customer. Each feature will drive an iteration cycle that's intended to be two to four weeks long. XP, specifically, uses a technique where the development team estimates the amount of time to implement each feature, requiring each feature be granular enough that it can be completed within one week of "ideal programming time" (a day without any interruptions—phone calls, meetings, and so on). Features that take longer than this have to be broken down further before an estimate can be provided, while features that can be handled in less time are aggregated.

Of course, not everyone lives in an ideal world, so XP proponents suggest mapping one "ideal" programming day with three actual work days. This mapping, of course, is a suggestion—your experience with development as well as with estimating could impact how you map ideal and actual days. Furthermore, the correlation will change as your experience on this particular project, with this particular customer, advances.

A big advantage of an Agile Methodology is that, while the big picture estimate is still hard (well, "impossible") to come by, the smaller estimates, those on a feature by feature basis, actually become easier and easier to do. Furthermore, there is less risk on both the part of the developer and the customer. Why? Suppose you miss an estimate on a million dollar gig by 30%. Either the customer's going to be unhappy to the tune of $300,000, or the developer is going to be unhappy by a similar amount.

If you miss your estimate on the first feature of a million dollar gig by 30%, but that feature was only $10,000, then someone is only out $3,000, and you've missed your delivery date by a few days. The customer can shoulder that much easier than the 100 times that, or, if the developer quotes a fixed price, they can shoulder that with a bit of overtime for a week or two. The key difference is that the customer and developer can then do a post-mortem on that feature and figure out what went wrong, and fix it for the next feature (or perhaps the one after that, depending on timing). The ability to make mid-course corrections after small errors means that it's much more likely that big errors can be avoided.

Indeed, part of the process of Agile Methodology projects is a debriefing after the delivery of each feature in order to examine performance and critique successes and failures. The results of these meetings should allow the team to further refine the ability to specify and estimate a feature, and identify errors made and steps that can be taken to reduce or eliminate those in the future.

Summing up

Depressed? Convinced that it's time to start cruising the want ads again, looking for a more rational choice of career—perhaps "in the fast food or personal housekeeping industries"? Well, cheer up, buckaroo, I've got a few tricks up my sleeve.

You *can* put together Functional Specifications that are useful to all members of the audience—it just takes rigor. You must be firm in asking the question and writing down the answer when the rest of the situation—company politics, changing and uncertain technology, looming deadlines, vacillating decision makers, and so on—is trying to persuade you to gloss over the issue and give it a superficial treatment.

The rest of the chapters in this section are going to describe what a Functional Specification should contain, and then how to go about putting one together, including the all-important process for costing the application once it's been spec'd. I describe the FS first, simply because it seemed inappropriate the other way around. If you were hunting for elephants, wouldn't you like to know what one looked like first, before you went on your search? Same thing here. So I'm going to describe what the elephant looks like before I put together a hunting party.

But before I begin, remember—you don't need to quote fixed price for a structured development application, but if you are going to quote fixed price, you must have the first four things mentioned earlier. And, even if you are not going to quote fixed price, your customer will want an estimate, and thus the more work you can get done on those four items, the better off you'll be.

Chapter 14
An Agreement to do Work

"Sign here, Sir."
"What is this I'm signing, Radar?"
"Nothing important, Sir."
   —M.A.S.H.

You've finished your sales call, and "Where do I sign?" are the next words out of your prospect's mouth. They love you, and can hardly wait. But no matter how lovey-dovey the relationship may be now, it's incumbent upon you to act in a professional manner from the very start. In this chapter, I'll discuss the three documents I use before beginning work—the Engagement Letter, the Attachment, and the Customer Setup Form.

I'm going to assume that you've made a sales call and the result of the meeting is that your prospect wants to turn into your customer. The first step agreed upon at the time of that decision was that you would send them an Engagement Letter for services.

This Engagement Letter actually consists of three pieces. The Engagement Letter itself is a two- or three-page letter that briefly describes the services that you propose to provide to your newfound customer, and is where the customer agrees to pay for those services. These services are usually consulting for either analysis and design of an application, or evaluation of an existing system. If you're using an Agile Methodology, these services would be for the whole shooting match—the analysis, design, development, testing, and delivery of an identifiable piece of the project if not the whole project at once.

The Attachment accompanies the Engagement Letter and explains the "rules of the road" for the software development process. The customer is often ignorant of specific issues that we software developers deal with every day; this document is our method of bringing up those issues and describing how we deal with them.

And, finally, the Customer Setup Form is how you gather information from the customer so that you can start the project properly.

If you're a corporate developer, then you probably wouldn't use a set of documents as formal as these. However, you should still put together a memo that touches on these same points and send copies to the main players (your supervisor, the supervisor of the department you're working with, and your contact(s) in that department). The key is to set the expectations of the folks you're going to be working with.

The Engagement Letter

The Engagement Letter is the next step in communicating expectations to the customer. In it, you should detail what you are going to do and what it is going to cost. Clearly, it is impossible to describe every nuance of a relationship in writing, but by putting the major points in writing, you can lessen the chances of misunderstandings. A sample Engagement Letter is included in the *DevGuide* downloads.

Purpose of the Engagement Letter

The purpose of this letter is to describe to the customer the types of services you are going to provide, and make it clear that from now on they will pay for what you are doing. The sales call was free. During the sales call, you should have informed them that you don't work without a signed Engagement Letter.

Before I start describing the details, I should mention that it's really easy to get tangled up in one's shorts by writing complex prose that eventually serves to confuse rather than clarify. Keep the description of your proposed services simple and to the point. Short sentences, short paragraphs, simple sentence construction, and none of those five-syllable words.

General format

I'm old-fashioned, very conservative, and so the materials my company sends out are designed to reflect that bent. I want my company to look like it's been around for 100 years.

That's why I make all of my printed literature—business cards, brochures, flyers, and so on—look pretty conservative. The message I deliver may not be quite as conservative, but the underlying theme is that this message is coming from an established, fundamentally solid firm. Some people may argue that that's a mixed metaphor and that it's confusing. Argue away. Marketing is not exact. I prefer to think of it along the lines that I am providing somebody with a conservative business foundation yet, where it counts, I'll be creative. The customer gets the best of both worlds.

You may choose to emulate that approach, or you may prefer to project a more modern or "far-out" image in order to attract attention. Whichever way you go, be sure to be consistent.

My letters start off something like this:

```
April 1, 20xx

Michael Austin-Thor
The Very Large Software Manufacturing Company
One Very Large Boulevard
Milwaukee WI 53202-1234

Dear Mike,
```

What are you going to do?

As every writing course you've ever taken has stated, put the most important thing first. And the most important thing is to describe to them what you're going to do for them. This only takes two short paragraphs. You're trying to sell them on something, and their attention, at this point, is tentative. Get to the point immediately. If it takes you a whole letter to describe what you are going to do, you don't have a clear idea, and they're not going to hang around while you try to collect your thoughts.

```
I am pleased to present this letter of engagement regarding custom database
software development services for your firm. The ultimate intent is to
completely replace and significantly enhance the functionality of your internal
knowledge base access system with a new one written in Software Studio's
Internet Programming Language. For the purpose of this letter, this new system
will be referred to as KBAS (Knowledge Base Access System).
```

```
The purpose of this letter is to outline the functionality of the system
and describe the services we propose to provide toward the development of
the system.
```

First off, tell them that this is a letter of engagement for services and describe what those services are. Usually, you're going to create a new application (or significantly modify an existing one). In either case, first make sure they understand what type of process you're going to use. You may not have opened that discussion with them—you may have decided which process you were going to use yourself—but even so, you need to make it clear to them how the process is going to proceed.

If you're going to use structured development or RAD, you're going to need to do a design first, and that's the purpose of this letter—to describe this design phase. If you're using an Agile Methodology, then you need to explain that you're going to do the entire design-through-delivery process on a piece by piece basis.

Next, tell them what they're going to get. They're spending their money, after all—so you want to make it very clear what they're going to get. Although you've done this 100 times, your customer probably hasn't.

If you're using a structured or RAD process, it's possible that they're still unclear about the two-phase process—design and specification first, then actual coding and a working app next. If, on the other hand, you're going to start delivering usable applications shortly, you want to make sure they understand that they're going to be responsible for taking part in delivery and acceptance testing in short order. In both cases, you put this in writing here just in case so that you have something to fall back on in case of trouble later. You'll also want to remember that the people reading this document may not have been in any initial meetings or discussions (in some cases you can count on it—the person signing the document may not have been involved at all up to this point). Thus, this document needs to stand on its own in explaining the whole process and what's coming up. They need to be able to understand the status of the project at this point without having to have a briefing session first.

Make it clear what the end result will be—are they getting just a specification? A prototype? Working software? In this situation, clear, concise writing will help you sell the end product to you customer more than any bells and whistles you may dream up later.

Describe the company and the pain

The "pain" I talked about during the phone call and the sales call needs to be stated in the letter as soon as possible. This puts that stake in the ground by which you're going to measure the success of the project.

While you and the customer both know the context in which the pain is being described, it's often useful for others to see the relationship between the company and their perceived pain spelled out clearly. These "others" include co-workers in the customer's company and employees in your company who are going to do some of the work.

Without burying the reader with jargon, it's appropriate to use company and/or industry specific terminology to describe their situation and environment. For example, in the following two paragraphs, "on-demand" has a specific meaning to the potential customer.

```
The Very Large Software Manufacturing Company is in the business of design,
development, and installation of automated manufacturing software. The Very
```

Large Software Manufacturing Company has offices throughout North and South
America and does business throughout both continents and the Pacific Rim.

The current knowledge base access system is an antiquated DOS-based application
that has a number of deficiencies in its multi-user and multi-tasking
capabilities. The purpose of KBAS is to provide a simple, `on-demand" tool for
employees to find information on a variety of development topics - along the
lines of a comprehensive help system. KBAS will be completely multi-user and
will be accessible across LANs and WANs and through the company intranet and
from outside the company via the Internet.

Again, being concise here is a virtue. You don't have to spell out reams and reams of
information about the company. Just show that you weren't nodding off during the sales call.
You also need to be able to identify in one or two sentences why they're spending all this
money with you, and what they expect to get for their bucks.

Describe a bit about what their company does so that you can reference this system in that
context. This gives them an idea of how important the system is and what role it plays. There
are two kinds of systems: 1) ones they have to have but would rather not, and 2) ones they like
because it helps them do their job and crush the competition.

A payroll system is an example of the first—it's rather boring but it's a requirement (sorry
if I've offended all of you accounting types). An example of the second type of system would
be one that allows them to pull up the order history of a customer in a nanosecond, something
no other firm in the country can do. Therefore they can provide better customer service—and
the system thus provides them with a competitive advantage.

The application

The customer is generally not very interested in buying software. They're much more
interested in buying new or improved functionality. They want to be able to do something that
they can't do now. These may be new functions, or existing functions, except that they work
faster, more efficiently, or with more features.

So as soon as possible, the letter has to tell them what they'll be able to do. (If you're
having a hard time envisioning this, picture the announcer from "The Price is Right" exhorting
someone to "Come On Down!")

Specific functionality includes the ability:

- For a user to access the system through the same interface regardless of
their physical location.

- For a user to find information in any of the knowledge base repositories,
including the internal documentation files, external documentation on products
and tools, abstracts or full magazine text, external knowledge bases, and
archives of newsgroups, forums, and e-mail collections.

- For administrative personnel to be able to update the knowledge base
independent of their location.

- To track usage statistics for items in the knowledge base.

This can be rather tough to pull together in a short period of time. It's even tougher if the customer has been yakking up a storm for hours about all the things they've had on their wish list for the past five years.

A trick I use is to pretend I'm issuing this software in shrink-wrap to sell at 'Puters-R-Us. Then I try to come up with the 10 bullet points that would be found on the back of the box that the user is going to read and then exclaim, "Oh! I want this one because it does X and Y!" If you do this, your customer is going to be able to take this list of "things it can do" to their boss or to their users and say "See! See all the cool things it can do for us? Isn't this going to be great?" Those are the items that make up this list of bullets in your Engagement Letter.

The development tool
Next, you'll need to tell them how you propose to do this. Be reasonably straightforward, but you can slide a bit of salesmanship into this area if you like.

```
The system will be written using Software Studio's Internet Programming
Language. It will include conversion of all old knowledge base data into a
new master structure, interfaces for access from inside and outside the
company, and administrative components for maintainance. It will be built on
a security-enabled foundation, and include a flexible reporting utility for
user-configurable reports, online Help for each function in the system, and
system utilities. The system will be developed using industry-standard,
state-of-the-art software development techniques including data normalization,
professional code documentation, and discrete alpha and beta testing to ensure
the production of a solid application that will require minimal maintenance.
Installation and training at The Very Large Software Manufacturing Company for
a group of primary users will be included.
```

Some people do not know what development tool they're going to use at this point. By all means, feel free to delete this section if this is the case. You may want to include some sort of description about when you will decide and how the decision will be made.

The software development process
The people who are buying this custom software from you could very well be new at it, and they're almost certainly new at doing it correctly. Thus, you have to educate them about how to go about the process. These next paragraphs describe the steps, from writing a specification to actual implementation.

Since they're going to be spending a lot of money for an extremely intangible item— a specification of software—it's important to give them as much information as possible about "what they're going to get."

For structured development and RAD systems, something like the following would be appropriate:

```
Development of custom software applications is done in two stages. The first is
the system analysis and design, with the resulting product being a Functional
Specification and an accompanying prototype. The Functional Specification is a
written document that serves as the "blueprint" of the system. It consists of
the following items:
```

This tells the customer right away that the end product of these services—what they're going to get—is a written document that describes what this system does.

It also tells them that there is a value to this. You are going to design this and engineer that, and these services are not trivial or inconsequential.

It's the rare customer, though, who understands what a Functional Spec is, so it's a good idea to paint a picture. Since it's a document, give them a rough outline.

```
Overview
· Purpose of the entire system and how it integrates into the business
· Description of the functionality of each module in the system

Technical Specifications
· Application architecture (directory structure, original data, logon and
security, interface mechanisms, and maintenance screens)
· General interface (maintenance screens, common buttons, toolbars, listbox
controls, and notes buttons)
· Screen descriptions (purpose, access, objects, and usage)
· Report and output layouts (detail entities, detail fields, calculate fields,
sort orders, grouping)
· Data structure (data dictionary, entity relationship diagrams)
· Test data set requirements
· Data validation rules
· Throughput analysis (for example, how many transactions would be entered into
the system on a daily basis, how many users, etc.)
· Environment and system requirements (definition of the network, what hardware
and software the system will be working with, and what, if any, additional
hardware or software will be required)

Implementation
· Installation
· Deliverables
· Testing methodology
· Test plans
· Modifications
· Milestones and delivery
```

Here, you're showing them the components in your specification. There is no single commonly accepted format for what a Functional Specification of a software application looks like. To one customer, a specification means a page and a half of scribbles they did at 6:15 one evening; to another, it means three binders of unreadable documents that were probably assembled by a committee. What you want to do is to tell them what they can expect in your specification.

If you're using an Agile Methodology, this looks a little different, as the Functional Specification plays somewhat of a different role. Not that it doesn't exist; rather, that it's used differently. With an Agile Methodology, the specification is a living document intended to facilitate communication, rather than to be the controller of the process that has to be signed off on and adhered to every time someone turns their head.

In this case, then, a long detailed description of the specifications document is inappropriate because it isn't a fixed entity. As a result, you would want to spend more time describing how the requirements collection and specification development is going to work, rather than what the end product is going to look like.

Are they going to understand all of this? Do you understand all of this yet? Some things may be new or phrased in an unfamiliar manner. Not to worry. The purpose is to reassure the customer that you are organized and thorough. They are buying your expertise as a project leader more than as a programmer at this point, and that's what you want to sell them on. You also want to give them a road map that they can follow through the journey, and know what's coming up next.

You want to give them enough detail so they understand this is not a trivial undertaking. They need to see the benefits of what their system is going to do without overwhelming them, or giving away the store for free. You could give them a 12-page outline of the specification, complete with boilerplate and instructions, but then they would have gotten the benefits of your knowledge without paying for it. You would like them to hear the sizzle and smell the aroma, but you don't want to give them the steak for free.

Structured development jobs require detail!

Some customers will try to avoid making the big decisions, and try to delegate responsibility—to you. Part of this avoidance includes the assumption that "You know what we want" and the command "Just make it happen!"

This can be a dangerous trap, so it's important to explain that this is a structured development job, and the details must be spelled out precisely. Sure, you could iterate through the project, figuring things out as you go—but then this process becomes RAD or Agile, not structured development, which is different from what you and they decided upon at the beginning. If they want to change the rules of the game, that's okay, but there is a different set of rules for that game.

And, oftentimes the lure of structured development is a fixed price—you can't give them a fixed price if you don't know what it is that they're buying. If you have a full grocery basket and you only allow me to peek into one corner of the basket, I can't tell you how much it's going to cost. Same thing here—you can't give them a fixed price, or even a reasonable estimate, without being very specific about what it is they're buying.

If you're going to provide a fixed price, tell them so. If you're not, you should still state how you're going to price the final application, and you may want to describe the benefits of structured development's approach as it relates to pricing.

```
It is important to note that this Functional Specification will contain a fixed
price and delivery quote for the system as described in the Specification.
Thus, it is important that the Specification clearly describe the functionality
and operation of the system as The Very Large Software Manufacturing Company
requires. Changes to the system after the completion of the Functional
Specification may result in additional costs and delays in delivery.
```

Depending on your preferences, you may want to change the last sentence to read "will result" instead of "may result"—it's up to you.

Now that you're done describing the spec, it's time to review what you're going to do with it—to tell them why you're going through all this work, and to make it clear that you're proposing to use the spec to build the system described therein.

```
The second stage is to use the Functional Specification to code, test, and
install the system. The Functional Specification will cover this process
in detail.
```

Naturally, the Functional Spec will describe the process, but you want to reassure them that you're not leaving once you're done with the spec.

Now it's time to get back to the specification process. Tell them what to expect, in general terms. Every project is different (although it has been argued that the more you do, the more they're all the same), so it's difficult to be exacting about the specific steps a particular project will require.

```
During the development of the specification, I will meet with you and other
members of the firm involved with the system multiple times in order to
determine the specific requirements (functions, data elements, operational
procedures, user access, etc.) of the system. I'll outline the rules for data
importing and validation, create prototypes of the menus and screens, and mock
up the reports that make up the system. At each meeting we will review the
progress made and view prototypes as they've been developed.
```

The key point in this section is that you'll be meeting with them over and over again, and that you'll be requiring regular feedback from them.

RAD projects require customer buy-in!

The primary difference between structured development and RAD is that structured development is a much more formal process, with authorization and sign-off required on each step of the process, while RAD is somewhat more free-wheeling, using the prototype and frequent customer meetings as a substitute for determining customer requirements. As a result, RAD projects require significant customer buy-in throughout the life of the project.

A recalcitrant customer can easily derail a RAD project by being too busy to meet with you regularly, so it's important to explicitly state the level of expected involvement in writing. Again, you're used to this process and you know what to expect. They don't, so make it clear.

Agile development projects are priced differently

Documentation for Agile projects is done concurrently with the development of the software. As a result, there isn't any place in the development cycle where you can draw a line and identify the price for the rest of the development.

Thus, the entire engagement will be done on an hourly basis, and your Engagement Letter needs to make it clear that the clock will start immediately.

How much will this spec cost?

Ah, yes, now to the crux of the matter. For structured and RAD projects, the customer will want to know how much is this specification going to cost? For Agile projects, the customer will similarly want to have at least an idea of the cost of the project. Unfortunately, there isn't a black and white answer to this question—often, there isn't even a good guess. Nonetheless, the customer is going to want one. So you have to explain to them why they're not going to get as good an answer as they'd like.

```
The development of complex software systems is an iterative process through
which discovery of new requirements is a normal and expected part. As a result,
the scope of the system will change during the specification process.
Accordingly, it is not possible to provide a fixed cost or even a reasonable
timeframe at this point.
```

The first sentence in that paragraph is a gold mine. Not only does it explain to them why you're not going to be able to provide a price this early on, but it explains to them that the iterative process that they're about to encounter is a normal and expected part of the deal. They may be expecting a miracle—a complete spec after a single meeting. (In my experience, this happens more often than not.)

The next stage—after you deliver the Engagement Letter (and they sign it)—is to actually do the work described in the specification. Since the spec is a finished product, I tell the customer that they can take this spec to other places and have them bid on it as well. This doesn't often happen, but it gives the customer a sense of security that they've got a way out if they don't like how development with us is going.

However, the intent from my point of view is that the customer will take our spec to another development house and get surprised. First, the other place will likely give the spec a cursory glance, since they're going to assume that the originator of the spec already has a lock on the work, and the customer is just going through the motions. Second, by virtue of their inattention, they'll provide the customer with an outrageous number—either way high or way low—and a shaky feeling to boot. After all, I've spent the time getting to know the customer's business, and the other guys are coming in cold. Furthermore, while I've documented the application thoroughly in the spec, I've still got two advantages over the competition—no matter how hard you try, you can't document everything, and, by virtue of all of the face-to-face meetings, hopefully I've developed a bit of chemistry with the customer. Finally, I've found that it's still pretty rare to run into a competitor that has a well-defined methodology for costing accurately.

In order to go about this process, I have to meet with several of their people many times. Each time we'll build more material out of the prototype and flush more material out of the document and so on. Tell them that this iterative process is normal, because again, these people may be new to this.

It's kind of like the pregnancy preparation book that has been so hot for the past 10 years—*What to Expect When You're Expecting*. Software development, while not quite the same as creating a child, is still a scary process. It's complex, and there are a lot of twists and turns on the journey that you may not be able to predict. A lot of this has to do with people's desires, wants, or expectations. People are human so they change their minds. I tell them and make it clear to them that this is a normal state of affairs. It's an iterative process because to iterate is in our nature. Therefore, I am comfortable with that process and I move with the current instead of fighting it. However, it's important to explain that process of discovery and iteration to them.

Thus, this statement reminds them that you know this, have seen it before, and are used to it. Thus, when the project seems that it's beginning to spin out of control, you can reassure them that you know how to deal with it—it's a normal aspect of the iterative process, and here's how we go about bringing it back under control.

For Agile projects, of course, this doesn't work quite the same way, but some of the techniques will work similarly. The key is to educate your customer that iteration is a normal course of development, not a sign that you don't know what you're doing.

Payment methodology

Just like everything else in the Engagement Letter, I've already verbally discussed with the customer how I'm going to charge, but it's a really, really, really good idea to put this part in writing. I particularly like being explicit about the "extras" that will show up on the bill in addition to straight consulting time.

```
Development of this Functional Specification is done on a time and materials
basis. Rates for various Hentzenwerke personnel range from $<rate> to $<rate>
per hour, depending on the experience of the individual. My time is billed at
top rate; other developers range from $<rate> to $<rate>, and administrative
and testing personnel cluster at the low end. Time includes time spent meeting
with you and other members of your staff and other firms involved in the
production of the system, preparation for meetings and work resulting from
meetings, including the design of the prototypes, and travel and phone time.
Materials include straight reimbursement of long distance phone charges and
mileage between Hentzenwerke's offices in Milwaukee and your offices at the
standard IRS rate. All billable personnel track their time against specific
modules and invoices reflect this level of detail.
```

Since this letter comes from me, I write in the first person; you'll need to change the wording to suit your particular situation.

I try to be very clear both about *what* I'm going to charge and *how*, so that there are no misunderstandings down the road. Of course, there always will be misunderstandings, mainly because the customer wasn't listening, and then didn't read this as carefully as they should have, or because they forgot—but if you have it in black and white, it'll be easier to reconcile the misunderstanding correctly—in other words, in your favor.

For example, suppose the first invoice shows up on the customer's desk, and 10 minutes later you get a call asking, "How come you're charging me for travel time?" You can simply say "Umm, that should have been covered in our Engagement Letter. Let me pull it out to make sure." Of course, you know you didn't forget, but this approach is an easy way to point this out to the customer without being abrupt or insulting. The customer, in this case, has made a mistake—the last thing you want to do is make them feel bad about it. Naturally, you didn't really think you forgot it, and you can, without being a jerk, point out to your customer that 1) it was in there, and 2) he agreed to it.

Describe the initial deliverables

One of the questions they're always going to ask is "How much will this cost?" (If they don't ask, be afraid. Either they're not serious, or they don't care—and in the second case, that's probably because they're not real worried about getting around to paying you.) It's pretty hard to give them any kind of reasonable answer unless you have some sort of idea of what it is they're going to buy. I do this by listing the basic components of the system.

Remember the homework they were supposed to do in preparation for the sales call?

The result of that was a list of modules, forms and reports—at least a first pass at them. From that, you can extrapolate the size of the application, and then assign some rough numbers based on that first set of assumptions.

```
At this point, the proposed deliverables include the following items:

Screens
< listing >
```

```
Reports
< listing >

Processes
< listing >
```

You may choose to list the details—the names of each screen, report, and process—right here, or you may want to simply tally how many of each, and include the specific list as an attachment. I can go both ways on this—on the one hand, it seems to flow better if you include the list as part of the body of the letter, but on the other hand, that sort of technical information can seem to interrupt a business letter—particularly if the list is long. Your call.

How much?
Okay, finally, down to the answer to the "How much?" question.

```
I estimate that, based on these deliverables as well as our experience with
other systems of similar magnitude and scope, the development of the Functional
Specification will take between 220 and 250 hours and the Implementation of the
system will take an additional 1,800 and 2,100 hours. Please note that this
time estimate is framed in terms of working hours and not in calendar terms.
```

Now, how do you figure out what these numbers are? What I've done is go through past projects, look at the amount of time I've taken to put together a spec, tally up the number of forms, reports, and processes for those specs, and run through a few what-if scenarios to determine the average cost to spec out a form, a report, and a process.

Given those numbers, it's easy to come up with a rough estimate for talking purposes. You, of course, may want to pad those numbers some right off the bat to give yourself some leeway as the application grows.

Remember that this is an estimate! It'll be very tempting for a customer to see a number, and to try to hold you to that number, no matter what the results of the iteration end up as. Thus, if you're going to include any sort of number, don't forget to include this next paragraph as well!

As a result, you'll want to include the following paragraphs to warn them.

```
It's important to remember that these figures are estimates, not maximums, and
will most likely change during the development of the specification as new
requirements are discovered and existing functionality is modified.

However, you will be informed in writing should it appear likely that the
estimate will need to be exceeded in order to finish the development of the
specification.
```

Of course, I discuss the fact that these are estimates in person as well, but no matter how well you cover the topic, 99 out of 99 people will remember the number you provide as an estimate and somehow forget that it was "an estimate." If the design goes over the estimate, they'll generally be upset. When you've detailed the basis for the estimate, it's a lot easier to explain why the initial estimate was for $5,500 but the final price for the spec ended up being $8,200—it's because you started out with a spec for 12 screens and 4 reports but the final design has 19 screens and a half-dozen reports.

Naturally, this doesn't prevent a customer from becoming irrational and making some sort of ridiculous argument about why the Final Specification price should have been what was stated in the Engagement Letter, but it helps your chances more than not stating anything at all.

The best way to avoid problems is to keep the customer informed about the state of the bill as it grows. I'll cover this in more detail in the next chapter.

By the way, another advantage to starting out with a list of actual components is that you can quickly tell (or find out) whether you're off track. Nothing is more frustrating than to spend hours and hours (days and days? months and months?) on a spec only to find out that you've gone down a blind alley or missed a critical turn way back there.

Describe the payment method

Now let's get down to the good part—how are you going to get paid? There are two basic methods—either get paid up front, or get paid after the fact.

Retainer

If you choose to require payment in advance for the work you do, this is called a retainer. As the language in the letter shows, you request funds in advance; the work you perform draws down those funds. When the funds are low or depleted, you send an invoice to replenish the retainer.

Here's an example of how the first option can be worded.

```
An initial retainer in the amount of <Amount> is required to start work, time
will be posted against the retainer as noted above, and monthly statements will
be rendered. Invoices will be used for replenishing the retainer as necessary.

Funds remaining at the end of the development of the Functional Specification
will be returned to The Very Large Software Manufacturing Company or applied
toward the implementation of the system as requested by The Very Large Software
Manufacturing Company. The Functional Specification and prototype tables,
menus, screens, and report layouts [but not the supporting libraries and design
tools] are the properties of The Very Large Software Manufacturing Company
as delivered.

We can begin work immediately upon receipt of a signed copy of this letter and
the attached customer setup form.
```

Invoice

You may wish to invoice the customer after doing the work. Don't think that you have to invoice after the entire job is done—invoice on a regular basis or after you've completed identifiable tasks. Here's an example of how you could set up the terms.

```
You will be invoiced every two weeks for work completed to that point; invoices
are due in 10 days. Work will be stopped in the event an invoice becomes past
due. The Functional Specification and the prototype tables, menus, screens, and
report layouts [but not the supporting libraries and design tools] become the
property of The Very Large Manufacturing Company upon payment. We can begin
work immediately upon receipt of a signed copy of this letter and the attached
customer setup form.
```

The decision, of course, is which method to use. You can talk to 20 developers and get 30 opinions. Some refuse to do any work without a retainer; others have worked successfully for years on an invoice basis. As much as I'd like to be able to provide guidelines for when to go which route—I simply can't. There are too many variables to create a set of fixed rules.

A small company may be perceived to be more risky. It seems that it would be easy for the owner of a small firm to get all hacked off for one reason or another, and simply announce one day, "I'm unhappy and I'm not going to pay you." Once you have a PO from MegaCorp, it would seem a lot harder for an individual to arbitrarily cut you off.

On the other hand, larger companies treat their payables as simply another business issue, and if cash gets tight, it's no problem for the board of directors to unilaterally declare, "All invoices will be held for 60 days from now on." And one or two large companies have been known to go bankrupt, leaving their creditors with tears and bad memories.

Meanwhile, most small business owners treat their payables as an extension of their word—and regardless of their financial position, they will pay what they owe—period.

There are no rules—you need to decide for yourself. The only advice I have is to listen to your gut. Every time I've been burned by a customer, hindsight shows me that I really should have seen it coming. This is a business decision, and not a developer's decision. Put on your businessperson's hat. A 15-day billing cycle may work out well for Acme Large Manufacturing, but a firm with a lousy credit rating may need to work on a deposit basis. You may need to make this call on a case-by-case basis instead of setting a single absolute rule. Follow your gut and common sense.

Expiration period

Presumably, you've wowed your customer to such an extent that they're going to sign and return the Engagement Letter via overnight courier (if not earlier). However, there's always the situation where a customer, hot to trot, suddenly disappears from the horizon, and repeated phone calls go unreturned. After a few tries, you get the message—and go onto bigger and better things.

Then, three months later, the customer reappears, and is ready to go—right away. But now you're in the middle of another job, or perhaps several of them, and you simply don't have the manpower to take this one on like you did three months ago.

Or, even worse, they sit on the Engagement Letter for a year or two, or more, and then one day, long after you've forgotten about them, a signed copy shows up in the mail, and you get a call later that day wanting to schedule a meeting for later that week.

And the problem here is three-fold—not only are you currently maxed out in terms of schedule, but your rates have gone up, and the language or toolset you proposed to use in the Engagement Letter has been revved twice (or been discontinued). Yet the customer, off in their own little world, could very well expect you to honor all the terms in the Engagement Letter.

And the longer it's been, the more likely they are to expect so. Why? If they've been sitting on a proposal for several years, and after all that time, they still find it applicable to their business, that means that their business hasn't changed much, if at all, and that they've likely got a moribund bureaucratic management as well. Thus, they're most likely not going to be in tune with the fast pace of the high-tech business, and not understand how your business changes rapidly.

Thus, you may want to consider including language—an escape clause, so to speak—that tells the customer that the terms in the Engagement Letter are good for only a certain period of time.

```
The terms in this Engagement Letter are good for 30 days from the date of this
letter. If this letter is not accepted within this period, we reserve the right
to requote.
```

The Attachment

The next part in the Engagement Letter covers the Attachment. You haven't beaten around the bush in the past, so don't beat around the bush now. There are a lot of hacks and amateurs and "I want to learn on your nickel" folks out there. Furthermore, since there aren't any government-imposed licensing or accreditation requirements, or mandatory membership in a professional society, there aren't any standardized practices in the software development world.

What does that mean? That means that customers don't know the questions to ask—they don't know what to expect—and they are at the mercy of their computer consultant. Being ignorant of what to expect means that the computer consultant can then sell them anything he wants, whether or not it's of value. A lack of reasonable expectations also means that the customer will develop their own—which very likely aren't going to be reasonable, and thus, sets the stage for conflicts. Thus, you want to provide them with a better set of expectations. This attachment gives them a baseline from which they can begin. In it, you explain about standard business practices in this industry, and how your company in particular operates. If they need more information—great. If they want or need to have changes made, that's okay too. The bottom line is to bring forward these issues and explain how you usually handle them.

```
Software development is a complex process that, due to the ethereal nature of
the product, lends itself to misunderstandings and miscommunication. Attached
to this Engagement Letter is a document that describes our view of the software
development process and explains how we handle issues that typically arise
during the custom software process. If you have any questions or differences of
opinion, please feel free to bring them up with me.
```

The contents of the Attachment are contained in the next section of this chapter.

Call to action

As any good sales manual will tell you, always close your letter with a call to action. Don't just wait for the customer to "get it" because they might never do so. Prompt them—make it easy for them to figure out what the next step is. And, as the sales manual also says, "Ask for the order." Ask them to sign this letter and get rolling!

I've included two ways to word this, depending on whether you're going to use a retainer or an invoicing scheme.

Retainer:

```
To confirm that these arrangements reflect your understanding, please sign one
copy of this letter and return to me together with the attached Customer
Information sheet and the aforementioned retainer in the amount of <amount>.
```

Invoice:

```
To confirm that these arrangements reflect your understanding, please sign one
copy of this letter and return to me together with the attached Customer
Information sheet and a company purchase order if required.
```

Finally, close the letter and allow a place for the customer to sign and date in order to signal their acceptance.

Note that I am asking the customer to actively agree that "Yes, the contents of this letter is what we talked about." If they have differences, they're more than welcome to give me a call and discuss what changes they want made.

There shouldn't be any substantial modifications, since each of these items has already been discussed during the sales call, but you need to be ready just in case.

The key point here is that they have to act in order to get you to start work. Simply calling up and saying "Yeah, sounds good, go ahead" isn't enough. In the case of disagreements later, you'll be on firmer ground if you've got a signed Engagement Letter in your hand. If you don't, the customer can always claim they never got it, or didn't read it all, or any number of other excuses. Once they've signed and returned it to you, they've made an easily identifiable contract with you.

Of course, this isn't a one-sided agreement. You've also committed to performing certain services for which you're going to get paid. There are plenty of documented cases where companies have made commitments to perform services that they weren't actually able to provide, and this type of contract thus also helps protect the customer from disreputable vendors.

When can you start?

The customer is probably quite interested in getting going. So tell them when you can start.

```
We can begin work within a week of receipt. We're all looking forward to
working with your company. If you have any questions, please call me at
your convenience.
```

This can be a tricky item to state. As described in the section "Expiration period" earlier in this chapter, you can't leave the Engagement Letter open-ended. Thus, in addition to the expiration period described earlier, you may want to include additional language that changes the start time if they don't sign right away (and you define what "right away" means).

I've found that I don't need to, and for two reasons.

First, I always have several gigs going on at a time, so it's good to get another one going regardless of the cycle. And, second, particularly in the early design phases, I've found that there usually isn't enough work to keep busy full time—on many projects, there's a lot of breathing room while waiting for the customer to find time for the next meeting, or to get back to you on issues you raised at the last meeting, or whatever.

The close

As a business owner, I'm also quite picky about the close of a letter. The letter is from the company, so the company signs it: Sincerely, Hentzenwerke Corporation. However, you're acting as a representative, and so you sign underneath, with your title as related to the company. This is important—you are signing as an agent of the company, not in a personal capacity. It may seem like a small point, but take another look at the various letters that you've received from the various professional firms you've engaged. I suspect you'll see a similar pattern from them.

You must make sure the customer signs and dates the letter. What if they don't? I'll get to various scenarios you might run into in Chapter 19, "Scenarios Encountered During the Specification Process."

```
Sincerely,
Hentzenwerke Corporation

Whil Hentzen
President


_____
Accepted By Authorized Representative


_____
Title


_____
Date
```

I've seen various Engagement Letters that include stricter wording to the effect of "I testify that I have the power to make this Agreement on the behalf of my company, and agree to be personally bound by this Agreement otherwise." I feel that's pretty strong, but you may be in an arena where that type of language is perfectly reasonable. Consult your own lawyer about specifics in your own situation.

The Attachment

 The Attachment is where you spell out the rules of the road, as your company sees them, for the software development process being undertaken. As I mentioned earlier, there are no commonly accepted practices or procedures for the industry, and it's an environment where misunderstandings are easily come by. While you can't anticipate every possible situation that may arise, by spelling out the most likely ones, you can generate a lot of good will that may come in handy when unanticipated difficulties arise. A sample Attachment is included in the *DevGuide* downloads.

General

The purpose of this first section is to deal with some legal issues. In the event of an IRS audit, this makes it clear why the other company is contracting with us. In the next section, I'll spell out more precisely what services are being contracted for.

```
Customer: The Very Large Software Manufacturing Company, Inc.
Vendor: Hentzenwerke Corporation
Custom Software Development Issues

General
```

The Very Large Manufacturing Company, Inc. ("Customer") is looking for a vendor
that will perform software development services for internal computer systems
that will run on a PC platform due to the shortage of time and personnel at
Customer, and has approached Hentzenwerke Corporation ("Vendor") to do so.

The purpose of this document is to spell out the terms and conditions of this
working arrangement to ensure that the expectations of both parties are
understood up front.

There's something subtle in the way I've structured the first few lines of this Attachment. This document is basically all boilerplate when it's first submitted to the customer. Thus, the standard mechanism is to simply cut and paste the text from the last Attachment (or from a directory that contains all of your master documents) you sent out.

However, doing so opens you to the risk of forgetting to search and replace the previous customer's name with the current one—and that's pretty embarrassing, particularly right off the bat when you're trying to make a good impression.

As a result, instead of using the customer's name throughout the document, I just define the customer and vendor once at the top, and then refer to the generic "Customer" and "Vendor" for the rest of the paper.

Of course, you may find that to be too impersonal, but I've found it to be much less of a problem than the problem of making an incorrect reference.

Services

The purpose of this section is to spell out that I am an independent contractor doing a work for hire—not an employee. The IRS has created a set of "20 questions" that they use to determine whether a consultant is acting like an employee. In this document, I explicitly address a number of those questions. If you're an individual, this section is important; as your firm grows, this section becomes less and less necessary.

Services

Vendor agrees to perform for Customer services ("Services") to generally
include, but not be limited to, design, development, coding, testing,
documentation, installation, training, and maintenance of software programs
("Programs") as specified in this or a future Proposal.

Customer is hereby contracting with Vendor for these Services and Vendor
reserves the right to determine the method, manner, and means by which the
Services will be performed. Vendor is not required to perform the Services
during a fixed hourly or daily time or at a specific site. If any or all
Services are performed at Customer's premises, then Vendor's time spent at the
premises is to be at the discretion of Vendor.

Vendor shall take appropriate measures to ensure that their staff members who
perform Services are competent to do so and that they do not violate any
provision of this agreement or subsequent Proposals.

Vendor shall supply all equipment, software, peripherals, and supplies required
to perform Services, with the general exceptions of installation and training,
and when requested otherwise by Customer.

Vendor represents that it is an independent contractor and as such agrees to
indemnify and hold harmless Customer from any and all liabilities for claims,

```
judgments, or losses and all lawsuits including the costs, expenses, and
attorneys' fees of any judgment for injuries to or property damage of any
person or persons including parties hereto and their employees or agents, and
third parties, arising from or caused in whole or in part by any operation
incidental to the performance of the contract performed by Vendor for Customer
under the terms described herein.
```

```
As a condition of this contract, Vendor agrees to carry the statutory Worker's
Compensation coverage on any employee engaged in work on the premises of
Customer within the purview of this agreement.
```

Support

One of the biggest fears a customer has is hiring a developer who disappears, leaving them hanging with a system that is badly (or un) documented, buggy, and hard to maintain. Almost as bad is the developer who, once having developed the application, holds the customer hostage, demanding unreasonable sums to make the most trivial of changes.

In the "Support" section, I alleviate some of these fears by explaining how I'm going to support their application.

```
Support
```

```
Vendor will make its best effort via alpha testing, integration testing, beta
testing, and Customer testing to provide a defect-free application. Customer is
responsible for providing a Test Suite of Data (with the assistance of Vendor)
that accounts for all scenarios and cases of data that the system may process.
```

If you're going to follow my approach, you must define what a "defect" is. A ton of credit goes to Pat Adams for her wonderful description of a defect: something that does not perform as specified in the written specifications or subsequent Change Orders. I cite this definition in all Specifications and rely on it throughout the development process.

```
Vendor warrants that Customer will not be charged for fixing "defects" that
slip through the testing phase. A defect is defined as:
```

```
- an operation that does not perform as specified in the written specifications
and/or change notices, or
```

```
- an error that causes the program to stop and display an error message that
says "An application error has occurred" and
```

```
- must be reproducible upon demand.
```

Be sure to state that a defect must be reproducible upon demand. It's extremely annoying to go on a defect hunt with a customer only to find that they can't show you what's happening in person. "I swear this happened to me five times yesterday," they wail, but as you and I know, we can't fix what we can't see.

We'll be happy to sit with them for days and days (well, maybe "happy" isn't quite the right adjective) and work with them to find out what is happening, but if it's not reproducible, that time is billable.

This helps the user focus on defining what the problem is—filling out our defect report forms, being clear in their descriptions, and so on—if they think that by providing a clear description, they might get the problem fixed without charge.

Too often (well, okay, all the time), a customer comes to expect that any unexpected behavior by the system can be called a "bug." It must be made excruciatingly clear to the customer that we are talking about defects (more on this in Chapter 24, "Bug Reporting and Application Feedback"), and that "It doesn't do what I want it to do" is not a defect—only behavior that is at odds with the written specification is a defect.

I probably explain to every customer at least three separate times that there are a million design decisions that cannot be anticipated, and, accordingly, we constantly have to make judgments about a myriad of issues during the course of development. It is simply impossible to document each and every issue in the written specifications—it would be too costly, and, given the state of development tools, technically impossible. As a result, the Attachment spells out that I reserve the right to make those judgments on the fly.

```
Non-inclusion of options, behavior not specifically delineated in the written
specifications, and operating system and environmental problems are not
considered to be defects. If the problem can be resolved without changing
application code, if it is not reproducible upon demand, or if it occurs in a
module that has been working for three months and that has not been changed,
then it is not considered to be a defect.
```

The key part about defining what constitutes a defect is that I will fix defects for free for the life of the application, but I will charge to do work that is not a "bug fix." Since the issue of money has been raised, it's important to be clear about what is a bug and what isn't.

I've found that I like to reserve the right to charge for bugs after a certain period of time. It's possible that the user hasn't really tested the system, and then, at year-end or just before plant shutdown, they run into something. That's pretty annoying, and while I might give them the benefit of the doubt, I'd like the option not to.

```
This does not mean that Vendor will not resolve these issues; this means that
Vendor will not resolve them without charge. Note that Vendor reserves the
right to interpret interface and performance issues that are not specifically
described in a written specification as it sees fit.

Customer will be charged on a time and materials basis at Vendor's rates then
in effect for time spent to investigate perceived bugs and to repair the
problem if indeed the problem is not a bug as defined above.

Customer will be charged on a time and materials basis at Vendor's rates then
in effect for services outside the scope of the proposal, including but not
limited to:

- additional training,

- modifications to the system, such as screen or report layouts, after they've
been accepted by Customer personnel,

- modifications to formulas or calculations to account for scenarios or cases
that were not part of the proposal or Test Suite of Data, and
```

```
- any services relating to modifications made to the application by non-Vendor
personnel.
```

There's a large gray area having to do with environmental issues. Suppose the application runs fine on all of the Win98 machines, but one day while you're out of town, they load it on a Win2000 box—and the printing that's clearly defined in the spec doesn't work the same way. Or even worse—it works on Al's machine, but not on Bob's—and they're both the same make and model, even purchased at the same time.

I handle this in the written spec by describing that I'll install the application on their server and a machine that represents the typical configuration—but that I won't install and test on every possible machine at the customer's site. If they need me to do so, or if they run into problems later on, I'm happy to troubleshoot and fix—but I can't possibly provide that level of service for a fixed price.

The first edition of this book was written in 1996; at the time, technologies like COM and CORBA, and the resulting distributed applications that were the precursor to Internet applications, were just starting to become visible. In the better part of the decade that's passed since, the development and deployment of applications has only become more complex; interdependencies have grown to the point that they can't easily be troubleshooted anymore. After upgrading every driver on a system, often the only solution to a problem is to simply reformat and reinstall Windows and "see if that works."

As a result, be sure that you don't open yourself up to an infinite support burden by blithely assuring that the application you're developing will work everywhere. This is not to say you won't help your customer—simply that you won't do it for free.

Ownership

If there is any issue raised by the customer, this is usually it, and, oftentimes, it's the only issue they mention. Who owns the code? People want to make sure that they are not indebted to you for the rest of their lives. They want to have freedom to do what they have to do in their business. So there are actually two concerns that people can raise here.

The first is whether or not somebody else can come in and modify the code that I've developed. My answer is "absolutely." I retain ownership, but they have a license that lasts forever. They can use it for any reason, but I must retain ownership of it (as explained below).

The second issue is pure ownership of the code—for whatever reason, they feel they have to own the code outright. For example, they may have a custom product that this code is incorporated into, or they may have licensing restrictions that require absolute ownership, or maybe they just like to play hardball. My short answer here is that I have invested thousands of hours in creating common code that I use across many applications, and if they must own all of the code in their application, I'm going to have to either rewrite all of this common code for them, or I'll have to sell them my libraries for an amount that will pay for me to be able to rewrite them myself.

Do they really want to spend the money for thousands of hours of work if there isn't that much benefit to it? Probably not. In the event that you are writing a custom app for another company who intends to resell it, it might be worth it to them, but that is a business decision that they have to make.

You want to protect the customer's interest, but not to the point of relinquishing your own interest. Here is how I've decided to make this a win-win situation.

Ownership

Except as specifically set forth in writing and signed by both Customer and
Vendor, Vendor retains all copyright and patent rights with respect to all
materials as described in "Deliverables" developed under this Agreement and all
subsequent Proposals to Customer. Therefore, Vendor grants to Customer a
permanent, non-exclusive license to use and employ such materials within their
business. Customer further agrees to execute a non-exclusive license agreement
should Vendor deem that said execution is necessary.

Materials delivered under this and subsequent proposals include five types
of program code (where "Code" refers to program code, design surfaces, and
other objects such as libraries and classes needed for complete generation
of an executable):

1. Generic code already developed by Vendor and used in applications delivered
to Customer. An example would be a user log-in screen that requires the user to
enter their name and password, and that is part of Vendor's standard foundation
already in existence.

2. Generic code developed by Vendor in response to a request by Customer during
the creation of applications for Customer, but that is added to Vendor's
standard foundation. An example would be an error logging routine that uses a
public domain routine to capture a screen shot of when the error occurred. This
functionality does not currently exist in Vendor's standard foundation, but
would become part of the foundation upon development.

3. Custom code developed by Vendor during the creation of application for
Customer that may have use in a noncompetitive application for another customer
of Vendor. An example would be a mechanism to populate a screen with data from
multiple mutually exclusive tables to give the appearance that all data came
from a single location. While the implementation of this mechanism may have a
specific use in the Customer's application, it could be applied in applications
developed for other customers without infringing on the intellectual investment
in the application by the Customer.

4. Custom code developed by Vendor during the creation of application for
Customer that is strictly proprietary to the applications that Vendor is
developing for Customer. An example would be in the case of an application used
by Customer for scheduling events. Custom code, algorithms, or interfaces
developed by Vendor or by Customer that give Customer a competitive edge or
comprise proprietary knowledge on the part of the Customer make up this fourth
type of code.

5. A variety of third-party tools, foundations, and other elements that are the
property of a third-party company, that are being used by Vendor for the
purpose of development of this application, for which licenses are owned by
Vendor, and which may or may not be possessed by Customer in order to run
and/or maintain System.

In order to provide Vendor with the flexibility needed within their business
but at the same time to provide Customer with protection for the investment
made in custom application development, Vendor retains all copyright and patent
rights with respect to materials described in the first three areas, and grants
to Customer a permanent, non-exclusive license to use and employ such materials
within their business.

Vendor assigns all copyright and patent rights with respect to materials that
fall under the fourth area to Customer upon full payment. Modules or routines
that fall under the fourth area will be designated as such in the Functional

```
Specification and a specific copyright notice indicating such rights and
ownership will be placed in the header of said modules and routines. Items that
fall under the fifth area remain the property of the third-party company, but
Vendor will supply Customer with information necessary to license said tools,
foundations, and other elements should Customer desire to do so.
```

In short, I declare that I own all source code (with one exception), but that I provide a non-exclusive, perpetual license for the customer to use that code in their business. Let's look at each of the points raised here.

First, I describe each of the types of code that could end up in an app—all the way from generic code written a long time ago and solidly planted in your common library to custom code that deals with a confidential business process or algorithm.

Non-exclusive. I reserve the right to use my code again and again. I am able to provide robust, feature-rich, bug-free functionality at an inexpensive price because I reuse code that I've written for other applications. If I were to write their application from scratch, it would cost a fortune.

I must have the ability to continue to reuse that code in the future, and that includes items that I specifically wrote for this customer. Note that this is subject to the second paragraph in this section.

Perpetual. They have this right forever. They don't have to pay an annual maintenance fee or be subject to any other requirements down the road.

Use in their business. They can use this code in their business, but they can't resell my code elsewhere. They can't go into business to compete with me, nor can they resell the application outside of their business without talking to me first. Of course, if the definition of the application is that it is to be distributed as a product or service of the customer, then this doesn't apply.

They can also have others come into their company and modify the code, but those individuals are not allowed to use the code outside that customer's business. As a matter of practicality, this is unenforceable. I've found that the issue of someone coming in to take over for me hasn't been a big worry either.

Common code. It's important for the customer to understand the benefits that they realize from my use of my common code libraries—and so that they can then make a wise business decision depending on their needs. But the company that requires complete ownership without paying for it is being unreasonable, and that spells problems for the entire relationship down the road.

Non-compete agreement

Along the lines of code ownership comes the issue of non-compete. A fair number of customers are developing custom software with the intent to develop or maintain a competitive advantage over their competition. It doesn't make sense for them to spend tens or hundreds of thousands of dollars on a new custom application, only to have the vendor turn around and resell a similar application to each of their competitors. Even worse would be for the vendor to sell the application for a reduced price, thus putting the first customer at a disadvantage—not only do their competitors now have the same software, but they paid less for it!

Thus, I agree that I won't approach competitors (or allow competitors to approach me) with the intent of infringing on the investment that the customer has made in their software.

Note that this language still allows me to work with a competitor on a completely different application; if I thought there was a potential conflict of interest, I'd first check with my first customer.

```
In addition, Vendor recognizes that Customer has made a significant investment
in the development of System, and hereby agrees not to resell, duplicate to any
significant degree, or otherwise infringe on the investment Customer has made
in the development of System. This includes not approaching competitors of
Customer with the intent of duplicating System.
```

Confidentiality

I have a standard confidentiality clause in my documents, but if the customer is really concerned about this, they may well ask for their own confidentiality agreement to be signed. Typically, they will present those and have a specific issue that they're concerned about—and I haven't found one yet that I've declined to sign. You, of course, would want to check with your lawyer before you sign a document with which you're not familiar.

```
Confidentiality

Each party shall hold in trust for the other party, and shall not disclose to
any nonparty to this Agreement or subsequent Proposals, any confidential
information of the other party. Confidential information is information that
relates to research, development, trade secrets, or business affairs, but does
not include information which is generally known or easily ascertainable by
nonparties of ordinary skill.

Vendor acknowledges that during the performance of this Agreement, Vendor may
learn or receive confidential Customer information, and therefore Vendor hereby
confirms that all such information relating to Customer's business will be kept
confidential by Vendor.
```

Customer representative

One uncomfortable situation that sometimes occurs is that of being bounced around from one person at a company to another during the decision-making process. Eventually you will get caught in the middle. This paragraph simply states that there will be one person with ultimate authority.

```
Customer Representative

Customer shall designate one employee to represent Customer during the
performance of this Agreement. Said employee will be the primary contact for
this Agreement, and will be authorized to make financial and legal commitments
on the part of Customer. No other Customer employees will be authorized to act
in such a capacity unless such authorization is made in writing to Vendor.

This agreement will be revisited and may be renegotiated in the event that the
Customer Representative materially changes during the development and/or
implementation of System.
```

This person is identified in the Customer Setup Form described next in this chapter.

I've also encountered the situation where a customer representative is changed partway through the project. This can cause all sorts of havoc—the new contact may decide they have to make the project their own, and thus throw out the work of their predecessor—and your work. Since I work on a written specification basis, this isn't as much a danger as when work is being produced on the fly, but even subtle changes in leadership can affect the project.

This situation is covered to some extent in the above phrasing, but you might include a clause that handles this type of situation if you're worried about it.

If your customer is sharp, they might ask you to provide the same sort of clause for the primary player at your company for this particular project—anyone who has contracted with a "big consulting firm" has no doubt been bounced around from project manager to project manager, experiencing exactly the same types of frustration that you're trying to avoid with this clause.

Disputes and liability

This is where the lawyers start to salivate. The fundamental rule here is to keep them out of the picture. Once lawyers get involved, the only people who win are the lawyers. Keep your customer happy, and if they ask for something that is unreasonable, part ways.

A contract, and that is what this is, is not really a tool to enforce behavior without the interference of lawyers. Rather, I view it as a tool to define what will happen when the parties agree to disagree. If one of the parties doesn't want to agree and insists on calling in the lawyers, then no contract is going to be enforceable.

```
Disputes

Any dispute that arises between the parties with respect to the performance of
this Agreement and subsequent Proposals shall be submitted to binding
arbitration by the Better Business Bureau's Good Sense Arbitration Program, to
be determined and resolved by said association under its rules and procedures
in effect at the time of submission, and the parties hereby agree to share
equally in the costs of said arbitration. Arbitration will be undertaken and
concluded within 15 days of commencement.
```

Similarly, you want to assure your customer that you're going to do the best job you can, and that that performance is appropriate for what they're asking for. In other words, that you're qualified and competent to do the work for which you're being paid.

On the other hand, people make mistakes, and you want to protect yourself from catastrophic events.

```
Liability

Vendor warrants to Customer that the material, analysis, data, programs,
and services to be delivered or rendered hereunder will be of the kind and
quality designated and will be performed by qualified personnel. Special
requirements for format or standards to be followed shall be included in a
specific Proposal. Vendor makes no other warranties, whether written, oral,
or implied, including without limitation warranty of fitness for purpose
or merchantability. In no event shall Vendor be liable for indirect,
incidental, special, or consequential damages, whether or not the possibility
```

of such damages has been disclosed to Vendor in advance or could have been
reasonably foreseen.

Vendor's liability for Customer's actual damages will be limited to the actual
amount paid by Customer for aforementioned Services. This limitation shall
apply regardless of the form of action, whether such liability arises from a
claim based on contract, warranty, tort, or otherwise, including negligence.
This limitation does not include liability due to claims by Customer for bodily
injury, damage to real property, or damage to tangible personal property for
which Vendor was found legally liable.

You may also want to have a cancellation clause that specifies exactly how the project can
get cancelled, either due to the desire of the customer or you.

The Customer Setup Form

 The Customer Setup Form is an attachment to the Engagement Letter, and must be
filled out along with a signed Engagement Letter. A sample Customer Setup Form is
included in the *DevGuide* downloads.

Purpose

The purpose of this form is to make sure I have all the information I need to work with this
customer—and to get paid.

Procedure

It should be filled out and returned at the same time as the Engagement Letter. Nothing more
to it than that.

Contents

There are two parts to this information. The first part is the regular demographic data—
address, phone number, that sort of thing. The second part is the information I need in order to
get paid—yes, I'm always interested in getting paid.

Customer Setup

1. The primary contact, authorized to act on the behalf of the customer in all
matters, is:
Name _____
Title _____
Phone _____

Company agrees to notify Vendor in the event that this person changes.

2. Please provide the name and address where invoices should be sent:

Name _____
Company _____
Address _____
City/State/Zip _____

3. Please provide the name and phone number of the person to contact in the event of a question regarding an invoice:

Name _____

Phone _____

Available Hours _____

4. Is a Purchase Order Number required on invoices?
___ Yes ___ No

If Yes, please provide the PO # for this project: _____

5. Work is invoiced every two weeks and our terms are net 10 days. Work will be stopped in the event an invoice becomes past due.

6. Our Federal ID # is <number>. We are a Wisconsin Corporation.

_____

Authorized by

_____

Date

You may want to change item #5 if you're using a retainer instead of invoicing.

Again, what this form does is make it easy for them to pay you—because you're asking how to submit invoices to them properly.

Small company owners will occasionally look at you funny, saying, "Well, duh—send everything to me," but in general, people look at this form favorably—noting that I seem to have my act together.

With larger companies, it's important to find out exactly where invoices should be sent.

Just as important is the name of the Accounts Payable person—and when they can be reached. This way, you don't run into the situation where the invoice is due Thursday, you call them on Thursday afternoon—only to find out the Accounts Payable department is only open Tuesday through Thursday, from 8 AM to 3 PM. You don't want to have to wait until the following Tuesday to follow up—that's an additional five days—because when your terms are net 10 days, another five is an eternity.

Also find out whether you need a PO number. Once in a while someone at a larger company will try to get the project kick-started—that is, begun without the paperwork having been approved. I've had enough projects get postponed or canceled that I won't risk spending time on it until I get the official okay. Of course, this doesn't prevent the project from being canceled later, but at least you have a better chance at getting paid for the time you have already spent.

Finally I tell them the terms and that work will be stopped if invoices go past due, and have them sign this. It's easy to have problems with an invoice and to suddenly be waiting for that $7,900 check a lot longer than your cash flow plans had anticipated. I find that payment problems get resolved quite quickly once they hear the magic words, "Can we pick up a check today or should I have <name of developer> stop work until you can send the check out?"

This is the most valuable form that I've put in place to ensure that I don't have problems down the road. If somebody is going to take advantage of you, you can have them fill out forms for the next three days and you're not going to get around it, but in order to solve ordinary misunderstandings, this seems to work out quite well.

Using these forms

It is unlikely that you'll make a second in-person visit to deliver the Engagement Letter; in fact, I rarely even mail these—faxing them the same day as the sales call has been the most effective technique for a couple of years now. The customer gets the contract while it's still fresh in their minds, and you get an item off your To Do list quickly.

Getting these documents into the customer's hands as quickly as possible is important, of course, because, as with most things, the longer they have to wait, the more likely their interest is to wane.

Along the same lines, you should expect an answer almost immediately. The longer you have to wait, the less likely you'll get a positive answer back.

Chapter 15
The Process of
Developing Specifications

"Yeah, I called her up, she gave me a bunch of crap about me not listening to her, or something, I don't know, I wasn't really paying attention."—Harry
　—*Dumb and Dumber*

Describing how to go from a list of 12 bullet points to a 200-page Functional Spec is, along with estimating the size and scope of a project, another of the "big questions" in software development. Unfortunately, there are a lot of books with fancy diagrams, thousands of equations, and a bunch of $50 words—but they seem pretty far removed from reality. No sample template, no "how to" instructions for running a design meeting, and certainly no mention of the people—the irritable IS managers, distracted project leaders mooning over a lost boyfriend, or nonchalant users concentrating more on the weekend's football game pool than the meeting at hand. I sat down one Saturday afternoon, cleared off a table, put a blank sheet of paper on the desk, and asked, "How do my customer and I get from A to B?" Here's what I came up with.

This book began as a result of two questions. One was "How do I figure out how much an app will cost?" and the other was "What should go in a specification?" As I built up a specification skeleton, I found myself going by the seat of the pants, each one adding more good info, but still being built more haphazardly than methodically.

I tried to figure out how to improve my process a number of ways. First I looked at how other developers did it. I ran into some pretty horrific scenes.

One experience was following another fellow. I had been asked in to provide a quote for a new system at a furniture rental company that had been using a friend of the nephew of a neighbor of the owner (you know that story!), and the relationship had increasingly deteriorated over the years, to the point where the system was barely meeting the minimum business requirements.

I spent a good day working on a proposal for the company, and then spent nearly two more days over the next week revising it according to "newly discovered" requirements. We finally all met and I presented the proposal—which by that time was closer to a mini specification than a proposal, including several scenarios with various sets of functionality at different price points.

The owner of the company turned to the last page, scanned for the lowest price, and said, "We'll take everything in this," pointing to the document, "but we want 20% off of this price." I politely refused, and over the next two months, they looked around and eventually contracted with another developer who promised to meet that price. A couple of years later I heard from the controller of the company who had initially brought me in, and he asked if I would still be interested in the project—at the original price the owner wanted to pay. It turned out that the developer they turned to had developed some "issues," such as having to ride his 10-speed bicycle to the customer's site after losing his license twice in six months on DUI charges. Another issue was that the developer looked at documentation as unnecessary, and so did as little as possible, and the company continued to flounder.

I also had an experience with one of those "big consulting firms" that's been spun off from a 100-year-old accounting firm—one with the oak doors and a reception area the size of a football field on the 60th floor of the newest office tower in town. They had the process down pat—one of their senior managers would wine and dine a client while subtly selling them on the virtues of their firm. At the same time, his (or her) boss would fill the client's boss with platitudes about quality, teamwork, and "people being their most important asset."

Then, the moment the ink has dried on the contract, that senior manager would turn the client over to an arrogant 25-year-old Harvard MBA in a brand-new suit who, charging $250 an hour, condescendingly performs sterile interviews while filling binders and binders full of scenarios, plans, and studies and all of the aforementioned fancy diagrams (and a bunch of 8x10 color glossy pictures with circles and arrows and a paragraph on the back of each explaining what each one was). By the time they're done, the business has changed and the specification has been turned over to a suite of programmers who are given old tools, no training, and unreasonable deadlines—and who are not allowed to question a single item in the 200 pounds of specifications dumped on them.

Am I being harsh? Are all of the big consulting firms like this? Hell, no. But running into this shop was one of my first experiences, and it, together with the absurdity of the furniture rental company expecting me to pay for the mistakes of their replacement developer, forever scarred me, impressing upon me the need to deliver real value from the first meeting. Both experiences, at the extreme opposite ends of the spectrum, convinced me that a specification 1) was not a trivial item to be taken for granted, and 2) was an item that needed to deliver real value to the customer.

Next, I looked in books, figuring *someone* must have done this before. And of course I have dozens of books from folks like Watts Humphrey and Capers Jones. The ones with millions of equations and lots of $50 words. Unfortunately, despite looking through a lot of books, I didn't find a lot of help. Maybe for big projects (millions of dollars), these books might be useful, but for that $35,000 gig, or even the one for $120,000—ones where the company expected results, and a lot of them, for their money—there seemed to be a lot more overhead and theory than practical "here's how you do X" instruction.

But I was still stuck; none of these options did it for me. Somewhere out there I knew there were shops that built usable specifications; I just wasn't able to find one. So I built the process myself, relying on other people's advice and war stories, as well as tens of thousands of hours of experience myself, and here's what I've come up with.

Doesn't it seem that it could be more efficient? More productive? Dare I say… useful? I became more and more firmly convinced that it's up to us to deliver real value as soon as possible.

After I thought about it for a while, it dawned on me that it was pretty simple. I had a problem that the customer wanted solved. And a skeleton for a Functional Spec that defined the ultimate solution already in place. All I had to do was fill in the blanks.

Now, that may seem a little flip—it's more complicated than that, for sure. But having a good idea of where you're heading helps you keep on track during the journey.

The basic process is to start with a single idea, and flesh out the details until you have the functionality completely defined.

What is a Functional Spec?

The first thing we have to revisit is exactly what a Functional Spec is.

When you contract with a builder to design and build a custom house, the first person involved is an architect who designs the structure according to your wants, needs, and budget. The first pass of documentation of that design is a series of elevation drawings and blueprints where you can see what the house is going to look like. In more complex structures, the architect might even build a scale model of the house.

Similarly, when a software developer designs a system, the defining document is a Functional Specification—a document that describes what the user will be able to do with the system. These requirements include user interface appearance, behavior of the interface, data validation, business logic, and even how the user will perform the tasks they expect to use the system for. The Functional Spec doesn't, however, define how the programmer will build the underlying software.

Functional Specs are the end result of the analysis and design phases in both structured development and RAD. Specs for Agile Methodologies aren't much different—they, too, focus on describing the user's requirements in enough detail that the user understands how the system will work as well as so that the programmer can implement the physical manifestation of those requirements in code. The difference for Agile Methodologies is that the development of a Functional Specification is repeated for each individual feature that is implemented.

In Agile Methodology projects, the specifications will most likely be more informal, both in terms of the format as well as the process used to arrive at them. With structured development, the format for each screen, report, and function is tightly scripted, and the approval process is similarly controlled. The RAD process is looser, relying on the prototype to serve as part of the documentation.

The pain

The first thing you asked your customer during the sales call had to do with the pain they were experiencing. I emphasized that you needed to work with the customer until they were able to describe their pain in a single sentence or two. They're going to spend a lot of money (and time, and brainpower) on you and your application, in an attempt to change the status quo that they have a problem with, so you'd better get it right. If you haven't internalized their pain yourself, now's the time to do so.

The bullet points

Assuming that the solution to their pain involves a new or modified custom software application (that's what this book is about, right? Developing custom software applications?), it's time to define the major pieces. Again, this should have been covered in the initial sales call. However, having been through a few of those sales calls where the customer runs wild for an hour and a half, I understand it's possible that you came out of the meeting with a list that you don't feel all that comfortable with.

Roll up your sleeves, review those bullet points, and make sure your customer agrees that these are good descriptions of the buckets that you're going to use to categorize specific functionality. If he doesn't, then revise these bullet points until you're both happy with them.

These bullet points are to help you put some structure to the application, and I'd like to stress that you want to keep this list to a dozen or so. It's easy to start scribbling down specific features and functions, and before you know it, you've got a list of 70 or 80 items, and that's too many. The idea here is to group the functionality into a handful of subjects. A human can't keep track of 70 or 80 modules, and thus, trying to assign specific functions correctly when you've got so many modules to remember is bound to lead into chaos. A dozen is doable; 50 or 150 is not.

Given that this book is addressing a wide range of applications—from the $10,000 scheduling add-on for a small machine shop in the next town to the multi-million dollar production management system that will run a small Fortune 2000 company—I can't provide a single laundry list of how these bullet points should be put together or organized. The size of the app determines the scope of each bullet point.

Samples

For example, in the aforementioned scheduling add-on for Bob's Machine Tool Shoppe, the bullet points would be fairly granular.

- Create a new schedule

- Modify an existing schedule

- Print a schedule

- Run a variance report between planned and actual production

- And so on

In contrast, the production management system would have many components and modules, and each of these modules would be many times larger than the entire machine tool scheduling app. So, your first job would be to simply identify what the modules are.

- Product maintenance

- Part maintenance

- Vendor maintenance

- Customer maintenance

- Sales Order processing

- Exception reporting

- Batch scheduling

- User and security handling

- And so on

There are some, myself included, who believe that a multi-million dollar application is simply too big to successfully develop as a single entity, and that it should be broken down into more manageable pieces. Thus, I'd write a separate Functional Specification for each of these modules, knowing that part of the job would be to integrate dataset definition and interface data transfer between modules, and that continually changing requirements in each module would regularly impact other modules.

Each of these Functional Specifications, then, would start out life with a series of bullet points, and we're back to where we started with the machine tool shop app. (You could go ahead and define the pain for each module, but I don't think that's necessary.)

As another example, halfway between the two just given, take the knowledge base application described in Chapter 14, "An Agreement to do Work." The problem is that the old DOS-based application severely limits access to the information in the knowledge base to people who have desktop computers, who are attached to the local area network, and who have the application running on their computer. The customer has oodles of documents and other information, and wants to provide access to that information through a larger number of vehicles—laptops only intermittently connected to the network, remote computers whose only access is through the Web, handhelds that connect through a wireless mechanism or via a cell phone—and each of these may be running a different operating system.

The first pass at the bullet points for the new system, then, may look like the following.

- Information maintenance

- Information updates

- Information annotation by users

- Dynamic formatting of information

- Secure access across multiple platforms and hardware mechanisms

- User validation and authentication

- Multiple levels of query

- Memory of previous queries

How do you know whether you've got them right? You'll be able to go back later and check off whether or not that bullet point's functionality was met.

Creating and winnowing the list

Reviewing a list of bullet points that someone else created is easy, and, if done properly, the list looks like it was easy to do. But that's not quite the case—the synopsis of hours of meetings and stacks of file folders on the conference room table into a dozen phrases can be a challenging task even in the best of environments. With the wrong mix of people, it's possible to spin one's wheels for meeting after meeting if you're not careful.

If you're having trouble achieving consensus on the top-level bullet points, here's a trick my technical editor offered up. At a meeting of the players, brainstorm a list of areas they want to talk about and put each idea on a Post-it Note. After the first pass of brainstorming is complete, organize the notes on the wall by functional area, starting with Accounting on one end and Sales (or Zookeeping) on the other.

Next, prioritize each item as very important, sort of important, or "nice to have but not very important," and reposition the notes vertically on the wall according to these priorities, with the most important being placed higher on the wall.

Most likely, there will be a wide variety of items, some very broad and general, while others go into excruciating detail. Since this is a brainstorming session, now's not the time to evaluate the ideas—simply organize and categorize them. When you come across very detailed items, attach them to an appropriate higher-level item, so as to not lose the idea, while still not getting overwhelmed with too many items.

If you have your users actually get up from their chairs and do the moving around of the pieces of paper, they begin to take ownership right away.

The end result is a visual representation of the business from the customer's point of view, and it helps them to see quickly what might be missing or improperly emphasized.

The big challenge is to keep items on the same general level of granularity, not being too general and vague while at the same time not drilling too deeply too soon. The point of this exercise is to get an idea of the overall scope and identify the big wins for the system.

Requirements

Once you've identified the dozen or so bullet points, it's time to move into the requirements gathering stage. Requirements take the dozen bullet points to a deeper level. Remember that list of 70 or 80 or 210 items that you were tempted to come up with when listing your bullet points? Those are requirements. More specifically, they're the detailed description of things that have to be functional—but not how those items are going to work, nor when and where.

The requirements will end up being a detailed list of all of the "whats" that need to be done, and some developers include the "whats" that were considered but postponed or canceled altogether. This is not as much a "CYA" action as much as a means to communicate fully about items that users might otherwise assume are included or are part of another item. If you draw boundaries from both "will do" and "won't do" perspectives, communication is clearer.

If your bullet points were created properly, your requirements can easily be assigned to a specific bullet point. If, on the other hand, you keep coming up with requirements that don't fit under any of the bullet points, then either the requirements aren't appropriate, or you need to revisit the definition of your bullet points. That's okay—you may recall the word "iterate" used once or twice in earlier chapters…

What is a requirement?

It seems simple but in the heat of discussions with a customer, it's easy to move from the "what" you're trying to accomplish with a specific type of functionality to the "how" it's going to be accomplished. If you are told that your customer needs to "track taxable status as part of customer information," the next thing you will probably hear is "and put the check box on the main customer screen next to the customer ID number." While you may not want to lose this information, it's not a requirement in and of itself. What you will want to track, though, is the "why."

How do you tell whether an item is a properly framed requirement? One acid test is whether or not the statement can be tested. Ask your customer how they will know whether or not you've delivered the requirement to their satisfaction. In the previous example, suppose they answer the "testable" question by saying, "We want to separate customers according to their taxable status and level of taxation."

This tells you that they're expecting a flag for whether or not they're taxable, and a second entity that holds the level of taxation. Since the level of taxation isn't identified or described in the initial requirement, you now know that the requirement has to be amended to include a second field. And think of how much easier it will be to add this second field now, than after the screen (or whatever) has been coded and tested internally!

So, a requirement 1) is a statement of what is to be done, 2) can be tested, and 3) does not indicate how something will be implemented or used.

Let's run through this again with a larger example. Let's say the client identified "Process Credit Application and Track Lending Decisions" as a high-level requirement. I would ask them to describe how this works today or even if they do such a thing. They say yes, we do this, and the manual process works as follows:

1. A customer submits a credit app by fax.

2. A clerk stamps it with received information, date, and time.

3. It is forwarded to a credit clerk.

4. The credit clerk notes what time they got it.

5. They review the app to see whether necessary information is completed:

    - If it's incomplete, they return it to the receiving clerk, who notifies the customer.

    - If the information is complete, they run a credit check on the customer.

6. They then score the person's application and give the decision (accept/reject) and documents back to the receiving clerk, who notifies the customer of the decision.

Some customers can readily give this sort of process overview while others could not for all the money in the world. For those others, an alternative technique could be to draw a flow chart on a white board, with boxes identifying each step and lines connecting the boxes. Note that this works best if the organization already has this process in place. If they're creating a new process, they very likely will have a hard time giving you this sort of context since it's new to them as well—so they're making it up as they go. In this type of situation, you will have to resort to really leading them through how something might work.

The other thing you should be doing at this time is to review documents, materials, forms, and other items that they use during the course of executing this process—again, in order to identify requirements—the WHATs and WHYs, not the HOWs, WHEREs, or WHENs. You should not have had preceding discussion without having at least an example of a credit app and hopefully also a credit bureau report sample. What "whats" do you now have?

- Input of credit application

- Calculation of credit score

- Acquisition of credit bureau report

- Integration of credit bureau information

- Tracking of events including receipt, decision, and response

- Credit application processing statistics report

Note that "obtain credit report through the Internet" is not on the list. That's a HOW, not a WHAT. The credit report might be downloaded from the Internet, but it also might come in the mail, or via fax.

Now, what about the possibility that you are enhancing an existing system such as the one just described? Now they want to put up a Web site where potential customers enter a credit application. So the WHATs in this case might be...

- Customer enters credit application information.

- Application completeness is verified before it is sent.

- Customer is sent a message that we have received application.

- If more than one hour goes by and a decision has not been made, customer is sent another message telling them it is still being processed.

- Application information is directly fed into existing application and receipt information is noted.

If these techniques don't work—you know, the customer stares with a blank look when asked how something is done—then you can start from the end and work your way forward. Ask them what reports the system should provide. If the process is one that's in place, they will probably have samples of these reports already available (or they can get them). Once you can get them to define the output, you can work your way back to the input required to produce that output. You can also use this technique to confirm the completeness of their describing what needs to be done. It is possible they could describe the whole application processing process and it might never come to light that a monthly application statistic report is required.

In addition, this section is where you start identifying system capacities and throughput requirements. For example, statements like "A new record must be committed within two seconds" or "Ninety-seven percent of queries must return a result within four seconds" as well as "The system must be able to handle at least 200 concurrent users" and "The system must be up between the hours of 5 AM and 2 AM" are also requirements. You can think of these as constraints, rather than features. They may map to specific bullet points, such as the requirements about commit and query time, or they may apply system-wide, such as the concurrent user and downtime requirements.

The Use Cases

The next step is to develop a more detailed set of user expectations.

What is a Use Case?

Use Cases are a way to organize the bullet points, requirements, and process descriptions already discussed in this chapter to create a detailed description of how the user wants to use the system in the course of their business processes. By examining and expanding upon these documents, you end up with a series of nouns and verbs that map to singular tasks that the user can perform. These tasks become screens, reports, and processes.

Purpose

The requirements specify the functionality of a system—the WHAT—while the resulting Use Cases describe the HOW of that same functionality. The Use Case is also the basis for testing and acceptance.

The Use Case methodology consists of two elements—the actors and the Use Cases themselves. The actors are external actions or stimuli that influence the system. The Use Cases are the responses of the system to the stimuli of the actor. This type of mechanism easily separates the internal structure and operation of the system from the external usage of the system, as it should properly be.

The Cliff's Notes version of how a Use Case works

Formal Use Cases have a graphic notation that includes icons for actors (stick men), Use Cases (ellipses), interactions (arrows), and the system itself (a box). There are just a few rules to be followed when creating a Use Case.

- Each actor has to interact with at least one Use Case.

- Each Use Case has to interact with at least one actor.

- Use Cases have no interactions with other Use Cases.

- Actors have no interactions with other actors.

- The user must be outside the system; the Use Case must be inside the system.

A simplified example of the Use Case model for a video store is shown in **Figure 1**. The example shows the interactions of three actors (customer, store employee, and video tape supplier) with the system. Note that the rules just described are all followed. For example, if a customer were to ask a store employee where the water fountain is, that would be an interaction between two actors, but that interaction isn't part of the system.

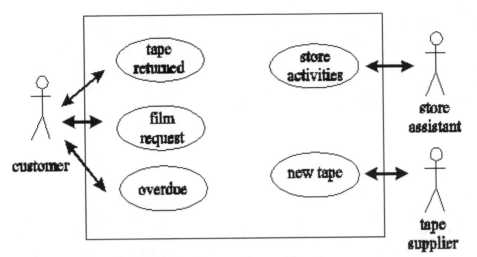

Figure 1. *A sample Use Case diagram for a video store.*

Actors
Actors specify an entity that exists outside the system and interacts with the system. Note that an actor is not the same as a user. The user is an actual person who uses the system, while the actor represents a role that a user (or even another system) can play.

Use Cases
A Use Case is a specification of what should be performed by the system as a response to the stimuli provided by an actor.

Interaction
An interaction shows the transaction flow between an actor and a Use Case. An interaction may be a process like a data flow or it might be a physical action like pushing a button.

Creating a practical Use Case
While there are a number of third-party software tools that help you model Use Cases, it's a good idea to start simple until you get the hang of it, and then use a tool to help automate the drudgery and ensure that the steps are all followed properly.

Most people start out Use Cases on a 3x5 card, each card representing a single Use Case. They'll identify the Use Case by name, and the actor(s), and then list the interactions (transactions) between the system and the actor. These interactions are the Use Case, and become the basis for the test plan as well.

Current Situation
Input of Credit Application Use Case

(Clerk) Credit applications are faxed in by a salesperson. I check the fax machine every 15 minutes. I inspect the application to make sure information is complete; if it's not I call the salesperson and have them update the application and resend it. Once I have a complete application, I request a credit report using our terminal that is connected to the credit bureau. I print the credit report and staple it to the application. I then enter the application into our tracking database. The database gives me a tracking number, which I note on the credit application, and then I give the paperwork to the supervisor.

(Supervisor) I review the application to see whether we want to grant credit to this customer. To make this decision, I consider the person's outstanding debt, amount to be financed, and collateral. If they are creditworthy, I assign a finance rate, also based on credit worthiness, and indicate the application is approved. Otherwise, I indicate the application is denied. I return the paperwork to the clerk.

(Clerk) I fax a form letter back to the salesperson advising them whether the credit was approved or denied. I update the tracking system with the approval/denial status. I then file the paperwork.

Prototypes

The next step after building Use Cases, for RAD systems, is to build prototypes. One of the major differentiating features of RAD (vs. structured development and Agile Methodologies) is the use of prototypes during the specification process.

What is a prototype?

A prototype is a seemingly live version of the software application that the user can work with in order to see how it functions. A prototype isn't actually live, though. It's a version with limited functionality—very limited functionality—that is made to help the user envision the application. A structured development specification would be akin to looking at a car's brochure, while a RAD prototype would be getting behind the wheel of a car, slamming the door, and taking the wheels for a 10-minute test drive, and the live system would be loading up the car with four kids, groceries, and soccer gear, and schlepping around in the rain for an afternoon.

Unlike structured development, where the most that a user will see is mocked-up screen and report layouts in a 200-page spec, a prototype can actually be run on a computer. Prototypes can vary in sophistication and complexity. At the low end, a prototype may simply be a slide show of screens loaded with dummy data, so that the user can visualize how the application is started, what the menu structure looks like, how the screens are displayed, and what screens come after others.

At the high end, a prototype may actually exhibit some functionality within screens, showing data choices, interaction between controls, and so on.

A sample prototype

For example, let's suppose we have an order entry system. The main menu would have choices for Orders, Order Support, Quote and Project Maintenance, Invoicing, Forecasting, Cancellations, RMAs (Return Material Authorizations), and Reports.

The Orders menu item may break down further into Order Entry, Company Defaults, and Customer Defaults (each of which is explained shortly). A simple prototype may just display each of these screens with hard-coded values in each field. The user of the prototype can navigate from screen to screen but can't change values in any field, add or delete records, or see the dynamics of how a specific screen works.

Let's further suppose that the company for whom this particular order entry system is being written has a number of specific design requirements regarding default values. For instance, when a new customer is added to the order entry system, the company has a number of default values that are to be used to populate the new customer's record, such as Shipper, Shipping Method, Payment Method, and Credit Terms.

Each customer record, of course, may be customized, so that Customer A uses the company's default shipper and default shipping method as Customer A's default shipper and shipping method, but Customer B has a different shipper and shipping method as their defaults. Okay, that's wordy. In real terms, the company prefers to use UPS Ground, so when Customer A (a new customer) is added to the order entry system, Customer A's default shipper is UPS and the default shipping service is Ground.

When new orders are added for Customer A, the order will be shipped via UPS Ground by default, but can be overridden at the order level.

Thus, when Customer B is added, UPS also is the default shipper and Ground is the default shipping service. However, in this case, the company wants to use a different shipper for Customer B (or maybe Customer B wants to use a different shipper). So the default shipper for Customer B is changed to Airborne and the default service is changed to Overnight. Orders for Customer B are automatically shipped via Airborne Overnight—but again, this can be changed at the order level.

What all this means is that the Orders menu option may further break down into Order Entry, Company Defaults, and Customer Defaults. The Company Defaults screen is where the default values that are used to populate a new customer's record are added (in this case, UPS and Ground Service), while Customer Defaults is where Customer B's defaults are changed to Airborne and Overnight.

Since this setup can be confusing—even after the explanation, it may not be clear—showing this menu structure and sample screens from each menu option makes sense.

In an even more complex prototype, examples of functionality and interaction and representative data may be built into the demo.

For example, the controls enabled on a screen may change according to the choices a user makes elsewhere on that screen. In the same order entry application, a customer may qualify for a discount based on participation in a special promotion. If the user enters the customer's participation code, the Discount Percentage field becomes enabled and the user can select the appropriate discount.

A second sample prototype

Another example comes into play when the controls visible on a screen may change according to the selection of a control on a previous screen. For example, in an order entry screen, the user may select the type of payment a customer is going to make—via a check, credit card, invoice, or on consignment. These choices could be presented via a group of option buttons. After choosing the type of payment, the user would move to a second screen where additional information is entered. The fields available on that screen would vary according to which choice was made on the previous screen—a place for entering check amount, number, and date would be visible for a check payment, while credit card number and expiration date would be visible for a credit card payment.

Another example would be showing the choices that populate a list box or combo box control, and how those items vary according to a previous selection. For example, suppose the user had a choice of which shipper to use for a shipment. The screen could present the choices in a combo box—UPS, US Postal Service, Federal Express, Airborne, and Customer Pick Up. Depending on which of those shipment choices was selected, the choices in the Bill Who combo box would vary. For UPS, the available choices might be Shipper, Customer, and Third Party, while for US Postal Service, there might not be any choices—the only possibility would be for the Shipper to pay for shipping, so that choice would be displayed and disabled so the user couldn't change it.

A prototype might also have a certain type of functionality working in one area of the application but not others; the specification would then refer to the area where it was implemented as an example, and then describe the specific implementation in the second area just in the spec.

For example, in the aforementioned order entry example, a requirement might be for the ability to assign default values for customers. Customer A always wants to ship via UPS, while Customer B always wants to ship via Airborne. Additionally, Customer A wants to use UPS Second Day, while Customer B wants to use Airborne Overnight. Furthermore, if Customer A wants to change from UPS to FedEx, they want FedEx Overnight as the default FedEx service, while if Customer B wants to change from Airborne to FedEx, they want to FedEx Second Day as their default service. Each of these rules is stored in a table, of course, so the procedure would be to describe how the rules work, not what the specific rules are.

This same behavior, where one default value attached to an entity would then control another default value, but choices other than the default value also have subsequent default behaviors attached to them, could be found in other places in the application. How to package an item might be one example. The product that a customer usually buys would be one example—with how that product is packaged or delivered being a second default. But other products possibly purchased by that customer would also have default packaging choices.

Instead of demonstrating all these choices in a prototype, simply discussing the fields and what they are dependent on would be sufficient, pointing to the default shipper and shipment service default mechanism as a live example.

These actions are examples of how a more sophisticated prototype would work in front of the customer.

The specification process with prototyping

The process of developing a specification when prototyping—from gathering requirements through delivery of the final wad of paper—is much like that of structured development, only better. Structured development is sort of bland when compared to the development process when you have the ability to demonstrate prototypes.

And it's a lot of fun. I never fail to get "oohs" and "aahs" during this stage of the game. Demonstrating a prototype is our version of performing magic before the client's eyes—making, literally, something appear out of nothing.

While prototyping is an essential part of the development of a Functional Spec, since it allows the user the best chance at seeing the application "in action" (and, again, "in action" is what you're aiming for), there are a few tips and tricks you should employ to take best advantage of it.

Sometimes, a customer's previous experience was with a mainframe style development process, where the programmer followed the structured development process, and the only thing the customer saw during the specification was rough sketches of screens on pads of paper. And the idea of iterating on the computer screen was completely foreign—it was a lot of hard work to make the sketch on that pad of paper appear on the screen—so to request a change once it'd been programmed was akin to asking the programmer to start over from scratch.

And many other times, it seems as if the current program being designed is replacing a version running either on a character-based screen or on a DOS-based PC. As a result, the customer has been through the process with another developer who always seems to have spent most of their time saying, "No, that can't be done" or "No, that would be too hard." To have the current crop of RAD tools for GUIs, such as Visual FoxPro or Visual Basic, at one's fingertips, ready to make a customer's desires appear on the computer screen, is a wonderful feeling.

Beginning with the "pain"

Much of the specification process is the same. Your first question to your user is "Where does it hurt?" More specifically, you'll take those dozen or so bullet points that you got from the sales call, and work from there as explained earlier.

First, you'll expand each of the bullet points into a series of requirements. From that, you generate Use Cases. Use Cases create user interfaces for input ("screens") as well as output interfaces—reports of one form or another. During the discussion of the Use Cases come ideas for screens and reports, and here's where prototyping kicks in.

Let's run through the development of a typical bullet point.

Getting started

Let's suppose the bullet point is a flexible customer default screen for order entry as described in Chapter 31, "Your Secret Weapon: An Administrative Assistant." Here's the pain:

- Custom customer requirements generate lots of exceptions, each of which has to be handled manually, creating a costly administrative burden.

This generates a series of requirements. Here are a few of them:

- Must be able to store company defaults that are assigned to each new customer.

- Must be able to override those defaults at the customer level.

- Must be able to override those defaults at the order level.

Here's an example of the beginnings of a Use Case for the first requirement:

The Company Defaults screen will contain one or more values for each of the following fields: FOB, Terms, Discount, Pricing Details, Packing Instructions, Documentation Required, Ship Type, Shipper, Ship Method, Service, and Payment Method.

The user will be able to select one of the values for each field and designate it as the default value for that field. This selected value will be used as the default value for the related field in a customer record added to the system. Note that if the user changes the default value for a company default field at a point in time, all customer records added up to that point in time will retain their original default values—the system will not update the values in those customer records.

For example, the Ship Type is set to "Bulk—Short Haul" and the Shipper is set to "UPS" on January 10. Customer A is added to the system on January 12. The default Ship Type for Customer A is "Bulk—Short Haul" and the default Shipper for Customer A is "UPS." On January 15, the Company Default is changed to "Bulk—Long Haul" and the Shipper is set to "Yellow Freight." On January 17, Customer B is added to the system, and Customer B's record has "Bulk—Long Haul" and "Yellow Freight" as the default values, but Customer A's record still contains the "Bulk—Short Haul" and "UPS" values.

From this basic description come more specific instructions on how the functionality will work for the Company Default screen.

The following values will initially be included in each of the following fields:

```
FOB: Milwaukee, Des Moines, Winona
Terms: Net 30, Net 10, Net 5 1%, COD
Discount: None, 1%, 2%
Pricing Details: None, Per Sales Rep, Per Order Dept.
Packing Instructions: Wrap and Stack, Individual, Per Pallet
Documentation Required: Standard, None, Per Location
Ship Type: Bulk - Short Haul, Bulk - Long Haul, Parcel Post, Pick Up
Shipper: UPS, FedEx, Airborne, Yellow Freight, Roadrunner, Burlington Northern,
USPS and Sales Rep
Ship Method: Standard, Overnight, Two Day
Service: Ground, Next Day Early AM, Next Day Priority, Next Day Economy, Two
Day Express, Two Day, Standard
Payment Method: Bill Shipper, Bill Receiver, COD, Third Party Charge
```

The user will be able to add additional values for each of these fields from the Lookup Maintenance form.

And from these instructions comes the first prototype screen for the Company Default Maintenance form, as shown in **Figure 2**.

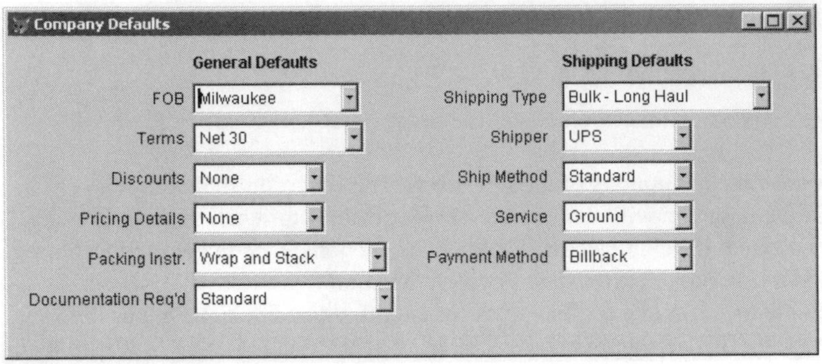

Figure 2. The first iteration of the Company Defaults screen.

As soon as the user runs this form, they'll discover new requirements. Now we're iterating.

Iterating

The whole point of prototyping is to give the user the ability to test drive the application. In fact, if they didn't try out the application and find things lacking the first time out, wouldn't you be sort of disappointed? It would mean the user wasn't very demanding, since in all but the most trivial applications, it is pretty hard to get things right immediately.

So when presented with this application, the user goes to the Company Defaults screen and sees a couple of problems that weren't apparent when the functionality of the screen was discussed at the previous meeting. Note that I'm presenting somewhat of a simplified example here—hopefully the issues raised in this first iteration would have been discovered by a skilled developer during the first round of analysis, but they may not have been, given how the problem was posed by the customer.

So let's look at a couple of problems that may be encountered during the iteration of this supposedly simple screen.

The first situation that the user will discover is that the values in some combo boxes need to depend on the values in other combo boxes. For example, there are four shipment types— Bulk—Short Haul, Bulk—Long Haul, Parcel, and Parcel Expedited. Not all shippers provide services to handle each of these shipment types. Federal Express, for example, solely handles Parcel Expedited, while UPS handles all four. Thus, the contents of the Shipper combo box vary according to the selection made in the Shipping Type combo.

Continuing along this line, how the Service combo box is populated depends on which Shipper is chosen. If UPS is chosen, then the Services may include Next Day, Two Day, Three Day, and Ground, while if FedEx is chosen, the services would simply be Overnight by 10:30 AM, Overnight Standard, and Second Day.

As the user works with this a bit, they will realize that they need to be able to specify a default shipper for each of the shipment types. There isn't just a single default Shipment Type—there are four shipment types, and they need to specify a different shipper and shipment method for each of those types.

Another item that the user will eventually run into is that the available choices in each of the combo boxes in the Company Defaults screen are populated from minor entity tables that are maintained through a Lookup Values Maintenance form. This means the domain of possible choices can change. An experienced analyst should recognize this problem at the outset, and ask the user how to handle this situation as soon as the ability for the user to change the domain of values is made available. However, we're all human, and it may not become apparent from the user's initial statement of requirements that this will be the case and the analysis may miss the requirement given the usual commotion of a design meeting.

The ability to add and delete values to the domains that populate each combo box will create one of several dynamic situations. The first question that has to be asked is whether a value added to a domain can truly be "deleted" or if it is simply marked inactive and unavailable for future use.

Suppose the value can truly be deleted. Further suppose that when a customer record is added, the actual value from each of these combo boxes is stored in the customer record. (I know, theoretically that's bad design, but it could happen in the real world.) That is, when Customer C's record is created, the value "UPS" is stored in the Shipper field in Customer C's record. What should happen if, later on, UPS is removed from the domain of available shippers? It can either be left in Customer C's record as a legacy value, or it can be changed to a different value (or set to a blank). All of this has to be done in the logic of the Lookup Value Maintenance form. What a mess!

On the other hand, suppose that when a customer record is added, a foreign key that points to the value of the combo box (via a lookup table) is stored in the customer record. When Customer D's record is created, the primary key for "UPS" in a Lookup table is stored in the customer record. This case is nearly as bad—if UPS is removed from the domain of available shippers, the foreign key has to be reset to 0 or set to the primary key of a different shipper, but it's marginally better because you're not messing with the actual values.

A better choice is for a value in a lookup domain to be marked as inactive, unavailable, disqualified, or some such moniker.

In this situation, no additional logic needs to be added to the Lookup Value Maintenance screen; instead, it's added to the Company Defaults screen, which is where it belongs. (Or, for the OOP purists among you, to the Company Defaults business object.)

As a result, the scenario changes. When Customer E's record is created, the primary key for UPS is entered in to Customer E's record as a foreign key. When, later on, UPS is marked as inactive in the Company Defaults screen, the business logic for the Company Defaults screen disables the availability of UPS from then on, and provides an interface for the user to determine what to do next. According to the requirements, the user may be able to keep UPS for Customer E, even though UPS is no longer available for future use. Alternately, the user may be required to select a new default shipper for Customer E (and every other customer who has UPS currently selected as their default shipper).

The second iteration of the Company Defaults screen, then, becomes something like shown in **Figure 3**.

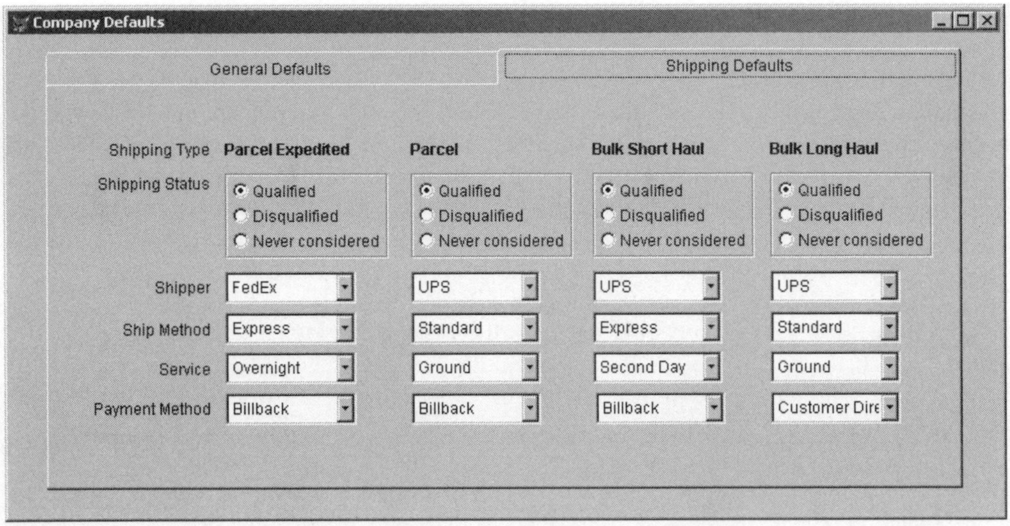

Figure 3. The second iteration of the Company Defaults screen.

It's not difficult to imagine how this functionality may continue to evolve. For example, the customer may discover a new requirement—that of being able to see a "snapshot" of all shippers and their qualified/disqualified/never considered status in a single list, as shown in **Figure 4**.

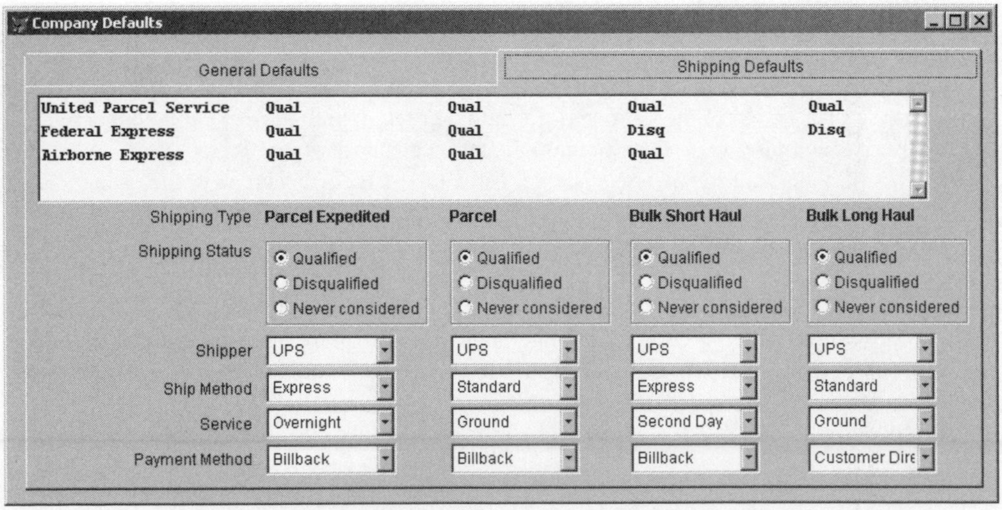

Figure 4. The third iteration of the Company Defaults screen.

Particularly given the extraordinarily flexible capabilities of today's RAD tools, to iterate functionality on this screen several more times is easy. In fact, it could be argued that it's too easy—many readers have probably run into the situation where the customer keeps asking for more and more changes as they learn how broad the capabilities of today's tools are. At some point, you have to tell the customer to stop.

The point is that RAD allows the customer to test drive the application before a lot of work goes into the actual development—the three screens shown in this chapter took a total of perhaps five minutes to whip up.

Tips on the politics of prototypes

I usually develop the prototype off-site, on the basis of what has been discussed at a design meeting, and then demonstrate the prototype at the next meeting. I don't strive to make the prototype as robust as possible. Instead of actually putting a lot of code in the prototype, I put as little as possible so there's as little chance as possible that something is going to blow up. This means hard-coding sample data, instead of trying to play tricks and showing off live data in a few places.

Depending on the progress of the meeting, I may put together a very rough prototype while the customers are watching, merely to demonstrate the look and feel of an idea, instead of using a whiteboard. This doesn't happen very often, because this activity is subject to one of those "20-80" rules—80% of the work is done in 20% of the time, and it's often difficult for the customer to understand why it took another three hours to "finish up" a prototype that they saw fleshed out in just 20 minutes before their eyes. What they don't see is the review of the screen that was thrown together, making sure that pieces weren't missed, impossible situations weren't constructed, and that needless or wasteful functionality wasn't added. Nor do they see the minute tweaking—aligning of controls, correct phrasing and spelling of prompts and labels, populating of controls with fake, and temporary, data, and so on.

One common refrain I hear, upon the viewing of repeated prototypes, is "You must be just about done." This can easily be addressed by indicating that the prototype is simply smoke and mirrors—no code, no data, just a few simple hard-coded routines to demonstrate the flow of screens and processes. Many customers can become quite a nuisance at this time—you might even consider displaying messages like "Placeholder for mortgage calculation routine" and "Placeholder for report output mechanism." The key is to show the user what is supposed to happen at a given time, but also emphasize that it doesn't actually work at all yet.

Another issue that comes up occasionally has to do with ownership of the prototype. First of all, the prototype is represented in full by the Functional Spec—all menus, screens, and so on have screen shots in the spec. Second, since the prototype is built for the customer, and they're paying for the time spent developing it, it of course belongs to them. However, often the prototype is built on top of my foundation of common code, and they don't get that. I'll give them the EXE and any support files, but not the code itself.

Tips on creating prototypes

In order to build a prototype, you'll need prototyping software. If you're using a RAD tool like Visual FoxPro or Visual Basic, you can do this easily. Hopefully, you're using a framework that puts a lot of the basic stuff together for you. The one thing you aren't going to create at this point is your data tables.

So you build screens with dummy data coded in them. Data comes later—what they can put in controls and what they can take out. It can be a pain to have to manually type sample data into forms over and over, however.

Thus, for common functions, consider having a set of dummy tables with values that you can plug in, instead of having to hard-code the values each time. For example, everyone has a customer table. I have a table with Al Anxious, Bob Boisterous, Carla Cunning, Dave Dashing, and Ellen Eager (and so on) as customers, and use those values instead of typing them in each time. It's just as fast to dig up values from that table in the Init() of a form as it is to type them manually into an array that populates a control.

Also prototype your reports, even if you hand sketch them and dump them via ASCII to a report writer. Your reports, perhaps more importantly than anything else, will control what data shows up.

Use the same values in your screens and your reports so the user can see the linkage between the two.

Make it obvious that your screens and reports are prototypes—mark them with a watermark of "prototype" as a background for each screen. Or use a legend in the corner of each screen and report that says "Prototype 2003."

And, gosh, document your source and your tables in your prototype. And when I say document, I mean WHY, not WHAT/HOW—it's very important because you're capturing business rules.

Tips on demonstrating prototypes

At some point, though, you're going to *demonstrate* your prototype. Here's how.

Package up your prototype and test it. How many times have you heard "It worked fine on my machine" or "The demo ran fine last night"? This experience doesn't set well with a customer—having them see that you can't even package a prototype properly won't exactly inspire confidence in your ability to deliver functioning software later on. Remember, we're still in the specification phase—you don't necessarily have the job. It's not unheard of for a design/build firm to create a design for a building, and then have the client go to another shop to have the building actually constructed, because the design/build firm demonstrated a lack of capability during the design phase.

Scripting your demo

Write out what you're going to demonstrate. In other words, create a script that you're going to follow, and that your customer can use to follow along as well. A script helps give shape to your presentation, but also helps keep your customer on track. If they start to get sidetracked, it's easier to get them back on course by pointing out how much more there is to demonstrate.

The script also serves as a checklist of functionality—if you don't demonstrate a function, it'll be difficult for them to claim that the final app is missing something.

Where does this script come from? From the Use Cases, of course! If, at some point, they discover that your demo is missing some key feature, go back to the Use Cases and look for that feature—if it's not found, it means that the Use Cases aren't complete.

Finally, the script serves as the start for the tutorial portion of your user manual or Help file.

Once you've prepared your script, send your customer a copy in advance if you can, so they can be prepared for what you're going to cover. Oftentimes they're not going to read it, but if they do, so much the better. And in the worst case, they've got a copy that they can follow once you start your demonstration.

At the demonstration of your prototype, follow your script. It's so easy to get sidetracked; having a written checklist of items to cover is the easiest way to keep your customer (and yourself, if you're a chatty kind of person) on track. As you go through the script, make notes on your copy about changes, questions, and so on.

Changing your prototype on the fly

It's tempting, when demonstrating your prototype, to want to react to requests immediately. "That field needs to be bigger" or "Those items need to be in reverse order" or "We need a second field for a purchase order number suffix."

One word: Don't.

Don't try to make changes to your prototype on the fly. You'll get distracted, trying to make things look "just so" as you're playing in the development environment, and your customer may well get distracted too. And it's easy to try to make "one little change"—but after the first attempt, something goes wrong, so you try to fix it, and that doesn't work, so you try to fix it again, and again, and before you know it, you've spent 15 or 20 minutes making that one little adjustment. You'll blow your customers' confidence in you (it's probably better that they don't see how sausage is made) as well as the budget for the meeting.

Tips on "keep overnight" prototypes

At some point, you may want to provide a prototype that they can "have overnight." Well, let me try to talk you out of this. You may think that you're just leaving a prototype at the customer's site for them to test drive in a more leisurely fashion than if you were to hover over them, watching every move, but in reality, you're shipping software. To you, it's a prototype—but to them, it's the first cut at the app, and they're not going to be nearly as forgiving as you would expect given that this is pre-alpha-level software.

Okay, given this disclaimer, and that you're still interested in providing them a prototype—or, perhaps more accurately, you've been badgered into providing them a prototype even though you didn't want to—here are some tips.

Preparing

First of all, as I just said, keep in mind the whole time that you're delivering software. You'll need to smooth out all of the rough edges—you'll have to test every function and feature so that the user doesn't end up in a morass of error messages for which the only recourse is to kill the task, or, worse, shut down the machine.

This doesn't mean that you have to employ a full-blown testing department—rather, you should be developing the prototype from the ground up so that there is no functionality except that which you specifically build in. That way, when they open up a menu item that isn't attached to a screen yet, they either get a dummy screen stub that's the same for every unfinished menu option, or they get nothing at all, because there is no code attached to the menu item at all. The one thing you don't want to do is attach the menu item to the start of a screen that doesn't work because there is unfinished code in the Init(), and when the user runs it, they get a recursion of errors. Their first thought will be that you're a rotten programmer, not that they're working on a prototype.

Second, when I say "smooth out the rough edges," make sure that it's clear that this is a prototype. You don't want errors to occur. That's it. You don't have to create new and clean functionality to make the prototype look finished.

It's your call as to whether you want to align all of the labels, test the tab order of controls, and other cosmetic items. Personally, I do, because I don't want the user to subconsciously get the idea that a choppy UI is my idea of "finished."

On the other hand, I do take care to include a simple dummy stub screen for every menu item that simply says "Not enabled in prototype." That tells them that they're not encountering an error while at the same time providing no functionality that they can end up breaking.

Next, you'll need to provide a user manual. This doesn't have to be a fancy document, and it may not even be on paper, but you need to provide some preliminary documentation on each feature or function that the user can work with. This documentation is the beginning of your spec as well as a place to document questions that have come up so far during the analysis phase.

If you don't want to provide paper documentation, consider building the stub of your Help file now, and connecting the hooks to each feature or function. If you do so, you'll need to allow the user to print each topic—and be sure to identify each topic so that when the user gives you handwritten notes on one of those printed-out topics, you'll be able to identify which topic it is.

Fourth, you'll need to provide a way to document feedback from the user. Chapter 24, "Bug Reporting and Application Feedback," covers one way to document a variety of types of feedback from the user; now is a great time to get them used to that mechanism.

Finally, you'll need a delivery document—something that confirms that they got something of value from you, when they got it, what they're supposed to do with it, and when they'll be done, or will "return" it. If you simply e-mail them a ZIP file and rely on them to get around to doing it on their own, you'll find yourself getting calls like "It seems that this ZIP file is corrupt" at 4:48 in the afternoon on the day before your next design meeting. Even if you're around to get the phone call, and can walk them through whatever problems they're having, they're sure not going to be able to provide enough quality feedback as if they are given formal instructions on how to use the prototype and what they're expected to do with it.

Installation

Once you've got all of this put together, you need to think about how you're actually going to deliver it to your customer. The first issue is the actual installation mechanism. Your choices are, generally, to use a professional installation program or to hand-install it on a single machine. Depending on the type of software you're developing in, that choice may be already made for you. Assuming that you've got the choice, there are pros and cons for both methods.

If you use an installation program, your customer might be tempted to install the prototype on a variety of machines that don't meet the minimum requirements for your software. I remember once providing a demo where the stated minimum was 16 MB of RAM (okay, this was a loooong time ago); he called a few hours later complaining that it wasn't running very well. I stopped in the next day only to find that he had installed the program on his own personal desktop that had the bare minimum—16 MB of RAM. However, he had two instances of my program running—in addition to copies of Word, Excel, a terminal emulation program that accessed the mainframe, and a date book/calendaring application. No wonder my app was running slowly!

It's also possible that they might try to install the demo on a machine that isn't fit for it at all. These days, you can specify which platforms (that's spelled "versions of Windows") an application is going to be installed on—if you don't check Windows 95 or Windows 98 and they try to install it on that type of box, you might end up with more support calls than you had bargained for.

Thus, a hand install may allow you to restrict what machine they run their demo on, so that you're not faced with those types of support issues.

On the other hand, a hand install doesn't always look very professional, and may require a great deal of tweaking, getting files in the right locations, components registered properly, and so on.

And if you deliver your prototype via the installation program that you're going to use for your application, you get an earlier shot at working out any problems with it as well. Your users get used to seeing what their final application is going to look like, and you can determine early on additional requirements—like the need to support platforms that you didn't think were going to be needed.

The bottom line is that you don't want to spend time troubleshooting installation issues for a prototype—and that type of scenario can injure their confidence in you.

Purposes and scripts

Providing a script for the user to follow with your prototype is just as important—arguably, more important—when you're leaving it with them to work with on their own. I've seen users act in the most random of behaviors when left to their own devices. Sure, you can't guarantee that they'll act in a completely rational manner when you walk out the door, but you can give yourself (and your app) a fighting chance.

So, the first thing you'll need to provide is a defined scope and purpose for the prototype. This may be simply a list of Use Cases that are available for testing with this particular version of the prototype. You don't want to have the user complain that they can't look at the purchase order screens when the prototype you're delivering doesn't have the purchase order module provided at all.

Next, you'll need to provide scripts for them to follow. As with the script that you would follow yourself, you'll create a script for each Use Case, illustrating how to go about following the Use Case using the prototype. As mentioned, this script will provide the basis for the tutorial for that feature or function. It won't be complete, of course, because the functionality isn't complete—it's just a start.

You'll also need to provide a way that they can provide feedback, similar to the AFI report described in Chapter 24, "Bug Reporting and Application Feedback." This is a good time to indoctrinate them in the proper way of providing feedback—identifying the exact steps to reproduce the problem, describing what happened, and what they were expecting to happen.

Finally, you'll want to provide a time limit so that they get around to the work—if you leave the prototype with them with the suggestion that they call you "when you've had a chance to work with it a bit," you may never hear from them again!

Calling it quits

The advantage to the prototyping process is that you can go through multiple iterations and hone in very precisely on what functionality they're looking for. This advantage, however, is also the downside—it's possible for the user to iterate to death—that you'll never been done with the project.

I had a customer with whom this happened a few years ago. They started out with a simple conversion of an existing application to a newer version of the software it was written in. They were adamant that there would be no new functionality added to the system, as it was working quite well for them. The only major change was that the data source for part of the application was going to be changing from one third-party contact management software package to another one.

You can probably already guess the rest of the story. It turns out that the data store for the new contact management package was SQL Server instead of the DBF file structure of the old package. Shortly after we started the design of the conversion, the customer decided to replace their accounting application with a new package that also used SQL Server as the data store (replacing a proprietary file store). Given that the majority of the system would now be in SQL Server, didn't it make sense to move the rest of the application's data to SQL Server as well?

This "small change" to a client/server architecture thus necessitated redesigning the interface to many of the screens of the application being converted. And as those screens were being redesigned—they figured it wouldn't be a big deal to tweak "just a little bit" of the functionality of the system while we were at it.

And a little bit more. And one more change. And another.

Ten months later, two months after the conversion had originally been slated to go live, we were about 70% done with the design of the main system (but two ancillary systems hadn't even been touched yet). You get the picture. With each new request, the customer's eyes were opened even wider as to the possibilities available. Capabilities were now available in the software that couldn't even be dreamed of when the original system was written eight years prior. And scope creep invaded the project in a big way.

This particular project had an abrupt termination to the design of the project, interestingly enough. When we began discussing the conversion, it looked like a six to eight month project. This was at the end of 1998—plenty of time to get the system up, running, tested, and data converted to the new system before the Y2K turnover (remember those days?). Well, when we hit the 10-month point, it was discovered that the old accounting system was going to die a hot white death on 12/31/99, taking the previous eight years of data with it, so we were suddenly faced with a crash program to code and go live with the mostly designed system in about two and a half months. It was a rather trying period, but we got everything done on time—in fact, early enough that we were live and running on December 20.

Unfortunately, most projects don't have a hard deadline like a Y2K date looming, and so projects can go on iterating well beyond any sort of reasonable means. How do you call it quits? Here are some choices, in order from worst to best.

First, you can just keep prototyping until the user grows tired of the process. I don't know if I can think of a situation where this is a good idea, but technically, it is an option.

The next option is to keep iterating until a predetermined time frame, and then stop. The problem with this is that you may miss specific required functionality—building a system where everything is done, except the reports, is probably not a good idea.

The third option is to stop once the initial requirements are handled. While this has the potential for terminating the iteration sooner rather than later—you put requests for changes to the prototype that go above and beyond the initially stated requirements into a change request for a later version—it also kind of defeats the idea of RAD—using iteration as a means of discovering additional requirements during the design phase, instead of later in the development process when those changes are generally more costly.

A fourth option is to stop when you see that the changes being requested in subsequent iterations are either really picky ("Maybe we should make the width of this field bigger by five chars") or starting to vacillate ("Maybe we should change this back to the way it was originally"). At this point, it's time to suggest that the development move on, and that those requests be saved for the next version.

And, finally, you can stop iterating when you find yourself asking for information about features or functions, and find that you're not getting answers back. This indicates a lack of interest in the project or the inability to find that information—in either case, you can't continue to iterate if you're at a dead end, so it's time to call it quits.

Drawing the line at including functionality

You may be wondering where to draw the line between including actions in a prototype and the real deal—in both of these examples, it may seem that the code required in the application is done. This is not necessarily so—the idea behind the prototype action is to give the user the idea of the action, not the complete functionality.

For example, in the example of the payment type, the prototype wouldn't necessarily enable and disable all of the controls for each payment choice. The first option button maps to certain controls being enabled, but the second, third, and fourth option buttons don't do anything. Which controls are enabled and disabled would be defined according to the spec.

In another example, the prototype wouldn't show all possible choices. Those choices would be defined in the spec:

- Choice 1 has X effect (enabling/disabling controls, allowing values to be chosen, and so on).

- Choice 2 has Y effect (enabling/disabling a different set of controls, populating those controls with a different set of values, and so on).

- Choice 3 has Z effect (enabling/disabling a third set of controls, and so on).

When is a prototype not a real application?

All of the time, of course.

The line drawn earlier—that the complete functionality is not provided—between a prototype and the real application may not seem to be much of a difference. You can almost hear the customer yelling, "You're almost done!" Here is a complete breakdown of what a prototype is vs. a real application.

First, as I noted, the prototype has sample functionality, not all of it. While all the controls are shown on a screen, the controls only show some of the choices, and those choices are hard-coded. The existing choices don't do everything—many times, they don't do anything.

Second, data isn't part of the equation. Data is hard-coded in the application. Typically, there are no data tables at all—any data that is displayed in the prototype is hard-coded in the source code. These fake data sets are usually set up in the Init() of a form so that they're available for the life of the form. There are no data tables.

Third, data-oriented functionality isn't built at all—Add, Delete, Edit, and so on. Validation isn't done either.

Prototypes don't connect to real data—either local data sources or remote sources like Microsoft SQL Server or MySQL.

Prototypes don't have the fit and finish of real applications—while you'll probably spend some time making your forms look nice, so the customer doesn't think you're a total nincompoop when it comes to screen layout, at the same time, you don't want to spend a lot of time making every control perfect, because some of it will likely change.

Finally, prototypes aren't tested like real applications, with thorough test plans and complete documentation. Why? Because they're prototypes—they're likely to change, and, as a result, their only measurable functionality is "proof of concept" and "demonstration of desired functionality." They don't have to actually "work."

The use of a prototype can be a powerful tool to determine and hone in on functionality. People who don't visualize well (which is most people) identify with a prototype much better. And if functionality isn't well defined in the customer's mind, iterating through multiple prototypes can be the best way to identify that functionality.

A final word about design meetings

This doesn't all happen in a single meeting, of course. The best way to handle this is to identify major modules, and take each of them in turn. As each task is identified, a task can be prototyped and demonstrated. At a meeting, I typically take down requirements and document Use Cases. I'll often use a whiteboard to draw pictures of what screens would be like—a design meeting without a whiteboard is much more difficult to hold. One nice tool is an electronic whiteboard that records what's been written down and can produce hardcopies, somewhat like a fax machine. At the next meeting, I'll demonstrate a polished (more or less) prototype, solicit feedback, take down requirements, and document Use Cases for the next task or module.

The trick is to keep the meeting focused on a specific topic or two—and to not let the topic wander. You should maintain a list of topics to address later, and put issues that arise but that are not directly related to the current meeting topic on that list.

Note that the first meeting to develop Functional Specifications for the first module or function or task is an opportunity to define and quantify those specifications that will be used throughout the entire project. These are items that provide the look and feel of the application, such as screen fonts and point sizes, use of color, whether command buttons that close a form should be captioned "Close," "Exit," or "OK," whether forms are always in "edit mode" or if some user action is required to edit data.

Similarly, the first meeting that discusses output should establish specifications that apply to all reports. How should the date, time, and user be identified on a report—on the first page, or all pages? Should reports indicate the version number of the application? Should reports always include a title and summary page? What about fonts, margins, watermarks? Should the network ID of the person requesting the report be included on the report?

Occasionally you may run into a situation where a discussion at a meeting seems to go around and around—while you're just sitting there watching like at a tennis match. Best to interrupt, identify the issue, and suggest that they address it "offline" (at another meeting where they're not paying your high-priced fees).

How far do you go during specification development?

Possibly the stickiest issue having to do with specifications is when and where requirements gathering ends and design begins. This relates to the granularity issue on requirements discussed earlier in this chapter. If you are working on a brand-spanking-new system, then it is easier to focus on the WHATs and not charge into design issues (the HOWs) too quickly. At the same time, though, requirements for enhancements to an existing system nearly always lead into specifications of HOW, WHERE, and WHEN. Look at this quandary from the point of view of the user—it is almost impossible to discuss what they want without adding, "I want this field added to this screen and I want it to perform X function."

Even for developers who have been in this business for decades, there is no clear-cut line here. I've done projects where requirements lasted forever, resulting in an application that could actually be put together rather quickly because all the thinking through had been done. But I've also seen projects where the requirements gathering was truly done while I was writing p-code during development.

One measure you can use to decide when you're done with requirements gathering and analysis is whether or not you have enough information to produce a reasonably accurate estimate. As you'll see in the next chapter, pricing an application requires a certain amount of information, but as the spec is fleshed out more and more, the amount of information available to produce that estimate is nearly complete.

People you may meet

Chemistry between the players is an important part of the specification development—more so than in any other part of the process. Thus, let me address a few common situations you may run into.

First of all, getting the right people involved is key, but you often don't have control over this. It is important to designate a single key contact—and it's also important that this person actually be a champion for the project.

One aspect you might have control over, or at least a fair amount of influence, however, is how many people can get involved. I've found that even as few as five people gets to be too many. It's ideal to have a single key contact, plus a couple others who have a lot of knowledge about the process being discussed. One person has to be the final arbiter of conflicts, and able to make the final decision.

On the other hand, what if you gave a meeting and nobody came? You can help attendance by people who are already busy, and don't want to, or don't feel they can cram "another meeting" into their already jam-packed day, through the following mechanism. First, send a preparatory memo to all those who are expected to attend the meeting—and explain what the meeting will accomplish, why they need to attend, and how they need to prepare and what to bring. If you can have the project champion (or another individual with "clout") deliver this memo, it will highly increase the chances of the meeting being well attended.

The dynamics of the possible participants in these meetings could fill books. Here are some types to watch out for.

The Wheel Spinner

When you find yourself going over the same ground again and again, you may be facing a wheel spinner. This could be someone who does not understand the process, or it could be a person trying to delay implementation of the project for fear of losing their job or position in the company.

The Perfectionist

This is the person who is never satisfied with a proposed solution. This behavior can be countered with a tapping of a finger on the watch—or a discussion of the current actual design cost of a particular module compared to the original estimate. People have to be willing to say, "Good enough for this version" and move on. If they won't, it's time to bring the champion in to call a halt to the nitpicking.

The Expert

"My job is too complex to describe to you." Again, often a reaction due to being threatened, the way to answer this is to explain that the part being automated is the "menial" or "boring" part of the job. Once the drudgery has been automated, the person will be free to concentrate on the challenging parts of their job.

Micro-managers

There will always be those who will, again, due to feeling threatened, insist on managing every aspect of the design, down to the size of screen fonts, and positioning of buttons on the forms. This is an exercise in patience, and can kill a ton of time, so if you run into one of these folks, you should consider having a specific meeting where you decide on "standards" that can be reused throughout the design process.

Cowboys

These are the guys on the team who insist on doing "their own thing"—not following standards, missing meetings, and generally being a pain in the neck. They're the ones who will insist that their own clever, although unproven and untested, technique, since it's 3% faster, should be adopted, in defiance of proven standards and development techniques.

Seekers of the Silver Bullet

Page through any magazine targeted at IS managers and you'll see ads for the latest developer tool that promises to save a development team from one disaster or another. And there will always be a few managers who decide that the ads speak the truth, and want to try out a couple of these new tools on a time-sensitive project, perhaps forsaking tried and true methods and tools that the development team is experienced with. There will always be people wanting to do this—again, it's up to the rational champion who, hopefully, can see that this is a poor choice.

Curmudgeons

There are always those who will insist, "We've always done it this way."

I like to tell the story of the captain of a battleship who was showing off his ship to an admiral. The captain had a gun crew fire off one of the big guns on the fore of the ship, demonstrating the efficiency of the men. However, as they fired the gun, five of the six men were frantic, loading the gun, preparing to fire, and issuing the command to fire. The sixth man, however, stood at attention the whole time. While impressed, the admiral couldn't help but ask what the sixth man was doing. The captain admitted he didn't know either, but they'd "always done it that way" and he'd look into the matter. A week later, he reported to the admiral, "I've found the purpose of the sixth man, sir. His job is to hold the reigns of the horses." This story usually nudges people into realizing that they can't hold on to the past forever.

There's always somebody...

The personalities involved in a project are very important to understand. Your customer community, as a whole, probably doesn't share your enthusiasm for this new application. Some will hardly be able to contain their eagerness; others wouldn't mind if you walked out the door and never returned. Your application implies change—and that's often an uncomfortable situation for people to consider.

Conclusion

The final piece of advice for this chapter is to always ask questions until you completely understand the issue. It's always easy to assume you understand all the pieces, or that you can figure out the last 10% yourself. But don't—you'll have to eventually make it work, so you'd better understand every little bit.

Chapter 16
The Specification

"We have analyzed the plans and have found a weakness."—Soldier to Lord Vader
  —Star Wars

This chapter is the longest one in the book. In it, I will describe the contents of a complete Functional Specification for a typical database system, and explain the purpose and use of every section. A sample Functional Specification is available as part of the downloads for this book.

The meat of this chapter describes the contents of a Functional Specification. The first order of business is... The order, of this chapter and the one previous, where I describe how to build a spec, is one of those chicken and egg situations—do you need to know what a specification looks like before I can describe how to build it? Or vice versa? Obviously, I've decided on the latter. Bear with me, and read both chapters a couple of times.

Second, unlike a balance sheet or a plumbing schematic, there is no generally accepted way to put together a specification. I have nearly 20 years of experience putting together various types of specifications, and I've never been able to find anything close to a standard or a suggested guideline.

As a result, I've had to come up with my own ideas on what to put in there. Thus, this whole chapter is a suggestion—a place to start—not a set of rules that you must follow "or else." I wish I'd had this chapter 10 or 15 years ago, and I'm looking forward to seeing what this chapter will look like 10 years hence.

The third thing to keep in mind is that the specification is not a static document. As I started doing specs, I kept on adding, changing, adjusting—the specification has truly been a living document. Even today, each successive specification has something new as a result of more experience with new customers, applications, and technology. Thus, if you've read an earlier version of this book, you'll see much that's the same, but there are some new pieces that weren't there before.

This growing, living being is much like an application foundation that you continually improve upon. However, unlike that foundation, a specification skeleton doesn't have to be rewritten from the ground up every time that a development tools vendor ships a new release of the tool. Some of the items in this specification of 2001 and beyond could be found in specs I wrote in the mid-1980s.

Yet another thing to remember is that both the structured development and RAD processes require a written specification. Period. If you don't have a written spec, you're just winging it. Actually, all development requires a specification—even if you start coding after an hour-long discussion with a customer, you've got a specification in mind. It's not written down, it's not very thorough, and it'll start to change as soon as you hit Save in your text editor, but it's technically a specification. All I'm doing here is formalizing much of the specification work—creating a template for a specification that will end up on paper and forcing changes to be documented as well. And that's a big advantage of the structured development and RAD processes.

After developing just a couple of dBASE II systems for the nascent IBM PC in the early '80s, I learned that written descriptions were just as valuable for the ethereal world of custom software as they were for multi-million dollar industrial robot installations. In fact, maybe even more valuable, since software seemed to be so much more victim to the whim of a customer changing their mind or a user not having the same vision after listening to a verbal description.

You're less likely to get burned if you've got it in writing. And I've found that the act of documenting the functionality of an application helps clarify things in my own mind. Often, by trying to describe the application, I find places where there are holes, or where I'm not satisfied with some-thing (the "gut feel" is all wrong), or where I can pin down something for the user that they weren't clear on in the last face-to-face meeting.

Finally, this is a functional description, not a technical one. You'll see some technical details included at the end, but the target audience of this document is, primarily, not a programmer. Sure, the programmer will read it too, but this document is intended for the end user who has helped you design the system, the boss who's going to sign off on the dollars, and the testing department that has to make sure it performs—er, as specified. (Hmmm!) Each of these people wants to know what the system is going to do—not how primary and foreign keys are going to be optimized or which subclassed methods are overridden.

They want to know what this thing they're buying will do, how it will solve their problems and ease their pain, and what the impact on them will be—what they have to do and what the schedule is as it relates to them. That is all. So let's provide them with this information as easily and succinctly—but as thoroughly—as possible.

This particular example is based on a desktop database application, but don't think that these are the only types of applications that can be put together using a specification. Some developers argue that different types of processes are more suited for specific types of applications—for example, that non-data-intensive systems are better candidates for XP because the discovery of a new data requirement halfway through the deployment of an application can make a major negative impact on the system. I'd argue that Agile Methodologies are too new to make that kind of argument, one way or the other.

Furthermore, to a large part, the sample specs I am providing are just that—samples. The way you design and develop applications is bound to be different. These specs are starting points for your own development.

Finally, many of the pieces of this specification apply regardless of what you are building. The most important aspect of a Functional Specification is to completely document what the system does. If you have done so, the rest of the job becomes considerably easier—you can determine the cost, you can turn over the production (the coding) to someone else, and the application can be tested. Without a detailed Functional Specification, everyone is just guessing.

You may be wondering who actually writes a specification. I used to write most—but not all—of the specs at my shop over the past few years, because I'm generally the one who gets called in to do the analysis and design. However, that's evolved somewhat since we've now got a pretty good template, and lots of examples. Thus, this has been an area that I've been able to delegate to others on occasion—with my role being that of a "review committee" more than anything else. And that's pretty rewarding—watching and helping others develop new skills in the software development process.

 A complete Functional Specification may be as short as 40 or 50 pages for a small app, or take the better part of a 500-page ream of paper. In this chapter, I've excerpted some specific sections from a sample spec for discussions of the sections for such a document. The complete sample Functional Specification is included in the downloads area of the Hentzenwerke Web site.

The Executive Overview

The Executive Overview is one of the harder, and, in my opinion, one of the more boring, pieces to write. Its purpose is to explain to the person who is going to give approval to the project just exactly why they should do so. It's a big picture of the system, spells out the benefits, and describes the dozen bullet points of "what can I do with this system." The key message to communicate is how this system will ease or remove the pain currently felt in the organization. You can often do this by describing the status quo, what the system will do, and how life will be different after implementation of the system.

General description

The general description does two things. First, it describes, in a few sentences, what the system does. We geeks know that we are writing a custom database system that's going to track a variety of data for a trade association's Political Action Committee. So does our primary contact at the organization. But that's not necessarily true for someone else who has to get involved with the system—volunteer users from companies who belong to the trade association, a high-level management person, an executive new to the industry who has to approve the money. They could be coming in cold, and they might not be quite sure that this application is that good of an idea. We need to give them the big picture idea, and this description does so. Don't let them assume anything.

Next, the general description describes the current business environment, how their business works, special terminology, what the pain is, and how the new system will solve those problems. I'll often use very explicit language that states exactly what the customer is looking for. This description is the piece you would give to somebody else in order to explain to them why the customer called you in the first place. Whether or not this project is a success and meets the needs of the customer is measured by how much pain it relieves.

In many industries and companies, there is a whole suite of terminology that is particular to that industry and/or company. This is the place to define those terms so that you can make sure you and your customer are communicating correctly. There's the famous line about "If you call a tail a leg, how many legs does a dog have?" "Five." "No, a dog still has four legs. Calling a tail a leg does not make it a leg."

It's best to describe each one of these terms and define what they mean. Don't just use a description of that term—provide live examples. This ensures that you really do understand what they mean and you're not making incorrect assumptions.

Suppose you're describing an entity that receives medical care at an urgent care facility. If you simply describe that entity as "people" or "patients," you haven't made clear a possible distinction between insured individuals and dependents of an insured individual. However, if you then provide an example of an individual and their entire family as being maintained in the same screen, your intent and plans for overloading the person table with both insureds and dependents becomes obvious.

If there is a large amount of special terminology, you may want to break out the terms in a table, or, if needed, even a special "definitions section" that would wrap up this section.

Functionality

The functionality is the list of bullet points that describes major functions. You're providing the description on the back of the shrink-wrap box that's going to help sell the software. I'll usually just list them as such unless the situation with the customer requires further elaboration on each. After all, the whole rest of the specification will be spelling these bullet points out in detail, so there's no need to beat the horse to death while it's still in the starting gate.

How detailed should this section be? One page is sufficient—no one is going to read (or remember) more than about a page. You want a digestible chunk of information. If it is absolutely necessary to have more than a page, break it into groups, modules, or other categories, or combine multiple types of functionality into the same description.

Remember that a person is going to be using the system, so phrase the bullet points in terms of actions—verbs—things the user can do. They don't care about architecture or capacities right now—but what they can accomplish with the system. And make sure that you phrase each bullet point in the same way—noun/verb/object, or verb/object, or whatever style suits you best. If you are inconsistent, the reader will get confused.

Sample use scenario

As systems get larger and more complex, it's more likely that parts of the system will be used by more than one person, and at several different times throughout the course of their business. Thus, it's important to show how the system integrates with their operations. This shows again that you understand how their business runs and what part you and your system is going to play in it.

Functional description

This section is the meat of the Functional Specification. In it, you'll describe the general look and feel of the system, how the user will install and load the app, and how each element—screen, process, and report—in the app will function.

General interface notes

This section describes the general look and feel of the application. In the olden days, operating systems and applications used to come with a manual that spent the first few pages describing what a command button is and how you operate a combo box. This section is similar—it covers both standard operating system functions as well as anything that is tailored for this application.

General Windows interface notes

First, you describe the interface functionality that is common throughout the app. I muddled along for a number of years just adding items as they came up from one project to another. When I started deploying on Windows, I used the information that is found in the Windows Interface Guidelines as a start. (If you're using a different operating system, such as Linux,

Palm, or Mac, check to see if there is a set of guidelines provided by the manufacturer.) A surprising number of applications (much to my aggravation) used by individuals don't follow the standard Windows interface, and so the users have unusual expectations. For example, many users are accustomed to using the Enter key to move from field to field. While this works when moving from one text box to another, it doesn't work with check boxes, combo boxes, and so on. This is where you spell out that you use the Tab key to move from control to control, that you use the space bar to pop open a combo box, and how you make choices in an option group.

Many users are accustomed to Quicken, which arguably has the best user interface on the planet. Unfortunately, that raises their expectations to an unreasonable level for a custom designed application that's written in a higher-level language than C. When users ask me why my app doesn't have all the gizmos that Quicken does, I explain that they didn't pay me $25,000,000 to write and debug seven versions of C code.

It's important, then, to explain exactly what will happen. Else, the user is likely to claim a certain behavior is a bug, when it's simply behavior that they're not used to since they commonly use an application with a non-standard interface. The following rules apply to the entire application. Exceptions are noted in the particular screen, process, or report.

As customers ask more and more questions, and as you add more and more standard features, this section continues to grow.

There are a number of advantages to including this section in your specification. First, you don't have to repeat certain information every time the issue comes up. For example, a common mechanism in database applications is a mover dialog, where the user can click or drag items in one list box in order to place them in the other list box. Instead of explaining how all the controls in a mover work each time you use one somewhere in the app, just explain how the mover works once, and then refer to "a standard mover" everywhere else in the specification.

Second, it's a means of protection from the aforementioned user who decides that pressing the Enter key shouldn't change the value of a check box—and raises holy hell about it. Explaining up front what the rules are takes care of those situations. It also provides a place to identify where you choose to implement non-standard behavior.

Third, it fattens up the specification by another 10 or 20 pages, and this makes customers who want to feel they got their money's worth by hefting around a fat document feel better. Remember that one of the biggest mistakes in business is assuming the other guy is going to act in a rational manner all the time.

Finally, since I basically include all of this in every spec, it's a simple cut and paste (oh, to have inheritance in your word processor!) operation, and this saves the customer money. They don't have to pay to have every word of the specification customized.

Lookup/code maintenance

I've been a fan of overloaded lookup tables for years. As a result, a lot of lookup table maintenance can be handled with a single screen. This screen contains a drop-down that allows the user to pick which lookup table they want to work with, and that choice then populates the rest of the screen with the values of just that lookup table. This can be confusing to a user who is used to separate screens (and menu options) for every picky little lookup table—in fact, they often don't even think of them as lookup tables. This was a "write once, use many" tool in my application framework, so it makes sense to also make its description "write about it once, use it many times."

Query screens

Client/server applications require a different interface than a traditional LAN app—I've run into too many developers who brought a system to its knees by trying to query the entire 205,000 records.

A better way is to have the user select which record set they want—and to do so, you provide them with a query screen that allows them to determine which records they want to see. A simple query screen might just display a few key fields, but I've found that making this screen powerful makes it much more useful for a wide range of users. And, like other common tools in the application, I would much rather write it once and make it very flexible instead of writing a dozen of them, each just 3% different.

Maintenance screens

A lot of my screens have the same look and feel. They have the Next, Previous, First, Last, Search, and Find features. It's efficient to describe key functions in one place. Furthermore, since all of this functionality is part of my foundation, describing all of it raises the bar for competitors. Suddenly they have to duplicate all of this functionality—and most likely have to write a fair amount of it from scratch.

I am not saying all of the functions described are included in every application, but if the user sees a multi-column list box, they can find out how it works in the description here.

Error dialogs

If you're going to provide a standard, robust method for providing error handling and feedback, discuss the mechanism here so the user understands what will happen with an error and how to deal with it. Error handling and processes are covered later, but discuss the interface here.

Buttons and toolbars

This section explains how buttons and toolbars work, by themselves and in concert with the menus. ToolTips, status bar text, and why items are sometimes disabled, and at other times disappear completely—these are covered in this section.

Controls: Combo boxes, list boxes, pick lists

Combo boxes, list boxes, and pick lists are all controls that an experienced user is comfortable with, but that a new user—or at least new to a GUI—might not be. This section discusses what these controls are for, and how they work. I provide pick lists through an application—and the incremental search feature is not intuitive, but very appreciated once explained.

Notes button

Users often want to add free-form text to a record, but there's often not room on a screen to do so. Thus, one common interface feature is a "Notes" button that opens up a full-sized editing window. In the olden days, the button used to just say "Notes"—now, the system checks to see whether there's data in the field, and sets the prompt to "Add Notes" or "Edit Notes" as appropriate.

The Done button

Unlike the stupid Windows guidelines that throw out a bewildering set of choices for buttons that close a screen—Close, Cancel, OK, and, sometimes, no mechanism at all except the close box in the title bar—I prefer to have a single Done button on every screen. It's pretty clear what that button does, isn't it? When you're done with the screen, press the Done button. Period.

Naturally, I trap for users performing inappropriate actions—like pressing Done when the user has pending changes. It's easy enough to throw a "There are unsaved changes—Save or Abandon?" dialog at them—the same one they see if they try to navigate to a new record without saving changes.

But there are also screens where there isn't the need to save—like the standard Windows Print screen. I put a Print button on the form, and you can tell what it does. When they're done with their output request, since, after all, they may be "printing" to the screen, or to a text file, they press Done.

Occasionally, a screen will close itself when a user has executed an action—those specific instances are noted in the specification for that screen.

Quick-add

Windows isn't always associated with quick, heads-down data entry screens—indeed, most applications that require banks of clerks just slamming data into tables use a character-based or very sparse GUI. But I've run into many situations where the customer needs a "quick-add" feature to an existing app. This mechanism is different from the standard maintenance screen—but it's also pretty common, so I describe the whole tool here, and then when one is needed in the app, that section can simply refer to a "standard quick-add screen."

Report front end

Reports are probably the least rewarding part of an application, and at the same time, about the most important part to the user. Remarkably few people are interested in jamming data into a system and then not retrieving it—data entry screens are a necessary evil in their quest for output. I've found it useful to make the reporting mechanism of an application as robust and flexible as possible, while still trying to do as little custom work as possible.

The FoxPro world has long had a tool that provided the ability to load a database with metadata that a user could use to generate their own reports; VB developers have their choice of several reporting tools that do, to some extent, the same thing. Still, many developers choose to roll their own. In any case, the front end used for reporting is explained here—since it never changes—and the Reports section later in the specification describes the actual reports that will be provided with the app.

Year 2000 issues

I started including a section that dealt with Year 2000 issues in 1995, and it fit in this section because the initial result was that all date fields displayed four digit years. Occasionally it was a battle, when a customer was trying to squeeze every bit of data they could on a screen and didn't want to use two additional characters for every date field. Over the past few years, I've added and enhanced the language that discusses my care and feeding for Year 2000 issues.

Now that the majority of the issues are past, this section isn't as important, but it's still important to address certain items. Perhaps you will want to call this "Year 1999 Issues," clarifying that your application will also work with dates "in the last century."

Customer-specific interface notes

It's a rare customer who doesn't want something different. One of my customers wanted every "Done" button changed to "OK"—against my advice, of course, but they wanted it so. Thus, I put in a note about this—and, as you'll see, I was then able to cost out how much this fellow was going to pay for this idiosyncrasy.

Other types of interface changes might include particular colors, wording (another customer wanted to put "© 1999 Intergalactic Machinery Company. All rights reserved." on every screen), and handling of multi-lingual requirements.

This may seem awkward—but later on, you'll see that I reserve the right to do anything that isn't spelled out explicitly in the specification. There are 1,000 minute design decisions you're faced with as a developer and programmer, and it's simply impossible to spell out every single item in an economical and timely manner. Thus, it's important to spell out specific items that the user does want handled.

Installation and setup

As you well know, it's frustrating to open up a box and not know where to start. Some of you may remember the infamous dBASE IV box from 1988 that included more than 20 pounds of manuals, and three different cards that each said, "Start here."

Furthermore, it's easy to plunge into the meat of an app—sketching out table structures, designing screens, and hundreds of hours into it, find out that the user is expecting distribution and availability to be handled in a manner that negates much of the work you've done. For example, users who are expecting to run an executable off of a server, like they did in DOS, NetWare, and Windows 3.1 environments, may be dismayed to learn that an app has to be installed on each NT or 9x workstation. An application that uses external components as part of the user "experience" poses other requirements during installation that need to be made clear as well. And setup and login can be sticky points—such as if your application uses a custom login screen, but your customer is expecting the app to capture the network username for authentication.

Delivery method

Application delivery used to be easy—throw an EXE and maybe some data files in a directory. If you were clever, add a batch file so that the app could be launched from any DOS prompt. These days, the deliverable is more likely to be a group of setup files created by a setup wizard, InstallShield, or something else.

To the old-timer in the MIS department who is used to getting a pair of floppy diskettes with perhaps a ZIP file containing their application, these setup files may be a new and frightening world. Furthermore, the setup files probably won't fit on a few floppies—25, 50, or 100 MB deliverables aren't uncommon. Perhaps you're burning a CD, or maybe you're just providing a CAB file on your FTP site. In any case, explain how you're going to deliver the files so they know what to expect.

Installation process

These days, there's a whole range of installation possibilities. First, obviously, is a stand-alone app on a single machine—not common, but it still happens occasionally.

More common is a traditional network app—despite all the hype coming out of Redmond, this is where a significant chunk of most shops' bread and butter is still coming from. That's often easy—throw an EXE and the data on a server, and point the workstations to the server. Or perhaps include a mechanism that automatically copies the EXE down to each workstation, and automatically updates the workstations when the master EXE changes.

A third possibility is a client/server system, where the application might be installed as with a LAN app, but where configuration of data connections has to be taken into account.

A fourth is a Web application, either intranet- or Internet-based, so that installation on the Web server, connections to a separate database server, perhaps, and even end-user browser issues have to be dealt with.

And, finally, there are road warrior types of apps, where traveling salesmen or other personnel have one copy of the app on their notebooks, handhelds or palm PCs, while the home office has another copy of the app. Keeping them synchronized adds a whole new level of complexity to the system.

However, given the new configurations of operating systems and tools, installation can get more complex regardless of the type of application. And your customer needs to know this information in case they need to tweak settings such as security and user access, handle backups, and so on.

In this section, the process of installation is described, in detail. Describe each step, both for the data (on a server) and for each user, since you're likely not to have users running a remote executable off the server anymore. If you've done things cleverly, perhaps you can do a single install on each workstation and then have the server install updates by itself so the company just plunks a new EXE on the server and the user auto-downloads that new EXE the next time they run the app.

Does your customer have to create an icon, or run other processes as well? Custom applications are expensive, and I've had several requests for an app that's going to be distributed to a population of uncontrollable or loosely regulated users—and as a result, the app had to run a routine during install that would verify who was using the system. For example, one app of ours was distributed to about 1,000 dealers throughout North America. However, in order to control the use of the app, the installation process had to run a registration routine to at least discourage piracy.

If you're building an n-tier application, you very likely have components running on multiple boxes that could be geographically disparate. Identify each piece of the application, where it goes, how it gets installed, how it gets updated, and how to handle reinstallation in the event that something breaks.

Make sure the customer understands what their part in this installation routine will be— again, helping get their expectations in line with yours.

Startup

Once the install is done, what does the user do to launch the application? Usually, they'll just have to click on an icon. But in some cases, the app might be provided as an operating system service or daemon, or available through the Web or an intranet, or a machine might be running it as a dedicated function. Be explicit, and you won't run into problems later when you find out the user was thinking they were going to have Herman from Accounting use the same PC that you were going to use as the database server.

Logon

How is the user going to get into the application? Is there any security or authentication involved at all?

If so, do they just have a username or will they also be required to have a password? Or perhaps you are going to snarf the network username and give them transparent access—perhaps the Windows desktop presents an icon that loads the app based on permissions set in the OS.

At this point, you're starting to show screen shots—pictures—of the application's interface. They won't remember the demonstration of the prototype five minutes after you leave their offices—but they'll refer back to the specification to look at the pictures over and over.

Configuration (if applicable)

Sometimes, particularly with larger applications, or apps that are distributed among a large number of users with varying environments, the user will have to (or may want to) configure the application to suit their needs. This may be as simple as providing a screen where they can enter their company name, address, phone number, and other demographic data so that reports, invoices, quotes, and exported files are customized.

However, it may be more complex. The next level of configuration would be for a variety of parameters that affect how the system operates, and one customer may want these set up differently than the next. A couple of years ago, I shipped an application that has a 12-tab configuration screen; the preferences file contains more than 120 fields. Furthermore, this app is going to be used by folks in a variety of geographical areas—one whole screen is used to define how taxation is going to be configured. Another screen allows the user to customize how RFPs and invoices should be displayed—including which fields should be presented, what level of detail should be presented, and whether or not a generic name and address or the customer's own scanned-in logo should be printed.

But it can get even more sophisticated. In another app that I've done, each site could set up parameters for the defaults for the query screen to best suit their organization. However, the site could then override those defaults for a particular form. For example, the query screen for the invoice table may require an exact match on invoice number, and a range match on dates—all of the other options, such as "nearest" and "top N matches" would be inappropriate. However, the query screen for the patient table should allow for considerably more fuzzy searching—since they may search on partial last names (which are of indeterminate spelling due to illegible handwriting), as well as a number of other attributes.

Furthermore, each user at that site could then override those defaults for themselves. One user only accesses the invoice table to search on invoice number, while another needs to look up date ranges and thus needs more ability to be fuzzy in criteria selection.

All of this is explained here in the spec, or, if the configuration is normally done later, the specification now points to the configuration topics.

Custom interface elements

Now that I've covered the standard stuff that comes in the box, it's time for the main show—the custom part of the application. This next section will be somewhat specific to the way I design applications. I am presenting this as one possible way to do it—you are certainly most welcome to present the information to your customers differently. Nonetheless, you will need to, at some point, define the specific functionality of your application and what the operating rules are for each function. If you don't, you're not going to be able to take advantage of the pricing methodology later in this section, and that would be a shame.

Types of application functionality

Despite the variety of software applications, there are remarkably few categories of "things you can do" with an app. In fact, there are basically three things: Put data in, run processes on data, and get data out. The first function is performed with data entry or manipulation forms, the second function is performed with menu options or toolbar buttons that launch processes, and the third is performed with a reporting or output tool.

This section of the specification walks through the menu that allows access to the rest of the app, and then through each screen, process, and report in the system.

Menus

I have used a standard CUA menuing system that is displayed after a successful logon for years. For those of you who don't know the term, a CUA menu has a set of common menu pads—File, Edit, Tools, Window, and Help. And, ordinarily, there are a few menu pads stuffed in between Edit and Tools. In my case, I have two pads—Operations and Reports—that show up in just about every app. I'm not saying this is the only way, or the correct way, but it's just turned out that I've never done apps that required a different front end. However, many users aren't used to this menu structure, so the specification spends a little time describing what each menu pad does and why it's there.

The menu should be comfortable and familiar—if the user is somewhat experienced, they should expect it to behave just like every other application running on the same operating system. They will expect to see File, Edit, Help, Tools, Window, and Help, and each option should work the way they have been conditioned to expect it to. They know Ctrl-X, Ctrl-C, and Ctrl-V work for cut, copy, and paste. They know they can do a Find and a Find/Replace, and that Exit is found under File.

On some systems, I may provide a pick list that allows them to choose a subsystem that is then used to create a subsystem-specific menu. This is becoming more common as my systems are getting bigger, but it still fits in with my general paradigm.

Screens

Underneath File, there are menu options for every data-centric form in the system. Some of these forms visually or mentally tie to a specific table or set of tables—the invoices, the parts, the patients, and the transmographers (it's a technical term—don't worry about it unless you're a six-year-old kid with a tiger named Hobbes) that the application handles. I call these forms "maintenance forms" because they are often used to perform routine add/edit/delete operations, but are sometimes used only to provide supporting data that is usually interacted with on other forms.

These other forms (still under the File menu) are more task-oriented, and don't have a high correlation to specific data structures. These screens usually map to forms they use in their business to do work, whether they update customer status, discharge a patient, fill out shipping label information, or enter transaction dates.

For each form, I show a screen shot of the form and describe what the form is, how it works, and how they will use it. This is where the rubber meets the road. If you scrimp here, you are going to be one seriously unhappy camper down the road. There is a ton of work to be done when describing each screen, but doing the work now will produce significant benefits in the future.

Screen shots

The first thing I do for each form is to provide a screen shot of the screen being described. These screen shots come from the prototype that I've built during my iterations of the Functional Specification with the customer. The old adage about a picture being worth a thousand words holds true here. The screen shot should be a sketch of the form if you're using structured development, or a picture of the form as it appears in the prototype that you're building for RAD projects.

One thing I've found very helpful, if you can do it, is to populate the prototype with real data from the customer, instead of made-up values like Bugs Bunny and Daffy Duck. You obviously need the customer's cooperation to get that information, but this act significantly enhances communication about how this form will look and act. It also helps ward off errors—if they see the letters "SW" in a text box labeled "Region Code" but their region codes have recently been changed to three-digit numbers, they're more likely to notice the difference than if the entire screen were filled with X's.

Purpose

Most specs don't include this description because it often seems obvious after you use the form for about 10 minutes. But if you haven't used the form, it may not be obvious what this form does, and thus this information can be pretty useful. Remember how confused you were when you had to first turn on a computer and didn't know where the On button was?

What will the form allow the user to do? What is its mission in life? This doesn't have to be a long section. It's not a tutorial, simply an explanation of what they can do with it and why it's important.

This description is particularly useful when the app is turned over to a new user, or to someone who hasn't used a particular part of the app. This section often becomes the lead-in for training materials and Help files.

Access

This section describes the answer to the question "How does a user get to this screen, and which groups of users have permission to do so?" Never more than about two sentences.

Usage

Now we get to the good stuff. In this section, you cover how the form works and how the user is going to use it in their day-to-day work. For example, in order to perform function X, you must do Step 1, Step 2, and then Step 3.

This is a process-based description, not an explicit description of each control. Those get covered next. For all but the most rudimentary of forms, it could very well not be apparent how to use the form itself. It might also not be obvious how the form is used in the bigger picture of a business process. By providing a usage description, three groups of people now know what to expect (and what not to expect): the user, the programmer, and the Quality Assurance group.

Screen objects

Next, I get into the reference part of this section—a description of every "thing" on the form. The most interesting objects are those that perform actions—push buttons, data entry fields, drop-down list boxes, and so on.

Every object on the screen that is not a dumb label, shape, or graphic image needs to be described. In order to make sure that the user doesn't expect behavior that isn't listed, I start out with the following most wonderful phrase:

`All fields are editable and no validation is performed except the following:`

If the form contains a text box in which the user can enter 26 characters, no description is necessary. The data dictionary listing (later in the spec) shows that this field is 26 characters long. The user should expect to be able to enter all 26 characters in any form that this field appears on.

However, if the data in that text box has to be converted to capitals automatically, that's specified. If a red dot is supposed to appear if the data entered is invalid, that's specified. If the field holds more characters than can be displayed in the text box on the form, I say that.

The key is to ensure that the customer understands how the form works and what the validations and rules are behind each object.

There are a number of objects that have a relationship with particular sets of data that may or may not be evident. For example, a list box may be populated from a table but the records that appear depend on a rule, such as who has access to that table, or whether a flag was set elsewhere in the form.

You need to explicitly identify how each one of these works and how it will be presented. For example, "List box A displays the last five transactions for this customer. It will be sorted by transaction date, and then by transaction code within transaction date. If the customer doesn't have any transactions, the list box will display <None> in the first row." This makes it clear what will happen. The user can choose to change the contents of this list box, but that request is definitely a Change Order.

Another example would be a radio button populated by the contents of a field. What happens if the contents of that field are empty? Do you have a radio button that says "None" or do you leave all of the radio buttons unchecked? The key here is that these rules are tied to a specific object and thus belong in this section.

Form-level rules

There are several types of rules that are tied to a form. An example is the enabling of one control based on the user changing the value of another—selecting a certain radio button enables a text box elsewhere on the form. Another example would be special record-level validation upon saving a record. You could argue that this rule would actually be a data engine validation, or a trigger. It might be, if any type of save function on that table required the rule to be fired. But it might not be a trigger if the rule was specific to this form, or if the development tool you were using didn't know what a data engine or a trigger was.

Two benefits of describing your rules in this manner are that 1) the user has a checklist of what is going to happen during the operation of the screen, and 2) your Quality Assurance group (or person) can use this guideline to test.

Now that you've gone through this process, you know what makes up the form. You know how many things (labels, text boxes, spinners, list boxes) are on the form and how many behaviors (validations, rules, triggers, function calls) are attached to the form. This information will be used to cost out the application. If you started the costing process with bad data, such as what might result from incomplete specs or vague descriptions about the form, you might as well go back to throwing darts at a cost dartboard.

User acceptance testing criteria

The final section for each screen is to identify the user acceptance testing criteria. This is a good way to have the user confirm that what you say it will do is what they want done. Identify what the user will do to test this particular feature or function—and you've both helped out the user as well as provided yourself a safety net if the user comes back and insists that "X" doesn't work right.

Processes

The Process menu contains menu options for functions where the primary motive is to perform data manipulation that doesn't require much, if any, user input, and may involve tables and processes that the user is not aware of.

Examples of processes include import and export routines, transaction updates, posting processes, and calculation type operations.

It is significantly more difficult to explicitly describe a process. Therefore, the Processes part of the specification contains a wider margin for error. Some people might even argue that it's impossible to define a process well enough to be able to determine a fixed price for it. It's easy enough to see all the objects on a form, and to count the number of rules attached to the form. But a process can be anything, and, they argue, it would be impossible to categorize a routine into a discrete set of objects like a form can. I beg to disagree. Let's take a look at how we might approach "what goes into a process."

Over the years, I've probably written a couple hundred process routines of one sort or another. In thinking over these, it's become apparent that there are perhaps only a dozen types of operations that go into a process, regardless of what kind of process it is. These operations are the building blocks that can be used to build virtually any kind of process. The ones I've identified include:

Create temp files.

This is the operation that creates a temporary text file, a temporary table, or a temporary cursor that will be used during the process. Typically, you'll have a generic function to handle the dirty work for you, so this would often be a simple function call or a small number of lines of code.

Delete temp files.

Why are they called temp files? Because they're not permanent—and that means that you'll often have to take care of cleaning them up, either deleting them off of the disk or simply closing the cursor.

Match two files.

In many processes, you'll need to look for the key ID of a record in one file in another file.

Update one file with data from another file.

If you are successful in the aforementioned match, you may overwrite one file's data with the information in the other one.

Assign data values with a calculation.

A process often updates a file with a value that is calculated. This value may be calculated any number of ways—a combination of fields, fields and memory variables, or even with standard "magic numbers" (proprietary algorithms).

Add a record to a file.

If the aforementioned match wasn't successful, the solution is often to add a new record.

Set a flag for later use.

When handling validation, you'll often need to "keep your place" and refer to that placeholder later.

Set up a countdown.

If you're ripping through a file, it's often polite to let the user know how much processing remains. I often do this through a simple countdown window in the corner of the screen that tells the user how many operations needed to be handled and how many are left.

Write a record to an exception file.

If you found a match when you weren't supposed to (duplicate records) or didn't find a record when you thought you would (missing keys), you may want to record this information in a file that the user can later access.

Write an alert to the user for immediate processing.

If something Very Bad happened, you might want to stop processing until a user can intervene.

Now that I've defined some of the building blocks, let's determine how we might describe the process that uses these building blocks in order to accomplish something useful for the user.

I don't have a foolproof way to make sure I catch every step of a process. (If we did, only the fools would use it, right?) But this set of questions tends to catch most of the "what if this happened" events—see the "Process rules" heading later in this section.

One of the things I do most often during a process is to handle things that go wrong—in other words, validation. Most processes can be handled with reasonably straightforward procedural code—until you start considering what could go wrong.

Given this description, you can begin to identify each of the types of building blocks that are needed at each stage. That's what you'll need when you determine the cost for the app.

Screen shot (if applicable)

Most of the time, a process has to be kicked off by the user, and they'll do this by executing a menu command. I always provide some sort of interface for that menu command so the user has the opportunity to cancel the operation just in case they picked the wrong menu command by mistake. They'll also often have to select a file (or at least confirm that the default that the system will process is correct), and so, for these two reasons, a user interface for processes is a good idea. Thus, the specification for a process invariably needs a screen shot.

Purpose

Just like with screens, the Purpose section describes, in a sentence or two, what this process will do. Note that this description doesn't go into a lot of detail about prerequisites or usage—I'll hit those topics soon enough.

Access

Again, just like with screens, the Access section describes how to get to this function and who has access to it. Given that processes may interact with other systems, you may also want to explicitly state what type of access is required to other systems or datasets.

Usage

The usage for a process is on average more complicated than that of a screen, and so it's important to explicitly describe how the user will use this process (and screen, where appropriate). In particular, you need to put the operation in context with respect to the other processes around it—does the user have to do something else first, or does this precede another process in the company? Also, provide the "why" behind the "how"—the business reason that these steps are being taken.

File requirements

If you are describing a process that deals with importing and exporting files or otherwise works with external files, you need to explicitly describe what those files are, where they come from, and where they are going. The actual file layouts are described in the Technical Specifications part of the spec, but you need to address the environment in which the process is operating here.

If you are describing a completely internal process, this section isn't as long, but you still need to explain which logical elements are involved in the process, and any special requirements there might be. For example, you may need to lock a file while you are posting to it—and you can make sure that the user knows that access to that file from elsewhere in the system will be prevented during this process.

Process rules

This is where you document what is going to happen during the process. It's tough, because you actually have to work through each of the rules, and you're often working with data that is not clearly defined by the user.

All you're really doing is writing pseudo-code for the process. This is a pretty good idea here, particularly because you must document your assumptions and explain to the user what is going to happen when things awry.

Let's take the example of a file import. First, you need to explain how the table(s) in the system will be matched up with the file being imported—on what key or set of fields. Next, explain what happens when there is a match—are all fields in the system overwritten, or just some of them? What if there isn't a match—is the record always added to the system, or does it have to be validated first?

Another very, very important issue to consider, and document, is the data that's being imported. How clean can you assume the imported data is? You can't! In literally hundreds of processes that have had to do with importing data, I don't think I've ever run into one where the actual data was perfectly clean the first time I tried.

If you're working with someone else's data, you will run into bad data, and you need to identify what you will do when that happens. If you don't, you'll end up fixing something or other, and your customer won't want to pay you for it, guaranteed.

Thus, identify what testing you will perform against the data being imported, and what you will do if that testing fails. Next, how do you handle lookups? Often, files being imported are not normalized, so you'll have to break out fields that you've got stored in lookup tables from the main file being imported. If the value in the import file is also in the lookup table, great. But what if it isn't? Do you kick out the imported record, or do you add a record to the lookup table?

When you review this set of rules, you see that you can identify the types of common operations described earlier, and literally count how many of each is needed.

This sounds like a lot of very detailed work, and it is, but really not any more so than describing every validation and form-level rule for a data entry screen. And if you don't go to this level of detail for a process now, you'll have to later. However, if you wait until later, you won't know how much work is involved in doing the process—which means you can't accurately cost it.

And finally, if you don't do this work now, you're at risk for missing important relationships between data in another system and data in this system. As I wrote the '99 edition of this book, I was working on a file import routine where the system was going to be updated every night from a national organization. The initial import file had about a dozen fields that didn't appear to be in the current system. If I had ignored those while writing the spec, I wouldn't have asked questions about the entities those values represented, and thus would have missed designing a much-needed part of the application.

What would have happened? I'd turn the application over to my customer, they'd install, roll out the app to a half dozen or so sites, and then someone would ask, "How do you handle <terse description of situation>?" and everyone would start pointing fingers at everyone else. Eventually, they'd all end up pointing at me.

User acceptance testing criteria

Similar to forms, you need to identify what the user will do to test the process to make sure it works as they want it to.

Reports

For the better part of the past 10 years, I've been using a third-party tool that provides a lot of the reporting functionality for my customers. As a result, I architect my applications and, more importantly, describe output knowing that I am going to use this tool to produce the output. Fortunately, many of the techniques I use are equally valid in other environments, or can be adapted to your specific requirements.

For example, instead of trying to be clever about stretching a report writer's capabilities to the very ends of the earth, I go to the other extreme. Every type of output I provide consists of two parts. The first part is a routine that creates a single flat file that contains all of the data I need for creating the report—including columns for all aggregations, like group and report totals. The second part is a simple report skeleton that the file is run through. This skeleton organizes and formats the data as the user wishes to see it.

This technique is a great idea for several reasons. First, it's a lot easier to debug a report where a subtotal isn't coming out correctly. Just examine the routine that creates that subtotal value. You don't have to rely on making sure every property is set for some arcane grouping or subtotaling object buried deep in the report skeleton.

Second, when the user decides they want the output in a different format—perhaps a text file dump, or formatted for a browser, or exported to a spreadsheet format—you've got all the data—just use a different skeleton. If you rely on calculations and logic built into the report skeleton, you'll have to duplicate that work for the new output mechanism.

And third, it's a lot easier to determine the cost of the report because the elements that go into creating the report are more clearly identifiable.

Thus, there are two steps to building the report—creating the file and creating the report form. Each of these has a number of discrete components, just like a process can be broken down into a small set of identifiable building blocks.

I need to note here that having a data model is critical—and makes creating the flat file much easier as well. It's pretty easy to gloss over specifics of an area of a report, not realizing that two of the fields that are to appear on the report aren't actually anywhere else in the system. A completed data model will help you avoid this type of mistake.

How to describe a report

You need to describe the data file that is going to populate the report and then describe the report skeleton that you're going to run the data file through. The data file is described in the Detail Entity, Filter, and Order/Group sections, and the report skeleton is described in the rest of the sections.

When you join the tables, you have to apply a variety of filters, specify the order in which the result is created, and perhaps create calculated fields or group on expressions in order to create output data at the appropriate level. When you produce the actual output, you have to identify each object that shows up on the form as well as any special levels of grouping or aggregation, headers and footers, and title and summary pages. Each of these objects also represents a "thing" that you can count and cost.

General report disclaimer

There is one very important paragraph to include in the report section. If you are specifying a fixed price application, you need to limit the number of iterations that the user performs on the final deliverable. There will always be a few tweaks that you'll probably throw in for free—I know we do—moving this field over there, changing the name of a menu option, and so on.

But reports are one of those things that can be tweaked forever, and that can break you if you're on a fixed budget of time. Our reporting tool includes a mechanism for allowing the user to modify the appearance of reports we've already set up, so we include the following wording to limit the number of tweaks that they expect of us:

```
Since the appropriate appearance of reports is a highly subjective and personal
matter, it is possible to make modifications to reports ad infinitum. Since
this is a fixed price proposal, we will create data items for the detail fields
listed above, produce the data file to populate the report, and mock up a
sample report layout based on the examples provided. Additional modifications
to reports can be made by customer through the reporting utility provided or by
vendor at additional charge.
```

I should also mention that our reporting tool also handles printing automatically—so we never have to worry about specifying a certain printer or handling weird print setups. The tool is configured for these cases automatically. It also allows us to set user permissions on a data item or report basis by flipping one switch.

Report template

Before getting into the description of a specific report, your specification should have a report section that describes the "report template." It should show the company name, logo, page numbering, and other print information, such as system-generated fields, like page numbers, report date, and user ID, that would be used on all reports unless otherwise specified.

Sure, some types of output, like a customer welcome letter that includes the customer name, address, account number, and credit limit, would not have some of these elements, but those special cases will be handled specifically for those reports.

Attached sample

I've found that one of the first acts of most customers during the specification phase is to drop a couple of pounds of paper on you saying, "These are the reports we need." When applicable, attach those reports as samples of what you're going to produce—or, what you're not going to produce, in favor of something else/different/better. Just like screen shots are worth a thousand words, it makes sense to include a report sample.

Purpose

Yes, I know—you're probably thinking, well, "Duh…" Do you really need to specify the purpose of a report, for Pete's sake?

Well, yes; otherwise, I wouldn't have put this here. It's often good to put the purpose of a report down in writing. However, there's a difference between screens (or processes) and reports. The ultimate recipient of a screen or process is the system—the database is getting something.

But the ultimate recipient of a report is a person—and here's where you identify who will be getting the report, and what they use it for. It seems a little simplistic, but you can actually do your customer some good by insisting on this information. Often, they'll discover that out of the 26 reports they thought they wanted, they only needed 18—and, furthermore, three of those are similar enough that they can be rolled into one. Now you've just saved them about 40% of their report costs—and they haven't even started to use the system!

Detail entity

Typically, a data file consists of fields from at least one, if not several tables, but at the same time, usually not all of the fields from every table. The key bit of information here is to identify what the most granular level of data is—what represents the "detail" band of the report. If you were cranking out an invoice report, the detail entity would probably be an invoice header. However, if you were reporting on back orders, you'd need to include line item rows so you can identify which items have shipped and which have not.

Within a detail entity, you'll have data items—fields, combinations of fields, or user-defined functions that create a value that can be placed on a report as a field. When you join a pair of tables, you'll need to identify how the tables are joined—by what column or columns in the two tables.

You'll need to identify both of these items—data items and joins between tables—in this section.

Calculated fields

You'll find yourself creating fields that consist of the combination of two or more other fields from the database. For example, you may have stored each part of a name—First, Middle, Last—in separate fields, but on the report, you want a single field that concatenates these fields. The Detail Entity might include each of the name parts by themselves because you need them for sorting—but you also have to identify the combination as a calculated field because you need to place this calculated field on the report skeleton.

Filter

Just as the Detail Entity describes a limited set of fields that are going to be produced in the result set, the Filters section describes which set of records will end up in the result set.

Order/Group

Once the entire result is created, you'll want to identify how it's going to be sorted—alphabetically? By date? By a combination of fields? And, often, you're going to want subtotals in the report, so you'll need to include columns with group subtotals. These "Group By Expressions"—key values that create aggregations of data—are separate from fields identified in the Detail Entity because they don't usually exist in a table by themselves.

Fields/objects

A report skeleton (or form) has "things" on it just like a screen—and so they can be defined and counted. The things are somewhat different in nature, but they can be discretely defined just as well. These things include:

- Labels—Either text or graphical.

- Fields—Straight from the data file.

- Calculated Fields—A combination of one or more fields from the data file in concert with other operations.

- Group Bands—A feature specific to our report forms, but there are similar features in many other reporting tools.

- Subtotals and Totals—Either in group bands, page bands, or title/summary bands.

- Rules—I don't use them often, but you can even attach processing rules that are applied when the report is executed.

- Exceptions to system generated fields (such as page numbers, report date, and user ID) that are part of the report template.

Each of these things plays a special role in handling the data file that is sent through the report form.

Additional notes

This description covers many of the common situations you'll run into for reports, but as with everything, there's always an exception or two. Here's where you identify any special circumstances or "not elsewhere mentioned" items. For example, perhaps you have to include graphical images or parts of other files on a report. You would identify these here—and describe where those images or parts are going to come from.

Now that you have a data file with a certain number of "things" and a report form that also has a definable number of "things," you have accomplished two tasks. First, you have explicitly described what the report is going to look like and what's going to be in it to the user. Second, you can determine the cost of this report.

By the way, this method of describing output can be used regardless of the destination of the output—the screen, a printed report, or a file.

Standard components

In my shop we have a number of standard functions in our foundation that are included with every application as part of the package. We've written each of these functions once and from then on, we don't touch 'em—the options that need to be configured for each application are all data-driven, so there's no work involved at all. However, we do describe how each function works in the specification for two reasons.

First, the specification is a description of how the system works and what functionality it possesses—just because we include it as part of our standard foundation doesn't mean it has any less utility than a custom designed screen or report for the user.

Second, if the customer should send this specification out for competitive bid, we've just raised the bar because now the other companies will have to match this functionality—and they likely do not have the same capabilities built into their systems. And furthermore, even if a competitor could come up with a competitive bid, we've been using our utilities for years. Which do you think is more bug free?

Password maintenance

High on the list of standard components is a password maintenance screen. There are a number of twists to this capability, so it's good to describe how yours works. For example, how often does the password have to be changed? Can a password be reused later? Can the same one be entered again? What are the length requirements of the password value? Are there restrictions to the types of characters that can be used in a password? Is it case-sensitive?

Is there a list of illegal passwords to validate against? For example, one password validation scheme I've seen matches the password against a dictionary of English words—so that a password can't consist of just words. And I know of another company that validates all passwords against a list of off-color language terms. This caused a bit of embarrassment when it was implemented, since users were suddenly running to MIS claiming they'd been locked out of their system, and MIS knew it was because the password no longer passed validation. One "sweet little old lady" in Accounting was discovered to have a vocabulary that would make a sailor blush.

User maintenance

This screen is simply the mechanism where an administrator can add, delete, and make changes to the list of users allowed to access the system. I actually don't encourage administrators to delete users unless they were created by mistake. Instead, I include an "Is Active" flag that is set to False when a user leaves the company. This way, any types of data that are tied to users (for example, accounts assigned to sales reps) don't get orphaned by mistake.

Configuration

I've discussed configuration fairly heavily earlier in this chapter. The only additional point to make here is that you might include two configuration choices—one for standard configuration options throughout the application that are standard in every app, and another for custom configuration options for this customer. Access to both screens would be restricted to supervisory-level type folks.

The standard configuration screen might include a number of items. The ability to set the time between incremental search keystrokes, various password maintenance restrictions (such as how often a password has to be changed), defaults for new users, and how the query screen that allows users to filter for data is configured could be just a few.

A custom configuration screen might include the location of data files to be imported or the directory names for exported files, how specific values in various screens are maintained (whether or not a company number is automatically generated), and items specific to how custom screens, reports, and processes operate.

User customization

As I mentioned earlier, you may also want to allow each user to have their own preferences. In the old days, this included custom color sets and printer drivers. Now that the popular GUIs usually control these items, you may provide the ability for the user to control how the interface works or to further customize items that were initially set in the configuration screens.

Data repair

Just about every database system I've ever seen has used data files on disk somewhere, and whenever software and hard disks come into contact, there's danger of data going bad. You should provide the ability for, at a minimum, a supervisor-level user to diagnose and possibly repair problems with data. Re-indexing, purging old data, and packing bloated files are all functions that you should consider providing as standard issue in your app.

However, it's not just enough to include them—explain how they work, and what situations might occur that would cause the user to need to use them.

Help

It used to be that there were three kinds of Help: non-existent, under construction, and not used. With the advent of HTML Help from Microsoft (I'm kind of a big fan—of HTML Help, that is), there's no excuse not to provide a reasonably robust, and useful Help system with your app.

I provide the entire Functional Specification online—and it's a simple matter to cut this file up into a bunch of HTML files and assemble them with the HTML Help compiler. A couple of hours, maybe half a day—and this is the type of work that a clerical-level person can perform quite nicely.

I've had to talk several customers into accepting a Help file built with HTML Help—until I showed them the results—and they admitted that not only was this the first Help file they felt they could actually use, but that it was actually "cool."

As I said, I put the entire Functional Specification (as well as any other info that's laying around, such as Use Cases or other documentation) into online Help. Later, when a customer asks a question like "Does the import customer routine convert mixed-case data into uppercase?" I'll answer, "Well, gorsh, I don't rightly remember. Howsabout you and I call up Help together and find out." After the third or fourth time, the user gets the idea that calling us isn't a quicker method than looking it up in the Help file.

Help can be taken further, of course. Back when Help files simply consisted of DBF or text files, we routinely included "user-defined" Help options where the user could append notes to an existing Help topic as well as add their own Help topics, and cross-reference Help topics to each other. With HTML Help, this isn't nearly as easy, but depending on your situation and preference for a Help file format, you may still include customizable Help. If you do, you'll need to describe how it works and how to use it. After all, a customizable Help system is simply another database management system. Hmmm.

Of course, your preference for Help files may differ, but in any case, you'll want to provide a description of how the online Help you're providing will work.

System info

It's a good idea to provide a screen that lists some basic diagnostic information about the application, such as which version, which directory it was installed in, the current system date, and machine information such as disk space and available memory. A System Information screen is a good place to put all this data.

But, you can do even better. Many Microsoft products ship with an applet called MSINFO. You can make a function call to it and display a ton of information—like operating system info, swap file data, a list of every DLL installed on the computer, and more data about stuff that lives in the Registry than you'll ever want to know. Provide a button that calls MSINFO if it's available, and describe what it does here.

About

You really ought to have an About screen, if for no other reason than to provide a hiding place for that Easter Egg you put in their system. You did put one in, didn't you? (The technical editor of a previous edition asked "at whose cost." I'm pretty certain that he was kidding.)

Technical specs

The technical specifications provide a description of how the system will be put together, what each function or operation will do, and how the user will use the system.

This section gets more and more technical—the casual user has probably stopped reading by now. Thus, I assume that most readers of this section are technically literate, although possibly not experienced with software development.

Environment

This is where I tell the user what the requirements for our app are. Just like on the box of software at MegaSoftCity, I list the minimum (and recommended) hardware configuration and additional peripherals required. This section also explains how our app is going to play nicely with the other software applications in the big sandbox that is the company's network and, specifically, the users' PCs. Finally, I describe a few requirements of how the user will maintain their system to keep it in good working order.

Hardware requirements

First, explain what level of processor, how much hard disk space, how much RAM, what type of network interfaces, screen resolutions, and other peripherals are required or desirable. I also state that this equipment will be purchased and maintained by the customer—it's not as common nowadays, but occasionally a software vendor will provide the box that their app is supposed to run on. I don't want the customer to assume that, just because the last vendor supplied a box, I'm going to as well.

The following text is a bit dated, but in these times, anything we would print in a book would be outdated before the ink was dry.

```
Operation of System will be performed on equipment purchased, owned, and
maintained by Customer. The workstations will be IBM PC compatibles containing
a minimum of Pentium II processors with 64 MB of memory, and 128 MB is
recommended. Machines with less than 64 MB of memory may not work reliably as
far as moving data between System and other applications.
```

```
All will be equipped with monitors capable of SVGA color display, will use at
least 800 x 600 resolution, and all will have hard disks with at least 500 MB
of disk space available. A mouse is required. Printing will be directed to
generic dot matrix and HP Laser-Jet and InkJet printers via parallel ports or
network connections.
```

Operating system and software

In the past, we have run into problems when a customer decides they are going to run our application somewhere we did not anticipate, has problems, and then expects us to fix it free of charge. We need to inform the customer what it should run on and how it will work. We also do a little CYA. Describe the operating system—including which version—as well as any other pieces of software that are required, such as DLLs, drivers, and patches.

```
The system will run on Novell NetWare 4, Windows 9x, Windows NT 4.0 Service
Pack 5 or later, or Linux kernel 2.02.781.
```

For example, in the olden days, we stated "FoxPro for Windows does not run reliably with less than 8 MB memory. If you want to run more applications, you will need more memory," in response to customers who would attempt to open up Word, Excel, PowerPoint, an e-mail program, and our application—all in 4 MB!

Nowadays, we often come across situations where the developer tools are not always compatible across all operating systems. For instance, Visual Basic 2.0 and Visual FoxPro 3.0 will run on Windows 3.1, Windows 95, and Windows NT. Visual Basic 6.0 and Visual FoxPro 8.0, on the other hand, are 32-bit only tools, which means they will not run on Windows 3.1. HTML Help requires pieces from Internet Explorer 4 or later to run successfully. These types of dependencies need to be specified. They cannot take this VB or VFP application and run it on the old 486 clunker in the corner with 8 MB of RAM. If we don't specify, they will run into all sorts of problems and argue that it's an application problem.

You'll also want to describe what software will be used to develop the application, including version number and level of product. A fair number of customers are interested to know which development tools are being used, in the belief that they will be able to take over the development of or otherwise contribute to the development project. It's good sense to keep the customer informed.

Third-party elements

Some products and projects are more suited for the use of third-party tools than others—but these days, it's a rare app that is built solely with a single development tool. Include the description of any third-party tools, libraries, controls, and other elements that are required to rebuild or recompile the application. Also include the name and contact information, and how licensing is handled.

You don't have to include tools that you use solely in-house any more than you would have to include which word processor you used to produce this specification. (Examples of these tools might be productivity tools, such as third-party debuggers, or design tools that allow you to generate end products such as CASE tools or flow chart tools.) You simply need to give the customer the information they would need in order to generate a new version of the application.

Interaction with environment

These days, it's trickier to keep a Windows application running than it was in the days of DOS—it's not uncommon for the customer to install another piece of software that clobbers some piece of Windows that your app needed. As a result, we require that, for smooth running, our app take precedence over anything else running on the machine. Naturally, this isn't going to happen often, but when problems arise that are caused by the interference of another app, we can charge the customer to troubleshoot and fix the troubles.

We also document additional requirements, so, should the customer run into network, hardware, viral, or data security problems, they won't expect us to fix the ramifications for free. We're happy to provide whatever support we can; we just make it clear that repairing their tables because a virus infected half of their workstations is not part of our fixed price proposal.

```
The equipment may be used for purposes other than running System, but System
will take precedence in terms of use, access by Customer and Hentzenwerke
personnel, and setup parameters. Data backup will be done according to standard
internal MIS procedures independent of System. In addition, Customer personnel
will take reasonable precautions that equipment is protected from outside
interference including, but not limited to, virus infection and use or access
by non-authorized personnel. System will not perform environment checking such
as looking for the existence of fonts, non-application-specific system files,
or available memory and disk space. Time spent on the resolution of problems
caused by the alteration of the environment once the System has been installed
is not included as part of this proposal and will be billed on a time and
materials basis.
```

Data

We're going to be installing the application onto some sort of computer. Since we're now invading someone else's domain, I like to describe what impact our application will have on their property.

Directory structures

We need to explain to the customer how we are going to set up the application architecture and how it is going to reside on their hard disk. This helps the MIS folks understand the requirements and demands we will place on their computer system. The other advantage is that we get to do a little bit of a sales job because most developers are, shall we say, not very sophisticated when it comes to handling application architectures. In other words, many developers still throw everything in one directory (including a dozen files with .TMP and .BAK extensions) and walk out the door.

```
In order to avoid the difficulties encountered by having hundreds of files in a
single directory, as commonly practiced, the files for this application are
broken out into multiple directories by function.
```

A healthy application has a number of requirements. For ease of maintenance, upgrade, and being able to keep things straight, I feel it's important to keep your program, metadata, and data in different directories. Depending on the size of an application, you may even want to do that for performance reasons.

Table summary

Even the most technically challenged customer is highly interested in their data and how it's going to be organized. However, trying to explain proper data normalization is sometimes difficult. I've found that the customers understand the description of a table when we explain it the following way:

```
A table is essentially a spreadsheet in which every row contains one example or
instance of whatever entity it is that the table represents, and every column
represents a single piece of information about that entity. If your table
contains pets, you might have a single row for each living or dead pet. Columns
would be: name, type of animal, type of species, date of birth, date of death,
date and type of immunizations, and gender.
```

When you describe each table, it's really important to provide an example of an instance within that table. In the pet description above, one would hope that an instance of a pet is pretty obvious—a single animal. However, if your table is for "cargos," you would want to describe what a "cargo" is—could perhaps the entire truckload of "stuff" be considered a single record in the cargo table? Or if you are shipping on a tanker, is there one cargo on board or could there be several?

This way, the customer understands the kinds of data that will go into the table. By explicitly saying that each instance of a pet has to go in one and only one row, you avoid the people who suddenly don't think linearly and think they can use three rows to describe a pet, because that's the way they would actually just type it in themselves if they were entering it into 1-2-3 or Excel. By giving them this visual conceptualization of a spreadsheet, they can help identify what is in the table in terms of rows and columns themselves.

The other thing that we must do is describe the relationships between the tables.

```
"If you have a bunch of people and a bunch of pets, how do you identify which
pets belong to which people (or in the case of cats, which people belong to
which pets)?"
```

It's pretty straightforward to make sure that we have an owner key in a pet table that ties that pet record back to the owner—but we have to verify this if the key is one that the user sees. We use surrogate (hidden) keys for all of our work, but in some cases, the user also wants to see a physical attribute that ties the two tables together.

The other piece of information you have to discover about relationships between tables is how many. For example:

```
Does every person have to have a pet? Possibly not.

Can an owner have more than one pet? Only if the pet allows it.

Can more than one person own the same pet? Possibly - in the case of children,
more than one person may be listed as being attached to the pet (so that each
kid could take the pet to school for Sharing Day).
```

As you know, in the case of many-to-many relationships, a third table is required to join them. While you and I know how to do this in terms of relational theory, it may not be necessary to describe the underlying concept of how this works to the customer. Still, it is important to document that there is a many-to-many relationship. When you are describing file structures, you may also want to provide some examples of typical data.

Table structures (data dictionary)

There are two parts to this section. The first is to describe our naming conventions for databases, tables, and fields, so that the reader can more closely understand the technical detail to follow.

```
Identical field names indicate the same attribute (data element) in different
tables. For example, the DINVOICE field in the INVOICE table represents the
same DINVOICE data element as in the JOB table.

All fields that begin with "IID" are unique, primary keys or foreign keys. All
keys are system generated and hidden from the user.

All fields that are named "CCREATED" and "TCREATED" are audit fields that
identify who added the record and the date and time of when the record was
added, while "CLASTMOD" and "TCHANGED" are audit fields that track the last
edit of the record.
```

Then, we list every table in the system, except the metadata tables, and describe what every field is going to be. This is one of those CYA kind of things—nothing is more aggravating than having a customer who, upon final delivery, produces a list of changes to the tables—field lengths, types, and so on—and expects you do so for free.

Hopefully, we have gotten a first draft of field lists (and, hopefully, what tables they might belong to) from the user. They should specify whether the customer number has to be seven characters long and the PO number has to be 14 characters, but sometimes they don't; therefore, we have to make it up. If the customer comes back with a set of requests like "Oh, that has to be another character wider" or "This has to be numeric," they're going to expect the change to take 10 seconds. However, it's a lot more work than that, because you have to change the actual table, the data dictionary, screens, reporting metadata, and possibly other things.

Sure, we'll be happy to do so, but we are going to charge them for that. Therefore, we document what we are going to provide and should they need changes, we will provide those changes for a fee. This is no different than if you asked your home builder for a different type of light switch or to have the sidewalk by the side of the house moved six inches so you can plant another row of flowers next to the house.

File layouts (non-table)

When users read about the processes that the system will perform in the Functional Spec, they don't want to see detailed file layouts—and that's why those layout definitions belong back here. First, much like table structures, describe what the file is, where it comes from, and where it's located on disk, if the user can't selectively go get it.

Next, identify the type of file—comma delimited, ISAM, fixed length, whatever. And then provide the exact layout—describing each field, its size, its type (if applicable), allowable values, and an English description of the field.

Be aware that as applications become more sophisticated, the data that it will be accessing often comes from a wider range of sources, such as binary files for multi-media and non-sequential file formats for mail files. You may not want to (or be able to) specify the file layouts in these cases, but you'll need to define the version of the file format and give whatever other information you can in order to clearly define what you're working with.

Image files come in a wide variety of formats—just because two files both have the same GIF, TIF, or AVI extension doesn't mean they've got the same internal format!

Original data

This is really an important point—but one that most developers either don't think about, or just plain forget about. I've found from reader feedback on previous editions that this one tip was more than worth the price of the book by itself.

If you don't identify where the data for the system is going to come from, the customer is going to assume something very bad—they are going to think that the new system will just magically show up. The customer *always* assumes a replacement system will come with the data from the existing system.

From their point of view, what good would an accounting system be if it didn't have any data in there? You couldn't do comparisons or postings. You couldn't run most reports. You'd have to enter each vendor and customer and employee again when it came time to enter POs and sales orders and time sheets. And the customer is not about to enter all the data from scratch, right? Thus, they're just going to think that you've got some magical way to get data from their old system into the new one. You're a software magician, after all. Thus, it is imperative to tell the customer how you will handle the original data.

What are your options? The first option is leave the tables empty. And this is okay, as long as you have told the customer up front (and reminded them several times) that this was going to be the case. If you do this, you should be sure to make it clear by helping them think about how they're going to enter the data. They might not have all the answers, but if you've gotten them to start to think about it, you can be more certain that they're not going to make the dreaded "data will just show up" assumption.

The second option is to provide a bare minimum data set—possibly some lookup tables and a few minor entity tables—but the guts will be empty. When the customer adds a new invoice, they can select an existing customer, for example, but the system will not be loaded with the invoices dating back to 1931.

The third possibility is to convert all of the existing data from the old system. Thus, unless the old system uses the exact same data structures (fat chance!), you will have to describe how you are going to convert the data.

Data conversion

If a customer has a boatload of information they want converted over to their new system, the technical specification needs to describe how that's going to be done. First, you need to provide a mapping of the old and new data, then you need to describe how the data is going to be moved from the old structures to the new ones (you know, that sorta sounds like a process that I described earlier in this chapter, doesn't it?), and finally, you need to define who will do what, and when it will be done.

Ordinarily, there is a lot of manual labor associated with this kind of thing. Why? One of the reasons an old system is being replaced is because it doesn't work well. One of the prime reasons a system is deemed unusable is that it doesn't care for the data very well. Therefore, the data that you moved from the old system to the new system may not be very good. This brings me to one of the fundamental rules of data:

People don't know their data. They do not understand what is in their current data, they do not know what holes exist, and they do not know if there is corrupt data in the system. Repeat after me: People don't know their data.

Never assume that the data will come over flawlessly—no matter what the customer tells you. I don't think I've seen a flawless conversion in the past 20 years. You may get lucky (if you do, write me!), but if you assume that their data is good, you're going to be unhappy. Make sure you describe what needs to be done to convert their data into a format usable by the system you are proposing.

Furthermore—and this is the important part—you'll have to describe what's going to happen if the conversion doesn't go smoothly.

There could be missing records, invalid entries, or holes in the data. Perhaps they are missing all of July's records. (Where did they go?) This would be a good time to ask if they really need the July transactions. Perhaps they should reconstruct the July transactions now so that you can get those records into the new system and allow the users to start off with a new robust set of data.

There could be invalid data. For example, suppose the valid codes are A, B, C, and D. But for some reason, there are 1,000 records with a "7X" in that field. Why is there a 7X? If you're lucky, you'll find Ed down there in the bowels of the Accounting department saying, "Oh, I remember what a 7X was." But that's if you're lucky. Otherwise, well, you'll need to have a plan for what to do when you run into unexpected data.

Thus, be sure to specify the rules used during import and conversion routines. You will need to do this in your specification so the customer understands what will be done and what will be left undone—and what they'll have to do before and after the conversion.

You need to identify, at a minimum, what data is required for a record to be valid in the new system. Next, find out where that data is going to come from—an existing source, a default value, or did it have to be entered manually with internal knowledge?

Next, write up your test scripts for running the migration, and for qualifying the results. Did the record counts come up as expected? How about dollar amounts or other totaling? Finally, rerun your tests and make sure you get the same results each time.

Data set size, throughput analysis

It's not difficult to put together a system that suddenly snowballs into several hundred megabytes (or gigabytes) of data, or to have data entry loads explode from 100 records per day to several thousand in the same period. Because the demands on a system are different depending on the number of users and the data set size, I specify what type of load—original and additional—the system can expect, as shown in **Table 1**.

Table 1. Initial and ongoing record loads.

Table	Original Load (# of records)	Weekly Load (# of records)
Pets	5000	200
Owners	3500	150

While not a commitment, it helps us make sure we have scaled the application to the expectations of the user. In other words, we're not using this to price the application as much as to communicate with the user so they don't come back in a month claiming the system is awfully slow—and upon investigation, we discover that they've increased the daily load twenty-fold.

Implementation

As systems get more complex, it's no longer satisfactory to throw a few diskettes at the network coordinator and walk out the door. This section explains how you are going to move from the "we are done writing code" phase to the "the system is up and running and the customer is happy with the results" phase.

By now, you may be wondering what this has to do with the Functional Specification. There are two points. I'll agree, this section doesn't tell the user "what" they're going to be able to do with the application, but, then again, yes, it does.

If you don't include information on testing, installation, training, and modifications, they aren't going to know how this will be delivered to them, and thus they won't know what they'll be able to use, or do, and when. It'd be just like if you had a house built for you, but were never told when you'd be able to move in.

And now back to the other reason for this section. The Functional Specification is also a sales tool for you. It's there to make you look good—to communicate to the customer that you know what you're doing, and that you're the very best to do it.

By including this section, you assure them that you're not a typical software developer, slinging code and bolting for your car, but that you're the "real deal" and that they're getting the complete treatment.

Test methodology

Most companies employ a testing plan that includes pushing most of the buttons at least once and then hoping the user doesn't find anything wrong late on Friday afternoon. While I'll be the first to admit that our testing methodology has room for improvement, our specs still draw a baseline for what types of testing we will perform, so that it is clear to the customer what we will do, and what we're expecting from them.

```
Hentzenwerke uses three distinct testing phases during system development. The
first phase consists of testing each action in the system (menu choices and
screen objects) to verify that it operates without adverse effects. The second
phase consists of verifying that each function point in the system (menu
choices, screen actions, screen data fields, and report objects) performs the
function or contains the data it is specified to. The third phase consists of
checking that the business rules of the system (logic and branching,
algorithms, special cases) are carried out through the operation of the system.

Each phase of testing is planned prior to the testing by the Software
Developer. This is referred to as the Test Plan. Upon completion of the Test
Plan, the Application Tester will perform the Test according to the plans and
record the results. This process will be followed for each Deliverable.
Hentzenwerke will perform all testing for each of these phases before delivery
of any working prototypes or final programs.
```

Test plan

The test plan does two things: 1) It lets the customer know we will be checking our work, and 2) it acts as a checklist for our QA department. Just as we need a blueprint for the developer to write the code, we need to provide a blueprint or a description for the QA department on how we are going to test the application.

What goes into a test plan? In the chapter on testing in the next section, I discuss test plans in more detail. The essential characteristic of the test plan description here in the specification is that we set expectations for the customer as to what work we will perform.

Test data set requirements

The next line in the specification is the following:

```
The customer will provide the following data sets:
```

Want a surprise? They never fill this in. They never provide test data. I had one customer provide us with a good set of test data once, but then that person was later fired from their job. (I swear I'm not making this up.)

Having test data provided is rare, but we do address it if for no other reason than to show that the customer isn't going to do it and therefore the application will cost more because we will have to do it. (Our metrics assume that we will be generating test data ourselves.) Regardless, it needs to be done. What might go into a test data set requirement description? Here are a number of check-off items we use:

```
How to populate minor entities and lookups.

How to populate the original tables in terms of having single records, 10
records, and 100 records.

Where will data come from - manually entered or converted from data provided by
the customer?
```

If at all possible, we would like to have data from the customer. As I mentioned earlier, if they see test results with real data sets instead of "Bugs Bunny" and "Road Runner," they'll be able to more accurately identify whether or not the system is working properly. Furthermore, you can write up test plans that demonstrate examples that they would be familiar with if they give you actual data available.

Deliverables

This section describes what we are going to provide and what the customer will provide. Particularly if you are a one-person shop, it is a good idea to describe what you and the customer will each provide. Partly this is to document that you are providing your own tools to do the work, thus satisfying the IRS that you are an independent contractor and not an employee of the customer's company. It's also nice for the customer to know what they should expect. Sometimes the developers forget to provide these things.

Installation

The best system in the world isn't going to do the customer much good if it stays on your development network. However, a significant number of problems can occur during the installation of the application at the customer's site. This final section (yes, we're almost done!) describes the last leg of our journey.

Most companies now have somebody who is their "PC person" or "Internet guru." We don't want to spend a lot of our time and talent doing things that their PC person could be doing a lot more economically.

```
System will be installed on the office server and on one PC that represents the
standard configuration throughout the office. Time spent installing and
configuring System to run on additional workstations, if any, is not included
as part of this proposal and will be billed on a time and materials basis.

Customer will provide remote access through modem dial-in software in order to
facilitate remote support.
```

We agree to install the application on the server and one workstation that represents the general configuration used in their office. We will install additional ones if they would like. Because it takes additional time, however, we charge them for it. We specify what we will do for the fixed price. If additional work is desired, the price will be adjusted accordingly.

If your application isn't a traditional network app, it's even more important to specify what services you will provide during installation and what you're expecting the customer to provide. For example, it can be a real hassle to arrive only to find out that the T-1 line was installed last week and their Web server was just plugged in this morning—and they're expecting you to load Linux, Apache, and everything else from scratch, in addition to your application.

Training

All but the most trivial of applications will require training of one sort or another. I personally try not to do formal training, relying instead on informal sessions provided during the delivery of each module of an application.

What if the application will be rolled out to a large number of users? This is a particular pet peeve of mine—if the application requires enough training for classes to be organized, I think the customer should do it. Having the customer perform training means that they take ownership of the app. I've run into too many situations where the customer wants to take a hands-off approach—they're busy, and since development is being done off-site anyway, it's easy for them to forget about it.

Getting them involved during training means they will begin to make it their own—they will need to know it well enough to explain it to someone else. Of course, this begs the question of who trains the trainer? First of all, since we typically deliver an application in pieces, there are one or two power users who have been working with the app for a while—and they are prime candidates to be trainers. Second, we've found it very economical to hold a "train the trainer" session—the customer gets a lot of bang for their buck, and you're not spending time explaining how to run Windows.

Some customers may want you to create user guides, training materials, or other things to assist them in rolling out the application. This is the place to specify these types of items. Be forewarned that these things may not be trivial—to create a CBT (computer-based training) CD can be as complex and expensive as doing the application itself!

Milestones and delivery schedule

It makes good sense to deliver pieces of the application as they are ready, instead of swooping in, dumping a bunch of CDs on their desk (remember the good old days when software used to fit on a single CD?), and saying, "Here it is! Work on it. Let me know if you have any problems." We want to deliver an application in pieces so by the time they have seen the entire application, they understand how the whole thing works. They have bitten off a bit at a time, have had a chance to digest each piece, and by the time the entire system is installed, they're comfortable with all of it.

How do we break up the milestones? We simply ask the customer how they want it delivered. They generally have requirements within their organization that will dictate the delivery schedule—they may have people going on vacation or someone not familiar with working with computers who needs more time to get acclimated. Asking the customer in what order they want modules of the application delivered is part of the design process.

Naturally, there may be some technical reasons that you can't deliver module C before module B, so this discussion of milestone delivery involves some give and take. But most people are reasonable, and they'll understand that the reporting module can't be delivered until you've had a chance to import data from the old system.

All of you who have absolute control over the entire application environment—system and situation together—please raise your hands. Exactly. Nobody has complete control. Thus, it is important to not schedule deliveries with hard-coded dates unless you have absolute control over everything required to deliver. Why schedule a hard-coded date that may get blown away because it's dependent on events outside of your control, or your knowledge?

You can state that you will deliver module X a certain number of weeks after each of the external events have happened because you do have some control over what you are doing.

Modifications

Modifications are a fact of life. This can be a bit disconcerting to some customers. They've spent a huge amount of money, expended even more effort, and made promises to probably everyone in the company. And as soon as the ink is dry on the Functional Spec, they discover that something has to be changed. New requirements come to light, a process was found to work differently than they initially thought, or someone down the hall just plain changed their mind.

And, gosh, they really are tired of spending money by now.

Here's the mantra we repeat to every customer who runs into this situation (and that would be all of them):

```
Useful systems are dynamic.
```

Businesses change, and it's impossible to anticipate all of those changes in advance. In fact, as I've said, both RAD and Agile Methodologies are set up, in varying degrees, to handle, even anticipate the ongoing changes and discovery of new requirements. Thus, instead of having them fight changes to the system, help them expect changes. One way of acclimating them to this idea is to provide a thorough description of how you work with changes. (Chapter

27, "Change Orders," deals with Change Orders in detail.) By doing so, you're going to look better, and give them greater peace of mind by showing that you're not only expecting this, but you have a well defined process for doing so to boot!

There are three important pieces of information in this section of the specification.

First, as I said, we're telling the customer, by addressing the issue of modifications at all, that modifications are part of the game. However, while we expect modifications and we are prepared to handle them—we will not perform unlimited modifications to a fixed price system for free.

```
The menus, screens, reports, table structures, and functionality described in
this Functional Specification are final.

It is not uncommon for modifications to be requested after such a point.
Depending on the type of modification, and the stage of development when that
modification is requested, the amount of work that the modification requires
may range from trivial to substantial.

Estimates for such modifications will be provided in writing on a Hentzenwerke
Corporation Change Order form and will need to be signed off by the customer
representative before they are incorporated into the system.
```

You may want to distinguish between modifications made during system development, and enhancements made in a subsequent release.

The next important point is to specify that the customer can't modify the system's source code while we are working on it. I've always been incredulous that a customer will want to accept part of the application, get their hands on the source code, and start making their own modifications when the entire application hasn't even been installed.

That's like changing the carpeting or painting the walls while the construction company is still putting up floor joists or laying conduit. But it happens, so we want to make sure to explain to the customer that this is going to cost them extra. Maybe it hasn't happened to you, but you'll want to spell it out so that you don't run into misunderstandings later on.

```
Customer agrees not to modify the source code and/or design surfaces during the
development of the System.
```

The last big point, and this is one of my favorite clauses, is that we reserve the right to interpret functionality and performance issues that are not explicitly defined in this specification. This way, we don't get dragged through the mud because a customer wants the tab order of a screen to be different, or the position of labels on a screen to be left aligned instead of right aligned (like they have been on every prototype we've shown).

For example, we typically display a countdown message in the upper right corner of a screen when processing a file. We had one customer who went through several prototype demonstrations, only to have them insist that the processing message should be displayed in a progress bar centered on the screen—and that "we should have known to do that" because that's what they've seen in other applications. If they have specific performance requirements, then they should have noted this (and we should have asked, of course) at the particular stage in the specification where appropriate.

```
Hentzenwerke Corporation reserves the right to interpret interface, behavior,
and performance issues that are not specifically described in this Functional
Specification, as it sees fit.
```

If you don't include a statement like this, the customer can request changes ad infinitum—which is death for a fixed price application. It's much like a furniture mover quoting a fixed price to move the piano from the den to the living room, only to have the parents request to have the piano moved to one corner, to another, then back to the first corner, on and on, for hours.

Error handling

You're probably not going to believe it either, but I've heard of applications that have defects in them—after they're shipped to the customer! And it's likely that you'll produce an application that will, sometime, behave in an undesirable manner in front of the customer as well (kids, software—nothing behaves the way you would like it to, eh?). Instead of sweeping this possibility under the carpet, explain to the customer what's going to happen.

First, describe the error handler you've got installed in your application (you've got one, right?) and explain what's going to happen when the application encounters an unexpected event. These events can be grouped into three categories.

First are programming errors that throw an error dialog. A routine running past the end of an array, or the attempted use of a table or data source that isn't there, are two such examples.

The second are business rule errors that cause a visible error message, such as dividing by a tax rate that was set to zero, and thus causing a divide overflow.

And the third are environment conditions that need to alert the user, such as printers out of paper or ODBC connections that have been broken.

Finally, explain what the customer is supposed to do when an error is encountered. Some error handlers trap, display, and log errors that the user can then forward to the developer; others are, well, less graceful. Make sure the customer knows what you expect them to do. Yes, there's that concept again: setting expectations. The interface for the error handler that the customer interacts with is described earlier in the spec, but the process for handling errors in a macro scale (reporting them to your tech support department, for example) is described here.

Application feedback

Errors are not the only type of feedback a user might want to provide. Actually, there are three types, and since this is coming from a customer, we are very rigorous about tracking it.

The first type of feedback is the reporting of a defect—and that might be generated from an error message, or just anomalous behavior from the app. The second type is an Enhancement Request. While the app is working as specified, they want something different, or new. And the third part is just a question—they don't remember how something is supposed to work, or it isn't clear, or a new situation that hasn't been covered comes up.

The whole Application Feedback scenario is covered in detail later in this book, but in the Functional Spec, we provide a brief description of how the user should communicate this information back to us.

This is a great section to have in the specification—by the time they finish reading back here, they're tired, hungry, and cranky, so they probably will forget before they turn the page.

However, they'll eventually ask about reporting bugs or providing other types of feedback, and it's then that you can point back to this section in the specification. And more often than not, they'll look up from the specification and exclaim, "You guys have thought of everything, haven't you?" And you can sit back and smile.

Support

This last section is where we set expectations for being able to contact us after delivery. Some firms provide 24 hours a day, 7 days a week support, and require their developers to carry beepers. In some situations, this is imperative—a company with a mission-critical app that goes down Saturday afternoon can't wait until 9 AM Monday for a return phone call. However, some customers want their developers to be "on-call" just for peace of mind, when the app doesn't really require that level of support.

I've never been one to carry a beeper, and in fact only take on jobs that don't require 'round the clock support or instant response turnaround. But that's my personality—and as long as I've communicated this about my company to the customer, and they accept it, the expectations for getting in touch with us have been set.

If your circumstances are different, you should specify your hours of availability, how to contact your company after hours, and what type of turnaround time for a phone call or page will be provided—and, of course, what the charges are for these types of services.

Conclusion

That's the specification. Sure does seem like it would be a lot easier if you would do time and materials, doesn't it? Well, at the outset, sure, but it is much easier to deliver high-quality applications with a fully documented specification because you know what you are suppose to deliver. The customer knows what you are supposed to deliver. You have fewer arguments and disagreements, and, frankly, it is also easier to write the code if you understand exactly what is supposed to happen.

Is this complete? Is this the be-all and end-all of specifications? Obviously not. There may be a time somewhere down the road when we want to add something to it. In fact, I think it may happen next week. This specification is, despite years and years of experience, still a work in progress.

You have other experiences, other situations and requirements, and, therefore, you may decide to make changes to this and do things a different way. My hope is that I have provided you with some ideas you haven't seen before and some reasoning for doing some things that you already had put into place but didn't exactly know why.

This is the way we do things, partly because of the way we write systems but also because of our set of experiences. Your mileage probably differs, and I would love to hear your experiences and what you think belongs in a specification.

Chapter 17
Calculating Time and Cost
for a Specification

"Excuse me sir, but just exactly how obscene an amount of money were you talking about? Just profane or REALLY offensive?"—Store Manager
"REALLY offensive."—Edward
  —Pretty Woman

Of the five big questions in the software development world, determining time and cost for an application is probably the single toughest one. Mankind has put men on the moon and squeezed a million transistors onto a piece of plastic an inch square. So how come we can't figure out how much time it's going to take to write a piece of software? In this chapter, you'll learn about a mechanism that you can use to get a better handle on the magic questions of "How long?" and "How much?"

Over the past few chapters, I've been stressing that you need to be able to define what it is you're going to build before you can provide an accurate estimate of the time and cost. But at the same time I've been taunting you about how it is that we were going to actually get there. Now the rubber meets the road. But before you find out what I've got up my sleeve, let's discuss the status quo.

It's very important to note that this mechanism works just as well for corporate developers. In fact, corporate developers can be divided into two camps—those who work for an MIS department and write software for internal use, and those who work for a corporation that produces commercial software that is sold to the corporation's customers.

In both cases, the only difference is that the "customer" of this time and cost calculation is an employee of the same company.

If it's an internal app, then you, the developer, are probably dealing with a department head or group manager. If it's a commercial app, then you're working with a "product manager" or "program manager."

Regardless, you're going to be running into someone who needs to justify the business expense. That business expense may end up assigned to overhead or "cost of doing business," or it may be used to determine whether the potential market for the proposed product can support the expense. In both cases, some idea in advance of "how much" and "how long" is needed. Sure, the way the money flows from the "customer" to the "developer" is different, but the ability to accurately determine time and cost is just as important.

Methodologies for estimating

First, how do people generally estimate and price software projects today? Over the years, I've found that six methods are commonly used.

- **Guessing Randomly**. Probably the most common, scarily enough. The one advantage to this method is that it is fast, and no special training is needed.

- **The Knowing Eyeball**. This is where the developer simply looks over the information provided and a few minutes later, after eyeballing the ceiling with a knowing gaze, announces a price. When pinned down, the developer explains with a condescending snort, "Because I *know*." The big consulting firms are particularly good at this, but I've also run into more than a few individuals who are "legends in their own minds."

- **Price per Page**. The next step, of course, is to produce a specification or document of some sort, and then charge by the page—much like your history teacher did, handing out grades based on how thick your term paper was. (You always suspected that's what she did, didn't you?)

- **Double and Increment**. A bit more sophisticated, this methodology requires specialized knowledge of the calendar and the ability to do arithmetic. The first step is to come up with an initial estimate, usually using one of the first two methods. Then, the value is doubled and the unit of time measurement is bumped to the next level. Thus, a two-day job would be projected at four weeks, and a six-month project would be estimated at 12 calendar quarters.

- **HMDILY**. We wouldn't be software developers if we didn't have a few acronyms to throw around, and this is the first of two, pronounced "Hum-dilly." This one hearkens back to the days of a social studies teacher of mine who was explaining his grading system—"35% for the final, 25% for the mid-term, 20% for four quizzes, 10% for class participation. And the last 10%? Well, that depends on 'How much I like you.'"

  Similarly, this pricing methodology's acronym stands for "How Much Do I Like You?" Come on, admit it. You've always charged a couple customers a bit more because, frankly, they're just not that much fun to work with. I'm just confirming that this is a valid and common pricing technique that's in use all over the world.

- **HMDYH**. First used by attorneys and the IRS, this mechanism goes by the "HumDuh" moniker, which stands for "How Much Do You Have?" It's a great way to estimate—if you can do it—and if you can look yourself in the mirror the next morning.

These techniques are all in use today—but the end result is really still just an estimate for a price (and, possibly, timeframe) for the project. But enough jokes.

Obviously, these all fall short of the goal since, bottom line, they're all just guesses. None of them use any methodical mechanism for determining the end result, and thus the end result is not reproducible. This means that the same application could end up with three different prices on three different days. Which one is correct? Is the developer at risk of losing money on one or more of these prices? The point is—no one knows!

Ways to charge

Just because you've got an estimate for the project doesn't mean everything is finished. You still have to decide how to charge your customer. There are two basic themes—Time and Materials, and Fixed Price.

Options

"Time and Materials" takes its name from other types of hourly work where the vendor charges both for their time and the materials they use. For example, someone coming in to repair your chimney would charge you for the labor as well as any materials—bricks, mortar, rags, and so on. Same thing for repair shops of all sorts—they charge you for the labor as well as the cost of parts and any miscellaneous materials they use.

The alternative is "Fixed Price," and this is what it sounds like—a flat amount for the work, period. Implicit in this method are three assumptions. First, the vendor has made an estimate of how long it will take to perform the work (and any materials that might be needed) and factored in their usual hourly rate to come up with a fixed price. Second, if the actual job takes longer than expected, the vendor will accept a resulting lower hourly rate. And, third, if the actual length of time is less than what the vendor estimated, the vendor receives a greater hourly rate.

A rotten combination of these two is the "Not To Exceed" mechanism—where the vendor charges the customer at an hourly rate, but agrees not to exceed a predetermined ceiling.

Advantages and disadvantages

Let's explore how each of these options treats the players.

Time and Materials

This is the safest route for the developer in that the customer shoulders all of the possible risks.

One risk is scope creep, where additional features are added to the system, usually at the behest of the customer. Clearly the customer should bear this risk, since they're the ones who asked for the extra goodies.

Another risk is that the developer will use inexperienced or incompetent developers, who end up charging the customer for their learning curve. In this case, the unit of measure is an hour of the developer's time, and the customer becomes hostage to how competent the developer is. The developer may provide an estimate and try to stay within the estimate, but in the end, the customer will pay for whatever time the developer actually spends.

Who should bear this cost? At first blush, you might argue that the developer should—but when it comes down to it, the customer will eventually, one way or another, pay for the cost of a new developer's learning curve. This may not be paid directly; rather, the customer will see the bite indirectly through higher hourly rates for experienced developers, as they increase their rates to cover the expense of a developer who isn't earning enough to justify their own share of the expenses.

The risk doesn't end with inexperienced or incompetent developers, however. An experienced developer may just screw up the estimate, or intentionally underestimate in order to win the job, knowing that the final number will be measurably higher. And a firm may create a good estimate, and intend to staff the project with the appropriate people, but then be unable to assign the intended people to the job when it's delayed, or personal issues affect the availability of those people.

At any rate, the bottom line is that the customer initially bears all the risk. However, the vendor isn't insulated from danger. There is a possibility, since most customers ask, at a minimum, for a good faith estimate for a Time and Materials project, that if the invoices submitted exceed the quoted amount by too much, the customer will become unhappy.

On the other hand, the customer does benefit if they work with a skilled developer and the scope of the project is kept in check—the customer will pay the least possible amount and the developer will get paid for all of the hours they put in. But as a wise soul asked, "Just exactly how often does this really happen?"

Fixed Price

This is seemingly in the best interest of the customer, since the risks all fall on the shoulders of the developer. The issue of inexperienced or incompetent developers working on a project is moot, since the cost is now born by the vendor. Forcing the customer to pay extra due to misrepresentation or mistakes won't happen in this case. The risk of inexperienced or incompetent people being part of the project, then, is borne by the developer.

A second risk occurs when the developer used one of the aforementioned estimating methods and, as a result, has a number that is significantly smaller than what will actually be needed. If the difference is big enough, the developer may bail on the project, or even go out of business. This risk, then, is borne by the customer.

On the other hand, the developer shouldn't bear the risk of scope creep, but often does. The customer, when faced with a fixed price and a three-inch specification, is inclined to believe that all the functionality they saw demonstrated, discussed, or even just briefly thought about while in the shower will be included in the final application. No matter how good the specification is, the client will always find one more feature they "absolutely positively must" have, and will be reluctant to pay for it. Cagey clients will play this game to the hilt, in order to maximize the amount of "stuff" they get for their dollar.

As a result, the developer is often faced with a continuing series of demands to "add this" and "include that" because the customer insisted that they were part of the fixed price. The developer may agree to provide additional functionality or provide things for free in hopes of winning additional business.

At some point, though, this becomes unprofitable to do, and, in some cases, the developer will simply walk away from such a situation. You've seen instances where a company has been left holding the bag on a project they claimed was "90% done" but had been at that stage for months and months as the customer kept adding items to the final To-do list. In other cases, the developer will finish the job, but with such ill will generated that the customer will be forced to find a new developer for any subsequent work on the project.

However, the customer isn't safe either. In order to handle all of the possibilities for variances—both known and unknown—the vendor is likely to subject the customer to an unreasonably large "contingency factor" within the estimate in order to obviate any—or as much—of the risk as possible.

All in all, the Fixed Price contract can initiate an antagonistic relationship, because the developer has an incentive to do as little as possible for the fixed price, while the customer will normally try to "get as much as possible" for the same amount.

The benefit, when all of the factors come together, is that the customer knows how much a predefined entity is going to cost—and the vendor can make a healthy profit if they have skilled developers working on the project and are efficient at producing it.

Not To Exceed

The Not To Exceed compromise is simply a way of getting the developer to shoulder, unfairly, in my opinion, both risks without any of the possible rewards. The customer gets to pay the lowest amount possible, with a guarantee of a ceiling, although, oddly enough, the customer seems to think they can add feature upon feature and make changes ad infinitum without consequence. The developer, however, doesn't get paid extra for a skillful job, but can get badly burned for a project that goes way out of scope or runs into other unknown issues.

Function Point Analysis—and its problems

You would think that, in the 40-some years that people have been writing software of one form or another, some company, somewhere, would have figured out that it was in their best interest to solve this problem. Well, someone did—and who else but the world's largest software company: IBM. (In the late 1970s, IBM wasn't only the largest hardware company on the planet, but they also produced more software than anyone else—after all, they needed operating systems, applications, and tools to run on those boxes.)

The technique's purpose was to determine the size (and thus, cost) of software projects across a broad spectrum of needs, and was named Function Point Analysis (FPA). It addressed the initial issue—sizing a specific software project—but also provided a means to compare that "size" across languages, platforms, and applications. Function Point Analysis approaches the sizing of software from the end-user (customer) perspective. It can be used to measure any type of software project—custom database systems, real-time process control, operating systems, virus scanning tools, and the assembly code that runs your toaster, watch, and heart monitor.

I first learned about FPA from presentations made by Bob Kehoe and Ken Florian of Geneer in Chicago. Following is a synopsis of what I've learned about FPA. (If you ever get a chance to hear anyone from Geneer talk about any topic related to software engineering, don't miss it!)

Traditional methods of measuring the size of software projects used artificial categorizations of measurable items that could be impacted by external factors. For example, one classic metric for measuring the size of a software project was "lines of code." However, the number of lines of code can be affected by the type of language used (including the version), the style of programming used, and the skill of the programmer.

For example, a program written in machine code would take more lines of code than the same program written in C++. A new version of a language or tool may include language constructs or features that allow a particular goal to be accomplished with fewer lines of code—a single expression replacing what used to take a dozen lines or even an entire subroutine.

A typical programming style may dictate "one entrance, one exit" for all modules. While this can always be done, at times, depending on the language, adhering to a "one exit" strategy can require more layering of code, thus producing more lines of code than if "exit" statements were allowed in a couple of strategic locations.

And, finally, the skill level of the programmer can affect the number of lines of code drastically. One example would be when an unknowledgeable programmer writes their own routine to accomplish a task, not knowing that the language already has a function built in to do that task, thus bumping up the "lines of code" metric unnecessarily.

Furthermore, unscrupulous developers could even manipulate the metric in order to make themselves look good, by producing huge volumes of code in an amazingly short period of time (oh, how wonderful line continuation characters can be!), or by making the project look extremely difficult, requiring a measurement that was actually easy to reach, by artificially inflating the number of lines of code required to perform a standard task, and thus getting an easier multiplier for the rest of the project.

Another example would regard the use of object orientation in a system. One programmer who developed and correctly implemented a good set of class libraries would ultimately generate an application with significantly fewer lines of code than a programmer who didn't reuse any code at all. Yet, by using the "lines of code" metric, the two applications would be seen as significantly different in size even though functionally they were the same.

Each of these factors means that the "size" of the project may change due to factors outside of the control of the customer, which then puts the risk of changing costs unfairly on the customer.

Function Point Analysis is a synthetic measurement, meaning it is not specific to a single language or family of languages. This is the same as your using the synthetic measurement tool of a "square foot" to measure the floor in your living room, the amount of trunk space in your car, the amount of rain forest destroyed last year, or the size of your grandfather's forehead. Thus, an application written in COBOL could be compared, using its Function Point count, to a completely different system written in C++. An accounting module written in RPG for use on a System/32 could be compared to a process control system written in assembler for an injection molding machine.

Why is this synthetic measurement better than the alternatives?

Unlike those techniques, Function Points gave an independent yardstick of size, and thus, cost and time requirements. So when we say one system is 500 Function Points, while another is 800 Function Points, we don't have to know what language they are written in, what platform they're running on, or how good the programmer is—we just know that the one is about 1.5 times the size of the other. Therefore, assuming all other factors being equal (the same development tool and skill/experience of the developer), the one should obviously take about 1.5 times longer and cost 1.5 times as much to develop.

Finding Function Points

A Function Point is a unit of functionality delivered to the end user. How do we find Function Points? Essentially, in order to arrive at the number of Function Points in a system, one counts the number of system inputs, the number of potential outputs, the number of inquiries, the number of internal and external logical files, as well as evaluating approximately a dozen other General System Characteristics to determine the overall system complexity. General System Characteristics (GSCs) include things like data communications, distributed processing performance, heavy use configuration transaction rates, online data entry designed for end-user efficiency, online updates, complex processing, installation ease, operational ease, and multiple sites.

After each of these characteristics has been counted, they're mashed through a formula, resulting in a final number of Function Points. How is that translated into dollars? Here's the "Oh no!" part of this explanation. You need a historical baseline of costs for projects, which is used to determine the costs for future projects. If a project in the past had 300 Function Points and cost $300,000, then the cost per Function Point is $1,000. The next project, but with 500 function points, would then cost $500,000.

This explanation is somewhat simplified (well, actually, it's simplified a lot), but you get the idea. You can think of this as similar to the square foot measurement. You could compare the square footage of two structures, but if one is to be built over a swamp with marble floors and the other is to be built on level ground with pine floors, the *costs* per square foot are going to be different. Similarly, to be able to do some sort of screen design in a tool like C++ may take a fairly long time because it's a low-level language—and it might actually take even longer to do it in something like assembler. However, if you were using a language like Visual Basic, it would be easier and faster to put that screen together.

Thus, there are factors that affect the cost per Function Point—such as tools used and skill level of the developer(s). But again, those multipliers are strictly used to determine the cost. The number of Function Points in a system is the same regardless of what tool you are going to use to build it.

The "most excellent" thing about Function Point Analysis is that this provides a mechanism to price the work according to what the end users see—what they are buying—functionality! If they decide to add four more screens, you simply recount the Function Points, run it through the formula, and come up with a new cost. It's just as if you were going through the line at the grocery store and said, "Hey, I need another two dozen eggs!" You put those in your basket, you count those along with whatever else you bought, and you have a new final price.

The key is that the user determines what they are going to buy. If the ultimate price is so much more than what they are prepared to spend, then tell them to take some stuff out of the grocery basket. Maybe they didn't need that second box of Cap'n Crunch with Crunch Berries or the fancy graphical reporting system, did they?

You may be wondering, "Who does the counting?" Well that's an easy one to answer—Function Point Counters! Seriously, when I alluded to the watering down of the process a few paragraphs ago, it was for a good reason. Function Point Analysis is a complex process that has a large body of knowledge behind it. As a result, there is an international organization, the International Function Point User Group (**www.ifpug.org**), that defines how to count Function Points, and trains and certifies companies and individuals to be able to do it properly.

Thus, you can hire a consultant to do Function Point Analysis consulting for you and provide an independent count of Function Points in an application. While you can train your own staff to count Function Points (and many large firms do), Function Point Analysis doesn't rely on the client having to take the developer's word. The customer can have an independent count done if they like, so there's none of that "Uh, yeah, there are 1,156 Function Points in there somewhere, but you wouldn't understand the formula, so you'll just have to believe me" nonsense from a shady developer.

In big systems, the customer and the developer might hire separate organizations to do counts and measure and come up with numbers. If the final results vary (it's a science, but it's not an exact science!), the contract between the client and the developer generally has a mechanism for resolution.

What's wrong with FPA?

So why don't we use Function Point Analysis at my shop? Because, in the immortal words of Andy Griebel, "That would be too hard." FPA is a complex methodology—Geneer is a multi-million-dollar development shop, and IBM is even larger. If you're writing $10,000, $50,000, and $100,000 applications, FPA is most likely to be overkill. If, on the other hand, you're involved in a four-man-year project that's going to span 2,000 users and three continents, then the alternative to FPA that you're going to read about next is probably not going to be robust enough. (Of course, if you have no methodology in place, then any method is absolutely better than that!)

Simply stated, Function Point Analysis isn't going to do you much good for a project that's going to take six weeks or four months, but you still need some sort of method to price applications of that size. A six-week application that ends up taking four months could put you under the table—forever.

The alternative: Action Point Counting

Faced with the amount of overhead that Function Point Analysis involved, I took the ideas out of Function Point Analysis and modified them to suit my company's needs as a smaller development shop. What did I call this? My first name for it was "Function Point Lite," but, not wanting the Function Point people or Miller Brewing to get mad at me, I opted for a replacement—Action Points, and Action Point Counting. It's rooted in the same basic concept but the implementation and process differ.

Intent: Sizing

The purpose of Action Point Counting is to provide the ability to determine the approximate, relative size of a project, and the ability to do it quickly and easily, and to reliably repeat the results. I'll discuss each of these goals briefly.

Approximate size

As mentioned earlier, even Function Point Analysis isn't an exact science, and it isn't the intent of Action Point Counting to create a complex mechanism that gets down to the last nickel and dime either.

First of all, it isn't a reasonable expectation to be able to pin down the size (time and dollars) of a software application to an exact number. There are a large number of unknowns involved in a software application, and you simply can't expect to know, and properly account for, all of them ahead of time.

People have been putting up buildings for hundreds of years, and it's still not uncommon to have a construction project go significantly over budget. Why? Projects are still subject to many variables that can't be controlled. Weather shuts down a site for a week. A supplier misses a delivery. A union goes out on strike. The foundation people find an enormous rock or a rusty oil tank where the basement is supposed to be, and removing the item wasn't budgeted for.

And that's with a well-defined project that has a blueprint drawn to timeworn standards, that involves bricks, steel, and glass, and is done by people who have been performing the same actions with the same materials for years. With software, we're faced with specifications of uncertain origin or precision, developers with widely varying skill levels, using tools that are new, untested, and probably buggy, for customers who don't really know what it is that they want. Cost overruns? Big surprise!

The same issues of variables interrupting what otherwise would have been a smoothly developed system always pop up during software development. An OCX that works fine on a specific operating system behaves in a different way once a service pack to the OS is applied. The format of the data file described in one of the import processes turns out to be wrong—and a considerable amount of work is required to cleanse the data before it can be brought into the system. The company buys another plant, and the network infrastructure at that location introduces new requirements—or incompatibilities—and both of these are spelled "P-R-O-B-L-E-M-S."

Size is an indication of "how many things do I have to do," and each of these variables changes the size of that "To-do" list. And we often don't know how many more things are going to end up on the "To-do" list, nor are we going to know how long those new tasks are going to take. For example, getting the OCX to run with a new service pack may simply require a query of the vendor's knowledge base to find out that a property, heretofore ignored, needs to be set a certain way. But it might also take two weeks of spelunking with the development team to determine precisely what the cause of the problem is, and then waiting for a complete rewrite of the OCX by the development team.

Second, the purpose of Action Point Counting was to develop a cost—and that cost would be marked up. Whether the cost was $23,105 or $23,220 didn't really matter. The important thing is to know where the cost was, so that you don't mistake the cost of a $55,000 project to be $35,000. Marking up a $35,000 project to $45,000 won't do you much good if it still actually costs you $55,000 to produce it, right?

Quickly

What good does it do to have an excellent costing methodology if it takes you three weeks and costs you $10,000 to do it for a project that ends up with a final cost of $15,000? Why spend more on the estimate than on the development?

That cost is going to have to get folded in, somewhere, and it's likely the other guy isn't adding another 10 grand for their estimating overhead. If you do, you're going to be operating at quite a disadvantage. By the time the Functional Spec is done, you want to crank out the cost as quickly as possible, and be done with it. If an estimating methodology takes a long time, you're liable to cut corners, which kind of defeats the original purpose, right?

You can count Action Points for a $100,000 app in a couple of hours.

Easily

Another aspect of Action Point Counting is that, well, it's not that intellectually challenging. And that's a good thing. Wouldn't it be ideal if you could get someone else to do the routine work of counting and tallying and all you'd have to do would be to double-check their work?

Action Point Counting is very easy, and can be done by a technical assistant or other semi-skilled individual.

Repeatable

A methodology that doesn't produce the same results each time is useless. Imagine if you gave the same Functional Spec to two of your developers, and they each arrived at different values. Not very helpful. Like the saying goes: A man with a watch always knows what time it is; a man with two watches is never sure. If you have two calculated costs, what do you do? Use the higher cost? You may not want to if you're bidding against other firms. And besides, how do you know that one is correct? What if they both made mistakes, and the actual cost was even higher than both of those?

Once you've got your metrics—the multipliers for specific types of objects, based on your company's historical performance—done, you can give two people the same project to count, and they'll both produce the same result, because there's very little subjective judgment involved.

How Action Point Counting works

Action Point Counting requires that you have a rigorous specification—that's why this is discussed in the section for the waterfall method of software development, why I've gone through the trial and agony of the last few chapters. The specification has to spell out exactly what the system is going to do, the rules that must be followed, and the components in each screen, process, and report.

The basic idea for APC is similar to Function Point Analysis: Go through the specification, and count the number of "things" on each screen, in each report, and in each process. Then, multiply the "things" times a "weight" factor, based on what type of "thing" it is, to arrive at the total number of Action Points. Finally, multiply the number of Action Points by a cost per Action Point to get to the final cost. I'll get to specific details on what constitutes a "thing" shortly, but for now, just take it on faith that a "thing" is one of those technical concepts that your spouse and kids wouldn't understand.

Count things

Let's look at an example. The form in **Figure 1** looks like it has five "things" on it—two labels, a command button, a check box, and a list box. Also, unbeknownst to us casual observers, but obvious to anyone who has taken the time to read the spec, there are two validation rules and one form-level rule attached to this form as well. The validation rules belong to the check box and the list box, and the form-level rule is fired when the "My Button" is pushed or when the form is closed.

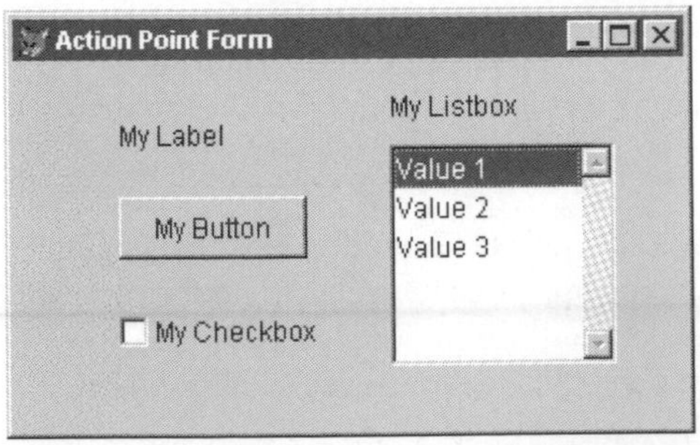

Figure 1. Sample form for calculating Action Points

This form may appear fairly simple, and, actually, it is for Visual Basic, C++, and Visual FoxPro developers. But if you're writing Web apps, this is about as fancy as a single page can get, right? And if you're working on a handheld platform, this form may be too complex already! (Well, just kidding about that last part, but you get the idea.)

Anyway, this form has all of the components needed for you to see how Action Point Counting works.

When you count the "things" on this form, you get a spreadsheet that looks like this:

Form Name	# of Labels	# of Buttons	# of Check Boxes	# of List Boxes	# of Valid. Rules	# of Form Rules
Form A	2	1	1	1	2	1

Form A has two labels, one button, one check box, one list box, two validation rules (you can't see them on the screen, but you know they're there—behind the check box and the list box—because you read the Functional Specification), and one form-level rule.

If you're using any type of framework, application generator, or reusable modules, you're probably wondering how doing so gets factored into this process. For example, what if the "My Button" control was part of a form class that was used to create the "Action Point Form" in Figure 1?

The short answer is that this discussion does not differentiate such factors. I'll explain more when it comes time to determine the actual cost based on the total number of Action Points.

Weight things

Each type of "thing" has a weight because some things are more complex than others. For example, a label is pretty easy to put on a form—and pretty hard to screw up. A list box, on the other hand, involves a lot more work, and is easier to screw up, so it's going to take more time for the "put a list box on a form" item on the "To-do" list. Just for argument's sake, let's suppose that a label has a weight of 1, buttons and check boxes both have a weight of 2, a list box has a weight of 4, a validation rule is weighted at 6, and a form-level rule has a weight of 10.

Multiply number of things * weight

So the preceding counts then get multiplied by factors, like so:

Form Name	# of Labels	# of Buttons	# of Check Boxes	# of List Boxes	# of Valid Rules	# of Form Rules
Form A	2*1	1*2	1*2	1*4	2*6	1*10

We multiply the number of objects by the weight of those objects to arrive at a total number of "Action Points."

The form itself also receives a weighting, according to the type of form it is. Types of forms may include simple maintenance forms, minor entity "quick-add" forms, complex data entry forms, and pick lists. Each of these has a different weight. In our example, I've assigned a weight of 0.1 because it's a pretty simple form. The counts are multiplied by the factors and the results are summed to a subtotal. The subtotal is multiplied by the form weight to come up with a value for the form itself.

Form Name	# of Labels	# of Buttons	# of Check Boxes	# of List Boxes	# of Valid Rules	# of Form Rules	Form Type	Form Weight	Action Points
Action Point Form	2*1	1*2	1*2	1*4	2*6	1*10	Simple	0.1	3.2

There isn't an "absolute" range for weights—they're all relative. You may decide to assign a simple message box dialog a weight of 1.0, and then increase the weights from there, or use 1.0 for a simple data entry form, and then use decimal multiples for simpler forms. There isn't a "maximum weight" because it's hard to say, at some point, just how excruciatingly difficult a form could get.

This same basic process is performed, in more detail, of course, for every screen, report, and process in the application, resulting in a total number of Action Points for the application.

Eventually you'll have a complete list of forms, reports, processes, and so on. This still is "for internal use only"—eventually you'll give the customer a list of modules, and prices assigned to each module. But you don't break out items in the module any more granularly for the customer.

The next step is to multiply the number of Action Points in the system by the cost per Action Point, and arrive at a total cost. Simple enough? Read on!

Cost = Action Points * cost per Action Point

We're just about done! The last step is to multiply the number of Action Points in the application by the cost per Action Point to arrive at a total cost, like so:

Form Name	Action Points	Cost/A.P.	Total Cost
Action Point Form	3.2	$100	$320

As you can see, this form would cost $320. (Kind of a rip off, wouldn't you think? Not so quick, now. You don't know what those rules are, do you?) Note that this isn't the final price. That comes later. The purpose of Action Points is to determine the cost. Given this methodology, you can now cost out each piece of an application.

Once you go through a couple of these exercises, you'll be able to compare and contrast parts of your application. You will find it pretty amazing that the one form with the nasty page frame and multiple grids is still actually less expensive to produce than the simple, single table maintenance form, but that has to pull data from several different data sources, eh?

You're probably wondering about a few things. First, I promised a more technical definition of a "thing." Next, you're undoubtedly curious about how the weights for each type of "thing" were arrived at—and you're dying to know how that magic $100 cost per Action Point was figured. For the time being, it's enough to know that I made up the numbers used in this example—for the sake of discussion. I'll cover how to get real numbers that you can use in your own business in just a little bit.

What is a "thing?"

Okay, you've been patient long enough. Let's get into more detail about these "things." Those of you with good memories or small children already know that a "thing" is a little furry biped of indeterminate sex and age whose main function is to make even a bigger mess than The Cat in the Hat. But we can get more specific.

Screens

A screen (also known as a "form" in some development tools) is any type of window-based user interface that is displayed on the computer's monitor. If you design software that doesn't use a windowing-style GUI, then you'll have to adapt these techniques for your own use.

The types of "things" that can show up on a form vary according to the capabilities of the development tool you're using. You've already seen what a basic form looks like and how a few typical types of "things" would be counted and weighted. How about some more detail about the types of things on a form—and how they might be weighted?

The "dumb" things, such as labels, images, and other "view only" types of things, have a minimal weight, because once they're placed on the form (and they're spelled right or their size is scaled correctly), there isn't much to do, and not much can go wrong. If there is some odd requirement to have an action fired from clicking on a label or an image, or to have the text of the label or the image displayed change according to some other event, then those would be considered either validation or form-level rules.

The next group of things that can be put on a form includes text boxes, edit boxes, option groups (or "radio buttons" to some of you), toggle buttons, check boxes, and so on. The similarity between each of these is that there is probably a relationship to a field in a table, and so some work is going to have to be done in order to make sure that relationship works and is sound, but this isn't usually difficult work.

The third group of things that can be put on a form includes complex types of objects like list boxes, drop-down combo boxes, grids, spinners, and other kinds of controls. There may or may not be rules attached to things like these, but simply populating them requires more work to begin with.

The fourth group of things is "action controls" like command buttons and page frames—data isn't bound to them, but invariably there are rules attached to them. I'll cover their rules in a minute—but don't forget to count the controls themselves as well!

Okay, now how about the magic—the code underlying the objects that the user doesn't see, but feels the effects of anyway? This code generally takes one of two forms—a validation rule that is tied specifically to a single object, or a form-level rule that spans multiple objects.

Once you're done with all of the things in and under the form, you can evaluate the form as a whole—how complex is it? For the framework that my company uses, I've generally broken down forms into five or six basic types, and used those as general "buckets." I found this was easier than trying to specify every imaginable type of form, and then applying weights for each type that only differed slightly. We also have an "adjustments" column that can be used to add or subtract Action Points from the form as a whole, in order to account for those situations where the counts, weights, and form weighting don't tell the whole story.

Finally, there's a multiplier column for the form as a whole. Multipliers that affect the entire screen—as opposed to simply adding a few Action Points to the form—are based on a number of factors. These include, but are not limited to, the following items:

- The complexity of the user security required by the form.

- Whether or not the user provides test data (or you have to create your own test data set for the form).

- The number of platforms the form will display on (a screen that has to run in DOS, Windows 3.1, Windows 95, and on a Mac will be considerably more of a pain than a simple single-platform screen, or even a screen that must run identically on both Win 9x and NT systems).

- The number of operating systems (which is slightly different than just platforms).

All in all, these weights and multipliers allow you to determine Action Points for any type of form, regardless of its complexity.

Processes

A process is an operation that runs without user intervention, and thus does not require an interface. Note that some processes may require a form in order for the user to provide parameters to control the direction of the process, but once initiated, a process generally needs no further interaction. The form that launches a process is counted as a form, not as part of the process.

Processes are tricky—they kind of seem like one of those "none of the above" types of categories. There's still more work to be done on making the counting of the Action Points in a process more accurate, but at this point, we've got a stake in the ground that has served well even as it undergoes additional refining.

So far, as you've seen in the Functional Spec, processes can generally be broken down into the following operations:

- Match two records in different tables. For example, when importing a list of parts, match the incoming part record with the existing part, using part number as the key.

- Do a lookup. For instance, when importing a hospital transaction, look for the diagnosis code in the diagnosis table.

- Make an assignment. Assign the value of one variable to another for the purposes of stuffing the new value into a table (either overwriting an existing record or creating a new record), including creating a value from a calculation.

- Insert a new record. When doing an import or a posting, for example, add a new record to an existing table.

- Create a new file. An example would be creating a temporary file for intermediate processing.

- Delete a file. An example would be deleting that temporary file that you just recently created.

- Write an exception. You typically write a record to an exception file when encountering an instance of data that shouldn't be there. For example, when importing a file, you write an exception if a foreign key field is empty.

- Set a flag. In many processing routines, flags are set for a variety of reasons.

Does this cover the entire gamut of possibilities in processes? Probably not. But over the past five or six years, I've found that it hits a lot of the things that are routinely done, and gets us a lot closer to sizing a processing module than simply saying, "Well, ya know, Ed, I think importing that patient file is gonna be about a three-day job."

You may also be wondering how to count each of these "things" without actually going in and writing the code itself. Well, in order to accurately describe the process in the Functional Specification so that there is no confusion about what will and will not be done, you need to be pretty detailed about the operations that will occur. For example, you need to describe whether exceptions will be written, whether a new record will be created, which fields will be put in that record, and so on. So, for the most part, these types of "things" have proven to be the types of operations that needed to be collected—and they were collectable as well.

And remember—both the spec and your estimating mechanism can always be changed!

Reports

A report is any type of output requested by the user. The output may take the form of a printed piece of paper, but it may also be displayed to the screen, or result in a file created on disk or transmitted to another computer. As I discuss the various "things" that can be put on a report, it may help you to visualize a printed report.

The first type of thing, like those found on a form, is a dumb object, like a label or a box or a shaded background. Generally, these will be simple, but occasionally you'll find a rule that needs to be attached to one, such as "The background should be shaded only if the percentage is over 10%."

The second type of thing is straightforward output—data from a field in a table is printed on the report. This does not include calculated fields or rules that result in specific output (like the shaded background). The reason that straight output is differentiated from calculated fields is that for the most part, our process for creating reports is twofold. First, we create a temporary cursor that contains a denormalized table with all of the data required, grouped and sorted as desired, on the report. Second, we place each of these fields on a report, and that's a simple matter. If the nature of the report is such that additional work needs to be done, like calculated fields or special rules, those things are counted separately.

The third type of thing is the aforementioned calculated field or rule.

The fourth type of thing is the actual number of groups required in the report. The reason this is counted is 1) fields usually have to be placed in special positions, and 2) calculated fields and subtotals sometimes have to be flagged as belonging to a group band.

For years, I've used a third-party reporting tool in my applications that requires a special type of setup, so I also include a place to count the number of report "things"—the items in the tool's data dictionary—that have to be set up with this tool.

Foundation

Robust applications generally use a data dictionary, and require test data sets, a menu, a Help file with topics and indexes, and other items that have to be built. Your particular tool and development style may include other items, and that's fine. The key is to itemize and count all of these "things" that are included in laying the foundation for a new system.

There are a few other things you might consider. What if an application has a toolbar? Are the buttons on a toolbar the same as the buttons on a form? What about rules that are embedded in a data dictionary? What about triggers? What if you have to be able to deploy across multiple platforms? How about if the application has to use multiple menus according to who is using the system? How is security implemented—user level, permissions, form or control level?

Database handling

If you're writing a database application, you probably have to deal with data. Thus, you've got work to do with setting up the database structures, handling test data, and so on. Just like dealing with screens, processes, and reports, you can "count" the number of things you have to do with a database in order to get it ready for shipping with your code.

For example, here's a list of things you may have to do, depending on what programming language and database you're using.

- Create a database (the container itself).

- Create tables.

- Create fields.

- Create indexes.

- Create stored procedures and triggers.

- Populate each table with data as required. You may want to ship lookup tables fully populated but major entities may ship empty (wouldn't it be disconcerting if Quicken showed up on your doorstep with a year's worth of transactions already entered?)

- Duplicate databases and contents for test vs. production setups.

- Create test data.

These are all items that you can count, and if you can count, you can measure, assign weights, and determine your costs. Some of these items may seem to be trivial—add a field? Set an index? But each one of these things is going to be important to your customer when it comes time to search on a field, index on an expression, or ensure that a primary key is properly populated with a unique value. And just like in the military, where a billion here and a billion there ends up becoming real money sooner or later, the 30 seconds it takes you to create a field, name it, set its length, set an index flag, and set its NULL property adds up when you have to do it for the 97 tables, each with an average of 22 fields.

Not elsewhere classified

Now you're probably asking, "How do you handle the myriad of things in an application that don't fall into the categories listed above?" For example, many Windows applications include ActiveX controls, have hyperlinks to Web sites, depend on NT Services to be available, and so on. Where are these included in the cost? Is it time to guess?

Actually, there's a better answer. I have taken a concept—counting, weighting, factoring, and summing the things in an application—and applied it to my way of developing custom software. I have a style and a philosophy of developing database applications that rely on my common libraries, the use of certain third-party tools, and I tailor my Action Point Counting with those habits in mind. I also use specific tools with certain capabilities.

Since you may develop using different tools, and you're undoubtedly using a different application framework than mine, you'll need to modify the technique outlined here—add different types of things, include the capability to count depending on your style of application development, and so on—to suit your needs.

However, don't confuse a difference in the tools you use within your applications with things that you haven't used before. For example, suppose your customer wants you to generate Web pages from your app and deploy them on a remote server. The Web page generation sounds pretty easy—you can probably count "things" based on a process of generating a standard text file. But deployment on a remote server? Read on.

Dealing with "Research and Development"

What if you're required to use a third-party HTML generator that you haven't used before, and that was actually only released about three months ago? How are you going to be able to "count things" in this situation? Or what if you're including an ActiveX control that you've never seen before—but that you found through some searching on the Web and need to include because it's the only one you've found that has the capability your customer wants?

This is, essentially, R&D—Research and Development—and you can't provide a fixed price for it. Period. Any more than your customer can develop a new process for curing paint or develop a new pressure-less light switch for a fixed price. By definition, R&D is undefined, and you can't provide a fixed price for something that's not defined.

So what do you do?

First of all, separate the request for R&D from the rest of the spec—make it clear that this particular component or module or whatever requires R&D, and thus isn't included in the costing process. Second, you have two choices. The first is to perform the development on a Time and Materials basis until it's finished to the customer's satisfaction. And that might be a defined physical result, or when the customer is tired of spending money and declares, "Good enough."

The second choice is to develop until you run out of money—in other words, make an estimate, and use that as a cap, declaring, "We will use whatever comes out of this fixed amount of money." Remember, your customer is a business, too. They have some sort of idea how much that feature being researched is worth—after that threshold is reached, it's not worth it to include it in the application anymore.

Bottom line: Identify and break out R&D separately. If your customer insists on a fixed price—and declared functionality—for an unknown or undefined process, find a new customer.

Weighting for "things"

Obviously, one of the key parts of this methodology is the weight used for each type of "thing." And, I'll admit it—I don't have a scientific algorithm for determining that a label has a weight of 1 while a check box has a weight of 2 and a list box has a weight of 4.

If you go to a factory that churns out hair dryers or lathes, you'll find out they've got a dweeb in a white coat and Clark Kent glasses who carries around a clipboard, a stopwatch, and the important sounding title of "Industrial Engineer." His job is to define the tasks required to produce a particular widget, and then time the line workers performing those tasks. After a few days or weeks, the dweeb comes up with a set of standards. It takes 3 minutes and 50 seconds to assemble a hair dryer—and every second of that time is accounted for: 14 seconds to pick up a plastic shell off of a pallet and place it in a vice, 22 seconds to insert an electric motor and hand-thread a mounting screw, 7 seconds to use an electric screwdriver to finish threading the mounting screw. And so on.

Well, believe it or not, we don't have one of those dweebs timing each developer, recording the amount of time it takes to put a check box on a form, and comparing that with the amount of time it takes to populate a combo box on a form. Let's be a bit realistic—where in the world would you find someone who is so desperate for a job that they'd actually agree to do this? (Actually, I never figured out why anyone would want be an Industrial Engineer in a factory either, but that's ancient history.)

Instead, we just looked at the way we go about putting together forms, and estimate the approximate differences between one type of object and another. Is it exact? No. Is it good enough for our purposes? Yes.

Can we have your weights?

Everyone wants a shortcut, and I sure wish I had a couple of nickels for every time someone has asked me for a copy of our weights. Sorry. You will have to come up with your own set of weightings, based on your style of developing and your skill level with the development environment. An expert developer may have a smaller range of weights across multiple controls because they've got a number of automated tools that help build forms—as well as understanding the tricks and traps of using specific controls. A not-so-experienced developer, on the other hand, may use the same weight as us for a simple control but a much higher weight for controls that are more complex.

As an analogy, suppose you were learning to do the long jump. You could watch other long jumpers, pick up on their techniques, and emulate them. But it wouldn't do you any good to try to copy their steps down the runway, because each person is different, and their steps are suited for them—with their stride length, leg strength, speed, and tendon snap. Unless your physical attributes were identical, copying their steps en route to the long jump pit would end in a less than optimal jump.

Application-wide counts

Now that you've got all of these Action Point counts for the various forms, reports, processes, and other types of things, it's time to look at what the Function Point Analysis people call "General System Characteristics."

If you're going to put this application on a simple four-node Novell LAN, it's going to be a lot easier than spanning three continents, deploying on notebooks and handhelds, and running a remote service on the mothership's EvilAlienOS on Independence Day. (Don't laugh. It could happen…)

So there needs to be one final multiplier for the entire application, based on its relationship to the rest of the company's environment.

Again, how you handle this depends on the types of apps you have done. If the majority of your work has been client/server applications with Visual Basic front ends running against

Oracle back ends, but a few of your projects were single-user systems that were deployed on an armada of notebooks, then you will have two application-wide multipliers. If you then try to build a new type of application, such as for handhelds, or for a distributed architecture on a new OS, then you'll need to come up with new multipliers.

Handling "Not-Brand-New" projects

So far, everything I've discussed has come from the perspective of "I am working on a brand-new system." What if you're working on enhancements to an existing app? What if you're putting together a band-aid for an app written in an older version of a tool, and you're both tweaking some of the existing code and adding some new functionality, albeit in the latest version of that tool? How are the counts and weights handled in these cases?

You can use this methodology to build components of an application just as easily as you would build an entire application—and when you spec enhancements to an existing application, you'll also use this technique.

As far as enhancements to an existing system written in an older tool, or integration with an application, well, I can't answer this question through empirical experience, since my company rarely does this type of work.

The basic process would be to go through the same analytical process, identifying functionality and counting and weighting actions that have to be done. I'm not saying this is easy; it feels a lot like the work I've done for performing Action Point Counting on processes—but sitting down with a clean sheet of paper and breaking apart the pieces would be the way to approach it.

Additionally, my technical editor has assured me that the process is basically the same. Some items have already been decided and so it's up to you to deal with them—things like system architecture and data structures. Thus, some of your work will disappear, since it's already been done (if you're making behavioral modifications to a system that doesn't require any database modifications, then the database structures section rounds out to a big zero right away).

Some of your multipliers might be lower—if you already have a test plan written for a module and you just modify that module, then you can probably just update the test plan and re-execute it, instead of creating a brand-new one from scratch.

What happens if the project is partway done, and suddenly a new manager comes in and axes half of the Action Points in the project? Does the project cost get halved as well? Obviously, you can't just cut those Action Points out—you probably have to provide clean termination or stubs for pieces that are no longer going to be developed.

This request—chop off the arms and one of the legs of the application while it's being built—falls under the category of "change requests" and needs to be specified, and quoted, using Action Points, just as any other enhancement would. You should be aware that it may be a bit of a tough sell—if the application is being downsized severely, there are probably some uncomfortable political currents floating around, and the people involved are probably not going to want to hear that they can't simply "turn off the spigot." You might use the analogy of mothballing a battleship or nuclear reactor. When a power plant is going to be shut down, they don't just turn the switch to "off" and lock the door behind them.

Getting the cost per Action Point

The other magic number I used earlier is that $100 per Action Point. And it's probably the more interesting one, since anyone can come with some initial "guestimates" for weights for different "things." Well, here's some tough news.

The need for historical costs

The next question—now that you know "how many things" (Action Points) are in the application—is "How much is this going to cost?" The answer is rather unpleasant for many people, because it requires a piece of information that they don't have—an accurate record of how much it cost to develop similar software in the past.

Software developers, as an industry, are remarkably immature in this respect, in that we really don't have any idea of what our historical costs have been. I can think of a dozen good-sized MIS shops, part of well-established manufacturing companies, and each of which has been around for two or three decades, that even now do not collect any type of data on how long it took to develop applications in-house. These are the same companies that have an army of the green-visor folks counting every penny that goes into the particular brand of widget or thingamabob that the company manufactures. And at the end of the year, the VP of MIS throws up his hands and wonders why all these software projects are over budget and late. Why? I'll tell you why—because their estimating techniques are all built on quicksand—the quicksand of having no historical records of what they did yesterday.

You must track your costs—the amount of time it took to develop projects in the past—if you are to have any hope of assigning a time value on an Action Point. I've been fortunate in that, before I even had any inkling of what I would do with the data, I had every developer keep detailed records on the time spent on various components of each project done since about 1993. And they say it doesn't matter whether "anal-retentive" is hyphenated or not!

As a result, when I came up with this idea of counting Action Points, I was able to get realistic values from the work we'd all done in the past. The first time I did this (in late 1994), I took about a dozen applications, totaling about 4,000 hours of work, and counted the Action Points in each one. The actual amount of time spent (not the time they estimated or quoted at the time!) was matched to the number of Action Points in order to produce some rough multipliers from Action Points to Hours.

From these numbers, we now know that an Action Point takes an average developer about 20 minutes. (That's actually just a made-up number—because our time per Action Point is irrelevant to anyone else, because the skill level of the "average developer," the application framework, and other factors are unique to my shop.)

I then took the average hourly rate of an average developer to determine the cost per Action Point. A skilled developer could make more, obviously, because they can crank out more Action Points per hour than an unskilled (or incompetent) developer could.

What about those frameworks and reusable components?

Earlier the question of how to factor frameworks, application generators, and reusable components into Action Point counts was raised. There are two parts to this.

First, you may be thinking that using tools like this gives you an accelerated jump into the production of an app, and thus, simply counting "things" and applying standard weights will produce a number that doesn't fairly reflect reality. For example, suppose you use a form class with a half dozen buttons and a bunch of default code to build a form, and that new form's functionality largely rests on the classes' functionality. You might end up with 50 Action Points for this form, but in reality, all you did was drop a few text boxes on the form and tie a table to the form's data environment—an effort equivalent to about 10 Action Points. "Charging" 50 Action Points doesn't seem right—kind of smells like those windfall profits the oil companies were accused of during the oil price shocks of the '70s.

Well, if you're so smart that you can use an automated tool to make your manufacturing more efficient, then shouldn't you make more money? Suppose there were two bicycle manufacturers. One built them by hand, had costs of $500, and thus charged $600 for each bike. The other, however, had made an investment in automating their factory, and could, as a result, make a bike for $200. Should they sell their bikes for $300? Or should they sell them for $595, and make healthy profits in return for being better at building bikes inexpensively?

The answer, of course (well, at least it's obvious to me), is that they should sell them for $550, and take away the entire market from the other company, while still making healthy profits.

You may be thinking that while you don't disagree with this philosophy, you also feel that assigning a count of 50 Action Points to a form that is actually only really worth 10 is a bad business move, because it doesn't truly reflect your costs. After all, when a competitor comes into the picture, using the same tools, and prices their application lower, you wouldn't have any idea of what your actual costs were, and thus you couldn't react appropriately. This brings us to my second point.

Remember that your history is based on your using the framework as well, right? So gains using a framework are, to some extent, factored in when you analyze costs based on your historical performance.

If you don't have history

First of all, it's probably quite unlikely that you have no history—it is probably just not kept to the level of detail that you now realize you would like. You can count the number of Action Points in a bunch of your applications, and then look up how many hours—or at least, how many dollars and which developers—it took to put that app to bed. Given even this minimal amount of historical costs, you can develop a couple of rough benchmarks. One would be trying to relate the number of forms, reports, and processes with some time and dollar numbers. Are they going to be exact? No, but the numbers you'll get are better than the wild guesses you were making yesterday.

The accuracy of your results will improve as you include more projects in the database you work with. Remember, "once is not a trend," and twice is not much of one either. But if you can look at one or two dozen projects, you'll have enough data points so that if one or two projects went south, that data won't skew your results as badly as if you just looked at three projects.

However, just because you didn't have history in the past doesn't mean you're going to get off the hook—it's time to start collecting that history, and today would be the best time to start!

Getting started with metrics

The easiest way to get started is to make each developer track the time they spend on each project and turn in a daily time sheet. If you want to get a bit more sophisticated, you can buy a software package, such as TimeSlips (**www.timeslips.com**), TraxTime (**www.spudcity.com**), or Time Trakker (**www.west-wind.com**). If you're really picky, you can develop your own time-tracking tool.

There are two things that are important. First, don't try to do too much too soon—start tracking the basics—you can always add more levels later if you like. And, second, start doing it now.

Gather something—all the time

I'm often asked about the types of tasks to be tracked. My shop gathers everything that is work-related—not just tasks that are related directly to coding. Travel time, development of a specification (analysis and design, writing the spec, doing Action Point Counting), tracking down bugs, writing memos and letters to customers, backing up projects—all these are part of a project. Presumably you are paying your employees for performing these types of tasks, so they are definitely part of the cost.

However, we go even further. What about time spent at user group meetings? Reading books? Searching the Web for a new utility? We track it all. You may not be able to bill the time spent looking for a copy of a magazine that has some interesting techniques, but it's part of your cost structure.

One particularly sticky point is whether or not to track time that someone spends "fixing" something, or "playing with something" on their own time. For example, suppose that one of your developers just likes to goof around at home, and they regularly take home parts of an application just to try different techniques out. However, they resist tracking that time. What do you do?

First of all, you may need to track it for legal reasons—but consult your lawyer on that one. Depending on how you categorize employees, the time they spend "on their own" may still be counted toward their hours, and you may be required to pay—or be specifically exempt from paying—overtime and benefits on that overtime.

More importantly, while you may be getting a "bonus" from the goodwill of an employee doing things on their own time, the firm is ultimately benefiting. It behooves you to identify how much time that R&D takes, in case you had to have someone else do that—while on the clock. You need to know how much extra time that takes, so you can factor it in.

Suppose you didn't track it, but began to rely on some of your developers putting in extra time. You would then begin costing your projects not including that time, while at the same time depending on this extra time. It would be like factoring in free raw material in the widget you're producing. Sure, you're getting a short-term benefit, but in the long run, you can get burned.

And, of course, if you know how much extra someone is putting in, it probably wouldn't hurt to give that person an appropriate bonus.

Are you going to get them to track every minute? Probably not. Even the most disciplined software developer is a bit of a cowboy at times—and they're just not going to bother writing down that 24 minutes they spent installing a new Help authoring tool before the in-laws came over for a birthday celebration. But the closer to reality your data is, the better off you're going to be.

Levels of detail

Okay, now the $25 question—to what level of detail do you track time? I'll cover this in more detail in the section on Manufacturing. For now, though, I'll tell you how detailed we get, and you can judge from that. In short, I've broken down development work into four levels, and have found that this is plenty.

The first level is "Customer"—and you can define that as you wish. Generally, I've defined a "Customer" as an entity with a primary contact and that pays bills from a single place. You may work with a large company and have several projects going with them—if you send all your invoices to the same PO Box, though, you might consider them a single customer. On the other hand, sometimes divisions of a company act as if they're on different planets, and you might treat them as two different customers. It's simply a bookkeeping issue, and whether or not you want to tally up at the end of the year how much of your business was from InterGalactica Widgets, Inc.

The second level is a "Project," and this has to do with a PO Number. Each project that requires a new PO Number becomes a new project in our system. If a company doesn't have PO Numbers, I make an educated guess as to whether or not they might be using separate accounting for Project A vs. Project B.

The third level is a "Module"—which is a deliverable item in a Project. A module may consist of a single process or report, or it may be a collection of several forms, a process, and four reports. Basically, whatever is delivered to, and accepted by, the customer at a single time is a module.

The lowest level is a "Task"—a single form, process, report, or other low-level entity against which we can count Action Points. Thus, a Foundation might include three tasks: Data Dictionary, Menu, and Help. An R&D project might also be a single task, or it might be a module with several identifiable tasks.

Direct vs. indirect costs

Through our historical records, I have determined how long it took a developer to write an application, and I know the cost of that developer—their wages, benefits, and other pieces of their compensation.

I also know how much I spend on running the firm—rent, non-billable personnel, magazine subscriptions, goofy screensavers, and so on. The combination of wages and overhead, plus profit, has to equal the dollars brought in through software development.

Manufacturers have been doing this for 200 years—including the cost of running the firm—overhead (some firms refer to it as "burden")—as part of the price. Remember, we're producing a product—a widget—and good old cost accounting requires that you include both fixed and variable costs. As your firm gets bigger, you'll need to include things like brand-new 5 Gigahertz PentaAthalons (won't that reference seem dated in a year or so!), subscriptions to *Dr. Dobbs*, *Software Development*, and *Object* mags, a fancy phone system with voice mail instead of a $19 answering machine, administrative support, and all that free junk food in the kitchen.

Handling variances in developer productivity

This can get really tricky.

Note that the multipliers also relate to the developer who worked on the specific project. If more than one developer worked on the same project, we tracked the Action Points delivered by each developer separately, and figured their current salary. We ended up with a chart that looked like this (numbers shown are totals for each developer across multiple applications, and they're all simply relative):

Developer	Hours	Action Pts	AP/Hr	Pay/Hr
A	100	2,900	29	$27
B	180	3,000	16	$26
C	215	21,500	100	$49
D	240	9,100	38	$41

There are a couple of issues demonstrated by the data in this chart. First, current salaries may not be related to skill level—in fact, they probably aren't. How are people paid? In one situation, people are plugged into salary ranges based on titles, and those titles have little to do with actual skill levels. In another situation, people are paid whatever it took to lure them from another job—again, their wages having very little to do with their skill level, or their productivity.

This, then, is a difficult situation. For example, Developer B is the least productive—whether that's due to experience or skill level—but his rate per hour isn't that much lower than Developer A who is considerably more skilled.

Let's take a project that comes in the door—and ends up at 1,000 Action Points. If the project is assigned to Developer A, the cost is $931 (1,000 AP / 29 AP/hr * $27/hr). If the project, however, is assigned to Developer B, the cost is $1,625 (1,000 AP / 16 AP/hr * $26/hr). Depending on who you assign to the project, you might want to change your pricing accordingly.

Second, what about developers who have a high level of reusability in their software? Wouldn't they get the short end of the stick because they would end up with a low Action Points/Hour number? Actually, no. The Action Points in an application are based on the number of "things"—buttons, validations, report subtotals, temp file creations. Whether these are done "automatically" (through the use of a tool or robust classes) or manually doesn't matter at the point that you're counting Action Points. (They come into play when you're assigning time and dollars based on history.) Thus, a developer who takes advantage of reusability and automated tools will actually see their Action Points/Hour go through the roof.

What about the developer whose code is of higher quality, and thus requires less maintenance? I'm discussing developer productivity, and, strictly speaking, maintenance down the road isn't an issue in current developer productivity. You're probably shaking your head at this, but you'll see that I'll address this issue—encouraging code that requires less maintenance—in the section on Manufacturing.

Third, the disparity in skill levels might be such that it would be impossible to adjust pay to reflect that productivity. Developer C is three times as productive as any other developer, but it's going to be difficult to pay her three times as much—both from a financial point of view as well as politically.

However, given this data, it's possible to be more objective about pay scales, raises, and bonuses. For example, if someone's performance of 16 Action Points per hour corresponds to, say, $26 an hour (yes, I'm just making up numbers here), then the developer who can produce 32 Action Points per hour should be paid $52 an hour. In practice, the disparity between production rates is higher, but you get the idea.

You might be asking right about now, "So, you're saying that if a screen has 50 Action Points, and you've got a multiplier of 1.5 hours per Action Point, it should take 75 hours? But doesn't this depend on the developer as well?"

Well, there's a bit of a jump in this question. Remember that each developer has a different productivity measure—a skilled developer should be able to do this screen in less time than a rookie developer because they can crank out more Action Points per hour. Note, however, that this skilled developer is also more expensive, right? So their cost—their compensation—would be higher per unit of time. So in an ideal world, the cost of the screen would be the same regardless of who did it. If you've got a highly skilled developer at $200/hour who can crank a module out in a day, your rookie developer, at $50/hour, should take four days.

I'll cover developer productivity and wages in more depth later in the book.

Benefits to Action Point Counting

Is this all too much to do in one step? Probably. If it's all new to you, the first thing to do is give this "Action Point Counting" a whirl on a few apps, just to determine the raw size of the systems. The numbers you come up with aren't that important—it doesn't matter if your app is 200 Action Points and someone else's is 380. What matters is that you can now compare the relative sizes of the various projects you've done, look at the actual time you spent producing them, and then get an idea of the dollars involved. Furthermore, simply by going through the steps here, you're significantly less likely to miss something—particularly something big.

And that's a huge benefit right away. Oftentimes an application goes out of control not because the developers aren't skilled, or because they're goofing off, but because that one little button the customer asked for turns out to drill into another huge set of complex screens. Not including that button at all is going to cost you a lot more than figuring that the screens would take 68 hours instead of 88.

From this, you can try to price an application—or even just a single screen or report—based on the hard data you've got instead of yet another SWAG. Worry about the sophisticated cost accounting once you've got the basics down first.

There's more, though, so don't stop reading yet! As you are undoubtedly aware, a highly skilled developer can easily be 10 times as productive as an ordinary developer, right? In fact, to say that an extremely skilled developer could be 20 times more productive than a hack isn't a stretch, isn't it? But even the most awful hack (and we have some of them in our business, don't we?) can get away with charging, oh, $40 or $50 an hour. How many highly skilled developers do you know who are charging 20 times $40 an hour—yes, $800/hour? Well, I can't think of more than two or three dozen myself.

But by using Action Point Counting, you can take advantage of the high productivity of a skilled developer and charge appropriately. (See the next section!)

Another benefit is better data to assist in scheduling. Since you now have the number of Action Points for an application, as well as the productivity of a developer in terms of Action

Points per hour, it's easy to determine how much time a given developer will need to complete that application.

The final benefit to this technique is that you can discuss how you determine your costs with your customer—which will be a far cry from the usual smoke and mirrors and waving of hands over the black hat that they likely hear from your competitors.

Determining the cost for the application

Okay, so this has been a great discussion in a theoretical sense. But what happens in real life, when the customer has signed off on the specification, and a developer starts working on it? The developer is compensated based on the amount of billable work they do, and the company is going to bring in a fixed amount of funds, regardless of how long it takes the developer to do the work. How does this scenario play, depending on whether the developer is skilled or relatively new?

Suppose we charge $100 per Action Point. Thus, the screen with 50 Action Points is worth $5,000. A highly skilled developer may only need 25 hours to do it, resulting in a rate per hour of $200, while a rookie developer may need 125 hours, resulting in a rate per hour of $40. As the rookie developer gains skill, he can produce more billable dollars per unit of time, and generate more revenue for the firm and earn more compensation for himself. The highly skilled developer also realizes a higher compensation, although it may not be exactly proportional to his hourly rate, due to having to factor in the company's fixed costs.

The customer pays the same for the specified functionality, regardless of who is doing the work. The highly skilled developer is able to earn significant income, because he is no longer tied to an artificial ceiling of "no one will pay more than $90/hour for a programmer in this market." And the company's costs are proportionally the same for producing the application—while the less experienced developer will take longer, he is compensated less as well. The total cost for that $5,000 screen is the same whether the highly skilled or relatively new developer worked on it. The difference is that the less skilled developer will take more hours, and thus, will take longer, in calendar time, to deliver the screen.

The cost is not the price!

I've said it before, but it is extremely important to stress that this number is the cost, not the price! The goal for Action Point Counting is to determine how much it is going to cost to build this project, not how much the customer is going to pay for it. There is a difference here. You want to make sure that your price to the customer is more than your cost—how much more is a different topic—or you'll never make any money. Just trust me—you'll never "make it up in volume."

So how do you determine the value to the customer, and thus, how much you're going to price the application? Well, here is where the art comes in. You need to have a proper relationship with your customer so that you can determine, to the best extent possible, what the value is. If you've done your homework properly—identified what their pain is and what it's worth to them to ease that pain—you already know the answer.

How do you translate your discussions regarding functionality and value to a cost that the customer is going to pay? Unfortunately, there's no magic answer for this process. Perhaps they've given you a budget from which they're working. Perhaps you can frame the application you're building in terms of what it's going to do for their company—will it save them money somewhere? Will it generate money for them? If so, how much?

You may need to have a frank discussion regarding "How are you going to justify this project?" You're not necessarily asking what their numbers are, but just what the process they're going through is. Are they counting heads that are going to be laid off? Are they looking at enhanced revenue streams? Are they looking at incremental cost savings throughout the process? Are they just making wild guesses? You can use questions like this to get a better idea of where their concept of value is priced.

Fixed Price vs. Time and Materials—revisited

Now that I've discussed the Action Point Counting concept in detail, you should be pretty comfortable that you can, eventually, deliver a fixed price for an application. There are three prerequisites: a sufficiently detailed spec, sufficient historical costs, and developers skilled with the tool(s) to be used.

So how does the Fixed Price vs. Time and Materials argument play now?

First of all, you're not required to quote a fixed price to your customer, even though you have the wherewithal to do so. Action Point Counting simply gives you a better handle on your costs—so that you don't mistakenly produce a price that is too close to, or less than, your cost.

Second, one of my motivations for implementing Action Point Counting was to be able to deliver a fixed price—because I felt we could make more money than simply by billing on an hourly basis.

I should, however, provide a few caveats before you rush headlong into a bunch of fixed price jobs. First, make sure that you're completely comfortable with the three prerequisites listed earlier—a tight spec, a solid handle on your costs, and a realistic assessment of your developers' skills. If you're working with a vague spec, or you really don't know how much it costs you, or your developers aren't that skilled, then you're just asking for trouble.

Next, remember that many customers will try to push you into a fixed price, most likely before you are ready. They need a number to put in their budget, or to tell their boss, or to present to the IT committee. Having a number—the more "exact" the better—makes them look better when they're in front of their people.

Action Points work for both the developer and the customer—just as with the shopping cart, the customer determines how much they're going to buy. If you deliver a price higher than their comfort level, it's a lot easier to simply ask, "What do you want to take out of your shopping basket? The bag of apples or the six-pack of beer?" When you have a clearly defined methodology for costing (and then, presumably, pricing) the application, it's not as easy for a customer to badger you into "dropping your price some."

Once accepted, you need to keep your customer on the straight and narrow. Even though you're working from a detailed spec, many customers still feel like they walked into an "all you can eat for $9.99" software buffet. And it isn't!

Like I said earlier, they may not read through the spec thoroughly, simply assuming that, since it was mentioned in a conversation six months ago, "it's in there, somewhere." They will have forgotten that even though you showed it on three prototypes, they later changed something else that made that feature too costly, or too time-consuming, and thus asked you to take it off until Version 2.

Finally, as the saying goes, "Changes happen!" Just because you gave them a fixed price for "X" doesn't mean that they are not allowed to change their minds. I'll cover Change Orders and the Change Order process in a few chapters, but for now, it's important to remember that they're more than welcome to make changes. Just not necessarily for free.

Handling ill-defined projects

Part of the purpose of this chapter is to simply give you the fortitude to tell a customer that you can't quote a fixed price until you have a completely defined spec, and to stand your ground when they start badgering you. It's easy to back down when a customer pushes and pushes; hopefully I've given you enough information for you to say, "No, the line is drawn here." And I think you'll be surprised when you find out how many times a customer will back down first. The first time you try this, it's scary, but each subsequent time, it gets easier and easier. I'm not saying you'll win every time, but you'll never win if you don't try.

The more you think about this, the more ridiculous it becomes to provide a fixed price on something if you don't know how much it's going to cost or without knowing what types of unexpected things might happen. Doing so would be like offering to dig a hole in someone's backyard for a fixed price of $100, when you've never dug a hole before, or you've just dug really tiny ones, and you don't know what might be under the surface.

So, remember, you don't know how long it will take because you don't have any history and you're not experienced enough to "guess." You may not have the right kind of tools. And if you didn't do your research to make sure there isn't a Leaking Underground Storage Tank, or a Really Big Rock or a subway tunnel down there, you could be in for a very tough time when unexpected, but not unreasonable, issues appear.

But the customer is still going to ask you, given an imperfectly or incorrectly defined project, for an estimate. Remember the old "I won't hold you to it—I just need some sort of number for my boss" promise that turns out to be an ironclad number? It will happen again.

And this doesn't just apply to a "true" customer—it can also apply to the corporate vice president in charge of technology who wants a number on the new database for the corporate Web-site—after first telling you about the project earlier today. Boy, can some people be unreasonable!

So, how would you handle this situation? You can't "just walk away" from the project for any number of political considerations or, perhaps, because the person asking the unreasonable question has a lot of weight or power that you've got to watch out for. What do you do?

The best you can do is to define what you do know, mark parameters for the project's scope, and offer to provide "estimates" pending further information—and as more information comes in, fine-tune your estimates. And all the while, document, document, document. Each time you're able to change your estimate, whether from fine-tuning or from making a major modification, be sure to explain it in writing to your customer.

Remember expectations? Each time new information comes out, you're potentially in a position to change their expectations (either in a good way or a bad way), and if you don't explicitly try to do so (change their expectations), you could be setting up future problems.

However, in the eyes of the corporate vice president, this can come across as "covering your ass"—and it's important not to appear as a whiner. Instead, present this method—incremental estimates—as the only way you know to do it. Simply asking for a solid number without enough data is something you don't know how to do.

And if they ask you to guess, give them a really unreasonable number, explaining that you simply don't know, and so that's a guess. If they buy it, you're safe. If they don't, and they ask for a new one, then what's happening, behind the scenes, is that they already have a preconceived notion of a number. You're going to have to get that number out of them (or, conversely, they're going to tell you what your guess should be). I'd look for another job in that situation.

But providing a fixed price—when the project doesn't meet the prerequisites—is asking for trouble, no matter how tempting it may be, or how sincerely you think it will be different this time.

Because it won't.

Chapter 18
The Cover Letter and
Delivery of the Specification

"Thanks for your letter. It was great. You sound neat. We're very excited about meeting you in New York... and seeing if we are MFEO."—Annie
"MFEO?"—Becky
"Made for each other."—Annie
  —Sleepless in Seattle

The Cover Letter that accompanies a Functional Specification is a separate document and thus merits its own chapter in this book. If you're writing specs for internal use, or where the recipient is not expecting a price and delivery quote, then this document changes somewhat, but you still will have the same goals of summarizing the proposal you're delivering. But if you're at all in the position of trying to sell the specification, then pay close attention.

The spec is done! You've slaved over it for weeks or months, gritted through the costing, and you're finally ready to turn the official document over to your customer. Let's take a look at the Cover Letter that should accompany the spec, and consider different ways that you might deliver the specification to your customer.

The audience for the Cover Letter

I've discussed who the Functional Specification is addressed to—it's a good idea to revisit who will be reading the Cover Letter.

Although you've addressed the Cover Letter to Michael Austin-Thor, he could very well not be the only person reading it. There may be others involved in the decision-making process, particularly as the price gets larger. It's likely that some—if not all—of these people are not as involved in the development of the specification process as your contact. In fact, some of them may have a copy of your Cover Letter and Functional Specification sandwiched between a request for a new copier machine and a proposal "to retrofit the waste holding tanks at the North Road Facility."

For this reason, you'll want to avoid a lot of—or any—technical jargon. You'll also want to spell out the salient points quickly and clearly.

The contents of the Cover Letter

 When you deliver a Functional Specification, you can't just heft a 300-page binder on their desk, shake their hand, and walk out. The spec requires an introduction, a greeting, and the Cover Letter serves this purpose. However, you can accomplish several very important tasks with a well-crafted Cover Letter. A sample Cover Letter is included in the *DevGuide* downloads.

Purpose

The Cover Letter accompanies the Functional Spec and serves as its introduction. It is always a one-page letter that "summarizes the deal." Why one page? Because there are only two things that the customer cares about when reading the Cover Letter: how much and when. They don't want to wade through 23 pages just to get to the price. Make it easy for them to get to the heart of the matter. You, as the vendor, need to provide two more things—the terms and a place for them to agree to the deal. These four items all fit on one page quite nicely. Past that, shut the heck up! You have a 3,000-page spec attached to the back of this Cover Letter— tell them everything else back there.

This letter is a formality, not brand-new news, and so you want to make it easy for them to sign off and get going. I feel pretty strongly about this, so let me say it again here (and I'll say it again, one more time, later). They do not want to page through an 80 or 200 page document just to find out the final cost and delivery schedule. They're going to find out anyway, so why try to bury it? The easier you make it, the quicker they'll get past the sticker shock and move on to more important items like "When can you start?"

They should already know, roughly, how much it's going to cost, and what type of timeframe you're looking at because you've been working with them during the development of the spec, sounding them out about where their price points lie. Still, they're going to want to make sure you didn't pull a fast one and add another 25% to it.

Why the Cover Letter is a separate document

The Cover Letter is always a separate document to which the Functional Spec (and anything else, if need be) is attached. Why? Because the Cover Letter is the only place where actual money is described. This way, you can keep the financial arrangements separate from the rest of the application. Virtually no one except the person whose budget this falls under and the person cutting the check cares how much the app is going to cost (or, rather, no one else needs to know).

By keeping the Cover Letter apart from the rest of the spec, the recipient of the spec can send copies of everything except the dollars to others in the organization for their review, input, or reference. Furthermore, your customer may end up sending copies of this spec to other developers for competitive bids. Again, the competition doesn't have to know, and shouldn't know, what your pricing is.

Of course, you'd probably prefer that your customer not shop the proposal around, but this way, you've made it easy for them to do so with a minimum of fuss. If you've got dollars buried in the middle of the spec somewhere, or, worse, scattered throughout the spec, it's going to be difficult or impossible for them to distribute copies of the spec to others without also showing your bid. If it's difficult, they'll end up making a mistake and your deepest, darkest secrets will be laid wide open for the competition. Isn't that information you would rather keep confidential?

Format

As I've stated before, I aim for a conservative image at this point. I want it to look like I've been around for 100 years. Thus, the letter looks like it has come from a traditional firm, one that you can trust and depend on.

```
January 1, 2000

Michael Austin-Thor
The Very Large Manufacturing Company
The Very Large Manufacturing Park
Milwaukee WI 53202-4104

Dear Michael,
```

A note about the salutation—you may want to consider how you address your contact. Do you need to be formal about it—"Dear Mr. Austin-Thor"—or can you be more casual—"Dear Mike"? Just remember that this is a business relationship—you don't want to confuse being friendly with being friends.

Introduction

At the company where I worked when I got out of college, the department I was in delivered proposals to customers for highly technical kinds of equipment configurations. The first line always read "We are pleased to present this proposal…" and I've continued using that line ever since. Why? Because I am, and so should you be! I'm *delighted* to be able to offer a proposal to a customer.

```
We are pleased to present this quote for the Beer, Alcohol, and Spirits
Inventory Control Application (BASICA).
```

After all, what else are you going to say anyway? You have to have some kind of lead in, and this phrase is really nice and classic and comfortable. You've also already given the thing you're trying to sell a name in the first sentence so that you can refer to that from now on.

Proposal components

Next, I explain that an attachment is provided with this letter. Normally, it's the specification, but if you need to vary the thing you're attaching, you can say that right here. Then I describe what the Functional Spec is.

```
Attached is the Functional Specification for BASICA. This includes (1) the
BASICA main application, including the foundation directory structure,
login and user/group permission maintenance, the BASICA functionality, and
(2) the BASICA Reports. This Specification contains discrete descriptions of
the functionality of each piece but each description references the other
when applicable.
```

Again, what you're doing is repeating to the customer what they already know, but you're putting it down in writing and you're saying it formally. Someone else might be reading this Cover Letter and they may never have heard of a Functional Spec before.

Price

The next thing is to tell them how much it costs. People want to know how much it's going to cost, now!

```
The total for the entire application is <$amount>. As requested, I've broken
out the price and delivery for each piece separately. The Reports module can be
viewed as an "add-on" to the main system, but can't be provided independently.

Main Application              $
Reports                       $
```

I learned this from one of the first jobs I worked on. I had delivered a 20-page specification and proposal where the price for the various configurations was on the last page, and the first thing the customer did was rip through those pages, looking to see how much it was going to cost.

Project components

This is also the place to tell them how the project is broken out as far as required and optional segments go. Tell them how the system is configured—a main application and a number of smaller pieces, or a shell and multiple plug-ins, or whatever.

Note that these segments are not the same as the modules that you are going to deliver. These segments are the various "things" that the customer could buy. It is still possible to have an application be comprised of a single purchasable segment but yet be broken down into many deliverables scheduled on several distinct dates.

Price escalation terms

This next section is one that you may have never seen before. On occasion, we give the customer a discount if they sign off on the application within a given period of time.

```
If this quote is accepted within 15 days, the price is subject to a 6%
<$amount> discount, resulting in an early acceptance price of <$amount>. We
reserve the right to re-quote price and delivery after 60 days.
```

Before you get too upset at "giving something away," it's important to understand the positioning of this offer. I had considered providing a price and then adding a "penalty" if they don't sign off within that period of time, but felt that gave the customer a bad message. Instead, I want them to perceive that they're getting a deal for acting fast. However, I take our original price—the one that they would pay if they bought the next day—and add the discount amount to it. In other words, if the price you're looking for is $100,000, then 6% is added to this, for a price of $106,000 that is quoted to them. If they accept immediately, in order to get their discount, they'll pay $100,000. This new price is the price they see, together with the discount if they sign off quickly.

The next question is—why bother at all? Here's my reasoning. We have just lived in this application for a while—designing, discussing, documenting, and so on. Right now, we know it pretty well. It is part of our being. We could recite functionality and validation rules by heart. If they have to go through 15 rounds of approval and end up sitting on the proposal for two and a half months, we're going to forget everything we know. It's going to take additional time to get back up to speed—and, well, hey, that additional time is going to cost us money.

Additionally, getting them to act fast also implicitly discourages them from shopping the specification around to other shops. It may not be a big deal, but depending on the type of app, they may figure the discount is a significant enough incentive to not monkey around.

Furthermore, we don't make cans of tomato soup, where one comes off the line every second and a half. Our business consists of great big projects and we need to be able to schedule people for them. We can't just have people sitting around waiting for a project to be approved. Thus, it's in our best interest to get that project moving and signed off on. A little financial incentive helps focus the customer's attention on getting this proposal approved. Does this bother the customer? It shouldn't. It's the job of the developer to help them along during the development of the specification so that they are ready to sign off as soon as possible after they get the final document.

The cardinal rule throughout this whole process is, as Steven Tyler put it so well, "No surprises." The customer doesn't like surprises, you don't like surprises. They should know what to expect and if they don't, the developer has made a mistake. The Cover Letter and specification are put down on paper to just remind them of what they already know.

Delivery

Tell them when you can start work, and when they can expect to get their stuff. Given the Price Escalation Terms just discussed, you may assume the customer will ask why they have to pay an additional amount if they don't approve the proposal quickly enough, but that, on the other hand, you can't begin work for another period of time after that. The simple answer is that this lead time before you can get started is already figured into the price—the discount is to encourage them to get things rolling just that much quicker.

```
We can begin work on this project within <TimeFrame> weeks of acceptance. The
final system can be delivered approximately <TimeFrame> working weeks later.
```

Rules of the road (including change of personnel)

We need to make it clear to the customer—right up front—that this fixed price proposal is given for the work only as described in the specification. However, during the course of application development, it is normal for new requirements to be discovered, or additional functionality to be requested; either must result in modifications to the spec. When this happens, we go through our standard Change Order process. Modifications to the spec— including the corresponding price adjustments—are provided to the customer in writing. The customer then has the opportunity to accept or refuse such modifications.

```
This is a fixed price quotation for the functionality described. Please read
carefully and confirm that the functionality described meets your requirements.
It is extremely important that every function and operation you are expecting
is listed here; this document supersedes all verbal discussions - any
modifications or changes requested after acceptance will alter price and/or
delivery and will require written confirmation by both parties via the Change
Order process described in the appendices to the specification.

Note that this is not an estimate but has been determined using our Action
Point Counting system. Our methodology requires an accurate specification of
functional capabilities for the system in question and relies on statistical
analysis of historical performance to determine actual costs for each component
of the system.
```

Those changes become a part of the application just as if they had been a part of the original spec. We also employ a bit of salesmanship here by explaining that we have a methodology for quoting prices—not some "pull a number out of the air" trick. By itself, the customer may not care, but if they're going to send this proposal out to other firms for competitive bids, we've now just raised the ante. The customer is now prodded to wonder how the other firms create their quotes, and those companies are put on the hot seat, having to come up with some sort of explanation for their "wild-ass guess" technique.

Terms—price, delivery, deadline

Finally, we cover the terms of how we expect to be paid. This goes in the Cover Letter because it's the document the customer signs, and thus commits to. We've discussed the issues of getting paid earlier, so there's no need to do so again. Just make sure you state your terms in the document they're going to sign. On a personal level, what we're saying in our own Cover Letter is that we are going to invoice the customer after we ship a module, and that we expect to do so on a reasonably regular basis.

Our goal is to invoice every two weeks for the modules that we shipped those two weeks. This philosophy has two benefits. First, we need to keep paying attention to delivering things so that the customer sees progress. We may not always make a shipment every two weeks, but we try. The benefit is that the customer sees regular progress and they can start working with the app quickly. We don't deliver the whole app in one fell swoop, but rather, in parts, so they can learn it incrementally.

The other benefit is that it gets cash in the door faster. And that's a pretty clear benefit to everyone.

```
Payment terms consist of invoices rendered every two weeks for the work
completed to that point, payable 10 days after presentation. Work will be
stopped in the event an invoice becomes past due. For specific information on
how the work completed is broken into discrete deliverable components, see the
section on Milestones at the end of the specification.
```

Some firms also impose a financial penalty for invoices that go past due. I've rarely run into that situation, since stopping work ends up generating a check rather quickly. You may want to also include an additional charge for late payment.

Ask for the order

I've been through this with the Engagement Letter, but it doesn't hurt to remind you. Don't just assume they know what to do—tell them what they'll have to do to start the process, and then ask them to do it!

```
In order to accept this proposal, please sign and return one copy of this
letter. I'm looking forward to working with you and the rest of the crew
at your firm on this system. If you have any questions, please call me at
your convenience.
```

Then make sure they know you want them to feel comfortable to call you.

Sign off

And again, as with the Engagement Letter, give them a place to sign the letter and return it to you in order to commit to starting the project.

```
Sincerely,
Hentzenwerke Corporation


Herman Werke
Executive Vice President
_____
Accepted by (Authorized Representative of <customer>)

_____
Date Signed
```

Delivery of the Functional Spec

By the time you've been through 100 analysis and design meetings, another dozen prototype demonstrations, and spent countless hours writing and revising the spec, the last thing you want to do is spend several hours delivering the final product. At least that's the way I feel. I'm exhausted, I've probably pulled an all-nighter putting the final touches on the thing, hoping the printer doesn't jam on page 285, and I just want to be done with it.

However, this spec is for a project that could cost anywhere from $25,000 to $500,000 or more. You don't treat it the same as the proposal for a $250 printing job at the local copy center. There are a couple different ways to deliver a proposal, assuming you're not answering one of those government "Sealed bids must be delivered to the county clerk's office by 4 PM on the first Monday of the following month" type of RFPs.

"Drop it off" vs. "Detailed walkthrough"

The first option, and sometimes the most tempting, is to drop the whole package off at the front desk of the company, or even messenger it over, thus not even risking accidental contact with folks involved with the project. The trouble with this method is that, well, it can be impersonal and insulting. However, there is one scenario under which it's actually a viable option, given some considerations described in the next section under "Iterative acceptance."

The second option is to schedule a meeting where you walk through the entire specification, page by page. The trouble here is that few human beings have the mental (or physical) strength to last through a meeting where a large proposal is presented. Either the meeting is going to last for several days, or the contents are going to get short shrift in the attempt to cover the entire spec in an hour or two.

As a result, I've opted for a third option—iterative acceptance.

Iterative acceptance

As we develop prototypes for parts of an application, we also deliver working copies of the spec that they can review and comment on. Just as we deliver a project in pieces—module by module—so as to not overwhelm a user with the task of having to accept 73 screens, 21 processes, and 102 reports, we deliver the spec in pieces as well. Some of you might note a similarity between this and Agile Methodologies. Hmmm!

By the time the spec is complete, they've already been through each page in fair detail, and thus the delivery of the whole spec is a simple act—one that might even be accomplished through the use of the "Drop it off" technique mentioned earlier.

If you should decide to employ this method, of course, you may still need to make a formal presentation to "upper management," but that becomes a "dog and pony show" as opposed to an in-depth presentation of every feature and capability. You'll also want to make sure that you've covered the big points—such as price, delivery, and implementation issues—earlier, so that they don't get surprised partway into the delivery process.

Follow-up

So they've got the package in their hot little hands, and they promise, "We'll get back to you." What do you do then?

You could simply wait until they call you. You could, of course, be waiting forever. No matter how firm the deal seems at the time of delivery, there are 100 things that can hang a project up. Some are external—the company goes into merger discussions, and all "big ticket" spending is put on hold. The company's market tanks, they lay off 10% of their workforce, and they postpone purchases. A new line of business suddenly crops up, forcing a sudden re-evaluation of the application's purpose, scope, or usefulness. Or it could simply be a political issue inside—a manager gets promoted, and wants to push your application aside in favor of her choice of a solution.

This is a bad idea, because until you hear from them, you simply don't know, and you need to determine whether or not to make future plans based on that app selling or not selling. So it's smart to get an idea of when you should be hearing from them, and then to follow up a few days after that date.

The other choice is to follow up on your own schedule. I tend to not do this because I really don't think that my phone call is going to force them to make a decision on a large, important purchase. They have other players involved in the game, and they have to make sure each of them is satisfied. When it all comes down to it, I'm just the vendor.

So at this stage in the relationship, I take my cues from their actions—if they need me to be aggressive and follow up regularly, I will, but generally, I'll wait for their action, and nudge them if they haven't acted when they said they would.

Chapter 19
Scenarios Encountered During
the Specification Process

"You know, some single people don't consider it to be a good party unless the cops have been there at least a dozen times. Same scenario every time: 400 drunks tryin' to act like they're not drunk. One guy is the spokesman for the group... 'Shh! Shh, I'm talking to the cops! Shut up!'"—Jeff Foxworthy

The specification process will produce the most customer contact per billable hour during the life of the project. I've been in this business for nearly 20 years, yet I still don't think I've seen it all. Nonetheless, there are a number of fairly common situations that crop up again and again. In this chapter, I'll discuss the more common of these scenarios. However, be assured that we've just scratched the surface of encounters with customers—the rest is left as an exercise for the reader.

As with Chapter 12, "Scenarios Encountered During the Sales Call," the purpose of this chapter is to help you see and practice for situations that may come up in the future, or to give you ideas on how to handle situations that you've run into in the past but weren't happy with how you handled.

And I want to remind you about the tone of this chapter—the negativity is rampant because it's the bad situations that you want to be able to handle. Sure, you might want to do a post-mortem on situations that worked out well, but it's not as important to prepare yourself in advance for those cases.

Getting started with the gig

While I've tried to draw a very clear line between the time you walk out of the sales call and the time you start billable design work, in reality it doesn't always work out so neatly. The plan is for you to have come to agreement with your prospective customer that you'll send them an Engagement Letter, and after they sign and return it, you'll begin work. Here are some situations you can encounter during this period, and how to deal with them.

Additional meetings

You can think of 100 scenarios where the customer would like more information but they don't want to pay for it. They want to decide whether they should do it in DOS or Windows. (Hopefully that's not a big issue anymore.) Or maybe it's Linux or Windows. Or they're thinking of moving to the Web and are trying to sort out the options. They want to determine whether they have enough capacity, or enough hard disk space, or whether their app can be ported to a client/server database that the company president read about in *Forbes* last week, or... yes, the list goes on forever... And they want you to come in again for free to do more analysis before they start paying for your time.

Guess what? That's knowledge—your knowledge—that they're asking for. You are not giving that away for free. Repeat after me—you are not giving that away for free! They want you to evaluate something. They want you to look at something. They want your opinion—to bounce a few ideas off of you. Again, these are services that you provide on a professional, for-hire basis. Would your customer expect to be able to call a lawyer and say, "I would like your advice on something" without getting billed for it? If they would expect it for free, perhaps they're not your kind of customer.

What types of lines might you hear from a customer, and how might you answer them?

"We need to have you come in and talk to our manager before you start anything." It depends on why they're asking this. If you didn't make it clear that the first visit was for the purpose of their being able to evaluate you, then you screwed up, and you may have to bite the bullet on this one. But if you were clear that the first meeting was for that purpose, it was their mistake not to have taken full advantage of that "freebie."

How do you say this? There isn't a great way to phrase this, but if they made this blunder, it's time to be a bit firm with them. "Well, <your manager> really should have been in that initial meeting. I've had prospects who have wanted me to go through four or five meetings with various personnel—and that's not the way I work. However, why don't we make this next meeting a working meeting, where I meet with your manager but we can also start in on the initial needs analysis."

"We would like to see more examples of your work." More? How many more? For how long? Again, this could go on and on. You can answer, "As we go through the design process, I can demonstrate similar things I've done that map to specific situations that we encounter."

"We would like your opinion on <this matter> before you start." And after that matter, they'll want your opinion a third time? Then a fourth? But how do you counter this?

I often remind potential customers that we might want to do some exploratory work first. "You don't have to commit to a $20,000 Functional Specification right now. What might be a better approach in this situation is to do four or five hours of consulting first, in order to resolve these issues that you've brought up. These aren't the sort that can be handled in a single meeting or over a couple of 10-minute phone calls." Most people will respect your time when you make it clear that you expect to get paid for consulting time.

And if it's "just one more meeting," then they shouldn't have any trouble with "just a couple hundred dollars."

The key point to remember—and to continue to explain to them—in each of these situations is that they are not committing to the entire app by opening up their checkbook. Sure, once they've developed a "for hire" relationship with you, it's tougher to say no, but any good salesman would tell you that this is the point of a sales call—to get them to buy something!

What if they ask you to look at an app during a sales call?

This shouldn't come up during a sales call if you made clear what the purpose of the meeting was. That said, people aren't blessed with perfect memories, and they're not above getting off track.

I'll try to beg off in this situation, first explaining that to pay proper attention requires more time than we (they or I) have available. Then I'll mention that we do offer the service of

thoroughly auditing an application, that we have documented procedures and formal
checklists, and that it usually takes a couple of hours to do a complete job. And—of course—
we'd be happy to perform that service for them if they'd like.

The missing Engagement Letter

Just for fun, let's walk through a situation where the Engagement Letter mysteriously
disappears yet you are expected to start cranking out work. How do you respond?

The call came in on Tuesday. They need some work done, and they'd like to see you next
Monday morning. Sounds good. You explain the way you do work, they agree, and you fire
off an Engagement Letter.

Friday's mail comes, and no EL has been returned. The fax machine is similarly empty.
You don't know these people, but have heard a rumor or two that they might play a little fast
and loose on occasion. And the situation that you're being called in on sounds like it might be
indicative of poor management as much as anything else.

Call your contact up—lo and behold! They're not in today! But they'll be back Monday.
What do you do?

The first choice is to blow off the appointment since you don't have a signed agreement.
You could do this if you've decided to make future meetings after the sales call completely
conditional on the return of the Engagement Letter. The way you phrase this is that you
explain that since you hadn't received a signed Engagement Letter, the deal was either
postponed, or off completely. If they protest, simply claim innocence—"But that's what the
letter said—in order to agree, sign and return—and since you didn't return, I figured you
didn't agree!" Now the monkey is on their back to explain why they didn't keep their end of
the deal.

Or do you place your trust (naïve and foolish as that may be) in humankind once more
and make your visit on Monday morning? Perhaps you trust your fellow man, and barring any
other unusual circumstances, keep your meeting on Monday.

But before you hang up the phone, leave a message gently asking about the Engagement
Letter. "You may not have been able to get to it before the end of the week—no problem. I can
pick it up on Monday." Again, don't blame, don't accuse, but make the point that you do
expect it to be ready when you show up on Monday.

Come Monday morning, the first question is to double-check on that Engagement Letter.
"Did you get that EL I sent you last week? Just wanted to keep our paperwork in order." Nine
times out of 10, your contact will have it on his desk, waiting for you. But what about that one
other time?

My answer is to treat this as an extended sales call. If you end up getting burned for a few
hours of work, well, that's the breaks. But generally you can provide some help, generate
some goodwill, but also be sure to get that letter immediately. Let's look at some specific
situations that may raise a variety of red flags.

"I need someone to check it out/my boss to sign it." The response is to explain that
you can't do the work without the paperwork. If they couldn't get their end of the paperwork
done, then they weren't ready to have you come out to see them. Treat this as a sales call to
determine in more detail what they're looking for.

"I lost it/never got it." You should have a second copy of the letter right there for them
to sign. If they can't sign it, see the previous response.

"It's in the system but we're really in a hurry—we need to get started today!" "Great! We want to get going too, but we never start work on a job without the paperwork in place. We've found that if we start work without the paperwork, we end up forgetting and then it comes time to invoice and we can't because the Engagement Letter contains information we use to set the customer up in our system. Then we have to stop work and it delays everything. Let's plan out what we're going to do and investigate what we'll need to do first."

"I don't see why I have to sign this. I'm good for the money." Here, the funny feeling in the pit of your stomach grows. Ask them if there is something objectionable or unclear. If the answer is no, but they still resist having to sign something, walk away. The person you need to watch more than anyone else is the person who has to tell you how honest they are.

"We need to get a PO Number for you, but we're in a real hurry." Again, see the previous argument. Every time I've been coerced into doing something because they were in a hurry, I've regretted it. Every single time. And if their company needs a PO to get started, then shouldn't we wait?

It might seem that I'm making a big deal out of this, so let me play through a typical scenario. Suppose you go in on Monday and do a half-day—or, worse, a full day ending around 6:30 PM— worth of work, with no Engagement Letter. You leave with more things to do than you had when you arrived—the project has mushroomed—and, naturally, they're in crisis mode—this has to be done by Wednesday, or Friday, or the end of the month, or heads will roll! So you're pressured to come back the next day—again, for a full day of work. And your contact had to leave early that day, and there's no Engagement Letter waiting for you.

But they're desperate, and so you come back the next day. Your contact isn't in—"He'll be in around 10"—but a surrogate has been appointed, and you buckle down to work. Your contact ends up never showing up—a meeting at the district office took all day—and you end up staying late on Tuesday to get this one last piece done. And, of course, you end up being asked back on Wednesday.

Meanwhile, you're in up to your ears on this project—despite the rocky start, it's pretty interesting—and you forget that you don't have an Engagement Letter.

You show up on Wednesday, your contact mutters something as he passes you in the hall—you're almost part of the staff by now—and shortly before normal quitting time, you're done. Nine and a half hours on Monday, 13 on Tuesday, and 7.5 on Wednesday. But the project is done and things look good. Thirty billable hours. Your daughter will eventually forget that you missed her rehearsal on Tuesday night. You sit down with your contact, indicate that everything is in order, and you're on your way. You send an invoice—and it's sent back with the terse explanation that "we never okayed this expenditure" or "our agreement was for four hours on Monday—not 30 hours. We're not going to pay your inflated bill."

All because you allowed yourself to be pressured into working without a written agreement.

How do you handle this? Come Monday afternoon, if no Engagement Letter is available, explain that, "unfortunately, despite the critical nature of your project, I have a prior engagement for Tuesday, but will check back with you on Tuesday to schedule more time. And, by the way, when will you have that Engagement Letter ready?" You allow your customer to save face, but at the same time, you don't put yourself at risk.

Arguing about the Engagement Letter

While I've tried to draw a very clear line between the time you walk out of the sales call and the time you start billable design work, in reality it doesn't always work out so neatly. The plan is for you to have come to agreement with your prospective customer that you'll send them an Engagement Letter, and after they sign and return it, you'll begin work. Here are some situations you can encounter during this period, and how to deal with them.

Resistance to signing the Engagement Letter

One of the most important things you can do during the initial stages of developing a customer relationship is to make sure they actually sign the Engagement Letter and send it back. Without a signed agreement, you are opening yourself up to a world of hurt. There is no good logical reason that somebody can't fill this form out. However, there are several reasons that they wouldn't want to—they don't want to open their wallet yet, they want to get "some more stuff" for free, or they're not ready to make a commitment, but they need to start getting some work done. As a result, it's not uncommon for people to try to avoid signing the letter and try to have you begin work on a non-billable basis. Let's look at some of the situations you might find yourself in.

Resistance to the customer setup form

On a rare occasion, you may get the Engagement Letter signed, but encounter resistance to filling out the customer setup form. It sounds silly, to be sure, but it happens. And, in this case, it's not ordinarily overt   "We're not going to fill this form out!" Instead, it's mild—the form is forgotten, and then a phone call or two isn't returned, and then it's "lost" and so on.

Again, instead of trying to ram the form down the customer's throat, find out why. You may learn that they're not ready to begin the work, or that your contact doesn't have the authority that they said they had. Or perhaps there's a misunderstanding—better to clear this up now.

Their contract

Occasionally, they'll want you to sign their contract instead. (This is a completely different situation than when they just want modifications to your contract.) While this may be okay, it's good to be aware of a few things. First of all, their contract is to protect their interests, and likely isn't written by people (lawyers) who are experienced with software development issues. Oftentimes, there are items in their contract that are totally irrelevant or just plain wrong.

Instead, offer to add their clauses to your contract. Bottom line—their contract can't be as effective as yours, because they don't know as much about software development as you do. Many times (not always, but often) they want a specific issue covered, and they're happy to have their wording included in your contract.

How do you actually say this? How about an exchange like this:

Customer: "We've reviewed your contract, and we've drawn one up of our own that we'd like to use instead," or "We have a standard contract that we use in these situations." [In any case, they're proposing their own contract.]

You: "Hmmm, I've never run into a customer that wanted to substitute their own—ours is pretty inclusive for a whole host of software development issues. Is there a specific issue that is missing or that you need covered in a different way?" [Find out why they are proposing their contract.]

This gives them a chance to explain what the issue is—are you dealing with a rigid bureaucracy, the kind that requires you to "direct all shipments to the shipping dock at Plant 7" so that their purchasing department can track that it was actually received? Or is your customer concerned about one specific issue but they're agreeable to alternate ways of putting it in the contract?

Second, remember that your "contract" (the attachment) is not a device for providing terms for a lawsuit; rather, it's simply to bring up issues and document them so that you can avoid misunderstandings down the road. You want to show them that you are professional and that you mean business. If the deal goes to the lawyers, you'll lose because your pockets probably aren't as deep as theirs.

Third, don't forget that contracts can always be negotiated! Each item in a contract has a price. If they want something in a contract that you don't care for, you can always include it for a high-enough price. I mean, if there were enough zeros at the end of the price, you could put up with a lot of onerous terms, couldn't you? If they insist on having everything in the contract but don't want to pay for any of it, that's pretty much the same as wanting the app for free, right?

We were once asked to sign a contract of a customer before beginning development. The general manager, new to the firm, apologized for the hassles that their legal department was putting us both through, but explained, "Evidently we like to be able to sue the people we do business with." I never got around to returning their calls after that.

Resistance to paying for design

I haven't seen it much anymore, but you will occasionally run into people who don't want to pay for the design of an application. Their reasoning is that you're supposed to "get paid" for the design if you win the contract for the coding of the application itself. I guess that works in some industries, but not in ours. Here are some of the scenarios you may run into, and how to respond.

"The design is sales work—we don't pay for it in our industry, and we won't pay you for it either." The answer to reply with goes like this: "The first visit was a sales call—but the rest of the work is professional, technical work. Just as the first visit to an architect or a lawyer could be considered a sales call, but from then on, you would expect to pay for their services. The expertise you're paying for here is the ability to design a system specification for your system."

"We don't need your expertise to do this." If they feel they have the expertise in-house to do the design, then by all means let them have at it. The only danger is that you'll have to be very careful about not laughing in their face when they show you what they think passes for a system design and specification. It's highly unlikely that they'll be able to provide a document that really provides the information you need, but since they're unskilled at this, they won't see it that way. I've seen more than one customer confuse effort with competence. "But we worked for two weeks on this! It's three inches thick! What do you mean it doesn't contain the information you need?!"

I'll also often explain, "If you want me to provide a fixed price (or reasonably estimated) quote on the final spec, then it will have to be in a format that I can use—and we use a specific methodology that requires a large amount of information described a certain way." Then, I throw out a few of those items—such as report definitions, database sizing, and so on, and see how quickly they decide that they don't have the expertise after all.

For example, and this is kind of wicked, you can ask them for a complete database schema, a screen shot of every user interface object, and a list of control-centric validations and form-based rules. Have you ever met a customer who could get past first base with such a request?

"We need to know how much the specification will cost before you begin. We understand that the development will have a fixed price, but we need to know how much the specification will run." Our answer is simple: "The price depends on how long it takes to determine what you need. We can't tell you how much it will cost because the specification process is an iterative process—we are discovering your needs and requirements. The quicker we can complete that discovery, the sooner we'll be done and the lower the cost will be, but we can't tell you how long because we don't know how much we have to do.

"What we can do—right now—is write out a rough draft of how many screens, processes, and reports you have, and then we can provide an estimate of how big this specification will be—and how much it will cost. But please note that there is still a lot of room for unknowns.

"For example, suppose you need a screen to maintain information about doctors. Depending on your needs, we may be able to spec this out in an hour—because it's a simple screen with name, address, specialty, medical school attended, and a couple of phone numbers, and this is all raw data entry.

"On the other hand, it may take us several days because your requirements might include the ability to maintain multiple addresses—home, a couple of offices, several hospitals, and an office in another state. Furthermore, we need to track what days the doctor is at which address. And we have many phone numbers, and we need to track which are active and at what time. And we need to be able to dial the phone by clicking on any phone number. And we'd like to be able to drag a file from a list of files onto the phone number and automatically fax that document when applicable.

"Furthermore, the specialties for a single doctor can vary from hospital to hospital. And we also select the hospitals from a pick list—instead of just typing in the name in a non-validated field. And once we've figured all this out, the specification for this screen has to be approved by someone else, and they see some things they want changed, so we go through another round of changes.

"Thus this doctor maintenance screen could take anywhere from an hour to several days, and we don't know this up front. We can make estimates, but until we're done, we won't know.

"Finally, our business is to continually ask you questions so that you consider things that you may not have thought of before—that's our job and we've seen things like this before. We can give you an estimate based on the number of screens, reports, and processes, but it's just a rough idea. "

At this point, they may intellectually see your point. However, emotionally they may not want to sign what they feel is an "open-ended" contract, or they may be required by corporate policy to have a number for whatever expenditure form they have to fill out.

Backed against a wall, what do you do? Here's where your initial estimate from the sales call comes in handy. Take out that number of screens, reports, processes, and other items. Have them assign a complexity from 1 to 5 for each. Finally, have them guarantee that they will have all the answers to your questions in one iteration, and that any changes to those answers later will involve extra charges. Once they do so, you can give them a fixed price for the specification. You'll probably want to, er, adjust the fixed price you would give them accordingly, since, if they're being this adamantly unreasonable here, they're likely to develop a memory loss later on when it comes to that "all the answers in one iteration" part.

"The price of the specification will be folded into the app, right?" This question comes from folks in industries where up-front work usually carries a charge not on its own merits, but to act as a qualifier for the work. An example would be an application fee for a mortgage. The mortgage company may typically charge an application fee, but if you qualify, and accept the loan, then the application fee is folded into the complete price of the loan.

We explain that the specification is a separate product with a separate price. They are not required to buy the app from us—and, in fact, are encouraged to shop around to make sure they are getting the best price on the app that is described in the specification. But the fact that the price of the spec is separate is spelled out in the Engagement Letter.

"This is such a big job, we want a volume discount." This one is remarkably easy to counter. The job is bigger, yes, but it also requires more skill because it's bigger. It takes more skill to build a skyscraper than a doghouse, and the rates charged for those higher-level skills are larger as well. Furthermore, there's more to a bigger project than just "more hours." A skyscraper that's 100 stories doesn't cost 10 times more than a skyscraper that's 10 stories— it's more complex to build and the building process is more involved as well. So while you could well expect a volume discount on the bricks and steel you'll use to build that 100-story skyscraper, you'll have to pay considerably more for the know-how to do so.

Changing the contract

Suppose you're partway down the road of development and your customer requests changes to the contract. They want you to work on site full-time, or they insist on complete ownership of all source code, including your library routines, or they even want a reduction in the quoted price. How do you answer requests like this?

Usually, these are posed because of a change in their business environment that they hadn't anticipated. For example, suppose a larger firm purchases their company, and the new owner has a policy of owning all source code and associated libraries. Or perhaps new management has been brought in, and those individuals need to have greater control, to the point of daily status meetings.

In these situations, it's up to you to decide what requests you want to accept, and which you don't. In the case of changes that you'll agree to, be sure to get something in return if necessary. For example, if they want source code ownership, make sure they pay for it!

The tougher situation is when they want a change that you're not willing to agree to. This should be treated just as if it had been brought up in the beginning of the relationship—if you feel strongly enough about it, it's a deal-breaker. At this point, of course, you'll need to agree to disagree. This type of circumstance is the reason you don't want them to get behind in paying their bills, or be otherwise on the hook.

Limit to design charges

A customer may accept the premise that you're not going to be able to determine how much the specification is going to cost up front, due to the unknowns inherent in the specification process. However, they may still have a business requirement to have a cap on the design expenditures. In this situation, it's important to know this information going into the project. Furthermore, it's critical to organize the design to make sure you don't run out of money and have a partially finished design. That may seem contradictory—after all, you can't necessarily force someone to stop iterating before they're done. Doing so means that end product is not going to be all they wanted.

The strategy here is to be 100% done with 80% of the modules, instead of 80% done with 100% of the components. You can again liken this to a house. Given the choice between a house that has a roof over every room, but doesn't have a garage at all, or a house with the garage, but where every room is missing the entire roof, which would you choose?

You can always add a garage later when you find more money, and so can the customer. They can add that fancy competitive analysis module next year after the new budgets come out. But they're going to be very unhappy if every module is missing the ability to save data.

How much is this going to be?

This is a variation of "How much will the specification cost?" and, in fact, is more common. First, the customer may not have been prepared to ask about the cost for the spec, but is definitely thinking about how much the app itself will be. Second, the price tag is going to be significantly more.

The quick answer is "It depends." Here are a couple of analogies you can use to explain that it is impossible to provide a fixed price for an entity that is undefined. The first is the grocery cart scenario. I'm going to go to the grocery store for groceries for my family. How much will that cost? It depends on a multitude of factors, and it is difficult, even in this relatively simple example, to quantify all of those factors sufficiently to come up with a reasonably accurate price. For example, some of those factors include:

- the number of members in the family,

- how old they are,

- how big they are (your 21-year-old daughter who just got signed to the Women's NBA may eat considerably more than your 23-year-old son who is a jockey),

- how long a period the groceries are to last for, and

- the family's eating habits.

My favorite analogy is to answer "about as much as a car" when faced with this impossible question. It's a wonderful experience to see the light come on when someone realizes what I'm trying to explain here. (And if the light doesn't come on, then you've gained a valuable insight as to the intellectual horsepower you might be dealing with during the project.)

And if they don't ever quite "get it" then here's the explanation. "I could describe a car to you for quite a while, and go into a lot of detail about many of the mechanisms and features that this car has—but even after hours of description, you still couldn't give me the price of the car with any reasonably accuracy. I can describe the number of doors and how the steering works and the functions on the radio and what the inside of the trunk looks like and what every dimension of the interior is. But you still wouldn't know whether I was describing a bottom-of-the-line Taurus, a mid-line Lexus, or a top-of-the-line Bentley. However, you could probably determine the price pretty quickly if *you* were able to ask *me* a number of specific questions.

"Same thing here—you can describe to me aspects of your system for hours, but that won't necessarily give me enough information. However, I can give you a price if you allow me to ask you a number of specific questions. The difference between a car and this software system is that a car has a relatively small number of options from which to choose. A software application by nature has an infinite number of options from which to choose. The process to determine the correct choices is an iterative one—choices made early on influence choices that become available later—and if it turns out that some desirable choices are no longer available, then backtracking and further iterations are required."

By the way, there are times when the question is not "how much" but "how long"— particularly in the corporate world, where developers usually aren't billing their time in the traditional "consultant" sense. You can use the same type of tact: "How long does it take to build a house?" "Until I know a lot more about what type of house, I can't say. But I can guide you along so that you can give me the information I need to give you an answer."

Cheapskates

Every once in a while, you'll run into a customer that is incessantly looking for the next angle to save a buck. Examples abound. Here are actual lines I've heard from potential customers:

- "How much will we save if you don't do any testing, but we do it instead?"

- "How much cheaper will it be if we don't write out the whole specification? I'll have my secretary take dictation at the design meetings."

- "What if we force the user to enter everything in uppercase—will that save any money?"

- "If we agree to give you the entire project today, how much of a discount on your hourly rate will you give us?"

- "Documentation is included with this, right? At no extra charge, right?"

- "We're a big company and if this project goes well, you're going to see a lot more business from us—so we need to see a more competitive price from you."

- "I know it looks like we have a lot of money because of all the marble floors and expensive furniture, but I'm not going to let you jack up your rates—I expect you to use your sharpest pencil on that quote!"

- "My nephew was in here last weekend—he goes to MIT—and he thinks you're over-designing this system. We don't want to pay for an over-designed system."

Need I say more? Listen to your gut. Do you really want to be involved with a company that's going to look over your shoulder and complain that putting those comments in your code is costing them too much money? Run away.

In your nicest fashion, explain that, unfortunately, you're not the cheapest firm in town, and they can probably find a less expensive route of having their project approached. Perhaps someone who is just starting out, and thus has lower rates, or maybe a moonlighter with a full-time job who doesn't have to charge as much. Just remember that, when they call next year for you to pick up the pieces, your price won't be any cheaper!

How do I know you'll be around next year?

If you're a smaller shop, you may well run into this objection when trying to close the deal.

Instead of trying to convince them otherwise, I meet them head on: "You don't. Any more than you know that the local supermarket you shop at is going to be there next month, or that your boss will still be your boss next year.

"Size and longevity are no guarantee that a firm will be in business next year. Who would have guessed in 1984 that Drexel Burnham Lambert would disappear from the junk bond market a couple years later? Chrysler—one of the 25 largest companies in the nation—nearly went bankrupt—twice. Digital Equipment Corporation—the company that invented the mini-computer and was the second largest computer manufacturer for decades—is gone. How many billion-dollar savings and loans vanished in the 1980s?" As I'm writing this, the accounting firm, Arthur Andersen is going through trial on a felony count of obstruction of justice. If found guilty, one of the most revered companies in the world will likely disappear within the year.

"The best you can do is to make educated bets based on the current knowledge you have, and safeguard yourself in the event that your bet doesn't pan out.

"So this is what we do to protect you."

Then I explain some of the procedures we follow to make sure that if we were to disappear tomorrow, either because of that errant beer truck that sent us to our maker, or because we're hiding out in the Caribbean from the Feds, our customers would be protected.

These include regular drafts of the specifications sent on to the customer for their review, source code put in escrow (where a third party keeps a copy of the source code until the application is delivered, accepted, and paid for), and documented standards to enhance maintainability.

Naturally, the procedures you follow may differ. The point is to make sure that they feel that they're not going to be left in the cold if you're not around next year. By doing so, you're more likely to continue the relationship—how many of your competitors are making sure that they can be replaced if necessary?

We're considering either language X or language Y. What do you think?

First of all, figure out why they're asking. If a company expects to maintain, enhance, or deal with interfaces with the application, they might have more of a say in the choice of language. But many companies don't, or farm that work out as well, so it really doesn't matter.

Another situation that they might run into is determining whether the cost of the project is going to vary significantly based on the tool. Suppose developers for one language are a dime a dozen but developers for a second language are hard to come by, and thus much more expensive.

Over the years, I've had more than one customer ask me this question. Considering that I've been a "one-trick pony" for most of my development career, I've often thought this was an odd question to ask me—I've always come in from the very beginning with a very clear bias toward my tool of choice, and they invariably know that up front. (In fact, in the introductory call, when we ask them "Are you looking for someone to write custom software for you?", I also confirm that they're interested in my language of choice.) If all of their systems to date have been written in Visual Basic and I've been writing Java for the past decade, then it's highly unlikely that I'm going to be a suitable candidate for them. Other developers have widely differing experiences, but I've always seemed to run into potential customers who contact me because of my language expertise.

Given all that, this is a tough one to answer. As the saying goes, "Some people treat the choice of language as if it's a matter of life and death. But in reality, it's much more important than that."

It's uncommon for an individual to possess a high level of skill with more than one language, to the extent that they can be fair about evaluating which language is the best candidate for a project.

I'll admit my bias, and then explain that it's not the tool as much as the hands of the craftsman using the tool that determines the end result. A rotten developer with a tool perfectly suited for the project will produce a much poorer application than a highly skilled developer with a mediocre tool.

Other developers have completely different experiences, where the customer doesn't really care what tools and language are used—they just want a solution to their problem. As a result, the developer is free to pitch their language of choice, presenting their best side, so to speak.

The specification process

Once you've started to work on the specification, the variables multiply exponentially. Not only do you have the technical issues to deal with, but all of a sudden everyone and their brother is an expert on software development—although, funny enough, no two people at the company can agree how the inventory restocking process works! Here are some situations you might encounter during specification development, and how to deal with them.

Customer participation

Once in a while you may run into a company that expects you to do all of the work; they show up, nominally, at a couple of meetings, but then their key people begin to miss meetings, but expect you to make continued progress on the specification. Sometimes a customer has slashed much of their staff, and expects you to provide not only the technical side of the system, but also just infer how the business works from a couple of high-level meetings.

Sometimes they can even be as brusque as "You're the expert, you should know what to do" or "If you are such an expert, why can't you tell me how an inventory system should be put together?" Of course, if you attempt to do so, they'll suddenly come up with 101 exceptions, because "we do things differently around here."

I've found when responses aren't forthcoming, I'll start sketching out the specification, leaving holes to fill identified, and then provide them with a copy of the spec at that point. I'll also provide a list of questions for which I'm awaiting the answers. This makes it very clear that I'm waiting on them for answers, and I'm not going to do anything else until I hear from them.

Resistance to design—just start coding!

How many times have you seen a variation on this cartoon? "You guys start coding—I've got a meeting scheduled for next Tuesday with the users so we can find out what they want."

Everyone thinks their situation is unique. "We've never done a design before—we don't have time! We have to start coding now! You don't understand our company [our industry]. "

I once was in a meeting where the bright young college kid stood up, defending the lack of standards, including any comments at all, in any of his programs, and claimed, "Look at every single program in this company. How many of the good ones have comments? None of them! That just goes to show that we don't need comments!" This fellow conveniently ignored the facts that this company had had three software development managers in four years, and experienced 200% turnover in 18 months. Moreover, less than a year later, the company fired the development department (more than 30 people) and outsourced the entire software development effort because their software projects were in such a mess.

You're the professional in this situation. Sure, you can start coding now, and make changes as additional requirements are discovered. Then you could make more changes as even more requirements are discovered, and then rip out entire modules when yet more requirements are discovered, until the entire project has taken three times as long and cost five times as much as it should have initially.

But it is your responsibility to hold your customer's feet to the fire. They wouldn't build a building without blueprints—they shouldn't build software without proper specifications either. It doesn't matter whether you use structured development, RAD, or an Agile Methodology—you need to size and scope the project in all three cases.

The desire to "just start coding" can be more intense in a corporate situation. One of the immediately perceived advantages of specifications is lower cost in the long run—but in a corporate environment, the work that an internal department does is often seen as having "no cost" (to the user, at least). Furthermore, the various political machinations that can grind away in a company are often hidden by the time a vendor is brought in—but they're in full view of an internal development department, and the department can often end up in the middle of the political wars. In such a situation, rationality disappears, and the "you start coding now" command takes its place.

If they insist—how badly do you need the job? I've walked away from every job where the customer insisted on putting the cart before the horse.

Rush jobs

I've just described one scenario of a rush job, and I can't be firm enough. Being in a rush is no excuse to skip steps. You've probably heard the saying, "Good. Fast. Cheap. Pick any two." I've modified that line to read "Good. Fast. Cheap. Pick any one." Fast just doesn't belong in the equation. When time gets short, something is going to be short-changed.

Frankly, every job is a rush job these days. Whether people are trying to beat a deadline based on a new product rollout, or just trying to get the project done before the start of the golf season, there's always a deadline. And rarely is that deadline as firm as it's made out to be.

That's not always the case, of course. We once wrote an application that scored the results of the National Football League for the calculation of statistics in a "rotisserie" league that had upwards of 100,000 participants. Of course, we were called in at the last minute when the original development firm went belly-up over the summer. This was a deadline—the NFL wasn't going to delay the start of the football season for a couple of weeks just so we could test the software some more.

But most of them aren't like this. And even this project had some flexibility—we had to get online scores up immediately, but printed reports that were going to be mailed out didn't have to be ready until the third week of the season.

It's tough to tell a prospective customer that their target deadline is unrealistic—after you've finally come to the realization yourself that "it just ain't gonna happen." But you will pay for it one way or another—more often than you'd expect, they'll appreciate your candidness, and work with you to determine what a realistic schedule is—and what they can do to help you meet it.

Aborted confidentiality

My company agrees not to resell or duplicate the work that we've done for the customer to a competitor. They're spending a lot of money to build custom software; it would be wrong to go and approach a competitor and do the same thing. That's all there is to it.

There is a touchy issue here. We are more than happy to sign a confidentiality agreement. However, what's going to happen if we start with somebody, we sign a confidentiality agreement and begin work, but two meetings later, they bail? Is that confidentiality still valid? What if you've done a complete specification, but before programming started, you and your customer parted ways? And then a month later a competitor approached you?

The answer lies in applying a bit of common sense and the golden rule to the situation. (No, not the golden rule that states "The man with the gold makes the rules." The other one—the one that goes "Do unto others as you would have them do unto you.")

First, what exactly does the confidentiality agreement state? Good confidentiality agreements cover information that isn't generally known or easily discerned. Suppose that after two meetings all you've learned about your customer's application is that it deals with a new way of tracking the way water purification filters are distributed and maintained, and that their sales force relies heavily on this procedure. You don't have access to the specifics of the tracking mechanism, nor do you have the algorithms and formulas, and you don't know the details of how their sales force is organized.

When a competitor calls you two months later, and they have already thought through the same approach, and have their own tracking mechanism (that may well leapfrog that of the first company), how obligated are you? You're obligated only to the extent that you can't divulge confidential information from another company. Your safeguard would be to document what the second company reveals to you, and your contributions along those lines, at least until you're far enough from the original company's work.

Second, what would you think is fair? Put yourself in their position, and determine what you would feel comfortable with, and what you would agree is confidential. Then, provide a bit of a buffer as a margin of safety, and use that as your proposed realm of confidential information.

The basic guideline in this scenario is to not give away the store at the first meeting. If they want you to sign a blanket agreement upon walking in the door, they may not be the best customer for you. Instead, work a piece at a time, much like a series of increased security levels.

For example, using the example just described, your initial meetings might discuss the existence of a new tracking mechanism, but not go into any detail. Instead, you would treat it as a black box, and work on other pieces surrounding it—putting it in the context of its use in the company. This context placing would conceivably not be as secretive an issue, since the implementation of a piece of software with a group of outside sales reps is a reasonably common process.

Once you're ready to get into the nitty-gritty of the tracking mechanism, you could introduce that into the confidentiality agreement.

When either you or the customer decides to not go further in the relationship, I would suggest that you document the termination of the relationship and describe what is being kept confidential. That way, it will be more difficult for them to come back later and claim that you breached the confidentiality agreement.

Sure, you can run into people who are unreasonable. They might feel that an hour-long meeting where they discuss what they think is a brand-new idea for pricing after-market motorcycle parts then prohibits you from working with any part of the motorcycle industry for the rest of your life. In a case like this, your best bet is to make sure that the initial agreement isn't overly inclusive. If it is, use that as a warning sign that you don't want to do business with them.

And when it comes down to a situation that you're not sure has been spelled out, ask yourself—if the tables were turned, how would you like to be treated?

Changing the primary contact

Suppose you're partway down the road of development and your primary contact—the project champion—leaves or is replaced? This can spell serious trouble, and I know some developers who insist on the entire contract being renegotiated when this happens.

The reason is that, depending on circumstances and personalities, your new contact may well come in with a new agenda. That new agenda could include all sorts of nefarious plans, such as sabotaging the project just to show their predecessor was incompetent, or making heavy modifications just to show off their newfound power. And on the other side of the pendulum, the new contact may have little interest in or concern for the project—and your champion has become ambivalent or careless—also a less than desirable position to be in.

If you're a corporate developer, this is probably even more important, because the new contact may not only have their own agenda as well, but it's more likely that you won't have a way out of the project if (when?) things turn ugly. And there may actually be more pressure applied due to changes in politics with new players in the game. For example, you never know when the new contact will turn out to be the best man for the guy who initially lost the project to you in the first place.

How you want to deal with this situation is up to you, and may vary according to the specific project. But you may want to provide yourself with an out in the event that personnel changes make successful completion of the project less and less likely.

Scope creep

Finding a competent developer who is personable, has the time to spend with them, and understands their business can be a giddy experience for a customer. They could react by going absolutely bonkers with their wish list. "You can do this? Great! Can you do this too? And this? Wow! How about this?"

Pretty soon that $40,000 app has turned into $90,000—and there are still a couple of really important pieces that haven't been addressed. If the customer has an unlimited source of funds, well, good for you! But more likely, they've still got to deal with a budget of some sort.

This issue is called scope creep (or feature creep)—where the list of features gets bigger and bigger. This is different from another issue I'll bring up later—where the customer keeps changing their mind, but the scope never really changes. The identifying characteristic here is that most of the requests are additions to the original list of bullet points.

How do you reel a customer in? How do you get them to shut up, bring closure to the spec, and let you start coding? Here are the magic words: "That's a great idea, and I think your users would love it—but I think that's getting beyond what we set out to do in our initial meetings. How about if we jot it down on a list for Version 2?"

It can get kind of silly if you have to say this over and over, but most customers will eventually start catching on themselves—and start to answer their own question with, "I know, I know—put it on the list for Version 2."

If they don't, however, you should discuss the financial impact of the continued additions. You had a ballpark price for the spec, way back in the days of the sales call and Engagement Letter (or, perhaps the first design meeting or two). You should be able to break that down, proportionately, against the list of bullet points you put together. You can raise a red flag if you can show that you've already spent 75% of the specification development budget, but haven't even covered half of the items on the bullet point list. At this point, you might even want to provide additional documentation, in the form of a letter or memo, indicating the "current status" of the specification development.

```
As of Monday, July 20, we have spent $X, and are about Y% along - at this rate,
the specification will end up costing approximately $Z.
```

You could even extrapolate that to a new estimate for the development itself.

If you do regular status reports—more likely for corporate developers than independents—you can provide a regular measurement of what you've accomplished against what the plan was. The danger to guard against, of course, is that the plan is just that—a "plan." It may vary for any number of reasons—but you still may not be off schedule. The issue of scheduling is one that I haven't addressed heavily in this book; you may want to look for Steve McConnell's *Software Project Survival Guide* (Microsoft Press).

What they decide to do about it, of course, is up to them. The earlier you can identify scope creep and force them to deal with it, the better.

Informal specs

It's a case of "love at first sight." You and the customer get along well—really well. The chemistry is really good, but other factors are so intense that your customer asks you to begin work before the spec is done, regardless of which development methodology you've chosen. Or worse, to bail on the spec completely—and to work with a rather informal set of documents that has a number of holes and is rather vague in other places. You decide to take them up on their offer, but there's that nagging voice, warning you to do a complete spec first. That intractable deadline that you're hearing about every day may not be so ironclad after all, and some of the other pressures seem intense to them, but really not that unusual to you.

Should you? There's no rule that says you can't do a project with ill-defined or incomplete specs. Sometimes the situation simply dictates that you begin work now—before all the details have been figured out. And that's where an Agile Methodology might serve you very well. However, you can't provide a fixed price for that job, nor can you guarantee that all defects will be fixed for free. Why? Because you don't have a complete blueprint.

If they want you to start before the spec is done, you can't provide a fixed price. Period. They can't have it both ways.

Using their specs

I've run into a couple situations where the customer insists that they've done the specification, and just need us to develop it. And you may run into a situation where they will offer to do the spec themselves (although it isn't done yet), so that they're really just asking you to write the code.

Of course, they're going to want to know how much it's going to cost—and, after hearing your sales pitch about how you estimate jobs, they're going to expect a fixed price.

This is pretty easy to counter—simply go through a specification of yours with them, and explain the level of detail they'll need to provide. This single act is usually enough to dissuade them from trying it themselves. I've never run into a customer that has the necessary combination of resources, skills, and desire to go through this process. Furthermore, even if the spec is perfect, there is a significant learning curve on the part of the developer to "become one with the spec." Given all these factors, your customer will probably see that it's better for you to develop it with them.

Welcome back, my friends, to the spec that never ends

Ever run into one of those situations where the customer (or user) can never come to a consensus on anything? This isn't the same as "scope creep"—the differentiating factor is that the functionality has been pretty well defined—it's just that the customer can't quite come to closure on anything.

For example, you've submitted a screen shot of a form, and they've come back with a few changes. Mostly cosmetic, but a couple data-oriented issues as well—the "Assigned Rep" field has become a combo box, not a free-form text entry field. But after you've submitted the revision, the combo box has become a pick list with last name, first name, and region. Then the column order in the pick list is changed. Then the font is changed. Then another column is added. Then the width of the columns is changed. You get the idea.

How do you get away from this—particularly when this "nickel and diming" of the spec leads to thousands of dollars of charges for virtually no benefit?

Same answer as the scope creep issue—draw a line in the sand, and suggest that further changes wait until Version 2. Then, when additional issues come up—that have to, have to, have to be included in Version 1—simply ask which is more important, changing the width of the column or shipping this year?

If you can bring up a list of 10 or 20 or 30 minor changes that have been made this way, you can often get them to see what is happening—and they're much more amenable to the line in the sand you've drawn.

Of course, you will be writing these other suggestions down—see the chapter on Application Feedback for more details.

Payment issues during specifications

Once in a while you may run into a situation where the Engagement Letter is returned on time, the specification is developed without bloodshed, and you start to congratulate yourself that this is looking like the perfect job. There's one small hitch, of course—the check is a couple days late, well, a week late, well, they're running into some "cash flow issues and could they get another 30 days on the invoice?" Harrumph. Remember the sign on the wall of the pizza parlor—"We have a deal with the bank. They don't make pizza and we don't cash checks." You're not a banker, and you're not in the business to extend credit or loan money. Here's how to deal with payment issues.

Payment mechanisms during spec development

You have two choices when deciding how to get paid for the development of a specification. Either get paid in advance—on a retainer—or present invoices for work already done. I've done it both ways, and there are pluses and minuses to both approaches.

When you get paid in advance, obviously, it's nice to have the money up front. You also run somewhat less of a risk of not getting paid. However, I've always found it tricky to replenish a retainer, because you're always estimating how much work is left—and you have to factor in how much time it takes between the submission of a retainer replenishment and when the check arrives.

The alternative is to invoice, and the danger is doing work and not being paid for it. This is particularly likely during the development of a spec, because the customer can feel that they haven't received anything "tangible." It's difficult to withhold delivery of the "final product" since most of the product has been design documents and prototypes that the customer has seen in progress—particularly with my philosophy of iterative acceptance.

The first piece of advice is to invoice on a regular basis and keep your payment terms short—invoicing every two weeks with a due date 10 days hence works for us, and I know of some firms with weekly invoicing and terms of seven days. However you choose, the key is to avoid getting hung out for 45 or 60 days of billable time. That can happen all too easily.

The second piece of advice I have for you is to deliver valuable goods regularly. That's one of the advantages of an Agile Methodology. A customer is much more likely to withhold payment if they feel they're not getting their money's worth. I'm not accusing you of going through the motions or spinning wheels. Rather, I'm suggesting that you make sure that your customer perceives that you're providing value. You may have written 70 pages of a rough draft, but if you don't show the customer progress, they don't know what you've done and may be hesitant to pay for unseen work.

Discounting in the early stages

You may be tempted to discount your services early in the game, either because you're relatively new at the software development game, or because you want to get your foot in the door with a particular customer.

You can do this one of two ways. For time and materials work—such as the development of the Functional Spec—you can either lower your hourly rate, or provide a defined number of hours for free. I always advise people to give away a few hours instead of discounting their rate. It's much harder to "raise the rate" because it is always perceived as a price increase. The net effect is the same—the customer received the same "discount"—but once the initial honeymoon is over, it's back to business as usual.

You may be wondering why this is effective—can't the customer simply ask for more stuff for free? In the situation where you gave a number of hours for free, the understanding that this was an "introductory discount" is explicit. With a rate change, it can be easier for a customer to claim that they didn't realize that a lower initial rate per hour was going to go up. They may even claim that their boss (or some committee) has put the kibosh on any price increases—and all your arguments that this isn't a price increase are likely going to fall on deaf ears.

You can do the same for development work—provide a number of Action Points for free, instead of lowering your "cost per Action Point."

"Why did you charge us for a meeting we canceled at the last minute?"

It's the rare consultant who doesn't show up for a meeting at a customer's office only to find out that the meeting has been postponed or canceled due to some event outside of the consultant's control. Some customers will not expect to be billed for this time, since nothing was accomplished. However, unless the customer's office is down the hall, you still have to take the time to prepare for the meeting, maybe don a suit (I've heard that some of you still do that), drive to the customer's site, wait around, and then drive back. Explain that, even though the application will be fixed price, the specification work you are doing now is on a time and materials basis. You had to spend your time on the meeting, even if the body of the meeting didn't take any time.

Calculating time and price

Sometime during the specification process, you'll have to start talking about money—not the money they're going to pay you for specification development, but the money the application is going to cost. Since it's their money you're talking about, things can get tricky. Here are some pointers.

Dealing with "Not to Exceed"

The customer on the other side of the table fancies himself a pretty shrewd negotiator, having taken that $99 course at the Holiday Inn just last month, and conceives of this clever "deal" that ends up being your basic "Not to Exceed" pitch. What do you do in this situation?

While you and I can discuss the difficulties, you can't very well accuse your customer of trying to cheat you, or of trying to play both ends against the middle. To be sure, there are those who think that "a win-win situation is where they win twice" (this line came from an experience that Chick Bornheim of Micromega Systems in San Francisco had).

I guess you just have to ask yourself, "How hungry am I?" Being willing to say no, while anathema, is a necessary skill in our business—if you don't learn it, you'll eventually end up working for someone else who has.

Refusal to state a budget

What do you do if they refuse to give you a budget? This can be very frustrating, since you don't know where to head. It would be like trying to build a house for someone without any idea of what price range they're thinking of.

Working in this environment requires a great deal of people skills—but here's one way to go about it. First, since they haven't given you any guidelines, assume you've got an unlimited budget. Then, start your analysis, and starting scoping out their project. Take as much time as you need—it's unlikely to be more than 20-40 hours. By the end of this span of time, you should have a much better idea of how big the system is going to be, and how much it's going to cost. From that, you can find out from them whether you're in the ballpark.

If, on the other hand, they want you to go through a full-scale "interview everyone in the company for two hours and then write up recommendations" process, you're doing consulting, not software development, and that's gotta be done on a time and materials basis.

"We need to see the algorithms and formulas you used to calculate this price."

Yeah, right. It's amazing how people's common sense and perspective go out the window as soon as they get in a room with a software developer. Think about what it is they're asking. Would they provide one of their customers with their detailed formulas for pricing their own products? I think not... But somehow, it doesn't occur to them that this is what they're asking for.

I simply explain that our "weights, price/point, and algorithms are proprietary company information—just as I'm sure that your costing formulas are confidential for your company." They may counter with an argument that the price is too high and they need to shave some dollars off, and so they want to do some "what-ifs" for various pieces of the app.

Our specifications break down a price on a module-by-module basis, but that's as far as we'll go with a customer. We explain that the algorithm that builds the price for even a single module is too complex to provide the ability to break down the price any further. A module, as defined in the spec, is as granular as we go, period.

Customers occasionally think that they can re-engineer modules by lopping off two screens or getting rid of a report. In some cases that might be true, but in many others, it's not. For example, other parts of the system may depend on the entry or manipulation of data that can only be done in that screen—and that may not be immediately apparent to the user. In other cases, a number of screens may be similar enough that the multiplier for each screen is lower than a single instance of that screen would warrant. In other words, there are some economies of scale by having six screens that use the same custom base class. If they get rid of two of those screens, they don't save a third of the price—the costs for developing the base class now needs to be spread over the four remaining screens. There's simply no way that a customer would be able to handle that kind of situation.

A customer may even more mistakenly think that they can perform surgery on a single screen or report: "If I take this list box off the screen, will I save $50?" While that may work if you're taking those two decorative lights on either side of the fireplace to save $200, it's not going to work for software.

When people are trying to save a few bucks, they can come up with all sorts of unbelievable lines. For example, they might argue that they want to see whether you've done the calculations correctly. This is just plain silly. If someone tried that line on me, I'd just look at them real hard, and suggest, gently, that if they have a concern about my ability to add up numbers, then perhaps their trust in our ability to develop software is misplaced. Or perhaps they think they might be overpaying. In this case, their attitude will be manifested through the development of the spec—every time a decision point for performing a task one way or another arrives, the first words out of their mouth are, "Which way is cheaper?"

You probably don't want to work with this type of folk—because, sure as shooting, regardless of what the spec says, they'll try to push the other side of the equation, expecting you to make all sorts of changes, insisting that gray areas in the spec be interpreted in the most unreasonable of ways, and so on.

In short, it's time to stand firm when a customer tries to push you around about this topic. It's simply none of their business, and by even allowing a discussion of the issue, other than explaining why it's not open for discussion, you're already starting to play their game.

"How many hours does this dollar figure equate to?"

This may well be a valid question, but you need to determine what they're really asking. They could be trying to figure out "When can you deliver," but they may also be wondering "What hourly rate did you use to figure this out?"

You can answer the first question—and already should have—without having to go into a detailed discussion of how many hours are in this job.

If, on the other hand, they're actually wondering whether they're paying some sort of exorbitant rate per hour, then you need to approach this differently. First, make sure that you've explained the general idea behind the Action Point Counting that you performed, and that, given that method, there isn't a straight correlation between hours and dollars. You can even offer the information that the concept of "hourly" isn't part of the deal at all. "The salaries of our developers are part of the cost, to be sure, but we have a lot of other factors that make up the cost as well, just as if we were building widgets. The hourly rate of the factory worker is one cost, but there's a lot more than just his hourly wage that goes into the cost of a widget."

They may argue that the cost of software is highly dependent on labor, while making a widget is heavily dependent on the cost of raw materials. But that really doesn't hold water in many industries. The cost of the raw materials for many products is a remarkably small percentage of the final price. What else goes into the price? Sales and marketing, engineering, R&D, plant and equipment, and so on.

Same goes for your firm. The uninformed customer may feel that all you need is a PC and a copy of MegaBase. But we know there's a lot more than that—all the time spent developing a common code library, a foundation, and utilities and tools for development and testing, the expenses of general office staff, new machines every couple years, education expenses, and so on. Good development shops spend a lot of money providing support for their developers, and that all has to be figured into the final price.

They may ask you to guess at "an average rate per hour." I've certainly been asked this a number of times—and I just throw up my hands, claiming ignorance. I explain that while big consulting firms simply assign exorbitant hourly rates to inexperienced 23-year-olds, and then run them through the billable hours ringer, we don't. And, thus, to guess at a "rate per hour" would be like asking what the average rate per hour is for the line workers at a company that manufactures automobiles. They know what they pay for time and materials work, for tasks such as developing a spec, but past that, it's just not a number we have.

"We really can't quite afford that. Can you come down a bit?"

A number of different scenarios can occur here, but let's look at two in particular. In both situations, we play the game just like the copier salesman—offer to take away features that would be "nice to have" but aren't absolutely essential. But there are variations on how to do it.

In the first case, we have a cost of $30,000. For whatever reasons, we believe that they have a value attached to this of $45,000, so we price at $40,000. But wham! The customer comes back with the statement that the app is too expensive. Perhaps they mean it (we might have made a mistake in assuming that $45,000), or perhaps they're just trying to bargain. In any case, they're not going to buy at $40,000. Obviously we don't want to lose the job, but we also can't just say, "Oh, gorsh, since you're such nice folks, we'll knock $10,000 off!"

Suppose they say they've only got $35,000 in their budget. How do we come down since we've got the extra margin, without appearing to be open to negotiation? One way is to take something really simple or trivial off of the app, but indicate that it was really expensive to do, so we give them virtually the same app but knock off some of the money. Another way is to ask for something in return—perhaps a longer delivery cycle, so that "we can use one of our newer (read 'less expensive') people on it." The sharp-eyed reader may wonder how this works, since the cost was supposed to be the same regardless of who does the work. What we're offering to do is to eat some of the cost by using part of the app as a training exercise for one of our people. While that will save some money, it will likely take longer.

The second possibility is that we priced the app such that we don't have any extra room, and it's still too expensive. In this case, it's time to get them to prioritize the features they need vs. those they want. Then we can start removing the "wants" until we get the price down to an acceptable level.

In either case, it's important to remember that your cost isn't your price. The only reason to lower the price is if you are lowering the costs as well. And in most cases, that means cutting features out.

"We don't have time to go through all this song and dance with a specification. Just tell us how much it will cost!"

There's always the arrogant, rude, abrasive prospect who won't want to spend the time working on a spec. Instead, they'll insist, while folding their arms across their chest and biting down on their cigar, "You're the programmer—you should just know how much it costs!"

There are two things this person might be doing. First, he might be irrational—fully expecting you to price a three to six month application based on a 40-minute phone conversation. There are a lot of them out there.

In this situation, you'd be best served by walking away from this person. He's the same person who will insist he told you that the application needs to run on a Mac and a SPARC-station as well as the creaky old 386 in the corner, and he's going to sue if you don't spend the next three months making it work.

On the other hand, the customer may simply be naïve, not knowing that writing an industrial-strength custom database application is not the same as a really long WordPerfect macro.

But before completely giving up, remember that they might be having a bad day, or testing you to see if you've got some backbone. We explain to the customer that we deliver production-quality, ready-to-run applications, and that in order to do so, we need to test the applications. If we don't have the rules of operation for the application written down, we won't be able to test, and that will prevent us from delivering a complete application. We can deliver one, but we will not guarantee a defect-free product, since we can't define what is a defect and what it isn't. A lot of folks really like the sound of "All defects are fixed for free" and will then go along with you.

Delivering the specification

Finally, it's time to deliver the spec. And, as with every other contact you have with your customer, this encounter can engender some situations that you should be prepared for.

"Wow! From the looks of this prototype, you're just about done with the app. Why are you telling us you're only 20% finished?"

Any developer using a prototype will run into this question sooner or later. It's usually posed out of naiveté, not malice. Bringing up the imagery of the old Wild West (which may be more appropriate in our industry than one would care to admit), with the grand, multi-story buildings on the main street usually does the trick. "The prototype you're seeing is constructed just like these buildings—an impressive facade, but nothing behind them. There's no data, no code, no nothing. Just a few hard-coded values to make it look pretty."

If they still resist, arguing that the prototype appears to operate as it is supposed to, I further bring up the minefield analogy. "There is a very limited amount of functionality in this prototype—and I know what works. I'm stepping very carefully to avoid pressing the wrong button."

"We've gone through this with a fine-tooth comb and it looks great."

Once in a while, you'll come across the customer who swears that they're memorizing your every word. Yet you know that, based on your interactions with others, you're just not getting the cooperation that you need to do the specification accurately. They either just don't get it, or they're paying it lip service.

Sure, you're going to make sure that they sign off on the spec, but often that's too little too late. When you develop with a spec that they haven't really looked at, you'll run into change after change. In each case, you'll have to go back to the spec, explaining that what they're requesting is a change from the original spec. Sure, you're right, but the reality is that you've caught them in a big, probably expensive mistake, and that's going to make them look bad, no matter which way you cut it. So even though you could have them dead to rights, you really want to keep it from happening in the first place. It can be so tempting to let them take their lumps on this, but in the end, you need to care now because if you've got the specification wrong, it's going to cause problems later when you build what's in it. This is one of those situations where the customer will become irrational (if they're not already), and that's never a good situation.

If this is happening, I have a trick to focus the customer's attention on the point that reading and understanding the spec is important. In two or three parts of the document, I will deliberately put errors in the spec. I mean very obvious errors—like misstating a crucial business rule or assumption—things that are pretty clearly wrong or missing.

Then, upon meeting with the customer for final sign-off, I'll direct their attention to a couple of these points. A blank look or some fancy footwork tells me that they've never seen this page before, and I can suggest that maybe they might want to re-read the spec before signing off completely. How do you word such a request? Just admit that you know how exhausting a spec like this can be—to read—and that it's completely understandable if their eyes glaze over in places. It's not meant to be a "spy vs. spy thriller" where you can't help but keep turning the pages.

You can't make them read it, but if they're not even reading the spec, you can be sure they'll miss other points, too. You may want to reconsider taking them on as a customer. On the other hand, if you do take the job, you'll certainly know to deal with them carefully in the future.

Conclusion

By now, you've hopefully seen a trend in my approach to tricky situations. There are a number of things to do.

Consider what the underlying situation is—are they really bothered about something else but having trouble talking about it? Consider what brought up the situation in the first place. It's easy to get so involved that you can fool yourself into ignoring the big picture—and the warning signs.

Let the customer save face. This is a tricky business, and it's easy for the customer to make a mistake that could embarrass them. Help them out of potentially embarrassing situations, just as you'd like to be.

Be careful. Watch your backside. There are a few folks out there who won't hesitate to take advantage of you. One great gig won't make a company, but one bad gig can ruin a company.

Section V:

The Development Process

You've now got a description of the software that you're going to build. There's still a long way to go, though—you have to put it together, test it, and deliver it.

In this section, we'll explore the environment, tools, and processes you can use to produce your software in a reliable, repeatable fashion.

Chapter 20
The Development Environment

"You'll dress only in attire specially sanctioned by MIB Special Services. You'll conform to the identity we give you. You'll eat where we tell you, live where we tell you. From now on, you'll have no identifying marks of any kind. You'll not stand out in any way."—Zed
  —Men in Black

What should your software development factory look like? In this chapter, I'll talk about the actual building, office, and infrastructure for a software development group. Note that I said "group" and not "company." In firms where "software development" is just another department along with the mailroom and the receiving dock, they'll often build cubicle farms and enforce corporate policy without exception—using the argument that "we're not a software company." Nonetheless, software developers everywhere are subject to the same dynamics, and thus these ideas apply for you regardless of what type of company you call home.

Much of the reason for the popularity of the Dilbert comic strip is because it's true. We see those things happening in companies all over. And while these events look absurd to us, they usually seem perfectly reasonable at the time to the people involved. People generally don't set out in the morning with the idea, "Hey, I'm gonna make a fool of myself today."

Nonetheless, a little common sense would go a long way at most companies—and development firms are no different. While I've pulled more than my share of bone-headed stunts at the shop, I've also tended to spend an inordinate amount of time thinking about the environment that my people work in, and trying to make it better for them.

Before I go on, I'd like to attribute many of my ideas to two sources. Geneer, formerly known as RDI Software Technologies, is a custom software developer in Chicago with several hundred people. Due to their proximity and to the fact that I know a fair number of people there, I've been to their shop enough that I feel like I'm not getting an artificial view of what the shop is like. I've formed a lot of opinions about how a development environment should be organized by seeing how they do it. Doug Grimsted, Ken Florian and company do things right. I think most anybody would do well to emulate them.

The other source I have to acknowledge right away is a pair of books: *Peopleware* by Tom DeMarco and Tim Lister, and *Constantine on Peopleware* by Larry Constantine (now out of print, superseded by *The Peopleware Papers*, also by Constantine). If you implement only 10% of what's in these two books, you'll be well ahead of most shops in the country.

The bottom line in software development can be summed up in one simple sentence. *Let people do their jobs.* Another way of saying that is "Get rid of the roadblocks for them." I'll talk more about that in the "People" section, but right now, part of this philosophy is relevant to the environment that you and your developers work in. How is anyone going to do their best if their surroundings and tools are inadequate? We are trying to facilitate the developers' ability to do their work—develop software—and get all their roadblocks out of the way. What kinds of things could we do to the factory that would help them do their work better?

In this chapter, I examine a variety of ideas, in no particular order, that you may find helpful in improving the productivity of your "manufacturing personnel."

Working off-site

The majority of this chapter presumes that your folks do not do their work "on-site"—at the customer's site—but, rather, at their place of employ—your company's offices. For corporate folks, that's pretty much a forgone conclusion, but for software development shops, it's not. I'll address this issue first, and then go into the optimization of the software development environment.

I've rarely sent people out to work on-site—only in very special cases. This is in direct contrast to a lot of firms that will send people out on-site to work all day, every day, for weeks, months, or years. I'm not saying that this practice is bad or wrong—far from it. In the first place, having people on-site can be very profitable. Second, you get instant feedback on the performance of an employee—if the customer becomes unhappy, that employee gets a pink slip at the end of the day, not after three months of off-site development has been completed. And some developers thrive on the on-site gig. They love being in different offices, meeting and working with a wide variety of people, and excel in the fire-fighting mode that much on-site work entails. If it works for them, fine.

But it's not my philosophy, and here's why.

Simply stated, I believe my people can do a better job—and enjoy their work more—if we work at my place. We write applications. We don't fight fires and tweak existing apps six ways from Sunday. Our offices are better suited to do the "heavy lifting" that big-time application development requires. We have better tools, we have better resources, we can control the environment, we have other developers around, we can control our hours. Simply put, we are masters of our own destiny if we work at our place. Software development is an intellectual process, and putting up an artificial barrier such as "all consultants must be out of the building by 4:30" essentially says "Turn your brain off at 4:20 and get ready to leave." Oh, if it were only that easy!

I feel it's similar to asking a garage mechanic or a dentist to make a house call to fix your car or replace a filling. It's not simply a matter of throwing a hammer and a wrench (or a mirror and some dental floss) in a bag and making a visit. The professional has a great deal of equipment and reference material at their place of work that isn't portable. The same should go for you—as a professional software developer, you're offering more than just a brain and a pair of hands to tap away on the keyboard.

On the other hand, in my experience working on-site, we are completely powerless to do anything. We don't control our equipment, our resources, the environment—our productivity is going to plummet and that's going to make both the developer and the customer unhappy.

Okay, that's painting an unnecessarily bleak picture, but you get my drift.

I'll describe a scenario. At my shop, we keep as near to state-of-the-art equipment and resources as is practical. At the customer's shop, the developer will as likely get an out-of-sync 15" monitor on a Pentium 100 without a cover or CD-ROM that's been put on a table next to the coffee machine. The chair will be missing two screws on one leg and the keyboard pad of the phone will be covered with two years' worth of goop and dust.

They'll have to get to get to work at 8 AM and leave at 5 PM. They'll have to wear a suit and won't be able to take work home (violation of company policy). And listening to Nirvana is a no-no. Again, it's against company policy.

The person in the cubicle on the left won't stop talking to their spouse, their mom, or whoever. The person on the right comes over every 10 minutes to ask about changing color sets in Windows and setting up a driver to play the newest version of DOOM while the boss isn't looking. And within a week, every weenie in the company is going to be coming over to say, "Oh, here's the new computer guy. Can you come over and take a look at my printer sometime?"

Okay, I've painted a pretty bad picture, but each of these events is from my own personal set of war stories. Sure, there are ways to deal with each of these situations, but why? These are *gumption traps*! Why set up artificial roadblocks that will inevitably occur at a customer's site when you don't have to?

Of course, let's look at it from the customer's point of view. There are several reasons that a customer might want a developer on-site.

The customer doesn't trust the developer to actually do work. In the case of fixed price jobs, why should it matter? They're paying a fixed price for a hunk of software—it should be totally irrelevant how the developer gets it done. In the case of time and materials work, do you really want to work with a customer who has so little trust that "face time" is a better measuring stick than the actual results produced?

The customer has to be able to meet with the developer on an ad-hoc basis. Again, why? Assuming you have a complete spec, this argument doesn't hold water—certainly not for fixed price jobs, but even for time and materials work. This argument tells me that the customer is poorly prepared and isn't planning out their work properly if they need to drag the developer into a meeting at a moment's notice. Then there's that "long blocks of uninterrupted time" thing I mentioned before. Ad-hoc meetings are nothing more than ad-hoc interruptions.

And frankly, a lot of these issues can be reconciled via e-mail, telephone conversations, and even the occasional teleconference.

The customer's application, data, and/or systems are so specialized and/or confidential that they can't be taken off-site. I'll accept this to some extent. However, it should be possible to create test data sets with dummy data that can be used for most development and testing. Shells or emulators that mimic the performance of the systems can be used for some parts of the system. In the rest of the cases, I still think that working on-site is so miserable that I'd turn down the work. But—that's my opinion. Some people love working on-site for the constant variety.

What if a customer insists that they will provide all that stuff? I'd love to see the customer that can. I haven't had the experience of a customer saying, "Yes, we'll supply you with the latest machine with 2 GB of RAM, a monster hard disk, and dual flat screen monitors. In your private office, you can shut the door, turn off the phone, we won't ever bother you, you come in when you want, wear jeans, and listen to Buddy Holly or Smashing Pumpkins." First of all, if that's the case, why are you on-site after all? You might as well be in your own office. And second, how long do you think that's going to last? About three days—maybe?

If the customer still gives you a hard time, simply explain that you have the tools you need to do your job correctly back at the shop and it's impossible to bring those tools in. You could use the comparison of someone asking an auto mechanic to come to their house to fix their car. The mechanic could only bring a hammer, a screwdriver, and something to gap the plugs. All the fancy diagnostic stuff would have to be left at the shop. How effective would that mechanic be? It's the same thing.

The bottom line for me is that we can be more productive if we develop at our shop. We've put a lot of money and effort into making our factory efficient and good to work in—we're going to use it because we believe it's the best way to do the job.

Working on-site—counterpoint

Okay, I have to be fair. Much of this book is based on my own personal experiences, and this chapter is no exception. However, during the writing of this book, I was brought to task on this particular issue—and so I should say that while these have been my experiences, it doesn't mean that they will be yours.

A friend of mine described several situations that she's been in where she was "treated really well—great digs, brand-new equipment. The client considered us a combination of guest/high-paid consultant, and they made sure we were comfortable and had everything we needed."

Additionally, the capacity and capabilities of a mobile office have changed since I first wrote these words. A notebook computer with a 50 GB hard disk and a 15" active matrix screen, an internal DVD player, and a 10/100 Ethernet port can be found at nearly any office supply store for a couple grand. You can take much of your office with you these days. Access to power and a high-speed Internet connection are the two most limiting factors.

Furthermore, flexibility in work hours, location, and ancillary factors such as dress code have increased in many areas. Some of the looseness varies in relation to the tightness of the job market—as the demand for skilled professionals increases, the "terms" that those professionals can dictate get better. In contrast, a glut of professionals means that companies can enforce stricter working conditions.

Finally, before you take my words as gospel, consider that this is Milwaukee, after all. Your mileage may vary.

The Jungle—circa 2003

I've seen development shops with conditions that should provoke a sequel to Upton Sinclair's famous "expose" of the packinghouse industry, *The Jungle*. Let me regale you with a couple of stories to get you warmed up.

There was the aforementioned "big consulting firm" that wouldn't allow their developers to have computers on their desks. They had to do everything by hand—yes, with a pen and paper. The developer—actually, titled a "programmer"—would start out with the three-inch binder created by an analyst, and put together flow charts, and write out code on specially designed forms constructed by a weenie at "corporate." When finished with everything, and after it was all approved by a "manager," the developer would pack all of his materials up, go down to the basement of the building he was working in, and sign into a room where 15 or 20 PCs were set up on folding tables.

The developer would then enter his program in the computer, compile, and put the result on a floppy disk. This floppy was turned over to others who were responsible for installing on a user's machine where it would be tested. Feedback on the application was sent back to the developer (and a "manager," of course), and the whole process would start over again.

I guess this made sense in 1978, when the developers were writing programs in COBOL for IBM S/32 style boxes. It was just plain stupid in 1996—a testament to upper management who did it that way in the 1970s, and, by God, if it was good enough for them then, it was good enough for the developers of today! And while it didn't get software done very efficiently, it sure racked up billable hours for the consulting firm!

There's another company in middle America with several thousand employees and an MIS staff of more than 100 programmers and analysts. The company built a brand-new headquarters, and put together a gorgeous MIS department with a raised ceiling, windows at a variety of angles, and brand-new everything. They stuffed this enormous room with aisles and aisles of cubicles with six-foot-high walls. Along each permanent wall were the manager's offices. It looked like a modern company cafeteria, and, truly, you wouldn't mind eating off the floor of this place.

The trouble is that the place sounded like a cafeteria. You could literally tell when Jack, six cubicles down and two over, had a cold—because you could hear him cough. Of course, you felt like you were in a cave, with maroon cubicle walls high enough to keep you isolated from anyone else—but the sound traveled beautifully above the walls.

Shortly after the company built this headquarters, they fell on hard times, and let go most of their support staff—leaving the developers and analysts to answer their own phones. It was pretty amusing to hear one phone after another in a row of cubicles ring, as someone tried to reach someone in the department. People either were out, on another call, or just ignoring the phone, hoping the person in the next cube would be fool enough to pick it up. It was amusing to me, since, after all, I didn't work there.

Interruptions, iterations, and gumption traps

The single most important factor in developer productivity is long blocks of uninterrupted time. Repeat after me: *The single most important factor in developer productivity is long blocks of uninterrupted time.* And, as you'll see, just about everything I believe in centers around this truism. That's why the two stories I told earlier just make me shake my head.

A corollary to this tenet is that developer productivity is directly tied to the percentage of time that the iteration time of development is shorter than the developer's attention span. In geek talk:

```
Developer productivity = (Attention Span - Iteration Time) / (Attention Span)
```

You always want the iteration time to be shorter than the developer's attention span. This sounds a little silly at first, and, when I heard this line from Alan Schwartz at a conference many years ago, the crowd laughed. But it's a fundamental truth in our business.

Take two developers with the same attention span. The first one is interrupted in the middle of an iteration half the time. The other is almost never interrupted in middle of an iteration. Who do you think is more productive? Clearly the second developer. Thus, the goal should be to keep the iteration time shorter than the attention span. You can do this in one of several ways—and if you can accomplish all three, you'll be well ahead of the game.

The first way is to decrease the iteration time. You can do this by providing state-of-the-art equipment, tools, and techniques that let the developer crank through iterations quickly.

The second way is to increase the developer's attention span. Sure, I suppose chemicals might have a part here, but I'm talking about reducing (to the point of trying to eliminate) interruptions. The longer the developer can concentrate on a project without interruptions, the more productive she'll be.

The third factor to keeping developer productivity high is the elimination (or, at least, the significant reduction) of what author Robert Pirsig (*Zen and the Art of Motorcycle Maintenance*) calls "gumption traps." A gumption trap is an environmental situation that drains your will to overcome obstacles. A machine that constantly GPFs is a gumption trap—pretty soon you're so annoyed at the machine that you've forgotten about the application you're trying to develop. A chatty co-worker in the next cube with a Fran Drescher-like laugh is another gumption trap. And so is a chair whose armrest keeps skipping down a notch. Sure, they may seem like trivial things that "adults" shouldn't let themselves get worked up over. But there's really nothing magical about being "grown-up." Adults are simply kids who have to pay the bills every month.

If you can keep your eye on these three factors—long blocks of uninterrupted time, short iteration turnaround, and the reduction of gumption traps—you're well on the way to keeping your developers productive and happy. Let's look at some factors that can have a positive impact on these factors.

Where do they sit?

Just so you don't think this is a completely ridiculous question, I'll give you the short answer right away. They sit on chairs. In offices.

I used to let everybody choose their own desks and chairs. My approach was to give a new developer a budget, and they could get what they want. One person wants a modular unit; another wants a traditional desk and bookcase. Fine! People are different; why make them all conform to some impersonal standard—particularly when there isn't any specific reason to do so? My thinking has changed somewhat—as the company has experienced some turnover, new developers usually inherit what someone else had chosen, and there has been some squabbling and trading of equipment and gear. But when new stuff has to be purchased, I'll leave the decision up to the person who is next in line for that new gear.

It's a perk of seniority, and the only tradeoff is that new gear has to go into an empty office—does the senior developer want to go through the hassle of moving out of their current digs? It's up to them—much like a bunch of kids who trade bedrooms every few months. I'm not going to spend my time playing referee.

Regardless of whether you do this, or if you have company standards that everyone follows, the one rule you should religiously follow is this: Don't scrimp on chairs. Your developers are typically going to be sitting for 8 to 16 hours a day—make sure that they're comfortable. It's a no-brainer to spend an extra $250 for a chair if it means that the programmer won't be walking around the office every day at 2:30 holding his back.

The other thing that works well is to provide every technical person with their own private office. These are software developers we're talking about—providing them with the ability to control their own peace and quiet so they can concentrate is an extremely good investment.

So now maybe you've got a bunch of private offices with furniture that wasn't quite coordinated by the furniture police. Perhaps the office kind of looks like a bunch of college dorm rooms, but it becomes personalized. The office becomes a home instead of a prison cell.

A developer's office can be outfitted for between $500 and $1,000 depending on the area of the country you're in. A remarkably small amount considering the money spent on computer hardware and software, compensation, and other ancillary expenses.

Equipment

The technical infrastructure for the firm is critical—you're writing software, after all. It never ceases to amaze me to see how cheap some firms are. They have highly paid developers writing critical software applications and they try to scrimp and save a couple hundred bucks on a machine because the bean counters say so. The average investment for a factory worker is well into six figures, but a firm will scrimp on the $3,000 or $4,000 machine that is the developer's most important tool.

My company has two practices that have served us well with respect to equipment. The first is that we always buy nearly as much machine as is possible at the time. Typically, this is one level below the current state of the art. When the best box available was a 486/66, we picked up 486/50s. When the best was a 1 GHz box, we purchased 900s. I've found the performance difference between the very fastest and the next fastest isn't that significant compared to the premium being charged for the faster machine. Instead, we spend that money on supporting equipment such as additional memory, or a bigger hard disk.

Some development shops argue that they don't want to get high-end machines for their programmers because their customers use tired, old machines and they have to make sure that their software will run on those machines as well. Well, in most development shops, old machines are not scarce. The technical assistants get machines lower on the food chain, so their machines are more likely to match what a typical customer might be using. And, just in case, we've got a couple of real clunkers in the back room that we can use in case specific testing requirements come up.

If you decide to keep your developers' hands tied by giving them low-end machines, an inadequate amount of RAM, and a poorly configured network, you're just costing yourself a ton of money. Every time a developer has to wait a minute and a half for a build instead of four seconds, it's going to cost you money. Since PC-based software is created on an iterative basis, you may build a project 10, 20 or more times an hour. If each build takes 30 seconds instead of five, that's 5-10 minutes of dead time an hour.

And the second problem with pokey machines has to do with this issue of rapid iteration. I'm sure you've made a change to a program, started the build, and by the time you were ready to test for the change, you'd forgotten what it was that you had changed. If you invest in a reasonably high-end machine, your developers can iterate and not lose their train of thought. Given the natural state of offices, it's pretty easy for any kind of interruption to make their minds jump track. Try to minimize those interruptions in any way possible.

Another good reason for investing in high-end boxes is that it shows that you care. Your typical software developer may not be that interested in Gucci loafers, Rolex watches, and flashy vacations—but they'll all crowd around in the office of the developer with the new dual Pentium with a 2 GHz processor, a 100x DVD, drive and a 27" monitor. High-end machines are status symbols and provide tangible evidence that the boss cares about the staff. It emphasizes the importance of the staff by giving them the best tools available.

The second habit of ours is the practice of, er, inheritance. When we bring in new machines, the developers with the most seniority have the option to grab them, so that the newest developers are getting "hand-me-downs." This rewards developers who have stayed around with an additional perk. This doesn't mean that the new developers are getting inadequate machines—when the slowest machine in the office isn't sufficient for a developer, it's time to buy a new one. But when a new employee joins the shop and a new machine has to be purchased, the developer with the most seniority gets it—and the other developers switch around machines as they want.

This doesn't always happen—I no longer automatically get the newest box, even though, technically, I have seniority. It's just too much of a hassle to set up a new box just the way I want it every few months—just for the sake of a few additional processor clicks.

I'm sure as time passes, we'll run into additional situations—the hot shot who, as part of his terms for joining the company, required a bunch of gear that would put him at the top of the pecking order, or the individual who spends all her time comparing seniority to CPU speed. I don't have any advice here—I guess I'll run off that bridge when I come to it.

Over the past couple of years, another factor has entered the situation—the fact that notebook computers are generally powerful enough to act as desktop replacements. As a result, we're not buying desktop machines for anyone anymore—the convenience in being able to pick up your machine and cart it down to a conference room for a meeting or to a customer's site or home on the weekends far outweighs the few MHz difference in the current state-of-the-art desktop and a similar notebook.

You may also want to consider giving your developers more than one machine, depending on the type of work they do. Again, a machine is inexpensive—$2,000 gets you an awful lot of horsepower these days. A friend of mine related the story of developing a data migration set of routines—that would take hours to run a cycle. She picked up a second machine that could be dedicated to development/unit testing and then used her regular machine that she did documentation, mail, and everything else on so as not to bog down development processing. In her words, "IT WAS AWESOME! For the time I was doing this having two machines really upped my productivity and quality of life." She also noted that both machines were laptops so she could again work anywhere. (When you see someone else carting around two notebooks, you're tempted to shake your head, thinking they've got to get a life. But the first time you try it yourself, you can get dangerously hooked. Now if only Microsoft could figure out a way to boot Windows in less than two minutes.) Having two machines might not be the norm but could be appropriate under particular circumstances.

Configuring the network

Things in the networking world have changed considerably since the 1997 *Developer's Guide*. (Was that really just five years ago?) Back then, I recommended one of two strategies—either keep everything loaded on a server with big hard drives, or stock up every developer with a powerful machine that could run stand-alone if the server should fail. What a difference a couple of years make!

First of all, a centralized server, not just a peer-to-peer network, is much more a requirement now than it was back then. Even the least sophisticated shop is probably dabbling with Web applications and group e-mail—both functions that, while able to run on a workstation, really need a server for optimal implementation.

Second, the cost of powerful boxes just keeps plummeting. So my advice has changed somewhat.

Now, I suggest three or four servers. These days, you can get a pretty powerful box for a couple thousand bucks. At the time of this writing, my kids have a 1 GHz home machine and a 20 GB hard disk that cost well south of a grand. Spend another thousand bucks by stuffing it with a big hard disk and 256 or 512 MB of RAM, and you've got a server that will do fine for many tasks.

Also, it only costs a couple hundred dollars a month to get a reasonably fast data line—an ISDN, partial T1, DSL or cable, depending on your location—into your office. You can set up your own Web server quite inexpensively, but if you do, put a second, identical box next to it to use as your test server and to be able to swap with your main server should the box fail.

Third, do the same thing with your company server—make one your primary database server, and make the second one a test machine that can be swapped in should the primary box go down. This is no different from having sets of test and live data available to an application. Instead of messing with a bunch of tape backups (I have always hated tape because of its history of not being random access), a simple Xcopy of all data to the secondary server provides immediate backup—with tape or Jazz drives allowing you to take additional backups off-site.

Give each individual a great, powerful box, and, since applications are running locally once again (instead of off an application server), they'll be able to do most of their work even if the server should go down. However, with a spare server, that downtime should be minimal.

Organizing the server

I've found that organizing the server drive(s) according to customer works out quite well for us. The reason I bring it up is that I'm continually amazed at the number of shops I see that have no rhyme or reason to their development project setup.

First of all, consider setting your network up along the lines of a Linux box, where the operating system, applications, common data, and user directories all reside on different partitions, instead of the stupid, brain-dead methodology of Windows, where they intermingle operating system DLLs and user configuration files in the same directory structure. (I believe that architecture was created by the same guy who stated "640K of RAM should be enough for anyone.")

First of all, the operating system should sit on its own partition so that when (not *if*!) you have to reformat or reinstall, you're not putting your applications, common data, or user information at risk. Consider a program like Norton Ghost where you can set up the operating system partition with a minimum of fuss.

Next, if you can, consider putting your application programs on a separate partition. If you're using Windows, this may not be that easy to do, given that many programs must be installed in C:\PROGRAM FILES and furthermore have to mess with the Windows Registry (another Microsoft idea, the stupidity of which, with .NET, they're starting to realize). We've had limited success with this, so we put the OS and application programs on a single partition and then Ghost the whole thing before we make any updates to the image, such as Windows Updates and service packs, new application installations, and so on.

We then have separate partitions for 1) customer applications, 2) common data, and 3) user directories.

Customer applications

We have a dedicated partition (Windows users can think of that as a network drive) for customer projects. Each customer has their own root directory; each project for that customer resides under the customer's root directory. If we have information specific to the customer (documents or other non-project specific data), it is placed in an "OTHER" or "DOC" directory directly under the customer's root. In some cases, we've also set up a directory for customer-specific libraries that are used across multiple projects.

Under a specific project, we have a directory for project-specific information, such as quotes, memos, documentation, and other non-technical data, called "DOC." Sometimes we have another directory, called "OTHER," for "all that other stuff."

Each project also has directories for source code, metadata, and multiple data sets. All of this information is drive non-specific so that it can be moved to another server and remapped with a minimum of fuss.

Common data

A second partition (or drive) is used for common data. This includes framework libraries, developer utilities, the customer database, mail files, the company's MP3 collection, and so on. Source code control files might be another type of data you'd put on a separate partition.

This includes any type of data that anyone (or at least subsets of people) at the company would have access to.

User directories

The third partition or drive is for individual user directories. Everybody has a need to have a place for "their own stuff." Do make it clear that, much like high school lockers, user directories are the company's property and thus subject to search and monitoring. Check with your lawyer on the details of this, of course.

Resources

One of my favorite lines from the Addams Family movie is when the little girl demands the salt shaker from her brother. "Pass me the salt." Her mother, Morticia, scolds her, saying, "Wednesday, what's the magic word?" The little girl appends to her initial request in a dark, cold, threatening voice, "Now!"

Similarly, when a developer wants an answer to a question, they want it NOW! So... make it easy for them to find that information! Spending 10 minutes looking for an article or a book not only destroys the iteration cycle, but it can be a significant gumption trap.

We get just about every magazine on the planet related to software development; we have bookcases upon bookcases filled with magazines. Since the very early days, we have maintained a database of every article of possible interest. As a result, we now have more than 6,000 articles online and available "at the touch of a key."

We also subscribe to every kind of service we can find, including all the Internet newsgroups, TechNet, and a customized knowledge base of internal development practices. This is all administered by a "librarian" who is responsible for keeping the resources up-to-date and consistently accessible.

The cost of downtime

When I got out of school, I worked for the largest robot manufacturer in the world. One of our hottest sellers was a spot-welding robot—one of those big arms that hefts a 300-pound spot-welding gun. The scene has been in every movie that has anything to do with Detroit. As the steel gray automobile frames come down the assembly line, a half-dozen robot arms on each side of the line do their mechanical dance, the spot-weld pincers tacking pieces of steel together with yellow sparks flying around—you get the picture.

Spot welding is a really tough job—it's hot, the guns are very heavy and unwieldy, and it takes a certain amount of skill to do it properly. Robots are an easy sell for this application. However, even robots go down—and, as Murphy's Law dictates, they usually fail when inside a car, holding onto the frame.

These robots are big, powerful machines—three to four tons, bolted to the floor with anchors an inch thick—and so if the robot stops and the line keeps going, the robot is going to rip the car right off the line and cause quite a mess. As a result, when a robot fails, the line is automatically stopped at that instant.

That's a long introduction, but it was necessary to explain the next part.

One day, one of the robots goes down, and the line is stopped. If I hadn't made it clear before, as bad as ripping a car off the line is, it's only marginally worse than bringing the line to a complete stop. (If you're fuzzy on this "bad" thing, refer to the first Ghostbusters movie.)

There are enough robots on this plant that the company I worked for always had a technician on-site in order to be able to quickly respond to machines that went down. So, the technician runs over there and within 45 seconds, he's got the robot computer control open and is fiddling with the controls, trying to start the robot arm up so they can get the arm out of the car and get the line going again.

Suddenly the technician hears a "Whooosh!" sound behind him. He turns around and one of the maintenance men from the factory has just ignited a blowtorch. "Get away from here. This is computer equipment. What are you doing here with that anyway?"

And the guy responds, "I'm going to cut the arm of that robot so we can get the line moving." The technician says, "What do you mean, you're not going to cut the arm off of this robot. This is a $100,000 machine! You can't do that!" Blowtorch man says, "We produce one car a minute and these cars are worth $10,000 each. If this line is stopped for 10 minutes, we've lost $100,000 that we're never going to get back. So if you don't have that robot arm out of that car in the next 90 seconds, I'm going to cut it off. It's less expensive to replace the arm than to wait for you to screw around for more than two minutes."

The moral of the story—think again about the cost of downtime. (And, as an aside, the technician did get the robot arm up and out of the way in time.)

Virtual offices

As this book is being written, in 2002, it's much more common to incorporate a "virtual office" as part of a development environment. Some companies, in fact, are structured with people physically located all over the globe, using a variety of electronic tools (and the occasional plane trip) to communicate.

Some of the big consulting companies, in fact, have reorganized their entire physical infrastructure to deal with the idea that many of their professionals do not have fixed offices. Rather, they are on the customer's site most of the time, and when they return to the office, they reserve a cubicle or an office, and set up shop out of their laptop bag, complete with a name plate for the door, pictures of the spouse, kids and dog for the credenza, and an ID on the company network indicating that they're in the office for the day.

Technology has advanced to the point where this type of setup is readily accessible; between high-powered notebook computers, VPNs, wireless connections, and so on, the case can be made for some types of consultants to have less and less need for a dedicated office in a centralized building.

This is all fairly new, however, and it remains to be seen what the long-term aspects of such an arrangement are. I know of many developers who work out of their homes and do not need to share physical proximity with other developers, finding that relying on e-mail and the phone is sufficient.

If you're doing a pair programming project, such as with an Agile Methodology, of course, this won't work as handily, if at all.

Conclusion

When all is said and done, the bottom line for the environment is that it ought to help the developers do their job, not get in their way. And the best environment that will satisfy that requirement varies according to the developer's personality, the type of development process, the specific gig, and the customers' requirements. Keeping gumption traps to a minimum and allowing for long blocks of uninterrupted time are the two key aspects of a development environment to watch for.

Chapter 21
Tracking Time and Other Metrics

"Everything depends on billing—how many hours you spend even thinking about a client. I don't care if you're stuck in traffic or shaving or sitting on a park bench."—Avery
—The Firm

If you're running a software development group, you are running a factory. Full of four-eyed craftsmen who coordinate their plaid shirts with striped pants that are hiked up to their ribcage, perhaps, but still a factory, where you have inputs and outputs, and need to turn a profit. Tracking time spent during development is of paramount importance—it's the essence of your cost of goods sold and without it, you can't determine what your historical costs are. There are two separate issues related to tracking time. The first is simply defining what you track, in, shall we say, a theoretical sense. The other is the nitty-gritty of how you actually get people to do it.

When you're an independent developer, it's reasonably easy to track your time against specific projects so that you can bill customers and determine how much time you are spending on other tasks as well. Many people just log time against a project, perhaps recording the start and end time, the billing rate if it varies from customer to customer, and a description of the work done. And if all you intend to do from your time-tracking system is invoice the customer, then that's all you need to collect.

However, the type of data you collect and the manner in which you organize the data is increasingly important as you expand the uses of your time database. The goal of time-tracking metrics is to determine your cost of producing software and give you the information you need to analyze bug production.

What do you track?

There are as many ways to track time as there are ways to design software applications. Instead of dictating what you "should" do, I'll explain how our time and billing system came about, what we do, and how it works. Then I'll describe some alternative methods I've seen that you might want to consider.

Take none of this as gospel, but simply as a starting point for deciding how to gather your own time.

How TABET came about

Our internal time and billing tool, TABET (Time And Billing Entry and Tracking), evolved over several iterations, much like many home-grown systems, but from the beginning, it was designed to perform two purposes.

The first was to track the time spent on projects, and to provide a reasonable level of detail so that we could provide descriptions of the work we performed for a customer. This was more useful when we were doing time and materials work, and still serves us well for those types of situations, such as during analysis and design, and other odd jobs that are done on an hourly basis.

Nowadays, however, the value of this detail actually comes from the hierarchy of where time is applied—the detailed description isn't as necessary since time is tracked granularly enough already.

The second was to automatically generate invoices from those time entries, and that continues to work for us today.

In the beginning (in the mid-1980s), I simply had two tables—one for customers and another for time entries. Since I was usually only working on one project at a time, it was a simple matter to enter the name of the project for each time entry. The invoice was simply a report grouped on project, ordered by date, and filtered by the lack of an invoice date.

Even at this point, I was able to go back and find out how many hours were actually required to do a project, and thus, was able to determine my cost per Action Point.

As I worked on more and more projects simultaneously, and had to go back to projects that were already shipped to do modifications or upgrades, keeping track of which project was which became more and more of a task. In turn I broke out projects into a separate table.

A couple of years into the '90s, I landed two large projects that were going to require a great deal of ongoing work. Winning both of them meant I also had to hire my first full-time employee. Keeping track of tasks to do across literally dozens of pieces of these projects (in addition to the other smaller projects I was working on), and for more than one developer, became overwhelming. Thus, three more tables were added to the mix—Modules, Tasks, and Users. Shortly after that, we decided to formalize the tracking of our bug reports, so we added another table that tied bug reports (AFIs) to specific modules of an application.

At this point, it's probably going to get confusing, so I'll describe the relationship between each of these tables, and how we distinguish between each entity.

The internal structure of TABET

We've broken our time-tracking system into six primary and four ancillary tables: The big hitters are Customers, Projects, Modules, Tasks, Action Points, and Activities. The supporting tables are Time, Invoices, AFIs, and Users.

Customers

A Customer is an independent billing entity. Thus, if we work with four different divisions of Exxon and send invoices to four separate locations, we enter Exxon four times. Yes, we could probably normalize this as well, so that we could roll up data into primary organizations, but we've yet to have that need. Once we get to 7,000 employees across three continents, we'll reconsider it.

Projects

A Project is defined as work that needs a separate PO Number or a new Functional Specification. A Customer can have one or more Projects. The customer's view of the work you are doing may also have some impact on what constitutes a Project. They may want you to break down various chunks of work into separate identifiable entities so that they can track costs against each of them. We have several customers for whom we maintain the systems they use to do work for each of their customers, thus we have created separate projects for each customer system of theirs. This way, even though they don't strictly require POs, they can track the monies spent for each of their customers.

Modules

The third table is Modules. One Project can have one or more Modules. The distinguishable attribute of a Module is that it is a deliverable. The Module is considered complete when it has been installed and signed off by the customer. The nature of the project determines what makes up a Module, but we typically break out a Project into at least six Modules: the Specification; the Data Structures and underlying foundation upon which all screens, processes, and reports are going to be run; and then separate Modules for Screens, Processes, and Reports. The sixth module is Enhancement Requests.

Depending on the size of the system, each of these Modules is usually broken out further. For example, we may actually have two Modules for output—one for custom, standardized reports, and another for an ad-hoc reporting system. Again, like Projects, we may also define Modules according to what the Customer wants delivered.

By now, you may have noticed how nicely this demarcation works regardless of the type of development process used—a Module is a deliverable, whether you use structured development and deliver an A/P module, or you use an Agile Methodology and deliver a single piece of functionality over a period of three weeks.

Tasks

The fourth table consists of Tasks that are attached to each Module. The need for this table grew out of the overwhelming amount of work and the difficulty in tracking (both for us internally as well as for reporting back to the customer) what we needed to do to before delivering a module. While a Module is a deliverable entity, it may consist of one or more separate programmable entities—such as a set of screens, a process, or a list of reports. Each of these entities—screens, processes, and reports,—can be priced out using our Action Point Counting method, and as such, has a specific dollar amount associated with it.

The specific Tasks depend on the type of Module. For instance, a Specification Module would have Tasks for Design Meetings, Review, Prototype Development, and Functional Specification development (the actual write-up). Modules that consist of application components have Tasks for each component. A Module that has three screens and two reports in it would thus have five Tasks, and time would be tracked against each of those five Tasks separately.

We also identify what it is we're doing on that Task: Coding, Review, Integration, Test, Help and Documentation, Internal Bug Fixing, Installation, and Maintenance after Installation.

The fundamental differentiation between Modules and Tasks is that Tasks have Action Points assigned to them, and thus, tie to a project schedule, since the Action Points determine both dollars and amount of time allotted for that Task.

Activities

The last table in this hierarchy consists of Activities—discrete action items that can be scheduled during a day, such as writing a process or creating a screen. A Task can be broken down into one or more Activities. This can then generate a To-do list for the day. The tricky part of making this work is to not get too granular—else a developer will spend more time entering their To-do list than actually developing.

At this level, the Activity is to help the developer more than anything else. We try to keep an Activity mapped to a Task on a one-to-one basis when practical, in order to keep the overhead down, but some developers like more details on their To-do lists than others.

When faced with a decision on how granularly to break down a Task into Activities, an Activity should be between 0 and 4 hours—if you end up with an Activity that's more than a day long, then it's probably not granular enough. At this point, the Task should be looked at to see if it needs to be broken up into more discrete steps.

For instance, let's take a processing module that has a "Coding" Task attached to it (as well as Review, Integration, Test, and Documentation Tasks). A big processing routine could well take a week or more to code. You don't want to have a Task for coding the routine, and a single Activity that also says "code the processing module" and has 34 hours assigned to it. If you end up spending 110 hours on it, you'll never know where you went wrong, but we've all had situations like this where something you thought you'd slam out in a few days ended up taking *forever*.

So, in this case, we'd break out the Task for writing the code for the processing module into several Activities, each taking a few hours. One Activity might be to define the data structures for importing some data, a second Activity would be to write the import routine, a third Activity would be to process and validate the imported data, and so on. If it turns out that the Task has 15 hours of time records attached to it but only one of these Activities, slated for three or four hours, has been completed, you can already tell that this Task might be a candidate for spiraling out of control, and thus take a look at why it's over budget.

Action Points

The last important table, although not strictly in the Customer-Project-Module-Task-Activity hierarchy, consists of the Action Points for a Task. As you saw earlier, Action Points are counted for each screen, report, or process (as well as other things) in a system. We enter those in a table that is related to the Task, and the fields in the table, obviously, differ according to the type of Task.

Time

The first ancillary table is Time. As time is spent on a Task, we create a new Time record. You may be wondering why we don't track time against Activities. We use Activities strictly to manage our personal To-do lists—but we don't have the need to break down the time we spend that granularly. We just care about how much time we've spent against a Task—a screen, a report, or a process. Eventually, we might want to bring that guy in the white lab coat and Clark Kent horn-rimmed glasses in and have him measure the amount of time needed to put a list box on a form. But probably not.

In TABET, the user picks the Customer, Project, Module, and Task, and enters the start and finish for a Time record. The interface is set up so that they can quickly enter a series of Time records for a single project, or for multiple projects for different customers. There is no official "standard" of what amount of time can be entered as a minimum—I ask the developers to use their common sense and how they would feel about being on the receiving end. Would they want to see time detail records for three- or four-minute chunks?

Generally, 10- or 15-minute chunks seem to work out okay—for a one-minute phone call, it's probably not worth entering a separate record, but for a five- or 10-minute phone call, there's probably something else involved that warrants the entry of a Time record. And if someone calls a half dozen times for a minute each time, then that all gets entered as a single Time record.

Invoices

The next table is Invoices. We attach Invoices to Customers, of course. In order to create an invoice, we display a pick list of available items that have been shipped—either Time records in the case of a Time and Materials project, or Module records in the case of a Fixed Price project. (The Module records that appear are only those that have been shipped.) The user then selects which records to include on the invoice, and those records are automatically marked as having been invoiced.

AFIs

You probably have figured out what each of the other tables is just by the name. This one probably doesn't ring a bell. "AFI" stands for "Application Feedback Incident" and it represents all the types of feedback we can get on an application.

I'll cover AFIs in more detail in a later chapter, but the point here is that feedback is attached to a Project, but we also identify which Module or Task the AFI pertained to if possible. It's just that it's not always possible—or practical—to tie an AFI to a more granular entity. For example, suppose the user reports a bug that turns out to be a corrupt database definition. Where does it get attached? The specific screen or report where the error was noticed? Or the Task where the database definition was created? Or somewhere else?

Users

Each developer has their own record in TABET so that Time records can be attached to the appropriate developer. This record also contains their login name and password, their hourly rate for time and materials work, and a few other fields.

We've considered being able to attach multiple billing rates to a person so that we can accommodate special situations, but so far, just being able to override calculated amounts for a specific task has worked well enough. I suppose we could set up one person who has more than one user to have them assigned different rates, but then they'd need multiple logins, since TABET's user records are tied into the network login. If your situation differs, you may want to build this into your time-tracking system.

Increasing sophistication: Capturing metrics

As you see, the initial "Customers and Time Entries" data structure for the 1980s has gotten considerably more complex. But it didn't get there in one jump. I saw that I wanted more than just a history tool that allowed me to invoice easily. I wanted to gather data that would allow me to plan for the future. I didn't know exactly what needs the company would have, but the information wasn't likely to change much between two developers and 20. It was simply a matter of organizing how that information needed to be gathered and then presented. I found we had three immediate needs.

Tracking time against tasks

As any manufacturer will tell you, if you don't know what the costs of your materials are, you won't be able to cost the product, and thus won't be able to price it. Since time is the single largest component of custom software, we needed to be able to track time against specific tasks. From this data, we are able to determine what our history is, and thus cost out future projects.

Tracking type of time

As I added people, more than one person began to work on a single project—for example, a developer would do coding, QA would do testing and tracking paperwork, and I would do analysis and design. Other tasks that fell to various people included code reviews, installation and acceptance, and ongoing support.

We need to be able to determine what percentage of the time we spend on each type of time. All the books (the ones with 10 equations per page) say that design should take up 30% or 60% of a project's allocated time. And that testing should be at least another 30%. Is this true? We don't have enough data yet, but we're tracking that information now so that, in the near future, we'll be able to generate these statistics.

We could have broken down the project into another category—within a Task, create sub-Activities for Testing, Coding, Design, and so on—but felt this really made the hierarchy too complex. Instead, we decided to flag a Time record as to the type of time being spent.

Application feedback

One of the reasons we track bugs is to determine where we need to improve our development processes. If we find a certain developer has an inordinate number of bugs related to a specific technique or process, we can consider some sort of action to correct that. This action might be better training, it might be changing the architecture of that technique so that it's less prone to creating a bug, or it might simply be the assignment of the developer to a post in northern Greenland.

Accordingly, we track feedback on each application and attach the feedback data to the most granular level known. A request for an enhancement to the system (say, some new functionality not related to the existing modules) could only be attached to the project, while a bug report (say, about an incorrect calculation) would be attached to the screen or report it was found on.

Since we know who has done the work on a system, down to the Task level, we can then count bugs, questions, and enhancement requests (ERs) per developer, and get an idea of the productivity and error-prone-ness of a developer as well. This has worked out well—on one project, we found out that nearly a quarter of the reported bugs from the customer were due to the poor design of a particular user interface mechanism, and the correspondingly faulty implementation of that mechanism. We redesigned the mechanism and provided better documentation for using that mechanism, and virtually wiped out bug reports in future modules of that project.

Eventually, we'll be able to put additional processes in place based on the defect count per developer.

Each of these was added on as our needs evolved. I've got a wish list item to track time spent on Activities automatically—perhaps through a handheld computer or some sort of "punch-clock" tool.

You don't have to become this sophisticated immediately—tracking time against Projects, and perhaps one more level of detail, such as Module or Task (but not both), is probably plenty right now. We added Modules into the mix just to keep 70 or 80 Tasks straight, and to provide us with some discipline in shipping identifiable pieces regularly. Your needs may differ.

Home-grown vs. commercial tools

I should close this discussion by mentioning that TABET is strictly an internal tool, and I don't plan on making it available publicly. You're welcome to use any ideas described here, but I can't provide the software itself for a variety of reasons.

You may be wondering why I went through the pain of creating an internal system instead of buying one of the many commercial time and billing packages out on the market. As with many things, "it just sort of snowballed." These days, TABET contains data since 1992, and trying to convert that data, including old projects, customer information, and so on, just doesn't seem worth it. Even if I was able to find a package that provided the project hierarchy, fixed price vs. time and materials itemization, and invoicing flexibility, we're certainly not going to find any package that can natively support our Action Point data.

In hindsight, of course, I think I would have taken a different tack, and suggest that you consider a commercial tool, and then spend your "custom time" writing an interface to talk to the tool you use to maintain Action Point data. If I was starting over again, that's what I would do. I doubt it would be difficult to find a commercial tool that would allow you to break down projects according to several levels of a hierarchy, and to attach time to the most granular of those levels.

How do you get employees to do it?

I dunno—sometimes I think maybe it's just me. But over the years, I've heard enough stories to make me think that it isn't. I'm talking about getting employees to track their time regularly. For some reason, it seems that people just won't unless threatened with punishments worse than death. Cleaning out the office refrigerator comes to mind. It's been a big enough source of frustration for me that I think it's worthy of some discussion here.

Before I begin this discussion, I should make a distinction clear. There are actually two pieces of the task. The first is to accurately track what they do, during the day, as they work. This is called contemporaneous record keeping, and it is critical. Even trying to remember what you did during a day when you're looking back at 5:00 is tough—if you skip a day or two, you'll never do it accurately.

The second is the entry of their time logs into the time and billing application. For some reason, employees—developers and technical assistants alike—don't like doing the three minutes of data entry needed each day to keep the database current.

Why don't they enter their time?

There are several reasons someone may resist tracking their time. First, of course, is the possibility that they're nervous about their work being measured—the number of hours they spend on X (or don't spend on Y) may come back to them, in a negative manner. And, if they're not working very hard, they should be worried. But management is going to find out sooner or later, with or without a time-tracking mechanism.

Another reason is that they find it a nuisance—having to remember what Project or Task they're working on, and writing it down. It's just so much more fun to cruise from one part of a project to another, cowboying one's way through the day. Tracking time just adds too much structure and discipline to the job.

A third reason is that the process used to track time isn't easy—it gets in their way. Filling out forms with lots entries, dealing with secret codes that have to be looked up, or entering data into a computer program that's hard to use or crashes a lot—these are all gumption traps. So, naturally, people are likely to avoid them, if possible.

Some ideas for getting people to track their time

I'll discuss a couple ways around the problems just listed, and then offer a stick or two if the carrots don't work.

If you have an employee who is afraid of what the data is going to be used for, then either you've got a management problem or an employee problem. In the case of the latter, the employee might have to go. Explain to them that the company can't get paid unless their time is recorded and the customer billed for it either directly or indirectly. If the company doesn't get paid, eventually, they won't get paid either. If they still refuse to accept that, then they need to find a job where tracking time isn't necessary.

The second and third reasons are somewhat similar, and can be lessened (or avoided entirely) by providing an exceptionally easy-to-use interface. I've experimented with a number of mechanisms where the user simply keeps a small application running all day long, and punches in and out of various projects during the day. The application keeps track of everything else—date, time, user, and so on. This data is then posted to the main database at the end of the day. It's about as easy as it gets.

If these techniques don't work, however, you have to bring out the heavy artillery. First is a formal declaration of policy that: 1) contemporaneous time tracking is company policy, and 2) neglecting to enter their time, or falsifying time entries, is grounds for dismissal.

A second plan but one that also includes a carrot is tying bonus money to successful time entry. For example, bonus money would be proportional to the number of times they successfully entered their time. If they missed four days out of 20 for a month, they'd only see 80% of their bonus for that month. That can provide a significant incentive.

The last solution is simply tying their paychecks to the time entered into the system. If someone misses a day, they don't get paid for that day—because you can't bill your customer for that day.

You might also point out that keeping detailed track of time is usually to the employee's benefit. First of all, most developers do work more than a standard 40-hour week—if they can point out the three 60-hour weeks they put in last month, they're much more likely to win a day off for chaperoning the school field trip to the zoo. Second, if they are indeed running into trouble, they'll be able to use their time records to identify the problem areas, and get to a better resolution than if they're simply perceived to be slow on everything.

Finally, the good employees already know this—and will willingly go along. It's the folks who are dragging the curve down who will resist. You might simply point out that the folks who don't want to track their time are often trying to hide something.

Metrics are not a punishment tool

It is critical to ensure that, as you capture metrics on your development, you do not use that data to punish people. Critique, coach—absolutely. Punish—never. There are two areas where the system could easily be abused.

The first is the simple tracking of time. Some managers will insist that their developers track every minute of time, and then will rain holy hell on them if the time logs show any deviation from perfection. Well, funny enough, we kind of figure that people are human, and that their time records will not be perfect. People will come in late, leave early, have a two-hour lunch, write off a morning because of something stupid they did—the whole ball of wax.

The same goes for bugs. We pretty much assume our developers will write code with bugs in it. We want, and need, to sensitize everyone in the process to the concept that we're here to learn from our errors—not to use the discovery of those errors as a tool for punishment. Pro football players spend all day Tuesday watching game films from the weekend—and while the coach may occasionally berate a player, everyone knows that the purpose of these sessions is to discover mistakes and determine how to avoid them in the next game.

What I'm interested in is using the information in TABET as a means to correct behavior and activities that I don't want to see. If I see bugs, I work with the developer to determine how to reduce those bugs—I don't scream and yell and make a lot of threats. If I find someone billing an unacceptable amount, I'll find out why, and see what I can do to get them back on track.

I've found in my own experience that people will go the extra mile on their own more readily if they know they have your support and your help.

This is a situation where actions speak louder than words. If you claim that you'll never punish someone due to data that's entered into the time-tracking system, but then Friday afternoon you go on a witch hunt to find out who came in to work late that week, you can be sure that everyone will have entered 8:00 as their start time each day the following week.

I don't care if someone shows up at 8:00 or 10:00—as long as two conditions are met. First, since customers and other developers do rely on that person, it's only a courtesy to inform the office if they're not going to be in during "usual working hours." Second, they have to get their work done. I've had employees who have taken advantage of the flexible hours I offer, but when it came to reviewing their performance, suddenly their failure to get their jobs done became everyone else's fault. Fortunately, those folks didn't stick around long once they found out that I really expected performance—not just face time.

Another selling point for employees is that if an organization wants to pursue some sort of certification such as the Capability Maturity Model (CMM), that organization will have to at some point track metrics and use them in managing and improving the process. If employees don't want to participate, then they're working at cross purposes to the goals of the organization.

To sum up, metrics are the tool you use to determine your costs—and it's as ridiculous to try to run a business without accurate time records as it would be to manufacture something without keeping track of how much it cost to buy it.

Chapter 22
Manufacturing Instructions

"You're the closest thing I have to a father."—Anikin Skywalker
"Then why won't you listen to me?"—Obi-Wan
  —Star Wars, Attack of the Clones

Writing software is still very much an intellectual activity, and, unlike other such activities, there are no "generally accepted practices" for writing code. Sure, attempts have been made, either on a macro level, aimed at "programming" regardless of language, or on a language-specific level, aimed at standardizing various methods for performing specific functions. But give 10 programmers the same problem and the same tool, and you'll end up with 15 solutions—all of varying quality and functionality. Contrast this with other industries that have generally accepted ways of doing things— you'll end up with similar, if not identical, results from the same 10 workers.

This presents a problem. How do you ensure that quality is being "built-in" during the programming, instead of merely being "added on" at the end, through code reviews and testing?

My first cut at solving this problem was "Manufacturing Instructions"—an itemized list of how a particular screen, report, or process is going to be built. In this chapter, I'll discuss how MI came about, what they look like, and how to use them.

If you walk through a typical factory floor, you'll see three distinct entities used in the manufacturing process. The first is the "blueprint" for what is being manufactured—a cylinder head, the headboard for a waterbed, a bicycle frame, or Cap'n Crunch cereal. Sometimes this isn't actually a blueprint as you and I think of it. If the product being manufactured is paint, the "blueprint" is actually a formula sheet. If the product is a circuit board, the blueprint is a schematic. But in each of these cases, this first entity is a specification of what is being made—similar to our specification that describes in detail what we're developing.

The third entity, obviously, is the hunk of metal that's being manufactured—or the vat of paint, or the circuit board, or the cereal mix.

But I said that there are three entities. What's the middle one? The middle entity is what the worker uses to actually "make" the product.

In the case of a cylinder head casting, you don't just take 200 pounds of iron, drill a bunch of holes in it willy-nilly, and—presto!—have a complete engine block, ready for cylinders and pistons and whatnot. The engine block has to be machined in a very specific sequence of steps, else you'll end up with an Escher-like device, where either it doesn't work or, at the very least, it takes a great deal longer to produce.

The same holds true for that vat of paint. In this case, it's mixing instructions. As anyone who has done more than boil water in the kitchen will attest, you can't simply throw all the ingredients of a meal into a pan and be happy with the result. Same with paint—you don't just throw everything into a vat and "stir vigorously." You have to know what to put in first, what to put in next, how much, how long to mix, and so on.

Manufacturing Instructions provide several advantages/benefits. First is quality. Imagine getting 90% done with a 10,000-gallon vat of paint, only to find that the second to last step requires you to mix two of the remaining chemicals for an hour and add it to the rest of the batch as it is mixing. In other words, you have to do two mixings simultaneously. But you didn't know that, so now the first batch will go to waste because it's going to coagulate before the other mixing is done. That's several thousand dollars of raw materials, as well as your time and the time you've tied up the equipment, all wasted.

Or suppose you were just about done with that cylinder head, only to find that you needed to machine a flat surface before boring a set of holes because they all had to be measured from the same plane? There goes a $20,000 casting into the scrap heap.

Sounds familiar, doesn't it? Ever dive headfirst into a screen, with a vision in mind of how it's going to look and work, and then, partway through, realize that the lovingly crafted Create-Cursor method isn't going to work in one case? It has to be broken out into four separate methods, and as a result, the past two hours have been for naught. Or, you've spent a half-day writing a new routine to perform a specific kind of data conversion. After submitting it to the librarian for common code, you find out that a routine that does this is already in the library—and it is considerably more robust, with two additional features that you immediately recognize as valuable but that you hadn't thought of during your piddling around—and has already been through thorough testing.

So—why do software developers, even if given the luxury of a spec (admittedly, rare), just jump into programming? Shouldn't they also have the rigor of "Manufacturing Instructions" ("MI") so as to accrue the same benefits as manufacturers?

It's because we don't have an apprentice relationship like many tried and true industries. We software developers simply throw a newbie in the water and hope that the half-hour of instruction we gave them last week was enough. Our industry has not recognized that we're lacking in this sort of rigor. Some companies use certification exams as a substitution for rigor and structure in coding practices, but that's not going to be the case (see the chapter on Certification for more on this topic).

The Chiefs, as well as all of the Indians, feel that such rigor and structure would kill the creative process that's part of software development, but that's not true—it would simply kill the dead ends and rotten coding that's produced because someone hasn't thought through what they're trying to accomplish well enough.

I'm going on this tirade early in this chapter to impress upon you the importance and value of some sort of rational, logical, structured instructions for going from the Functional Spec to working code. Simply sitting down and winging it, while fun, is a bad idea. Imagine if your doctor adopted the same attitude—"I don't have to wash my hands or prep up the materials—I'm just going to cut you open and see what I find inside!"

How MI came about

A long time ago, I hired a programmer who had spent a number years as an independent consultant. This person brought with him a wide array of credentials, including a number of certifications and an expertise I had seen demonstrated at a number of user group and marketing presentations.

However, as defect reports on the first few modules he had worked on came back to me, I began looking at his code. I was horrified.

Just about every possible programming sin one could commit could be found somewhere in his code. He had sat through group code reviews of other developers' work, and, given his experience, I had assumed that he was using our standards, learning new techniques, and adopting good practices. It had all fallen on deaf ears—he had achieved "success" in the past using his own "ways" and dadgummit, he was going to continue to use them. While he wasn't arguing that the techniques we were using weren't valid, and he did use them at times, he simply had a fundamental lack of knowledge of how to write code.

I cast about for a handbook of basic programming techniques and practices—"PPP" for "proper programming practices"—and found nothing. Sure, there were a lot of books that touched on one topic or another, but I didn't find anything short of a two-year textbook on general-purpose programming. And even that was too generic, and too tilted toward C and Pascal, to be of much practical use.

Nonetheless, I had an immediate problem to solve—this person was writing code for our customers, and it wasn't very good. The end result was laden with defects, and more importantly, the code inside was so convoluted and poorly constructed that maintenance or extensions would have been nearly impossible.

However, he did have a good programmer's mind, he thought logically, and he was willing to learn. Hence, I came up with Manufacturing Instructions for software.

Using Manufacturing Instructions

Here's how to use Manufacturing Instructions in your development. When starting a new task—a screen, a report, or a process—write up an MI for the task before starting to write code. A sample of Manufacturing Instructions is included in the *DevGuide* downloads.

First, read the entire spec and related documents for the task. For example, the Functional Spec may refer to other parts of the spec, as well as other reference materials (such as materials from the customer).

Next, write down all questions and areas that are unclear. These will probably fall into three areas: terminology, functionality, and operation. It is helpful to document these shortcomings so that you can see where the spec and other materials have fallen short.

Third, obviously, you'll need to get an answer or other resolution for each item in the previous step.

Fourth, outline how the user will perform the Task if the Use Cases and Functional Spec's Usage sections are not sufficient.

Fifth, list the tools required for this Task:

- What foundation tool will be used, if not already decided? For example, for a screen, which base class will be used? For a report, which type of report—detail, parent-child, and so on. We should eventually have skeleton procedures for common types of processes.

- What library functions are needed?

- What application-wide or library-wide properties are needed?

- What application-wide functions are needed?

- What tables will be used? What temp tables will need to be created?

- What internal functions will need to be created? Just list what they are—the purpose and header information, but not the pseudo-code or anything further.

- What properties for the Task that are internal to the Task (for example, form properties or local variables in a stand-alone subroutine) are needed?

Sixth, create a map—on paper—of how the Task will work. In the olden days, this was called a flow chart. (Quaint, eh?) This map will list all of the properties internal to the Task as well as each function. Each function should be pseudo-coded (or flow charted). The key is that once this map has been created, you should have a complete list of properties and methods needed for the Task.

Seventh, get these manufacturing instructions approved, or at least reviewed by someone else. In our shop, a new developer is not to start coding until this happens. This means that they'll want to have several things in the fire at the same time so that if they have to wait for approval for a while (a day, perhaps), they're not sitting on their hands.

This approval process is key. If you're having a developer write up MIs but not having anyone review them, then what's the point in the first place? Yes, it does get the developer thinking through all of the technical requirements before starting to sling code, but, particularly when they're new, they need review to make sure that they're doing things the right way. Otherwise, they're simply developing bad habits that will be harder to break later on.

You may be wondering how to handle the "approval" process. To answer this, take a step back and remember the purpose of this documentation. It's not simply to get in the developer's way, or to tie their hands behind their back. Instead, the purpose is to get the developer to think through the architectural details before starting to code. Thus, you may want neophyte programmers to have their MIs approved while experienced developers do their own review. There isn't any single "right" or "wrong" answer, nor is there a point at which it's clear that the MIs are "finished," and it's a judgment call as to when you have developers do their own reviews.

Obviously, submitting a set of Manufacturing Instructions for approval wouldn't mean that they're automatically approved. Similar to a code review, the reviewer will go through the document, and perhaps suggest changes or, more likely, identify items that aren't as clear or as thorough as they ought to be. The programmer will revise the Manufacturing Instructions, and, if the revisions are significant enough, submit them for approval again.

Finally, once approval has been given, start coding.

A different take on Manufacturing Instructions

This may seem like a lot of work—both unnecessary for the developer and time-consuming for the manager or other reviewer. I've also heard that this smacks of "micro-management." However, it really doesn't work like that, so I spent some time trying to figure out how to explain why this works.

Then I realized that I was simply using, in large part, a different term for a document that many of you are also using, and this document is called "technical specifications." A well conceived technical specification eliminates huge coding problems down the road. Just like code reviews (covered in the next chapter), MIs are one of those things that seem redundant ("We don't have time for MIs on this project!") but pay off significantly by the end.

Just like with Functional Specifications, there is no set standard for a technical specification. If you talk to 10 developers about their technical specs, you'll again get 15 different answers. Our Manufacturing Instructions try to formalize what a technical spec looks like, on a very granular level. You may argue that technical specs need to be done at the same time as, or right after, the Functional Spec is done. On a theoretical basis, I guess I'd agree, but in the real world, I would argue that it just isn't going to happen.

A technical spec can't be written until you've defined the functionality, so the Functional Spec must be done first. And I've found in my experience talking to developers over the past few years that a reasonably thorough Functional Spec is rare enough—to expect a thorough technical spec on top of that is an unreasonable expectation.

I would love to hear from you about your experiences on this matter—while I've been writing Functional Specs for years, the formal technical spec as a successor to the Functional Spec is a fairly new piece of the puzzle.

Chapter 23
Code Reviews

"Does anyone else here think this is a really stupid idea?"—Jack Burton
   —Big Trouble in Little China

Code reviews are a lot like the weather—everyone talks about them but no one does anything useful after the discussion. Most references on software quality will tell you that code reviews are one of the more valuable practices that you can implement. However, these tomes then spend pages and pages quoting statistics to prove their point, and leave the actual implementation up to you. In this chapter, I'll show you how to get started with code reviews quickly and painlessly.

Λ code review is a means by which you can evaluate the work that you or your staff is doing. It's the story of the football place-kicker all over again. You can meet with your programmers time and time again, but, eventually, won't you want to open a code window and see what they've been doing? Kinda makes sense, doesn't it?

Once you've been sold on the idea, though, what's the next step? Where's the "how to" manual? There are all sorts of questions and issues with a new process like code reviews.

First of all, what does one look like in the real world? Is it a checklist, an essay, a form to fill out? Does it cover just lines of code, or can other items be included, like screen design and reports? How about other deliverables, like a scope statement, requirements document, design doc, test plans? What roles are required, who is involved—and who plays which roles?

Next, how do you implement them? Where does it fit in between meeting with customers, cranking out code, calling the building superintendent to fix the heat, and interviewing new employees? The challenge of incorporating it into your day-to-day schedule needs to be met. The best of intentions may win you plaudits in some places, but the hustle and bustle of customers hollering for their work somehow tempts developers to cut corners and shorten delivery cycles. Since you can still ship modules to customers without doing code reviews, code reviews are often one of the first things to go. So, even though they are scheduled in, how do you make sure they'll actually happen?

Since a code review is a process without a specific deliverable (to a customer), it often becomes a collaborative effort—without a leader, or an owner. And as Plato said, that which is owned by everyone is cared for by no one. Again, another reason that they won't get done.

And, finally, what do you do with the results? If a half dozen highly paid professionals spend an hour and a half on a code review, but the meeting notes are filed in a binder that gets placed on a dusty shelf somewhere, what's the point, other than some short-term pep-talk motivation?

Purpose

The purpose of a code review is not, as you might first assume, to find bugs. That's what Quality Assurance does.

Well, that's sort of a flip answer. In a later chapter, I'll explicitly define a "bug" (or a "defect," or a "boo-boo"—whatever you want to call it) to mean functionality that isn't described in the Functional Specification. For example, the Functional Spec might say that selecting a particular choice in a combo box will cause a certain business rule to fire such that a value on that screen is recalculated. If that value doesn't get recalculated, or is recalculated incorrectly, that's a bug. A code review isn't supposed to find that type of bug (although it may, if someone in the back of the room asks, "Why are you dividing by zero in the third case?").

A code review is to make sure the developer follows the rules of coding. Not following the rules may not cause a bug—it may just result in code that is more likely to allow the developer to write bug-laden code, or it may result in inefficient, bloated, or hard to maintain code.

This big picture can be broken out into three more explicit purposes. The first is to provide a mechanism for sharing techniques between developers. As a reviewer looks over the actual work of another, the person being reviewed is bound to pick up ideas, tips, tricks, and so on. You can read all the golf magazines you want, and play all the rounds you can stand, but until someone else watches you play, you're not going to reach your full potential. Of course, it's especially helpful if that someone else is better than you are.

Along the same lines, seeing your work "in public" provides a different perspective than when you're just looking at it yourself in the privacy of your own office. This is one of the reasons that pro football teams review game films on the day after—so that players can see their performances in a different light. They may convince themselves that a certain play wasn't that bad, but when viewed in the community film room, the flaws—and the successes—become obvious.

The second function is to encourage proper coding practices. It's easy to, er, well, you know, get lazy. You know you should explain that magic formula, but you just couldn't. You did comment the code when you first wrote it, but then you kept finding bugs, and it took you all morning to get it right. By the time you were finished, you were just too tired to change the comments again.

Knowing, however, that this code might be the subject of the Defending Your Life meeting on Friday afternoon often provides an incentive to finish up the last 5% of the code— the comments, the indenting, the deleting of old versions of the program, and so on.

The third reason for a code review is an offshoot of the second—it provides a mechanism that encourages developers to write maintainable code. Simply following the "rules" doesn't ensure maintainable code. It's easy to follow the letter of the law but break the spirit. One typical coding guideline is that a procedure or function shouldn't ever be longer than a single page—25 to 50 lines long. It's easy to find a 20-line routine that is virtually impossible to understand, much less modify, while it would be equally easy to put together a function of 100 lines that is crystal clear and trivial to maintain. The 20-line routine keeps to the letter of the law but breaks the spirit, while the 100-line routine does the reverse.

By demonstrating this function in a code review, the developer hears from others how good or bad their code is. If the rest of the room hoots and hollers, or starts cutting side deals to avoid getting stuck with this code, the developer knows they've written a maintenance nightmare.

This also forces the developer to be accountable to the group. If you see someone else's routine and say that you don't know how it works, it's more likely that the routine will get cleaned up.

Definition and types

A code review can take one of three forms. The first is a mechanical review, where a technical assistant looks over things, using a checklist to evaluate what's been done (and what hasn't). The second, more in-depth type of review is a one-on-one review, where a developer's code is reviewed by someone of equal or superior ability—preferably the latter. The last is a group review, where one developer shows their code to a group of several developers who then critique it in public. This group review is referred to in our shop as "Defending Your Life."

(By the way, while I'm referring to "code" reviews—this doesn't mean that I'm only referring to long listings of lines of commands. "Code" in this context means all of the development work that makes up a system—design issues, projects, programs, forms, reports, libraries, classes, and so on.)

Marquis of Queensberry Rules?

It only stands to reason that if someone's code is going to be critiqued by another—whether that "other" is a technical assistant, another developer, or the whole team—there should be some sort of commonly accepted standard against which the critique is performed.

Thus, the first element of a code review is a set of development conventions, guidelines, standards, or whatever you want to call them. This is the framework within which each developer performs and against which the development is measured.

For example, you may likely have a standard Functional Spec (by this time in this book, I would certainly hope so!). You also probably have a few tried and true methods for handling business problems that come up over and over—parent-child relationships, queries against many-to-many table joins, and so on. Instead of each developer in your shop figuring out their own special tricks to handle these situations, share those techniques and methods by documenting them.

In a more nitty-gritty sense, you may want to provide guidelines about the actual coding techniques—how variables are named, how code is formatted, and so on. Instead of letting each developer figure out their own styles, you can help them adopt "best practices" that your firm has decided upon.

Just like a prewritten checklist in an application audit acts as an independent arbiter of judgment, so does a set of predefined standards in a code review.

If you don't have standards

The purpose of a code review is to make sure a developer follows the rules. This begs the question: What are the rules? Obviously, a worthwhile code review assumes a set of predefined guidelines that the developers should be following. It's pretty hard for a developer to write good code if there has been no predetermined definition of what "good" is prepared.

Remember the angst with which you approached the question regarding "What if we don't have historical costs of development recorded? How are we going to determine our cost per Action Point if we don't have any history?" You may be dealing with the same angst now—thinking, "We don't have any standards!"

First of all, that's probably not true—you do have some sort of standards, you just may not have documented them very clearly yet. But think through how you do your work—you've undoubtedly got a number of standard techniques and processes you use on a regular basis, and that's an excellent place to start. In fact, when you start out with code reviews, "less" probably is better than "more," in terms of being useful. After all, you can probably remember a dozen guidelines to consider during your first code review—but not 20 pages worth.

Next, what you'll want to do is collect what you do have in a simple document that can be easily absorbed and followed by everyone on your staff. If you don't feel it's complete, don't worry, it will gradually become so, as regular use prompts contributions based on holes in the original document.

If you're still freaking out about the prospect of having to create a standards document, I've got a sample set of code reviews later in this chapter that you can use as a starting point.

There's a hidden benefit to starting out small and having each team member add to the document. As they make contributions, they buy in to the concept of using this document in their own day-to-day work. Developers, and particularly day-to-day programmers, can often be difficult to corral—they like to take their own route, instead of traveling one that's been trail-blazed by another. That's why managing programmers is often referred to as similar to the process of "herding cats."

But what if your standards really are, er, sparse? Does this mean that you have to spend hours, days, and months putting together a set of guidelines before you do your first code review? It depends. If you don't have any documented company standards, it probably means that you've got a number of cowboys who each do things their own separate way. You're going to have to spend some time to get them to agree on at least a minimal set of commonly accepted rules.

You don't have to stop the presses for a year in order to do so. If your company guidelines consist of a half page of notes taken from a seminar someone attended three years ago, here's a trick that will get your guidelines up to industrial strength in a surprisingly short time.

You can gradually build a set of guidelines by having one person document "good ideas" as you go through your code reviews. (Yes, you still have to do your code reviews! You're not getting off that easily!) We started with a fairly detailed set of standards and guidelines, but we still add items to the list as we go through group reviews. This is an excellent way to build or enhance a code review checklist, because it achieves buy-in while it's being put together.

Your checklist does not have to be a 90-page manual and, in fact, probably shouldn't be. If it's that long, no one will pay attention to it—who could remember all of it? And how in the world would you bring a new developer up to speed?

One more thing about the guidelines—the term is "guidelines," not "absolute rules that must be followed or we'll cut off your hand." There are always situations where a standard doesn't make sense. Forcing people to mindlessly adhere to the standard produces code no better than had there been no guidelines in the first place.

Implementation

Code reviews are difficult to do because no one is waiting for the end result. So you've got to have some tricks up your sleeve to make sure they get done. But code reviews aren't just hard to do because of business pressures pushing them aside. They can also be difficult because of personality conflicts between the players—developers are typically pretty smart people, and have egos to go along with their IQs. When you throw two or more into a room, some interesting fireworks can take place. Here's how to handle both situations.

Scheduling

The biggest hurdle to getting code reviews done is getting them started. As I mentioned earlier in this chapter, no one is waiting for the results of a code review—you can ship that "critical module" to a customer without a code review, and no one will ever notice. It's not like not including the reports or the Save method, both of which will be noticed in fairly short order by the customer.

The first trick is to treat a code review as just another task for a module, like design, coding, documentation, testing, and so on. If there's a place on the schedule for a code review, it's easier to get it done than if it's expected to happen "by magic."

Next, how often do you schedule them? Totally up to you. You might do one every Friday afternoon, assuming that you have enough code going through your shop to warrant a code review that often. Or you could have a formula that defines that for every N Action Points, you will have a review of a certain type (code, design document, test plan, whatever). Each review would require X days of effort for preparation (preparation of materials, time spent by the reviewers, actually conducting the review, and disposition of the review) and span Y for execution (time to prepare, time to review materials prepared, the review itself, and then to resolve outstanding issues).

Again, code reviews should not have to be shoehorned into the schedule, presumably at the expense of something else; rather, they should be scheduled when the project schedule is created. Bottom line—they should not be a surprise at all.

How far do you go?

A common question that comes up is simply, "Do you have to perform a code review on every snippet of code produced in your shop?" No, absolutely not, and, in fact, asking the question almost begs whether or not you understand what a code review is for. The purpose of a code review is not to find defects, so, no, you don't have to review every piece. It's to get better. If you want to improve your game, you don't have to review every minute of every game film. You may want to just review the big plays, or the critical last two minutes of the quarter, or when you're up against a player who gives you a lot of trouble.

And even if you wanted to, it just wouldn't happen. Why wouldn't it? Well, we're human. We make impossible schedules, commit to deadlines that are silly, and once in a while, people get sick or forget. But we do track which pieces of an application have been through a code review and which haven't. At some point in the future, we'll have enough data to do some meaningful analysis. I'm terribly curious about the effectiveness of code reviews—do the modules that have had code reviews reflect the effort in terms of quality? In other words, have our code reviews really reduced bug counts?

Okay, maybe what you meant, since you really knew that you weren't going to review every piece of code written, is "How much—what percentage—do you review?" It depends on which type of review you're talking about.

All modules go through the mechanical review; this helps the newer programmers develop good habits, and regular vigilance helps prevent the veterans from getting sloppy. A smaller percentage goes through a one-on-one review; and a smaller percentage yet undergoes a full group review.

As you can intuit, you'll eventually run into diminishing returns. When? I suggest you let your gut tell you in a one-on-one review, and I argue that the group will tell you in a group review.

However, that doesn't help answer the question regarding *what* to review. You've got five projects, each with 5-20 MB of source code. Just where in the world do you start? Here's a trick: Just as I said that you might want to review the game films focusing on a player who gives you trouble or a key timeframe of the game, focus on areas that cause people problems—or that create a lot of bugs!

For example, a module that involved several go-arounds with the customer, with additional requirements being introduced each time, or the functionality whipsawing back and forth would be a good candidate for a code review.

Another consideration you may use in determining how rigorous a review something requires is its impact on the system. Here are three areas where you might want to consider implementing a full review: 1) If it touches data to a significant degree, 2) if it's a library routine that will be used over and over not just by the current system, but by other systems as well, or 3) if it's going to be critical to production support, such as financial reports or night-time batch processing.

And you might want to use a review for training purposes—a module might be fairly small and/or simple, but if the standards that apply to that piece of code have changed or significantly evolved, and you want to acquaint your team with those changes/updates, a review on a less complex module would allow you to easily illustrate those changes.

And as you get more sophisticated, another way to identify modules to review is to examine your defect history. As 80-20 rules go, programming and defects are no different. You'll find most of your defects concentrated in just a few modules. If you can, you may even identify certain types of modules that are more error-prone than others—these are excellent candidates for review.

As you perform reviews, you'll often find that the incident of defects in those types of modules goes away as people learn what they're doing wrong, and what the proper way is. Other times, you'll decide that the approach being taken just screams out as being defect-prone and, in a group setting, you'll figure out a new approach to tackle that problem that isn't as fragile.

Criticisms

People in general don't take criticism well, and programmers are, in this respect, no different from anyone else. Well, actually, they are—since programmers have landed in their position by virtue of being generally "the smart one" in the crowd, they're used to being right much, if not all, of the time. Thus, they're not used to being told they've done something wrong.

Furthermore, given the social difficulties that many in our industry experience, many aren't well equipped to provide constructive feedback in a manner that's easy to take. Thus, particularly with group reviews, but even, to some extent, with one-on-one reviews, things can get tense between participants.

At a juncture like this, you may want to step into the fray and remind people of the benefits of code reviews—what the developer can get out of the review. If you can draw on specific experiences in your shop, even better.

There's a lot to be said for high-spirited camaraderie, to be sure. I remember doing a training class for a group of regional sales managers years back. They all got together several times a year for various company events and knew each other well. Thus, when introduced to computer training for a set of customized applications, they all bonded together, with the computer (and the instructor—me) being the common enemy.

They all walked into the training center on Monday morning, wearing dark suits, white shirts, and Ivy-League style ties, except for one unfortunate fellow whose luggage had been sent to the South Pole and who had to attend the first day in his casual clothes. It of course didn't help that this fellow was from California and had come into town wearing bright green slacks and a screaming yellow golf shirt. Despite his repeated denials, all of the other reps decided that green and yellow must be the new business dress code for California, and gave him a hard time for the rest of the week.

Similarly, this type of good-natured ribbing can work wonders in a potentially tense environment like one where one's work is being critiqued—and it's important to keep it on that level.

Let me stress this point again. This is training—not a veiled opportunity to rip someone's heart out. So while it's great to have a lot of active give-and-take, it's not acceptable to be mean. It's the boss's responsibility to put an immediate stop to any of that—because, the first time it happens, everyone else will be much less likely to stick their neck out next.

Have you ever written a piece of code that was perfect? I mean, one that was longer than four or five lines. Of course not—none of us have. There's always room for improvement—better comments, improved performance, more robust error trapping, whatever. Take the comments and criticisms in a code review as an opportunity for learning how to solve problems better.

That said, I should add that the developers being reviewed must understand that they will have to meet a certain level of expectations. If they come into a review unprepared or present a module that's a piece of junk, they shouldn't be surprised to have their head handed to them on a platter.

Code review formats

It's time to get into some sample code reviews in more detail. Note that I've just provided samples for reviews of code—if you want to review test plans, design documents, and the like, you'll need to determine their contents yourself. Yes, the old "the exercise is left to the reader" ploy!

Mechanical

 The mechanical code review examines the nuts and bolts of a chunk of code, using a checklist to ensure that certain standards and practices are followed, and that identifiable "gotchas" are avoided. This type of review leans right up against the edge of Quality Assurance, except that it isn't output or functionality-oriented. A sample Mechanical Code Review Checklist is included in the *DevGuide* downloads.

This review is performed by a technical assistant or perhaps an entry-level programmer, and does not even need the concurrent participation of the programmer whose code is being reviewed.

This situation is similar to that of an insurance company that uses nurses to review medical histories and claims. They know what the procedures are well enough to identify whether or not they were followed, and to flag unusual circumstances for further review by someone more technically qualified (a physician). It would be a waste of a physician's time to do a lot of the review themselves.

Once complete, the reviewer will discuss the results with the programmer in an effort to train the programmer about proper techniques. You may feel this seems funny—a non-programmer training a programmer. But it's often difficult for new programmers to get their arms around the entire set of standards—they'll learn some, but not others. The mechanical code review helps them learn those pieces that they haven't picked up yet, or are having a difficult time with.

Some companies use a position as a "technical assistant" as a stepping-stone to a programming position, and so these reviews, performed by an individual in that position, can also help the tech assistant learn about programming while performing a valuable service for the company.

Sample checklist

These items can be examined without even opening up a code window:

- Does the system compile without errors?

- Do all of the functions work (has anything been stubbed out)?

- Are all of the files (programs, screens, reports) and procedures used, or does the project contain things that aren't used anymore?

Now it's time to make sure the code inside follows the rules:

- Does each routine have a proper header?

- Is the header updated to reflect major changes in the routine?

- Are parameters described in the header?

- Are required parameters checked immediately upon entering the routine, both for their presence and their data type?

- Are there comments in the code? A good rule of thumb for knowing when there are "enough" comments in the code is to remove the code and just read the comments. Is it still clear what the routine is doing?

- Do the comments explain why? A second item of note—the comments should not simply answer "what" the routine is doing, but why. If there are episodes of "magic" throughout the code, they should be explained in the comments. Conversely, it's a foolish programmer who decorates the following line of code with a comment like "determines if the amount is non-zero":

```
IF nAmountTax > 0
```

- Is the code formatted with indenting and white space?

- Does each logic structure check for the "in all other cases" structure? For example, does each IF have an ELSE, each DO CASE have an OTHERWISE?

- Are variables named consistently and according to your standards?

- Are long or complex calculations commented?

- Are there complex nestings—many levels deep, or structures that look very elaborate?

- Are there comments that indicate code has been modified (this is good, by the way)?

- Are there chunks of code that have been commented out (with no explanation of why the code was left in place)?

- Is a return value always returned?

- Are all possible return values of the same data type?

The next group of things to check can be checked by a highly skilled technical support level person, or by an entry-level developer:

- Are string comparisons handled properly—both with respect to exactness and case? For example, which do you see:

```
upper(cString) = "HERMAN"
or
cString = "Herman"
```

- Are file locations hard-coded or is the application portable?

- Are similar but not identical functions used as if they were interchangeable?

- Does arithmetic performed on dates handle the turn of the millennium gracefully?

- Are divisors tested for zero?

- Are variables initialized?

- Does the code contain "magic numbers," or are they 1) explained, or 2) DEFINED as appropriate for the language?

- Are there blocks of repetitious code?

One-on-one

The programmer mentoring code review involves either a senior developer and one at a junior level, or two senior developers of equal or comparable skill levels. If possible, a third, disinterested party will choose a module to review, and the two will either walk through it together or the reviewer will make a first pass by himself and then walk through it with the developer. The third party will often be a member of the QA team, because they have the knowledge of the developers' defect history and can pick a module that would more likely benefit from a code review.

This is an excellent opportunity for training the junior developer. It's also an opportunity for the reviewer to re-examine both the company's standards as well as their own styles and techniques.

Sample checklist

Finally, we get to the items that generally need the expertise of a developer to look at:

- Can custom code be replaced by common code or library functions?

- Is code in the proper place in the hierarchy of the call stack?

- Are variables scoped and released when appropriate?

- Are the more common cases tested first in logic structures?

- Do routines have one exit or does each exit call a single termination routine?

- Is the code contained within loops absolutely necessary?

- Are external device accesses trapped appropriately?

- Are files checked for existence (before creating, writing, or updating)?

- Is the environment returned to the same state at the end of the routine?

- Is there an implicit target environment (development language, operating system, machine/hardware)?

At this stage, it's also time to look at specific algorithms, techniques, approaches, and other items that generally fall more into the "bigger picture" than granular rules.

"DYL"

Ah yes. Lock a half-dozen programmers in a room, make one of them serve up an offering of his code, and let the others tear into him. Sounds like fun, eh? For everyone except the victim, right?

We jokingly refer to these group reviews as "Defending Your Life" because the developer being reviewed is on stage in front of a crowd. It's a dynamic situation—imagine a training situation where a group of developers has a chance to look at, examine, critique, admire, and improve a chunk of real-life code! What an excellent opportunity!

Often done over the lunch hour or in that oh-so-unproductive 3-5 PM Friday afternoon time slot, each developer in the group gets their shot in front of the group, but they don't get to choose which module they show off. That way, it keeps each developer honest—making sure that the code is "real-life" and not especially tuned for a review.

While time-consuming, the group review is a lot more valuable than a one-on-one. I've covered several of the reasons, but there's one more. Even the most senior developer is subject to a DYL code review. Having the others in the shop ask the old pro why she didn't delete a temp file at the end of a routine is good for everyone's egos ("Hey, even she screws up sometimes!") and it keeps everyone honest.

Sample checklist

I haven't found a "one-size-fits-all" checklist. At this point, the review is an intellectual exercise where anything might happen. First, the authors describe what the application, module, or procedure being reviewed does. Then they will walk through the data structures, the object model, and other supporting entities that are specific to the thing being reviewed. Finally, they'll walk through the specific code. As this happens, questions invariably come up, either in the guise of "why" or "how."

As each segment is being discussed, each reviewer should keep in mind several general questions:

- Would I be able to modify or extend this module in an efficient and timely manner, or would the learning curve be overwhelming?

- Would I be able to feel confident about modifications I made to this module, or do I feel that the module is "fragile" and I'd be afraid to touch anything for fear of breaking it?

- Would I feel comfortable handing this module off to someone else after I made changes to it?

If no discussion comes about as a result of the review of this module, it may be an indication that it wasn't a very good module to select for review in the first place.

Disposition

Naturally, as the review is being performed, the results should be written down and included with the project binder. You may wish to include a status for the review, including such levels as "Outstanding," "Acceptable," "Acceptable with reservations," "Failed," and "Review not made." The date that the module is reviewed, and the date that the module passes the review (which could be two separate dates), are recorded in the project binder as well—because it's part of the project schedule.

The tricky part here is assigning reviews to be done—every module should go through a mechanical review as part of QA, but only a small percentage goes through the other types of reviews. Once a review is assigned and made part of the schedule, it's a lot more likely that the individuals involved will prepare for them, and that the reviews will get done.

Chapter 24
Bug Reporting
and Application Feedback

"I'm going to take a bath, Hobson."—Arthur
"I'll alert the media."—Hobson
  —Arthur

As I've mentioned before, as much fun as software development is, it's still encapsulated in the object of a business, and a good business wants to get feedback from its customers. Here's how to get feedback—all sorts of feedback—from the users of your application.

Once someone other than the original developer sees the application, defects are going to appear. More accurately, that first user is going to provide feedback. This feedback may identify a defect, but it may also be a question or an enhancement request. And it is possible that the user making the report can't necessarily make the distinction.

Ordinarily, a developer fixes the defects, answers the questions, offers to make the changes requested, and that's that. When I first decided that my company needed to track this feedback, I came face to face with four issues. First, when do you start tracking application feedback? Second, how do you categorize it? Third, what mechanism do you use? And fourth, what information do you track about each feedback incident?

The initial assumption: Do you want feedback?

First, let's talk about that initial assumption—that you want to formally track this feedback at all. Isn't it much easier to just deal with each communication from a user and be done with it? There are three distinct benefits to formally tracking each Application Feedback Incident (AFI).

First, you can provide better customer service. AFIs should be numbered and entered into a database (you've got a spare database laying around somewhere, don't you?). As a result, this feedback doesn't fall through the cracks. One of the steps in the tracking process is to provide resolution to the customer.

Second, you can improve your process. One of the attributes to be tracked for each defect is the type of defect and where it came from. From this, you can determine where your weak spots are, and thus, determine where you need to improve your development processes. The AFIs are a tool from which the developer can learn.

Third, you can help improve user acceptance of your system. Everyone has seen the "perfect" system that was rejected by the user community. Well, "user feedback" might not be about a bug. It may simply be a question or a request for a modification in disguise. It can raise a red flag that end users don't understand what the application is supposed to do. You (or your customer) can adapt end-user training and/or documentation to combat this and head off user rejection of the application.

Finally, as I said, user feedback might not be about a defect. It may simply be a question, or, better, it may be a well-disguised request for a modification or enhancement. If you heard the cash register echo in the background, yep, that's right—more business! You can think of user feedback as a very specific, narrowly focused version of market research. You can show a consumer all the pictures of a car you want, but until they get in and drive the car around the block a few times, they won't really know what they think of it. Same thing here—feedback from the user after the application was delivered can't be gotten any other way.

Bugs, defects—you say tomato...

I'm sure that you've already noticed that I'm using the term "defect" instead of "bug." There are a couple of reasons for this. First, it conveys a more accurate impression of what is being discussed. Manufactured parts don't have "bugs"—they have defects. And a defect is an instance of something that doesn't conform to the specification against which it was manufactured.

A "bug"—when you get right down to it—is really just a programming problem. A misspelled variable name, an improper calculation, an out-of-bounds array, or the use of the wrong function. A (programming) bug is the cause of a specific type of defect. Unfortunately, the use of the term "bug" has grown way out of proportion, to the point that many users tend to run out into the street screaming, "It's a bug! It's a bug!" as soon as they encounter something that doesn't behave just the way they wanted it to. It's hard to talk them down into understanding that it's not a "bug"—since the term "bug" has significant emotional connotations.

My business, in particular, is heavily tilted toward manufacturers, and they all understand the concept of a "defect" because they run into them in their own business as well.

Furthermore, being realistic, they also know that they have to send out their own product even when it's not defect-free—one unit may have a blemish on the paint job, another may be missing an eighth screw on the cover assembly, and yet another may have a gap between two doors that's a sixteenth of an inch too wide. But these aren't "show stoppers" because the product can be shipped and successfully used by the customer without problems.

In a similar vein, we need to help the user realize that software has defects as well, and that while some are critical and must be fixed, others aren't as important, and can be ignored, or at least rectified at a later date.

So I always use the term "defect" because it means something is not operating according to how it's specified. And this makes the rest of the job—both fixing as well as, possibly, charging for that work—easier.

When to start tracking feedback

Assuming you have a formal testing process (see the next couple of chapters), you should start tracking feedback as soon as modules go into internal testing. There are three reasons for this: The first is that you want to fix it, right? If you don't document each bug that your QA department finds, it's going to be really easy to lose track of them, and if you don't keep track of them, some will get lost—and they won't get fixed.

The second reason is that, based on what you "fix," you need to determine what testing needs to be redone in order to confirm that the "fix" lives up to its name. You don't want to go through the work to fix something only to find out that there was a deeper-seated problem causing the defect, and that the fix didn't really do the job, or, even worse, to introduce additional defects with the fix. If the fix is to correct a typo on a screen or the order in which items are displayed in a data control, then a simple visual inspection would be enough. But if you changed a calculation in a large invoicing routine, you may have extensive unit/integration/system retesting to do.

The final item has to do with the way you should be trying to improve your development process. "Quality Assurance" has to do with making sure that you're not sending junk out the back door. If you can improve the process you're using up front, you will end up producing fewer defects in the first place.

Thus, you want to track each defect and find out why it occurred. In the case of a programming bug, you want to find out who is putting bugs in the code, and why. Once you find out, you can not only fix the defect, but also take corrective steps to fix the source of the problem. Perhaps you'll provide better training, or develop better coding techniques to make a specific mechanism less fragile, or even learn to avoid certain types of interfaces, processes, or techniques that prove to be more fraught with peril than other types.

Gathering application feedback—the process

When someone encounters a defect in an application, I highly suggest that you require that person to fill out an Application Feedback Incident form and e-mail or fax it in. (I know of some companies that provide a reporting tool over the Web as well.)

Do not—DO NOT—take the report over the phone, or via an informal e-mail or face-to-face discussion. First of all, by making them write down the steps required, they're much more likely to discover that what they perceived as a defect was actually a mistake in their steps. Or, by repeating the steps so they can write them down, they might answer their own question. Or, they might even discover they can't repeat the purported "defect" and thus save you the time and aggravation of trying to reproduce it as well.

The reason for the long name of this form is that frequently the users are not sure what they are reporting. They may think that it's a defect when in actuality it's simply a question about a capability they are unsure of.

Perhaps it's really a request for a new feature or a twist on some existing functionality. They will phrase the request in terms of a defect ("The Framboozle report doesn't break out the prior year and current year values"). But when you review the "defect" report with them, and refer back to the Functional Spec, you can show them that the Framboozle report was never designed to break out the yearly values like they want. Of course, I'm sure that you'd be happy to write up a Change Order and modify the report so that it does so!

Other times, they'll interpret a native behavior in Windows as a defect—such as pressing the Enter key does not advance the cursor from one control to the next, depending on what type of control it is. Or they'll even report behavior that is specified in the Functional Specification as a defect because they're not that familiar with the system and didn't read the specification. For example, we had one customer who, against our advice, wanted the cursor to stay in the field even when it was filled in. However, some of their users reported that behavior as a defect—and when the customer saw the amount of feedback regarding this behavior, they recanted their position.

So, use one form to enter all types of feedback, instead of blanketing the users with a series of forms that they'll either lose or that will just confuse them. The AFI form has spaces for defects, for questions, and for enhancement requests. I'll discuss the contents of the actual form shortly.

Once you receive the application feedback form, your QA department will enter it into the database, and the internal process is started. The developer is notified of the receipt of an AFI form, investigates, produces a fix if necessary, and sends the fix off to QA. Once the fix passes, the fix is given to the customer, and the defect is closed. If the AFI is actually an enhancement request (and the customer wants a Change Order), the developer begins the Change Order process. (See Chapter 27, "Change Orders.")

Each week, QA produces reports for all bugs, questions, and enhancement requests that haven't been closed, and follows up with the developer as to their resolution. Whether the AFI is an actual defect or not, you should report back to the customer as to the proper resolution.

It may be tough to get your customers into the mindset of filling these forms out at first, but often they'll begin to enjoy the challenge of trying to break "your" code. As they become more familiar with the system and spend more time with it, their confidence in the system grows because the rigorous testing and reporting process helps them to realize how sound the system is. And, as an added benefit, the people who test become the "super users" of the system and make your support of the system easier down the road. For some of them, it's a chance to learn new skills, and if they become a system expert, it can enhance their position and standing within their organization.

You'll notice that I don't discuss the testing process itself—and you might be thinking that a well-defined testing process would help alleviate some of the issues raised when getting customers on board with respect to filling out the AFI. The reason I don't is that AFIs can be used at two times—both during formal testing by folks specifically tasked with testing, and during use of the system where issues will undoubtedly crop up. I'll cover testing in more detail in the next two chapters.

Categorizing feedback

I've briefly alluded to the fact that there are three types of feedback: defects, enhancement requests, and questions.

The first kind of feedback actually identifies a defect. Again, if I haven't beat on this enough, a defect is a behavior that doesn't perform as it's described in the specification. As the attachment to the Engagement Letter stated:

```
A defect is defined as an operation that does not perform as specified in the
written specifications and/or change notices, or an error that causes the
program to stop and display an error message that says, "An application error
has occurred." A defect must be reproducible at the developer's site. Non-
inclusion of options, behavior not specifically delineated in the written
specifications, and operating system and environmental problems are not
considered to be defects. If the problem can be resolved without changing
application code, if it is not reproducible upon demand, or if it occurs in a
module that has been accepted, and has been working for three months and has
not been changed, then it is not considered to be a defect. This does not mean
```

```
that Vendor will not resolve these issues; this means that Vendor will not
resolve them without charge.

There are a multitude of interface behavior, application performance and
general system characteristics for which it would be cost-prohibitive to
explicitly delineate. Vendor reserves the right to interpret these and other
issues that are not specifically described in a written specification as Vendor
sees fit.
```

The second type of feedback is an enhancement request. This is where they want something added to, changed in, or removed from the application. The AFI does not handle the entire change—it's simply a flag that indicates more work needs to be done. It initiates a Change Order form, which then has its own process, including a specification, a price, a delivery, acceptance, and so on.

The third type of feedback is simply a question. Sure, they could just call up and ask, but that's usually an unsatisfactory process. First, the person who can answer the question may not be available. Second, the question may require an answer more involved than what a simple phone call can provide—the developer may have to investigate something first, or find someone else for more information.

Third, the act of writing down the question often forces the user to think through what they're asking, and they can sometimes answer the question themselves. And, finally, having it written down and formally submitted means, again, it's not going to get lost. It's all too easy for the developer to talk on the phone for a few minutes and promise, "I'll get back to you on that." But, before they have a chance to do anything about it—including even writing it down on their To-do list—all hell breaks loose and it's suddenly forgotten about. Until, of course, the customer, now angry, calls two weeks later, wondering where the answer is.

The Application Feedback Incident form

Remember that your prime motivation should be to avoid getting defect reports at all, and while some of you may think that the best way is to write flawless code, I personally have found that technique to be too hard. Instead, you can just make the defect reporting process a real nuisance—and this starts with a long, intimidating name for what is otherwise known as "The Bug Report."

The header of the AFI has a place for today's date, the name of the customer, the system they're working on, and the personnel involved.

It also has a place for two tracking numbers. The top number is for your own tracking number—and you'll note that it's not pre-numbered, because customers will often just make a bunch of copies and distribute them to users. Even if you gave them pre-numbered forms, they'd lose them, run out of them and then use the backs of envelopes, and so on. Once a form hits your office, have the "Keeper of AFIs" number them while they're entering them into the database.

The Customer Tracking # is for them to keep track of the AFIs that they submit. They may want to track their own reports before submitting them, or otherwise use it for internal tracking. Your tracking number and theirs often don't coincide—while you'll have all of theirs, they won't always have all of yours, because your internal staff will likely be generating AFIs as well.

Of course, if you deploy this type of application electronically, such as on the Web, or even in a separate application you provide to your customers, you can populate the AFI # yourself each time they complete a new AFI.

The rest of the AFI form is dedicated to capturing specific information from them. The fundamental rule about user feedback is that "Users don't tell you what is going on when their software breaks." It's quite a challenge to get this feedback in a manner that is usable. In creating the layout and instructions for this form, we've adopted the format used by Microsoft in its public beta testing.

Type of AFI

First, have them identify whether this AFI is a defect, a question, or an ER. 'Nuf said? Not really. In my experience, I've found that anywhere between 25% and 50% of AFIs classified as "defects" by the customer are actually misunderstandings about the functionality of the system and/or ERs. So don't freak out the first time you implement this type of system and find, of 45 AFIs in your system, 32 of them are marked as "defects"—it may well not be as bad as that!

Is it reproducible?

Second, if it's a defect, ask if it's reproducible. Many times you'll find a user discovers that the problem they are having is not a bug, but that they forgot step five in a seven-step process. We had one customer who installed a new version of a program three times in a row on three different machines, and each time, encountered the same problem. We had provided step-by-step instructions on a single piece of paper—explicit enough that you could have given them to your 10-year-old to follow. They weren't all that happy about having to use the new version in the first place, and so when the install didn't work flawlessly, they got madder and madder with each new attempt.

We finally walked through these steps with them, on the phone, waiting for minutes each time he fumbled to insert a new floppy or for a file to copy, and lo and behold—when he got to step five, he grunts, "Huh. Never saw this step before." Needless to say, the installation went fine after that.

Of course, it's a rare AFI where the user will circle No in response to this question. They always circle Yes, even if they didn't try to reproduce it. Of course, this doesn't make the defect reproducible. What it does do is give you ammunition when you try to reproduce it and can't. Our position is that we should get paid for spending our time on dead-ends like anomalous behavior that can't be reproduced. When they tell you they can reproduce the behavior, but then can't, it's substantiation for charging for the time spent on that AFI.

What are the steps?

Next, if it is reproducible, describe the steps to reproduce the bug. This is the hardest part for the customer to fill out.

Unfortunately, a common example of "steps to reproduce" looks like so:

```
"Add some data with a number in it to the system."
```

An ideal response to this question is along the lines of:

```
1. Select File, Parts to bring the Parts form forward.
2. Press the Add button.
3. The cursor is in the First Name field.
4. Enter a name with some digits in it, such as "herman444".
5. Press the Tab key twice.
```

I've found that providing a couple of examples of "good" and "bad" sets of steps to your customers or users will help them create better reports for you.

What happens?

After the user has described what they did, ask them what the result of those steps was. It's amazing the number of times that the user will fill out the steps to reproduce and the last line will provide absolutely no useful clue about the results.

There are typically two similarly useless responses here.

The first that you'll often see is "And see what happens?" This is an unsatisfactory answer because the user is assuming that the same thing is going to happen on your system. But what if it doesn't? What if the behavior is environmentally related, or perhaps has to do with specific data they entered? (Why would they have entered a negative invoice number?)

The other reason this answer isn't acceptable is because while the results may be the same on both the user's system and your system, they may be the correct results, and the user doesn't understand this. So, in this case, simply saying, "See what happens?" would evoke a "Yeah, I see what happens. That's good—that's what's supposed to happen," from the developer or tester.

The second response is along the lines of "Then the system died." What do they mean by "died"—did the current form disappear and return them to the main menu, did the system lock up, did they get the blue screen of death, did the power go out or what? More information would be very helpful here as well.

What did you think was supposed to happen?

The fourth part of this form is "What did you expect to happen?" Occasionally, they will indicate that they expected something to happen which reveals that it is not a defect, but a misunderstanding of the way the system actually works. For instance, we received this AFI report once:

"Add a record without pressing 'Add' button. Record not added."

We were not particularly surprised at the result. The problem was that the user was in "live edit" mode, but thought that simply entering new data would add a new record instead of changing the current record. So while we still charted this as a defect, we marked it down as attributable to training.

Of course, when we received four more AFIs from this same user over the next month about this same issue, we realized that it wasn't a training error after all.

The more specific the user is about what they expected to have happen, the better off you're going to be when it comes time to hunt this one down. Even the most dutiful of users will miss a step now and then, but if they're explicit about the results, you'll still be able to read their mind.

What do you want us to do about it?

No, this isn't the smart-ass question it seems to be.

There are several different avenues of action available to you once you've received an AFI, depending on what type of AFI it is. If it's a defect report, they may want it fixed right away—particularly if it's a serious issue. However, if the application is a large one, and the defect is trivial, or if the application has been delivered to a large population, they may just be notifying you for repair in a future version.

If it's an ER, they may want you to submit a Change Order immediately, but they also might just want to put it in the queue for discussion for the next version's specification.

And, finally, they may just be providing information for you, but don't expect any action.

In any case, it's important for you to understand what the customer expects of you. If you're thinking, "Wow! That's a huge amount of work..." and that you'll get to it in the next release, but they're perceiving the defect as minor, you're going to have a problem resulting in "differing expectations" when they ask, "Why haven't you fixed this yet?"

Determining what to do can be a point of conflict, and how you handle this can have a substantial effect on customer satisfaction and confidence in the system—and the developer. Some give and take is often wise.

Other information

Finally, you'll want to get any other information you can. There's no telling what type of information you can dredge up with this question, and sometimes that's the one piece of the puzzle that will help you figure out what's going on. After all, getting a properly filled out AFI is just the first step in what could be a very complex puzzle.

The AFI database: What information do you track?

Obviously, you'll enter your AFIs into a database.

The complexity of your AFI database can vary greatly. Some people find it sufficient to enter them into a simple spreadsheet, just tracking a few items, such as the name of the customer and the system, the date the AFI was reported, a description of the AFI, and when it was handled. If one person is in charge of maintaining this entire system, you probably don't need much more than this.

However, with bigger systems, in companies with more than a couple of developers, and in order to be able to run the occasional statistical analysis, you'll need more information. Here are some suggestions—you can pick and choose as you desire.

- Who submitted the AFI. This could be an internal person or a customer.

- The type of AFI—defect, ER, or question—and, if defect, whether it was reproducible.

- The specific Module and Task within a Project. You may not be able to pinpoint every AFI to this extent. For example, a toolbar may exhibit undesirable behavior when focus is shifted from one form to another. Is that to be attached to the first form? The second form? Or the toolbar? At times, the user may not be able to identify which Module, depending on the behavior exhibited. This is particularly true for questions and ERs, since they may encompass a process, not a specific form or report.

- The initials of the person responsible for handling the AFI. In other words, the developer who is going to fix a defect, answer a question, or issue a Change Order for an enhancement request.

- The date the AFI was reported closed (fixed, answered, and so on), and when its closure was reported back to the customer. Also, in the case of a defect, the date and the initials of the QA person involved in signing off on the repair.

- The severity and priority for handling the AFI. In the surgical field, this is known as "triage." When there is more to do than can be done in a given amount of time, someone has to decide who gets taken care of first. Same thing here—which are the high priorities, and which can wait? You will probably have to work with the customer to assign these—since they can tell you what's most important to them, and you can tell them the tradeoffs, given your not unlimited resources.

- Who was responsible for the development of the Module or Task that ended up generating the AFI if it was a defect.

- One piece of data that we don't collect but that my technical editor does is determining where in the process a defect was introduced. Was it a missed requirement, poor design or improper coding, or something else altogether? This is actually done during reviews that are performed at each step in the process, and the purpose is to see how long it takes to find a defect and then to see whether they need to do something different earlier in a project to have better deliverables.

- Resolution. It's often handy to document, particularly for the customer, what the resolution of a specific issue was. Humans aren't perfect—they'll submit the same AFI more than once, they'll change their mind again and again, and they'll even withdraw AFIs that were submitted earlier. Standard responses, such as "Fixed," will be entered in specific date and "Fixed By Who" fields. You can document each of these resolutions most easily in a text field.

- Finally, as described earlier, you should define what testing needs to be re-executed in order to ensure that the fix is indeed a fix.

One tricky situation is when a customer puts multiple items on the same AFI. If they're all going to be handled as a group, you can simply enter one record in the database, but if different pieces will be handled separately, you may consider breaking up their AFI into multiple pieces, and assigning a separate AFI number of yours to each piece.

For example, if they find three typographic errors on the same screen, that can all be lumped under one AFI, but if they include a typo on a control's caption, data not being saved for that control, and a request for the field to be made bigger, those become three separate AFIs. The first is easy and trivial to fix, but at the same time, not critical, while the second is critical, and may or may not be easy to fix, and the third lies somewhere in between—easy to deal with, but may or may not be critical.

Categorizing defects

I think it makes sense for all but the smallest development shops to be very exacting about categorizing defects. Most people think that there are two kinds of bugs: those that the customer finds and those that they don't. You can get much more precise. As an example, here is how we categorize them.

Analysis

This means that you made a mistake in the analysis phase of the project. Examples of an analysis bug would be the situations where the way a customer process worked, or how they recorded data was misunderstood.

I've mentioned earlier about the application where I understood the term "part" to mean a component of the product that the customer was shipping, while they used the term to refer to a component of a machine that was used to make those products. We spent several weeks of iteration before realizing this—if we hadn't realized it at all, and had implemented a system based on our poor understanding of the term, we would have recorded it as a bug in analysis.

True, it's pretty hard to document something like this, but you need to have a mechanism in place. It may not be that important to track if you've only got one or two people in the shop doing the analysis, but once you have 38 analysts at the shop, you'll want to track these bugs just like any other.

Design

Two obvious examples of design bugs would be mistakes in data structure design and screwups in designing forms. A data structure design bug would be the incorrect normalization of a set of tables, the use of an overloaded table when it was inappropriate, or the use of data attributes as keys when the instances of that data weren't going to be unique. (Of course, if you didn't realize that the data wasn't going to be unique, that might be an analysis bug.)

An example of a bug in form design would be the creation of a form that required the user to hit four keys to save a record, and then three more keys to start the Add process for a new record—when the form in question is specifically a heads-down data entry tool.

Again, if you heard this in analysis and didn't design the form to be able to do so, then it's a design bug. If you didn't catch on to the customer's requirements, then it would have been an analysis bug. If a customer calls and asks you the same question four times, it could be a design bug. If they have to ask you incessantly, then there was probably a better way to have designed the interface or process that the user is asking about. But it could also be an end-user training bug—that you need to do a better job explaining something to a user, or perhaps find a different way altogether.

Coding

The third type of bug is a coding bug. We're all familiar with these. Syntax errors, mistakes in algorithms, incorrect usage of commands; a coding bug is defined as "We knew what to do (analysis and design were correct) but didn't properly create the code to do the function properly."

Environmental

This category flags a situation when the application runs fine on your system, and runs fine on their system, but when they add another machine to the network the app comes crashing down. Turns out they didn't configure memory properly, or the network card is conflicting with something, or they installed an old set of DLLs, or whatever. In any case, the bug is resolved either by changes to the environment, or by adding features to the code that make checks for the environment problem at hand. The key is that you didn't have to change your code, and, in fact, may not have had to do anything at all.

Installation

Installation issues are the fifth type of defect we track. These obviously only happen at one point during the cycle, but it's important to note them. This bug is flagged whenever an application runs fine at your site but somehow it's not installed to the point of proper operation at the customer's site. This could range from technical issues like bad drivers, lack of disk space, or bad media to human problems like forgetting the media when they visited the customer or overwriting files by mistake.

Training

This next type of bug is a bit of a gray area (perhaps not as gray if you're using computer-based training), but it's worth paying attention to anyway. If a customer has to ask a question about the application that they should have known after you were finished installing the system, then it gets marked down as a training bug. For example, a question like "Why don't I see all of the transactions in the list box?" indicates that we didn't do a good enough job documenting or explaining how the list box is populated. The reason that it's a gray area is that we might have documented it and felt that we did a good enough job, but sometimes users need a bit more clarification than we need.

The important issue here is to make sure that you're taking care of the customer's learning curve—the best application in the world isn't going to do any good if they don't know how to use it.

Data

The next category is my most favorite and least favorite at the same time. I lump these issues under the heading "Data." Suppose the user imports a file and suddenly every list box in the system has garbage in it. Or they turn the system on and are getting intermittently screwy results and a lot of processing errors. Perhaps the records in one table are missing most of their children. In each case, the error is not fixed by changing code, because there are problems associated with the actual data in the tables.

What might have happened? The import file was not in the correct format. Or the user went into the file manually and deleted all the fields with surrogate keys. Or it could just be that a "helpful" administrator from another department restored a backup and overwrote the lookup table with an old lookup table without the most current values.

On the one hand, "it's not our fault"—but on the other, these are issues that we should consider when enhancing the system and making it "idiot proof."

Irreproducible

Finally, the most famous category of them all: irreproducible. "It's just one of those things." This could be traced to a flaky network card, an errant video driver, or just plain magic. I know of one installation where the notebook of a certain executive would flake out and just die every once in a while. It turned out that his office backed onto the freight elevator, and every time he had his modem on and the elevator went by, some sort of interference crashed the system.

Reporting back to the customer

In any but the most trivial project, the list of AFIs you receive from a customer will be sizable enough that you won't be able to keep track of them in your head. And neither will your customer—so they're going to want a report of AFIs that they've submitted. Most likely, they're going to want several reports, or at least one report broken into multiple sections.

These sections are 1) outstanding AFIs (those that haven't been fixed), 2) AFIs that have been taken care of in the most recent build, and 3) all other AFIs. Depending on personalities and needs, the first section may be broken down further—organized by priority. Some AFIs (both defects as well as ERs) might be scheduled for a future version, while others may be serious enough to be scheduled to be handled in the next build.

We've found that we need two types of reports—those that are produced for the customer, and those that are produced for use internally.

The customer reports include our AFI number, the customer's AFI number, the date reported, the priority, the date fixed or dealt with, the description of the AFI, and the resolution of the AFI (if any).

The internal reports also include who's responsible for handling the AFI, the date that the AFI fix was reported back to the customer, and the module the AFI belongs to.

Where next?

Now that you have a mechanism to capture feedback from users, and a process to do so reliably, it's time to examine testing. But before I do so, I'd like to say one last thing about application feedback. Requiring users to fill out these forms and send them in has been a significant benefit to our operations. It enforces discipline on the part of the user, allows us to batch process defects instead of getting interrupted every few minutes with the odd phone call, allows us to charge for more of the odd time we spend with customers, and even reduces time as the users solve some of their own problems. Sure, it can be politically tricky to get users to do so, but if you introduce the requirement as part of the initial specification, it becomes a lot easier to train the users to do so regularly.

Chapter 25
Testing—Who Does It?

"Hey guys, we're going on a national bikini tour and we're looking for two oil boys who can grease us up before each competition."—Girl in bikini
"You are in luck! There's a town about three miles that way. I'm sure you'll find a couple of guys there."—Harry
  —Dumb and Dumber

It's often been said that the worst person to test an application is the programmer who wrote it. This isn't actually true—the worst person is that programmer's mother, because mothers never want to find fault with their son or daughter. But now that we've eliminated two people, there are still about 6 billion potential candidates remaining. In this chapter, I'll discuss the options you have at your disposal, the pros and cons of each, and then give you a third option that has worked well for me for years.

There are three reasons behind the truism stated in this chapter's introduction.

First, the programmer knows how computers work, and thus wouldn't try something illogical or out of sequence. Every programmer has had the experience of listening to a user describe a set of steps they followed, and shaking their head, thinking, "Why in the world would you do that?"

Second, the programmer's natural mind-set is to make something work—not to try to break it. And when it's their own baby they're testing, they're definitely predisposed toward being faint of heart when it comes to intentional demolition.

And, finally, despite their best intentions, the programmer has a vested interest (if only subconsciously) in not finding any bugs in the application.

Regardless of which is true, it's clear that someone other than the programmer should test the application. Or is it?

There are basically three sources of testing personnel:

- The programmer who developed the system (despite what I just said a few paragraphs ago)

- A dedicated testing staff

- A select group of end users

The purpose of this chapter is to discuss the pros and cons of each source of testing personnel. Before I get into that, however, let's define more fully what "testing" means in the context of this discussion.

What is testing?

For the purposes of this chapter, I'm assuming that these are desktop applications—either stand-alone, LAN-based, client/server, or Web-based systems. Testing process control systems, missile-guidance applications, and the like require a whole different level of sophistication and are way beyond the scope of this book.

During the development of desktop applications, testing takes various forms, and in most of them, testing isn't very sophisticated. There's a whole discussion on the proper forms of testing, how it should be structured, and why most desktop platform applications aren't tested this way. I'll discuss those details in the next chapter.

For now, let's just define the testing we're talking about as the last stage of application development where the application is tested to determine whether it works as defined in the Functional Specification.

Using the programmer as tester

There actually are mechanisms through which you can use a programmer as the first line of testing—that is, to test a module to ensure it works by itself before integrating it into the rest of the system. In some companies, the developer is given responsibility for unit testing, and then has the opportunity to fix problems found without the overhead of the company's formal defect-tracking system. As part of this process, defects are not counted, so the developer is spared the publicity of a visible record of boo-boos at that stage.

As a result, developers are much more interested in this first level of testing. They've found that if they find problems at this stage, they're still relatively easy to fix, and they have only limited administration and paperwork to deal with. For some developers, those benefits outweigh any negatives of having to do rigorous testing.

Advantages of using a dedicated testing staff

If the development team has a dedicated testing staff that runs through the final testing themselves, a number of advantages accrue.

First is the control—they can be more confident of getting the testing done. If they're responsible for the testing and also control the resources needed to do the testing, they can be assured that the testing will get done. If the customer is responsible for testing, it may or may not get done, depending on other demands on the customer's time.

Next, a dedicated testing staff will more likely know how to perform testing. Proper testing isn't as simple as placing a warm body in front of a keyboard and telling them to "play with it for a while." Just as with any quality control function, a technically oriented person has to lay out the proper procedures—something rarely done in the PC world to begin with. Then the QA staff must follow those procedures and document their work accordingly. Simply handing over an application "to see if they can break it" is likely the result if it's given to the customer.

A corollary to this is that a dedicated staff will also become increasingly skilled at testing. They'll learn the tips and tricks. They'll know the ins and outs. A dedicated testing staff will become more skilled at it than people who are thrown into the task for a one-time shot.

For example, given the dynamics of our industry, techniques that worked last week won't necessarily be sufficient or even applicable this week. If the staff continues to accumulate skills, they'll be able to pick the most appropriate testing methodologies. In other words, they'll be able to pick the best tool—the best testing methodology—for the job. This is something that the customer's testing team wouldn't be able to do.

And furthermore, a dedicated testing staff, used to working in tandem with the same programming team, develops specialized knowledge of the way the programming team works—their styles and attendant flaws. This leverages the knowledge of testing procedures in general and makes the skilled testing group incrementally more valuable.

A dedicated testing team will also acquire special tools and resources, in addition to the growing level of skill. A customer isn't ordinarily going to acquire specialized software tools for a one-time use, while a dedicated team may find them a valuable investment, both for their own productivity as well as turning out higher quality work.

And as they learn how to use them, subsequent uses will be less expensive than if the one-time user were to ambitiously undertake the same effort. Other resources, such as a range of test beds of data, specialized machines that allow testing in a variety of environments, and so on, are also more likely to be available to a dedicated testing staff than to the customer's user.

The last advantage is that the programming team can be assured that the testing was done properly and completely. When the testing team works "for" the programming team, the programmers can confirm and audit that the testing was performed as it was supposed to be. However, whether the user of the application is an actual customer of an outside firm, or simply another department in the same company, there is a line that the programming team can't cross. Thus, the programming team can only go so far to verify that the testing is complete. Given the multitude of pressures due to their regular job, testing personnel from the user side often run into problems completing the testing as it should be, despite the best of intentions.

Disadvantages of a full-time testing staff

There are some downsides, of course, to having a full-time testing staff. First of all, just like any other employee, they're subject to doing substandard work, leaving in the middle of a project, and 100 other things that you've undoubtedly seen yourself. But these things aren't reasons in and of themselves to avoid a full-time testing staff.

A second disadvantage is that they are often expensive. It's not as easy to invoice a customer for "testing"—the perception is that testing is part of the project, and thus should be "included" or, worse, "free." But at the same time, it's hard to itemize the 34 hours of testing on a couple of modules as "programming." If you've gone the fixed price route, then testing needs to be factored in. This additional factor adds complexity, and thus, uncertainty, to the mix.

A third disadvantage, and one that I find most compelling, is that it's simply difficult to find and retain talented testing personnel. By its nature, testing is repetitive work and can become boring quickly. At the same time, it's still "processor intensive"—meaning that testing personnel have to be bright and motivated—qualities that are at odds with repetitive, boring work.

One solution—to use testing as a training ground for potential programmers or other technical staff—sounds ideal, but often those people can find full-time development jobs at other firms without having to go through "an apprenticeship."

So while there are a number of advantages to having a full-time staff, it's not without its downsides either.

The advantages of having the users do the final acceptance testing

While the possession of a full-time testing staff may present a compelling argument, there are variations to consider. Let's look at the advantages of the customer becoming involved as the primary testing resource at the end. First, though, you must understand that the crux of this argument is based on the assumption that the customer should, and is going to, provide daily and ongoing support for the application.

Why make that assumption? Just as a manufacturing company would hire a contractor to build an addition, but use their own maintenance people for tasks like moving office partitions, a user department would likely contract out—either to an internal MIS staff or an outside vendor—for a large custom software development project. But they wouldn't want to rely on that staff for daily support of the application such as adding users, changing vendor code numbers, or instructions on how to run the monthly posting transactions in two parts.

As a result, it's important for the users to fully understand how to use the application and what's behind it. Then, when business conditions change, they can take full advantage of all of the flexibility in the application, instead of having to assume nothing works the minute that the environment changes.

This understanding can be communicated via training, but it's a long and expensive process, and is generally not very effective. Due to a variety of constraints—such as scheduling people together at the same time—training on a large, complex system is often done in a few full-day sessions. This is often not enough time to cover a system thoroughly enough, and people come away with only a cursory understanding of the functionality. Furthermore, full-day training takes its toll on people, and absorption rates can be surprisingly low by the end of a week like this.

The alternative, then, is to have the users who will be working with the system become involved in the testing. By doing so, they'll be able to spend more time with the system— perhaps by spending a couple of hours a day over several weeks or months, instead of a week-long crash course. Thus, they learn exactly what the system was intended to do, and they become expert in running the system through all its paces.

Another advantage to the users doing the final testing is a lower dollar cost. Generally speaking, staff at the user's site will be less expensive on a dollar-per-hour basis than the corresponding technical staff on the programming team's side. Technical talent on the programming team, be it from the MIS department or from an outside firm, will continue to become more and more expensive over the next few years.

Meanwhile, their existing staff is already paid for in the daily operations budget, so it "appears" to be free. After all, those people have already been scheduled to be doing some work on this project. And even sophisticated customers still balk at spending many tens of thousands of dollars for the "Testing" line item for a custom software application.

The disadvantages of having the users do the final acceptance testing

By now, the disadvantages of having the users perform the bulk of the testing should be fairly obvious. Are they going to do it? Can they do it well? Will they do it on time? How can the developers depend on the testing being done properly?

Users have other jobs, and because of this, are prone to being less than reliable in terms of getting the job done correctly and on time, if at all.

The answer to this dilemma—the third horn?

And what a dilemma it is. In addition to describing how the developer can participate in the initial testing, I've laid out several solid reasons for having a dedicated testing staff on the programmer's team do the testing, but there is a compelling argument for using end users as well. What's the answer?

It may seem as if you're impaled on one horn or the other of a charging bull. The one thing you can't do is ignore testing altogether. But there is a third choice.

The answer is to have bright high school or college students do a lot of the grunt work of testing. One of the smartest things I ever did, next to proposing to my wife, was to hire part-time high school and college kids to do testing for me. At the time, I was working out of my house but was still delivering applications that were big enough that I needed to have them tested.

I lived in a suburban kind of environment, so it was easy to find kids in my community to come over to my house and help. I went to the local high school and explained to the calculus teacher that I was looking for some kids who were pretty bright, had a good work ethic, and wanted to do some part-time work that would be more stimulating than cutting lawns, flipping burgers, or baby-sitting. And to my advantage, I would have some useful resources available for several years that might also be interested in short-term assignments—vacations and holidays—and would feel particularly flattered when I called.

This was something the calculus teacher had never heard before and she got pretty excited about it. She gave me a list of four or five names, and I ended up with several good candidates who were able to come in afternoons, evenings, or weekends during the school year. In summer, they could work during the days as well.

These were very bright high school kids who had been accepted to very good colleges and were motivated to do a good job because this job was a lot cooler than what their friends were doing. I also tried to provide a good work environment—flexible hours, casual dress code, and so on—and treated them with respect instead of as if they were 12 years old. In retrospect, I think what I did was just spoil them. Once they got out of school, they had to find real jobs, and they're starting to realize that they will be living in Dilbertland for the rest of their lives.

Another benefit to them was the fact that they were actually doing something important—that the results of their work were going to impact the people at another company—my customers. Some of their friends were sweeping the floor at Pizza Heaven—if they quit, so what? Another kid would be plugged into the job in about five minutes. With this job, they could actually see the effect they were having.

On the other hand, these were high school students. They may or may not have had experience with computers, and they definitely didn't have more than a passing look with the tools I was using, relational database structures, or custom database applications.

They needed training. The first thing I did was to make sure they were comfortable with DOS, Windows, and all the usual things with a computer that you and I can take for granted. I always had some type of "grunt work" around, and so I'd have each new kid just crank out some of that for a couple of weeks, getting familiar with everything. There was a second reason for this work as well.

You know how when you're performing some task and suddenly you get this feeling that "something's not right"? You can't quite put your finger on it, but you just have this gut feeling that something wrong has happened. This simply comes from experience. When you're testing, you need to have some sense of a gut feel that something doesn't feel right. I wanted the kids to get comfortable enough that they would develop some sense of how the development environment operated.

I've used this technique now for about six years, and continue to be pleased with it. Moving into an office that's some distance away from the community has caused some problems with commuting, but not as many as I had feared—several of the students were able to drive themselves or catch rides with friends or parents. Weekends were less of a problem—they would have had to drive to another job anyway.

Furthermore, as students have gotten more sophisticated, it's become more and more likely that they'll have a computer at home where they can do some, if not all of their testing—and with the Internet, communication via e-mail and Web sites has made this vehicle quite workable.

Depending on your relationship with a specific customer, you may be able to suggest that they use this trick instead of carrying the burden yourself—they might dedicate a summer intern or other part-time person to concentrate on it. In fact, this could well be a great position for someone getting back into the commercial workforce—folks who stayed at home with their kids for a while, military personnel who have finished their term of service, or even people released from prison and looking to get back into the real world.

Putting the pieces together

Now let's look at how these elements fit together.

Obviously, your particular business environment and the way you develop custom applications will dictate, in large part, which of these factors are most important. That will, in turn, drive your decision on how to structure your testing and which resources to use.

I think the optimal solution is a combination of all three. The best application of your limited resources—and technical talent is just that—is toward the design and programming of systems. Bring in high school and college students to do some of the functional testing, and then partner with the appropriate customers who can and are willing to join in at the final stage to do the functional testing.

And have someone on staff whose primary responsibility is testing. You could even think of that person as being the QA department—for the most part, testing, but with other responsibilities as well. These other responsibilities could involve the monitoring and handling of your processes. Once development stretches past a few people, the number of forms and mechanisms to track grows. Engagement Letters, Customer Setup Forms, Functional Specs, AFIs, Change Orders—it's starting to feel like "paperwork city." But every manufacturing facility runs on paperwork—potential orders, specifications, requisitions, Change Orders, QA results, and so on. If this paperwork (or the electronic equivalent) is missing, you can't get things through the system. Verbal communication simply does not work. This QA person makes sure that this process is running smoothly—in effect, performing QA on a macro scale as well as with the details of a specific app.

Including the customer in the functional testing doesn't mean that the programming team just disappears upon shipment of a late-beta CD. Their role during this phase of final testing becomes that of "training mentor" and "technology transfer guide."

As training mentors, the programming team is still responsible for developing test plans and instructing the customer's testing staff on how to test properly.

In the technology transfer role, they're responsible for training the testing staff as to the functionality designed and implemented. As detailed as a Functional Specification is, it never seems to cover every imaginable scenario. The programming team is also responsible for training the customer's staff about the internal technical details of the application.

This division of responsibilities allows you to take best advantage of what you do best, and allows you to provide the customer with a more complete solution—not just a pile of CDs and a manual, but a staff that understands the application and has taken ownership of it.

Chapter 26
The Process of Testing

"I just fixed that!"—Harrison Ford
—Star Wars Episodes IV, V, and VI

So now that you're done with the previous chapter, "Testing—Who Does It?" you've got some testing folks lined up and ready to "have at" your app. But what does their job description entail? What does their day-to-day work look like? This chapter will open the door to the QA department.

There are four discrete phases to testing, and in all but the rarest of environments, most of the steps get ignored. As a result, it doesn't make a lot of sense to spend pages and pages covering processes that you're likely not going to do. I'll address each one; showing you where they fit in the grander scheme, but concentrate on those that are more likely to be addressed in the day-to-day life of your shop.

The five phases of testing

While every development shop has its breakdown of the testing process, the phases can generally be grouped into five categories.

Unit testing

The first phase is "unit testing." This is where the functionality of an individual task or module is compared against the specification.

Step 1: Push all the buttons

Yes, this sounds really stupid, but how many times have you gone to a customer and said, "Oh, and by the way, if you click on this... oh no! I thought that was working!" We've all done it. This is QA's first responsibility—to make sure that every one of those buttons does something.

QA first creates a list of every menu and submenu option, and verifies that each one either operates as expected, or has been, at the current time, stubbed out because that task hasn't yet been finished.

Then, QA creates a list of every object on a screen, and checks off each object as it's tested. All the buttons are pushed, all the check boxes are checked, and data is entered into each of the fields. Tab order is another item that is checked in this phase—when you tab through the screen, does the focus shift appropriately?—and, do all the keyboard shortcuts work?

Step 2: Test the functionality

The second step is to verify that the basic functionality of each object is in place. When they press the Add button, enter data into every field, and then press Save, is the record actually added? Does all the data get added? Did the entire entry in each field get saved, or did the last five characters in the invoice number get chopped off? This is why QA has to be comfortable with the underlying tool—they need be able to verify what is happening in the application down to the raw table level.

In a practical sense, steps 1 and 2 are usually performed together, but these make up two separate columns in the checklist.

Step 3: Test the rules

There are three general types of rules in an application—those attached to a field, those attached to a screen, and application-wide rules. In all three cases, these rules have to be identified and then those rules have to be tested.

Identifying those rules is easy; they're in the Functional Specification! Yet another advantage to writing the spec out beforehand, no? However, simply having a list of rules isn't enough. The real work here falls on the shoulders of the QA staff, since they're the ones who have to write up a detailed test plan that will verify those rules. Ideally, the test plan is also in the spec, but in the real world, the test plan is usually glossed over during specification development.

Once QA writes the test plan, they'll pass the test plan by the developer to make sure it's robust and fairly covers the functionality. QA and the developer may work together to put together a case chart to handle all of the possible options within a program and provide test data or require a test plan to handle these cases. Finally, QA will execute it. As QA tests each option, they should be able to check off which options were tested and what the result was.

Step 4: Break it!

As developers, we know our application works. Right? We don't need anybody to prove to us that it works—we've run the application after writing the code and we've seen that it works. Of course, we've only seen that it works one time—why would we waste our time trying it more than once?

Up to this point, QA has simply been verifying functionality—much like an inspector would verify that all the items on the packing list are indeed in the box. But the ultimate mission of QA is not to prove that the application will work—their mission is to break the application.

So the final step in the testing process is to repeat the first three steps, but this time, pulling out all the stops to be devious, conniving, and downright evil in trying to find ways to break the application. The greatest fear of a testing person is that there's a bug in the system that they didn't find.

System testing

This phase is defined as "do all the pieces work together," and the level of detail and amount of effort will be proportional to "how many pieces" you've got. Just as with unit testing, you have to have a definition of what the app is supposed to do and how it's going to work. In this case—what are the pieces in the game, and what are the rules and expectations of how the pieces are supposed to interact?

Integration testing

Does the app work in the production environment? I know of shops that actually set up test environments that mimic the production environment of the customer, and do a separate round of system testing in that environment. As you can imagine, I think this is quite a luxury, both in terms of having the resources to do so, and the time (and money) to do yet another round of testing. After all, someone is paying for the testing, and, ultimately, it's the customer.

However, no matter how much you try, it's going to be nearly impossible to precisely duplicate the customer's environment. As an example, witness the fragility of Windows after a decade of use all over the world. Optimally, your application will have to have some bodacious exception handling for unexpected environmental conditions and situations—and I mean something better than the "Blue Screen of Hieroglyphics and Death" that every Windows NT user has seen.

Acceptance testing

This is where the customer checks over what you've delivered, and pronounces it fit. This maps directly to the inspection department in a factory, where boxes from the receiving dock are opened and the parts are examined to make sure they meet the standards of the customer.

It's a rare customer who will actually perform full-blown acceptance testing; even rarer is the customer who, after doing a poor job of acceptance testing, will not complain about finding defects in the application.

You can help this situation to an extent by providing test scripts—even your own test plans, if you like—for your customer to use for their acceptance testing. If they feel that a lot of their work has been done for them, they may be more inclined to pitch in and do their part.

Be aware that if your users still don't use the materials you've given them, you'll have to run through them yourselves—you'll suffer in the end, regardless of "whose fault" it was that testing wasn't done.

If you don't have a model office as described in the "Integration testing" section, another option you might consider for user acceptance testing is a test environment at a customer's site. You have to be careful to isolate it enough so it can't impact their actual production, but not too much so you don't get a reasonable test.

Regression testing

Regression testing refers to the practice of testing an application after a change was made to the application to make sure that the change (or fix) didn't break anything else.

There is no magic formula, no silver bullet, for performing regression testing for the type of applications this book is covering. There are some automated test tools that perform some of the mundane testing—and they can prove very handy precisely in this situation. However, as I've already discussed, there are limits to these tools, and so the burden is still on the QA department to ensure that nothing has been broken.

Adherence to a couple of techniques can help to some extent. Modularizing your code so that there are distinct boundaries between functions is one useful procedure; using common routines and libraries as often as possible is another.

Doug Hennig of Stonefield Systems uses a detailed change log that documents every change made to an application in order to aid in hunting down the problems caused by changes to code. While this doesn't solve the problem up front, it makes a great deal of difference in tracking the problem down and determining where else the bug might manifest itself.

But the bottom line is that we, as software developers at the turn of the millennium, are still hobbled by Stone Age tools and techniques to handle regression testing in an accurate, timely, and cost-efficient manner.

Other issues

Weighting the time spent on each phase

The weight you put on each phase may differ, according to the skills and personalities of the developers in your shop.

For example, I've found that my programs generally need a lot of unit testing because I'm simply not as detailed-oriented a programmer as others are. However, once each task or module has been verified, system and integration testing go fairly smoothly, because I've got a good eye for the big picture, and can keep a lot of details in my head at once. One of my developers, however, is the exact opposite. He's a far better "nuts and bolts" programmer than I'll ever be—his defect rate per Action Point is considerably lower than mine. However, he's not as interested in the "big picture" and as a result, his attention to detail between interfaces of modules suffers.

Your mileage may vary. The important thing is to understand where your developers stand and what you need to concentrate on.

Regarding diminishing returns

Testing is the most difficult of activities, because you're never done. Unlike programmers, who can, at some point, identify when they have finished writing code that fulfills all of the requirements spelled out in the Functional Specification, testers can never be sure that they have found all of the defects. As a result, the testing process becomes an exercise in dealing with diminishing returns: If you find 100 defects during the first week of testing, 50 defects during the second week, 10 during the third week, and then two during each of the next three weeks, how many more weeks do you want to continue to test?

This is your call, and the decision has to do with the quality requirements of the application. As I discussed before, quality is a relative term, depending on the use of the application. An application that measures the GNP of the country probably doesn't have to be tested very thoroughly, since the politicians are going to screw with the results anyway. On the other hand, an application that tracks retrofit schedules of heart monitoring equipment needs to be considerably better, since errors have a potentially more catastrophic effect.

Techniques to make testing easier

Two very frustrating situations that occur during the testing process are 1) testing something that just worked a minute ago but doesn't any longer, and 2) having to restore the environment because the application blew up and took every special setting and switch with it. Here are some techniques that can help out with these problems.

Original data

One of the most common reasons that a routine works at 11:46 but not at 11:47 is that the data that was entered in the last test is causing problems. Either the data was bad, it got corrupted, it was incomplete, or it wiped out something else that shouldn't have been wiped out.

One of the two fundamental rules we've had for all of our application development was to create a clean set of original test data so that you have an accurate and measured baseline from which to start. Each time you are ready to run a test, you can refresh the data from the original test data environment (which might be a directory for some applications and a whole discrete database for others) into the current test environment and run off that clean set of test data.

If you are testing a long process, you may want to create several data sets that represent different points in the process or for different parts of the system. If you have a long process, and a problem is cropping up in step 7, it is time-consuming and laborious to wade through steps 1-6 before finally getting a chance to examine what's happening in step 7. Again, keep the iteration time shorter than your attention span. If you provide a set of "good data" that can be plugged in to simulate the completion of step 6, then you can test step 7 much more efficiently.

The cardinal rule for original test data: Make it clean, robust, and keep it in a location that can be accessed easily so that the scripts to refresh the working test data can run unimpeded.

Original environment

You also have to be able to restore the environment back to its original state. Even if you try your best to clean up the environment and keep things orderly during the execution of your application, a failure of the system will take the environment with it. For example, suppose your application always runs with the flag for exact comparisons set OFF. However, during one specific point in a routine, you need to have the flag set to ON, so at the beginning of the routine, you do so. At the conclusion of the routine, you set the flag back OFF.

But, somewhere in the middle of that routine, the system crashes. If you don't reset the flag, and simply run the application again, any comparison that was relying on the exact comparison to be off will now fail—and possibly send you down a blind alley for hours until you realize what happened.

Create a quick general-purpose tool that will automatically reset your development environment back to where it came from so that you're always starting with the same baseline, just as you did with a clean set of test data.

Testing tools

There are a number of other techniques that can come in very handy during testing in order to track down problems. Here are some of the tools you should consider using.

Track users

Even if you are creating a single-user system, include a routine that automatically tracks the user who is on the system. Often times, there will be more than one person using the system, and providing them each with their separate login allows you to determine who was using the system when problems occurred.

Track activities

Create a function at the start of every routine that logs the name of the user and the date and time that they called the routine. The table that this information is placed in is relatively small compared to the rest of the application, and you can clean it out at any time. (The file should be created on the fly if it's missing, so you can simply delete the file if you desire.)

Knowing who was in a routine (and when) provides valuable information when trying to track down particularly thorny or infrequent bugs. You will also find it useful when a customer claims they've been using a certain module or routine "for a long time," and that it "suddenly" broke. The contents of this log will tell you whether or not they're being straightforward with you.

Track errors

It's still amazing to me that people write applications that don't log errors to a file that can be picked up and investigated later, but I see it all the time. You should keep a very detailed error log that captures everything you consider valuable. For instance, you should capture the error message, the line of code that causes the error, the call stack of programs that led to the error, any parameters that were passed, the name of the user and the time stamp, and a host of environment information, including files open, libraries loaded, all memory variables, the current state of the environment, and so on. It's a very rare error whose cause won't just jump out at you when you have this information at hand.

Some developers grab a screen shot at the time an error occurs. They take a snapshot of the screen at a particular instance and store it to a file, and so can see what the user is seeing at the time of the error. The only difficulty is that these screen shots are pretty big—several hundred kilobytes—and an error that occurred numerous times could chew up disk space quickly.

Audit trail

Track the user and the date/time that a record was last changed, and, if you have the space, log this same information for when the record was added. Yes, this information takes another 30-40 bytes per record, but it is invaluable to being able to save to do detective work on what is happening later on.

A more involved version of an audit trail feature tracks every change to any field. While this log can get awfully large awfully quick, it can be useful to be able to turn this on and off on demand, in order to isolate a specific problem.

Error log access

Another tool you should have available is a one-step tool to access the error log because, unfortunately, you're probably going to look at it an awful lot. You could place this on your Developer menu so that you can access it at a customer site if you've logged into the app using your "super duper secret developer password."

You might not want to call this file an "error log" because it tends to unnecessarily worry some users. "What? You've got errors? What kind of hacks are you??"

Instead, use a name like "activity log" and explain to the customer that this file is used to store any kind of activity that you're not expecting. These could be errors, unexplained problems, data problems that shouldn't have happened—just anything out of the ordinary. They are free to send the activity log to us at any time. You should follow the same technique as with the activity log and allow the user to delete it completely—the next time an error occurs, the file is created if it didn't already exist.

Debugging tools menu

If you haven't already, set up a series of developer tools on a menu pad that is only available to the developer. These tools should allow you to suspend program execution, or cancel the program outright so that you can halt and investigate the environment at any time. Make sure all of your debugging facilities are available and ready to be enabled whenever you need them. These will differ according to what development tool you're using, but take full advantage of those as you can.

Chapter 27
Change Orders

"This is a fascinating little gadget. It's going to replace CDs soon. Guess I'm going to have to buy The White Album again."—K
—Men in Black

"Useful applications are dynamic." Those are code words for the reality that you are going to be asked to make changes to an application. Just as the original application had a detailed specification and costing process, so do changes to that application. You've already told your customer, in general terms, how Change Orders are handled; here are the details of what the Change Order process looks like.

If you've been following along, you've now gone to great lengths to document how an application is going to function. This has to be done for a number of reasons:

- To determine the cost.

- To determine how to test it.

- To provide user help.

- To determine whether a reported behavior is a defect or "by design," and thus, perhaps fodder for an enhancement request.

This work is relatively useless if the documentation process stops here. Once the Functional Specification has been accepted, there must be a mechanism to handle further changes to the system—whether those changes come from the discovery of additional requirements or simply from the user being wishy-washy.

Again, I come back to manufacturing as the model for software development. It's not uncommon for a part, a component, or an assembly to need modifications after it's been designed, prototyped, or even cast. In order to handle these change requests, manufacturing firms use a system of "Change Orders" (some call them ECOs—Engineering Change Orders) that document the request, much like the original blueprint.

This documentation includes the change itself, the cost and the ramifications, and is just as useful in our world, and, in fact, might be more useful. The ethereal nature of software development lends itself to misunderstandings between the user and the developer— seemingly simple changes that are verbally communicated can cause huge problems later on. A formal method to document even the most trivial of changes will pay dividends by the end of the project.

The need for Change Orders

We have gone through great pains to convince the user of the need for a formal specification—but, due to Murphy's Law, the user will call you up the day after the specs were signed off on, and ask for "just one simple change."

There are several things that could happen. Most often, all of them happen.

The first scenario that could unfold is that the change is simple. You agree to add it in, and do so. Months later, someone else asks why the system doesn't meet the specification—this one particular operation is different from what is described in the spec, and so, could you please change it so it meets the spec? For free, of course!

This second request to reverse the change could cause a problem because the original change was actually needed and the person making the second request didn't understand it. Changing back to the original specification will, in essence, "break" the system, and that will certainly come back to haunt you.

On the other hand, suppose that the original change wasn't needed. You heed the second request, and change the operation back to the way it had been originally. You've just performed the software equivalent of moving the couch from under the windows to in front of the fireplace, and then back to under the windows, just because the homeowner can't make up his mind. Both of these situations will cost you money (and aggravation).

The second thing that could happen is, now that the user has seen how nice you were to accommodate that change, they ask for a second "very tiny change." And then a third, and a fourth. Suddenly you're looking at your fifteenth request, and this last one is a big one. However, the user has seen 14 changes made without a fuss—or an invoice for the work. How do you explain that this one will cost them $1,000? Where do you draw the line? It's a rare developer who doesn't get caught in this trap sooner or later.

The third thing that could happen is that the change turns out not to be "that simple" after all. However, since you've agreed to "just throw it in" for free, you're committed to more work than you're comfortable with. Either you'll do it right, spending a lot of time, or you'll try to compromise with a quick fix, and end up shortchanging either the customer or yourself.

You can respond two ways to this state of affairs. Either you can get bugged about it and try to resist as much as possible, or you can accept that changes from the user are a part of nature.

Clearly, the latter is preferable. "Useful applications are dynamic," after all. So now that you have accepted the fact that they're going to ask for changes after the spec has been signed off on, you can get ready for them. Since the process is predicated on having things written down and documented, requests for changes are going to be documented in just as much detail as the original spec.

You must write out a Change Order for two reasons:

- Inevitably, the Change Order is going to have a cost associated with it. Even if any given Change Order doesn't cost the customer, it's best to write the Change Order up, and simply mark "No Charge." This both provides documentation of the change, and generates good will as the customer sees "pro bono" work being done for them.

- You need documentation that describes how the system is supposed to function. The Change Order acts as an addendum to the specification, and can be folded into online

Help at the appropriate time. (There's actually more to it than this, but this is the basic idea.)

The Change Order process

First, the customer contacts the developer, requesting a change. They typically do this verbally, but occasionally something will arrive in writing. You should accept their written Change Orders in the same manner that you would accept their written specs—use their information as a starting point to create your formal Change Order.

 Second, write up a Change Order, including description, test plan, ramifications, and cost. A sample Change Order form is included in the downloads. The Change Order is also entered in the project tracking system, as a new module, but with the flag "Accepted" turned off and the "Date Accepted" field left blank.

The written Change Order is sent to the customer, who then has to either accept or reject the Change Order, much as they would accept or reject the proposed Functional Specification.

If the Change Order is accepted, the Accepted flag is turned on, and in either case, the Date Accepted field is filled in. If the Accepted flag is turned off and the Date Accepted field is filled in, you know the Change Order was rejected.

Change Orders are often made in a rush mode, and we've often had customers call to ask about the progress of Change Orders while they've still got the original (and unsigned) copy on their desk. Make it clear that you will not begin work on a Change Order without a signed Change Order form—and don't accept verbal approvals, period. In this day of omnipresent e-mail, it should be no big deal to follow up on a Change Order with an e-mail, and you could even use a standard "signature" type e-mail that indicates acceptance—these e-mails can go in your project binder just like an original signed copy. There could still be a situation where you may have to accept a verbal approval, such as when your customer is calling from the airport just before being gone for a week. In that case, you need to make an annotation on your Change Order indicating that it was verbally approved on such and such a date, and who it was approved by, and you should still follow up in writing later.

In 95% of the situations, a verbal approval will work out fine, but it's the other 5% that make all this paperwork a necessity in the first place.

Generally, I've found that we don't have a problem with requiring a signed Change Order, but in the event that a developer is getting pressure from a customer to start work before the paperwork has begun, we've adopted the stance that the developer has the right to paint me as the bad guy: "Gee, I'd love to, but my boss won't let me."

It gets the developer out of a potentially sticky situation, and if the situation escalates, I'm more than happy to step in and take a firmer line with the customer. This helps the developer allow the customer to potentially save face.

You should charge for the "design" of the Change Order, just as you charged for the development of the original spec. Hopefully, they have asked for several changes at the same time so that you can do them all together; it's more efficient for you and thus less expensive for them. But you should always charge—they are asking you to do analysis and design, and that's intellectual work, just as the initial specification development was.

If you have a Czar (or Czarina) of Change Orders, it makes life a lot easier. Initially, I intended to have my administrative assistant help out with monitoring some of those processes. Unfortunately, she was so good at doing so many other things that monitoring the processes items tended to fall through the cracks.

I eventually decided that we would merge the monitoring of our processes in with our Quality Assurance group and have them handle all of the tracking processes. Other companies turn the Change Order monitoring over to the person responsible for the project schedule, since Change Orders can impact the project schedule and resource assignments.

Since Change Orders initially show up in our system as an ER, they get tracked in the AFI report that the customer gets. You may decide to include Change Orders as part of your project status report where you communicate progress on each module against the plan.

Yes, it is possible for things to slip through the cracks. If you're concerned about this, you can put together a set of "exception" reports that will call your attention to anything that is out of the ordinary. Furthermore, even if something does slip through—it's another example of the case of diminishing returns—it's still a lot less likely to do so now than it was before. Maybe your process is now only 95% fail safe, but considering the previous method you had in place was 0% fail safe, you've achieved a tremendous improvement.

Pieces of a Change Order

First, describe what the reason for the Change Order is. Just as you initially documented the "pain" that the application would ease, you need to describe why they are going to spend money (and time and other resources) on a Change Order.

Next, describe the change as the user sees it. The user doesn't really care what we're going to do inside, but they are interested in the change in functionality—much like with the Functional Specification. They are going to see an extra button on the screen, a new screen, a report that prints five times faster, or that the subtotals calculate differently.

The third part of the Change Order is a description, somewhat technical, of what the developer has to do. Since the developer has already spent time investigating the requirements of the change, they probably have done some brainwork in terms of what they will have to do if the customer accepts the Change Order. Do I have to add a field to a table? Do I have to change the indexes? Do I have to add an object to a screen? Do I have to change these rules? The developer will eventually go through this work to perform the change; you might as well document it now and save the developer work later on. We've also found that, in many cases, the customer can review this part and offer input. They may not be able to create this section, but often they can spot missing pieces.

The fourth part of the Change Order is ramifications. For example, you might need to explain that "This change is going to require an additional 4 GB of storage space" or "The entire application will have to be shut down while the database is converted to the new structure." The customer needs to understand what impact the change is going to have on their existing system.

The fifth part of the Change Order is the test plan. This is a To-do list for the QA folks, just like in the Functional Specification.

And the final part of the Change Order is the cost—how much, and how it's going to be determined—either via time and materials or fixed price. If the change is concentrated and large enough, you can often use the same Action Point Counting methodology that you used for the original specification. Remember, the purpose of Action Point Counting is not to determine the cost to the nearest nickel, but to make sure you don't forget a large piece, and end up eating part of the work.

If the change isn't large enough, I've found simply estimating high and providing a fixed price is pretty workable. If you think, after examining the Change Order, that it's going to run an hour or an hour and a half, set a fixed price for two and a half hours of time, and let it go at that. You may feel more comfortable providing an estimate and charging time and materials.

If you use Action Point Counting, you can choose whether or not to use fixed price or time and materials for presenting the price to your customer; if you don't, you will need to use time and materials.

The end of the Change Order also includes a place for the customer to sign off or decline so that you can be sure that that the customer has approved the work. If the customer decides not to go through with the Change Order, they'll still need to return it, noting that it is declined. Of course, this feels like a lot of paperwork, and we often get a verbal decline, so we note the Change Order accordingly.

You should follow up on all open Change Orders on a weekly basis to ensure that the customer has received it. Often times, a customer will not return a Change Order that they are not going to accept, figuring that it will automatically end up in the bit bucket. Developers are usually in close contact with the customer to find out whether it was accepted or not. You want to make sure that you don't let anything fall through the cracks.

If a Change Order requires a change to existing code as opposed to a new function or module, that code should be marked with the following items:

- Date and time of the change

- Who made the change

- Change Order number

- Release number or version number of the application that will next incorporate the change

That way, you can go back and find out more about the reason for the change. A two-line comment in the code doesn't always jog the developer's memory sufficiently.

You'll also want to include a basic note about the change in the "change history" of the header of the module or program that was changed, so that you can quickly see what was done without having to read through all of the code and mentally rearrange everything chronologically.

Tracking Change Orders

You can track a Change Order in a number of different ways; we do so as a separate module because it is a specific object that can be shipped. Remember, that's what you're doing with your project tracking system—tracking widgets that you can ship, and, of course, invoice for. Thus, you need to enter them into your project tracking system just as each module of the original project was. Given this, a Change Order has a unique number. Furthermore, the module screen has a place to record the Change Order number, as well as fields to track whether the Change Order has been accepted or rejected, when it's been tested, approved, and shipped to the customer. And, finally, defects and ERs can be tracked against Change Order modules just as they can be tracked against any other type of module in the system.

Coordinating Change Orders

Change Orders can come either in groups or one at a time. However, it's a pretty rare occasion that you're going to want to send out a new release of your system just because of a single Change Order. This, then, begs the question of how you coordinate multiple Change Orders and organize them into a single release.

After a version of an application ships, it's unlikely that the To-do list is completely empty. There are always tasks left undone—whether they are minor defects discovered at the last minute but not important enough to warrant the inclusion of their fix or "great ideas" that were proposed too late in the development cycle to be implemented for the release.

Thus, one of the discussion items on the post-mortem of the delivery of an application should be an evaluation of the open items on the issues list. These can be grouped into potential upcoming versions—defects and enhancements that are important or easy to do get scheduled for the next release; enhancements that aren't critical or that will take more time to develop than is available before the next release get scheduled for later releases.

As new Change Orders appear, they should be assigned to a specific release, giving consideration to the impact that the work has on the release schedule (and cost of the release).

Including multiple items in a release is a good idea whenever possible. There's a certain amount of effort to mentally getting in gear—for the developer who is going to do the work, for the testing staff who is going to send the modifications through QA, and for the training staff who is going to have to explain the new features or differences to the user community. Once a developer has their mental arms around a project, it's more efficient to make multiple changes than to make just one. Finally, there are also some economies of scale for administration—it costs just as much to send out an invoice for $2,000 as it does for $20, but the results are so much more worthwhile.

Addendums vs. specification updates

At the beginning of this chapter, I stated that "The Change Order acts as an addendum to the specification, and can be folded into online Help at the appropriate time." The real-world situation can be more complicated than this. Here's why, and what to do about it.

Suppose you have a 250-page specification, and you've started on production (that's the manufacturing term for "we're slinging code now"), and a request for a change comes in. A field has to be split into two, or the behavior of a screen has to be changed... whatever it is, you write up a Change Order and add it to the back of the specification. Then a second Change Order comes in, and you repeat the same process.

Well, suppose you eventually ended up with 40 or 50 Change Orders for this system—not an unreasonable number, based on both my experience as well as my cohorts in the business.

Now it's time to write test plans, and you have to figure out exactly how some specific screen is going to work—one with four or five Change Orders attached to it. It can get pretty confusing—you may end up rewriting the spec for that particular screen in order to coordinate all of the changes in one place so you have a coherent description again. And it's not unheard of for Change Order #4 to actually contradict part of Change Order #1, without referencing it just so.

So what do you do? The answer is… it depends.

One solution is to just "live with it" and do the best you can, reconciling the specification and subsequent Change Orders. Another solution is to incorporate Change Orders into the specification as they occur, so that at any given time, you've got a completely up-to-date specification. And the third answer—sort of a middle ground—is to update the specification "when it needs to be."

Manufacturing companies, despite being in business for hundreds of years, don't have any more formal a reconciliation of this issue themselves. Most often, now that CAD systems and word processors are standard tools of the trade, they'll update the documents at the time of each Change Order. They'll reissue a drawing for each change, and you'll be able to see in the bottom corner a description of the change history, and be able to view the detailed Change Order documents separately.

The key is that the Change Order still has to be written, as it contains details like who requested it, who approved it, and the reasoning behind the request, but the impact of the Change Order—the actual change to the system—is also incorporated into the Functional Specification so that there is always a single place that describes the entire system. Of course, the user then needs to approve the portion of the specification that's updated as part of the Change Order process.

Chapter 28
Delivery

"Bad dates."
  —Raiders of the Lost Ark

Yes! It's done! Whether you're finished with the first module of the application or the last, it's always a nice feeling to be able to ship something to a customer. If you've followed all of the steps to this point, this should be a relatively painless process. Here are some pointers for the transition from "development" to "in production."

The delivery mechanisms available for you to provide access to your application (or parts thereof) to your customer have changed a great deal in the past few years, and so the delivery process has changed some. Nonetheless, the same fundamental requirements still apply.

Delivery mechanisms

Although the technical issues are beyond the scope of this book, you'll want to spend more time considering how you package your application, and then deliver it to your customer.

It used to be that a developer would throw a bunch of files on a diskette (or two), drive to the customer's site, and copy those files onto the customer's system under their watchful eyes. Indeed, when I was writing the *1997 Developer's Guide* in late 1996, that was still a common modus operandi.

There are, in the early 21st century, several different ways to package and deliver an application to a customer.

Most Windows development environments include some sort of a "setup wizard" that creates a number of files that are installed on the target machine. If you are delivering to a single site, that may be all you need. But if you're creating an application that will be deployed at more than a few locations, you may want to avail yourself of one of the professional (and wonderfully flexible) installation utilities, like InstallShield or WISE.

Bringing a handful of floppy disks to a customer's site in person is virtually never used in the Windows world anymore, since modern applications often span a volume of disk space that wouldn't be practical to convey via 1.44 MB media. A newer mechanism is a high-capacity storage disk, like a Zip, Jaz, or SyQuest drive disk, or, more commonly, a CD-ROM or DVD drive, as long as your customer has the mechanism to read it.

Once you've established a rapport with a customer, it's often easier to provide online access to the files to be delivered, either Internet FTP or even just e-mail. Of course, the files would need to be encrypted or otherwise secured, but that's not a barrier to using this type of delivery.

You'll also need to provide a complete set of instructions on what to do with the file, starting with how and where to save it on their machine. I've found that the shorter the installation instructions, the better off your customer is going to be. If they have to go through all sorts of gyrations—saving the master file one place, unzipping into a second place, running a pre-install in a third place, and then copying additional files from somewhere else, and setting parameters, and standing on one foot while doing all of this, they're liable to get confused, miss a step, and both become unhappy and make your life more difficult.

Delivering the application

Upon delivery of a module in person, the developer takes one final form with her—the Customer Visit Report. This form (a sample is included in the downloads) lists all of the "widgets" that the developer is going to deliver, together with a sign off by the QA department and a space for the customer to accept (or reject) the delivery as well.

 The first column—the list of "widgets" to deliver—acts as a To-do list for the developer, both when assembling materials to take to a customer, and while at the customer's site. The second column—the sign-off—serves two purposes: an audit for you to make sure that the specific deliverable was okayed by QA, and to reassure the customer that your quality control procedures were followed.

You can also use this form to document what action items come out of the meeting—if, indeed, there are any remaining tasks—and who is responsible for those tasks. With some customers, you may end up with more to do when you leave than you had when you showed up at their door, even taking into account the pieces you delivered at the meeting.

You should also have a space for recording how satisfied the customer was with the visit. It's a good idea to document customer dissatisfaction immediately. Customers often delay this type of bad news until the invoice comes due, and by then it's too late. If they're forced to measure their level of satisfaction immediately, you can find out quickly, instead of having to wait. An added benefit is that you're less likely to have an invoice thrown back in your face with the excuse that "All the work you've done is unacceptable" if they've had to sign off at each meeting. It's not impossible—just less likely.

If you're providing builds to a customer electronically, then you need to change the way the Customer Visit Report is handled (as well as, probably, the form's title). In this scenario, you would provide a cover letter or memo detailing 1) what's included in this build, 2) how to install it, and 3) any known issues (that is, defects you weren't able to address before the delivery date) or other items remaining. With this letter or memo, you would include a copy of the Customer Visit Report, requesting it be filled out and returned within a day of install. Then, of course, you would follow up with the customer upon receipt of their form.

Skipping the process

This whole book has been about process—but nowhere is it easier to get sidetracked than during the actual delivery process. Customers are always in a hurry—during the sales call, they want to get moving into design; once the design has been started, they're anxious to see some code being cut; and as soon as screens are being tested, they want to start entering data.

Given that impatience is the norm, often it's worse than that—the customer is in a near panic, some deadline is always around the corner, and the developer is under the gun to deliver something, anything, as soon as possible—in 30 minutes, if that isn't asking too much.

As a result, it's tempting to forsake the procedures just described—because, "just this once," it's different. It's an emergency, this time. It won't happen again, of course.

Well, I've got some bad news—and some more bad news.

The bad news is that this time isn't different. Every customer is in a hurry. Every customer has a drop-dead delivery date. Every customer is a special case. You can't simply suspend procedures once, for a special case, because you'll end up suspending procedures again and again, until you've done it for every case.

I spent a winter working in a foundry, where the primary work was supplying castings for other divisions of the company. Since the foundry was a captive facility, they weren't treated terribly nicely—each division was extremely demanding, as if they were the only division of the company whose products and customers were important. One result of this attitude was that each division always expected their jobs to be expedited ahead of everyone else in the queue.

Once in a while, someone from one of the divisions was successful in badgering a foundry supervisor to bump their product up in priority. More often, the salesman from the division complained or sweet-talked a corporate vice president into calling the general manager of the foundry to get their job moved up in the queue.

Since the scheduling process was automated, the job tickets that determined which castings would be processed on any day were printed first thing in the morning, and that's how the shop workers knew what to do. Expediting a job became a problem, because the tickets for the entire day couldn't simply be rerun when the order came down from on high to move a specific job through the shop faster.

Finally, management came up with the idea of putting a red cardboard ticket on the casting to indicate that it was to be handled out of order. Human nature being what it is, eventually 90% of the castings on the floor were carrying red tickets.

One day, a salesman touring the foundry realized that the red ticket carried by his job looked just like the 270 others on the floor. There was no way his job was going to make the promised delivery date if the casting had to vie with the 270 others also carrying the "high priority" tag.

When the salesman left the foundry that morning, one job was carrying two red tickets—obviously indicating that it was much more important than those jobs carrying only one red ticket!

The second bit of bad news is that the more special the situation is, the more important it is to maintain the use of your procedures. Let's use the analogy of a hospital. One important procedure is to track what drugs have been given to a patient, along with when and at what dosage.

Now let's move out to the field—a MASH unit where the wounded are coming in faster than the door can be opened and the physicians and support staff rotate in and out of the unit nearly as fast. Given the breakneck pace, it would be easy to suspend some procedures because there simply isn't the time.

However, it's precisely due to the bedlam in this situation that the procedure of tracking the administration of drugs must be followed—and, in fact, is even more important. In a normal hospital setting, it's conceivable, if not particularly comforting, that the drug history could be reconstructed at some later date if it hadn't been maintained contemporaneously. The physicians and support staff could be interviewed, drug inventories could be checked, and the relative calm of the hospital (well, relative to a battle front) makes the process somewhat more stable.

It could likely be impossible to reconstruct that same history for a casualty at the MASH unit, due to hospital personnel being rotated through the unit as well as the loss of personnel due to their location in or near a war zone. As a result, keeping contemporaneous records would be critical in that setting.

I'll argue that this applies equally well to the special, rush-rush job when a customer puts you under the gun. You have to write down the work you're doing, you have to track Change Order requests, chart bugs, and keep the documentation in front of the customer. You can always find another 30 minutes in a day to do the paperwork—and if you can't find the time, you'd better make the time. Else, you're going to have to find the time at 8 PM or this coming weekend. I know—I've done it myself.

Past delivery

However, just because your work is done doesn't mean that you're completely finished. Remember—in the customer's eyes, they've only just begun. Thus, the handoff of the application to them is, hopefully, triggering the start of a process that they will undertake. This process begins with a standard way of installing the new application, deploying through their organization, training their users, and providing ongoing support. They'll also want to maintain an ongoing dialog with you when feedback on the application is warranted.

Your role here is two-fold. First, you want to hold their hand while they install, deploy, and train. You might consider helping them put together a set of standard procedures for installation and deployment, so that when parts of the infrastructure change, they know how to handle them. Showing them how to use the materials you've produced during the application development, whether they are online Help, printed manuals, training slides, or something else, is another step.

If there are a large number of people to train, a "train the trainer" session can be a popular and wise investment. You can impart the detailed knowledge of the application to your customer in an efficient manner, training those high-end folks who are most likely going to be able to absorb a lot of information, and they benefit by having several of their people learn the application in-depth so that they can then train others.

Your second role here is that of production support. I personally prefer the approach of "technology transfer" so that my customer can handle all of the day-to-day issues, needing to lean on my firm for particularly difficult or unusual issues. And even those issues become fewer in number as time passes and the customer becomes more knowledgeable about how to handle the issues.

Post mortem

Upon completion of a project or a major phase of work, take a little time to digest the work that was just completed. This does not have to be a week-long soul searching; perhaps just an hour or two with the team members you worked with on the segment being reviewed. And you may or may not want to include the customer depending on what you hope to accomplish. The purpose of a post mortem is to consider what went well, and of course, what did not. Did you select the best process for the situation? How can you make the same good choices, or better choices, for future projects? Did a new form or process that you introduced for this project have the desired results, or did it just get in the way? What could have been done more efficiently? What did the customer find to work smoothly, and what did they think was difficult?

Certainly there is nothing wrong with asking your customer how you can improve... although if the relationship is particularly poor this may be very difficult—but this is the one time where you want to listen more closely than ever. If you only listen to the customers who give you glowing reviews, you're not going to learn anything that will help you improve.

When all is said and done, your ultimate goal is to delight the customer, to make your engagement with them one that will stand out in their mind, that will give them stories to tell for years to come (and I don't mean those told around a campfire: "Do you want to hear something *really* scary?").

Chapter 29
Making Money

"Look. I ain't in this for your revolution and I'm not in it for you, Princess. I expect to get well paid. I'm in it for the money."—Han Solo
  —Star Wars

As much as you like software development, writing the code isn't the be-all and end-all of a project. Up to this point, we've worried about getting the software written so that it meets user requirements. But there's another requirement that the user usually isn't concerned about. The Engagement Letter spelled out the payment terms—here's how to make those terms turn into money, and profits.

The Action Point Counting mechanism described in Chapter 17, "Calculating Time and Cost for a Specification," gives you the ability to size a project. Furthermore, the "Historical costs" section in the same chapter showed you how to figure out what your cost per Action Point has been. From these, we can figure out some guidelines about how to price a project so that it comes in profitably. There's more to it than that, though. Differences in developer productivity and actual vs. planned results can affect the profit plan, and need to be taken into account as well.

The cost is not the price!

Our ultimate goal is profit. Profit is defined, in the big picture, as the difference between the amount you spend and the amount you take in. And, if you've done it right, you've spent less than you've brought in—so, as a result, your profit is a positive number.

Action Points have given you a mechanism for determining what your cost is regardless of which development process you eventually use. Don't make the mistake of equating the cost and the price. The price is the amount you're going to take in—the revenue side of the equation. If you simply reuse the cost number as your price to the customer, you'll end up without a profit, and that's bad.

In other words, the cost merely gives you a number from which you can more wisely base your price. The price is what the customer will pay—and if the project you're doing is a valuable project, that price will be more than the cost. Hopefully, significantly more.

Many developers make the mistake to equating the two. They feel uncomfortable asking for additional money past the cost, and so figure that they'll actually be able to shave their real costs somewhat, thus eking out a profit by virtue of skilled development techniques, while holding the price for the customer artificially low.

The purpose of this chapter is to continually remind you that this approach isn't valid. In a capitalistic society, profit is the necessary lubricant that makes the rest of the components work. Profit is the incentive required to undergo the financial risk involved in the business enterprise.

Determining the cost (reprise)

We initially figured out the cost per Action Point in Chapter 17, "Calculating Time and Cost for a Specification," but those formulas were introduced just to get you thinking about the mechanism. There are a number of ways to categorize and assign costs.

Fixed vs. variable costs

The first way is breaking costs down into fixed and variable costs. Fixed costs are things that don't vary according to your production. Office space, telephone expense, subscriptions, copier rental—whether you have eight developers or 10, and whether your team is cranking out 100 Action Points a day over five projects or just seven Action Points a day over two projects, these fixed costs stay the same.

If your staff is on salary, you may also consider them to be fixed costs—again, regardless of whether you're cranking on two projects or five, you still have to write that set of payroll checks each month.

The other type of cost is variable—those that vary according to how much is being produced. In a manufacturing environment, where you're turning rubber, coal, and sand into automobiles, your variable costs are the material costs for each widget you're cranking out.

Furthermore, since you can, to some extent, get rid of your labor costs if production requirements go down (through reduced overtime, furloughs, and layoffs), you could consider your labor to be a variable cost.

Conversely, then, you could consider your labor costs to be variable if your production went through the roof, since you would have to pay a known amount of overtime per additional unit of production. Your fixed costs, though—plant and equipment—would stay the same. Thus, you could spread out your fixed costs over a larger number of widgets.

In an endeavor like software development, where there isn't a lot of raw material, variable costs are usually fairly low. This model is difficult to reconcile with a non-manufacturing environment, since it appears that all costs are fixed. Let's look at the next method.

Direct vs. indirect costs

A second way of breaking down costs is into direct and indirect costs. Direct costs are attributed to a unit of production, while indirect costs, somewhat like fixed costs, aren't tied directly to how many widgets are produced.

Direct costs

In the case of software development, direct costs are the labor that went into a unit of production—an Action Point. We calculated the cost of an Action Point in Chapter 17, "Calculating Time and Cost for a Specification." To refresh your memory, we took a bunch of old, completed projects that had a minimal amount of data about how they were produced. We needed to know three things—a Functional Specification of the final, delivered system, the hours each developer and support personnel applied to that project, and the compensation for those people.

We counted Action Points for each project. We knew that those counts weren't going to be completely accurate, but figured that by averaging the numbers over multiple projects, the error variance in each project would be minimized.

Then we tallied up the number of hours spent on those projects, and multiplied the hours by the hourly compensation to arrive at a total cost for the projects. There's a bit of sleight of hand going on in that last statement—let's stop waving our hands quite so fast.

Cost per Action Point

We're first and foremost interested in the cost per Action Point.

Our initial calculations assumed that, say, a developer made $50,000 a year. Add benefits—medical insurance, employer contributions to wages, and so on—for another $20,000 a year, and you get $70,000 a year.

Now, let's suppose that developer was responsible for producing 2,200 Action Points over that year. That's $31.82 per Action Point. Or is it? Since I asked the question, you can guess, "Actually not."

The previous calculations assumed that the developer spent the entire year cranking out those 2,200 Action Points. But you and I know that there's a lot of down time (that's spelled "non-billable") involved in software development. There's 2,080 possible hours in a year, but let's say that the developer only billed 1,550 of those hours—about 30 hours a week. The rest were spent on non-billable tasks like vacation and sick time, attending educational seminars, filling out paperwork, reinstalling Windows, and so on.

You need to account for that time. You need to include the non-billable hours as part of the development cost for those 2,200 Action Points. After all, the developer was paid for 40 hours a week, not just for 30.

You have to think of the cost of vacation and sick time, and other "non-billable time" as a perk—one that has a cost just as insurance or employer-paid classes do. It gets included as part of your direct cost, just as you would the check you write for health insurance.

That's why it's important to track all time spent by developers—not just the time they spend coding, testing, writing specs, and so on. If you just track the actual time they spend on billable activities, you don't get the true cost.

On the flip side, though, it's a rare software developer who only spends 40 hours a week. Let's suppose that our theoretical developer also put in 490 hours of overtime—evenings, weekends, vacation days, and so on. You need to figure out the cost for the overtime that developer spent, even if there wasn't a paycheck cut for those extra hours. Why? Can't you assume those hours are free?

Absolutely not! They're part of the cost of building your software.

Our mythical developer—we'll call him Al—has produced his 2,200 Action Points during a total of 2,040 billable hours. So, while he ends up appearing to have produced 2,040 hours of work for the cost of one developer, you can't necessarily count on that happening regularly. Suppose he leaves or is reassigned elsewhere, and you need to fill his shoes with someone else who can't, or doesn't want to work another 10 hours extra each week. You may end up having to hire one-and-a-third people to produce that 2,040 hours of work. (Of course, I'm assuming that they're all similarly productive, and are paid the same, for the time being, just to make the math easier.) Thus, the true cost of those hours is off by a third.

It'd be just as if you were producing cars, and everyone on an assembly line snuck in on Saturday and built, in addition to the 750 cars they produced during the week, another 150 cars without telling anyone. It would appear that you could now produce 900 additional cars for the labor cost that it used to take to produce 750 cars. But as soon as those workers decide that they want to start attending soccer games with their kids on Saturday, you're back down to

750 cars a week. If you started budgeting a profit based on 900 cars for the labor cost of 750 cars, though, you're going to be looking at a loss—and probably for a new job.

Thus, you need to figure out your cost per hour, multiply that by the total number of hours spent to get your total cost, and then divide the cost by the number of Action Points to arrive at the cost per Action Point.

In this example, you'd take the $70,000 paid for a standard work year of 2,080 hours to arrive at an hourly rate of $33.65. Multiply that by 2,570 hours needed to produce the 2,200 Action Points, for a total cost of $86,480. Divide the 2,200 Action Points into that for a direct cost of $39.31 per Action Point.

Indirect costs

So far, so good. Now what about all those "other" costs? Costs such as office expense, telephone, non-billable personnel, marketing, and equipment and infrastructure. That's next.

Over the lifetime of the projects you're evaluating, you'll need to total the other costs involved in producing those projects. You may need a bit of a green eyeshade to figure this one—for example, suppose you buy a computer at the beginning of one project, and you figure the useful life of that machine is three years. Unless the project is exactly three years in length as well, you're not going to be able to assign the cost of the machine entirely to that project. So while your cash cost may be several thousand dollars, you can only assign a portion of that cash cost to the project.

If your company is involved in activities other than software development, then you need to decide how to apportion the overhead of your company to the software development side of things. You may use a formula as simple as calculating total overhead, and then dividing it according to the revenues each part of the business has generated. Alternatively, you might want to go in for a more involved calculation, such as determining the portion of square footage attributable to each part of the business, as well as percentage of use of assets and non-billable personnel.

It's probably wise not to go into too much detail—the bookkeeping could end up being more trouble than any benefits realized by a more precise calculation would be worth.

Eventually, though, you'll end up with a total indirect cost of the software projects you're evaluating. Divide that number by the number of Action Points in the set of projects, and now you've got your indirect cost per Action Point.

Total cost per Action Point

So, in order to determine your total cost, you need to sum up both your direct costs per Action Point and your indirect costs.

You can now use this number to figure out what it's going to cost you to send the next Action Point out the door.

Splitting the action

Note that I've been using the term "developer" as if they're the only people who do any work around the shop. I actually mean to include everyone involved—analysts, coders, testers, trainers—everyone in your shop who has a hand in cranking out that application. And that has some serious implications for the apportioning of the Action Points.

Here's what will really happen if you've got more than one person involved in a project.

First, let's assume that you've got three distinct groups of personnel involved—the analyst/designer, the programmer/debugger, and the tester/documenter. And they all contributed to cranking out those 2,200 Action Points.

If your history of time records has broken out these tasks across projects, you know more than just how many hours it took to produce a project; you know how many hours it took for each of these functional groups. You also know what each person who contributed to that project was paid, and what percentage of their time they're involved in productive (billable) work, and how much overtime they spent.

However, take one additional possibility into consideration. The discussion covering Al's billable, non-billable, and overtime hours assumed that his sole job was software development. It's quite possible that some of your people don't spend all of their time in the pursuit of kicking Action Points out the door. For example, you may have a QA person who spends part of her time on network administration.

You'll need to take that into account. If you've got someone wearing more than one hat, and one of those hats doesn't contribute to the software development effort, then you'll have to portion their time according.

Suppose that your QA individual, as posited earlier, did indeed spend two days a week on network admin. So she's only got 24 out of 40 hours each week devoted to software development activities. Furthermore, however, assume that she doesn't work a straight 40 hours a week. You need to add overtime and non-billable time into the mix as well.

Carrying this example further, suppose that your QA person records another 200 hours of overtime, and chalks up 420 hours of non-billable time throughout the year. This 420 hours, though, needs a bit of explanation. I'm assuming that your time keeping assigns billable hours during software development QA as well as time strictly devoted to network admin—and that this person had 420 hours of non-billable time across both activities together. It's all the non-billable time over the year for either activity—QA or network admin.

The 200 hours of overtime and the 420 hours of non-billable time, then, both have to be divided, proportionately, according to the amount of straight time spent as well. Thus, since she spends 60% of her time doing QA and 40% doing network admin, the 200 hours of overtime would be allocated thusly: 120 hours to QA, and 80 to network admin. Same for the 420 hours of non-billable time—252 to QA and 168 to network admin.

Use just the QA numbers, then, to figure out how the dollars for QA should be allocated toward the Action Points QA worked on during that time.

Thus, you can calculate the same numbers for everyone else involved in the software development project—specifically, the cost per Action Point by each person who contributed.

Let's suppose that we have, in addition to the $39.31/Action Point for the programmer, $52.40/Action Point for the analyst, and $22.75 for the tester. (And, of course, we have another chunk of money allocated for overhead and other indirect costs. For argument's sake, let's say it's $25/Action Point.)

As a result, it's going to cost a total of $140.46 to send that next Action Point out the door.

You may be thinking that we need to back off of the $39.31/Action Point for the developer—after all, since he didn't do all of the work for that batch of 2,200 Action Points all by himself, he shouldn't get credit for the whole thing, right? Not so. We're still assuming that he spent all of his time on the 2,200 Action Point project—but what we're also saying is that he wasn't the only one involved—other folks contributed some of their time as well.

In a practical sense, it's highly unlikely that it took exactly three people exactly one year together to produce those 2,200 Action Points. I just used these numbers to make it easier.

Furthermore, that developer could well have spent some of his time on other projects as well, but that's easy to figure—you just take the percentage of his time he spent on that specific 2,200 Action Point project to figure the cost.

It's quite possible, though, that your history of time records doesn't get that granular, or perhaps you didn't track one or more of those tasks (maybe testing just kept testing whenever they didn't have anything else to do). In that case, make a guess about what it costs for the other functions per Action Point. Even the worst guess is going to be better than the alternative—going without the information at all!

Determining the price (reprise)

I started developing applications in the 1980s—the same decade that Wall Street got famous for the merger and acquisition fever that was immortalized in movies like Wall Street. One of the byproducts was seeing lawyers making $10,000,000 for a few weeks of work of putting together a deal—averaging, say, $50,000 an hour for their work. That seemed a fairly lucrative business to me, and it's been distressing ever since.

The discontent is based on the premise that, as an hourly worker, you can't hope to earn more than a certain rate per hour, no matter what business you're in, nor no matter how skilled you become. Thus, as long as you're selling your time, your income has a very fixed ceiling, since, like real estate, "they ain't making any more of it." There are two ways to overcome this barrier.

The first is to get into the product business. Make a widget and sell it a billion times. If you can come up with a widget that doesn't cost anything to manufacture—like… software!— you can become quite wealthy. However, doing so requires a number of factors to all come into play at the right time—and a healthy dose of luck besides.

The other option, then, is to package your time into a discrete entity that you charge for, and that the amount of time it takes to produce that entity has little to no relation to the entity itself. This is what the lawyers involved in M&A do—they package a deal for, say, 2% of the price. The fact that it takes them just a few hours or weeks to do it doesn't matter—in the big picture, their fees are miniscule compared to the bigger deal. They're not getting paid for their time—they're getting paid for their skill level and knowledge, and providing value to the customer.

Fixed price software development can be constructed the same way.

What if you could, in a morning, produce a piece of software that would save a company $20,000 a year? Would it be fair to charge $5,000 for that software? Even though it only took you a morning to produce it? In the eyes of the customer, of course it would be—they're going to make their money back in a month.

But what if it took your competitor two weeks to produce that application—and so they had to charge $8,000. Remember that you were able to produce the same application—because of your greater skill level and knowledge—in only a morning. Could you legitimately charge your $5,000? Heck, you could even charge $6,000, or $7,000, and both save your customer a bit of money while making a healthy piece of change yourself.

As a result, the price you charge should have no relationship to your cost structure (other than, hopefully, being greater than your cost). It's strictly based on the value that the customer is going to receive.

You may run into a customer who argues differently. But where is it written that a business can only make a certain amount of profit? You could just as easily make the argument that they shouldn't be allowed to make back their money at more than a certain rate. If they spend $X on something, you could argue that they shouldn't see better than a 15% return on their investment—after all, that's what you'd make if you were to invest in the stock market or a well performing mutual fund, right?

Determining the value

Now, this whole discussion begs the question—how do you determine the value of this project to the customer? Unfortunately, as much as we'd like to think otherwise, most businesses do not have a good mechanism for determining the value of an automated system. Well, some people might argue that no businesses have a good mechanism for determining the value of an automated system. The closest they can come is some rough guess at how many people they're going to be able to replace, and thus, how much they will save on salaries and benefits. Well, at least that's how people used to think of automated systems. These days, that mode of thinking has largely been replaced—many systems are not put in place to replace people as much as they are implemented to enhance or add functionality or otherwise provide a competitive advantage to the company.

Still, despite however much you hear about people determining the price based on value, invariably you'll find they do a cost model and then tack on a margin, and the project ends up being handled on an hourly, time and materials basis again.

In 1970, companies installed payroll systems so that they could get rid of an army of clerks in the back room who used to calculate paychecks by hand. Thirty years later, companies install payroll systems so that they can provide a smorgasbord of benefits tailored to a variety of employee categories, mandated by law and necessitated by competition for talented employees.

So, given that even customers don't know how much a system is worth to them anymore, how do you go about figuring it out, so that you can price it?

The first way is to simply ask the customer. "How much is this system worth to you?" Just like with the section on estimating, many customers may be reluctant to answer, for fear (and possibly rightfully so!) that their answer will somehow magically become the price.

More likely, before the customer comes to that realization, they won't answer because they don't know.

Nonetheless, unless you're talking to the president of the company (or the ultimate decision-maker, whoever that may be), the person you're talking to undoubtedly had to get permission from someone else for the system they're contracting out for. So while they may not actually know what the system will *really* be worth to them, they still very likely have a number in mind.

Once in a while you'll get lucky and they'll tell you. I once had a customer who gave me a list of system specs for a potential system and—honestly—accidentally copied the budget for the system and included it in the stack of papers I received. But you shouldn't hope for that kind of luck.

Another way to go about this is to "help" the customer figure out what their budget is. This technique can work whether they actually know or not. Oftentimes, the budget or the requirements for a system are fairly flexible—so the process becomes one of negotiation.

This shouldn't be done at the end of the design, of course. You don't want to design a huge application only to find the customer has a $5 bill in their pocket. Remember, the idea is to price your application as close to the value that the customer is going to receive as possible—without going over. If you happen to go over, and the customer ends up stuttering on the final price, you can knock off a few features that are in reality not terribly expensive to produce, but knock off a disproportionate chunk of the price at the same time, in order to help the customer accomplish their goals while still saving face yourself.

The third possibility is to walk through the goals of the application, asking what the purpose of each is, and try to determine the cost/benefit ratio for each. This is technically the most difficult, but sometimes you can help both the customer and yourself by re-examining assumptions. Do you really need a customized programmable rate calculator, or will shelling out to another application via Automation do nearly as much for considerably less trouble? Force the customer to justify the application, and you can find out a lot about how much it's worth to them.

Making money

Theoretically, you can then subtract your cost from the price, and come up with the profit expected for this system. In the real world, of course, it's more complicated.

Sure, as the ink is drying on the acceptance of the Functional Specification, the expected profit is pretty clear. However, as soon as the staff begins work, things happen.

What do you want to know?

As soon as you start the project, you'll want to start tracking the dollars. You're going to want to know how long this project is going to take, and you're going to need to be able to track how much your project is actually costing day to day. While your specific requirements and interests undoubtedly vary from mine, here's one way to do so to give you a starting point and some ideas.

How long will it take?

In order to determine hours, you'll need to know two numbers—the number of Action Points for the module (which you already have), and the number of hours an Action Point takes. (Note that this is all done in conjunction with constructing a project schedule and determining who is available and applying the appropriate numbers for each resource. These calculations are designed to tell you how many hours you'll need—you'll then have to work those hours into the schedule for your people.)

You should have broken out your Action Point counts by module. Ideally, you've assigned each module to a single developer—it's pretty hard to track how many Action Points a developer produces when you've got a mismatch between how developers and Action Points are assigned. It'd be the same as if you were trying to measure how much cement each of two workers were shoveling into a foundation, but they were both digging out of the same trough, and dumping the cement into the same blocked out foundation. You simply couldn't measure the productivity of each worker individually without counting and weighing each shovel-full individually.

Okay, now that I've (hopefully) convinced you to assign just one developer per module (that means you make your modules small!), you need to know the rate of Action Point production for that developer.

As you'll recall from before, each developer has a total cost for an Action Point—their compensation, benefits, and so on—spread over the number of hours they spent to produce their Action Point total. You also know what percentage of those hours was billable.

From these values, you can determine the number of billable hours per Action Point. Note, again, that this is not the same as number of hours per Action Point. There's always non-billable time in a developer's life. Be sure to account for this downtime.

Using the same example we've been using, developer Al has cranked out 2,200 Action Points in 2,570 hours. As a result, he can crank out about 0.85 Action Points an hour, or 6.8 Action Points in an eight-hour day.

You may be tempted to extend these calculations by figuring that of those 2,570 hours, 530 were non-billable, for a productivity rate of 79.4%. Thus, he's productive about 6.5 hours a day, and thus can crank out about an Action Point each productive hour. Since that will inevitably introduce a Dilbert factor—pointy-haired bosses will then proclaim that all developers must be productive 7.5 hours a day, instead of 6.5 hours a day, but the work produced won't ever actually go up, so there's no point to it.

Similarly, you can calculate the Action Point productivity for other people—Analyst Bonnie may be able to crank out 0.42 Action Points an hour, while Tester Carl zips through 2.77 Action Points an hour. They all play a part in the process; their individual contribution histories show these levels of productivity.

However, we don't know how to merge these numbers together. What proportion do these folks contribute to the production of Action Points? In other words, suppose you've got a 150 Action Point module. How do you figure how to allocate Al's 0.85 AP/hr with Bonnie's 0.42 AP/hr and Carl's 2.77 AP/hr?

At first blush, you might just try adding them up—getting 4.03 AP/hr. You can't just add them up—that would assume that each of these folks contributes the same number of hours to the project, and upon reflection, that's highly, highly unlikely. You need to figure out in what proportion these ingredients—the amounts of time that Al, Bonnie, and Carl contribute to the project—are added.

Figuring the proportions

We could take the ratio of $/Action Point for each person to the total of dollars for the group. Thus, we'd assume that Bonnie contributes 52.40/(52.40+39.31+22.75), or 45.8% of the Action Points.

However, this isn't correct. After all, the dollars may be artificially set in the first place. Remember our discussion of how people are paid? There's no holy grail that automatically and perfectly correlates compensation with ability and productivity—in fact, the lack of such a correlation is one of the main reasons we're having this discussion at all.

To prove this point, suppose that one of the players got a significant raise halfway through the 2,200 Action Point project. As a result, that person's assumed participation in the project in terms of contributed Action Points went up. But did his productivity actually increase?

There's no proof of that whatsoever. Thus, compensation can't be used as the basis to calculate the percentage participation of each player.

A more accurate measure would be the hours they contributed. After all, that's eventually what we're going to be looking for in the end.

So, look at the projects they worked on, just as you did when figuring the cost per Action Point. Sum up the hours they each spent on those projects, and use the proportion, in relation to the whole, to figure out their participation.

For example, let's take that 2,200 Action Points project. How many hours did each of our players spend? We already know that Al spent... how many did he spend? After all, we threw about a bunch of numbers—1,550 regular billable hours, 490 overtime billable hours, and 430 non-billable hours.

Since we're trying to figure out what the proportions for those activities are, we'll use total hours again. If you assume that all three players just worked on this 2,200 Action Point project, you'll want to account for variances in billable percentages. In other words, suppose two developers worked on this project, not just one. We know that Al was billable 2,040 out of 2,570. Suppose the second developer was billable for 1,900 out of 2,080 hours. It's not fair to the second developer to throw 1,900 hours into the pot when in fact they were much more productive.

Thus, you'll put 2,570 hours against the project, knowing that Al did nothing but work on that project for the year. Now, it's plausible that the other players didn't spend their entire year on that project. Let's suppose that Bonnie logged 2,480 hours over the year, and a quarter of those (billable and non-billable) were for this project—620 hours. Similarly, Carl added 490 hours.

The three, together, then, put in 3,680 total. Of that, 70% was Al's, 17% was Bonnie's, and 13% belonged to Carl. These are the percentages you use to apportion Action Points.

So, given that 150 Action Point module, Al is responsible for 105 Action Points, Bonnie is to produce 25.5, and Carl gets the remainder, 19.5.

Multiplying these by the rate of Action Point production, we get:

Al 105 AP * 0.85 AP/hr = 60.7 hours
Bonnie 25.5 AP * 0.42 AP/hr = 123.5 hours
Carl 19.5 AP * 2.77 AP/hr = 7 hours

From these figures, we can determine what the project schedule should be, and in a larger sense, track the progress made from module to module.

Thus, we end up with a budget of about 60 hours for Al to do the programming for the module.

Now that you've got the estimated hours for Al to develop the app (as well as for the other players to perform their parts), you can match up actual vs. estimated, and see how you're doing. When those numbers diverge (and they usually do), it's critical to remember that these metrics are not a tool for administering punishment.

Rather, you're trying to catch big problems early—while they're still small problems. Suppose this module starts to go over—of the four screens, each of which is approximately equal in complexity, only two are done, yet he's already spent 60 of his hours. Now is the time to figure out what's happening.

Is it possible that the last two will actually get cranked out in short order, because there's some degree of reusability or commonality?

Or were there hidden requirements, additional complexity that wasn't documented? Just as a well-designed application shouldn't have bugs—those should be caught in the design phase, not while programming—a well-designed app should also not have surprises creep up at this phase. If they do, they get categorized as bugs—in the design phase. It's time to examine the design phase, determine why those bugs occurred, and re-examine other parts of the application to see whether that same type of design bug could have crept in elsewhere.

Finally, you can track the margins of your project, again, down to the module level. As pieces are delivered, you can track not only the direct costs, but the indirect costs incurred to that point, and see how your profit margin is coming along.

Tracking your project's schedule is just one part of the game, though.

Scope creep

The first danger is scope creep without a corresponding price creep. It's a rare salesman who can't resist throwing in a couple of freebies after the deal has been signed—much to the chagrin of the boss, who has to look at the profitability of the deal, not just the fact that the salesman has notched another chunk of revenue in his bedpost.

But it's not just sales reps who do this. Developers—indeed, most people—like to be "nice guys," and that desire often manifests itself in the reluctance to charge extra for something added to the project.

This is a bucket of groceries, and you and the customer have agreed upon a fixed price for the stuff in the bucket. You can't go putting more stuff in the bucket without adjusting the price for the whole purchase—but that won't stop the customer from trying, either consciously or subconsciously.

Remember, each time the customer asks for something, it's time to pull out the Change Order pad, and start figuring out the hit on the price. You're certainly free to give something away at no charge—but the act of producing a Change Order means you'll think twice about it, and it'll be easier to charge the customer for the next request.

Developer productivity

Another key part of the profit puzzle is developer productivity—and trying to adjust compensation accordingly. While it's highly unlikely that you'll be able to tie compensation to productivity directly, the effort you expend in attempting to do so will be appreciated.

The key is to have the rules firmly understood and documented. If they aren't, your staff will assume that arbitrariness comes into the picture, and everyone will feel slighted. If the rules are well understood, though, everyone knows what they have to do to get better compensated.

Take, for instance, a ball team. Everyone knows how much everyone else is making—but they also know what each ball player's numbers are. Want the next $10 million contract? No problem—just knock 80 balls over the fence next season, or win 25 games, or score 35 touchdowns.

Unlike many jobs, job performance in sports is pretty black and white. Either you win the tournament by keeping the ball in the middle of the fairway and making the tricky putts, or you don't.

Make the rules black and white for your development team, and they'll come to appreciate what they have to do to make the big bucks.

You don't have to make money the only compensation item. A bigger office, more toys, er, equipment, time off—these can all be powerful motivators. But so can the choice of new projects—the highly productive developers get first shot at new projects, for example.

Section VI:

People

I grew up in a second-generation family business: My father and his two brothers took over the business from their dad, and as my generation got old enough, we were drafted into service as summer and part-time workers at "The Factory." One summer evening at an extended family gathering, my grandmother leaned over to a cousin of mine who had just started at the plant, and asked in a stage whisper, "So how do you like working at the company?"

In the same loud voice, meant to be overheard by everyone at the long table, he replied, "It's awful! I mean, they gotta *pay* you to work there!"

And therein lies the answer to the next question in software development—how do you get others to help you produce software? Once you have enough business to fill more than one pair of shoes, you have to pay someone else to get them to help you.

The employer-employee relationship is much like the rest of the software development business—many people get into it by happenstance and without really thinking about what they're getting into.

In this section, I'm going to address the business of finding, hiring, evaluating, keeping, and getting rid of employees. There are, of course, a million books on this topic, and while this section will give you a good foundation for the issues involved, I recommend that you don't use this book at your only source of information. It's important that you consult an attorney as well. However, our business—custom software development—and the players in it—analysts, developers, programmers, technicians—have a number of particular nuances that make employee relations in our business unique. This section pays particular attention those issues.

Chapter 30
Setting Expectations: Revisited

"Marriage is hard enough without bringing such low expectations into it."—Walter
  —Sleepless in Seattle

I've talked about setting expectations with respect to customers; setting expectations is even more important with employees.

Your customers look to you for guidance on how to maneuver through the minefield of custom software development; you're the expert, after all. It is the same with employees. They're going to look to you, consciously or unconsciously, to define what the rules are, and to set an example of how to act and behave. After all, you're the boss.

As with customers, expectations with employees go both ways. You will have certain expectations of them, and they will have their own expectations of you. Unfortunately, while you can, and should, spell out your expectations of them, they're not always going to do the same. You're the one with the power—you're making the job offer, setting the compensation, handing out bonuses, parceling out projects, and controlling their reviews. Some employees approach the employer-employee relationship in an adversarial manner. They may well be very cautious in telling you what they're looking for and wanting, feeling that playing those cards exposes them to a less than advantageous bargaining position, or even to risk. They're not going to do anything that might jeopardize their employment unless they're no longer interested in maintaining that employment.

The best you can do, then, are the following:

- Define and state clearly your expectations. You are, in this situation, the customer. You're the one with the money who is contracting for work to be done. It's up to you to be explicit when describing what it is you're buying.

- Explain to them what they can expect as well. You have to be honest and open, even if the truth isn't as, er, optimal as you would like. They're going to find out you're very cranky before 10 in the morning, or that your spelling is atrocious, or that you don't return phone calls very reliably. Tell them up front what they can expect from you, and you will have fewer misunderstandings.

- Be fair and consistent in your words and actions. Make sure that you "walk your talk" and that your actions today are the same as your actions yesterday. Unpredictability and unreliability are two traits most employees despise in their bosses. You may be an S.O.B., but if they know that going in, and that they can rely on that, then it's up to them to decide whether they want to deal with it. It's much more difficult to work with someone who blows hot and cold at a moment's notice.

If your employees know what to expect, and then you deliver on those expectations, they have no one to blame but themselves if something goes astray. As the boss, you have to take the lead in setting those expectations. And setting expectations starts when you begin the hiring process.

Chapter 31
Your Secret Weapon:
An Administrative Assistant

"You're like one of those psycho cops who keeps getting his partners killed, and no one will ever ride with him anymore."—Harrison Ford to Melanie Griffith
  —Working Girl

I've started three companies, and each time, I've delayed on hiring a personal assistant—and each time, the delay was a mistake. Each time I waited, it was because I felt it was too expensive. However, I hope I've learned my lesson, and I'll try to impart it to you. You can do yourself a world of good by bringing in an assistant, at least part-time. Here's how. And, I'd advise you corporate managers not to skip this chapter entirely. You'll find out why soon enough.

Many of you are individual developers who may be thinking about getting an office and working with somebody else.

And if you're like most developers, you do not want to spend a lot of money for an administrative assistant because they are "non-billable" people. I've seen several companies where the head honcho has never made the jump to bring an administrative assistant on board, even after hiring a number of other people. Some people say they can't afford one. Others say that it's a meaningless status symbol, or a hallmark of earlier times, or some other such nonsense.

I understand where these thoughts come from. An administrative assistant can run anywhere from $20,000 to nearly double that, full-time, depending on the skill level, experience, and geographic region you're located in. You have to crank out a lot of work to pay for that—and it's difficult to work that much when not a cent of it lands in your pocket.

And in the olden days of conglomerates and empire building, one significant status symbol in corporate life was having your own executive secretary. It was one of those steps up the corporate ladder—a "supervisor" title, a private office, an office with a conference table, and a shared secretary. When you were "allowed" your own private secretary, you knew you had made it to that small elite circle.

But this is different from "corporate America." You're running a small custom software shop. It's important to keep in mind that your assistant will free up a lot of your time, doing those time-consuming but non-billable tasks, thus allowing you to do more billing. And if you're a manager of a department, the same issues apply, albeit in slightly different clothes. You may have to play a couple of games to get an administrative assistant on board when none of the other managers on your same level of the corporate organizational chart have one, but trust me—it will be worth it.

How to justify an administrative assistant

I've been faced with the decision of hiring an assistant three times in the past 20 years. In two out of the three situations, I was blessed with excellent admin assistants, and I repeatedly hit myself upside the head muttering, "Why didn't I do this sooner?"

It's somewhat difficult to hire an assistant if it's just you. You might consider bringing in a college student, or a parent who wants to work part-time. Three or four half days a week ends up being fairly inexpensive, but can pay enormous dividends—answering the phone, paying bills, searching the Web for stuff, running errands at the local computer store, and so on.

Probably the optimal way is to bring in a second billable person, get them up to speed so that they can be billing full-time, and swap the phone answering duties so that one of you always has long blocks of quiet time. One person does "grunt work" while answering the phone in the morning; the other does their "grunt work" while answering the phone in the afternoon. Once you have two billable people, you actually have enough administrative work to justify having someone on board at least part-time. Consider bringing somebody in from 9 AM to 1 PM. Then, you and the other developer will have four hours of reasonable peace and quiet before you are interrupted by the phone.

If you're a manager of a small department at a company, you may not be "allowed" to have what the corporate personnel department calls "a secretary." The trick here is to bring in a part-time person to whom you attach a moniker like "technical assistant" or some such thing. Given that you're working under the corporate veil, you're probably not going to have as much flexibility about the tasks you can set this person upon, but you can still have a fair amount of non-billable or administrative work done by this person.

The very most important point here is to make sure that you're making good use of this person. In other words, pretend that you were paying for this person out of your own pocket, which is what you'd be doing if the "department" were your own company. Don't hire an administrative assistant because it looks important—do it because you can make better use of your time. The scuttlebutt around the company should be that everyone is in awe of how much you and your department get done, not disdain for your having danced around corporate policy to "hire a secretary."

The right administrative assistant can almost act as a "foreman" for your factory, helping out with many scheduling and coordination tasks as well as personal tasks for you and the company.

The trick is getting somebody in as soon as you can. Having the right assistant is one of the most productive things you can do.

The goal

The goal of hiring an administrative assistant is to take the day-to-day tasks off of your back. There is so much mundane stuff to do when running even the smallest development shop— and your time is too valuable to spend doing it. I state it like so: "Your job is to help me be more productive." Anything within that description is fair game.

Once in a while you'll run into a potential administrative assistant who has a chip on his shoulder about "not getting coffee" or "running out to get a sandwich" for the boss. Puh-lease! This person should be eliminated from consideration even before the phone gets warm.

Given this goal, you'll be looking for someone who 1) agrees with this job description, and 2) can read your mind.

Simple agreement with the job description, however, really isn't enough. Don't accept tacit acquiescence when you're looking for enthusiastic participation. This person is going to be, in a sense, your partner. Chemistry is so important—you're going to be working with this person closely, possibly more closely than with anyone else in the company, and you're likely going to end up entrusting confidential personal and company information to this person.

The ad

There is a wide range of candidates that will answer an ad for an administrative assistant position, and, frankly, many of them won't be qualified regardless of how you state the qualifications. Thus, the idea is to cast as wide a net as possible, but to also be specific about your requirements, so that 1) at least some people will disqualify themselves, and 2) you can quickly, easily, and painlessly weed out those who are not appropriate candidates.

Explain the parameters of the position and the company so that people will weed themselves out, if possible. And, mention something to make your ad stand out. A great exercise is to read through the ads for an administrative assistant—and then write yours so that it stands out from the others.

A typical ad that you would place might read:

```
President of local software development company seeks an administrative
assistant. Full-time (8:30 - 5:00) position, casual dress code, downtown
location, paid parking. Excellent PC skills (Microsoft Office and Web),
fanaticism about details, and a sense of humor required. Database experience,
an eye for graphic design, and experience working for upper management all big
pluses. Cover letter and resume to <company name and address>.
```

Let's take this ad apart for a minute. The first sentence lays out exactly what you are looking for. More details about what an administrative assistant does really aren't needed—everyone knows. You'll get to provide specific examples ("get me a bologna sandwich every day at lunch") during the phone interview.

The second sentence spells out several important parameters—at least, important to me. Full-time—the hours are spelled out because folks who are used to administrative assistant positions are often used to working hourly, and will want to know the bounds. I've run into people who have worked in factories and have expected hours from 7:00 to 3:30—the only time they would run into a developer in our shop at 7 AM is if the developer hadn't left the previous night.

Casual dress code isn't the big deal it was a few years ago, but it's still good to list. You'll have to be more specific in the interview—"casual" means different things to different people. I've always had an office downtown—and some people don't like (or, even, are scared about) coming downtown.

The line about "Excellent PC skills" shouldn't have to be in an ad for a software development firm in this day and age, but I've run into individuals with some truly abysmal skills—here you need to set high expectations. The trouble is that 90% of the individuals who apply for this position think they're in the top 10%—and the other 10% think they're still in the upper half.

"Shouldn't 'anal retentive' be hyphenated?" reads a favorite T-shirt of mine. I can't work with a sloppy person, and you probably can't either. You'll be able to test for detail-orientation soon enough—again, you're setting an expectation.

There are a few people out there without a sense of humor. That's fine, but I don't want to work with them. More importantly, this helps my ad stand out from the rest. I've had a couple people interpret that phrase in the wrong way ("You need a sense of humor to survive there") but generally, it's viewed as a positive by potential employees.

And, just to draw in that special person, I'll throw in a few more attributes that I'd be interested in seeing.

I also request a cover letter and a resume, and give them an address, not a phone number. I'll explain why.

Resume city

You'll likely get a load of resumes—administrative assistants are plentiful, and the position is a fairly transitive one—many people use an administrative position as an entry into a company or an industry.

Reading through the resumes can be quite amusing. I remember a few classic examples that I have to pass along. There was the one person who claimed "significant experience" and was a "mature" individual. This person also listed one position at a county courthouse from 1865 through 1979. That was a bit more maturity than I needed.

Another person went on and on about how detail oriented she was—mentioning it twice in her cover letter and once in her resume. She also spelled my company's name wrong three times—and in two different ways—in the cover letter alone.

A third person actually landed an interview—claiming a "9" on a scale of 1 to 10 (most experienced) with his level of PC expertise. This person had never used Windows File Manager, wasn't able to locate a file given the name and the drive, wasn't able to copy a file from the hard drive to a diskette, and couldn't change the font of a paragraph in a document.

However, reading through all these resumes can also be distracting. Before you start opening up envelopes, write down a list of qualifications that potential candidates should have. Then, when you're going through your 40th resume, you can still be reasonably objective.

It's up to you to decide what should be on these qualifications, but here is a list I started out with a long time ago:

- Cover letter included? This was requested in the ad—doing so indicates they can follow instructions.

- Cover letter personalized to company? Doing so indicates that they're not on a fishing expedition, just throwing hundreds of envelopes in the mail. You don't want one of these people.

- Cover letter says something specific about the job? Doing so also indicates that they're not just throwing hundreds of envelopes in the mail and that they found something (or, at least, are pretending to have found something) particularly interesting about *your* company.

- Company name spelled correctly? Doing so means nothing, not doing so means a lack of detail-awareness. Tsk, tsk.

- Cover letter and resumes typed and printed professionally (no mimeographs, bad copies, or dot matrix printers)? C'mon, this is a position where the person should be skilled in cranking out extremely good-looking correspondence. If someone feels a poorly presented resume is acceptable, do you want them sending out correspondence for your company?

- Is their stated objective consistent with what you're looking for? If not, again, they're just throwing hundreds of envelopes in the mail. Furthermore, they may well be hunting for a job to "hold them over" until they can find the job they really want. No matter how skilled they are, you'll have to spend some time training them, and you don't want to waste your time doing so, only to have them leave three months later.

- Do they indicate that they have the specific skills you've asked for? If you need someone with Mac experience and it appears they've never seen one, send the resume to the bottom of the pile.

- What is their related job experience? I've gotten a number of applicants who have never been an administrative assistant before. I personally look for someone who has worked for an executive before, instead of someone who's coming from the typing pool or who performed some unrelated administrative type of work. They generally have a better understanding of working for someone who operates under a lot of pressure and can be very demanding, and they know when and how to keep their mouth shut.

There are more specific qualifications, but you get the idea. This book is about software development, not hiring. I just want to give you a head start on this process if you haven't done it before.

The phone interview

The interviewing process actually has three parts to it. The first is a phone interview, where I might spend up to an hour on the phone with a top-notch candidate. That may seem like a lot of time to spend on the phone—but it's a lot more efficient than bringing someone in for an interview only to find out they're missing some essential quality. It also helps evaluate someone more fairly—based on what they say and don't say. Everyone, regardless of how much one tries not to be, is influenced by appearance—and so I try to avoid an initial prejudice based on appearance by making a first impression on the phone.

This phone interview is a lot like the initial phone call with a potential customer. It's your first chance to set expectations with a potential employee.

Start out with a checklist of topics to discuss. I spend the first half of the conversation confirming information and asking questions about holes or interesting things on their resume, and the second half, if we get that far, letting them do the talking (and, really, the selling of themselves to me).

Confirm information and ask questions

First, identify yourself, tell them why you're calling, and ask them if they have time to talk for 20 or 30 minutes. You don't want to put a potential candidate in the position of feeling uncomfortable because they didn't realize this conversation was going to last a long time and they answered the phone while they had a kid in the tub or food on the grill.

Make sure you confirm all the basic facts—they're looking for an administrative job, they're interested in coming downtown every day, and so on. Find out whether they're currently employed. I'm not saying that someone who isn't working now isn't qualified—what I want to find out is how candid they're going to be. Someone whose resume states that they were at ABC Insurance Company from "<date> to Present," but actually left five months ago doesn't engender a lot of trust.

Ask them how much they're making and how much they want to make. Once in a while you'll run across an executive-level assistant who's currently making more than many of your developers—why spend an hour on the phone with them only to find out you can't afford them? On the flip side, you might want to be a little wary of someone making considerably less than what you're expecting to pay. This can indicate a serious lack of sophistication or other traits that aren't going to work for you.

Have them explain exactly what type of experience they have with a computer. You can usually tell within a couple of minutes if they might have the experience you need. A pretty telling sign is if they've been using a spreadsheet for several years, but they're not really sure which one—"Excel, I think—you know, the one that IBM bought."

Next, explain in more detail what your company does. Many people don't have a clue about what custom software development is. Also be explicit about what you're looking for. Here's where you explain that you need someone to make your life less frantic. They may balk: "Well, I'll have to tell you one thing. I don't do personal tasks for my boss. I don't get her coffee and I don't run out for lunch." That's perfectly okay—they just don't want to do the job you've defined. It's not their place to define what their job is any more than a waiter has the right to tell you what to order. You're the customer—you're the one with the checkbook.

Get them talking

It's pretty tempting to talk for the whole interview, but you're not going to learn anything about them if you do all the yakking. At some point, I usually interrupt myself and say, "Hey, that's enough of my voice. How about giving you a turn? Tell me about yourself." This both disarms the person on the other end of the line, and essentially turns the microphone over to them.

You should have a number of open-ended questions prepared. If you come up short on answers after the first few, that's probably enough of a clue to indicate that this person isn't right for you.

You can find oodles of books on interviewing—from both sides of the desk—and it's probably a good idea to read a book about "how to interview" from the point of view of a job seeker. Some possible questions include:

- What three things do you like most about your current job? If they like aspects of the administrative assistant position, that's good.

- What three things do you like least? Similarly, if they tell you that they hate aspects of their current job that are going to be key aspects of working with you, then that's a bad sign.

- What three things must you have in your next job? Here's where you find out about some of their expectations.

- Why are you leaving? Many times the reason is mundane—more money, different hours, personality conflict. But sometimes the reason is interesting, and more importantly, I'm interested to find out how they talk about their soon to be former employer. Do they bad-mouth them?

- Tell me about the coolest project you worked on. Here is where I'm looking for passion and deep interest in how they work, and what they're really interested in.

A key tactic is to ask about specific items on their resume—and see how much detail they give you. If they claim to have "managed a project" but can't talk in depth about it, they may not have been as much a "manager" as a spectator.

If things go well, you're probably going to bring them in for an interview. You don't have to conduct the entire interview on the phone. At some point you'll want to cut it off and schedule a time for them to visit. I used to send them some company information and an application form that they could fill out and bring to the interview with them. Nowadays, I'll suggest they visit our Web site and e-mail an application form. If things don't go well, simply explain that it doesn't appear that they've got all of the qualifications that you're hoping to find, thank them for their time, and that's that.

Office interviews

I don't hold just one interview—I hold several. You may think this is a lot of time to spend on someone, particularly an administrative assistant, but face it—you're going to spend a lot of time with this person. Would you marry someone after just one date? People are on their very best behavior on the first interview, and they tend to hold their cards close to the vest as well.

I've had several interviews where I thought the first one went fairly well. I was interested in having them back for a second interview and got the impression that they were likewise very interested—only to find that by the time I called them back a few days later, they had taken a job with another firm. People tend to keep their options open, and most feel no remorse in leading on a potential employer, only to drop them the minute something better comes along.

Understand, I'm not blaming them. I'm just saying that you need to be aware that this type of thing happens frequently, and so you need to be ready for it.

I want someone who has some level of commitment—and I find out more about that commitment through a series of interviews than just a single 45-minute yak-fest in a conference room.

The first office interview

The first interview is the initial courtship—showing them around, having a chance to determine in more detail what their skill levels are, and providing them a chance to sort you out as well.

First, briefly repeat the questions you asked on the phone. Like I said earlier, a lot of people like to keep their options open, and it's remarkable how loose with the truth people can be when trying to land a new job. Repeating these questions is simply common sense—

making sure that the basics are covered. You can get more in-depth on items of interest, or where their answers made you uncomfortable. And if there's a serious difference in the answers you get the second time you ask the questions, it's time to tread carefully.

Next, show them around the office, and briefly introduce them to everyone. Others in the office are going to be curious anyway, so let them in on what's going on. As you'll see in the next few chapters, they've all gone through the same process anyway, so they'll expect to see who the potential new recruits are.

The third item on the agenda is a skills test, but this isn't an ordinary skills test that you might find at a temporary help agency. As I've said before, the best way to evaluate someone's ability to do a job is to watch them do it. (Remember the football place kicker?) Thus, you should consider giving a potential administrative assistant a 15- or 20-minute obstacle course around the office. Possible items might include:

- Here's our fax machine (or laser printer or…). Change the toner/paper/whatever.

- Here's the number of a friend of mine in New Zealand. Call her.

- Twenty-nine out of 152 letters in this mailing are going to Canada. What percentage is that, and approximately how much is it going to cost to mail them?

- Tell me your favorite joke.

- There's a document named "Interview.doc" on this computer. Find it and open it in Word.

- How wide is Lake Michigan?

- Where is the ZIP Code 10001?

- Show me how you use your favorite search engine on the Web.

- Write a letter to a hotel requesting information about reserving a conference room for a meeting.

- Explain the steps in procuring all travel arrangements for me to go to Seattle and back, staying overnight for three days.

I've had excellent results with this type of test. You are looking for mental agility and general "smarts" through this process. You're also looking for the ability to think on their feet, and how reliant and self-directed they are. You can ask them "Are you detail-oriented?" all day long, but until you actually see them in action, you won't really know. I've had some candidates look at me with a dumb look on their face once this skills test starts, completely lost, while others dug in, relishing the challenge.

You want a go-getter and someone who isn't going to give you grief every step of the way. A test like this is an excellent way to find out first hand about their attitude and approach to unusual situations.

The second office interview

The purpose of the next interview is primarily to let them talk to others in the shop. I don't like hiring people without letting them meet as many others at the company as possible. I'm pretty casual about this process, preferring to let nature take its course instead of forcing current employees to follow a strict script. I try to talk about the recruit to employees as little as possible, so as to not color their opinion or impression of the interviewee.

This interview is a chance for the prospective hire to find out from others what the shop is like—and get the inside scoop on me. Of course, I'll talk to my employees afterwards—it's amazing what you can learn about what a prospective employee's real interests and fears are.

I'll also use this interview to quiz the interviewee about some major things discussed in the first interview. If we've talked on the phone and in a face-to-face interview, and they still don't understand, really, what it is that we do at the company, it's a pretty telling sign that this hire isn't going to be a good fit.

If things go well by the end of the second interview, I'll ask them how interested they are—point blank—are they interested in a job here? And, if so, how interested—on a scale of 1 to 10. I'm asking them to commit to their level of interest—and this is pretty valuable. They may have found, after two interviews, that they're just not that keen on the place—and by bluntly asking them, they're very likely to say so. Alternatively, if they're really interested, they'll waste no time in telling me so.

If they're extremely interested, I'll explain what an offer is going to look like, including start date, dollars, and other items. I don't make the offer yet, but I tell them what it's going to entail. It can be a little tricky to have this conversation—you don't want to "lead them on" but at the same time, you want to prepare them so that there aren't any surprises. I phrase the discussion as "This is what will happen if I make you an offer and this is what the offer will look like." I'm trying to get to a point where we've both agreed—"in principle"—that this is something we both want to do—I want them to come work for me, and they want this job.

I also make it clear now that at the time of the offer, I'm going to expect them to accept or decline at that time. Thus, this is their chance to ask questions about details like benefits, specific job responsibilities, and other little details that they would otherwise ask at the offer. The offer itself, then, should be simply a formality.

The offer, and how much to pay?

The third interview is just the job offer, and can be done pretty quickly. I give them a written offer—the one I described to them in the second interview—and I expect them to accept it or decline it on the spot.

This may seem harsh, and I've been criticized for it, but there's a specific reason. They should have had all the information they needed by the end of the second interview—and so they've had time to think about it. They could discuss it with their spouse, friends, whoever else. They should, by this time, know whether or not they want the job. If they don't have enough information, then they haven't done their part. I've explained up front what is going to happen. I've told them how this process works: that it's their responsibility to get the information they need to make a wise choice, that they'll be told about the offer, and that when I make it in writing, they'll be expected to accept it or decline on the spot.

I've had prospective employees take an offer and shop it around, and I think that's unfair. I've made a significant investment in this person at this point, and I expect them to take their part of this relationship seriously.

Of course, to counter this "harshness," I have a card hidden up my sleeve. The offer I've described to them in the second interview isn't actually the one they get in the third interview—I sweeten it ever so slightly. For example, I may have mentioned a figure like "$26,000 to $27,000" (and of course, they're going to be either expecting or hoping for the higher number), but the actual written offer will be $27,500 or $28,000. Then if they say something about it, I smile sort of embarrassedly, saying, "Well, I really want you to accept." This also tends to make it difficult for them to try to "negotiate" at the last minute.

What if they come to the final interview and try to bargain? For example, suppose the offer is for $30,000—$1,500 higher than what I had discussed in the previous interview. However, they then say that they really need $32,000.

I really have no patience with this. Remember that I've already asked them what kind of money they were looking for on the phone, confirmed that in the first interview, and confirmed what kind of money we were discussing in the second interview. For them to backpedal this late in the game indicates that they either don't listen or don't think things through well, or that they weren't being square with me in the first place.

This relationship has now taken the cast of one where a customer is always trying to get you to throw in "something for free." You know the one—they want a report modified, or a text box changed to a combo box, or whatever. But whatever the terms of the deal were, they just want a little bit more. It doesn't matter how generous the initial deal was—they just have to squeeze another couple drops out.

If they're beginning our relationship in this manner, I would fully expect them to continue to bargain and deal—wanting to get out of work early twice a week, or taking a longer lunch hour, or whatever. The funny thing is, this always ends up being a one-way street. They may want out at 4:00 three days a week for an aerobics class or to coach a softball team, but they never offer anything in return.

I'll show them the door.

I realize that this approach is a little off the beaten path. Nonetheless, I hope I've given you something to think about. Your style may vary.

Day-to-day life

Remember that your administrative assistant should be making your life easier—and she needs to be attuned to your needs. If you're not a morning person, she shouldn't dump a load of stuff on you at 8:30 unless it's really important. If you're under duress because of two big projects, trouble with the kids at school, and jet lag from a weeklong trip in Europe, she should know enough to detect this.

At the same time, an administrative assistant is not your slave. Don't treat her like a second-class citizen—remember that this person is, to an extent, your partner in making the company run better.

I think it's your responsibility to keep your assistant informed about what you're doing, your plans, and what she can do to help. Although she's supposed to be a mind reader, she's probably not, so make it easy for her to help you.

If you're not a boss

You may feel this doesn't apply to you if you're not a company president or a department manager. Even if you're simply a developer but you've got significant control over your earnings, I'd like you to reconsider. Suppose you had an assistant who worked for you part-time, and you and another developer together paid that assistant between $10,000 and

$15,000—pretty good wages for half-time administrative work. Could you increase your productivity enough that you could earn that money back?

Go through your day or week and see how much time you spend on non-billable work. Some of it is technical stuff—installing software, beta-testing, backing up files, writing and reviewing documentation—and some of it is just dumb administrative or clerical stuff—spell-checking documents, hunting down a new mouse when yours dies, getting that new copy of a book, and so on.

In both cases, your assistant can very possibly help with some of these chores. In fact, depending on the skill level of the assistant, he may even be able to do some billable work, just as a paralegal's time is billed out at a law firm.

In other professions, top producers often have one or more assistants who look after the details while they concentrate on doing the magic that they do. A stockbroker spends his time yakking with clients, not filling out order forms, updating address changes, or mailing business cards. He hires an assistant to do that work for him. A lawyer has a paralegal do the legwork for her cases, while she can concentrate on the client contact and the brainwork to support the case. You may be in the same position—if you're a top producer for your firm, you may be able to afford an administrative assistant after all!

Chapter 32
Finding:
Options for the Hiring Process

"What do you think the chances are of a guy like you and a girl like me ending up together?"—Lloyd
"Not good."—Mary
"You mean not good like one out of a hundred?"—Lloyd
"I'd say more like one out of a million."—Mary
"So you're telling me there's a chance..."—Lloyd
   —Dumb and Dumber

The truisms that applied to marketing—nothing works, but you must still do it all the time, whether you need to or not—also apply to finding employees. Given the work on your shoulders as a result of those marketing requirements, you may be tempted to throw your hands in the air again. In this chapter, I'll discuss a few techniques you might find helpful in finding folks to join your firm or department.

Software development is an intellectual activity. Despite the strides made in automated tools, it requires the unique talents of an individual's mind. And truly talented people are rare and must be sought after regularly—whether you currently need them or not. Furthermore, many of the great catches may not be actively looking for a new job. As a result, you have to change your mindset—even more so than when you're marketing—to always be on the lookout for potential employees.

You may argue that the difference is that you're *always* ready for taking on more work, but you may not be able to take on a new employee. That's okay—just because you're keeping your eyes open for a potential candidate doesn't mean you have to hire them the moment you run into someone. They may not be ready to move either—but if you keep in touch, there may well be a time when you need someone and they're ready to make a switch.

The recruitment mentality

Developers quickly find out that they must keep marketing throughout the year. If they land a job and then stop selling, they'll find out that when that job is over, they'll be up the proverbial creek if they haven't continued to market during the job. The same goes for finding employees. Most firms treat employee recruitment as a one-time activity, to be performed when a person quits or when the firm lands a job and needs additional people.

The first trick to successfully bringing people on board is to have your "people finder" radar turned on and running full strength all the time. I remember walking through a trade show one time, passing by a booth exhibiting equipment that was of absolutely no interest to me, but being hailed by the woman doing the demonstrations. Even after politely declining her sales pitch, she continued to pursue me, and in a few minutes, it dawned on me that she might be a good candidate for future work at my shop. I turned the tables on her, suggesting she give me a call sometime if she wanted a new position, and six months later she had become my star instructor.

So what avenues do you have when wandering around with your "people finder" radar? Let's examine some of the typical places, and then wander a bit further a field.

The Internet

Probably the easiest way to cast a wide net for potential employees, the various mechanisms on the Web allow you to perform a variety of employee recruiting activities.

One avenue is to post your position on various job boards and wait for potential job seekers to "wander by." Another is to register with various services, specifying what type of employees you're looking for (or what type of positions you're looking to fill), and have them send you "pre-qualified" stacks of resumes. A third is to log on to any number of resume services and do the scanning yourself.

None of these services are free, of course, and as an employer, the burden is on you to cough up the funds to support the service.

The primary advantages of using the Web to find candidates is that you can cast a wide net for relatively little cost, as well as being able to specify more exactly what you're looking for. The downside is that listings get stale easily and it may be difficult to find someone geographically appropriate—more and more, people don't necessarily want to uproot their life and family for a new job.

Want ads

As the type of position you are trying to fill becomes more and more sophisticated, or as the number of openings increases to outnumber qualified candidates, the want ads become less and less a viable option. Typically, you place an ad, get a few responses, and then fend off headhunters for a year. Nonetheless, it's an avenue that should be investigated, if only to turn it down later.

Don't forget that you have many possible venues for placing a want ad—not just in the big metropolitan paper but smaller papers as well—suburban weeklies, specialized publications, and so on. The trick to successful recruiting in want ads is to look at what your competition is doing, and beat them. As the pool of available candidates becomes smaller, they'll become more selective, and you'll need to do a better job of selling them on your firm.

Just like marketing, you want to set yourself apart from the others. Technical people are hard to find. Therefore, you have to be smart about attracting the few who end up scanning the want ads. You can't just say, "Programmer wanted; competitive wages offered" and be done with it. There are gazillions of those ads. Why should the superstar programmer out there answer your ad instead of someone else's? See what the other firms are saying and then tailor your ad differently.

Take a look at the local want ads—yes, now, particularly if you're not in the hiring mode. Read through a couple dozen—it kind of strikes you in the face as to how similar and bland they all sound, doesn't it? Once you've finished with the batch, try to recall the first one you saw—and if you can't, how can you expect the candidate pool to?

What can you do to differentiate your shop from the others in print? I've already gone over a couple of reasons why you do business differently (remember that chapter on

Positioning?). Tailor your ad so that your company sounds different, exciting, and attractive. Some questions you can ask yourself:

- Do you have a distinctive environment?

- Do you specialize in some particularly cool area of technology?

- Is there some other attribute of your firm that makes you stand out?

Here's a pretty bland ad:

```
Due to continued growth, leading software development firm seeks experienced
programmer with college degree and at least five years of Visual Basic, C++,
and Java experience. Windows 2000 and Novell a plus. Excellent communication
skills and a willingness to work as a team player a must. Competitive salary
and benefits. Send resume to Human Resources, ABC Bland Company.
```

Gosh. Could they have used more clichés? Here's how you might doctor it up to stress a few unusual attributes that are particularly attractive to the software developer type.

```
Local software development shop keeps on growing. In dire need of entry-level
programmers and experienced software developers. Full-time or part-time
available. Downtown location. Flexible hours. Casual dress. Private office.
Fully stocked kitchen. Sense of humor mandatory. E-mail resume and code samples
to alias@company.com.
```

What's new here? Okay, some of the same stuff, but stated differently. It doesn't sound like a suit in the corner office on the Human Resources floor wrote this one, does it?

Second, notice some of the attributes that might prompt one to take a second and third look. First, it makes a distinction between a programmer and a developer—and notes that part-time folks are welcome as well. Some of the other things as well—hours, dress code, private office—are benefits still fairly rare in the industry.

I've had more people respond positively to a line regarding the requirement for a sense of humor—and, as you'll see, I later ask them for their all-time favorite joke.

Show them that you expect them to be "with it" by having them e-mail their materials to you. Okay, this may sound silly in this day and age, but you'll get a quick sense of how technically competent they are—wouldn't you love to hear from a "programmer" who ends up e-mailing his resume 14 times, each time with a 12 MB attachment, because he didn't think to ZIP his code samples? I've seen it happen!

Finally, as I just alluded to, ask them for a code sample. It's again truly frightening to see what happens when you do. I've had people send me 50 pages of COBOL they wrote five years ago in school, and trivial six-line snippets of code that converted data from one type of data to another.

Part-timers

You can do yourself a great deal of good by ignoring conventional wisdom. Here's an example: One of the great hidden resources in this country is the huge population of parents who are now at home but would still like to continue working. They'd like to keep their hand in what they do so that once the kids are at school or out of the nest, they don't feel like they've lost touch. However, many of these parents can't or won't go back to work full time. Note that I say "parents," not "moms," —because it is very possible that mom is working full-time and dad is staying home—or, in their ideal situation, that's what they'd like to do, and are looking for the opportunity that will let them do so.

Most employers see this as a problem. They think the employee will leave work early to go to soccer games, or have to skip work because the kids are sick, or that the insurance premiums will be too high, or that the employees will be distracted with the multitude of kid problems, and so on.

Software development is one of those areas where part-time, flexible situations are a great match for the employee and the firm. This is the type of thing you can stress to candidates in your ad.

Now, let me take this one step further. In the previous section, I suggested not ignoring publications other than the big suburban daily. In many cities, there is a weekly or monthly publication that caters to working parents. In Milwaukee, there is a monthly called *Metro Parent* that is chock-full of ads for day care, playground equipment, diaper services, reused toys, obstetricians, and so on. Obviously, the readership is precisely your target. I placed just one ad in this paper looking for a part-time marketing professional and received several qualified responses.

It is important to stress three things in an ad in this type of media. First, if you have part-time work available, make a big deal out of it—that's still a rare commodity. Second, emphasize that your firm is "family friendly"—that you're not locking someone in a cubicle without a phone from 8 to 5. And, third, just to make sure the reader is "getting it," make sure they understand this is a professional position, not a $7 per hour job licking envelopes at home.

Customers—yes and no

It's pretty common to have an employee of a customer approach you for work. This sword cuts both ways.

I did some consulting at a firm a few years ago, and years later, one of their employees saw that I was running an ad. This person called me up and since I had already spent twenty-some hours of consulting time with them, I knew quickly where that person fit, how they interacted with others, and their technical skill level. Once I was able to determine what would happen at my customer's firm if they left and joined my firm (and that no bad feelings would occur), it was a pretty easy decision to bring them on board.

Of course, this begs the question—what would happen if an employee of a customer left and joined you? The first thing to consider is who approached whom. In the aforementioned case, since they approached me, and they had already told their boss that they were looking around, there were no hard feelings. One doesn't always get that lucky.

A long time ago, I met someone at a customer site who was extremely sharp and personable. We hit it off quickly and I, being somewhat less experienced then, asked this person if they'd consider coming on board with me. They were pretty interested, but wanted to think about it. While they were thinking, I called my prime contact at the customer to see if there would be any problem, and he consented as he didn't see any direct problem. What I didn't quite catch on to was the fact that the candidate I was pursuing wasn't a direct report of my contact.

Well, as you can imagine, word of this informal "OK" got back to the candidate's boss, and tensions between our contact and the boss were rather high for a while: "What do you mean you told someone they can go hire my people out from underneath me?" Yes, in retrospect, it was a stupid thing to do—one of those "What was I thinking?" kind of moments—but it sure seemed logical at the time.

Before you go after a customer's employees, or let them come after you, take a couple of steps back and reconsider the long-term ramifications.

Competitors

This can be a tempting possibility—luring a valuable employee from a competitor, or having them approach you first. However, there are both pros and cons to this situation. Obviously, they should be more familiar with the type of work you do than somebody off the street, but at the same time, you may have to retrain them if they've picked up bad habits.

Also, consider the possibility that your competitor may feel it's an unfair act—and target you with legal action—regardless of whether any infringement occurred on your part. And, of course, the flip side of that is having a competitor's employee spend some time in your employ only to accept a counter offer from their old shop—thus potentially opening the door for confidential information of yours to end up in their hands.

Community college classes

If you have the opportunity to teach classes at a local community college, such as a once-a-week night class, you've got a potential source of hot prospects. There are two advantages to this avenue. First, you are now in contact with people who are motivated and interested in learning more than what their daytime job will teach them. They're making an extra effort to attend a three-hour class once or twice a week while still holding down a full-time job. The other advantage is that you can evaluate them for potential—without them knowing that you're doing so! It's expensive in terms of your time, but you may get really lucky.

I taught a Visual FoxPro class at a technical college, and I spotted one person in the class who had a great attitude and incredible desire. She was working a full-time job and taking three night classes at the same time. I was able to see that she was the quickest in the class and had the technical knack of picking up things logically. This is normally a difficult attribute to evaluate because it requires a greater amount of time than just a one-hour interview. It is also difficult if the candidate knows you are watching.

At some point, you need to approach them. They are generally flattered, yet they also realize you know what they are really like. You hear them curse, you hear them complain about work and their spouse and see them in a bad mood. In general, you get to know what they are like in a way that you generally don't during the formal interview process. I'll discuss how important this is in the next chapter, but for now, I'll leave it at that. You can get a better evaluation of them if they are unaware of your interest for a while.

Employee referrals

Some companies get excellent results from having their employees be on the lookout for potential candidates, and go to the extent of paying bonuses for referrals that end up in an employee being hired, and who lasts a specified length of time.

This technique provides several benefits. You get a number of additional sets of eyes now on the lookout for potential candidates—at user groups, at church meetings, through alumni groups, and so on. The employees can actually be more rigorous about screening candidates, because they know they'll have to live with them, and if they bring in someone who doesn't pull their weight, they'll probably have to make up for it.

The reverse of this is that employees need to be savvy enough to handle delicate situations, and that they may still feel that they can propose their friends or relatives for jobs, not being concerned as to whether they're qualified for the job. In this case, it can be more difficult to turn such a person down.

Elsewhere

Keep your eyes open everywhere—everybody you meet—and everyone you see. You know how it seems that life insurance sales reps look at every person they meet as a potential sale? That same "I've always got my marketing hat on" attitude isn't quite as applicable for our business—lots of people buy life insurance; not quite as many spend $5,000 to $100,000 for a piece of custom software.

However, there is always someone you will know who knows a programmer or has someone in mind. A lot of people are turned off by the omnipresent salesperson, but not many are offended by a potential job offer. So they are generally not threatened if you say, "Well, what do you do for a living? Do you like what you are doing?" You are actually curious—and, hey, who isn't looking for a better job?

You should also investigate user groups and individuals in the same industry who aren't direct competitors. You may have a Visual Basic shop and your friend may run a PowerBuilder firm or do AS/400 work. You can both be on the lookout for each other. There are so many niches in our business that it's easy to keep in touch with other technically savvy people. Hook up with people who have the same types of needs but for a specific technical requirement that is not applicable to your business. It doesn't hurt to keep a network of people out looking for you.

Cold callers who don't fit

If you have developed any type of visibility at all, eventually you will get calls from other programmers asking for work. This is good—it's the reason you've got your "people finder" radar turned on 24 hours a day. However, you can't afford to talk to every person who calls— you don't have the time.

That is why you have recruiting procedures for handling such inquiries. The solution, of course, is to get them on the right track and have them send a resume and some sample code in. You can then evaluate them in the normal course of operations.

However, there will always be those who believe that they have such personality and smarts that your recruiting procedures don't apply to them. Instead, they will call and insist on talking to you. They want to "get to know you," to "do lunch," to "talk about some opportunities," or to "do some networking." There are dozens of job-hunting manuals and a number of placement firms that actively encourage this activity. This is a problem.

The problem is that they're going to waste your time. I don't mean that they woke up one morning and said, "Hey, I'm going to call this guy up and waste his time," but in effect that's what they are doing. Let's take a real-life example of someone who called me, oh, an indeterminate time ago. He called and wanted to talk about Internet, blah, blah, blah, FoxPro, blah, blah, blah, Visual Basic, blah, blah, blah, application design, blah, blah, blah, their cool home page with Java, blah, blah, blah. While he may have been smart and clever, he would have gone on forever if I had let him.

Just like with the 14-year-old who called your company wanting to buy a copy of the new version of Tomb Raider, you need to be able to get these people off the phone quickly—while still being polite and respectful.

I have a quick solution to get those people off my back and at the same time not offend them. It provides them with the ability to save face and does not burn bridges in the future. That guy may be a lousy Access programmer but he may know a thing or two about .NET (and .NET might actually work some day!). So don't lose the possibility of getting together with them at some later time.

A number of years ago I developed a set of "17 Questions" that were designed to give me a quick overview of a person's technical abilities with the language that we were using. They are wide ranging and yet, at the same time, very specific to the kinds of things that we do. We didn't do event-driven programming at the time, so we didn't ask about DEACTIVE WINDOW. We didn't write our own DLLs, so we didn't ask questions about C++. We do employ a rather sophisticated set of interrelated function libraries, so we ask about functions and procedures. When I get one of these guys on the phone, I pull out the list and start talking tech. "Can I ask you a couple of language-specific questions?" and he thinks he's already got the job.

Then I roll down the list of questions, each of which has a very clear-cut answer. At the end of the 17 questions, which has taken about one and a half minutes to ask, he's said, "I don't know" eight times, has given six wrong answers, and hit the other three on the head. Usually he's not aware of how he's done at this point. I tell him he has gotten three out of 17 correct, and then, as gently as possible, explain that "he may be highly skilled in some areas of the language but doesn't have the knowledge needed in order to be successful here."

Then I continue, "This means that I would have to bring you in as an entry-level developer, and since you consider yourself experienced, you are probably expecting to be compensated as an expert, so bringing you in as a rookie will not make you comfortable. It doesn't make sense for us to try to train you because we're not going to be able to make any money if you're being trained for six months and being paid an advanced developer's salary."

This is a pretty humbling experience, and gets the guy off of the phone quickly and at t he same time is able to help him save face. Instead of being told that he's a loser, the simple fact is that their skill set doesn't match our needs. It also doesn't wound our reputation by criticizing or badmouthing somebody about their abilities.

Furthermore, he now gets the idea that, "Wow, I thought I was good but there is an awful lot that I don't know." And by having this set of questions ready to ask, he is also surprised that I am prepared. He is now left with three good impressions of our firm: 1) We are highly skilled, 2) we are highly organized, and 3) we don't dump on people if they are not a match.

I've had more than one person come back to me six months or a year later, with an improved skill set, and ready to try again. That's an impressive ambition, and one worth appreciating.

The headhunter

The other nuisance call is the professional recruiter, or as they're more commonly known, the "headhunter." I'm sorry, but these folks are terrible. It's not really their fault; it's endemic to the industry, but the bottom line is that they're still of no use to a professional software development firm.

One of the perks of running a user group is getting calls from recruiters with a "once in a lifetime" opportunity—this programmer just became available but is liable to be snatched up at any moment. I offer a free one-paragraph ad for their position in the user group newsletter and that's it.

If he asks if I am interested in hiring this person—after all, "this programmer is probably just perfect for your firm"—I translate this into meaning that the person put the word "Microsoft" on their resume and even spelled it correctly.

The problem is that a recruiter is responsible for finding people for a wide variety of openings, and the skills required for those positions span a huge range. It's impossible for them to fairly evaluate how good a match is between the technical skills an individual possesses and the technical requirements of a position. It's difficult for one of us to stay up-to-date on anything past our own tiny specialty, so how is a recruiter going to learn—and keep current enough—to truly make good matches?

The best you can hope for, should you end up going with a recruiter, is to pick up a few leads—they're not going to be able to do any more than pick out keywords on a resume and set up an interview.

Nonetheless, a good recruiter will charge between 30% and 40% of the employee's first year salary. They'll try to justify this fee by explaining all of the services they provide—developing leads, evaluating candidates, matching up requirements, and then just picking "those special individuals" who are exactly suited for you. This is awfully expensive just for a lead, since you're really going to have to do all the evaluating yourself anyway.

As a result, I stay away from the recruiter.

Conclusion

Many projects go astray not because of technical incompetence, but because of people issues. A large number of developers either try to do too many things or simply don't learn a language well enough. As a result, they struggle to "make things work" as opposed to "making it work right." The time you spend in finding the right people is the best investment you can make.

Chapter 33
Hiring:
The Interview Process

"Why do you want to become an embalmer?"—Interviewer
"Because I like working with people."—Interviewee
  —Anonymous

If you've done your recruiting correctly, you'll soon be inundated by people wanting a chance at the brass ring—a job at your company or in your department. Unfortunately, the work has just begun—and this is a task for which many company presidents and department managers are woefully ill prepared. Here's a step-by-step guide to hiring software talent.

Whether you're the owner of a small development shop or the manager of a department in a larger company, you probably haven't gone through the hiring process that often. As a result, it's likely that you haven't developed as deep a level of skills as you have in other areas, and even if you had gotten reasonably skilled in the past, it's easy to get out of practice.

However, hiring is a critical step in growing your company—mistakes here will multiply further and faster than in any other area of business. While I can't guarantee success, at least I can point out some possible pitfalls along the way.

One of the early pitfalls is not having a plan, and that's primarily what this chapter is about. Over the past 15 years, I've hired my share of technical folks, and in doing so, I've put together a checklist for going through this process in an organized and methodical manner.

Getting resumes

The first step in hiring people is to get the names (and related information) of potential candidates. I'll cover asking for a formal resume in a few steps, but for now, it's names and contact info you want—and that's all been covered in the previous chapter. It's simply amazing to experience the variety of responses to your recruitment efforts. You will get people who call you up on the phone and leave a phone number. You will get people who e-mail you with a one-sentence statement, "I'm an experienced programmer and can add a lot to your team!" You will get scraps of paper shoved under your office door, or thrown over the transom. The end result is a stack of names with various stuff attached to it, which some may refer to as resumes.

The first thing to do is to look for some way to weed out the, er, rubbish. That's the one thing that most people looking for jobs have never figured out—that the guy on the other side of the desk is, first off, looking for a reason to get rid of a resume. He has too many pieces of paper and can't deal with all of them, so he is looking for any excuse to get rid of some of them.

However, you can't just use "any excuse"—they're too old, they're not the right religion or race or gender, they're handicapped, they're a member of the wrong club—whatever. It ain't legal, but more importantly, it ain't right. So how do you perform this "weeding out" process correctly?

I'll get into this in more detail shortly, but in brief, you define the qualifications that an individual must possess to do the job, you determine what qualifications each individual possesses, and then you disqualify those individuals who don't have the necessary qualifications.

In order to do a proper job, you'll want to start on as level a playing ground as possible, and that means getting resumes from every applicant. Everyone who has contacted you should be sent a "Sales Packet" so that they're at least starting out at the same place. It's then up to them to do the best they can in the contest once the starting whistle blows.

The Sales Packet

Once you've gotten a lead on a promising candidate, it's tempting to throw caution to the wind. However, remember that you're trying to accomplish two things during the recruiting process. The first is to evaluate them, and the second is to sell them on your firm.

We screen candidates by sending them a packet of information about the job and the company, a job application form, and a list of other things they'll have to return. Actually, that information is provided through a hidden URL on our Web site now, and people are instructed to find it as appropriate. They are told to go through this information and return the job application (and the other stuff) before we'll consider them.

This may seem like an additional, unnecessary step, but the advantage is that you get to weed out those who are not interested. A surprising number of initially promising candidates are actually just kicking tires, and won't bother to make any real effort. If they have to go to all the trouble of preparing for the interview, they probably won't. Do you really want someone like that? Obviously, no, you probably don't want them and so the process has already become self-selecting. Those who are truly interested will answer appropriately.

The second advantage is that you make sure you have the same info from everyone. Some people send in a resume that doesn't have all the facts you need, other people send in a cover letter, still others just leave a phone number. As you'll see shortly, it's to your benefit to treat every applicant as fairly—that means equally—as possible. And you can start doing so by giving them all the same chance to submit the same materials at the beginning.

Set up criteria for the job

The trick to organizing this race properly is to write out your evaluation criteria *before* you start looking at resumes. Actually, you probably should have done it before you started actively recruiting, but there's a limit to how far in advance you can prepare.

Think about the person who would ideally fill this position and what attributes they *must* have in order to be successful in this position. Then consider what attributes would be helpful but are not required. And finally, consider which attributes are "extra credit" but won't matter if the first two groups are lacking—these can be used as tie-breakers. Write this list of criteria down, and make sure to write down what date you prepared the list.

Writing this list down and dating it is important for two reasons. The first is that the act of writing it down clarifies in your own mind what you are looking for. It's easy to be swayed by resumes boasting of this or that when, really, you don't have a need for it.

The second reason is to protect yourself in the event of a wrongful lawsuit. When someone you interviewed three years ago comes back and tries to slap a lawsuit on you, claiming that you wouldn't hire them because they were X, Y, or Z, you can pull this list out as evidence of how you went about hiring.

For example, suppose they claim (falsely, of course) that you discriminated against them for some reason. Being able to answer "Actually, the reason why I didn't bring you in is because your resume stated that you wanted an entry-level analyst position with no programming required. Our job description, which you received in your Sales Packet on <date>, described an analyst position as requiring about 25% programming." This is annoying because you may feel you don't have the time, or the need, to go through this "busy work."

But you have got to protect yourself—and the first lesson to learn when you start hiring is that there are disreputable individuals out there and you only need one to make your life miserable. If you have shown that you have a methodical process for looking at and evaluating people and that those criteria are not biased, it will be easier for you to defend yourself against a wrongful claim. They'll see that you've done your homework, and they'll look for someone else to feed upon.

I'd like to come back to the first reason again. Writing out your criteria helps *you* to make a decision—in particular, a better decision. We are all influenced by irrelevant factors. If somebody comes in with great qualifications but they look like the creep who stole your girl just before Senior Prom, well, they're going to have a more difficult time finding work at your shop, aren't they? You want to provide an environment where the effect of those irrelevant attributes is minimized or eliminated.

Let's take a look at some possible criteria.

- What is this person going to be doing on a day-to-day, hour-by-hour basis? What actual skills do they need to possess? How far do they need to be able to kick a football?

- What experience does this person have to have? Is it something that they can learn, or do they need to be able to hit the ground running?

- What background must they have? Why must they have it? A lot of jobs "require a four-year degree" when, in fact, the work that they are going to do makes schooling irrelevant.

- Will other non-technical skills be required or helpful—customer management, writing, speaking abilities, and so on?

- What other factors are relevant? Do they need to be able to travel? Do they need their own transportation? Will they be working in specific environments that are dangerous or hostile? Is there a security clearance required?

Evaluating resumes

Once you've got responses to the Sales Packet described earlier, you'll begin evaluating them. However, just as you've set up criteria for the job, you'll also want to establish a base set of rules about the resumes you're going to go through. Suppose you've got a stack of 150 resumes—you will want to have an objective set of measures that will help you divide the pile into the contenders and the pretenders. These criteria might include:

- Is the package they sent you tailored to the position advertised? Or did they just mail out yet another stack of generic resumes after circling every remote possibility in the Sunday paper?

- Did they follow instructions? Is the package they sent you complete? Did they include a cover letter? Did they include code samples if they were requested? Did they send a complete resume or was it thrown together at the last minute?

- Is the package presentable? They are trying to sell themselves to you. The manner in which they present themselves to you can be indicative of the way they would present themselves to customers as your employee. This means original versions of a cover letter, a nicely printed resume, no typographical errors, reasonably organized, and easy to read.

- Does the cover letter indicate what they're looking for? Did they mention the job they're applying for or is it obvious that they're just using a shotgun approach?

- Did they do something, anything, to indicate that they have a real passion for the job? Did they possibly do a little research on your company, on the industry, on the business?

Given these types of criteria (please feel free to add your own!), you can quickly create three piles—the contenders, the "Well, maybe…" and the "Yeah, as if…"

Now that you've got a list of requirements for the job, you're ready to start pawing through the stacks of hopefuls.

As noted, you will get resumes from a wide range of folks. Some of these folks have been through the job hunt before and others are brand-new (or it will appear that way). So let's be really, really picky about what we see on a resume.

The cover letter

These are professional positions, somewhere above the level of assistant fry cook at Burger Boy. Applicants should have a cover letter that explains what they're looking for and why you should be interested in them, and contains a call to action. They should also spell everything correctly.

In the old days, when I had more time on my hands, I would occasionally take a particularly horrible resume, pull out my red pen, and grade the thing like it was a homework assignment. Yes, that's right—I'd circle spelling errors, correct their grammar, ask pointed questions like "How can you claim that you're an expert in C++ if you've only been using the language for three months?" and so on. Then I'd mail it back to them.

Unfortunately, I never received a follow-up to one, which kind of saddened me. I'm sure most people were either very angry or simply horrified that they got caught with their pants down—but I sure would have liked to have seen the individual with enough chutzpah to make the corrections and try a second time.

Next, I look for something compelling! They will all try to sell you on how great they would be for this position. You'll see claims that they're dedicated, detail-oriented, hard-working, and that they possess fantastic communication skills. It's all standard stuff that they likely read out of a resume preparation book or saw on a co-worker's resume.

So when you have 150 people beating their chest, each proclaiming that they're king of the programmer hill, what is going to set one apart from the others? There's just one correct answer at this point—"Passion." In his book *Dynamics of Software Development*, published by Microsoft Press, Jim McCarthy has this wonderful passage:

"The role of passion in software development can't be overstated. To some people, the computer represents the ultimate in self-expression and self-discovery. As the pen is to the poet, the palette to the painter, is a compiler to a software developer. When the passion burns out, the compulsive interest in pouring oneself into an invisible yet coherent and dynamic stream of bits goes with it."

If someone figures this out and communicates it to me, this tells me maybe there is something worth investigating further. Frankly, I have no place for people who are applying for a software development job but are treating it as if they were selling furniture in the evenings.

How might they communicate passion to you? Have they done their research to see what your company does? Do they have any motivation, ambition about finding out what it is you do and how they might fit in? Have they talked around town to see how your company is regarded? Have they checked on the kinds of projects you have worked on or talked to your employees? Do they have really more of an interest than "Oh, here's another company, I have nothing better to do so I guess I'll send them a resume"?

If any of this comes through in the cover letter, then they've risen to the top of the stack and they're much more likely to get a phone call. Further, the existence of passion will be a significant tie-breaker down the road.

The resume

I've seen literally thousands of resumes over the years, and have developed a critical and unforgiving eye. Let me offer some ideas on how you can evaluate a resume.

Basic information

Their resume should have a name, address, and phone number (day and night). An e-mail address is required these days as well—a computer professional without a computer at home and a $20/month account with an ISP really can't call himself a "professional," now can he?

Extra credit for the person who has an unusually spelled name and provides either a nickname or a phonetic interpretation of the name. This person has either been through difficulties before or has a bit of empathy for the reader—a sharp quality to have.

Objective

What are they looking for? Do they have an objective on their resume? When someone sends me a resume and goes into a list of jobs they've had and what school they've been to, but assumes I know what they're looking for, I get quite distressed. I can't read their mind, and I think it's an unreasonable assumption for them to think that I can. I want to know what they want to do.

Some people don't put down an objective because they are afraid they will be eliminated from some position. They're just throwing resumes into the mix and hope something will find a match. These days, given that those new-fangled "personal computers" are available all over the place, the expectation that they could tailor a resume is not terribly onerous.

School experience

If they have been out of school a long time, they will probably list their work experience first, while if they've only been out for a year or two, they may well place their school first. Let's tackle school first.

I don't care where they went to high school, and am not all that concerned with where they went to college unless it was a really high-end college or if they did spectacularly well. A 4.0 at most any school means they paid attention in class a little bit. If they went some place like Carnegie or Stanford, I would like to know that. Frankly, a 2.6 at "any old school"—I'm not really sure how relevant that's going to be to me. I guess I'd like to know what degree they have, whether or not it took them nine years to get through school, and so on, just to get a feeling for who they are and what types of life experience they have.

Work experience

Do they list their work experience in reverse chronological order? As an engineer and programmer I like to see this in black and white. Work experience should be listed from most recent to most outdated, for the most recent 10 years or so, and past that, perhaps a very brief summary.

A potential problem can arise when a person has a, shall we say, "checkered" job history. The resume books advise that in this type of situation, work history should be organized in functional order, showing a progression of increasing responsibility and expanding skill set. Of course, for anyone who has looked through a dozen resumes, this treatment is a red flag saying "I hopped from job to job and I'm trying to hide it." There isn't anything inherently bad about a number of jobs in a short period of time, but I want to know about it—and I resent it when someone tries to hide it.

Why? First, there *could* be something bad hiding in the wings, and it's up to you to find it. Somebody who says "13 years in a variety of positions in the food service industry" and lists a few of the companies he's worked for but doesn't list the dates could be concealing something. It could be something perfectly reasonable—perhaps he traveled with his spouse through Europe for a year, and the candidate is simply being shy about admitting it. Or he stopped along the way to have a child or two. Or maybe he had a couple of bad breaks—laid off from one job, then fired from another that he took out of desperation. This is a mobile, transient economy, and having a period of unemployment or having a period in which you switch from job to job is normal. I can understand that. But I want to know.

On the other hand, the person might have areas in his past he would do well to keep hidden—the three-year stint as president of the regional hate group that kept him away from a paying job, or the year spent in prison after going ballistic at a customer's site and then going home and beating up a neighbor's kids—yeah, maybe you'd want to put their resume aside for the time being.

Second, I detest being lied to, and this type of misdirection feels a lot like subterfuge. If you're trying to hide this from me, what else might you be trying to hide? Software development requires an incredible amount of trust, and you have to be really confident that you're getting the whole story from one of your developers.

This issue of honesty is another reason I like to see dates attached to all schooling and work history. Dates are very specific facts that can be checked, and if someone has a propensity for stretching the truth, this is an area that can be validated quickly. I have a responsibility to my customers, my other employees, and myself to practice due diligence during the hiring process.

The key points are that they have to be able to perform, they have to be dependable, and I have to be able to trust them. People with outside influences that make them incompetent, unreliable, or dishonest are not qualified for the position.

Professional societies

Many people list professional societies they belong to. This can serve as a valuable indicator, and on some occasions actually means something. In other cases, however, the person is just looking for another line item to add to their resume.

If someone has joined the ACM in order to gain access to their Digital Library, and they did this on their own initiative, that's pretty impressive. On the other hand, if that membership was required by their employer because it looked good on the company's marketing materials, well, then I'm not as likely to be impressed.

Here's another trick you can use when deciding how significant these types of items are. When they describe their part in professional societies (and other activities), you should be looking for action verbs and that they actually got something done as opposed to "was a part of a team and all I did was watch" or even worse—"all I did was to get in the middle and screw things up until I was moved somewhere else."

Hobbies

I like to see hobbies listed. It tells me that they have outside interests, that they are looking to expand themselves past sitting at home and watching TV, and that there might be some commonalties. It's nice to find someone else who is into body-surfing—particularly if you live in Kansas. It's also an opportunity to break the ice with them in a non-threatening way.

You can also use their hobbies to get a better feel for their level of passion and commitment to life. Looking for someone who has a drive for excellence in another field is a good idea—because these people are devoted to excellence in all aspects of their life. That generally carries through into whatever they do, be it raising kids, making furniture, or writing custom database applications.

You may be able to infer their race, political leanings, or religious affiliations through a hobby of theirs. Remember that blowing off a resume just because they belong to a religious or ethnic or political group not of your choosing is illegal. Period. End of story.

What if something on the resume makes you think they might not fit in with your crew? If their other qualifications look sound, keep your mouth shut. Trust in the team you've already assembled and let them pick up on the possible "team chemistry" issue(s) during the interview stage.

References

A lot of people list references on their resume. I personally don't care for this. A reference is valuable asset—I wouldn't offer it to a prospective employer until after an interview or two. Also, the sentence "References provided upon request" strikes me as unnecessary.

Code samples

I like to ask potential developers for code samples because most of them will not do it. When I put an ad in the paper, I expect people to follow instructions. If they are going to be belligerent and sullen about following instructions when they are starting to look for a job, I don't have a lot of confidence that they are going to be good employees later.

Why would someone not provide code samples when it was requested? Well, some of them don't have a clue what you are talking about. Others will think that they are above the ordinary candidate and that they don't have to comply with this requirement. Some will want to, but won't have the confidence. And some might cite seemingly reasonable excuses such as confidentiality issues. Yet some will send in a listing, or maybe even a diskette. And once in a while—yes, this actually has happened to us!—someone will send you code that works. The superior candidate will find something to send, and if confidentiality worries them, they'll "change the names to protect the innocent."

The kiss-off letter

By now, there are already a number of candidates that have not made even the first cut. It's tempting, and very easy, to just toss those in the wastebasket—but do yourself a favor and respond to every one of them. You can simply state that their qualifications don't match your current needs, or something similar—but it's a courtesy often remembered, and you can never tell when that person might become a potential hire—or a client contact—in the future.

```
April 1, 1999

Dear Mr. Joe Schmoe,

Thank you for your interest in the position of Programmer at Hentzenwerke
Corporation. However, your skill set does not match our needs at this time.
Your resume and materials will be kept on file for <period of time> in the
event that a position that requires your skill set opens up.

Sincerely,
Hentzenwerke Corporation
```

Due diligence

Before I go on, let me offer a few words of caution. Hiring is a tricky process. Once you start communicating with applicants, you must document your contacts carefully. By practicing due diligence, you are more liable to avoid frivolous lawsuits and other problems.

There are two fundamental rules to follow. First: See a lawyer to make sure you're doing things right. Second: Document, document, document. Document everything. This started with the written criteria you used to weed out resumes, and it continues with your first phone call to potential candidates.

Practicing due diligence can help defend you from three angles: from customer liability, against charges of discrimination or unfair hiring/firing practices, and from being defrauded.

Customer liability

You are liable for the actions of your employees. You will be sending them out to meet clients, giving them access to your clients' confidential information and charging clients for their abilities. You must make sure that your employees can be trusted and are capable of doing the work.

Charges of discrimination

Remember all your documentation of resumes and phone calls? By being able to show that you had consistent criteria to apply, you reduce your exposure in this area.

Fraud

Just like thieves, people who are out to defraud will look for an easy target. I once read a story of a person who started work at a company, and within two weeks, filed for workman's compensation as well as a civil suit using Carpal Tunnel Syndrome as the reason.

The company settled rather than litigate, despite the fact that the person had retained a lawyer to handle this claim—*before they started work*. But the company couldn't risk litigation, and ended up paying out just to get the case off their backs. If you make getting a job with you a bit more rigorous, they'll look for someone else.

The phone call

You never get a second chance to make a first impression, or so the saying goes. While this may not be the first contact your prospective employee has had with your firm, it will be the first with an extended impact.

Set the stage

The first 30 seconds or minute allows you to set the stage. A phone call is an interruption—and a phone call from a potential employer can be particularly stressful. Your first objective is to put them at ease.

Identify yourself

The first step is to identify yourself and explain why you are calling. You know who you are and what you are doing. You've probably just made 12 phone calls and so you're "in tune" with this process. However, they're probably not prepared. You may have caught them right after a 40-minute argument with their brother about who is hosting the next family get-together. Or just as they're about to get their third kid into the tub. Or while they're taking a break from hacking down the underbrush that's gathered in the back yard. As a result, their mind may be elsewhere, and they may not quite understand what you are saying right away. Give them a few minutes to get their bearings.

Ask them if they've got time to talk, and if they've got time to talk for 15 or 20 minutes. They might be in the middle of something and you will want their undivided attention. Also, you want to give them a shot at making their best impression. Make it easy for them to tell you they can't talk right now.

If they can't talk right now, ask when a better time to call would be, and then call them. I do not let them call me back. I usually make a series of calls like this in the evening, and as soon as I'm done with this call, I'm on to the next—so they're not likely to be able to get hold of me, and I usually do this from home, and I don't really want to give out my home number that indiscriminately,

Party manners

During the interviewing process, people naturally attempt to show themselves in the best possible light, and I refer to this façade as "interview manners" or "party manners." You know, saying "Thank you" and "Please," opening the car door, and so on. When people are on party manners, they don't get too comfortable or let their hair down. They're thinking, "What if they find out what I'm really like? They might not hire me!"

The whole key behind our interviewing process is to get people off of these party manners. People will be reticent to show their true colors during the interview process. My point of view is that I'm going to find out what this person is like sooner or later—and I want it to be sooner, before I make an offer. Furthermore, they need to find out what I'm like and what the company is like. Again, I want to show them sooner rather than later so we don't waste each other's time.

Hiring, to me, is a long, in-depth commitment second only to marriage and raising kids. In a lot of companies, people spend more time at their jobs than with their spouse. Yet they will spend years dating someone before getting married, but take a job on the basis of a single 40-minute interview. What are they thinking?

As a result, we want to find out what this person is really like because we expect to be living with them for a long time. If both parties are not compatible, we need to know as soon as possible. It does take a long time to really convey that attitude to somebody, and you have to be very good at it. As the advice to the budding actor goes, "The key to successful acting is sincerity. Once you can fake that, you've got it made."

Why 15 minutes?

So now, in the first 30 seconds, I've told them who I am and asked if they have time to chat for a while. Let's assume they said yes and we're now at the point where we're going to talk for 15-20 minutes. Why 15-20 minutes? Well, 15-20 minutes is still a short enough time that if after the first few minutes, you can tell that the chemistry isn't there, or that something is not clicking, you won't make them feel uncomfortable if you cut the conversation short. Yet, it's long enough that you can actually get some decent information—if you plan it out in advance.

Get a pen and some paper

The second thing to say after confirming that they can talk for a while is, "You may want to get a pencil and paper and take a couple notes." It also allows them to write down questions during the course of the conversation. One thing I get rather annoyed at hearing is "I had a question but I forgot what it was." Well, if they had a pencil and a paper right there, they could have written that question down and wouldn't have forgotten it! Seems like common sense, but you'd be amazed how many people decline your offer.

And it's intelligence and common sense that I am looking for. If someone says, "I wrote down a couple of questions earlier—can I ask them now?" this impresses me. It tells me that they are a little more organized than the average bear. And we want people more organized than the average bear, don't we?

What to expect during this interview process

Now that we're actually talking (I know, it's taken 20 minutes just to read about the first 30 seconds of this phone conversation), I explain the ground rules of the interview process with our company and what they can expect. They should understand that we don't hire on the first or second interview, and that we expect them to meet everyone else in the shop.

We want them to have enough opportunities to gather as much information about our company and the job as they need. If they're in such desperate straits that they need a job by Thursday, then they're not going to like our interview process. I tell them that they could have four or five interviews, and that if we get that far, it's not because we're flakes or indecisive, but rather, it is good news, because they've made it that far through the gauntlet.

The responsibility speech

Most companies treat employees like 12-year-olds. And while I can think of a few 12-year-olds who I'm very impressed with, I'm not sure I'd turn over a custom software development project to any of them.

We treat people like (gasp!) adults. This means that they are expected to be responsible, contributing members of the company and that we don't look over their shoulder every five minutes, micro-managing how they do every little task. At the same time, we don't cotton much to excuses. They have the responsibility to get the work done, and that's that. If they get stuck, it's up to them to get help because I'm not going to come around and check to see that they've done every problem on their arithmetic homework.

At the same time, I tell them, to the best of my ability, what they can expect from me and the firm. But I remind them that since I'm human and fallible—I forget things, I make mistakes—I'll also have them talk to others in the shop so they get a better, more rounded picture of the firm. It's their ultimate responsibility to gather the information they need.

Now, I've laid down the fundamental law in my company—you're treated like an adult and you're expected to act like one—and I will hold them to it. If they think they can get away with irresponsibility at some point, I'll remind them, and if push comes to shove, I can shove harder. At the same time, while this is a powerful stick, it's a more lucrative carrot, wouldn't you say? Which company do you want to work for—the one that assumes you're a 12-year-old or the one that actually treats you like a grown-up? Tough choice, eh?

This little spiel has taken about a minute of the conversation.

About the company and the job

Now that you've laid the groundwork for the phone call, it's time to tell them about the company and the job. They may not recollect off the top of their head which company you're representing. Remember, they may have sent out several dozen letters, or heard of your firm from "a friend of a friend," so don't be hurt. It's thus appropriate to spend a little time to bring them up to speed on your company.

About Hentzenwerke

Next on the list of things to cover is a bit about the company—what we do, company history, something about the glamorous founder, that sort of thing. I'd suggest having a written checklist of things to mention. If you don't, you'll yak for hours during the first interview or two, but then you'll get tired. By the time you're talking to the tenth candidate, you'll barely say two sentences about the company.

About the job

Next you'll want to discuss the job itself—what the position entails, the general environment, what they would be doing, and so on. Again, a checklist is a good idea here.

Well? Are you interested? This now should have taken between five and 10 minutes—depending on how chatty you are and how many questions they ask. At this point you may have already determined that you're not too interested in them, so you'll need to go to the next step to determine how to let them down gently. But it's usually too soon to find out. So all you're trying to find out is whether, given this additional level of detail, they are happy they contacted you.

Basic data

You're still lecturing, and while they might have asked a few questions, you have the floor for a bit longer. Now that you've discussed your company and the job, it's time to find out about them. During this segment, the mix of conversation will begin to swing more their way.

Confirm the ad

Now we get to the nitty-gritty. I go through the ad that they answered, and confirm every requirement listed in it, as well as a few more that aren't appropriate for the ad. There are weasels out there who will answer an ad that they're not qualified for. Just because they answered the ad doesn't necessarily mean they have each of the attributes listed.

When you're doing this, be careful—be very careful. You may even wish to have your attorney review your checklist of items to discuss. There are a lot of rules about what you can and can't ask. Here's a starting point.

Full or part time?

Are they looking for part-time or full-time work? Our ads often indicate an interest in both, but the candidate does not always identify which. However, you can't ask them why they want one or the other. For example, you can't ask whether or not they have children.

Location, location, location

Are they interested in working downtown? Some people, incredibly enough, do not care that downtown is where the lights are bright—and they want to stay out in The 'Burbs. In fact, I once lost a potential employee because he was scared of driving downtown. And this was Milwaukee! You can't ask them if they have a car, but you can make sure that they know where your office is, and that transportation is their responsibility.

Hours?

What kind of hours are they available? Will overtime pose a problem? You can't ask specifically about issues at home in this regard, but you can explain the requirements of the job, and ask if that poses a difficulty for them.

Are you working now?

A surprising number of people answering ads in the paper aren't working. If they say, "No, I'm not," there could be a lot of good reasons for that, and that doesn't particularly bother me. However, if they try to dance around the question, I start to get nervous. If they really hedge around, do all sorts of fancy talking and refuse to tell me, then I won't talk to them anymore.

If they are going to be evasive when trying to make a good impression, I don't want to have to deal with them as an employee. There are many good reasons that someone is not working. It's how they give you the answer rather than what the answer is that's important.

New questions

Now that you've got the basic demographic data out of the way, it's time to dig a bit deeper.

Why are they leaving?

Again, it's not really the answer that is important unless they say, "Well, I knifed my old boss and had to leave before they found out who did it," and even that may have extenuating circumstances.

Instead, it's how they deliver the answer. Are they comfortable and do their answers sound reasonable, or do they sound defensive, hostile, and wary? Do they badmouth their current boss or employer? People generally don't leave because they are thrilled with their job. They leave because they want something better, different, they're unhappy, whatever. I want to find out how they react in that kind of position. When things go wrong, when things go bad, can they keep their cool? Are they smooth with a customer during a difficult situation? There are always two sides to every story. I'd like to know what both sides of the story are.

How much are they making now?

This tells me expectations, and whether I can afford them. People generally don't take jobs with a significant pay cut. I once had a situation where the candidate called up and seemed pretty sharp; I thought I would like to speak with him some more. Then, I found out he was making well over three times what I had in mind for the position. While he may have been very well worth it, I simply couldn't afford that type of cash flow hit at the time. It would have been unfair for me to have talked to him for a long period of time, only to find out that he would have had to sell like crazy for three months prior to his employment here in order to produce enough for me to cover his first paycheck.

The reverse is also true, of course. Suppose the position you are offering is for $25,000 and a person is making $6.50 an hour right now. They are going to see $25,000 and fall over themselves, promising the moon to you because it's more money than they could ever conceive of in their life, and they simply may not have the skills or the abilities, regardless of their desire.

If someone refuses to tell you, end the conversation. That's all there is to it. You have to know and if they are not going to tell you, then how are you going to work with them? Some people think by telling you they will lose their negotiating strength. If they are going in to the interview process with that kind of attitude, then they should talk to someone else. It's not as if we are going to magically find a way to bump up their salary 40% if they play some fancy negotiating game. What we can pay is what we pay. If they are not going to believe that we will treat them fairly along those lines, then the relationship won't work.

How much do you want to make?

At the same time, people sometimes get put into situations where they are truly underemployed. For instance, they get downsized out of a job, they need to bring some bucks into the family, they take a job that is less than optimal, and as a result, they're underpaid. If this happens it's perfectly understandable. Suddenly, you see a programmer who's making $35,000 and you're thinking, this person has an awful lot of skills, and she states that she is expecting to make $68,000. That may be completely reasonable.

She may have taken her current job just to put bread on the table, but she really should expect compensation at a higher level. Frankly, if you try to save a buck by figuring she was making $35,000 and so you will give her $39,000, she may come on board, but she'll still be looking and she very well may jump ship at the next best offer.

Very few people will be nasty and aggressive about that, so it really isn't that big of an issue. But it is something I need to know because compensation is very important and if the expectations are out of line on either side then one of us or both of us are wasting our time.

What do they want to do with the rest of their life?

I tell them to suppose that they won the lottery, and were guaranteed approximately their current salary for the rest of their life. Then I ask them what they would do with their life? The money means that they could support themselves comfortably enough to get along without working, but that they wouldn't necessarily be able to buy yachts and condos in Switzerland.

Obviously, the first thing most people would do is drive their spouse crazy. But what comes next? I'm looking for an answer along the lines of "I'd write computer programs, I love writing computer programs. I would do it without getting paid at all!" That's the passion I mentioned earlier—the person who thinks computers are so cool that by the time the sun starts setting, he realizes he forgot to eat lunch again today.

There are so many people who go to work and just can't wait to get out of work at 5 PM so they can do something they really like. If you go to any office park or downtown office building, you'll see them blast through the doors at 5 PM. You can see in their eyes that they are finally free to do something else. Wouldn't you rather hire people who like what they're doing for a living?

I want to find the person who comes to work saying, "I do something really cool! I like my kids and I like knocking around on the bike, but I also really, really like computers." As the ad goes, "Life is short, play hard." It is far too short to waste time on doing things you don't like, so I want to find the people who have a passion for writing software. Not only are they going to have a better quality of life, but they will make life for everyone around them easier as well. And, not only are they getting compensated dollar-wise, benefit-wise, and so on, but they also have a job they love. Someone else will come along and offer them another 10%, but if they think this stuff is cool, we will probably hang on to them.

A turning point

These are the topics I hit in the first 15-20 minutes. At this point, I'm going to have an idea as to whether or not I want to continue talking to them, or let it go. You can continue to evaluate passion. Are they interested? (Of course, if they have any brains at all, they will act interested.) Have they been asking questions all along, or are they just listening to you yak?

It's important, while you're talking about how great you are and how smart you are, to be really jazzed about it. First of all, that shouldn't be hard because you really should be excited about it. You don't want to sound as if you are reading off of a checklist in a monotonous tone. While you're talking about the firm, you should also be listening—do they start asking questions, or do they just listen and say, "Uh-huh, uh-huh, that sounds interesting"? It's one of those subjective things. Do they sound like they want to hear more or are they really bored?

How to terminate a conversation

Okay, you've done your best sales job, tried to draw them out, but they're simply not interested. Or perhaps, unfortunately, they are interested—really interested—but the door isn't swinging both ways. The golden rule is to let them save face.

You want to give them a good reason that this relationship isn't going to work—that they're not a bad person but that "what they are looking for and what you are looking for are different things."

On the other hand, you could explain that "You just don't sound that interested, so let's not waste our time any further." This is a bit more of an "in your face" approach, but, if it's really true, then go for it. If they protest, explain what led you to that conclusion—for example, that in 20 minutes, they haven't asked a single question about the job or the company. Either this will shake them up into getting more involved, or you can save yourself the rest of a one-way conversation.

Get them talking

On the other hand, let's suppose that the first 15 or 20 minutes are successful. You've told them a little bit about the firm and about the position and confirmed some basic information about them. But during this time, they have also become involved, and it's time to move onto the next phase.

It's now time to evaluate them. If you're going to continue talking, ask them if they can still talk. Remember, when you first called, you said this would just take about 15-20 minutes. Make sure they can still give you their undivided attention. Then, start asking probing questions that allow them to do most of the talking.

How do you get them to talk? Easy. First, ask "So tell me about yourself." Then, shut up and listen.

(This reminds me of an episode of Cheers. Sam is talking to his date, and delivers the line, "Well, enough about me, let's talk about you. What do you think of me?")

Often, that's a difficult request—people in our line of work can sometimes be introverted (yeah, I know, you're shaking your head, muttering, "Not all the time?"). So what can you do?

Ask open-ended questions

What do you like about your current job? What do you hate about it? What do you do in your spare time? What kind of hobbies do you have? Tell me about what you've done at work? What have you actually accomplished?

You want them to start a conversation so you can find out what's on their minds. Can they initiate and hold a conversation? Now remember, we're talking to nerds, so they may not be all that outgoing, but even the most introverted, geekiest, nerdliest programmer in the world will have a hot button. What might this be? Ask them about the last hunk of code they wrote. Ask them about the last cool thing they did. Ask them about the last great project they worked on. Even the most introverted of them will get all fired up about this topic and you won't be able to shut them up for hours.

If you don't get a response to this, it means one of three things:

- You're talking to someone who simply can't communicate regardless of the topic.

- You're talking to somebody who isn't very interested in you or your firm.

- You're talking to someone who hasn't actually done anything and therefore can't talk about it.

The key is details. Some people may be, at first, a little reticent to talk because they're shy, because they're on party manners, or because they're nervous. This is only 20 minutes into the first phone call, after all. But by now you should have been able to draw them out to some extent.

Other topics and questions

There are a few other standard questions you can use to get the conversation jump-started if it starts to die. You can find many of these in any standard text about interviewing, of course. A few of my favorites include:

- Which development tools have you used, describe a project you did with one of the tools, and how would you rate your level of proficiency with each one?

- Describe three things you really like about your current job.

- List three things that you really abhor about your current job.

- Describe the ideal job—including the work environment—for you.

- Where do you want to be in five years? Yeah, this one is trite, but it's telling for a software development professional, since they often don't yearn for a career in management.

Finishing up the phone interview

Over the last 15 to 30 minutes, you should have formed an opinion on whether you want the person to come in for a face-to-face meeting.

Schedule an interview

At this point, it's not only important to set a date and time, but also to set expectations—an agenda—for that first meeting. "Well, I'm pretty happy with our conversation and would like to have you in for an interview. You'd get to see the shop, meet a couple of the people, and we can talk more in-depth about what this position entails and get to know each other better. How does that sound?"

If you don't bring them in for an interview

I've already discussed how to tell them that you've decided not to continue—you explain a factual reason that you don't feel there is a match so that you can help them save face. Most of the time, the candidate will feel pretty much the same way, and will accept this as is. However, there are times when they won't. Remember, they're programmers, just like us, and social skills are not always an abundant attribute.

If, after hearing the news, they start whining and begging for a second chance, you may simply need to be firm. No easy way around this one. You're the boss. At some point you just have to say, "Sorry, but this is my decision and that's that. Thank you for your time."

There is the possibility that they'll turn your opinion around in that last 30 seconds—the half-court shot, the Hail Mary pass from mid-field. I'm always open to a zinger like that—it impresses me that they have the tenacity not to give up, and to do it in an elegant and convincing way.

Post mortem

As soon as you hang up the phone, stop and jot down some notes about the conversation. What's your overall impression of the person, their potential with your firm, their interest? This is especially important if you are on a phone interview marathon. Write it all down while the individual is still fresh in your head.

The in-person interviews

There are two significant attributes to every good employee. I've covered one already—passion. The other is brains. Languages change so quickly that specific knowledge is sometimes irrelevant, or, at least, not as important. You need to find whether they have the brains to learn on an ongoing basis. During your numerous face-to-face interviews you will find out.

The face-to-face interviews, while they take a fair amount of time, are really expanded versions of the phone conversation. What you do during them is pretty much up to you in relation to the job requirements. As you go through the multiple interview process, the actual things you do at each meeting will change. I've already discussed at great length my philosophy about employees and how to treat people; the interviews are merely a chance to gather additional information on things that you can only pick up face to face.

First interview

So the door opens at 5:45 PM and a somewhat timid fellow (or gal) with tape holding their glasses together peers into the office. The very first thing to do is make them feel comfortable. Remember, they're still on interview manners, and just possibly they're playing games, so you want them to let down their guard and get to know better them as soon as possible.

The tour

Offer them a soda and some Doritos (you want to verify that they're really a developer), and walk them around the office. Show them your fancy file server upon which you sweated blood when installing a new 450 GB RAID drive, show them the refrigerator and microwave and the box of candy on top of the tape backup unit.

Poke your head in each developer's office, make some wise cracks about the decorations (or lack thereof), introduce them to the person in the chair, advising the candidate to ignore their grumpy demeanor—the developer probably just woke up and arrived at the office a few minutes ago. Finally, take a gander out the windows. The idea is to get them used to the "look and feel" of the environment.

Then pop back into your office, offer them a comfortable chair, and start yakking. A couple of rules here—I always try to keep my desk completely clean, so that there aren't any distractions, and I always try to be available at precisely the scheduled time. Nothing bothers me more than having to wait for an appointment (you should see me at a doctor's office!). I don't feel it's fair for someone coming to see me to have to wait.

Small talk

What do you talk about in your interview? A little small talk, of course, perhaps bringing up something that happened in the industry recently, or an event around town—whatever comes to mind. If it's not natural to make this type of small talk, then you shouldn't. Subjecting a candidate to artificially induced banter is worse than having to listen to it on the 10 PM news.

As soon as you can, review the agenda for the interview that you set out over the phone, and then proceed to check off each item.

Demonstration of some applications

It's usually a good idea to demonstrate the types of things your firm does, so fire up a machine and go through a few applications, explaining what makes your development style particularly unique, interesting, or special.

While you're doing this, be sure to note their reactions. (You are taking notes yourself, aren't you?) Are they paying attention? Do they understand what you're talking about? Do they ask questions? Are they good questions, or are they simply being polite?

The company

I usually spend some time during the first interview to bore them with more information about the company—how it got started, a few war stories, a lecture about the company values and philosophy, that sort of thing.

Their experiences

Now that they've been put to sleep, it's time to get them talking. Ask them again about the applications they've worked on, how they develop software, what their coding style is like, and things they like to do.

Get them to tell you some war stories of their own, engage them in technical discussions about specific applications or implementations, and go over some stuff that didn't work out all that well.

This last topic is particularly interesting, and if you can draw them into it without them realizing what you've done, so much the better. You're trying to get them to feel at home, so that you can get a better idea of what they're like, and if they can feel comfortable enough to share some failures as well as successes, then you've started to make some inroads.

The job application

You may or may not have a job application that you have them fill out; if you don't, it's probably about time to make one up or pick up one of those $49 Your Personal Lawyer pieces of software. I've found it handy, when getting bad vibes from someone, to have them fill out the job application twice at two different times. I simply explain that, "Silly me, I must have misplaced the first one—would you mind filling it out again?" Then, check the information they enter on both forms. If there are any significant discrepancies, it's time to verify all of the information on the form to see whether your gut feeling was accurate.

The 17 Questions revisited

If, after the phone interview and one face-to-face meeting, your gut still suspects that they're just talking a good game, now is a good time to bring out the 17 Questions.

The minutes of the meeting

The last thing I do at the close of each of these interviews is rather unusual. I ask them to write out the minutes of the meeting—of the interview. To a person, they look at me like I'm from Mars. It's truly a wonderful experience to see this response, and it's very telling. When they realize that I'm serious, they usually buckle down. I give them a few pieces of paper and a pen, and then leave the room. If they've taken notes during the interview, that's good, but it's also a rarity.

Why do I do this? First, I get to see them freak out to one extent or another. I've seen people totally lose their cool on this one, and that's been valuable information. One person actually refused to do it—and I promptly showed him the door. This may be an unusual request, but it's not illegal or kinky, and when this person showed such reticence, I found out that this was not the person I wanted to deal with as an employee.

The second benefit is that I get to see how they do brain work—how do they organize their thoughts, how do they communicate, and what do they do in a potentially stressful situation that requires them to think on their feet.

Third, I find out what they remember. This is a new job we're talking about—their career—and if all they remembered is touring the office, looking at some apps, and having a Coke, then perhaps they weren't that interested after all.

Finally, I get to see how poorly they write. Yes, that's an assumption made in advance, but it's right on the mark—most people write badly, and the rest write even worse. And while there are a lot of sharp programmers, not too many of them can communicate in writing. If this person has particularly abysmal (or, conversely, unusually good) writing skills, I want to know.

Closing

The goal of this first interview is to get a face to face sense of "are the vibes good" as well as to learn more details about their technical experience and how they do their work.

When they leave this interview, I want them to know what, in detail, we do for a living, what their daily job would generally be like, and what the environment is like. If you can get them to feel that their first day at work would be like "coming back home," instead of the first day of a strange new experience, you might have a match.

They should have a clearly defined set of expectations and you should be comfortable with their level of intelligence and passion. If things look good, you can invite them back or you may defer until you've had a chance to interview with some other candidates as well.

Second interview

At some point before the second interview, your candidate should have answered the 17 Questions (or your equivalent). These are good for providing you with a snapshot of their technical skills and general thinking abilities. The second interview is a chance to examine their technical skills more carefully, to get to find out more about them, and to let them sell you on them.

The technical exam

The second interview is used for a longer technical exam (the 67 Questions) that determines, in detail, what skill level this person possesses. This test requires them to know their way around the tool or development environment in question quite well.

The test includes a number of trick questions, a few without any answers, a few with multiple answers, and so on. I even make them (the horror!) write some code and defend it.

I also discuss the rules of the road—what it's like in terms of daily routine, what the sales call process is like, how we go about designing, coding, testing, and all of that magic. Yes, I've discussed this before, but most people are so nervous in an interview that they really don't pick up on most of it the first time around. By this time they've heard a fair amount of it for the third time, and I am starting to expect them to remember it.

Twenty really weird interview questions (and the reasons for asking)

Go into any bookstore and you'll find a bunch of books that help job hunters prepare for interviews—including a list of "typical interview questions." You don't want them to answer questions to which they've already prepared the answers, do you? Here are some off-the-wall questions that can prove much more useful than the typical suite of interview questions.

There isn't any rhyme or reason to the order or sequence, other than to keep them off balance and in a mode where they're not on party manners.

Give them a program in their chosen language without any comments and ask them what it does.

Here's where you get to bring out the football and see if they recognize it. First of all, they get to find out just how awful it is to work with a program that has no comments in it. Second, you get to see their thought process at work—how do they go about this, from scratch? And third, seeing as this is a reasonably pressurized situation, how do they react? If they freak out, what might they do in front of a customer who asks something really unrealistic?

If I had to fire you, what would it most likely be for?

The correct answer is "personality conflict." Most people have trouble on the job not because they are technically incompetent, but because they don't play well with the other boys and girls. Most people don't know this, and it's quite telling to see them squirm, trying to answer this question "correctly." You can almost see their mind churning, thinking out loud, "How do I answer this? Do I tell them the truth—that I'm completely useless before noon—or do I fabricate some sort of story, like 'I work so hard that the other people in my department try to sabotage my work'?"

How many people live in Wisconsin?

(You could substitute the name of your state here, or you could find out whether they've even heard of Wisconsin.) Here's a bit of factual knowledge—but it should also be easy to sort of figure out, or at least make some sort of ball park guess. If they give some ridiculous answer, it tells me that they may not be the most logical thinker in the world. How are they going to debug programs? Just random, wild guesses?

What do you do when you get mad?

I love this question, because it's not a common question, yet it's a very useful one. People tend to do one of two things—either they go ballistic, or they pout. In other words, they're either demonstrative or they withdraw. I don't really care which they are, but I want to know which it is, so that I can deal with a mood appropriately. If they come into work one day and they're totally withdrawn, is it that they're mad at something, hung over, or just concentrating on some really ugly problem? And I'm also interested in their level of self-awareness—do they even know the answer to this one?

Name three things about work that you really, truly, and passionately hate right now.

What are their hot buttons? Do they even have any? Or are they really basically level-headed folk?

What would lure you away from your job here at the company?

Right away, I find out what's really important. Is it money? Maybe their spouse gets transferred. Is their family out of town? Do they really want to be an aerobics instructor, and computer programming is just a way to pay the bills?

I also find out how quick they are on their feet, and how smooth they can be in a pressure-filled situation. If they answer this comfortably, I'm going to be more confident sending them to a customer who can be difficult to work with.

Are there right or wrong answers to this question? I'd say the more superficial the answer ("a bigger office"), the less impressed I'd be.

What is your favorite band, movie, and TV show?

Just trying to get to know them and provide some possible topics for small talk.

What's the one thing I can do that would keep you here?

Okay, this one doesn't require a lot of explanation. But it's good to hear them give you the answer.

What were the last three books you read?

The really smart ones will name one of my books as one of them <g>. I'll give them extra credit if any of the Calvin and Hobbes collections show up in their list, but they get docked big time if Judith Kranz or any Star Trek book shows up in the list.

Seriously, wouldn't you be frightened if the last book a potential employee read was a text required in a college course?

Describe a situation where you really screwed something up.

It's interesting to hear the situation they choose, as well as how "honest" they are in admitting it. The stupider the situation, the more believable it is. And I also enjoy finding out how they admit to weakness and mistakes—or if they can even do it!

Describe a good performance review format/method.

People often have some very good ideas about things but most companies aren't in a position to take advantage of those ideas. How much thought have they put into this? I'm always on the lookout for new ideas.

Twenty-eight people out of 147 did something or other. What percent is that?

You would be shocked at the number of people who can't calculate a simple percentage on paper, much less in their head. It should take any developer about a second to see that 28/147 is pretty close to 30/150, and to be able to come up with the rough answer (20%) in their head. If they can't, should they really be in front of a computer?

Give them a page of poor grammar and ask them to correct it.

Again, another pressure-filled situation, but this time with a slight twist—most programmers try to avoid writing a sentence if they can at all help it.

Tell me your favorite joke.

I'm always on the lookout for good jokes, for one. Second, a sense of humor is really required at our shop. Can they think on their feet? Funny enough, most "How to prep for a job interview" books leave this question off.

Here's the number of a friend of mine in Germany. Call him.

It seems like a trivial task, but one that most people don't know how to do. How do they go about figuring this one out?

What were your New Year's Resolutions?

Okay, this one is a little whimsical, but it's fun to see what the answers are. Again, I'm trying to see if they're on interview manners or if they have begun to feel comfortable.

Name the only band that declined an invitation to play at Woodstock.

Next to a sense of humor, the ability to win rock trivia contests is the most important asset at our company. And no one knows the answer to this question. What I want to know is, once they admit they don't know, do they let you go on to the next question without giving them the answer? Some people just go, "I dunno" and look at you. I'm looking for the person who answers, "Well? Who was it?"

Where are ZIP Codes 01010, 30011, 90210, and 98052?
If they've been doing anything with databases, they've had to have worked with ZIP Codes enough to have an idea of how ZIP Codes are distributed. And the last two are gimmes, aren't they?

Subsequent interviews
These next interviews all serve two purposes. As our shop is pretty small, I want each new employee to have met and spent at least a half-hour or hour with everyone else in the company. Yes, it's actually quite time consuming, but it does two things. First, you have a better buy-in from each employee in that they've all had a chance to evaluate this new person and provide their feedback. You don't have to follow their advice, but the grown-ups among them will realize that at least they've had the opportunity to provide feedback.

Second, the candidate feels more comfortable with your company, and more a part of the team (gag, I used that T word!). They've made it through the gauntlet—the initiation rite—the hazing rituals. They've been subjected to the torture test and if they're offered the job, they know they've passed. No, it's not actually all that bad, but this long process shows them that you actually mean what all the other companies just say—that employees are important and you invest a lot of time and effort in making sure you have the right ones on board.

Each of the other employees has been briefed on the topics already covered with the candidate, and gets an opportunity to quiz them, subtly, on some part of that information. If we've discussed Functional Specifications with the candidate three times but, when asked, he says, "I'm not sure what you mean by specification," then we can assume that this person is either really, really, really nervous, really stupid, or just doesn't care a whole lot.

Finally, it gives the candidate a chance to ask your employees questions—to verify some of the conclusions they've arrived at.

You're likely going to circulate the candidate's resume around, particularly to the people who will be talking to them. You'll want to make sure that you don't write comments on the resume itself—they can come back to haunt you. Better to use sticky notes for noting something on a resume that you wanted others to see, and to use a separate evaluation form to record post-interview comments.

Preparing them for an offer
At each of these interviews (there may be two or three), we cover topics such as compensation, benefits, holidays, billing expectations and the corresponding work load, and other general topics that would be covered in an interview situation, and that would be included in the offer.

At some time during the interview process, I make it clear that should we extend an offer, they will be expected to accept or reject it on the spot. This sounds pretty rough—shouldn't we give them the opportunity to at least go home and discuss the opportunity with their spouse or significant other or a friend or their current boss? Again, I liken this to the process of marriage. If you dated a person for several years, and got ready to propose to them, you'd expect that, given your relationship and the conversations that you've had with that person, they would answer on the spot. If you propose marriage and the person has to say, "I'd like to think about it for a while," then perhaps it wasn't a very good idea to propose in the first place.

Same thing here—this is a significant commitment of time and energy, you've discussed all the details, and have pretty much agreed to agree. The offer is simply formalizing what both of you already know—setting it down in black and white. If they can't agree on the spot, then something is wrong. Either you've done a bad job in making sure expectations were in line, or they're pulling the wool over your eyes and they're still playing games.

I've had the situation where a candidate has told me that they needed to take an offer back to their current employer. At this point, I terminate the relationship. Any number of studies show that a counter-offer is ineffective and simply a means to hold on to someone for a short time while they line up alternatives. And if the candidate would truly stay in their current job because they were offered another $1,500 or promised a promotion in six months, then it's clear that they don't want to write custom software with us.

The offer

If all goes well, you'll eventually want to give them an offer. If they're still alive by the time you've gotten through this marathon of meetings, they might want to accept.

I've already covered what an offer would look like in previous interviews. The offer itself is a mere formality to confirm what we've discussed over the past half-dozen meetings. It is my opinion that by this time, there shouldn't be any doubt.

The written offer should include their salary, a description of their benefits package, and a complete job description. I also specify their work environment—office and equipment. Put this in a format that shows them its total value. Salary is not the bottom line.

I make a written offer, as much for our records as for anything else, but I've found that putting it in writing makes them just a bit more comfortable, and I'm happy to do it.

Conclusion

This process is extremely valuable for you, of course, but for the right candidate, it can be just as valuable. Many people are intent only on selling themselves during the interview process, and don't pay attention to whether or not they want to work at the new digs, and whether they could be successful. The right candidate will realize that the interview process is a two-way street.

Chapter 34
Keeping:
Day-To-Day Operations

"So you guys work on Sunday now too!"—David
"It's Wednesday, David."—Linus
  —Sabrina

Can't you feel it coming? Another chapter full of clichés—"People are our most important asset" and other such slogans that end up as fodder for Dilbert cartoons. There are far better places to learn about employee relations than in a book about software development, wouldn't you think? I think so too, so I'll keep the general-purpose stuff short, and instead share some ideas specific to our business that you may want to consider.

It really is true, you know. Your staff is the single most important piece of the development puzzle. Great developers with mediocre tools will outperform mediocre developers with great tools every time. So why do people ignore the staff? I've just spent pages on finding and hiring people. Why spend so much time on recruiting if you're going to let them wither once they're on board? It makes a great deal more sense to spend a little effort to hold on to them once you've got them.

Why do people leave?

What can you do to keep employees once they've joined you? Take a look at what makes them leave! First of all, generally, people do not leave just to make an extra buck or two. If the financial difference is large enough, sure, most people will perk their ears up at a new opportunity. But unless their current situation has significantly changed, people tend not to look around just for a slightly larger paycheck.

Instead, they tend to get pushed out the door, either by work conditions or a job that makes them unhappy. If you can make them say "Life is good" four times a week, you'll likely never lose that person. You should focus on treating them correctly so that the grass will never be greener.

Here are five major questions that you should ask about your people on a regular basis:

- Are they being paid fairly for the work they do? Are their wages, benefits, and bonuses at the very least competitive with other similar positions in the area? Money is at best a short-term motivator. The best you can hope for is that they are satisfied with their job and thus don't spend a lot of time dwelling on whether or not they're fairly compensated.

- Are they doing work that they love? Do they get to do their job or do other things get in the way?

- Is the work environment comfortable? Is the atmosphere friendly? Do they enjoy walking into work in the morning?

- Is there an opportunity for future growth, either in terms of new types of work, or actual promotions within the company? Can they foresee doing something that they're going to enjoy five and 10 years from now?

- Do you listen to them? Are their contributions valued, or are they treated like machinery? The scenario where a company hires a consultant who ends up telling them the same thing the employees have been saying all along is regular fodder for cartoons—but that doesn't make it any less real.

Of these five, the fifth is probably the most difficult question for you to answer correctly—for two reasons. First, human nature makes it difficult, if not impossible, for people to critique their own performance—either you're going to be too easy or too hard on yourself. Second, since you're the boss, many employees—even those who have been with you for years, and with whom you think you have a good relationship—will sometimes not level with you. You hold the threat of firing over their head, after all.

Combine these factors with how busy you are. I've made that mistake many times—getting so involved that you can't see that you're a tornado blasting through the office. It's very likely that your evaluation of your relationship with them is not seen the same way from their point of view.

These five areas tend to generate the primary reasons for which people leave their jobs. If you make sure to pay attention to them, the details will take care of themselves.

Your job: The view of a coach

Despite portrayals in the popular media over the past 150 years, your job as a boss (either a company president, a division manager, or a department manager) is not to "make people do things." Your ability to "make people do things" ends about the time your kids become teenagers.

Instead, your responsibility is to determine the direction of your, ahem, team, to evaluate their performance, and to get obstacles out of their way so they can do their job. If you think of yourself as a coach, say, of a football team, instead of the all-powerful "boss," and then implement that viewpoint, you'll be much more successful.

This doesn't mean you can be wishy-washy; indeed, sometimes you'll wish you could yell at your employees like you see the head coaches in the locker room scream at their players after a particularly humiliating first half. Nonetheless, just as the head coach's responsibility is to determine the game plan, find and put the right people in the right jobs, and then achieve that performance, so is yours.

You need to leverage yourself, and you can do that best by helping them do their jobs better.

Get roadblocks out of their way!

Most companies throw so many roadblocks in front of their people that it's a wonder that anything gets done. Most people would like to do a good job—but they are hamstrung by rules and regulations and policies and a ton of ancillary tasks that get in the way of developing software. One of your missions should be to keep as much of that junk out of the way of the developer as possible. It is in your best interest to have your people working as efficiently and effectively as possible.

For example, it makes their lives so much easier if you have a contact person who can handle administrative tasks and managing the day-to-day tasks that get in the way of their real jobs. Yes, these days, it's quite fashionable to "downsize." What this means in the corporate world is that a company ends up with a lot of highly paid, highly trained people doing things like making copies and hunting down insurance forms instead of writing code.

Does it make sense to have a skilled software developer spend an hour every morning for a week trying to track down the right insurance claim form? I don't think so! In the book *Peopleware*, the authors relate the story of a memo being passed around to a group of software developers, scolding them for having their phones forwarded to the receptionist. "We know that you would like to have peace and quiet to do your work, but if you continue this practice, she won't be able to get her work done!"

It makes a ton of sense to have one person—even a part-time person—handle a lot of these things. Software developers are rare individuals with specific skills—and they should spend their time developing software. Your job is to help them do that.

Upward delegation

There is a danger, of course, lurking in the shadows as you announce your goal of eliminating roadblocks. Some people, either innocently or not so innocently, will take that to mean that they can shuck off any type of work that they don't want to do. You have to keep an eye out for two types of actions on the part of your people.

The first is the person who unconsciously asks other people for more help than they should. This type of person can be handled with a bit of firm management. The other, however, is more conniving—this is the subtle slacker, who finds ways of having others do work that is genuinely their responsibility.

In both cases, the biggest danger occurs when you're the target—instead of work flowing down the corporate hierarchy, it flows up. "I ran into this bug and I don't know how to do it. Could you look at it for me?" People will do that—it's human nature. When this happens, deflect the request by suggesting "Okay, let's do it together." Instead of giving them a fish, teach them how to fish.

Teaching them to fish

It's your job to train them (or make sure they get the training) to deal with this situation. For example, in the case of a bug, lead them through the detection process by asking more questions. Play devil's advocate, and get them to do the work. Ask "What is the behavior that is being exhibited?" and when they say, "I guess I really don't know," tell them to figure out what is happening and then come back.

There is no excuse for somebody saying, "I'm not sure" when they have the tools to find out the answer. This is simply laziness. Why go off on a wild goose chase with them, based on a wild hypothesis? Force them to be more rigorous in their request—"I don't know the answer and I don't know how to find out" is about the stupidest thing a software developer could ever say to me.

For example, suppose that they are running some sort of posting process but only every other value is being posted, and the rest are zeros. The process is fairly messy, involving a number of temp files being created, a number of subroutines that perform validation, and so on. Instead of diving into the middle of the code, trying out random changes (and you know developers out there who would do that, don't you?), have them start at the beginning. Is the original file full of the proper data? Is the data being flagged properly according to transaction type? Is the proper data being put into a temp file? Have you scanned the contents of a temp file? Are you sure of your assumptions?

You guide them, having them work through one step at a time. The key is that you're coaching, not taking the keyboard in your own hands.

If you have to do this for three years, of course, maybe your developer should be in another business. Many developers will go manic when faced with a nasty bug. They will try this, and that, and then a third thing, randomness seeming to be the operative method. Finally, they will get one that seems to work, be happy, and put it away. This is the way I would panel my basement—but it's not the way to develop software. The key is you have to help them do the work themselves. Yes, I know—it's a pressure situation and the bug has to be fixed right now, but, as you've found out, there is time to do it right—because you don't want to spend the time to do it over.

What else could you possibly do for your people? The idea is to enable them, which means training, coaching. Not doing their work for them.

Keeping your cool

Sooner or later, you'll run into an employee whose primary mission in life is to make your life miserable. The worst part is that they never seem to be bad enough to just outright fire—they delight in taking you to the edge, and then keeping you there. When you finally figure this out, you've already won the battle, but the trick is recognizing the situation.

I had an employee once who exhibited this precise behavior. Fortunately, she does not read books, so I'm not too worried about her seeing this. It turns out that I looked just like her father (yes, handsome hairline and all), and that she hated her father. Why she joined the company, other than to taunt me, I've never figured out.

Anyway, she'd misbehave just to the point where I was ready to knock her block off, and then she'd back off. Time and time again, until finally, I had enough. Remembering a rule from up above, I had documented her various difficulties. We sat down one afternoon, and I read her the riot act, indicating that her behavior had better improve. Yes, this was a formal warning.

Before I knew it, she was in tears. Evidently an uncle of hers had died over the weekend and she was still pretty broken up about it, and having this discussion with her at this time was just too much for her to bear. Well, naturally I backed off, her behavior improved a bit, and things were tolerable.

About six months later, things had deteriorated again. Yes, you guessed it. She again started yanking my chain, and we finally had to have a talk. I brought out the documentation, and had even prepared a written warning. I called her into my office, and again, the tears flowed. The airplane crash that had happened over the weekend? Well, naturally, she had known the pilot, and she was just beside herself with grief. This was a bit much, but again, I relented and things got better.

The written warning straightened her out for a number of months, and we were getting along quite well. Eventually, since her lifelong mission was to make me unhappy, she resorted to her old tricks. I guess I had kind of accepted that, in return for her outstanding performance in the classroom (the students simply loved her, and the other employees for the most part liked her as well), I was going to have to lock horns with her on a regular basis. So I started to get ready for another one of these meetings, and as I was doing so, my wife asked me, "Which one of her friends or family do you think you're going to kill this time?"

It was never a problem to confront her from that moment on. Finding absurdity in adversity makes any difficult situation much easier to bear.

Reviews

Reviews are one of the most dreaded parts of an employer-employee relationship. And for good reason—employers hate giving reviews as much as employees hate getting them. Thus, the employer tries to avoid it, doesn't spend much time at it, and, probably doesn't prepare until the last minute. Correspondingly, the boss probably isn't very skilled at it, precisely because they try to spend as little time as possible. And to compound this unfortunate situation, most companies don't tie compensation or any type of reward system to the review.

Reviews are almost like quarterly grade reports—think back to school (if you can remember that far). Who dreaded midterms and finals? Well, sure, everyone, because you had to stop drinking (or at least slow down) for the week. But really, those who were expecting good grades lined up to see the grades posted after the quarter—those who knew they had gotten clobbered took their own sweet time to find out how bad the new was.

Furthermore, reviews should be like quarterly grade reports—regular and reasonably relevant to the work you just performed. And you knew going in to the quarter what you had to do in order to earn a certain reward. Would you like to have attended class for an entire year before finding out how you did? To have had no hint about what your grade would be based on? And then to find out that your reward—your grade, or whether you were going to graduate to the next grade—was pretty much irrelevant to your performance in class?

It doesn't have to be that way, though, and here's a methodology that may help you (and your employees) look forward to them instead of want to call in sick.

The fundamental guidelines for reviews

There are three fundamental guidelines for reviews. First, your employees must know what the rules are—how they will be evaluated. Without this, the rest is irrelevant, isn't it? What if two ball clubs play a contest but neither knows what the goal of the game is, or how scoring is to be done? Yet that's exactly how most companies handle their reviews.

The second guideline is that the employee must be able to control the results. This isn't the same as having an effect on the results, though. Think about this for a minute. Reviewing an employee on the overall profitability of the firm, for example, is silly—in all but the very smallest companies or in very special positions, a single individual has very little control over the profitability.

If a senior VP neglects to insure the company limo and then crashes it on a joyride, profitability is going to take a hit, and the employee can't do much to change that. Or if you decide to buy everyone in the shop brand-new workstations, and load up the server farm with a bunch of great new equipment, profitability could also take a hit. Again, your employee, while possibly grumbling about it, can't control that action. However, they can impact profitability—by screwing up a big project, by figuring out a great way to reduce time spent on non-billable work, or by wrecking the uninsured company limo.

The third guideline about reviews is that they should be done frequently so that corrections can be made early enough. You need to provide feedback often—and formally, through a review, more than once a year. What good is it going to do you or your employee if you bring up an unsatisfactory incident from 11 months ago?

Before a new employee starts

Remember that job description you used during the hiring process? It wasn't just for hiring—but also for use during the employee's tenure. Take this list and transform it into a description of expectations for you to use lay out the game plan for that new employee. It's a perfect starting point—since the employee has already seen it (or at least part of it), and it is, after all, why you hired the person.

If this sounds like you've developed a specification, and are now working with the spec, measuring performance and all, you're absolutely right. Seems like a recurring theme, doesn't it?

New employees

If you have gone through the hiring process properly, the employee shouldn't really have to spend a lot of time doing the traditional "new employee" stuff like finding out where the bathroom is, who the person in the office next to theirs is, and so on—because they've already been around enough to be comfortable.

Thus, you should spend a significant amount of time on the first day going over the employee's job description, your expectations, and set them to work. The most frustrating experience for a new employee is to be shown an empty desk, be handed a stack of magazines, and be told, "Get acquainted with things. We'll find something for you to do pretty soon."

Touch base with your new employee every day the first week, and at the end of each week for the first month to make sure they understand what you expect of them, and to see how they are doing. This is also a good time to find out whether the job has turned out the way they expected, based on the interviews, or something has changed. You can use this information to improve your interviewing process.

During the first week, you should lay out, formally (by that, I mean in writing), expectations you have of their work and performance. You'll use this for the first review.

During the quarter

I don't want to presume so much as to tell you how to manage on a day-to-day basis—your actions will be affected as much by your personal preferences and current situation and environment as anything else. However, you wouldn't take off on a cross-country journey just by looking at the map once on Day 1, and then drive the rest of the way without consulting the map again. Similarly, you shouldn't assume that a quarterly goal-setting meeting is going to be enough.

Consider, at the very least, a weekly meeting (maybe every other week with more experienced folks) where you review progress made over the past week and set goals for the upcoming week.

All employees

At the end of each quarter, review the expectations that you set for the quarter and compare them with what the employee has actually accomplished. If the two diverge badly, you need to examine why, and what you can do to improve things. This is not rocket science, of course, but the trick is to do this on a quarterly basis and not wait until the end of the year.

It's important to mention at this point that you really shouldn't be surprised. There's a saying in our business—"How do software projects become late? One day at a time." You shouldn't ever be in a position where you review someone's performance and find any surprises—either on your side or from their point of view.

If you've done a decent job at your regular weekly progress reports and goal setting sessions, you know how things have gone. The quarterly review, then, isn't so much a discovery process as a means to make sure you get together with your employee regularly.

Why quarterly?

Notice how I subtly mentioned that reviews should be done quarterly? Maybe I caught you off guard, or maybe you're already rolling your eyes. Quarterly reviews, while not unheard of, are still pretty rare, but I think they're an extremely valuable tool. I'd like to discuss why I suggest a quarterly review, rather than some other periodicity.

Pros to quarterly reviews

Earlier in this book, I talked about tracking people's time. This means measuring the dollars they are bringing into the firm, the bugs they are producing, and the number of Action Points they are shipping. As a boss of mine used to say (I'm pretty sure he got it from someone else), "What gets measured, gets done." This is all fine and good, but what use are all of these measurements if the developer never gets any feedback? Or worse, they get feedback on something that happened so long ago that it's of no practical use? Most firms schedule an annual review, and to my way of thinking, it's one of the stupidest things companies do. No one can remember what they did 11 months ago.

Second, the idea of a review is to provide the opportunity to take corrective action. If they started screwing up on something 11 months ago, then they've had 11 months to get really good at screwing it up, right? It's a lot easier, and much more effective, to make smaller mid-course corrections than to try to make a big move once a year.

Of course, you should be giving slight nudges on a daily, weekly, and monthly basis. I've found that a quarterly review gives us a formal place to do a reality check. If I need to talk to you about something or nudge you along this line or give you a pat on the back for something else you have done, I can do it at any time. But a formal meeting every three months makes sure that I don't get so caught up in the day-to-day fever of running the business, chasing customers, cranking out code, and swatting bugs. It's a real danger for an issue to surface, but there never seems to be a good time to really discuss it—and suddenly it's been seven months and that issue you wanted to mention has now become a real problem.

Furthermore, another advantage to quarterly reviews is that in a fast-paced business, the environment could well have changed and therefore things that you thought were going to be relevant a while back are no longer important.

Finally, quarterly reviews let the employees know that you are really interested in helping them do a better job—that your admonitions about "Our employees are our most important assets" aren't just lip service. This is a coaching session to say, "This is where we are at—and three months ago this is where we said we wanted to be. How are we doing?" If there is a difference, what can we do to make some corrections? A lot of companies blab on and on about their "interest in people," but the action of quarterly reviews shows you mean it.

Cons to quarterly reviews

You may look askance at a quarterly review because, traditionally, reviews are tied to compensation adjustments. Thus, big companies use annual reviews so that they can provide annual raises. You don't have to do it this way. You needn't talk about dollars every time a review comes around, and, in fact, given the way I'm going to suggest you consider compensating your developers, the compensation sort of runs alongside performance all the time.

In a larger company, you may feel that there is too much work involved in quarterly reviews. I think this is a lot like regular automobile maintenance—sure, you might think you're spending more time if you take your car in for an oil change and lube job every 3,000 miles. But, in the long run, you're going to save yourself a lot of time—and money—if you can avoid having the engine overhauled, or replaced, because you hadn't changed the oil for 55,000 miles!

Same thing here—quarterly reviews actually go a lot quicker than you would initially imagine, because you're still thinking of the pain and agony you go through for an annual review. Not only do you get better at doing them (and your employees get better at "receiving" them), but there's not as much to discuss, since a habit of regular feedback tends to reduce or eliminate the big issues that annual reviews can sometimes focus on.

Reviews aren't just for corrective action

By the way, it might sound like I am constantly crabbing about things employees may do wrong, but I'm not really. First, the developer is being paid to do X, those are the expectations that have been laid out early on, and we're simply taking action if X hasn't been done. If X has been done, then we're in great shape!

Second, while I've been mentioning mid-course corrections, those aren't necessarily due to employee problems. The business plan might have changed, the customer requirements might have changed, or a host of other factors could have gotten involved. The key is that more regular, formal communication can provide substantial benefits.

Finally, a quarterly review is also an opportunity to praise—to "catch them being good." Even more powerful than a "mid-course correction" is a mid-course pat on the back. People need to hear that they're doing a good job—regularly—and you're the one person from whom praise means the most.

Compensation

As much fun as reviews will come to be, your employees are also going to want to get paid for the work they do. Simple fact of life—you won't be able to get around it!

People want security, generally, or else they would go out on their own. So you need to give them a salary and set realistic billing goals—but not scare them if they don't hit them. Your job is to make sure they can reach them. And to help them reach them.

This discussion covers compensating employees who are billable. There are other issues with folks who are on straight salary, but those aren't really unique to the software development biz.

First, let's presume that a billable employee can be billing both hourly and on fixed price work. I know, I've been arguing that fixed price work is the way to go, but, in a pragmatic sense, most billable employees will need to bill some hourly work—either from folks who refuse to work with fixed price jobs, or during work that can only be done on an hourly basis, such as the design of Functional Specifications and Change Orders, and some types of maintenance.

In general, a billing professional should be compensated at 40-45% of their billings. This may vary somewhat—in a big law firm, the grunt associates get a smaller percentage and the partners—what a surprise!—get more. But as a general rule, it's a pretty good target.

As the person's hourly billing rate varies, so does their paycheck. The person thus has a high incentive to increase their skills in order to raise their rate and the corresponding take-home. You can use this as a rule to pay your people, or you can use it as a starting point to create a more worthwhile pay structure. I don't view pay as a nuisance that must be handled in order to get something done, but rather as a tool that can be manipulated to get a better deal for both you and your employees.

Since the wages of the billable employees are a significant factor in the cost of developing an application, I have taken those percentages into account, and have gone much further. Here's how we work the compensation plan—and, please note that in all of this discussion, I'm referring to compensation as the total dollars earned by the employee. How it is split up into pre-tax benefits, gross wages, after-tax benefits, and take home pay is another discussion that is actually not specific to our industry.

A new employee generally comes into the firm with an expectation of earning a certain amount of money. This amount corresponds to a certain amount of billable work. For example, if a person wants to earn, say, $4,250 a month, they'd need to bill $10,000 per month. Their compensation expectation and the matching billable requirements—and what that translates into in terms of actual work—have been discussed during interviews. Through the long recruitment process, we've determined that they do have the skills necessary to produce the amount of work that corresponds to that billing level. Of course, we're quite conservative—I make sure that it is very likely that a developer will meet their monthly billable target.

As you can see, it's a simple matter to change a person's compensation based on their performance. As soon as they regularly bill more, they can be eligible for a raise. Now it's time for a few questions.

Bonuses: What if someone bills more than their monthly target?

We pay quarterly bonuses based on the amount by which an employee exceeds their monthly targets. A bonus is additional compensation that is earned according to performance of an individual or the team to which that individual belongs.

Going in to the quarter, the developer knows what their monthly and quarterly targets are. As they enter their time and task completion dates into our time tracking system, they can identify how much work they have "shipped," and thus, how they are doing against their targets.

If we were strictly billing time and materials, of course, this would be an easy calculation. Number of hours billed times their rate per hour. However, since many of our applications use fixed prices, it isn't as immediately apparent. Here's how it works.

First, remember that a project has a price associated with it, and, accordingly, a number of Action Points. That project, unless it's trivial, has been broken down into modules and tasks, and each of those has its own number of Action Points assigned—and, thus, its portion of the total fixed price. Thus, we can actually determine that the customer query screen is worth $750 and the regional sales analysis report is worth $2,000. Since the developer knows what their dollar target is, they know they need to get a certain number of modules or tasks that add up to their target done.

The more efficient they are, and the fewer defects they produce, the more dollars they can ship in a given period of time, and the quicker they can reach (and surpass) their target. This pay and bonus system then rewards the smart, efficient, productive developer for doing a good job—as it should!

Naturally, there are always booby traps and detours. This is software, right? The key to making this type of system work is, as I've been stressing all along, a detailed specification and clearly defined functionality, so that the developer doesn't fall into a "black hole" whereby a $500 report ends up taking six days to develop.

Effective bonuses

I've decided on a quarterly bonus system for many of the same reasons that I believe in a quarterly review. There are three basic rules for making bonuses effective—that is, using them as an incentive.

First, a bonus should be paid often enough to be seen and felt immediately—so that a worker can relate the bonus to the work that they've done. Quarterly is long enough for variations in billable time to even out. Billing on software projects, despite one's best intentions, can become somewhat cyclical, and a time span of three months allows the developer to ship enough work to make their targets.

But, on the other hand, they shouldn't be paid so often that workers begin to think of them as part of their paycheck.

In the early 1980s, General Motors workers began to regard their overtime as part of their standard pay package. Eventually, they made financial commitments based on expectations of that overtime pay lasting forever. It wasn't uncommon for a line workers with 10 years of seniority to have an expensive house, two new cars, a boat, and a vacation house—all bought on time, and all based on the assumption that their regular $50,000 a year would always be supplemented by another $35,000 in overtime pay. When cutbacks in the auto industry forced the reduction or elimination of overtime, these workers couldn't make their payments, and lost a lot of the goodies they had acquired.

Additionally, of course, the bonus that is regarded as part of their paycheck loses its value as an incentive. If the employee is performing at a higher rate on a regular basis, perhaps it's time to increase their salary.

Second, a bonus should be based on factors that the developer has control over. A bonus given because Herman over the Lab invented a new polymer is never refused, but is regarded as a "gift"—not as a performance-based bonus that will serve to motivate the employee.

Accordingly, the developer should also know the rules upon which the bonus calculation is based.

Third, a bonus should be big enough to matter. A quarterly bonus of $7 or $70 to a developer who's making $50,000 to $100,000 a year is going to be regarded as silly or irrelevant. Setting up a system where a developer can't make a significant (10% to 30% or more of their base salary) bonus will become self-defeating.

These guidelines don't prevent you from providing other types of incentives, of course. I've been known to hand out a $100 bill on the spur of the moment when a developer goes "above and beyond" the call. For example, one of my developers inherited a number of projects when another developer left. As things do, the paperwork's entropy had increased substantially over the life of the projects, and some of the files were quite a mess. She took all of the paperwork for those projects home and cleaned it all up over a weekend.

Cutting fingers off: What if someone bills less than their monthly target?

We monitor the amount a developer bills on a weekly basis, so we're aware of divergence from the monthly goal right away—we don't get an "end of month surprise." This means we can take mid-course corrections quickly, resulting in minor adjustments instead of panic swings to starboard (or was that port? I don't know! Eeek! Panic!) at the last second. And given the potentially cyclical nature of billable work, we also watch the cumulative amount billed, to make sure we're on track and stay on track.

However, it is still possible that at the end of a quarter, a developer's total billings are less than their target. What do you do then? It depends on the reason that they missed their target.

If they came in under the target because there wasn't enough work, it's not their problem. Selling is management's responsibility, not the developer's. (Of course, if the developer is responsible for losing accounts, then that must be handled, but that's a different issue.)

If, on the other hand, everyone else is backlogged and one developer is still way under target, it's up to me to determine why, and take action. However, as I said, I should have been doing this all along—I shouldn't have waited until the end of the quarter to say anything.

What reasons could there be for a developer not to make their target? The first one is that they're going over budget on a particular project—they're having technical trouble, the estimates were bad, they need better training, or there's a problem with the front end of the work, not necessarily the work that the developer has done.

The next reason is that the developer has a problem customer. If difficulties with the customer are causing the developer to miss their target, then it's time for me to step in and help out—by getting the customer back on track.

It is also possible that the developer is simply goofing around, and if so, then it's also my responsibility to straighten them out. If this becomes a trend, then I need to do one of two things—either adjust the compensation of the developer (which actually may be a reasonable alternative for the developer—as opposed to losing their job), or adjust the responsibilities of the developer, which may include termination. After all, for X amount of compensation, the developer is expected to produce Y results. If they're not able to or willing to do the work, then the other side of the equation has to be changed to keep in sync.

When a developer falls behind on their target, they're actually falling behind on their schedule. And as you are monitoring the progress of your developers, you'll want to keep in mind a very important rule about schedule slippage. When a schedule starts to slip, it's very difficult to make up lost time.

You've all seen a schedule where each of six modules is slated to take four weeks. And you've all seen the manager (or the developer) who, when faced with the first module taking two months instead of one, changes the schedule for each of the other five modules to take only three weeks instead of the original four, so that the project could still be completed on time. Ask yourself one simple question: If the first module, originally estimated at four weeks, actually took eight, why would you think that all of the other modules could be produced faster? Wouldn't it make more sense to double the estimate for each of those modules as well? The moral of this is to not believe the developer when they promise to "catch up"—more likely, they're going to fall further and further behind.

How do you set your hourly rates?

Hourly rates—those numbers charged on time and materials projects—are set to map to the employee's salary, using the aforementioned 40-45% proportion. Remember that our developers can do significantly better on fixed price work than on hourly work, and so the actual amount of time and materials work is still fairly small in comparison to the entire amount of work they do. We also revise hourly rates based on their performance on an annual basis.

Rates for entry-level employees are set around the third quartile of the generally accepted billing range for the geographical region. For example, if the general rate ranged from $40 to $80 in your area, your rate for entry-level programmers would be around $50 to $60.

What benefit is there to staying around and gaining seniority?

Monetary compensation is only one piece of a total compensation package. The most senior developers get the newest equipment, the best offices, and other related perks. They also get the first chance to go to conferences, and are often the best compensated. And, of course, due to their experience, they get the better, more interesting and higher margin projects.

Additional ideas

There are a number of additional twists to the compensation scheme just outlined. First, note that the total compensation for the developer depends on the billable dollars they bring in. As the developer's skill level increases, the number of dollars they bring in through fixed price work increases, and their variable compensation goes up.

Second, should a developer gain a certification of some sort—one that is marketable on the behalf of the company—you could consider a one-time bonus. And, of course, ideally that certification also translates into a higher skill level, which makes its way back to the previous paragraph.

Third, remember that the developer's compensation is a percentage of the amount billed over the quarter. This percentage can be changed for selected circumstances. For example, you could implement a mechanism whereby the percentage varies according to their rate of production of defects (well, varies inversely, right?). This type of approach has a two-pronged benefit, in that the lower the bug count and the higher the amount billed over quarter, the better the end result for the developer (as well as for the company and customer).

Unusual situations

Compensating people fairly is a difficult situation, and that's why we're so particular about hiring people in the first place. Here are a few situations you may find yourself in at one time or another.

Current skill level and compensation don't map

Most companies use completely ridiculous schemes to pay their employees. For example, you can bet that a secretary who's been with the firm for 12 years earns more, on average, than the one who has been there six years, and even more than the one who has been there three years. There is no taking into account the abilities or the actual amount of work done by any of these three people—their primary criteria for pay is the amount of time they've been with the firm.

Correspondingly, this means that it's easy to run across a developer with such a minimal skill level that you can't justify paying them any more than a rate that corresponds to an entry-level monthly target. However, since this person has already been out in the working world for a few years, they are thus making significantly more money than what their skill level maps to.

A common example of this situation is the corporate MIS programmer who hails from the mainframe days, but in these days of "right-sizing" finds himself pushed into PC-based systems. With 15 years at his previous employer, he had a healthy salary. To you, his skills with the PC-based languages would place him in the entry-level area. How can you justify bringing an individual like this on board? It's a tough call; perhaps you feel their potential and attitudes are such that you want to make the investment in someone who's not going to be billing up to snuff for a while—much like you would with a newly minted college graduate. Or perhaps you feel that his project management skills and customer management skills are worth adding to your repertoire.

There is not an easy answer to this situation. One possible way to handle it is to bring the developer in at the level of compensation they are expecting, and eat the difference for a while, planning to make it up once the developer is up to speed. However, this method is fraught with peril, as it is a distinct possibility that such an individual may leave the firm as soon as their skills have grown to the extent that they are more marketable and attractive somewhere else.

The second way to handle this situation is through fixed price work, and effectively splitting the difference with the developer. Since there is often a significant margin built into a fixed price project, this room can be used to pay for the developer's training time. While another developer may be able to do the work considerably more efficiently, the firm is still not losing money by assigning such a project to a developer still in training.

It's important, however, to know that you're bringing a person like this on purposely, not making a mistake blindly.

Moonlighting

On a related note, one other thing we do is make it explicitly clear that doing work on the side without written permission is grounds for immediate termination and basis for a lawsuit for recovery of wages that is equal to the time spent moonlighting. All side work must be okayed in writing. This is a direct conflict of interest and we won't tolerate it.

I have run into situations where a developer still has "old clients" for whom they have ongoing work, and they don't want to leave them in the lurch, but at the same time, those clients aren't appropriate for us to take on. In a situation like this, I've allowed for the developer to finish up a current project on the side, in a fixed time frame.

What if their outside work is selling Avon, or some other sideline in no way related to software development? I've not run into this personally, but I guess I'd treat it as an outside hobby—it must be clear to the employee that their full-time work comes first.

Encouraging teamwork

Suppose Herman and Olga both get individual bonuses. It can be hypothesized that Herman will not be inclined to help Olga if Herman perceives that by doing so, they will lose time on their own project and thus their billable work will suffer. This could happen if Herman is more experienced than Olga and thus, the tables will never turn—Herman would never have cause to turn to Olga for help.

There are two possible solutions to this. First, depending on the makeup of the developers in the firm, it is possible that Herman won't ever ask Olga for help, but Herman may need tons of help from Inga on another project. If Herman develops a rep for not helping out other developers, he'll most likely run into trouble when he needs help himself.

The second possibility to consider is to set up a company-wide bonus as well as individual bonuses in order to encourage teamwork. This may or may not work because 1) now management has to spend more time figuring out how to do this new, more complex formula, and 2) it is difficult to weight the components of a multi-piece bonus. For example, in an ideal situation, the company bonus will be $100 and the individual bonus will be $100. But what happens if it's possible that the company bonus will be $10 and the individual will be $200? A developer will still be less likely to help out because the perceived benefit is much less appealing.

Here, I feel you have to rely on your people to do what's right! If you treat your people fairly, they will be more likely to respond in kind.

Training

Training is yet another topic that is paid far more lip service than true attention, but is a valuable and well-received benefit to employees. Throw a couple of books and the tutorial in front of a new employee, spend an hour with them twice during the first week, and—*voilà!*—a new project has sold, better get Biff or Muffy cranking on it and—well, don't you worry, you can go back to the tutorial as soon as you finish the project, okay?

Yup, we've all seen it, haven't we?

There isn't a single magic answer for this; you could try to set up a formal curriculum and program, almost like a regular school-based course of study. Much like code reviews, this is tough to implement because there is no "end-customer" (other than the developers themselves).

There are the usual suspects—but I'm already assuming your shop is chock-full of magazine subscriptions, CDs, books, and so on. And you should provide all of your developers with online access to whatever tools they need. And hopefully you send your developers to conferences on a regular basis. But can you do more?

You might consider trying to institutionalize training. For example, Friday afternoons are generally known as the worst time to develop software. You might consider doing some informal training sessions, along with group code reviews, after lunch on Friday. We've experimented with a mechanism where each developer took a turn presenting a topic of interest to them. One person covered a set of utilities that he had been working with, someone else covered the new features of the mail server, and a third discussed a series of articles that had appeared in a popular magazine over the past few months.

A number of our developers have in the past become involved with a study group that the local user group formed in order to acquire certification with the Microsoft Certified Solution Developer designation. While this is done on their own time, they see benefits in improved skill levels and, frankly, better marketability outside the company, in the event that should happen.

You could also consider providing a "training budget" for each employee that they are free to use as they desire (with your ability to override, of course). Perhaps you could set aside $500 a year to spend as they want—they could decide on classes, conferences, books that interest them and are above and beyond what you might want them to go to or have in your own library. That way, if they are really interested in a class on testing techniques, they could pursue it in this way. The amount they are budgeted could be a standard amount or could be influenced by performance as a perk.

Chapter 35
Not Keeping:
When You Have to Fire Someone

"There's something wrong with this yogurt."—*Spike*
"It's mayonnaise."—*William*
   —*Notting Hill*

Firing someone is probably the most uncomfortable task a business owner or manager has to perform, and, due to the litigious world we live in, it's increasingly dangerous. While there are many reasons an individual may leave your company, the purpose of this chapter is to discuss how to terminate the employment of an individual whose performance is not acceptable.

The first time I had to fire someone, it probably took me a month to admit that I had to do it, and another two weeks to garner up the courage to actually go about it. This was partly due to the pain I went through, and the subsequent guilt due to the fact that I screwed up the exit interview and made the other person feel uncomfortable. Therefore, I decided that I would have to create some sort of process to make parting ways less painful.

Obviously, you'd rather not go through the same process I did. So how do you go about firing someone so that everyone comes out in as good a shape as possible?

Firing an employee: A definition

There are many reasons an individual may leave the employ of your company. First of all, they may choose to go, and give you a resignation letter. By the way, it's a good idea to require an employee who is quitting to submit a letter of resignation. This way, it's more difficult for them to come back later, claim they were fired, and demand compensation or other benefits.

Second, you may need to terminate them for reasons other than poor performance. They may have performed an illegal, insubordinate, or unsafe act, or otherwise violated a rule of behavior that spells out termination as punishment. Lying, theft, causing harm or threatening to do so to another individual—these are all examples of behavior that is cause for immediate termination.

Business conditions may necessitate your letting go individuals as well. A drop in sales, a drastic change in the skill requirements of your employees, or other types of outside interference may require you to let someone go through no fault of their own.

In this chapter, however, I'm only discussing the situation where an employee's performance is unacceptable, and you've found no other avenue than to terminate their employment. You'll want to consult generic employer manuals for those other situations.

Termination shouldn't be a surprise!

Terminating someone because of performance should not be a surprise to the person being let go. If it is, either you've not done your job right during the review process, or they've got such a problem with communication that you probably shouldn't have hired them in the first place.

Writing this chapter, I'm reminded of the "Cheers" episode where Norm Petersen was given the job of hatchet man for the company. He was so unhappy about the job that he couldn't get around to actually performing the act. He took the soon-to-be-unemployed person out to lunch, then to a ballgame, then to a movie, and finally ended up at Cheers seven or eight hours later, still not having delivered the bad news. When he finally got around to it, he was so broken up about it that the other person had to comfort Norm, attempting to cheer him up. "I'm young, Norm, I can find another job easily! And my wife has wanted to move to another city for years—maybe now is the time to make that move. And don't you worry, we've got some money saved up—we'll be fine!"

While this type of exchange might be a bit too much to hope for, an exit interview should not be a hostile, surprising encounter, any more than the actual job offer should be. If the groundwork has been laid properly, the exit interview should be a formality, rather than a shock.

It makes complete sense to me to approach the termination of an employee as a formality. First, it's less stressful on all parties involved. Bug-ridden development tools and irate customers churn up enough stomach acid as it is. Second, if you've done your job correctly, there is much less likelihood of things coming back to haunt you—wrongful termination suits, vengeful ex-employees, and so on. Third, the process by which you terminate a person will send an important message to the others in the company. If they see that you are fair and pleasant about a potentially hostile action, they'll feel better about their own job and working for you. I think this attitude is just one more part of providing a good environment for your people and allowing them to feel comfortable and happy.

Don't discount the impact a poor performer or disruptive person has on the total work environment. A problem person can become a roadblock for your other people and can drag everyone down. Your good people will resent it if you don't deal with a problem person. If you have a problem, deal with it swiftly and decisively and your good staff will respect you all the more.

Laying the groundwork through quarterly reviews

Remember those quarterly review meetings I encouraged you to consider earlier? The issues raised in these meetings become the genesis of an employee termination. If an employee regularly does not meet their goals, and is unable to formulate a plan or follow a plan laid out for them, then termination is one possible path.

However, it's not the only path. Let's suppose that a developer just isn't cutting the mustard. What could they be doing wrong? Well, let's set aside some of the more blatant problems—swinging at customers, arriving at work brandishing an automatic weapon, groping other employees in public, or stealing office equipment. Those types of concerns should be addressed by any standard employment manual and are really out of the scope of this book. As they say, "See your lawyer."

But what about the situation when a developer's bug count is stubbornly high, and in spite of all attempts to bring it down—training, code reviews, automated tools, team coding—it stays in the stratosphere? Do you just walk into their office one day, swing your thumb over your shoulder like a baseball umpire, and scream, "You're outta here!" Obviously not. (Well, maybe not so obviously—we've all heard stories of bosses whose only role model was Attila the Hun.)

In each review, you should be discussing three things: First, go over the performance that was achieved (or not achieved) over the past quarter. Second, lay out goals for the upcoming quarter. And third, identify specific tasks and responsibilities that the employee will undertake in order to correct any past deficiencies.

After two or three reviews, depending on how forgiving you are and what any extenuating circumstances might be, you might be considering termination, and that's certainly a possibility. After all, the two of you have identified performance that does not match expectations, and the employee has repeatedly failed to correct the problem, even with clearly identified steps to do so.

However, before jumping into firing mode, consider in a bigger picture why these problems are occurring, and investigate whether there are other avenues.

Well intentioned, poorly skilled

The easiest case to solve is when an employee is having problems that can't be solved, but is making a genuine effort to make things happen. The real problem may be that the person simply doesn't have the skills to do the work. This sometimes happens—bugs slip through the hiring process just as they slip through everywhere else, and it's possible that an employee can't hack the work.

In this case, however, try to evaluate what the person can do, and see if you can either change the job, or find a new position for that person. You've already invested a lot in this person, and it just doesn't make sense to lose them unless absolutely necessary. Sure, if you've got four people in your company, and one of the four isn't working out, it may be unreasonable to think that you can simply turn the company around on its ear just to accommodate one person. It doesn't make sense to bankrupt a company in an effort to keep one person employed. On the other hand, think outside the nine dots for a minute, and see if there isn't some creative solution to this situation.

Both that employee, as well as the rest of your employees, will take note of your efforts to make things work out.

Acceptably skilled, poor attitude

This situation is the reverse—their technical skills are, at a minimum, acceptable, but the rest of the picture is unpleasant. There's often someone in the crowd who has to complain about everything, who's always looking for the cloud under the silver lining, and who makes it a drag to be around.

Unlike the poorly skilled individual, it's much harder to isolate and identify behavior that is unacceptable. If someone has an attitude problem, oftentimes discussions about specific incidents end up as additional arguments, and instead of correcting the problem; they serve to add more fuel to the fire.

If an individual's attitude is bad enough, sometimes other employees will undertake a solution themselves. An employee with a bad attitude may be much more likely to listen to their peers than the boss.

If even this approach doesn't work, and an employee continues to refuse to admit they've got an attitude problem, the door is most often the only solution.

Poor skills, poor attitude

The last possibility is when the person is just not cut out for the position—in either department. They could simply be one of those "problem" types—despite having sky-high bug counts, they insist they don't have a problem, that the problems are all someone else's, and that if only "X" would change, they'd be at the top of the heap. Incessant denial of a problem and refusal to make modifications make this person a problem, and termination may be the only route.

While you're probably going to have to terminate this person, you should at the same time be examining the hiring process you followed (or didn't follow) for this person. It's very likely that something went wrong. Can you make a correction in your hiring process so that you don't end up making another mistake?

The three-step firing process

In any of these cases, when you've decided to include termination as a possible option, you must let the person know, in advance, that their job is in danger, and explain to them what they've got to do in order to keep their job. This sounds a little harsh, and I don't really like this language, but you've got to make it clear to them that this is not simply a cosmetic matter, but rather, it's serious. You have to make sure they understand the gravity of the situation. You don't have to be mean about it, of course, but you do have to be firm.

The first quarterly review might consist of identifying a number of potential problem areas, and then documenting the plan to resolve those problems. The plan has to include both 1) actions that the employee (and perhaps the employer) has to take, and 2) the way that the results will be measured in order to determine whether the employee has gotten back on track. If there isn't a concrete measuring stick, the potential for conflict increases, and that's when things get ugly.

In the next quarterly review meeting (if not earlier), review the progress that the employee has made, and evaluate how acceptable that level of the progress is. If their performance is still not acceptable, you need to impress upon the employee the seriousness of the matter and move to the next step.

The third step is to shorten the length of time between subsequent evaluation meetings, and get together regularly during the next quarter to correct the problem.

You should schedule formal monthly meetings with an employee who is on thin ice, and continue them until the employee shows marked improvement over an ongoing period. At the first one, a verbal warning, together with a discussion of steps to take to correct the situation, may be enough. If the situation doesn't improve, you may need to escalate to a written warning at the next meeting. If their behavior continues to be unacceptable, the third meeting would be where you make the termination. By this time, of course, all but the densest employees will realize that their time is limited, and they may well save you the aggravation of going through the termination, and find another job themselves.

If it has improved from one meeting to the next, you will still want to meet again each month for that quarter to make sure that the employee is truly on a new course and to encourage that behavior.

In each of these cases, you'll want to document (that means in writing) the meeting, the discussion, and the results and actions agreed to. If you give the employee a written warning, you'll want them to sign a copy and give it to you for their file.

Finally, talk to your lawyer regarding specific documentation and the actual termination meeting. Even the best relationships can turn sour, and you'll want to protect yourself and make sure you treat your employee fairly. This process is never a pleasant one, but it can be conducted civilly and properly if you plan ahead.

Post-mortem

This term is probably more appropriate here—after the termination—than anywhere else, isn't it? I mentioned you might want to review your hiring process to see if there was something you could have done differently to have avoided this person in the first place, or if there was something that came about during their tenure that caused the situation to deteriorate.

You might also want to query your employees—often they'll see the situation in a different light, or have information that you weren't aware of. I once had an employee who went through a particularly ugly divorce—and kept the entire matter from me. Months later, after performance problems I had experienced with her during the time had gone away, another employee mentioned her past divorce in a casual aside—and was shocked to hear that I had never known about it.

You won't be able to solve every employee problem, but just as with every other process in this book, it's worth reviewing your hiring and employment methodology on a regular basis for possible improvements.

Expectations, revisited one last time

Terminating an employee, like parting ways with a customer, is the result of differing expectations. If you're clear about your expectations as an employer and they choose not to (or can't) meet them, then the logical outcome is to remove them from that position. Of course, people aren't always rational, but if you do your part of the process in a methodical manner, then possible hassles associated with the termination procedure will be minimized. Good luck.

Index

You'll note that there is not an index for this book. "How odd," you might say to yourself.

The reason is that we're trying something new with this book. An index is by nature incomplete—unless you tried to cross reference every word in the book. In order to provide a better searching facility, we provide the entire book in PDF format. You can search the entire PDF for any word (use Edit | Find), not just a selected subset from the index.

You can download the PDF file for this book from **www.hentzenwerke.com** (see the section "How to Download Files" at the beginning of this book).

We realize this is a significant departure from the norm, but then the norm doesn't include the availability of an ebook with the printed book. We'd like to hear your reaction. E-mail us at **books@hentzenwerke.com**.